LLB

LAW OF TORT
Suggested Solutions

UNIVERSITY OF LONDON

June Examination 1991

HLT Publications

HLT PUBLICATIONS
200 Greyhound Road, London W14 9RY

Examination Questions © The University of London 1991
Solutions © The HLT Group Ltd 1991

ISBN 1 85352 977 X

British Library Cataloguing-in-Publication.

A CIP Catalogue record for this book is available from the
British Library.

Printed and bound in Great Britain.

Contents

Acknowledgement

The questions used are taken from past University of London LLB (External) Degree examination papers and our thanks are extended to the University of London for the kind permission which has been given to us to use and publish the questions.

Caveat:

The answers given are not approved or sanctioned by the University of London and are entirely our responsibility.

They are not intended as 'Model Answers', but rather as Suggested Solutions.

The answers have two fundamental purposes, namely:

a) To provide a detailed example of a suggested solution to examination questions, and

b) To assist students with their research into the subject and to further their understanding and appreciation of the subject of Laws.

Note:

Please note that the solutions in this book were written in the year of the examination for each paper. They were appropriate solutions at the time of preparation, but students must note that certain caselaw and statutes may subsequently have changed.

Introduction

Why choose HLT publications

Holborn College has earned an International reputation over the past ten years for the outstanding quality of its teaching, Textbooks, Casebooks and Suggested Solutions to past examination papers set by the various examining bodies.

Our expertise is reflected in the outstanding results achieved by our students in the examinations conducted by the University of London, the Law Society, the Council of Legal Education and the Associated Examining Board.

The object of Suggested Solutions

The Suggested Solutions have been prepared by College lecturers experienced in teaching to this specific syllabus and are intended to be an example of a full answer to the problems posed by the examiner.

They are not 'model answers', for at this level there almost certainly is not just one answer to a problem, nor are the answers written to strict examination time limits.

The opportunity has been taken, where appropriate, to develop themes, suggest alternatives and set out additional material to an extent not possible by the examinee in the examination room.

We feel that in writing full opinion answers to the questions that we can assist you with your research into the subject and can further your understanding and appreciation of the law.

Notes on examination technique

Although the SUBSTANCE and SLANT of the answer changes according to the subject-matter of the question, the examining body and syllabus concerned, the TECHNIQUE of answering examination questions does not change.

You will not pass an examination if you do not know the substance of a course. You may pass if you do not know how to go about answering a question although this is doubtful. To do well and to guarantee success, however, it is necessary to learn the technique of answering problems properly. The following is a guide to acquiring that technique.

1 *Time*

All examinations permit only a limited time for papers to be completed. All papers require you to answer a certain number of questions in that time, and the questions, with some exceptions carry equal marks.

It follows from this that you should never spend a disproportionate amount of time on any question. When you have used up the amount of time allowed for any one question STOP and go on to the next question after an abrupt conclusion, if necessary. If you feel that you are running out of time, then complete your answer in *note form*. A useful way of ensuring that you do not over-run is to write down on a piece of scrap paper the time at which you should be starting each part of the paper. This can be done in the few minutes before the examination begins and it will help you to calm any nerves you may have.

2 *Reading the question*

It will not be often that you will be able to answer every question on an examination paper. Inevitably, there will be some areas in which you feel better prepared than others. You will prefer to answer the questions which deal with those areas, but you will never know how good the questions are *unless you read the whole examination paper*.

You should spend *at least* 10 MINUTES at the beginning of the examination reading the questions. Preferably, you should read them more than once. As you go through each question, make a brief note on the examination paper of any relevant cases and/or statutes that occur to you even if you think you may not answer that question: you may well be grateful for this note towards the end of the examination when you are tired and your memory begins to fail.

3 *Re-reading the answers*

Ideally, you should allow time to re-read your answers. This is rarely a pleasant process, but will ensure that you do not make any silly mistakes such as leaving out a 'not' when the negative is vital.

4 *The structure of the answer*

Almost all examination problems raise more than one legal issue that you are required to deal with. Your answer should:

i) *identify the issues raised by the question*

This is of crucial importance and gives shape to the whole answer. It indicates to the examiner that you appreciate what he is asking you about.

This is at least as important as actually answering the questions of law raised by that issue.

The issues should be identified in the first paragraph of the answer.

ii) *deal with those issues one by one as they arise in the course of the problem*

This, of course, is the substance of the answer and where study and revision pays off.

iii) *if the answer to an issue turns on a provision of a statute, CITE that provision briefly, but do not quote it from any statute you may be permitted to bring into the examination hall*

Having cited the provision, show how it is relevant to the question.

iv) *if there is no statute, or the meaning of the statute has been interpreted by the courts, CITE the relevant cases*

'Citing cases' does not mean writing down the nature of every case that happens to deal with the general topic with which you are concerned and then detailing all the facts you can think of.

You should cite *only* the most relevant cases - there may perhaps only be one. No more facts should be stated than are absolutely essential to establish the relevance of the case. If there is a relevant case, but you cannot remember its name, it is sufficient to refer to it as 'one decided case'.

v) *whenever a statute or case is cited, the title of statute or the name of the case should be underlined*

This makes the examiner's job much easier because he can see at a glance whether the relevant material has been dealt with, and it will make him more disposed in your favour.

vi) *having dealt with the relevant issues, summarise your conclusions in such a way that you answer the question*

A question will often say at the end simply 'Advise A', or B, or C, etc. The advice will usually turn on the individual answers to a number of issues. The point made here is that the final paragraph should pull those individual answers together *and actually give the advice required*. For example, it may begin something like: 'The effect of the answer to the issues raised by this question is that one's advice to A is that ...'

vii) *related to (vi), make sure at the end that you have answered the question*

For example, if the question says 'Advise A', make sure that is what your answer does. If you are required to advise more than one party, make sure that you have dealt with all the parties that you are required to and no more.

5 Some general points

You should always try to get the examiner on your side. One method has already been mentioned - the underlining of case names, etc. There are also other ways as well.

Always write as *neatly* as you can. This is more easily done with ink than with a ball-point.

Avoid the use of violently coloured ink eg turquoise; this makes a paper difficult to read.

Space out your answers sensibly: leave a line between paragraphs. You can always get more paper. At the same time, try not to use so much paper that your answer book looks too formidable to mark. This is a question of personal judgment.

NEVER put in irrelevant material simply to show that you are clever. Irrelevance is not a virtue and time spent on it is time lost for other, relevant, answers.

EXAMINATION PAPER

UNIVERSITY OF LONDON LLB EXAMINATION
PART I
for External Students

LAW OF TORT

Tuesday, 4 June 1991: 10.00am to 1.00pm

Answer *four* of the following *eight* questions

1. 'Neither the liability of an employer to an employee on the basis of breach of statutory duty nor vicarious responsibility for fellow employees adds much to the liability resulting from the employer's personal duty of care.'

   Discuss.

2. What principles determine whether deliberate interference with another's business is regarded as tortious?

3. At a shareholders' meeting of the Newtown Football Club, Stanley made a speech accusing the six directors of the club of cheating the club by selling club land for their own benefit and adding that they were not fit to run the club and should resign. Stanley distributed a leaflet which stated that the directors were incompetent and the land had been sold to a business associate of the directors at less than half its real value. Stanley also wrote a letter to the Daily Courier newspaper in which he made a similar accusation and stated that the directors were not fit to run the club. The Daily Courier published the letter. Stanley is a large shareholder in the club and has told friends that he intends to remove its directors and take over the club by any means he can. It is true that the land was sold at less than half its value but it is not true that it was sold to a business associate of the directors.

   Advise the directors.

4. Harry's hobby was walking. He went for a long walk in the countryside. He did not take a detailed map with him and as a result he got lost. He saw a road in the distance and, to get to it, he climbed over

a locked farm gate and started to cross a farm field. There was a notice on the gate which stated: 'Gordon's Farm. No trespassers. Warning: farm land is dangerous. No liability for any injuries accepted.' Halfway across the field, he fell into a five foot deep hole which was hidden by grass and branches. Gordon had dug this hole two years ago when he was thinking of building a silo. Gordon had abandoned the silo project but forgotten to fill in the hole. Harry broke his back in the fall. He is 45 and will never be able to work again. He was a school teacher earning £15,000 per year. His wife, Jane, has had to give up her £8,000 per year secretarial job to look after him.

Advise the parties.

5. Alan is an old age pensioner living with Brian, his nephew, in Stoketon. Brian treats Alan badly, threatening to punch him if he leaves his room without permission. Alan is too frightened to disobey. Their neighbour, Clive, suspects that Alan is badly treated and tells Diane, the Stoketon social services supervisor. Diane tells Clive that social services will arrange a visit but they fail to do so and simply pass on the information to a local pensioner support group. Edward, a volunteer from the group, calls but fails to recognise the signs of age abuse which would be obvious to a professional. Alan becomes so depressed that he tries to commit suicide by jumping out of his window. He breaks his leg and is taken to Stoketon Hospital where Fiona, an experienced medical student working in casualty, fails to recognise the problems that can be caused by bone fractures in the elderly. As a result, Alan does not receive proper treatment and will always have to walk with the aid of a stick. If Alan had received proper treatment, he would have had a reasonable chance of making a full recovery.

Advise Alan.

6. Mary wished to buy a luxury yacht which was being offered for £80,000. To raise the money she needed to sell her shares in Zeta Ltd. Zeta's accounts had recently been audited by Olive. Olive had negligently undervalued Zeta's assets and, as a result, the market price of Zeta's shares had fallen by half. Hence, Mary was able to raise only £40,000 instead of the £80,000 she had expected. She applied to the Chameleon Bank for a loan of £40,000 secured by a mortgage on the yacht. Chameleon informed Mary that it would make the loan

provided that it received a satisfactory report from a yacht valuer, Pamela, whom the Bank had retained to provide a valuation. Pamela negligently failed to notice that the yacht had major defects. She gave Chameleon a report valuing the yacht at £80,000 and stating that she assumed no responsibility to anyone for the accuracy of her valuation. On receiving the valuation, Chameleon advanced the loan to Mary. Mary has now discovered that the yacht is worth only £20,000 because of its defects and that the market price of Zeta shares has doubled following a correction of the negligent undervaluations in the audit report.

Advise Mary.

7. Nigel started operating a saw mill in a small village. He has leased the premises for a ten-year period from Michael who had told him to be careful about the noise and dust. To complete a large order, he has had to work late at night for the last month. The noise prevented Joan, the wife of Ken who owns the market garden next to the mill, from getting to sleep at night. Nigel has installed the best wood dust extraction equipment available, but last week the equipment malfunctioned and blew dust over the village. Much of the dust settled on Ken's garden and ruined a large number of sensitive orchids which he was about to send to the flower market. Last night there was a thunder storm and lightning set fire to wood stored in the mill yard. Nigel had not had time to purchase any fire fighting equipment and, because of the way he had stored the wood, the fire quickly got out of control. It spread to Ken's property where it destroyed two tool sheds before the fire brigade brought it under control.

Advise the parties.

8. Mark is a first year student at Leek University. He has a ground floor room in a student block. Tom is a burglar who has been entering ground floor rooms on the campus for the last two weeks. Tom enters Mark's room through his open window while he is asleep. Mark wakes up, sees Tom and screams. Tom climbs out of the window, dropping Mark's stereo equipment which is badly damaged, and runs away. Paula, who occupies the next room, hears the scream, looks out of her window and sees Tom running away. Thinking that Tom might have injured Mark or stolen something from him, she climbs out of her window and runs after Tom. In the excitement of the chase Paula trips

over a tree stump and breaks her leg. Tom reaches the exit road and looks back to see if anyone is following. At that moment he is hit by a security van belonging to Slipshod Security, which is being driven too fast by Richard. Slipshod Security have a contract to organise security for the university. They knew about the recent burglaries, but decided to take no special security measures other than alerting their staff to the problem. Simon, the security guard on duty at Mark's block, is deaf and did not hear Mark's screams.

Advise Mark, Tom, and Paula.

SUGGESTED SOLUTIONS

Question 1

'Neither the liability of an employer to an employee on the basis of breach of statutory duty nor vicarious responsibility for fellow employees adds much to the liability resulting from the employer's personal duty of care.'

Discuss.

Suggested Solution to Question 1

General comment

This is an intellectually challenging question which requires a complete grasp of the conceptual distinctions between three torts: employers' personal duties; employers' breaches of statutory duties; and employers' vicarious liability for torts of employees during the course of employment.

Students tend to be familiar with the principles of vicarious liability but tend to have more sketchy knowledge of the other two torts. Some students overlook the continuing relevance of employers' personal duties at common law. Recent caselaw is available to assist with the discussion.

Skeleton solution

Employers' liability at common law; non-delegable nature;

Breaches of statutory duties; non-delegable nature and extent of such duties; pure economic loss;

Vicarious liability; effect of Law Reform (Personal Injuries) Act 1948, liability for dishonest employees.

Suggested solution

At common law an employer's personal duty of care to an employee comprises a 'threefold obligation' namely the provision: of competent staff; of adequate equipment; and of a safe system of work (per Lord Wright in *Wilsons & Clyde Coal Co* v *English* (1).

This definition is not exhaustive and has been extended to cover a duty to warn a prospective employee of inherent risks involved in the work before the employee accepts the job: *White* v *Holbrook Precision Castings* (2).

The burden is on the employee to prove that the employer either deliberately or negligently breached the personal duty of care and that as a result the employee sustained damage recoverable at law. The personal duty is a non-delegable (or primary) duty.

The injured employee may also be able to rely on two other forms of employers' liability which overlap but do not precisely coincide with the employer's personal duty. These forms are breach of statutory duty and vicarious liability for the torts of an employee acting in the course of his employment.

In regard to statutory duties, it will be a matter of construction whether the particular duty was intended by Parliament to be strict, such as in the case of the duty to fence dangerous machinery. If the duty is strict the employee is relieved of the burden of proving fault (though he must still prove a breach of the statutory duty and consequent damage): *Groves* v *Wimborne* (3) and per Lord Wright in *LPTB* v *Upson* (4), who emphasised the importance of the conceptual distinction between employers' personal and statutory duties. A statutory duty of the strict kind is, however, similar to the personal duty in being non-delegable in character.

The statutory duty may be interpreted to include a duty to protect the employee from suffering pure economic loss if that kind of loss is within the ambit of the relevant statute; for example an Act to protect the performing rights of film actors could protect correlative financial interests. By contrast the employer's personal duty does not extend to protect his employee from such loss because common law regards their relationship as being insufficiently proximate, with no assumption of special responsibility by the employer. This is consistent with recent common law hostility to the imposition of tortious duties to prevent pure economic loss, especially where a contract exists between the parties which may either expressly or impliedly deal with such loss in a more satisfactory manner than the law of tort: see *Reid* v *Rush and Tompkins* (5) where the Court of Appeal held no duty to insure an employee or to warn him of the wisdom of self-insurance in a case where the employee was being sent to work overseas.

In regard to vicarious liability there was a considerable expansion in the scope of such liability following the passage of the Law Reform (Personal Injuries) Act 1948. Before that Act the employer had a defence called common employment which prevented an employee suing him for the torts of a fellow employee. The Act abolished this defence so that where the employee can prove fault by a fellow employee a claim under the principles of vicarious liability will succeed. Nevertheless the continued existence of the employer's personal duty to provide a competent staff may still be of relevance, as where the injured employee cannot prove fault but can establish that the other employee was not suitably qualified or experienced to perform the job in question.

Further there may be one area where the personal duty is wider in scope than vicarious liability. That area covers dishonest conduct by an employee. As a general rule an employer is not vicariously liable for such conduct even though he may have placed the dishonest employee in a position where he had the opportunity to steal from fellow employees (or others), unless it was a special position of trust akin to an agency: *Armagas v Mundogas (The Ocean Frost)* (6). However an employer may be held liable for breach of his personal duty if he had knowingly employed a dishonest servant.

Finally, the personal duty is non-delegable and therefore constitutes an important exception to the principles of vicarious liability under which there is no liability for the acts of an independent contractor: see *McDermid* v *Nash and Co* (7) where the D employer had put the P employee under the control of a tugmaster who operated an unsafe system of work on the tug. It was held that D was liable for not providing a safe system of work. The House of Lords made it clear that the threefold obligation of the employer's personal duty was non-delegable in all of its three parts.

Hence issue is taken with the statement in question. There are sound practical reasons for the distinctions between an employer's personal duty, his statutory duties and his vicarious liability. Further, as Brazier points out in her 8th edition of Street on Torts, the conceptual distinctions between the three torts remain the basis of judicial thinking on the subject, and the developments and implications of the cases cannot be understood if this is not grasped.

References
(1)   [1938] AC 57 HL
(2)   [1985] IRLR 215
(3)   [1898] 2 QB 402 CA
(4)   [1949] AC 155 HL
(5)   [1989] 3 All ER 228 CA
(6)   [1986] AC 717 HL
(7)   [1987] 2 All ER 878 HL

Question 2

What principles determine whether deliberate interference with another's business is regarded as tortious?

Suggested Solution to Question 2

General comment

As with question one, there is an intellectual challenge to the student in discussing the conceptual distinctions between a number of the so-called 'economic torts'. It is an area ripe for critical analysis, particularly over the confused state of the tort of conspiracy which as recently as 1991 required fresh examination and formulation by the House of Lords. Academic research should be utilised and cited, eg Sales' brilliant analysis of conspiracy in the 1990 Cambridge Law Journal foreshadowed the conclusions eventually reached by the House of Lords.

Skeleton solution

Ingredients of tort of conspiracy; the anomaly of malicious conspiracy and the predominant purpose rule;

Ingredients of breach of statutory duty and damage to business; the modern narrow principle of liability established in *Lonrho* v *Shell* (No 2);

Ingredients of inducing a breach of contract: the definition given in *Merkur Island Shipping Co* v *Laughton*;

Ingredients of tort of intimidation; is there a tort of harassment?

Suggested solution

There are a number of torts which exist to deal with invasion of economic interests. The classic economic torts include:

a) *Conspiracy*

P must show that Ds intended to injure his business either through an agreement to use lawful means to achieve the unlawful end or through an agreement to achieve a lawful end by unlawful means. The two types of agreement constitute distinct categories. The first type includes malicious conspiracy with the result that an agreement deliberately to injure P's business can be tortious even though, if there were no combination, there would be no tort, ie a malicious act which is not actionable by one person acting alone becomes actionable if done in combination.

Since this first category of conspiracy is somewhat anomalous in character and less dangerous than the second category which involves unlawful means (such as intimidation of P's workforce) it is restricted by a requirement that P must show that the 'predominant purpose' of Ds' agreement was to injure P's business. For this purpose if the predominant purpose was the protection or promotion of either Ds' legitimate self-interests or of the public interest the combination will not be an actionable conspiracy.

The leading authority remains *Crofter Tweed Co* v *Veitch* (1) where it was held that the trade union's strike action was not a conspiracy because the main motive was to improve the wages and conditions of the union's members rather than to injure P's business. The latter injury was described as a 'by-product' or 'side-effect' of the agreement. Similarly in *Scala Ballrooms* v *Ratcliffe* (2) an organised boycott of P's dance club was held not actionable because the object was to end racial discrimination operated by the club and that object was in the public interest.

Some confusion was caused by later decisions which appeared to extend the predominant purpose rule to the second category of conspiracy involving unlawful means, but the House of Lords has recently re-affirmed the conceptual distinction between the two types of conspiracy and the law is as stated above: see further *Lonrho Plc* v *Fayed* (3) and article by Sales (1990) Cambridge Law Journal at p491.

b) *Breach of statutory duty*

At one time there was a broad principle that whenever violation of a statute causes damage to a person's business, a right of action accrues: *Couch* v *Steel* (4). However, subsequent caselaw restricted this principle by a requirement that the legislature must have intended to give a cause of action to the person whose business was harmed by the breach of statutory duty. In *ex parte Island Records Ltd* (5) Lord Denning attempted to resurrect the broad principle but his attempt has since been firmly rejected by the House of Lords: *Lonrho Ltd* v *Shell (No 2)* (6).

In the *Lonrho* case the P oil company had suffered heavy losses because they complied with government regulations prohibiting trade with the illegal regime in Rhodesia whilst competitors violated the regulations. It was held, inter alia, that the sanctions law was intended to bring down the illegal regime and not to protect particular businesses from unscrupulous competition. Hence the scope of this economic tort will depend on the construction of each particular statute and is likely to prove of limited effect in protecting businesses.

c) *Inducing a breach of contract*

The essential elements of this tort were explained by Lord Diplock in *Merkur Island Shipping* v *Laughton* (7) as follows:

    i)   that D knew of the existence of the contract and intended to procure a breach of it or interfere with its performance; and

    ii)   that D procured the breach or interference; and

   iii)   that breach or interference took place; and

   iv)   such breach or interference was the necessary consequence of D's act.

It appears unnecessary for P to show that D's predominant purpose was to injure P's business. However P must show that the primary obligations of the contract were prevented from being performed, so that it will not be enough to show an interference with the secondary obligations arising under many types of business or employment contracts: *Thomas* v *NUM* (8).

d)   *Intimi dation*

This tort was examined by Lord Diplock in *Rookes* v *Barnard* (9) who stated that it covers either intimidation of P himself or the intimidation of third parties where in either case the object was to injure P's business. The concept of intimidation involves wrongful compulsion. The wrong may be in the form of a crime, tort or breach of contract. Compulsion implies something more than peaceful persuasion, even if the latter is vigorous in tone, such as abuse, swearing and shoving: per Stuart-Smith J in *Newsgroup Newspapers* v *SOGAT* (10). Hence peaceful picketing and demonstrations do not constitute intimidation. It is unnecessary for P to show that D's predominant purpose was to injure P's business by the intimidation.

e)   *Harassment*

There is considerable controversy over the existence and scope of this tort. It appears to have been invented to deal with the effect of mass picketing during the coalminers' strike of 1984-5: see per Scott J in *Thomas* v *NUM*. Doubts about its existence were expressed by Stuart-Smith J in the *SOGAT* case (above) and, in a different context (domestic violence in the family), it has been held that no tort of harassment exists in English law: *Patel* v *Patel* (11).

References
(1)   [1942] AC 435 HL
(2)   [1958] 3 All ER 220 CA
(3)   [1991] 3 All ER 303 HL
(4)   (1854) 3 E & B 402
(5)   [1978] 3 All ER 824 CA

(6)   [1982] AC 173 HL
(7)   [1983] 2 AC 570 HL
(8)   [1985] 2 All ER 1
(9)   [1964] AC 1129 HL
(10)   [1987] ICR 181
(11)   [1988] Fam Law 213

Question 3

At a shareholders' meeting of the Newtown Football Club, Stanley made a speech accusing the six directors of the club of cheating the club by selling club land for their own benefit and adding that they were not fit to run the club and should resign. Stanley distributed a leaflet which stated that the directors were incompetent and the land had been sold to a business associate of the directors at less than half its real value. Stanley also wrote a letter to the Daily Courier newspaper in which he made a similar accusation and stated that the directors were not fit to run the club. The Daily Courier published the letter. Stanley is a large shareholder in the club and has told friends that he intends to remove its directors and take over the club by any means he can. It is true that the land was sold at less than half its value but it is not true that it was sold to a business associate of the directors.

Advise the directors.

Suggested Solution to Question 3

General comment
This ought to be familiar ground for the good Torts student, since defamation is a predictable examination topic. However, because it covers so much ground and comprises so much caselaw, the real challenge for the student is to identify the relevant issues from the facts given and confine the analysis strictly to them.

It is impossible to be familiar with all the authorities, but it does not matter if a student is unaware of a particular case on the precise point in issue provided he/she can argue by analogy with other relevant caselaw. For example, the case of *Parsons* v *Surgey*, which is cited in the solution, is tucked away as a footnote in most textbooks, if cited at all; but the point can be discussed by reference to the analogous and more widely discussed case of *Bridgeman* v *Stockdale* (or other similar authority on scope of qualified privilege).

Skeleton solution
Defamation; determining the 'sting' of the defamation; distinction between libel and slander; defaming a group/corporation; relevance of malice to particular defences; defence of justification; defence of fair comment; defence of qualified privilege; newspapers' defence under Defamation Act 1952, s4; defence of innocent dissemination.

Suggested solution
The directors need advice as to whether they have the right to sue in the tort of defamation in respect of statements made by Stanley (S) and published by the Daily Courier (DC).

The 'sting' of the accusations is that the directors are unfit to hold office because of incompetence and corrupt land dealing. It is advised that such accusations are defamatory on their face and that, subject to defences considered below, the directors have the following remedies:

a) *To sue for slander* in respect of S's oral speech at the shareholders' meeting. Although slander is not generally actionable 'per se', in this case the directors are not obliged to prove special damage because the accusations were calculated to injure their professional reputations as holders of the particular offices in question: Defamation Act 1952, s2. At common law words are actionable per se if they impute corrupt or

23

dishonest conduct in the performance of the office (whether an office of profit or honour) or if they allege incompetence in the performance of an office of profit: *Alexander* v *Jenkins* (1).

b)   *To sue for libel* in respect of the leaflet and letter to DC. Libel is actionable per se.

The above actions may be brought by the directors as individuals or in their corporate name. It is not possible to defame a group or class of people unless the group or class is so small that what is said of the group or class is necessarily said of each member of it: the ancient authority of *Foxcroft* v *Lacey* (2); see also in recent times *Farrington* v *Leigh* (3), where an investigating taskforce of seven police officers was the subject of a defamatory statement; it was held each officer had the right to sue. Clearly the six directors of Newtown FC form a sufficiently small group for this purpose. Further, they could sue also in the name of the club, which is a separate trading entity and which enjoys a commercial reputation distinct from the personal reputations of the directors: *South Hetton Coal Co* v *N E News Association* (4).

Relevant defences to the above actions will now be considered. Some of these defences will be affected by S's motives, which, if malicious, may cause them to be lost. It appears that S's position as a large shareholder and his ambition to take over the club 'by any means' raise the strong possibility that he was motivated by malice towards the directors. Malice involves non-belief in the truth of the accusations or reckless carelessness as to whether the accusations were true or false; malice also includes general spite or ill-will.

Defences

i)   *Justification*

This defence requires that the accusations must be substantially true; minor inaccuracies which do not damage reputation will not prevent the defence: Defamation Act 1952, s5. If S's accusations had been true he would have had a complete defence even if actuated by malice. For the purpose of s5 where separate accusations are made it may be possible to sever them so that if the major accusations are true any minor accusations which are untrue may be severed and reduce an award of damages. In the present problem the accusation of incompetence might be justified by relying on the fact that club property was sold at a serious undervalue. However, this accusation was closely linked to the accusation of corrupt dealing with regard to that sale, and this accusation had no factual basis. Since both accusations had a 'common sting' it is suggested that they are not severable and that consequently neither S nor DC can plead justification.

ii) *Fair comment*

This defence does not require the statement to be factually *true*. It is a defence that there was honest expression of opinion on a matter of public interest. There must be a *factual basis* for the opinion and minor inaccuracies in the factual basis will not destroy the defence: 1952 Act, s6. Honesty requires absence of malice, as defined above; mere prejudice will not constitute malice for this purpose: *Horrocks* v *Lowe* (5).

Since S appeared to have a malicious motive he will be unable to rely on the defence. It is debatable whether DC may be able to rely on it if they published the letter in honest belief that it might be true. There is a conflict of authority as to whether publishers are 'infected' by the malice of the authors whose work they publish; in favour of infection is *Adams* v *Ward* (6), but against it is the later and more fully considered decision of the Court of Appeal in *Egger* v *Chelmsford* (7) and *Lyon* v *Daily Telegraph* (8). Even if the DC is not infected by S's malice, it is questionable whether the conduct of the directors is a matter of public interest because they did not hold public offices. It is arguable that, as directors of a football club, they are more frequently in the 'public eye' than the directors of an ordinary small business, but whether this makes their conduct a matter of public interest is as yet undecided by authority. What is interesting to the public may not be the same as the public interest!

iii) *Qualified privilege*

A statement made on an occasion of qualified privilege will be protected from suit if the maker was not motivated by malice. S's speech to the shareholders' meeting, and the distribution of his leaflet at it, would be regarded as being made in the context of an occasion of qualified privilege because there was a common (shareholders') interest in the conduct of the Board (*Parsons* v *Surgey* (9)), analogous to the common interest of exam invigilators and candidates to stop cheating: *Bridgeman* v *Stockdale* (10).

However, since S was actuated by malice he cannot rely on this defence. Further, qualified privilege would not in any event have extended to the sending of the letter to DC because qualified privilege is lost if there is excessive publication: *Oddy* v *Lord Paulet* (11).

It is also very doubtful whether DC could plead qualified privilege because even if one leaves aside the doubts about the applicability of public interest and the infection of S's malice the law requires that newspapers have 'official' or 'reliable' sources if they intend to publish accusations of corruption in public affairs; the publication of speculative accusations is not protected: *Cork* v *McVicar* (12) and *Blackshaw* v *Lord* (13). Although S was a large shareholder it is doubtful whether he would be regarded as a reliable or official source since he was not on the Board.

iv) *Defamation Act 1952, s4*

This provides a special defence for newspapers. As a general rule it is no defence that there was no intention to defame, but s4 gives the media a chance to make an apology and an offer of amends for unintentional defamation, thereby avoiding an award of damages. However s4 applies only if the words were not defamatory on their face and since DC must have been aware of the risk of defamation from the contents of S's letter, it seems unlikely that s4 can be successfully pleaded by DC.

v) *Innocent dissemination*

This is a common law defence protecting newspaper vendors, distributors and the like provided they were unaware of the defamatory character of the libel contained in the newspaper.

References
(1)   [1892] 1 QB 797 CA
(2)   (1613) Hob 89
(3)   (1987) The TImes 10 December CA
(4)   [1894] 1 QB 133
(5)   [1975] AC 135 HL
(6)   [1917] AC 309 HL
(7)   [1965] 1 QB 248 CA
(8)   [1943] KB 746
(9)   (1864) 4 F & F 247

(10)   [1953] 1 All ER 1116
(11)   (1865) 4 F & F 1009
(12)   (1984) The Times 31 October
(13)   [1984] QB 1 CA

Question 4

Harry's hobby was walking. He went for a long walk in the countryside. He did not take a detailed map with him and as a result he got lost. He saw a road in the distance and, to get to it, he climbed over a locked farm gate and started to cross a farm field. There was a notice on the gate which stated: 'Gordon's Farm. No trespassers. Warning: farm land is dangerous. No liability for any injuries accepted.' Halfway across the field, he fell into a five foot deep hole which was hidden by grass and branches. Gordon had dug this hole two years ago when he was thinking of building a silo. Gordon had abandoned the silo project but forgotten to fill in the hole. Harry broke his back in the fall. He is 45 and will never be able to work again. He was a school teacher earning £15,000 per year. His wife, Jane, has had to give up her £8,000 per year secretarial job to look after him.

Advise the parties.

Suggested Solution to Question 4

General comment

The danger for the student is the temptation to launch into a discussion of the Occupiers' Liability Act 1957, when the facts clearly invite discussion of the Occupiers' Liability Act 1984 (trespasser, not visitor!). Nevertheless brief references to the 1957 Act will be useful to bring out the distinctions between the two statutes. Note in particular the application of the Unfair Contract Terms Act to the 1957 Act but its apparent non-application to the 1984 Act.

The assessment of compensation for the injuries in question requires a detailed analysis of the various heads of damage and of the way the computation for loss of earnings is made. Some students tend to overlook the law on compensation, probably because it usually comes at the end of their course and they neglect it in the panic to revise earlier topics! Recent caselaw and statute law, plus the continuing debate about no-fault compensation schemes, should make the subject essential revision for the Torts student.

Skeleton solution

Occupiers' liability to trespasser; the duty of care under Occupiers' Liability Act 1984, s1(3) and its factual application; exclusion of liability and effect of s1(5); the contrast with the 1957 Act and the questionable applicability of UCTA 1977. Defence of volenti.

Assessment of compensation; heads of damage; loss of earnings; the multiplier and discount for vicissitudes of life; deduction for State benefits, etc. Effect of contributory negligence, if any.

Suggested solution

The issues raised are whether Harry can sue Gordon for breach of the occupier's statutory duty of care to a trespasser and, if so, the extent of compensation payable by G for H's physical injury and consequent economic loss.

a) *G's liability as occupier*

Under Occupiers' Liability Act 1984, s1(3) an occupier owes a duty of care to trespassers if he is aware or ought to be aware of a danger on his land, knows or has grounds to believe that a trespasser may be in the vicinity of the danger, and if he might reasonably be expected to offer some protection to the trespasser against the danger.

In the present problem the danger was a five foot deep hole which Gordon himself had dug two years ago and which he had forgotten to fill in. Consequently, it would be difficult for Gordon to deny knowledge of this hazard. Further he must have been aware of the risk of trespass because he had put up a notice discouraging it. Since no effective security measures were taken to prevent trespass (such as an electric fence) the possibility that a trespasser might ignore his notice and come onto the land within the vicinity of the hole was one that Gordon should have been aware of. Since it would take comparatively little in effort and resources to fill in the hole or to fence it adequately, Gordon would have been expected to provide such protection against this particular danger, which posed a threat of serious injury to a trespasser who might fall into it. Consequently all the elements required for imposing liability on Gordon under s1(3) are present.

OLA 1984, s1(5) permits an occupier to exclude his duty by giving adequate warning of the danger to a trespasser, or by otherwise discouraging trespassers from incurring risk.

It appears that the warning need not be in a form so as to make the place reasonably safe for the trespasser to enter, in contrast to the duty to visitors under OLA 1957. Hence G's general warning notice on the gate may be sufficient to exempt him from liability although the court will have regard to all the circumstances.

It appears that OLA 1984 may not be subject to the provisions of the Unfair Contract Terms Act 1977 (which specifically apply only to the tort of negligence and the duty of care under OLA 1957), so that it is open to G to exclude liability for personal injury sustained by trespassers on his land: view, Brazier, 8th ed Street.

The defence of 'volenti' is not available to G because although H voluntarily entered land which he knew might be dangerous he was acting under the pressure of being lost and needing to find the nearest road; in a sense he was rescuing himself and not truly consenting to run the risk of injury.

b) *H's compensation*

This will consist of a lump sum for his pain, suffering, loss of amenities and loss of earnings. The case of *Housecroft* v *Burnett* (1) indicates that a sum of £75,000 is appropriate for a tetraplegia victim who is aware of his pain, suffering and loss of amenity. The same case allows H to claim for nursing care, including a sum to compensate his wife (Jane) for giving up her job to look after him.

A sum will also be awarded for H's loss of future earnings. Although Harry could have gone on working for another 20 years before retiring at State retirement age (65 for men) the court will take account of the 'vicissitudes of life' from which H may have suffered even if he had not suffered this injury (eg premature death from natural causes, illness, etc): *Jobling* v *Associated Dairies* (2). So the multiplier will not be 20 but more likely in the region of 12, which will be applied to his net earnings, ie how much he took home after deductions for tax, national insurance, etc. If the figure of £15,000 pa represents his net earnings he could expect a lump sum award of about £180,000 for his lost earnings. A similar approach will be taken to calculate Jane's lost earnings; assuming the same age and £8,000 pa net earnings this will be a sum of about £96,000, making a total award of approximately £351,000.

From this total award there will be deductions for certain State benefits which H may claim, such as unemployment benefit, attendance and mobility allowances and income support. The full value of these benefits must be deducted: *Parsons* v *BNM Laboratories* (3) (unemployment benefit) and the Social Security Act 1989 (other State benefits).

It seems unlikely that the court will find H contributorily negligent for not spotting the hole, since the hole was hidden by grass and branches and probably not observable even to one who was on the lookout for holes. Also, it is advised that the fact that H was to blame for getting himself lost in the first place is not sufficiently proximate to the incident of falling down the hole to be regarded as contributory negligence. However his decision to ignore the warning notice might count as contributory negligence so as to justify a reduction in the award of damages (it might even provide G with a complete defence, as advised above. There is no such thing as 100 per cent contributory negligence (*Pitts* v *Hunt* (4)); in reality such a finding would mean that the defendant has not caused the plaintiff's injury, the plaintiff is wholly to blame).

References
(1)   [1986] 1 All ER 332
(2)   [1982] AC 794 HL
(3)   [1964] 1 QB 95
(4)   [1990] 3 WLR 542

Question 5

Alan is an old age pensioner living with Brian, his nephew, in Stoketon. Brian treats Alan badly, threatening to punch him if he leaves his room without permission. Alan is too frightened to disobey. Their neighbour, Clive, suspects that Alan is badly treated and tells Diane, the Stoketon social services supervisor. Diane tells Clive that social services will arrange a visit but they fail to do so and simply pass on the information to a local pensioner support group. Edward, a volunteer from the group, calls but fails to recognise the signs of age abuse which would be obvious to a professional. Alan becomes so depressed that he tries to commit suicide by jumping out of his window. He breaks his leg and is taken to Stoketon Hospital where Fiona, an experienced medical student working in casualty, fails to recognise the problems that can be caused by bone fractures in the elderly. As a result, Alan does not receive proper treatment and will always have to walk with the aid of a stick. If Alan had received proper treatment, he would have had a reasonable chance of making a full recovery.

Advise Alan.

Suggested Solution to Question 5

General comment
A number of complex issues arise on the facts given. In particular, detailed knowledge of the rule on omissions in the tort of negligence, including the duties of public authorities to protect vulnerable citizens and even to prevent suicide attempts! Recent caselaw is available concerning the policy on these matters, and the general issue of the 'duty to rescue' has been the subject of academic research; probably the best is Bowman and Bailey's analysis in the 1984 Public Law Journal, which can be cited here. The problem also involves the law on medical negligence; students need to be familiar with the standard of care and its applicability to inexperienced staff. Probably most difficulty will be caused by the causation issue and the question of whether loss of a chance of recovery can be the subject of a claim in tort. A helpful analysis of the leading authority is provided by Hill in the 1991 Modern Law Review.

Skeleton solution
Alan v *Brian*: ingredients of torts of assault and false imprisonment;
Alan v *Stoketon Council*: vicarious liability for Diane; the law on omissions: is there a duty to rescue? the special rules for public authorities; causation; prevention of suicide attempts; 'novus actus interveniens'.
Alan v *Edward*: standard of care from a volunteer;
Alan v *Stoketon Hospital*: direct and vicarious liability for hospital staff; standard of care; inexperienced staff; causation; balance of probabilities test; is loss of a chance recoverable in tort?

Suggested solution
A number of possible claims arise out of the facts given and it will be convenient to consider them separately, although in some claims there will be similar or overlapping issues (such as causation).

Alan v *Brian* (A v B)
A may sue B for assault. Assault is any act (including words) which causes another person to apprehend the infliction of immediate unlawful force: *Wilson* v *Pringle* (1). B's threat to punch A falls within this definition.

A may also sue B for false imprisonment, which involves the unlawful imposition of constraint on one's freedom of movement from a particular place: *Wilson* v *Pringle*. B's confinement of A to his room under duress falls within this definition.

Both torts are actionable per se.

Alan v *Stoketon Council*

If Diane was negligent the Council will be vicariously liable as her employer for acts or omissions occurring during the course of her employment.

The first difficulty is in establishing that the Council owed A a duty of care. The failure to arrange the promised visit by the social services department is an example of a pure omission and the law of tort does not impose a positive duty to act (here, effectively, a duty to rescue) unless there is a special relationship between the parties in which one exercises control and the other is dependent on the controlling party.

Mere status does not imply control or duty to rescue; there must be also practical ability to control the particular situation, such as in the case of a lifeguard on the lookout for swimmers in distress: example given by Bowman and Bailey in (1984) Public Law at p277.

The courts are especially reluctant to impose positive duties on public authorities which may be faced with limited resources and difficult operational decisions, eg it has been held that the police are not under a duty to answer a burglar alarm or 999 emergency call in the absence of a contract or other special relationship with the plaintiff: *Alexandrou* v *Oxford* (2); see also *Hill* v *Chief Constable of West Yorkshire* (3) and *Knight* v *Home Office* (4).

However, in the present problem Diane had promised to investigate A's circumstances and such assumption of responsibility might be enough to give rise to the duty of care. If so, it is advised that the Council were in breach of that duty by 'passing the buck' to an unprofessional organisation.

The next issue is one of causation. If A had suffered further abuse from B as a result of the failure to investigate, there would be little doubt as to the Council's liability. However, A's actual damage is the broken leg caused by a suicide attempt at a time when he was depressed. Although the Council were under a duty to exercise supervision, it would be going too far to suggest that they were under a duty to prevent a suicide attempt, because they did not have sufficient degree of control over Alan's hour-by-hour movements. Even if they had had such control (eg, if A had been transferred into their custody) a suicide attempt would be unforeseeable in the absence of direct knowledge of A's clinical depression and suicidal tendencies.

For those reasons the present facts are distinguishable from *Kirkham* v *Chief Constable of Greater Manchester Police* (5) where the police had known of such tendencies in a remand prisoner but had failed to alert the hospital wing which would otherwise have taken protective action. The prisoner's widow was successful in suing the police for negligence (defences of 'ex turpi causa', and 'volenti' were rejected, and the plea of contributory negligence was also regarded as unavailable).

Hence, although the Council were in breach of their duty of general supervision, A cannot sue them for the damage to his leg, which was not caused by such breach of duty. The suicide attempt could be described as a 'novus actus interveniens' breaking the chain of causation leading from the breach of duty to the actual damage sustained.

Alan v *Edward (A v E)*

On the existence of a duty of care it has been said that if a person undertakes to perform a voluntary act he is liable if he performs it improperly: per Willes J in *Skelton* v *L & NW Ry* (6). Hence the issue here is whether Edward was in breach of the duty he undertook to investigate A's circumstances. The standard of care expected from him was that which would be expected from a member of a 'pensioner support group'. Since the objectives of such a group are wide-ranging and involve activities of a political nature rather than medical or quasi-medical the law would not impose on its members the standards expected from a professional social services worker. Since the facts indicate that the signs of A's age abuse were not obvious to a non-professional such as Edward, he was not in breach of his duty to A. Even if there were a breach of the duty of care, E would not be liable because of the causation issue, which would apply in the same way as in A's claim against the Council (above).

A v *Stoketon Hospital*

If Fiona was negligent Stoketon Hospital (SH) would be liable, either directly for failure to provide competent medical staff or vicariously for the individual act of negligence committed by an employee in the course of employment: *Cassidy* v *Minister of Health* (7).

On the issue of medical negligence the test will be whether Fiona failed to diagnose a problem which would have been diagnosed by a responsible body of medical practitioners: *Bolam*'s case (8). On that test Fiona is in breach of her duty of care to A and her inexperience will not affect her liability because a uniform standard of care is required from all those who undertook the practice of medicine in the casualty unit of the hospital, be they doctors of 30 years' experience or, like Fiona, a student 'learning on the job': *Wilsher* v *Essex AHA* (9). In the law of tort the duty is tailored to the act being performed and not to the actor performing it: *Nettleship* v *Weston* (10) (driving a car: learner-driver under same standard of care as qualified driver).

However, even though Fiona was in breach of her duty of care, the issue of causation remains: did her breach cause A's permanent disability? If it can be shown that it was more probable than not that A would have been permanently disabled in any event as a result of the suicide attempt, that will conclude the issue in the hospital's favour, because evidence that D's conduct may have caused or contributed to P's injury will only result in a finding that it did cause that injury if there is no or inadequate evidence of any other causal factor which on the balance of probabilities resulted in the injury: see *Hotson* v *East Berkshire AHA* (11) where it was found that there was a 25 per cent chance that the delay in diagnosis contributed to the development of D's condition but a 75 per cent chance that it would have happened anyway as a result of established other causes. It was held that the delay in diagnosis was not a cause of the injury on the civil standard of probabilities and so the hospital escaped liability. It was left open whether a lost chance of recovery which could be proved to result from a breach of duty could be compensated in tort, as it clearly is in contract law (*Chaplin* v *Hicks* (12): see further, article Hill (1991) Modern Law Review at p511.

In the present case the facts would seem to suggest that it was Fiona's negligence which prevented A's complete recovery and therefore A may have at least an arguable case for compensation on the basis of his lost chance of complete recovery.

References

(1)   [1987] QB 237 CA
(2)   (1990) The Times 19 February CA
(3)   [1988] 2 All ER 238 HL
(4)   [1990] 3 All ER 237
(5)   [1990] 2 WLR 987
(6)   (1867) LR 2 CP 631
(7)   [1951] 1 All ER 574 CA
(8)   [1957] 2 All ER 1
(9)   [1988] 1 All ER 871 HL; [1986] 3 All ER 801 CA
(10)   [1971] 2 QB 691 CA
(11)   [1987] 2 All ER 909 HL
(12)   [1911] 2 KB 786 CA

Question 6

Mary wished to buy a luxury yacht which was being offered for £80,000. To raise the money she needed to sell her shares in Zeta Ltd. Zeta's accounts had recently been audited by Olive. Olive had negligently undervalued Zeta's assets and, as a result, the market price of Zeta's shares had fallen by half. Hence, Mary was able to raise only £40,000 instead of the £80,000 she had expected. She applied to the Chameleon Bank for a loan of £40,000 secured by a mortgage on the yacht. Chameleon informed Mary that it would make the loan provided that it received a satisfactory report from a yacht valuer, Pamela, whom the Bank had retained to provide a valuation. Pamela negligently failed to notice that the yacht had major defects. She gave Chameleon a report valuing the yacht at £80,000 and stating that she assumed no responsibility to anyone for the accuracy of her valuation. On receiving the valuation, Chameleon advanced the loan to Mary. Mary has now discovered that the yacht is worth only £20,000 because of its defects and that the market price of Zeta shares has doubled following a correction of the negligent undervaluations in the audit report.

Advise Mary.

Suggested Solution to Question 6

General comment

This kind of question on pure economic loss is likely to become a regular feature of exam papers in Tort. It requires a complete grasp of the reformulation of and refinements to the principles laid down in *Hedley Byrne* v *Heller* (1964) brought about by the decision in *Caparo* v *Dickman* (1990). There is a wealth of academic analysis of the implications of Caparo appearing in such sources as the Modern Law Review and New Law Journal. Examiners would probably expect students to be familiar with some of this research, particularly if the standard textbooks are out-of-date in this area.

The case of *Smith* v *Bush* (1989) is important in identifying a duty situation with the necessary close degree of proximity; students would be expected to show sensitivity towards the factors that may affect the recognition of a duty situation.

Skeleton solution

Pure economic loss; the replacement of a general principle with pragmatic duty situations; the effect of *Caparo* v *Dickman* and its factual application; the effect of *Smith* v *Bush* and its factual application; effect of a disclaimer: the effect of UCTA 1977, s2(2).

Suggested solution

a) *Mary's claim against Olive*

The issue is whether the facts disclose a recognised 'duty situation' in which the law of tort imposes a duty of care to avoid causing pure economic loss (which, in Mary's case, consists of £40,000 for a negligent audit and valuation).

It is no longer appropriate to search for a general principle or formula to determine the existence of the duty of care. The imposition of the duty of care is a pragmatic task rather than one of legal logic. The duty to avoid causing physical damage will be different in nature and degree from the duty to avoid causing pure economic loss, because in the latter case the availability of a contractual remedy or insurance cover or other special factors may be relevant in restricting the duty that is owed: see further Martin (1990) Modern Law Review at p824.

In the present problem Mary's claim will fail because the factual circumstances do not create the 'duty situation' which is necessary to establish a successful claim. Mary cannot rely simply on the test of foreseeability, even though it was reasonably foreseeable that, as an existing shareholder, she might rely on the auditor's report in deciding whether to sell her shares or buy more shares in Zeta Ltd. It is not enough for her to prove such reliance or that the result was economic loss.

The above principles and conclusions were established in *Caparo* v *Dickman* (1) which can properly be treated as the modern leading authority on negligent misstatements which cause economic loss. In that case it was settled that the auditor's duty of care is owed to the shareholders as a group so as to make corporate decisions and not for the purpose of individuals, whether existing shareholders or strangers, to make personal decisions as to whether or not to buy or sell shares in the company.

In reaching this decision the House of Lords laid emphasis on two special considerations. The first was the classic 'floodgates' argument: no duty of care could arise where a party puts into general circulation a set of statements which might be relied on by others for any one of a variety of purposes, since otherwise the maker of such statements would be subjected to too onerous a duty, one which might involve indeterminate liability.

The second consideration was the effect of imposing such a duty on a professional or expert adviser: no duty of care should be imposed if it would constitute an unfair exploitation of the adviser's status, or if it would deter him from giving general advice.

Hence, in the context of pure economic loss, traditional tests such as foreseeability and proximity must be considered along with the question of whether it is fair, just and reasonable in the particular situation to impose the duty of care.

b) *Mary's claim against Pamela*
The facts of this situation contrast sharply with the previous one. Pamela had been asked to carry out a valuation of a specific object for a specific purpose. She knew, or ought to have known, that the bank would rely on her valuation when deciding whether to advance the loan to Mary. Even though she may have had no direct contact with Mary, Pamela should have foreseen that Mary would rely just as heavily as the bank on the accuracy of Pamela's valuation. Further, Pamela should have known the purpose of the investment, since there was only one purpose and it was clearly ascertainable from her instructions, namely the purchase of the yacht. This is in contrast to the previous situation where Olive, the auditor, did not

know what Mary had in mind in regard to her investment decisions when she relied on Olive's report.

These conclusions can be supported not only by reference to the general principles established by Caparo but also by reference to the analogous case of *Smith* v *Bush* (2) where the House of Lords recognised the existence of a 'duty situation' in the context of a negligent valuation of a house by a valuer engaged by the building society for determining a loan and where the purchaser had relied on the valuation to his detriment. The purchaser was an identifiable individual whom the valuer should have foreseen would be relying on his report for the specific purpose of buying the particular house. The necessary close degree of proximity was established, a degree which might be described as 'equivalent to contract'. Further, it was not unjust or unreasonable to impose the duty on the valuer because his liability was clearly determinate (duty being owed only to the building society and purchaser, and not, for example, to subsequent purchasers), and, further, imposition of liability would not amount to an unfair exploitation of the valuer's general status or deter him from giving professional advice: see further Horton Rogers (1989) Cambridge Law Journal at p367.

Finally, Pamela's disclaimer of liability will be tested by the requirement of reasonableness under the Unfair Contract Terms Act 1977, s2(2) and in the case of *Smith* v *Bush* a similar disclaimer by the valuer was found to be unreasonable and ineffective because of his expertise and close relationship with the party relying on his professional judgment. Consequently it is advised that Mary's claim against Pamela in respect of the £60,000 loss caused by the negligent valuation will not be defeated by Pamela's attempted disclaimer.

References
(1)   [1990] 2 WLR 358 HL
(2)   [1989] 2 WLR 790 HL

Question 7

Nigel started operating a saw mill in a small village. He has leased the premises for a ten-year period from Michael who had told him to be careful about the noise and dust. To complete a large order, he has had to work late at night for the last month. The noise prevented Joan, the wife of Ken who owns the market garden next to the mill, from getting to sleep at night. Nigel has installed the best wood dust extraction equipment available, but last week the equipment malfunctioned and blew dust over the village. Much of the dust settled on Ken's garden and ruined a large number of sensitive orchids which he was about to send to the flower market. Last night there was a thunder storm and lightning set fire to wood stored in the mill yard. Nigel had not had time to purchase any fire fighting equipment and, because of the way he had stored the wood, the fire quickly got out of control. It spread to Ken's property where it destroyed two tool sheds before the fire brigade brought it under control.

Advise the parties.

Suggested Solution to Question 7

General comment

Students tend to be very familiar with the tort of nuisance, because, like defamation in Question 3, it is a predictable topic in the average exam paper. However the challenge here is not merely to discuss nuisance but to distinguish it from other relevant torts such as negligence and *Rylands* v *Fletcher*. There is also the usual temptation to give a mini-lecture on the ingredients of these torts, rather than advise the particular client as to his/her rights by identifying the weight which the court is likely to attach to relevant factors disclosed by the facts.

Skeleton solution

Scope of negligence, nuisance and *Rylands* v *Fletcher*; factual application of tort of nuisance; licensing a nuisance; sensitivity of victim or victim's property distinguished from non-remote damage; liability for escape of fire; defence of Act of God; licensing an escape.

Suggested solution

The facts involve a number of indirect interferences with neighbouring land and consequently invite discussion of the scope of and relationship between the three relevant torts of negligence, nuisance and *Rylands* v *Fletcher* (1) (hereafter *R* v *F*).

The first issue is whether Joan has right of action for her loss of sleep. The tort of *R* v *F* is concerned with the escape of tangible things or natural products of tangible things, such as gas or electricity, but not noise, which is not a 'product' in this sense. Further it is doubtful whether noise can be said to 'escape' in the same ways as gas or electricity, fumes, etc.

It seems that Joan may be able to sue in both nuisance and negligence which are overlapping torts. Negligence will require proof of fault so it will be preferable for Joan to sue in nuisance because liability in nuisance is strict: per Lord Simonds in *Read* v *Lyons and Co* (2).

In order to sue in nuisance Joan must first show that she is either legal or equitable owner of the market garden property because the tort of nuisance is confined to the invasion of proprietary rights. As Ken's wife it is assumed that she has such an interest. Since she is complaining of interference with her enjoyment of the property a number of factors will be relevant in deciding whether a nuisance was committed. In her favour are the matters of location and duration; industrial noise in a small rural or suburban village is not as acceptable as in an industrial area, and the intensive nature of the activity for something like 30 consecutive nights must render it unreasonable on an objective viewpoint. Nigel was not being malicious in causing the noise, but nevertheless his selfish profit-making motives will not assist him in establishing reasonableness.

The only factor which may count against Joan is the question of why Ken did not also complain about loss of sleep, because if Joan had special problems about getting to sleep and a normal person would have been untroubled by the noise, then nuisance is not established: *Robinson* v *Kilvert* (3). But, assuming the point in her favour, it seems she will succeed in proving a substantial interference with her enjoyment of land because for this purpose the loss of just one night's sleep is a serious and substantial matter: per Lord Greene in *Andreae* v *Selfridge* (4).

Joan may sue Nigel, as creator of the nuisance, and also Michael, who leased the premises to Nigel knowing that noise is a natural consequence of using a saw-mill; licensors are liable for such permitted use and consequences: *Tetley* v *Chilty* (5). It might have been different if Michael had insisted on undertakings from Nigel not to use the mill at night since licensors cannot be expected to supervise the daily activities of licensees or prevent unauthorised activities: *Smith* v *Scott* (6).

If Joan can establish injury to her health as a result of the loss of sleep she will be entitled to damages; she will be entitled to an injunction preventing Nigel from using the saw-mill at night. The second issue is whether Ken can sue in respect of the damaged orchids. In addition to the actions in nuisance and negligence an action under the rule in *R* v *F* may also be relevant as the escape involved a natural product of sawn wood which Nigel had accumulated on his land.

In regard to negligence Ken would have difficulty proving fault because Nigel took reasonable care to prevent the escape of dust by installing the 'best wood dust extraction equipment available'; it may well be that Nigel was not responsible for the malfunction. Hence Ken is advised to sue in nuisance and/or *R* v *F*, where liability is strict.

In regard to whether the escape of the dust was a nuisance, an isolated or one-off escape may constitute a nuisance if it arises from a state of affairs, such as a factory site, and it is irrelevant that the escape was of limited duration if the state of affairs is continuing and not temporary: *Matania* v *National Provincial Bank* (7). Further, the sensitivity of Ken's orchids is not relevant to establishing the nuisance which existed by the time the orchids were covered in dust (dust had blown over the whole village): *McKinnon* v *Walker* (8) (also involving orchids!). This is in contrast to Joan's claim where any special sensitivity of Joan to noise was relevant to establish the existence of nuisance.

It follows that since the damage to the orchids was the non-remote consequence of the nuisance Ken will be entitled to compensation for such damage, but not for loss of prospective profits from their sale, which was uncertain and not reasonably foreseeable. The principles of remoteness in the tort of negligence apply equally to actions in nuisance: dicta in the *Wagon Mound (No 2)* (9). Ken can sue both Nigel and Michael. Ken can also sue under *R* v *F* (considered below), though the choice of action will make no difference to assessment of loss. The third issue is whether Ken can sue for the damage to the tool sheds caused by the escape of fire. Special rules have developed in regard to fire, which today is best dealt with under the tort of *R* v *F* which imposes strict liability for non-natural use of land involving the escape onto neighbouring property of things likely to do harm. (Hence the escape of wood dust is also caught by the rule). It is a defence under the Fires Prevention Act 1774 to show that a fire had accidentally begun on a person's premises but it had been held that this defence does not apply to claims under the rule in *R* v *F*: *Musgrove* v *Pandelis* (10). It is debatable whether today the defence of Act of God covers a common, predictable event such as a thunderstorm but even if it does the defence is lost if negligence also contributed to the escape of the fire: *Goldman* v *Hargrave* (11). On the facts Nigel was negligent for the way he stored the wood and the lack of fire-fighting equipment. It is advised that Ken can sue Nigel under *R* v *F* or in negligence, but that he cannot sue Michael under *R* v *F* because licensors are regarded as having insufficient direct control over the occupier's acts or omissions which have given rise to the escape: per Pennycuick V-C in *Smith* v *Scott* (though there are earlier conflicting authorities which have allowed licensors to be sued for an escape in the same way as being sued for licensing a nuisance; on balance the modern authority of Pennycuick V-C is preferred here).

References

(1)   (1868) LR 3 HL 330
(2)   [1947] AC 156 HL
(3)   (1889) 41 Ch D 88 CA
(4)   [1938] Ch 1 CA

(5)   [1986] 1 All ER 633
(6)   [1973] 3 All ER 645
(7)   [1936] 2 All ER 633
(8)   (1951) 3 DLR 577
(9)   [1966] 2 All ER 709 PC
(10)   [1919] 2 KB 43 CA
(11)   [1967] 1 AC 645 PC

Question 8

Mark is a first year student at Leek University. He has a ground floor room in a student block. Tom is a burglar who has been entering ground floor rooms on the campus for the last two weeks. Tom enters Mark's room through his open window while he is asleep. Mark wakes up, sees Tom and screams. Tom climbs out of the window, dropping Mark's stereo equipment which is badly damaged, and runs away. Paula, who occupies the next room, hears the scream, looks out of her window and sees Tom running away. Thinking that Tom might have injured Mark or stolen something from him, she climbs out of her window and runs after Tom. In the excitement of the chase Paula trips over a tree stump and breaks her leg. Tom reaches the exit road and looks back to see if anyone is following. At that moment he is hit by a security van belonging to Slipshod Security, which is being driven too fast by Richard. Slipshod Security have a contract to organise security for the university. They knew about the recent burglaries, but decided to take no special security measures other than alerting their staff to the problem. Simon, the security guard on duty at Mark's block, is deaf and did not hear Mark's screams.

Advise Mark, Tom, and Paula.

Suggested Solution to Question 8

General comment

This is the kind of problem question which sometimes causes confusion if it is not immediately apparent to the student what is required for discussion. A bungled burglary on a students' campus can tempt the student, under exam pressure, to discuss irrelevant issues such as the criminal law or the tort of trespass to goods (the latter is available in theory but consider whether it is usually practicable to sue a rogue!). Once attention is focussed on the 'true' defendants (the security firm) then the relevant aspects of the tort of negligence become perceptible, namely, the liability for deliberate harm caused by independent third parties; the forseeability of rescues and the application of the defences of volenti and ex turpi causa; the relevance of contributory negligence and so on. Sometimes students miss the opportunity to demonstrate their knowledge of these issues because they failed to spot them as being relevant! Such a pity! Thinking time is so important; even two minutes' calm reflection in the exam room would help overcome this problem, yet students erroneously believe that not a minute should be 'wasted' because there is so much to write down!

Skeleton solution

Mark v *Slipshod Security*: liability for acts of independent third parties; assumption of special responsibility; possible contributory negligence;

Paula v *Slipshod Security*: foreseeability of rescue attempts; was it a rescue or unnecessary interference? Volenti;

Tom v *Slipshod Security*: vicarious liability for negligent driving; is it against public policy to compensate Tom? Scope of 'ex turpi causa non oritur actio'; possible relevance of contributory negligence.

Suggested solution

a) *Mark*

Mark can sue Tom, the burglar, for trespass to goods but since it is not normally feasible to recover compensation from such a rogue (who is best dealt with by the criminal law) Mark would probably have a better chance of obtaining compensation for the damaged stereo equipment if he could sue Slipshod Security (SS) for negligence in safeguarding the campus from burglars.

In the law of tort there is no duty to prevent an independent third party from causing deliberate harm unless there is a special relationship in which one party accepts responsibility to another party for protecting him from the activities of a harmful third party: per Lord Goff in *Smith* v *Littlewoods* (1).

In the present problem SS had assumed a contractual responsibility to the university to organise security, but Mark is not a party to the contract and cannot sue under it. Can he sue in tort? The assumption of special responsibility for the acts of third parties depends on the degree of control and the degree of dependence existing in the relationship between a plaintiff and defendant. A sufficient degree of control exercised by the defendant and a sufficient degree of dependence of the plaintiff on the proper exercise of such control will give rise to the special relationship required by the law of tort; an example was the liability of the prison officers to local residents for the escape of the juvenile offenders whilst out on exercise in the *Dorset Yacht* case (2).

In the present case it is advised that the necessary degree of proximity existed between Mark and SS because SS had the ability to control security on the campus and had been alerted to the recent spate of ground floor burglaries; Mark was a ground floor resident at special risk. In *Dorset Yacht* it was suggested that a high degree of foreseeability is required to impose the duty of care on a party for the acts of independent third parties, but this was doubted in the later case of *Smith* v *Littlewoods*. Even if a high degree of foreseeability is required it is advised that the requirement is met on the facts given.

Since SS failed to take extra security measures to safeguard ground floor residents and also because of their failure to provide a suitable security guard at Mark's block (a deaf security guard is surely prima facie unsuitable), there should be no difficulty in establishing breach of the duty of care to Mark.

It is debatable whether Mark was contributorily negligent in leaving his window open when he must have been aware of the recent burglaries from ground floor rooms; if it was summertime or the room was always stuffy there would be a good excuse for leaving the window open. It is advised that it is unlikely that a reduction in Mark's award against SS will be made.

b) *Paula*

It follows from the advice to Mark, above, that SS had negligently created a situation in which a burglary might take place. A burglary creates a foreseeable risk that an occupier might be physically harmed by the burglar; it is also foreseeable that upon discovery of the burglar a chase might ensue. Mark's scream suggested danger and invited a rescue. The issue is whether Paula can be classified as a rescuer to whom SS owed a duty of care.

If she had gone to Mark's room to assist him and fallen over on the way there would be no doubt that this would have been a rescue act entitling her to sue SS, who would have been unable to plead 'volenti' (assumption of risk) against her: principle of *Haynes* v *Harwood* (3) (it is irrelevant whether a rescuer acted out of legal or moral duty). But can her decision to give chase to the burglar be classified in the same way? Should she have left it to SS or phoned the police? By chasing after Tom was she knowingly and voluntarily assuming an unnecessary risk of harm to herself?: see *Cutler* v *United Dairies* (4) (plaintiff had intervened in a dangerous situation which did not pose immediate risk to anyone present; held that plaintiff had voluntarily assumed the risk of injury, was not a rescuer, and could not recover for personal injury sustained as a result of the intervention).

It is advised that although her chase attempt was reasonably foreseeable, SS will have a strong argument for the application of the defence of 'volenti' against Paula.

c) *Tom*

Tom can sue SS who are vicariously liable for their employee's negligent driving (it is stated as a fact that the employee, Richard, was driving too fast). However there is an issue as to whether the courts will permit the action to be heard. This is because SS may plead 'ex turpi causa non oritur actio', ie that since Tom was injured during an escape from his burglary attempt, he is a wrongdoer who ought not to be compensated for matters arising out of his wrongdoing, because to do so would be an affront to the public conscience and contrary to public policy: *Holman* v *Johnson* (5).

However in the present problem there was a distinct cause of the road accident, namely Richard's negligent driving, which by itself is unrelated to the particular wrongdoing. It would have been different if, for example, Tom had got into a getaway car and had been injured by the negligent driving of the getaway driver, because that incident would have been 'part and parcel' of his wrongdoing and public policy would forbid the recovery of compensation: *Ashton* v *Turner* (6). But in the present case it is suggested that the public conscience would not be shocked by an award to

Tom for Richard's negligent driving, since the incident was not inextricably tied up with Tom's wrongdoing.

There may be a case for reducing the award on the ground of contributory negligence since Tom was not watching out for vehicles when he reached the exit road. The fact that he forgot to look in the excitement of the chase is not considered a reasonable excuse. However any reduction under Law Reform (Contributory Negligence) Act 1945, s1 is likely to be comparatively small since the main cause of the accident was Richard's negligent driving.

References
(1)   [1987] 1 All ER 710 HL
(2)   [1970] AC 1004 HL
(3)   [1935] 1 KB 146
(4)   [1933] 2 KB 297
(5)   (1775) 1 Cowp 341
(6)   [1981] QB 137

DETAILS FOR DESPATCH OF PUBLICATIONS

Please insert your full name below

Please insert below the style in which you would like the correspondence from the Publisher addressed to you
TITLE Mr, Miss etc.   INITIALS   SURNAME/FAMILY NAME

Address to which study material is to be sent (please ensure someone will be present to accept delivery of your Publications).

POSTAGE & PACKING
You are welcome to purchase study material from the Publisher at 200 Greyhound Road, London W14 9RY, during normal working hours.

If you wish to order by post this may be done direct from the Publisher. Postal charges are as follows:

UK   - Orders over £30: no charge. Orders below £30: £2.50. Single paper (last exam only): 50p
OVERSEAS - See table below

The Publisher cannot accept responsibility in respect of postal delays or losses in the postal systems.

DESPATCH All cheques must be cleared before material is despatched.

SUMMARY OF ORDER   Date of order: | |

					£
			Cost of publications ordered:		
			UNITED KINGDOM:		
OVERSEAS:	TEXTS		Suggested Solutions (Last exam only)		
	One	Each Extra			
Eire	£4.00	£0.60	£1.00		
European Community	£9.00	£1.00	£1.00		
East Europe & North America	£10.50	£1.00	£1.00		
South East Asia	£12.00	£2.00	£1.50		
Australia/New Zealand	£13.50	£4.00	£1.50		
Other Countries (Africa, India etc)	£13.00	£3.00	£1.50		
			Total cost of order:		

Please ensure that you enclose a cheque or draft payable to **THE HLT GROUP LTD** for the above amount, or charge to ❑ Access ❑ Visa ❑ American Express

Card Number | | | | | | | | | | | | | | | | | | |

Expiry Date .... Signature ....

ORDER FORM

✂ cut along dotted line

LLB PUBLICATIONS	TEXTBOOKS		CASEBOOKS		REVISION WORKBOOKS		SUG. SOL. 1985/90		SUG. SOL. 1991	
	Cost £	£	Cost £	£	Cost £	£	Cost £	£	Cost £	£
Administrative Law	17.95		18.95				9.95		3.00	
Commercial Law Vol I	18.95		18.95		9.95		9.95		3.00	
Commercial Law Vol II	17.95		18.95							
Company Law	18.95		18.95		9.95		9.95		3.00	
Conflict of Laws	16.95		17.95							
Constitutional Law	14.95		16.95		9.95		9.95		3.00	
Contract Law	14.95		16.95		9.95		9.95		3.00	
Conveyancing	17.95		16.95							
Criminal Law	14.95		17.95		9.95		9.95		3.00	
Criminology	16.95						+3.00		3.00	
English Legal System	14.95		12.95				*7.95		3.00	
Equity and Trusts	14.95		16.95		9.95		9.95		3.00	
European Community Law	17.95		18.95		9.95		+3.00		3.00	
Evidence	17.95		17.95		9.95		9.95		3.00	
Family Law	17.95		18.95		9.95		9.95		3.00	
Jurisprudence	14.95				9.95		9.95		3.00	
Labour Law	15.95									
Land Law	14.95		16.95		9.95		9.95		3.00	
Public International Law	18.95		17.95		9.95		9.95		3.00	
Revenue Law	17.95		18.95		9.95		9.95		3.00	
Roman Law	14.95									
Succession	17.95		17.95		9.95		9.95		3.00	
Tort	14.95		16.95		9.95		9.95		3.00	
BAR PUBLICATIONS										
Conflict of Laws	16.95		17.95				†7.95		3.95	
European Community Law & Human Rights	17.95		18.95				†7.95		3.95	
Evidence	17.95		17.95				14.95		3.95	
Family Law	17.95		18.95				14.95		3.95	
General Paper I	19.95		16.95				14.95		3.95	
General Paper II	19.95		16.95				14.95		3.95	
Law of International Trade	17.95		16.95				14.95		3.95	
Practical Conveyancing	17.95		16.95				14.95		3.95	
Procedure	19.95		16.95				14.95		3.95	
Revenue Law	17.95		18.95				14.95		3.95	
Sale of Goods and Credit	17.95		17.95				14.95		3.95	

* 1987–1990 papers only
† 1988–1990 papers only
+ 1990 paper only

HLT PUBLICATIONS

All HLT Publications have two important qualities. First, they are written by specialists, all of whom have direct practical experience of teaching the syllabus. Second, all Textbooks are reviewed and updated each year to reflect new developments and changing trends. They are used widely by students at polytechnics and colleges throughout the United Kingdom and overseas.

A comprehensive range of titles is covered by the following classifications.

- **TEXTBOOKS**
- **CASEBOOKS**
- **SUGGESTED SOLUTIONS**
- **REVISION WORKBOOKS**

The books listed above should be available from your local bookshop. In case of difficulty, however, they can be obtained direct from the publisher using this order form. Telephone, Fax or Telex orders will also be accepted. Quote your Access, Visa or American Express card numbers for priority orders. To order direct from publisher please enter cost of titles you require, fill in despatch details overleaf and send it with your remittance to The HLT Group Ltd.

CARAVAN
AND
CAMPING
BRITAIN & IRELAND
1999

Produced by AA Publishing
This edition published November 1998

© The Automobile Association 1998

The Automobile Association retains the copyright in the current edition © 1998 and in all
subsequent editions, reprints and amendments to editions

The directory is generated from the AA's establishment database, Information Research and
Control, AA Hotel and Touring Services

Maps prepared by the AA Cartographic Department
© The Automobile Association 1998

The contents of this publication are believed correct at the time of printing. Nevertheless,
the publishers cannot be held responsible for any errors or omissions or for changes in the
details given in this guide or for the consequences of any reliance on the information
provided by the same. Assessments of the campsites are based on the experience of the AA
Caravan & Camping Inspectors on the occasion of their visit(s) and therefore descriptions
given in this guide necessarily contain an element of subjective opinion which may not
reflect or dictate a reader's own opinion on another occasion. We have tried to ensure
accuracy in this guide but things do change and we would be grateful if readers would
advise us of any inaccuracies they may encounter.

Advertisements
This guide contains display advertisements in addition to the editorial features and line
entries. For further information contact:
Head of Advertisement Sales: Christopher Heard, telephone 01256 491544
Advertisement Production: Karen Weeks, telephone 01256 491545
Filmset/Reprographics by Avonset, 1 Palace Yard Mews, Bath BA1 2NH
Printed and bound in Great Britain by Gràficas Estella, SA, Navarra, Spain

Editor: Denise Laing
Cover Photograph Derwent Water, Brandelhow Bay, Cumbria

The Automobile Association wishes to thank the following for their assistance in the
preparation of this book.

AA Photo Library 14 (W Voysey), 16 (V Bates), 25a, 25b (V Bates), 26a (M Short),
26b (V Bates), 27 (A J Hopkins), 28/9 (V Bates), 30 (W Voysey), 30/1 (P Baker), 31 (V Bates),
32 (D Forss), 35b (V Bates)
Department of Agriculture, Dundonald House, Belfast 38a, 39a, 39b
Northern Ireland Tourist Board 3b, 8, 9a, 35a, 36a, 36b, 38b

A CIP catalogue record for this book is available from the British Library
ISBN 0 7495 1933 9 AA Ref 10187

Published by AA Publishing, a trading name of Automobile Association Developments
Limited, whose registered office is Norfolk House, Priestley Road, Basingstoke, Hampshire
RG24 9NY. Registered number 1878835

CONTENTS

Prize Draw
family weekend with the
Hilton Hotels directory   **Opposite the title page**

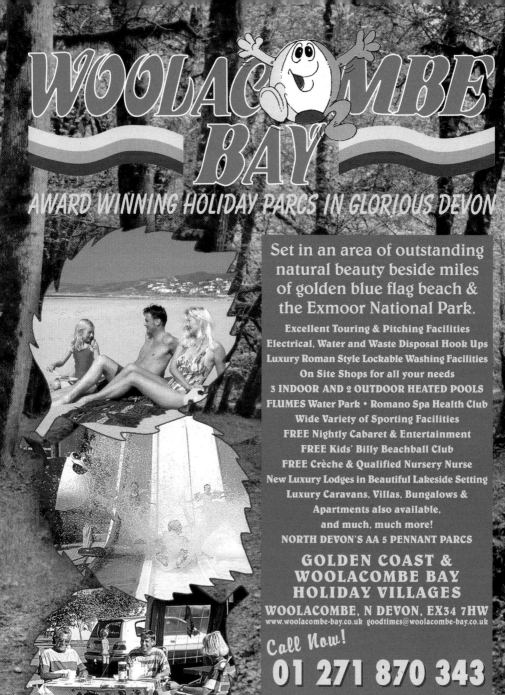

HOW TO USE THE GUIDE

Whether you are a newcomer to camping and caravanning or an old hand, it is probable that what attracted you in the first place was the 'go-as-you-please' freedom of being able to set off on the merest whim. However, in practice, especially during holiday periods, parks in popular parts of the country get dreadfully crowded, and if you choose somewhere off the beaten track, you may go for miles without finding anywhere.

When you do find somewhere, how do you know that it will have the facilities you need? How do you know whether they will be maintained to an acceptable standard? This is where you will find the AA guide invaluable in helping you to choose the right park. Please also read the section on the Pennant Classification Scheme so that you know what the classification symbols used in this guide mean.

The directory of parks is organised by county in England and Ireland, with locations listed in alphabetical order of location. Scotland and Wales, because of the many small counties, are divided into three regions: in Scotland, Highlands & Islands, Central, Southern Lowlands & Borders; in Wales, North Wales, Mid Wales and South Wales. The Channel Islands and Isle of Man appear between England and Scotland. Parks are listed in descending order of pennant classification. There is a location map for every county or region and the map normally appears after the county or regional heading; if it does not, there is a page cross reference.

Explanation of a Directory Entry

Town name
appears in alphabetical order within counties in England, within regions in Scotland and Wales

Name of Park
followed by 6-figure Ordnance Survey map reference. If park name is in italic type, details given have not been confirmed by the park. If the words 'Apply to' follow the map ref, this is the contact number for details and bookings.

Pennant Classification or Designation
See the section on the AA Pennant Classification scheme for an explanation of pennants. Parks with the highest ratings - four and five pennants - have highlighted entries, and so do Holiday Centres.

ANY TOWN

Pleasant Caravan Park SW8627281
Carnevas Farm PL28 8PN ac 01841 520230 Signposted
Nearby town: Padstow
➤ **Family Park** ⊕ £5 £8 ⊕ £5 £8 ▲ £5-£8
Open Apr-Oct lst Apr-Whit & mid Sep-Oct shop closed
Booking advisable Jul Aug A rather open site in a rural
settng near the North coast. Off B3Z76 Padstow-
Newquay road 2m SW of village. A 8 acre site with 195
touring pitches and 74 statics.
A working farm site with better than average facilities.
The very well converted farm buildings look purpose
built. Situated .5 mile offA389 on unclass rd to church.
A 3-acre site with 40 touring pitches.

🔣 🔣 🔣 🔣 🔣 🔣 🔣 🔣 🔣 🔣 🔣 🔣 🔣 🔣 🔣 🔣
🔣 🔣 🔣 🔣 🔣 🔣 🔣 🔣 🔣 🔣 🔣 🔣

Price Guide
for caravans, motor vans and tents. Not every park accepts all three.

Facilities
Symbols show amenities on site or (following the arrow) within 3 miles of the site. See the last page of the book for an explanation of symbols.

Credit/Charge Cards
See page 7 for the Credit/Charge Card symbols.

Important Note on Restrictions
In the caravan and camping world there are many restrictions and some categories of visitor are banned altogether. On most parks, unaccompanied young people, single-sex groups, single adults, and motorcycle groups will not be accepted. Most parks accept dogs, but some have no suitable areas for exercise, and some will refuse to accept certain large breeds, so you should always check with park before you set out. On the other hand, some parks cater well for teenagers with magnificent sporting and leisure facilities as well as discos; others have only very simple amenities. There is at least one park in this guide which does not accept children under 18 years old. Always telephone the park before you travel.

Special Offers
In the front of this book you will find a reply-paid card and details of how to enter our prize draw for a Luxury Weekend. Please don't forget to fill it in, with your name and address, and return it to us so that we can enter it in one of the draws.

Booking
It is advisable to book in advance during peak holiday seasons and at school or public holidays. Where an individual park requires advance booking, 'advance bookings accepted' or 'booking advisable' (followed by dates) appears in the entry. It is also wise to check whether a reservation entitles you to a particular pitch. It does not necessarily follow that an early booking will get you the best pitch; you may just have the choice of what is available at the time you check in.

The words 'Advance bookings not accepted' indicate that a park does not accept reservations. Some parks may require a deposit on booking which may well be non-returnable if you have to cancel your holiday. If you have to cancel, notify the proprietor at once because you may be held legally responsible for partial or full payment unless the pitch can be re-let. Do consider taking out insurance such as AA Travel Insurance to cover lost deposit or compensation. Some parks will not accept overnight bookings unless payment for a full minimum period (e.g. two or three days) is made. If you are not sure whether your camping or caravanning equipment can be used at a park, check beforehand.

Please note: The AA does not undertake to find accommodation or to make reservations.

Chemical Closet Disposal Point (CDP)
You will usually find one on every park, except those catering only for tents. It must be a specially constructed unit, or a WC permanently set aside for the purpose with adjacent rinsing and soak-away facilities. However, some local authorities are concerned about the effect of chemicals on bacteria in cesspools etc, and may prohibit or restrict provision of cdps in their areas.

Cold Storage
A fridge and/or freezer or icepacks for the use of holidaymakers.

Complaints
Speak to the park proprietor or supervisor immediately if you have any complaints, so that the matter can be sorted out on the spot. If this personal approach fails, you may decide, if the matter is serious, to approach the local authority or tourist board. AA members may write to:
The Editor,
The AA Caravan & Camping Guide,
AA Publishing,
Fanum House
Basing View
Basingstoke, Hants RG21 4EA.

The AA will look into any reasonable complaints from its members but will not in any circumstances act as negotiator or undertake to obtain compensation or enter into further correspondence. The AA will not guarantee to take any specific action.

Credit/Charge Cards
Most of the larger parks now accept payment by credit or charge card. We use the following symbols at the end of the entry to show which cards are accepted

Access/Masterchoice
American Express
Barclaycard/Visa
Switch
Connect
Delta
Diners

Directory
If the name of a park is printed in italics this indicates that we have not been able to get details or prices confirmed by the owners.

Electrical Hook-up
This is becoming more generally available at parks with three or more pennants, but if it is important to you, you must check before booking. The voltage is generally 240v AC, 50 cycles, although variations between 200v and 250v may still be found. All parks in the AA scheme which provide electrical hook-ups do so in accordance with International Electrotechnical Commission regulations. Outlets are coloured blue and take the form of a lidded plug with recessed contacts, making it impossible to touch a live point by accident. They are also waterproof. A similar plug, but with protruding contacts which hook into the recessed plug, is on the end of the cable which connects the caravan to the source of supply, and is dead.

These cables can usually be hired on site, or a plug supplied to fit your own cable. You should ask for the male plug; the female plug is the one already fixed to the power supply.

This supply is rated for either 5, 10 or 16 amps and this is usually displayed on a triangular yellow plate attached to source of supply. If it is not, be sure to ask at Reception. This is important because if you overload

Portable black & white TV		
50 watts approx.		0.2 amp
Small colour TV		
90 watts approx.		0.4 amp
Small fan heater		
1000 (kW) approx.		4.2 amp
One-bar electric fire		
NB each extra bar rates		1000 watts
60 watt table lamp		
approx.		0.25 amp
100 watt light bulb		
approx.		0.4 amp
Battery charger		
100 watts approx.		0.4 amp
Small refrigerator		
125 watts approx.		0.4 amp
Domestic microwave		
600 watts approx.		2.5 amp

the circuit, the trip switch will operate to cut off the power supply. The trip switch can only be reset by a park official, who will first have to go round all the hook-ups on park to find the cause of the trip. This can take a long time and will make the culprit distinctly unpopular with all the other caravanners deprived of power, to say nothing of the park official.

It is a relatively simple matter to calculate whether your appliances will overload the circuit. The amperage used by an appliance depends on its wattage and the total amperage used is the total of all the appliances in use at any one time. See the table on previous page.

Last Arrival
Unless otherwise stated, parks will usually accept arrivals at any time of the day or night but some have a

special 'late arrivals' enclosure where you have to make temporary camp so as not to disturb other people on the park. Please note that on some parks access to the toilet block is by key or pass card only, so if you know you will be late, do check what arrangements can be made.

Last Departure
As with hotel rooms and self-catering accommodation, most parks will specify their overnight period - e.g. noon to noon. If you overstay the departure time you can be charged for an extra day. Do make sure you know what the regulations are.

Maps
A map of each county, highlighting the locations, usually appears as near as possible to the county heading, or if one or more county maps have been grouped together, there will be a cross-reference under the county heading to the appropriate page. These maps will make a good first reference point to show you everything the AA lists in that county. If you have a specific destination in mind you can quickly see if we list any parks there, and if not, what alternatives there may be.

Please note that these are not road maps and have been designed to show you a quick overall picture of the county. When you are driving to a park, you must use a good road atlas - the AA publishes several - or the appropriate Ordnance Survey 1: 50 000 sheet map if the location is really remote. We give you the National Grid map reference (see 'Explanation of a directory entry', page 6) and outline route directions but space in the directory is limited and we cannot go into exhaustive detail.

Motor Caravans
At some parks motor caravans are only accepted if they remain static throughout the stay. Also check that there are suitable level pitches at the parks where you plan to stay.

Parking
Some park operators insist that cars be put in a parking area separate from the pitches; others will not allow more than one car for each caravan or tent.

Park Rules
Most parks display a set of rules which you should read on your arrival. Dogs may or may not be accepted on parks, and this is entirely at the owners' or wardens' discretion. Even when parks say that they accept dogs, it is still discretionary and we most strongly advise that you check when you book. Dogs should always be kept on a lead and under control. Sleeping in cars is not encouraged by most proprietors.

Most parks will not accept the following categories of people: single-sex groups, unsupervised youngsters and motorcyclists whether singly or in groups, even adults travelling on their own are sometimes barred. If you are not a family group or a conventional couple, you would be well advised to make sure what rules apply before you try to book.

Pitches and Charges
The number of touring pitches is included in the description. Charges given immediately after the appropriate symbol (caravan, tent, motorvan) are the overnight cost for one tent or caravan, one car and two adults, or one motor caravan and two adults. The price may vary according to the number of people in your party, but some parks have a fixed fee per pitch regardless of the number of people.

Please note that some parks may charge separately for some of the park's facilities, including the showers.

Please note that prices have been supplied to us in

good faith by the park operators and are as accurate as possible. They are, however, only a guide and are subject to change at any time during the currency of this book.

When parks have been unable to forecast their 1999 prices, those for 1998 may be quoted, prefixed by an asterisk. See also Directory above.

Campsites are legally entitled to use an overflow field which is not a normal part of their camping area for up to 28 days in any one year as an emergency method of coping with additional numbers at busy periods. When this 28 day rule is being invoked site owners should increase the numbers of sanitary facilities accordingly when the permanent facilities become insufficient to cope with extra numbers. In these circumstances the extra facilities are sometimes no more than temporary portacabins.

Rabies
Rabies warning: because of quarantine requirements (for instance, six months isolation for dogs and cats) it is not a practical proposition to bring an animal with you from your own or a foreign country on holiday to Britain. Penalties for trying to avoid this regulation are severe, and if you do have to bring an animal into Britain, you must have an import licence, obtainable from Ministry of Agriculture, Fisheries and Food, Hook Rise South, Tolworth, Surbiton, Surrey KT6 7NF. Tel: 0181-330 4411.

Restricted Service
Restricted service means that full amenities and services are not available during the period stated - for example a swimming pool or bar/restaurant may open only in the summer. Restrictions vary greatly from park to park, so you must check before setting off.

Shop
The range of food and equipment in shops is usually in proportion to the size of the park. As far as our pennant

requirements are concerned, a mobile shop calling several times a week, or a general store within easy walking distance of the park entrance is acceptable.

Signposted
This does not refer to AA signs but indicates that there is an International Direction Sign on the nearest main road, showing whether the park accepts caravans, tents or both. These signs have not yet been erected for all parks.

Static Van Pitches
We give the number of static van pitches available in the entries in our guide in order to give a picture of the nature and size of the park. The AA pennant classification is based on an inspection of the touring pitches and facilities only. AA inspectors do not visit or report on the fixed types of accommodation. The AA takes no responsibility for the condition of rented caravans or chalets and can take no action whatsoever about complaints relating to them.

Supervised
If this word appears in a directory entry it means that the park has someone in attendance 24 hours a day. Other parks may have less comprehensive cover.

Telephone
The telephone authorities are liable to change some telephone numbers during the currency of this guide. If you have difficulty in contacting a park, please check with Directory Enquiries.

Who and what *are* the
Best of British?

CARAVAN & CAMPING PARKS

We are currently a group of 39 privately owned prestigious Touring Caravan and Camping Parks who are all graded 5 ticks excellent by the Tourist Board, giving you your Guarantee of Quality.

We offer:
- A warm welcome from owners or staff at reception
- Attention to detail
- Scrupulously clean, award winning facilities
- Beautiful surroundings to pitch your caravan, autohome or tent
- At our larger parks all the leisure facilities that you would expect; our smaller parks naturally offer more tranquillity, but both will offer a relaxing quality family holiday.
- That extra 'sixth tick' giving just that bit more to ensure your stay, be it long or short, is a stay to remember and repeat.

- **Please see individual advertisements under relevant county**

From the lochs of Scotland...

1	BAINLAND	01526 352903
2	BEACONSFIELD FARM	01939 210370
3	BLAIR CASTLE	01796 481263
4	PARK OF BRANDEDLEYS	01556 690250
5	BRIGHOUSE BAY	01557 870267
6	BROADHEMBURY	01233 620859
7	BRYNICH	01874 623325
8	CENARTH FALLS	01239 710345
9	DRUM MOHR	0131 665 6867
10	FOREST GLADE	01404 841381
11	GART	01877 330002
12	GLENDARUEL	01369 820267
13	GOLDEN CAP	01308 422139
14	GOOSE WOOD	01347 810829
15	THE GRANGE	01206 298567
16	GRANTOWN-ON-SPEY	01479 872474
17	HAWTHORN FARM	01304 852658
18	HIGHFIELD FARM	01223 262308
19	HIGHLANDS END	01308 422139
20	HOME FARM	01248 410614
21	HUNTLY CASTLE	01466 794999
22	KENNFORD	01392 833046
23	LINCOLN FARM PARK	01865 300239
24	LINNHE	01397 772376
25	MERLEY COURT	01202 881488
26	NEWPERRAN	01872 572407
27	THE OLD BRICK KILNS	01328 878305
28	THE ORCHARDS	01983 531331
29	ORD HOUSE	01289 305288
30	PITGRUDY	01862 810001
31	POLMANTER	01736 795640
32	RAMSLADE	01803 782575
33	RIVER VALLEY	01736 763398
34	ROYAL UMPIRE	01772 600257
35	SEA VIEW INTERNATIONAL	01726 843425
36	TREVELLA	01637 830308
37	TULLICHEWAN	01389 759475
38	WILD ROSE	017683 51077
39	WOOD FARM	01297 560697

...to the heartlands of Britain...

...to the tranquil natural beauty of the east...

...to the mountains of Wales...

...to the rolling sands of the south coast.

The PRIVILEGE CARD

fantastic value at £10

...and gives you a **SAVING of £1 per night** off the tariff at any Best of British member park...

Any DAY Any SEASON

Available from any member park

Members Privilege

Beautiful Parks
Outstanding quality
Brilliant value

For an up-to-date brochure of all *Best of British* Parks please write to: Anthony Gent, The Paddocks, Little Barney, Fakenham, Norfolk NR21 0NL

THE AA PENNANT CLASSIFICATION SCHEME

The pennant classification scheme is based on annual inspection visits and incorporates both a facilities requirement and a quality requirement. The quality requirement is especially important at the higher pennant levels.

There is also a category of Pennanted Holiday Centres to represent those parks with a very high level of leisure and recreation facilities, which are able to provide a complete holiday on site. The Pennanted Holiday Centres must achieve a high level of quality before they are considered for this category. Please see the quick reference list on page 28.

How AA Pennant Classification Works

The pennant scheme is designed for touring holiday makers who travel with their own caravans, motor caravans, or tents. Our Officers visit Caravan and Camping parks to assess their touring facilities, but do not inspect any static caravans, chalets, or ready-erected tents available for hire on the parks. Although many of the parks in this guide will have static vans and self-catering accommodation, such accommodation is not taken into account for the pennant classification.

AA parks are classified on a 4-point scale according to their style and the range of facilities they offer, with a separate category for holiday centres which offer a complete on-site holiday.

As the pennant classification increases, so the quality and variety of facilities and amenities will be greater. The basic requirement for all Caravan and Camping parks in the pennant-classification scheme is that they reserve an acceptable number of pitches for the use of touring caravanners and campers, and that the facilities provided for tourers are well maintained and clean, and comply with our standards of classification. All parks receive an annual visit and report, and the pennant classification is based on this report. Many parks display a yellow and black AA sign showing their pennant classification, but not all parks choose to have one, and in some areas local authority regulations prohibit the display of signs.

Basic Requirements for AA Pennant Classification

All parks must have a local authority site licence (unless specially exempted) and must have satisfied local authority fire regulations. Parks at the higher pennant classifications must also comply with the basic requirements, and offer additional facilities according to their classification.

Please note that campsites are legally entitled to use an overflow field - which is not a normal part of their camping area - for up to 28 days in any one year as an emergency method of coping with additional numbers at busy periods. When this 28-day rule is being invoked, site owners must increase the numbers of sanitary facilities accordingly when these become insufficient to cope with the extra numbers.

Town and Country Pennant Parks

These offer a simple standard of facilities, and sometimes only drinking water and chemical waste disposal for the really self-contained caravanner. Other parks in this category are well-equipped with toilets, washbasins and showers, and might also have a reception area and dish-washing facilities. You are advised to check with individual sites at the time of booking to make sure they satisfy your own personal requirements. All Town and Country Pennant Parks should offer the following:
* Maximum 30 pitches per campable acre
* At least 10 feet between units
* Urgent telephone numbers signed
* Whereabouts of an emergency telephone shown
* First aid box

ANY TOWN

Pleasant Caravan Park SW8627281
Carnevas Farm PL28 8PN ac 01841 520230 Signposted
Nearby town: Padstow
▶▶ Town & Country Pennant Park 🚐 £5 £8 🚐 £5 £8
Open Apr-Oct lst Apr-Whit & mid Sep-Oct shop closed
Booking advisable Jul Aug.
Off B3Z76 Padstow-Newquay road 2m SW of village. *A working farm site with better than average facilities. The very well converted farm buildings look purpose built. Situated .5 mile offA389 on unclass rd to church. A 3-acre site with 40 touring pitches.*

🔧🏠🎁🐕✕ 🦮🔌🔦🛒⛵🌳🏕️🎣📷🏳️
📺 M ⚙️ T 🏔️ 🚭 🛒 🔫 ♒ PO

3-Pennant Family Parks

In addition to meeting all of the Town and Country Park requirements, 3-Pennant Family Parks guarantee a greater degree of comfort, with modern or modernised toilet blocks offering an ideal minimum of two washbasins and two toilets per 30 pitches per sex. Toilet facilities should include:
* Hot water to washbasins and showers
* Mirrors, shelves and hooks
* Shaver/hairdryer points
* Lidded waste bins in ladies toilets
* Uncracked toilet seats with lids
* Soap and hand dryer/towels
* A reasonable number of modern cubicled showers
* All-night internal lighting.

Family Parks must have evenly surfaced roads and paths, some electric hook-ups, and some level ground suitable for motor caravans. Buildings, facilities, services and park grounds should be cleaned and maintained to a high standard.

In addition to the above, these parks will ideally offer a laundry with drying facilities, separate from the toilets, and a children's playground with some equipment, fenced and away from danger. Details of nearest shops/chemist should be posted.

ANY TOWN

Pleasant Caravan Park SW8627281
Carnevas Farm PL28 8PN ac 01841 520230 Signposted
Nearby town: Padstow
▶▶▶ Family Park 🚐 £5 £8 🚐 £5 £8 ▲ £5-£8
Open Apr-Oct lst Apr-Whit & mid Sep-Oct shop closed
Booking advisable Jul Aug. Off B3Z76 Padstow-Newquay road 2m SW of village. *A working farm site with better than average facilities. The very well converted farm buildings look purpose built. Situated .5 mile off A389 . A 3-acre site with 40 touring pitches.*

🔧🏠🎁🐕✕ 🦮🔌🔦🛒⛵🌳🏕️🎣📷🏳️
📺 M ⚙️ T 🏔️ 🚭 🛒 🔫 ♒ PO

4-Pennant De-Luxe Parks

As well as meeting all of the 3-pennant requirements, 4-Pennant De-Luxe Parks are of a very high standard, with good landscaping, natural screening and attractive park buildings. Toilets are smartly modern and immaculately maintained, and offer the following:
* Spacious vanitory-style washbasins
* Fully-tiled shower cubicles with dry areas, shelves and hooks, at least one per 30 pitches per sex

Other requirements are:
* Shop on site, or within a reasonable distance
* Warden available 24-hours
* Reception area open during the day

* Internal roads, paths and toilet blocks lit at night
* 25 pitches per campable acre
* Toilet blocks heated October-Easter
* 50% electric hook-ups
* 10% hardstandings where necessary 4-Pennant De-Luxe Parks should also ideally offer a late arrivals enclosure, and some fully-serviced toilet cubicles.

ANY TOWN

Pleasant Caravan Park SW8627281
Carnevas Farm PL28 8PN ac 01841 520230 Signposted
Nearby town: Padstow

▶ ▶ ▶ ▶   **De-Luxe Park** ⚑ £5 £8 ⚑ £5 £8 ⚑ £5-£8
Open Apr-Oct lst Apr-Whit & mid Sep-Oct shop closed
Booking advisable Jul Aug. Off B3Z76 Padstow-
Newquay road 2m SW of village.
*A working farm site with better than average facilities.
The well converted farm buildings look purpose built.
Situated .5 mile off A389. A 3-acre site.*

🛊 🏦 🏠 🍴 ✗ 🛁 🔌 🎣 🏋 ∪ 🐾 🐓 🗑 🗝
🗑 Ⓜ ☾ Ⓣ 🏠 🚌 🚗 ♨ ♨ 🅿

5-Pennant Premier Parks

All parks in this category are of an award-winning standard, and are set in attractive surroundings with superb landscaping. They must offer some fully-serviced pitches or first-class cubicled washing facilities to the ratio of one per 20 pitches per sex; most pitches should also offer electric hook-ups. These top-quality parks will ideally but not necessarily offer, in addition to the above:
* a heated swimming pool (outdoor, indoor or both)
* a clubhouse with some entertainment
* a well-equipped shop

ANY TOWN

Pleasant Caravan Park SW8627281
Carnevas Farm PL28 8PN ac 01841 520230 Signposted
Nearby town: Padstow

▶ ▶ ▶ ▶ ▶   **Premier Park** ⚑ £5 £8 ⚑ £5 £8 ⚑ £5-£8
Open Apr-Oct lst Apr-Whit & mid Sep-Oct shop closed
Booking advisable Jul Aug. Off B3Z76 Padstow-
Newquay road .
*A working farm site with better than average facilities.
The very well converted farm buildings look purpose
built. Situated .5 mile off A389 A 3-acre site .*

🛊 🏦 🏠 🍴 ✗ 🛁 🔌 🎣 🏋 ∪ 🐾 🐓 🗑 🗝
🗑 Ⓜ ☾ Ⓣ 🏠 🚌 🚗 ♨ ♨ 🅿

* a cafe or restaurant and a bar
* decent indoor and outdoor leisure facilities for young people
* a designated dog-walking area if dogs accepted.

Pennanted Holiday Centres
In this separate category we distinguish parks which offer a wide range of on-site sports, leisure,

entertainment and recreational facilities. Supervision and security are of a very high level, and there is a choice of eating outlets. Any touring facilities must be of equal importance to statics, with a maximum density of 25 pitches per acre; toilets should be of a very good quality. Holiday-makers staying on these parks have no need to look elsewhere for their amusements.

ANY TOWN

Pleasant Caravan Park SW8627281
Carnevas Farm PL28 8PN ac 01841 520230
Signposted Nearby town: Padstow

⚑ £5 £8 ⚑ £5 £8 ⚑ £5-£8
Open Apr-Oct lst Apr-Whit & mid Sep-Oct shop closed
Booking advisable Jul Aug. Off B3Z76 Padstow-
Newquay road 2m SW of village. *A working farm site
with better than average facilities. The very well
converted farm buildings look purpose built. Situated .5
mile offA389 on unclass rd to church. A 3-acre site with
40 touring pitches.*

🛊 🏦 🏠 🍴 ✗ 🛁 🔌 🎣 🏋 ∪ 🐾 🐓 🗑 🗝
🗑 Ⓜ ☾ Ⓣ 🏠 🚌 🚗 ♨ ♨ 🅿

ISLAND CAMPING

SCOTLAND

The Shetland Islands

These are the farthest-flung outpost of the British Isles, taking 14 hours to reach by boat from Aberdeen. The archipelago of Shetland consists of over 100 islands and skerries (reefs of rock), though only 15 are permanently inhabited.

Campers and caravanners are welcome, the only restrictions being on Noss and Fair Isle, and the Tresta Links in Fetlar, where camping is not allowed at all. Elsewhere there are four official campsites, but visitors can stray into the wilds, provided that they seek permission to stay from the owner of the land. Caravans and motor caravans must stick to the public roads.

Camping 'Böds' are a good way of seeing Shetland on a budget as long as you don't mind a unisex dormitory. Some have no electricity, and none has hot water. You need your own sleeping bag and bed roll, camping stove and cooking utensils. What you get is a toilet, table and benches, and a roof over your head.

The Orkney Islands

Closer to the mainland of Scotland, the Orkneys are far less rugged and wild than the Shetlands. There are no restrictions on access for camping and caravanning, and plenty of beautiful spots to pitch camp.

Only on the tiny island of Fair Isle between Shetland and Orkney is camping not allowed, and there is no car ferry.

The Western Isles (Outer Hebrides)

These are a group of over 200 islands - only 13 of them inhabited - linked by a network of ferries and causeways. Most of the population

live on Lewis, with Harris, home of the famous tweed, being another major centre. That leaves miles and miles of spectacular mountains, golden beaches and rolling hills to explore. There are official campsites, but 'wild' camping is allowed within reason, and with the landowner's prior permission.

The Inner Hebrides and Other Islands

Tucked in against the mainland behind North and South Uist is that most nostalgic of islands, Skye. With its sister isles of Rhum and Eigg, it remains as atmospheric as when Bonnie Prince Charlie fled over the sea. These days he could also take the road bridge from Kyle of Lochalsh, which is less romantic, but there is still a car ferry from Mallaig for those who prefer to make a more traditional crossing. No such ferry goes to Rhum and Eigg, so the only camping possible is for the backpacker.

The Isle of Bute is tucked into the west coast of Scotland only 30 miles from Glasgow. Official camping is permitted at Rothesay.

The islands of Mull, Islay, Coll and Arran have official campsites, and caravan and motor caravans are welcome as are tenters. Offsite camping is also allowed , provided the usual permission is sought. Iona is car-free, and a backpackers' paradise, while Tiree does not accept either caravans or motor caravans, and has no official sites.

Colonsay and Cumbrae allow no camping or caravanning, though organised groups such as the Scouts and Guides may stay with official permission; Jura and Gigha allow no camping or caravanning; Lismore bans caravans but permits camping, although there are no official sites and few suitable places anyway.

(contd. on p16)

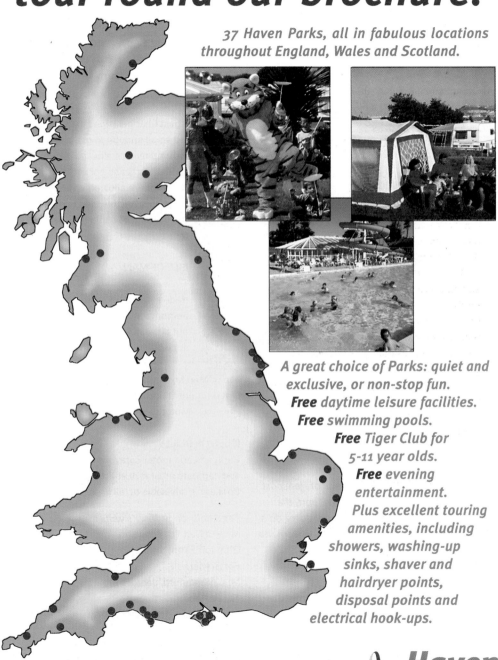

THE CHANNEL ISLANDS

The tightest controls are on the Channel Islands, because of the narrowness of the mainly rural roads. On all the Channel Islands you can hire tents on recognised campsites.

Jersey

On this, the largest of the islands, visitors are not allowed to bring either caravans or motor caravans, but tents and trailer tents are allowed, as long as you stay on a recognised campsite, and booking is strongly advised during July and August.

Guernsey

The same rules apply as on Jersey, except that motor caravans are allowed under certain strict conditions.

1. You must apply for and receive a permit in advance.
2. You may not use your motor caravan for sleeping but merely as a means of transport.
3. When not being used for transport, the motor caravan must be left under cover on a camping park with prior permission from the owner.

Herm and Sark

These two small islands are traffic-free. Sark is not part of the UK but the smallest independent state in the commonwealth. Herm is privately owned, with one hotel, a few shops and pubs, a handful of self-catering cottages and a small campsite. You can either hire a tent or pitch your own. Sark has three campsites and offers a more dramatic landscape. New arrivals are met off the boat by a tractor to carry both themselves and their luggage up the steep hill from the harbour. After that all travel is by foot, on bicycle, or by horse and cart.

Alderney

The third largest Channel Island is the closest to France and small enough to get around on foot for those who relish a slow pace of life. As on Jersey, neither caravans nor motor caravans are allowed and campers must have a confirmed booking on the one official camp site before they arrive.

ISLE OF MAN

Trailer caravans are only allowed for trade shows and exhibitions, or for demonstration purposes. They must not be used for living in. Written application for permission must be made to the Secretary, Planning Committee, Isle of Man Local Government Board, The Government Offices, Murray House, Mount Havelock. Motor caravans are permitted.

ISLES OF SCILLY

Caravans and motor caravans are not allowed, and campers must stay at licensed sites. Booking is advisable on all sites.

For details on St Mary's write to:
Mr and Mrs Ted Moulson,
Garrison Farm, St Mary's.
For Bryher:
Mrs J Stedeford, Jenford Bryer.
For St Agnes:
Mrs S J Hicks, Troy Town, St Agnes.
For St Martin's:
Mr C A Savill, Middletown, St Martin's.
Please note that strict control is kept on the landing of animals on these islands.

CAMPSITE
OF THE
YEAR AWARD
1998-1999

Our winners of the prestigious Campsite of the Year Award this year are a diverse and disparate collection of parks. Each in its own very special way has succeeded in blending a unique brew of quality, service and those many ingredients which go to make a holiday pleasurable and relaxing. Every one of them has already been marked out as distinguished, either because of its particularly enviable setting, its commendable selection of leisure and sporting activities, or its first class toilet and laundry facilities. Sometimes all three. We bring these winners to readers of this guide without any reservations, in the confident belief that your stay on any or all of them will confirm our judgement.

CAMPSITE
OF THE YEAR

NATIONAL AWARD WINNER

Merley Court Touring Park, Wimborne Minster, Dorset

Enter the precincts of Merley Court Touring Park and experience that satisfying glow that comes from having picked a winner. There is a reassuring excellence about this park that is immediately apparent from the well-kept landscaped grounds which open up beyond the imposing entrance. Once inside the park visitors can relax in the sure knowledge that everything will be just as they dreamt it might be. This sophisticated holiday park is one of the best equipped in the country, with tastefuly designed buildings offering immaculately-kept facilities. The Wright family take enormous pride in their high standards, and whilst their perfectionism might keep them constantly on their vigil, it means that their guests can unwind serenely and let the experts do what they are best at.

Ten acres of sheltered grassland and five acres of mature woodland comfortably envelop even the maximum number of allotted tourers without anyone feeling crowded. Tents can pitch within the woods or in the main areas as they choose, and there are plenty of fully-serviced pitches for caravans and motorvans, with large shrubs dotted about strategically for extra privacy. At this imaginatively planned park careful

consideration has been given to the needs of everyone, and there is an admirable variety of things to do, from swimming and tennis, to adventure playground and games rooms. A choice of eating outlets backs up the supply of food and other goodies in the shop, and evenings can be whiled away in the lounge bar or family room. Planned for the near future is a leisure garden which is being built on land adjoining the park. Will the restless Wrights rest on their laurels after that, and just enjoy the fruits of their labour? Our guess is, No!

BEST CAMPSITE FOR SCOTLAND

Springwood Caravan Park, Kelso, Roxburghshire

This attractive, peaceful holiday park shows little sign of the turbulent, bloody history which was enacted over a period of many centuries within its grounds. Nowadays the Springwood estate is home to a very respectable retirement village, and a caravan park which nestles quietly beside the trout-filled River Teviot. The two touring areas offer a delightful choice of remote seclusion and the slightly busier character of the riverside section close to the play area. Hundreds of acres of woodland and parkland are waiting to be walked through and enjoyed in this very rural park with its pleasantly relaxing atmosphere. Ownership and management is in the active and enthusiastic hands of the Elliot family who set and maintain standards that many parks could only imagine.

Springwood Park boasts a commercial laundry which takes the sting out of those tedious holiday chores, and the main toilet block offers combined toilet and shower cubicles in luxury surroundings. The historic ruins of Roxburgh Castle stand in the grounds, and for those who get tired of such countryside pleasures as are offered here, there are plenty of golf courses near at hand, and endless tourist opportunities in the Borders region. This gem of a site is the ideal centre for exploring the area.

BEST CAMPSITE FOR WALES

Brynich Caravan Park, Brecon, Powys

Set inside the National Park in the foothills of the Brecon Beacons, Brynich Caravan Park is a warm and friendly family site in wonderful natural surroundings. Such beautiful scenery as rings this touring centre takes some beating, and the Jones family who have farmed here since the Sixties have long capitalised on nature's gifts. There are boat trips on the Brecon and Monmouth Canal and the River Usk which form part of the boundaries of this park, and information is freely available on the many walks which can be enjoyed in this famous area. The Joneses understand that people come to the countryside in search of peace and seclusion, and they make spacious, sheltered pitches a top priority on their park.

The two camping fields are landscaped and attractively divided up by well-placed shrubbery, and from every part of the park there are those stunning panoramic views. Tarmac roads connect the sparkling luxury facilities with the camping and caravanning pitches, and the site is beautifully laid out for ease of use and to enhance its mountain setting. Nearby are many attractions and historical places of interest.

Lowther Holiday Park, Penrith, Cumbria

this proves to be a very popular activity with visitors.

Managing Director Sam Mackaness, ably supported by a well-qualified and devoted team, is sensitive to the needs of touring campers and caravanners, and strives to provide the best of everything. Toilet facilities are very modern and as spotlessly kept as you would expect on a park of this calibre. The Squirrel Inn is open all day for drinks, serving meals at lunchtime and in the evenings, and there are three adventure playgrounds, a games room and a supermarket to ensure that the needs of the whole family are met satisfactorily. All this, and the Lake District right on the doorstep offering many more recreational opportunities.

A long woodland drive, beside which fearless red squirrels can be frequently seen, leads from glorious Lake District countryside into this appealing, natural park. The level touring areas are well sheltered by mature trees, and the park is bordered by the River Lowther where fly fishing can be enjoyed on a day ticket along the park's two and a half mile stretch. A fascinating and important feature of this park is the conservation group which helps to preserve, among other things, the strong colony of red squirrels, and

BEST CAMPSITE FOR CENTRAL ENGLAND

Searles Holiday Centre, Hunstanton, Norfolk

More a small township than a caravan and camping park, Searles offers the ultimate in holiday entertainment based on over 50 years in the business of satisfying holidaymakers. Although this centre caters mainly for those renting static holiday homes, touring vans and tents are certainly not overlooked or ignored. Indeed the touring areas are extremely well equipped and elegant, and they are sensibly located apart from the statics and close to the long sandy beach which fronts the whole centre. Spacious level pitches are marked out with small shrubs and bushes, and the toilet facilities are kept to an impeccable standard.

The point of Searles, however, is the dazzling selection of entertainment, sporting and leisure facilities offered here, most of them radiating out from the town square at the heart of the park. An indoor swimming pool, fitness centre, shops, club, bar and restaurant are just some of these amenities, with fish and chip shop, tennis courts, large play areas, and even the centre's own riding stables. A full entertainment programme caters for young and old, day and night, and anyone staying here is unlikely to ever know a dull moment.

Carlyon Bay Caravan & Camping Park, Carlyon Bay, Cornwall

A touring park set in open meadowland, bordered by mature forest and just a few minutes' walk from an award winning beach on the Cornish Riviera needs little introduction. But Carlyon Bay does not just rely on its magical surroundings to entice holiday-makers to stay here. This top quality park is designed for the discerning visitor who rates cleanliness and order as highly as beauty and comfort, and is assured of getting all of these and much more besides. Run by the same family for nearly fifty years, our West Country choice offers a spacious and open atmosphere with some of the best facilities and amenities to be seen. The Taylors welcome their visitors personally, and go on to cater for their needs so successfully that complaints are almost unheard of.

While most people will spend their days on the beach or exploring the delights of Cornwall, there are plenty of first rate entertainments on site. A large heated swimming pool offers a warmer alternative to the ocean, and there is pool, table tennis, crazy golf and badminton. A large indoor complex called Ben's Play World speaks for itself, and children will delight in its many toys and games. What else? Oh, yes, a discreet and secluded naturist enclosure with its own facilities is located in the middle of the woods. Something for everyone, as they say!

BRITAIN'S BEST CAMPSITES

Listed below are all the parks with the AA's highest pennant rating and those nominated by our inspectors for the AA Campsite of the Year Awards for 1998/99. These entries are preceded by an asterisk* and details of the awards are featured on pages 17-24. Please see also the list of Pennanted Holiday Centres on page 28, and on page 30 the list of parks in this guide with David Bellamy Conservation Awards.

CORNWALL & ISLES OF SCILLY
Boswinger
Sea View International Caravan & Camping Park
Bude
Wooda Farm Park
Carlyon Bay
*Carlyon Bay Caravan & Camping Park
Pentewan
Sun Valley Holiday Park

CUMBRIA
Appleby-in-Westmorland
Wild Rose Park
Penrith
*Lowther Holiday Park

Windermere
Fallbarrow Park
Limefitt Park

DERBYSHIRE
Matlock
Darwin Forest Country Park

DEVON
Combe Martin
Stowford Farm Meadows
Newton Abbot
Ross Park
West Down
Hidden Valley Coast & country Park

DORSET
Chrristchurch
Hoburne Park
Wimborne Minster
*Merley Court Touring Park

HAMPSHIRE
Fordingbridge
Sandy Balls Holiday Centre
New Milton
Bashley Park

LANCASHIRE
Silverdale
Holgate's Caravan Park

NORFOLK
Huntstanton
*Searles Holiday Centre

NORTHUMBERLAND
Berwick-upon-Tweed
Ord House Caravan Park

OXFORDSHIRE
Standlake
Lincoln Farm Park

SOMERSET
Cheddar
Broadway House
Glastonbury
The Old Oaks Touring Park

SUFFOLK
East Bergholt
Grange Country Park

WIGHT, ISLE OF
Newbridge
Orchards Holiday Caravan Park
Sandown
Adgestone Camping Park

YORKSHIRE, NORTH
Harrogate
Ripley Caravan Park
Rudding Holiday Park

SCOTLAND
HIGHLANDS & ISLANDS
Aberfoyle
Trossachs Holiday Park
Corpach
Linnhe Caravan & Chalet Park
Fort William
Glen Nevis Caravan & Camping Park

CENTRAL SCOTLAND
Dunbar
Thurston Manor Park
St Andrews
Craigtoun Meadows Holiday Park

SOUTHERN LOWLANDS & BORDERS
Brighouse Bay
Brighouse Bay Holiday Park
Creetown
Castle Cary Holiday Park
Crocketford
Park of Brandedleys
Ecclefechan
Hoddom Castle Caravan Park
Kelso
*Springwood Caravan Park

WALES
MID WALES
Brecon
*Brynich Caravan Park

REPUBLIC OF IRELAND
COUNTY CLARE
Killaloe
Lough Derg Caravan and Camping Park

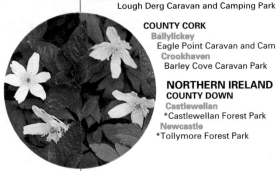

COUNTY CORK
Ballylickey
Eagle Point Caravan and Camping Park
Crookhaven
Barley Cove Caravan Park

NORTHERN IRELAND
COUNTY DOWN
Castlewellan
*Castlewellan Forest Park
Newcastle
*Tollymore Forest Park

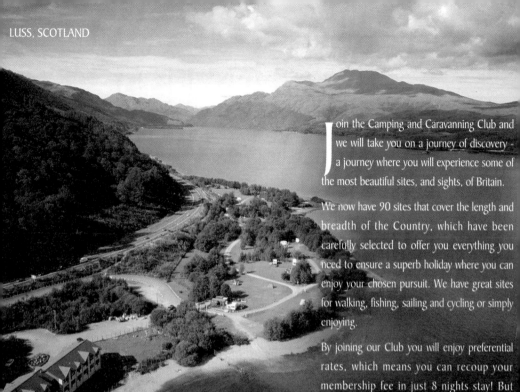

LUSS, SCOTLAND

Join the Camping and Caravanning Club and we will take you on a journey of discovery - a journey where you will experience some of the most beautiful sites, and sights, of Britain.

We now have 90 sites that cover the length and breadth of the Country, which have been carefully selected to offer you everything you need to ensure a superb holiday where you can enjoy your chosen pursuit. We have great sites for walking, fishing, sailing and cycling or simply enjoying.

By joining our Club you will enjoy preferential rates, which means you can recoup your membership fee in just 8 nights stay! But remember a vast majority of our sites are open to non-members.

THE CAMPING & CARAVANNING CLUB

Great Sites of Britain

YOUR MEMBERSHIP COMES WITH MANY MORE BENEFITS THAN DISCOUNTED FEES. AS WELL AS GUIDES TO THE GREAT SITES OF BRITAIN, WITH OVER 4,500 SITE LISTINGS, YOU'LL RECEIVE FREE A MONTHLY CLUB MAGAZINE AND GREAT DEALS THROUGHOUT THE YEAR, FREE ORDNANCE SURVEY MAP WITH ALL SITES PLOTTED AND OUR FREE GUIDE TO CAREFREE TRAVEL FOR OVERSEAS HOLIDAYS.

FOR A SPECIAL INSIGHT INTO CLUB MEMBERSHIP CALL

01203 856 797

QUOTE M9528 AND ASK FOR AN INFORMATION PACK.

Just one of our 90
Great Sites of Britain

Apply today and discover the Great Sites of Britain for just £27.50 per year (plus £4 joining fee*)

* Waived if you pay by direct debit or continuous credit card transaction

The Camping and Caravanning Club, Sites Department, FREEPOST (M9528), Coventry CV4 8JH

The Camping and Caravanning Club

The friendly Club

PENNANTED HOLIDAY CENTRES

Holiday Centres are in a class on their own, and must achieve a high level of quality and maintenance for their touring sections and leisure amenities to gain AA recognition. All those listed here have full entries in the directory. They have been designated as Pennanted Holiday Centres because they have a wide range of recreational and entertainment facilities to enable them to offer a completely self-contained holiday experience on site; they will also have high levels of supervision and security.
We must make it clear, however, that the AA does not inspect any static holiday vans or self-catering chalets, and these sections of the parks are outside the scope of our classification scheme.
Searles of Hunstanton at Hunstanton in Norfolk is the Winner for Central England of the Campsite of the Year Award for 1998/99. Please see the feature on page 23.

CORNWALL
Bude
Sandymouth Bay Holiday Park
Hayle
St Ives Bay Holiday Park
Holywell Bay
Trevornick Holiday Park
Mullion
Mullion Holiday Park
Newquay
Hendra Holiday Park
Newquay Holiday Park
Polperro
Killigarth Manor Holiday Estate
St Minver
St Minver Holiday Park
Whitecross
White Acres Holiday Park
Widemouth Bay
Widemouth Bay Caravan Park

CUMBRIA
Flookburgh
Lakeland Leisure Park
Silloth
Stanwix Park Holiday Centre

DEVON
Chudleigh
Finlake Holiday Park
Dawlish
Golden Sands Holiday Park
Paignton
Beverley Parks Caravan & Camping Park
Grange Court Holiday Centre
Woolacombe
Golden Coast Holiday Village

GLOUCESTERSHIRE
South Cerney
Cotswold Hoburne

LANCASHIRE
Blackpool
Marton Mere Holiday Village
Cockerham
Cockerham Sands Country Park
Morecambe
Regent Caravan Park

LINCOLNSHIRE
Cleethorpes
Thorpe Park Holiday Centre

Woodhall Spa
Bainland Country Park

NORFOLK
Great Yarmouth
Vauxhall Holiday Park
Hunstanton
Searles of Hunstanton

NORTHUMBERLAND
Berwick-upon-Tweed
Berwick Holiday Centre
Haggerston Castle

SUSSEX, WEST
Selsey
Warner Farm Touring Park

YORKSHIRE, EAST RIDING
Skipsea
Far Grange Park

YORKSHIRE, NORTH
Filey
Flower of May Holiday Park

SCOTLAND
HIGHLANDS & ISLANDS
Dornoch
Grannie's Heilan Hame Holiday Park
Nairn
Nairn Lochloy Holiday Park

CENTRAL SCOTLAND
Longniddry
Seton Sands Holiday Village

SOUTHERN LOWLANDS & BORDERS
Southerness
Southerness Holiday Village

WALES
MID-WALES
Tenby
Kiln Park Holiday Centre

REPUBLIC OF IRELAND
COUNTY KERRY
Killarney
Fossa Caravan Park

THE DAVID BELLAMY CONSERVATION AWARD PARKS

More than half of the 150 or so parks which have been distinguished by this innovative nature conservation scheme are also accredited with an AA Pennant rating. The awards are jointly organised by David Bellamy and the British Holiday & Home Parks Association, and recognise parks which make a positive contribution to conservation and the environment, such as recycling, landscaping, and waste management. Any small or large project which encourages wildlife to flourish makes parks eligible for an award, and we thought our readers would like to know which AA-recognised parks have been praised for their outstanding contribution to the environment. We list them here, alphabetically by location within county.

Cornwall

Maen Valley Holiday Park, Falmouth
Silverbow Park, Goonhavern
Croft Farm, Luxulyan
Mullion Holiday Park, Mullion
Penhaven Touring Park, Pentewan
Ayr Holiday Park, St Ives
Carnon Downs Caravan &
Camping Park, Truro

Cumbria

Skelwith Fold Caravan Park,
Ambleside
Cove Caravan & Camping Park,
Watermillock

Devon

Clifford Bridge Park, Clifford Bridge
Channel View Caravan & Camping Park, Lynton
Beverley Park, Paignton
Widend Touring Park, Paignton
Oakdown Touring & Holiday Home Park, Sidmouth
Ramslade Touring Park, Stoke Gabriel
Harford Bridge Holiday Park, Tavistock
Higher Longford Farm Caravan Site, Tavistock

Dorset

Rowlands Wait Touring Park, Bere Regis
Freshwater Beach Holiday Park, Bridport
Highlands End Holiday Park, Bridport
Golden Cap Holiday Park, Chideock
Sandford Holiday Park, Holton Heath
Beacon Hill Touring Park, Poole
Ulwell Cottage Caravan Park, Swanage
Merley Court Touring Park, Wimborne Minster

Essex

Waldegraves Holiday Park, Mersea Island

Gloucestershire

Cotswold Hoburne, South Cerney

Hampshire

Sandy Balls Holiday Centre, Fordingbridge
Doctors Hill Farm Caravan & Camping Park, Romsey

Lancashire

Mosswood Caravan Park, Cockerham
Claylands Caravan Park, Garstang
Regent Leisure Park, Morecambe
Holgates Caravan Park, Silverdale
Kneps Farm Holiday Park, Thornton Cleveleys

Lincolnshire

Foremans Bridge Caravan Park, Sutton St James
Bainland Country Park, Woodhall Spa

Greater Manchester

Gelder Wood Country Park, Rochdale

Norfolk

The Old Brick Kilns, Barney
Clippesby Holidays, Clippesby
Searles of Hunstanton, Hunstanton
Little Lakeland Caravan Park, Wortwell

Northumberland

Waren Caravan & Camping Park, Bamburgh
Haggerston Castle, Berwick-upon-Tweed
Ord House Caravan Park, Berwick-upon-Tweed

Shropshire
Stanmore Hall Touring Park, Bridgnorth
Mill Farm Holiday Park, Hughley

Somerset
Broadway House Holiday Caravan & Camping Park,

Cheddar
Westermill Farm, Exford
Halse Farm Caravan & Camping
Park, Winsford

Suffolk
Cliff House, Dunwich
Peewit Caravan Park, Felixstowe

Sussex, West
Southern Leisure Lakeside Village,
Chichester
Wicks Farm Holiday Park, West Wittering

Wight, Isle of
Heathfield Farm Camping, Freshwater
Orchards Holiday Caravan Park, Newbridge
Whitecliffe Bay Holiday Park, Whitecliffe Bay

Yorkshire, East Riding
Thorpe Hall Caravan & Camping Site, Rudston
Far Grange Caravan Park, Skipsea
Weir Caravan Park, Stamford Bridge

Yorkshire, North
Allerton Park Caravan Park, Allerton Park
High Moor Farm Park, Harrogate
Ripley Caravan Park, Harrogate
Rudding Holiday Park, Harrogate
Upper Carr Chalet & Touring Park, Pickering
Jasmine Caravan Park, Snainton
Wood Nook Caravan Park, Threshfield
Northcliffe Holiday Park, Whitby
Woodhouse Farm Caravan & Camping Park,
Winksley

SCOTLAND

Highlands & Islands
Glen Nevis Caravan & Camping Park, Fort William

Central Scotland
Trossachs Holiday Park, Aberfoyle
Blair Castle Caravan Park, Blair Atholl
Thurston Manor Holiday Home Park, Dunbar
Glendaruel Caravan Park, Glendaruel
Argyll Caravan Park Inveraray
Craigtoun Meadows Holiday Park, St Andrews

Southern Lowlands and Borders
Brighouse Bay Holiday Park, Brighouse Bay
Castle Cary Holiday Park, Creetown
Springwood Caravan Park, Kelso
Kippford Caravan Park, Kippford

WALES

North Wales
Bryn Cethin Bach Caravan Park, Abersoch
Bryn Teg Holiday Park, Caernarfon

Mid Wales
Disserth Caravan & Camping Park, Llandrindod Wells
Cenarth Falls Holiday Park, Newcastle Emlyn

READERS' INVITATION
– USERS OF THIS GUIDE

Nominate your Millennium Campsite of the Year

Every year, the seven AA Caravan and Camping Officers each nominate a park in their area as a candidate for the AA Campsite of the Year Award. All the nominations receive an independent visit, as a result of which the award winner for each region and the National Award Winner are chosen.

For the Year 2000 we would like to have nominations from our readers for AA pennant-rated parks or AA pennanted Holiday Centres, listed in the 1999 edition of the Caravan and Camping Guide. For this once-in-a-lifetime Millennium Campsite of the Year, your nomination should take environmental factors (does it fit into the landscape) into account.

Your nomination form will be entered in a Readers' Prize Draw.
Only one nomination form per household will be accepted.
Just award your marks out of 10 on the form overleaf and send it to:

The Caravan and Camping Editor,
AA Hotel Services, Fanum House, Basingstoke RG21 4EA.

To reach us not later than 30 May 1999. Don't forget to fill in your own name and address.

All entries that reach us before 30 May will be entered in a **Prize Draw** and the first 6 entries drawn will receive £25 worth of vouchers from a leading High Street Retailer. The draw will take place, and the winners notified within 14 days of the close date.

To qualify, your nominated campsite must be listed in this edition of the Guide.

I am nominating
(name of campsite)   _____

Address of Campsite   _____

                               _____

                               _____

AA Pennant Classification: _____

Please give your mark out of 10 for each feature below.
They are not listed in any particular order:

☐   Peace and Quiet

☐   Well Spaced and Well Screened Pitches

☐   Natural Screening and Landscaping

☐   High Standards Of Cleanliness

☐   Neat and Tidy Site (e.g. Grass cut, Rubbish disposal kept clear)

☐   Well Maintained Roads, Buildings with Attractive Exterior

☐   Facilities (e.g. Drinking Water Standpipes, Toilet Blocks,
     Waste Disposal, etc). within easy reach and generous for size of park

☐   Safe Children's Playground

☐   Attractive Reception and Entrance to Park

☐   Friendly, Efficient Management and Staff

Your name and address: _____

                               _____

                               _____

                               _____

**May we mention your name in any publicity for this award, and in the next edition of
this guide, as the nominator of the Winning Site?**   Yes ☐   No ☐

A COASTAL PARADISE

Exploring the Magical Coast and Forests of Northern Ireland

By DENISE LAING

The first thing you notice after crossing the border from the Republic of Ireland into the North is that almost nothing changes. The same greener-than-green hills and small, neatly hedged fields unfold all around, while the uncongested lanes and highways continue to make driving a pleasure. Later you will probably admire the province's smoother roads, its smarter towns and the general air of greater prosperity. But these cosmetic comparisons soon pale into insignificance when you realise that, as you travel northwards, the renowned warmth, kindness and natural hospitality of the Irish are qualities that also pervade the northern counties. Maybe it has something to do with attempting to overcome the world's prejudices, to counteract the belief that Northern Ireland is one big battleground. The truth is that most parts of the north have never witnessed sectarian violence, and, statistically, residents and tourists alike are safer than in most other parts of the world.

The North is Beautiful, Relaxed, Welcoming

The North is beautiful, relaxed, welcoming and well worth a visit, though the 'troubles' of the past thirty years have certainly scared off tourists. Even in May of 1998, as the people of Ireland prepared to go to the polls to vote overwhelmingly in favour of peace, foreign visitors were not very much in evidence. While tourist bodies work hard to reverse this situation and reassure people that the province is safe, it does mean that Northern Ireland is a very attractive place to visit without, at the moment at least, hordes of tourists to spoil its serenity.

Some factors across the border might jar, like the heavily defended police stations which lurk behind formidable wire or metal fences, but these are usually the only outward sign of

Come to the heart of Britain's wonderful woodlands for a holiday or short break.

Peace and beauty come naturally, all around you on our sites. There is an unhurried pace, with a chance to enjoy all kinds of outdoor sports and countryside activities, from hill walking to fishing, cycling to skiing or just enjoying the clean, fresh air.

We have almost 30 touring caravan and camping sites in scenic forest locations throughout Britain. From Balmacara on the Road to the Isles, to the New Forest, with a network of sites in between.

Brochure Hotline
0131 334 0066
Quote Ref. AA

Forestry Commission

the threat of violence. Memorials to soldiers killed in the two world wars are the chief reminder of what happens when neighbours fall out. In some nationalist or unionist strongholds, kerb stones are painted provocatively in red, white and blue, or green, white and gold, while the corresponding flags, tattered after long exposure, are flown in gardens and from telegraph poles.

Small is Beautiful

The province is very small - the size of Yorkshire - and most of it can be seen in a week or even less without clocking up more than 500 miles. Crammed into this relatively intimate area are enough different types of terrain to satisfy the most demanding tourist: several lakes and inland lochs, including the largest lake in Great Britain; a spectacularly rugged coastline that includes the Giant's Causeway; rolling hills looking out over serene farmland; and the deep and isolated valleys which cut into the coastal landscape to make up the romantic Glens of Antrim. Clearly, in spite of its smallness, this is not a place to rush through, but to savour, especially if you are lucky enough to have fine weather. Since this can change dramatically almost hourly, it is best to be prepared for all conditions.

Campsite of the Year for Northern Ireland

Campers and caravanners are very well catered for in Northern Ireland, with well over 100 parks of all shapes and sizes spread throughout the six counties. In our next edition of the Camping and Caravanning Guide - in the year 2,000 - we hope to introduce many more of these sites to our readers than we are currently able to include. This year, however, we would like to feature two outstanding forest parks which welcome touring vans and tents, and where some of the finest scenery imaginable can be enjoyed throughout the year.

Both Tollymore and Castlewellan Forest Parks, at Newcastle and Castlewellan respectively, are conveniently placed within easy driving reach of the ferry ports at Dublin (and Dun Laoghaire), Belfast and Larne; either makes an ideal first stopping place on a tour of the North. With only a few miles between them, the choice of which one to stay on might, in summer at least, be decided only by which one has vacancies. These forest parks are popular with walkers and climbers as well as campers and caravanners, and each offers four marked walks ranging between one and eight miles where visitors can vanish safely into remote and wildly beautiful countryside.

Tollymore Forest Park

The Mountains of Mourne, which famously sweep majestically down to the sea, rise up beside Tollymore Forest Park to form 48 peaks, including Slieve Donard, Northern Ireland's highest peak at 2,796 ft. This means the park offers panoramic views of both foothills and peaks, and the nearby sea is also clearly visible. It is not just the stunning setting which marks this park as special, however, even though it has long been admired as a beauty spot. The grounds form part of an old estate, once owned by a keen

florist and horticulturist who began to plant an arboretum with rare and lovely trees in the 18th century. His legacy has been added to and maintained, and today visitors are introduced by an avenue of imposing Himalayan cedars to the riches contained within the park.

The River Shimna wanders through the centre of the park, where it is crossed by several ornate stone bridges, many of which were built to commemorate friends and relatives of the various owners. Fishing is available by permit in season, with some hefty salmon being caught and recorded over the years. These can easily be spotted in the river's deep pools when the salmon are struggling up-water to spawn between June and November.

The camping and caravan parks are located at the end of the cedar drive near the main car park, and handily placed for the tea rooms. The facilities are housed in smart brown-stained wooden buildings, and Head Forester George Hanna sees to it that everything is kept spick and span even at the busiest times. Trees and shrubs offer

plenty of privacy if required, and there are open fields for tents, all with the same glorious views.

Castlewellan Forest Park

This similarly was a private estate until it was bought by the Department of Agriculture in 1967 and turned into a national amenity. The park is nearly as extensive as Tollymore, but this one is dominated by a large lake which is itself overlooked by a Scottish-style baronial castle, now used for retreats and conferences. This park boasts the presence of the National Arboretum, where magnificent trees and shrubs are set in landscaped surroundings with fountains, ponds, ornamental greenhouses and sweeping views.

The large open caravan and camping area is tucked away behind a series of Queen Anne courtyards, once part of a farmstead and now housing a coffee house and exhibition area.

Attached to this is the toilet building, where a new shower block has been provided courtesy of an EU Peace and Reconciliation grant. Picnic tables are sprinkled around the grounds and under trees, and barbecue areas help to make this an idyllic spot for the outdoor life. The Head Forester here is Sean Harrison who is a mine of information on the park itself, and can offer advice and guidance on how to make the most of the facilities and surrounding area.

Both of these outstanding forest parks are located on the coast of Co. Down, not too far away from the border with the Republic. Although many people will be tempted to linger here, finding enough to satisfy them in the nearby sandy beaches, the mountains and the forests, Northern Ireland has much, much more to offer yet. Still to explore are Strangford Loch with its amazing wildlife and birds, the coast and glens of Antrim, the causeway coast with the geological freak known as the Giant's Causeway, the Sperrin Hills and Loch Neagh, and the lakes of Fermanagh. And everywhere, because they are naturally friendly and kind, and because they want to put the record straight, the people of Ulster are ready with the warmest welcome which makes the spectacular scenery yet more memorable.

How to get there:
The quickest crossings from the UK to Northern Ireland are by high-speed ferry from Scotland to Belfast or Larne. There is also an overnight crossing from Liverpool to Belfast, and direct sailings from Wales to the Republic of Ireland. For details of ferries or flights, ask at a travel agents.

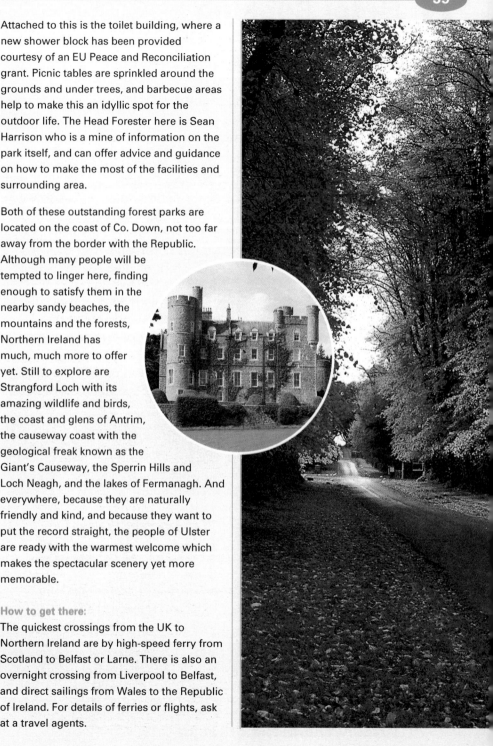

AA Hotel Booking Service

The AA Hotel Booking Service - Now AA Members have a free, simple way to find a place to stay for a week, weekend, or a one-night stopover.

Are you looking for somewhere in the Lake District that will take pets; a city-centre hotel in Glasgow with parking facilities, or do you need a B & B near Dover which is handy for the Eurotunnel?

The AA Booking Service can not only take the hassle out of finding the right place for you, but could even get you a discount on a leisure break or business booking.

And if you are touring round the UK or Ireland, simply give the AA Hotel Booking Service your list of overnight stops, and from one phone call all your accommodation can be booked for you.

Telephone 0990 050505

to make a booking.
Office hours 8.30am - 7.30pm
Monday - Saturday.

Full listings of the 8,136 hotels and B & Bs available through the Hotel Booking Service can be found and booked at the AA's Internet Site:

http://www.theaa.co.uk/hotels

Directory

ENGLAND

FORESTRY COMMISSION CARAVAN AND CAMPSITES

Forestry Commission sites which come within the scope of the Automobile Association's Caravan and Campsite classification scheme are listed in this guide. For a Forestry Commission brochure telephone 0131 334 0066. In addition there are entries for minimum-facility sites suitable for the camper or caravanner who prefers to be self-sufficient and carries his own chemical toilet.

ISLE OF

Places incorporating the words 'Isle of' or 'Isle' will be found under the actual name, eg Isle of Wight is listed under Wight, Isle of. Channel Islands and Isle of Man, however, are between England and Scotland.

BERKSHIRE

NEWBURY

Oakley Farm Caravan & Camping Park (SU458628)
Andover Rd, Washwater RG20 0LP ☎ 01635 36581 (2.5m S off A343)
► ► ► Family Park ★ ⚌ fr £6 ⚌ fr £6 ▲ fr £6
Open Mar-Oct Booking advisable bank hols
An open farmland site, well maintained and clean, S of Newbury. From rndbt S of Newbury on A34, take A343 Andover rd. About 300yds past Hants/Berks boundary bridge, turn left at car sales garage into Penwood Rd. Site on L. A 3-acre site with 30 touring pitches.
🔷 📞 ⊙ ▣ ⌑ ✳ Ⓐ ▮ ∅ ℃
→ ♨ 🝓

RISELEY

Wellington Country Park (SU728628)
RG7 1SP ☎ 0118 9326445 Signposted
Nearby town: Reading
► ► ► Family Park ⚌ ⚌ ▲
Open Mar-Oct Booking advisable peak periods Last departure 14.00hrs
A peaceful woodland site set within extensive country park, complete with lakes, nature trails, deer farm, boating and museum. Ideal for M4 travellers. Signed off A33 between Reading and Basingstsoke, 4m S of M4 junc 11. A 350-acre site with 70 touring pitches.
Boating & fishing.
🔷 📞 ⊙ ▣ ⌑ 🝓
→ ◎ ❄ ⌇ ♪

AA members can call AA Hotel Booking Service on 0990 050505 to book at AA recognised hotels and B & Bs in the UK and Ireland, or through our Internet site: http://www.theaa.co.uk/hotels

BUCKINGHAMSHIRE

For the map of this county
see BERKSHIRE

CHALFONT ST GILES

Highclere Farm Country Touring Park (SU977927)
Highclere Farm, Newbarn Ln, Seer Green HP9 2QZ ☎ 01494 874505 & 875665 (1.25m SW) Signposted
Nearby town: Beaconsfield
► ► ► Family Park ⚌ £10-£12 ⚌ £10-£12 ▲ £8-£12
Open Mar-Jan Booking advisable Last departure noon
A small farm park surrounded by pasture, and sheltered on one side by trees. Situated between Chalfont St Giles and Seer Green, 2m E of Beaconsfield. A 2.5-acre site with 60 touring pitches.
🔷 📞 ⊙ ▣ ⌑ ✳ Ⓐ ▮ ∅ ▣ Ⓣ ℃ 🛁 ⚲ 🐾 ⚹
→ ∪ ▶ ♨
Credit Cards 💳 ▬ 🔲 ⊙ 🔳 🔳

CAMBRIDGESHIRE

BURWELL

Stanford Park (TL578675)
Weirs Rd CB5 0BP ☎ 01638 741547 & 439997
Nearby town: Newmarket
► ► ► Family Park ★ ⚌ £7.50-£9.50 ⚌ £7.50-£9.50 ▲ £5.50-£7.50
Open all year Booking advisable bank hols Last arrival 20.30hrs Last departure noon
A secluded site on outskirts of Burwell with modern amenities including purpose-built disabled facilities. Signed from B1102. A 14-acre site with 100 touring pitches and 3 statics.
See advertisement under CAMBRIDGE
🔷 📞 ⊙ ⌑ ✳ Ⓐ ▮ ∅ ▣ Ⓣ ℃ ⚲ ⚹
→ ∪ ▶ ❄ ♪ ▣

See advertisement on page 44

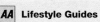

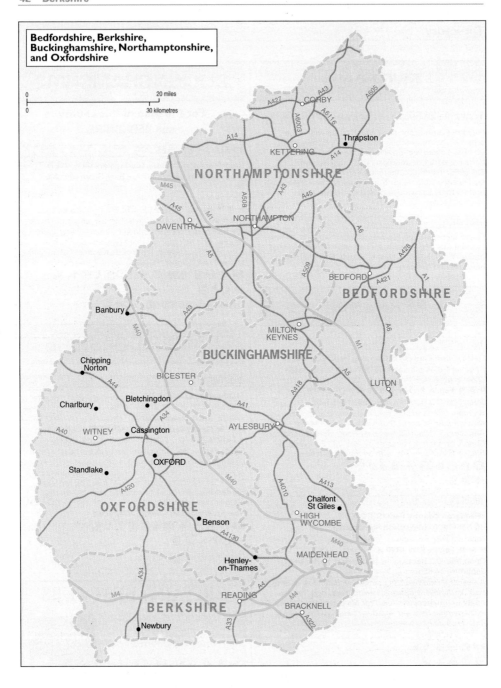

Bedfordshire, Berkshire, Buckinghamshire, Northamptonshire, and Oxfordshire

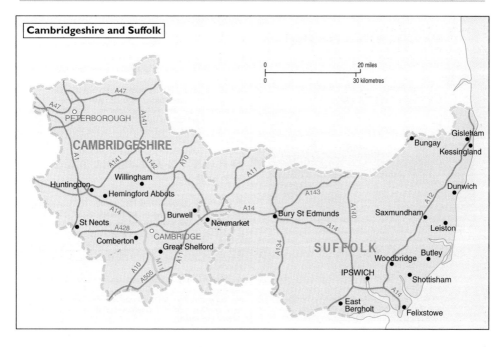
Cambridgeshire and Suffolk

Highfield Farm Camping Park

Comberton, Cambridge CB3 7DG
Tel/Fax: 01223 262308

A popular award-winning park with excellent facilities. Close to the historic university city of Cambridge, the Imperial War Museum, Duxford and ideally situated for East Anglia

Please write or phone for colour brochure

CAMBRIDGE

See **Burwell & Comberton and advertisement on p44.**

COMBERTON

Highfield Farm Camping Park (TL389572)
Long Rd CB3 7DG ☎ 01223 262308 Signposted
Nearby town: Cambridge

QQQQQQQQQ

► ► ► ► **De-Luxe Park** 🚐 £7.25-£8.50 🚐 £7-£8.25
▲ £7-£8.25
Open Apr-Oct Booking advisable bank hols wknds Last arrival 22.00hrs Last departure 14.00hrs
A first class site with good quality facilities, set in farmland and screened by conifers and hedges. 3m W of Cambridge between A45 and A603. From junc 12 of M11 take A603 Sandy road for .5m, then B1046 to Comberton. An 8-acre site with 120 touring pitches. Dishwashing facility, postbox & hardstanding.
See advertisement opposite

🔌 🐾 ⊙ 📷 🍳 ✳ ⚙ 🅿 ⊘ 🔲 🅣 📞 🐕 😊 🎱
→ ∪ ▶ 🎣

QQQQQQQQQ

GREAT SHELFORD

Camping & Caravanning Club Site (TL455539)
19 Cabbage Moor CB2 5NB ☎ 01223 841185 (in season)
& 01203 694995 Signposted
Nearby town: Cambridge

QQQQQQQQQ

contd.

STANFORD PARK

Cambridge ►►► AA

Weirs Road, Burwell, Cambs
Tel: (01638) 741547 & (0802) 439997

Conveniently situated at Burwell for visiting Cambridge, Newmarket and Ely. Several places of interest within easy reach, Wicken Fen National Trust, Newmarket Races, Ely Cathedral and Cambridge University. Camp site includes: modern toilet block with hot showers, hair dryer & iron, laundry room, electric hook-ups, fishing close by, disabled facilities. **Open all year.**

DISCOUNTED RATES FOR SEASONAL AND LONG TERM PITCHES

►►►► De-Luxe Park ★ ♥ £11-£14 ♥ £11-£14 Å £11-£14
Open end Mar-early Nov Booking advisable bank hols & Jul-Aug Last arrival 21.00hrs Last departure noon
An attractive site with good landscaping and excellent toilet blocks. From junc 11 of M11 take A1309, then R at traffic lights on to A309; site .5m on L. Please see the advertisement on page 27 for details of Club Members' benefits. An 11-acre site with 120 touring pitches.

🔌 ⌨ ⊙ 🗑 ⌇ ☀ ⚠ 🔋 ⌀ 🚽 📵 ✆ 🐎 ♿
➜ ⚓ ☕ 🐾

Credit Cards 💳 💳 💳 💳 💳

HEMINGFORD ABBOTS

Quiet Waters Caravan Park (TL283712)
PE18 9AJ ☎ 01480 463405 Signposted
Nearby town: St Ives
►►► Family Park ★ ♥ £8-£9 ♥ £8-£9 Å £8-£9
Open Apr-Oct Booking advisable high season Last arrival 20.00hrs Last departure noon
This attractive little riverside site is found in a most charming village just 1m from the A604 making an ideal centre to tour the Cambridgeshire area. Follow signs for village from A14. A 1-acre site with 20 touring pitches and 40 statics.
Fishing & boating.

🔌 ⌨ ⊙ ⌇ ☀ 🔋 ⌀ ✆
➜ ⛽ ⚓ ☕ 🐾 📵 🐾

Credit Cards 💳 💳 💳 💳 💳

HUNTINGDON

Park Lane Touring Park (TL245709)
Godmanchester PE18 8AF ☎ 01480 453740 Signposted
►►► Family Park ★ ♥ £8 ♥ £8 Å £8
Open Mar-Oct Booking advisable bank hols Last arrival 22.00hrs
Attractive little site with good facilities and a high standard of maintenance. Situated just off the A14 Huntingdon bypass. Follow signs into Godmanchester along Cambridge Rd then Post St, and turn into Park Lane by the Black Bull Inn. A 3-acre site with 50 touring pitches.
Enclosed dishwashing & preparation area.

🔌 ⌨ ⊙ 🗑 ⌇ ☀ ⚠ 🔋 ⌀ 🚽 📵 ✆ 🚿 ♿
➜ ⚓ ☕ 🐾

The Willows Caravan Park (TL224708)
Bromholme Ln, Brampton PE18 8NE
☎ 01480 437566 & 454961 Signposted
►►► Family Park ★ ♥ £7-£9 ♥ £7-£9 Å £7-£9
Open Mar-Oct Booking advisable bank hols, weekends & school hols Last arrival 23.00hrs Last departure 19.00hrs
A small, friendly site with a pleasant situation beside the River Ouse, on the Ouse Valley Walk. Leave A14/A1 signed Brampton, follow signs for Huntingdon. Site on right close to Old Mill (Beefeater) pub. A 4-acre site with 35 touring pitches.

🔌 ⌨ ⊙ ☀ 📵 ✆ ♿
➜ ⚓ ☕ 🐾 🐾

ST NEOTS

Camping & Caravanning Club Site (TL182598)
Rush Meadow PE19 2UD
☎ 01480 474404 (in season) & 01203 694995 Signposted
►►► Family Park ★ ♥ £11-£14 ♥ £11-£14 Å £11-£14
Open end Mar-early Nov Booking advisable bank hols & peak periods Last arrival 21.00hrs Last departure noon
A level meadowland site adjacent to the River Ouse on the outskirts of St Neots, well maintained and with helpful, attentive staff. Take B1043 N, crossing A428 into Eynesbury, cross small rndbt, then take first left. Please see the advertisement on page 27 for details of Club Members' benefits. A 10-acre site with 180 touring pitches.
Coarse fishing.

🔌 ⌨ ⊙ 🗑 ⌇ ☀ 🔋 ⌀ 📵 ✆ 🐎 🐾 ♿
➜ ⚓ ⛽ 🐾

Credit Cards 💳 💳 💳 💳 💳

WILLINGHAM

Roseberry Tourist Park (TL408728)
Earith Rd CB4 5LT ☎ 01954 260346 Signposted
►►► Family Park ★ ♥ fr £7 ♥ fr £7 Å fr £6
Open Mar-Oct Booking advisable bank hols Last arrival 22.00hrs Last departure 13.00hrs
A pleasant site in an old pear orchard, surrounded by peace and seclusion. Signposted between Earith and Willingham on the B1050. A 9.5-acre site with 80 touring pitches and 10 statics.

🔌 ⌨ ⊙ ⌇ ☀ ⚠ 🔋 ⌀ 🚽 📵 ✆ 🐕 🐎 🐾
➜ ⛽ ⌨ ◎ ⚠ ⚓ 🐾

CHESHIRE

For the map of this county
see SHROPSHIRE

CHESTER

Chester Southerly Caravan Park (SJ385624)
Balderton Ln, Marlston-Cum-Lache CH4 9LB
☎ 0976 743888 Signposted
▶ ▶ ▶ Family Park ⊞ ⊞ ▲
Open Mar-Nov (rs Dec-Feb open for caravan rallies
only) Booking advisable for periods of 1 wk or more &
bank hols Last arrival 23.00hrs Last departure noon
A well-tended site in rural area, on S side of city close to
the bypass, and just off the A55/A483 roundabout. An 8-
acre site with 90 touring pitches.
Duck pond & breeding cage.

🎦 📵 ⊙ 🖸 🖳 ✳ Ⅿ 🔋 🖉 Ⓣ 📞 🏪 🎣 🐾 ♿
➔ ∪ ▶ 🛆 🛉 🐾 ⌇ 🖊

KNUTSFORD

Woodlands Park (SJ743710)
Wash Ln, Allostovk WA16 9LG ☎ 01565 723307
▶ ▶ ▶ Family Park ⊞ ⊞ ▲
A very attractive park in the heart of rural Cheshire, and
set in 16 acres of mature woodland. 3m from Jodderel
Bank. From Holmes Chapel take A50 N for 3 miles, turn
into Wash Lane by Boundary Water Park, and site on
left in 0.25m. A 16-acre site with 50 touring pitches and
100 statics.

MACCLESFIELD

Capesthorne Hall (SJ840727)
Siddington SK11 9JY ☎ 01625 861779 & 861221
Signposted
▶▶ Town & Country Pennant Park ⊞ ⊞
Open Mar-Oct Booking advisable public hols Last arrival
dusk Last departure noon
Set in grounds and gardens of Capesthorne Hall in the
heart of the Cheshire countryside. The pitches are on
level ground close to the Hall, off the A34. Immaculate
toilets in old stable block. A 5.5-acre site with 30 touring
pitches.
Capesthorne Hall, gardens, fishing. Laundry room.

🎦 📵 ⊙ 📞 🐾
➔ 🖊 🐾

RIXTON

Holly Bank Caravan Park (SJ693904)
Warburton Bridge Rd WA3 6HU ☎ 0161 775 2842
Signposted
Nearby town: Warrington
▶ ▶ ▶ Family Park ★ ⊞ £10.50-£11.50 ⊞ £10.50-£11.50
▲ £9.50-£10.50
Open all year Booking advisable bank hols & wknds
Apr-Oct Last arrival 21.00hrs Last departure noon
Attractive site with spotlessly clean facilities. Just off
A57 close to the Manchester Ship Canal and convenient
to M6 and Manchester. From junc 21 of M6 turn E on
A57 to Irlam, in 2m turn right at traffic lights, and site
immediately on left. A 9-acre site with 75 touring
pitches.

Lending library.

🎦 📵 ⊙ 🖸 🖳 ✳ Ⅿ 🔋 🖉 ⊞ Ⓣ 📞 🐾 🐾
➔ ∪ ▶ 🛆 🐾 🖊

CORNWALL &
ISLES OF SCILLY

The total eclipse of the sun on 11th August at 11am is
expected to attract thousands of visitors to Cornwall
and Devon where this once-in-a-lifetime phenomenon
can be witnessed. While many extra touring pitches are
being set up over the period to cater for the sudden
influx, demand for places on parks listed in this guide is
bound to be dramatically increased. To be sure of
securing your holiday dates, please try to book well
ahead for the period around 11th August.

ASHTON

Boscrege Caravan Park (SW595305)
TR13 9TG ☎ 01736 762231
Nearby town: Helston
▶ ▶ ▶ Family Park ★ ⊞ £5.50-£11.50 ⊞ £5.50-£11.50
▲ £5.50-£11.50
Open Apr-Oct Booking advisable Jul-Aug Last arrival
22.00hrs Last departure 11.00hrs
A much improved site in an isolated rural area with very
good screening. From Helston take A394 signed
Penzance, turn right in Ashton on unclass rd, and follow
signs to Boscrege. A 4-acre site with 50 touring pitches
and 26 statics.
Recreation field. Microwave facility.

🎦 📵 ⊙ 🖸 🖳 ◀ 🚻 ✳ Ⅿ 🔋 🖉 ⊞ Ⓣ 📞 🍴 🏪 🎣
🐾 🐾
➔ ∪ ▶ ◎ 🛉 🖊
Credit Cards ⬤ 〓 〓 🅖

BLACKWATER

Chiverton Caravan & Touring Park (SW743468)
East Hill TR4 8HS ☎ 01872 560667 (jct A30/A390)
Signposted
Nearby town: Truro
▶ ▶ ▶ Family Park ⊞ ⊞ ▲
Open Good Fri/Apr-Oct (rs Apr-May & mid Sep-Oct
limited stock kept in shop) Booking advisable mid Jul-
Aug Last arrival 22.00hrs Last departure noon
A small, well maintained, level, grassy site recently laid
out and run by enthusiastic owners. Leave A30 at Three
Burrows/Chiverton rndbt onto unclass rd (3rd exit)
signed Blackwater. Take 1st right and site in 300yds. A
4-acre site with 30 touring pitches and 30 statics.
Covered sink area, drying lines.

🎦 📵 ⊙ 🖸 🖳 ◀ ✳ Ⅿ 🔋 🖉 ⊞ 📞 🐾
➔ ∪ ▶ 🛆 🖊

Trevarth Holiday Park (SW744468)
TR4 8HR ☎ 01872 560266 Signposted
▶ ▶ ▶ Family Park ★ ⊞ £5-£7.25 ⊞ £5-£7.75 ▲ £5-£7.25
Open Etr or Apr-Oct Booking advisable Jul-Aug Last
arrival 22.00hrs Last departure noon
A compact, well screened site on high ground adjacent
to A30/A39 junction. Leave A30 at Chiverton rndbt onto
contd.

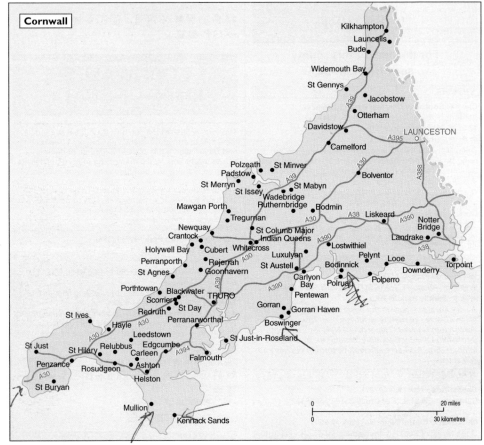

Cornwall

Kilkhampton
Launcells
Bude
Widemouth Bay
St Gennys
Jacobstow
Otterham
Davidstow
LAUNCESTON
Camelford
Polzeath   St Minver
Padstow   Bolventor
St Merryn   St Mabyn
St Issey
Wadebridge
Mawgan Porth   Ruthernbridge   Bodmin   Liskeard
Tregurrian   Notter Bridge
Newquay   St Columb Major   Landrake
Crantock   Indian Queens
Holywell Bay   Cubert   Whitecross   Lostwithiel
Perranporth   Rejerrah   Luxulyan   Pelynt   Looe
St Agnes   Goonhavern   St Austell   Bodinnick   Downderry   Torpoint
Carlyon   Polruan   Polperro
Porthtowan   Bay   Pentewan
Scorrier   Blackwater   TRURO
Redruth   St Day   Gorran   Gorran Haven
St Ives   Perranarworthal   Boswinger
Hayle
Leedstown   St Just-in-Roseland
St Just   Edgcumbe
St Hilary   Relubbus   Carleen
Penzance   Rosudgeon   Ashton   Falmouth
St Buryan   Helston
Mullion
Kennack Sands

0 ____ 20 miles
0 ____ 30 kilometres

unclass rd signed Blackwater. Site on right in 200 metres. A 2-acre site with 30 touring pitches and 21 statics.

[symbols]

Credit Cards [symbols]

BODINNICK

Yeate Farm Camp & Caravan Site (SX134526)
PL23 1LZ ☎ 01726 870256 Signposted
Nearby town: Fowey
► ► ► Family Park ★ ⊞ £6-£8 ⊞ £6-£8 Å £6-£8
Open Apr-Oct Booking advisable mid Jul-mid Aug Last arrival 21.30hrs Last departure 11.00hrs
A small, level grass site adjacent to a working farm overlooking the R Fowey. From A390 at East Taphouse take B3359 signed Looe and Lanreath. Follow signs for Bodinnick on unclass rd. A 1-acre site with 33 touring pitches and 2 statics.
Private slipway/quay, storage of small boats.

[symbols]

BODMIN

Camping & Caravanning Club Site (SX081676)
Old Callywith Rd PL31 2DZ ☎ 01208 73834 (in season) & 01203 694995 Signposted
► ► ► Family Park ★ ⊞ £9.20-£11.60 ⊞ £9.20-£11.60
Å £9.20-£11.60
Open end Mar-early Nov Booking advisable bank hols & Jul-Aug Last arrival 21.00hrs Last departure noon
Undulating grassy site with trees and bushes set in meadowland within urban area. Signed off A30 from Launceston. Please see the advertisement on page 27 for details of Club Members' benefits. An 11-acre site with 175 touring pitches.

[symbols]

Credit Cards [symbols]

BOLVENTOR

Colliford Tavern Campsite (SX171740)
Colliford Lake, St Neot PL14 6PZ ☎ 01208 821335
Signposted

► ► ► ► De-Luxe Park ★ ⚌ £8-£10 ⚌ £8-£10 Å £8-£10
Open Etr-Sep Booking advisable bank hols & Jul-Aug
Last arrival 22.30hrs Last departure 11.00hrs

*An oasis on Bodmin Moor, a small site with spacious
grassy pitches and very good quality facilities. Leave
A30 1.25m W of Bolventor onto unclass rd signed
Colliford Lake, and site on left in 0.25m. A 3.5-acre site
with 40 touring pitches.*

🔯 🛈 ⊙ ⚑ ✳ ⛾ 🛈 ⌀ ✕ ⌧ 🛒 🏇 🖼 🖳 ⚭
➜ 🌙

Credit Cards 💳 🈺 🆑 🈺 🔳 ⑤

BOSWINGER

**Sea View International Caravan & Camping Park
(SW990412)**
PL26 6LL ☎ 01726 843425 Signposted ✕
Nearby town: St Austell

► ► ► ► ► Premier Park ⚌ £7.50-£16.90
⚌ £7.50-£16.90 Å £7.50-£16.90
Open Mon before Good Fri-Sep Booking advisable Jul-
Aug Last arrival 22.00hrs Last departure 11.00hrs

*This level, grassy site has been colourfully landscaped
with flowers and shrubs and overlooks Veryan Bay.
Many times a winner of AA awards in previous years
for its beautiful environment and its dedication to high
standards of maintenance. 3.5m SW of Mevagissey
harbour and .5m from beach and sea. A 16-acre site
with 165 touring pitches and 38 statics.*
Crazy golf, volleyball, badminton courts, putting.
See advertisement under MEVAGISSEY

🔯 🛒 🛈 ⊙ 🖥 ⚑ 🔧 ⚹ 🔍 ✳ ⚠ 🛈 ⌀ ⊤ ⌧ 🛒 🚲
🏇 🐕 🛒 ⚭
➜ ◎ ⚠ ✢ 🌙

Credit Cards 💳 🆑 🈺 🔳 ⑤

BUDE

Sandymouth Bay Holiday Park (SS214104)
Sandymouth Bay EX23 9HW
☎ 01288 352563 & 0831 213932
Signposted

★ ⚌ £7-£12 ⚌ £7-£12 Å £7-£12
Open Apr-Oct Booking advisable Jul & Aug Last arrival
22.00hrs Last departure 10.00hrs

*A friendly holiday park with glorious and extensive sea
views. Many on-site facilities, and an extensive
entertainment programme for all ages. Sandymouth
Bay is signed off A39 approx .5m S of Kilkhampton, 4m
N of Bude. A 4-acre site with 55 touring pitches and 125
statics.*
Sauna & solarium.

🔯 🛈 ⊙ 🖥 ⚑ 🔧 ⚫ ⌧ ✳ ⛾ ⚠ 🛈 ⌀ ⊕ ⊤ ✕ ⌧
🛒 🍴 🏇 🛒 ⚭
➜ ∪ ▶ ⚠ ✢ 🌙

Credit Cards 💳 🆑 🈺 🔳 ⑤

Wooda Farm Park (SS229080)
Poughill EX23 9HJ ☎ 01288 352069 (2m E) Signposted

◖◗◖◗◖◗◖◗◖◗◖◗

▶ ▶ ▶ ▶ ▶ Premier Park ★ ⚍ £6.50-£10 ⚍ £6.50-£10
Å £6.50-£10
Open Apr-Oct (rs Apr-end May & mid Sep-end Oct shop hrs, laundrette/restaurant limited) Booking advisable Jul-Aug Last arrival 20.00hrs Last departure noon
Attractive park set on raised ground overlooking Bude Bay, with lovely sea views. From the A39 at the edge of Stratton follow the unclassified Coombe Valley road. A 12-acre site with 160 touring pitches and 52 statics.
Coarse fishing, clay pigeon shoots, pets corner.

🔌📻🔦⊙🗄🗑🛒⏰✳️⛱️⚠️🍴📱⌀⊞Ⓣ✗📞🐾
♿🏕️🐎🐾♿
→∪Ⓟ◎⬡⚓⚡☕🔋⌇

Credit Cards 💳 ▒▒ ▒▒ 📶 🔲

See advertisement on page 47

◖◗◖◗◖◗◖◗◖◗◖◗

Budemeadows Touring Holiday Park (SS215012)
EX23 0NA ☎ 01288 361646 (3m S of Bude on A39) Signposted

◖◗◖◗◖◗◖◗◖◗◖◗

▶ ▶ ▶ ▶ De-Luxe Park ★ ⚍ £8-£11 ⚍ £8-£11 Å £8-£11
Open all year (rs Oct-Spring bank hol shop & pool closed) Booking advisable Jul-Aug Last arrival 21.00hrs Last departure noon
A very well kept site of distinction, with good quality facilities. A 9-acre site with 146 touring pitches and 1 static.

Outdoor table tennis & giant chess. Baby changing.
🔌♿🔦⊙🗄🗑🛒⏰✳️⛱️⚠️📱⌀⊞🔋☕🚽🔲
🏕️🐎🐾♿
→∪Ⓟ◎⬡⚓⚡🔋⌇

Credit Cards 💳 ▒▒ ▒▒ 📶 🔲

See advertisement on page 47

◖◗◖◗◖◗◖◗◖◗◖◗

Willow Valley Holiday Park (SS236078)
Bush EX23 9LB ☎ 01288 353104 (on A39) Signposted
▶ ▶ ▶ Family Park ⚍ £5.50-£8 ⚍ £5.50-£8 Å £5.50-£8
Open Mar-Dec Booking advisable Jul & Aug Last arrival 21.00hrs Last departure noon
Small sheltered park in Strat Valley with stream running through. Level grassy pitches and direct access off A39 .5m N of its junction with A3072 at Stratton. A 3-acre site with 41 touring pitches and 4 statics.

🔌🔦⊙🗄🗑✳️⚠️📱⌀⊞Ⓣ🔋☕🏕️🐎🐾
→∪Ⓟ◎⬡⚡⌇

Credit Cards 💳 ▒▒ ▒▒ 📶 🔲

CAMELFORD

Juliot's Well Holiday Park (SX095829)
PL32 9RF ☎ 01840 213302 Signposted
Nearby town: Tintagel

◖◗◖◗◖◗◖◗◖◗◖◗

▶ ▶ ▶ ▶ De-Luxe Park ⚍ ⚍ Å
Open Mar-Oct (rs Mar-Apr & Oct swimming pool closed) Booking advisable bank hols & Jul-Aug Last arrival 21.30hrs Last departure 11.00hrs

A quiet site in the grounds of an old manor house. From A39 in Camelford turn right onto B3266, at T junc turn left and site on right in 300 yds. An 8-acre site with 60 touring pitches and 50 statics.
Skittle alley, boules.volley ball, tennis, badminton.

🔥 🚤 ⌑ ☉ ◙ 🦐 ⌇ ⦉ ⚫ ☀ ♀ ⼭ 🔋 🐕 ⊞ 🆃 ✕ 💧 ⊞ 🐎 ㉿
→ ∪ ► ♪

Credit Cards 💳 ▦ ▦ 🖼 🔄

○○○○○○○○○○○

Lakefield Caravan Park (SX095853)
Lower Pendavey Farm PL32 9TX
☎ 01840 213279 (1.5m N on B3266) Signposted
► ► ► Family Park ★ 🏕 £5-£8.50 🚐 £5-£8.50 ⛺ £5-£8.50
Open Etr or Apr-Oct Booking advisable Jul-Aug Last arrival 22.00hrs Last departure noon
Set in a rural location, this friendly park is part of a specialist equestrian centre, and offers good quality services. Riding lessons and hacks always available, with BHS qualified instructor. From A39 in Camelford turn right onto B3266, turn right at T junc, and site on left in 1.5m. A 5-acre site with 30 touring pitches.
Own lake & full Equestrian Centre.

🔥 🐴 ⌑ ☉ 🦐 ☀ ⼭ 🔋 🐕 ⊞ 🆃 💧 🐎 ㉿
→ ∪ ► ♪

CARLEEN

Lower Polladras Touring Park (SW617308)
TR13 9NX ☎ 01736 762220 Signposted
Nearby town: Helston
► ► ► Family Park ★ 🏕 £7-£8 🚐 £7-£8 ⛺ £7-£8
Open Apr-Oct Booking advisable Jul-Aug Last arrival 22.00hrs Last departure noon
A very rural farm site with good facilities. From A394 turn onto B3302 Hayle road at Hilltop Garage, then take 2nd turning on L to Carleen for site, about 2m on R. A 4-acre site with 60 touring pitches.

🔥 🐴 ⌑ ☉ ◙ 🦐 ☀ ⼭ 🔋 🐕 ⊞ 🆃 ㉿
→ ∪ ♪

Poldown Caravan Park (SW629298)
Poldown TR13 9NN ☎ 01326 574560 Signposted
Nearby town: Helston
► ► ► Family Park ★ 🏕 £4.50-£9 🚐 £4.50-£9 ⛺ £4-£9
Open Apr-Oct Booking advisable Jul-Aug Last arrival 22.00hrs Last departure noon
A small, quiet site set in attractive countryside. From A394 turn off onto the B3302 Hayle road at Hilltop Garage, then take second left to Carleen for site which is .75m on right. A 2-acre site with 10 touring pitches and 7 statics.

🔥 🐴 ⌑ ☉ ◙ 🦐 ☀ ⼭ 🔋 🐕 ⊞ 💧
→ ∪ ► ♪

CARLYON BAY

Carlyon Bay Caravan & Camping Park (SX052526)
Bethesda, Cypress Av PL25 3RE ☎ 01726 812735
Signposted
Nearby town: St Austell

► ► ► De-Luxe Park 🏕 🚐 ⛺
Open Etr-3 Oct (rs Etr-mid May & mid Sep-3 Oct swimming pool/take-away/shop closed) Booking advisable mid Jul-mid Aug Last arrival anytime Last departure 11.00hrs
An attractive, secluded site set amongst a belt of trees with background woodland. Winner of the South-West England Campsite of the Year Award for 1998/8. Off A390 W of St Blazey, turn left on A3092 for Par, and right again in .5m. On private rd to Carlyon Bay. A 35-acre site with 180 touring pitches.
Crazy golf, childrens entertainment in Jul & Aug.

🔥 🐴 ⌑ ☉ ◙ 🦐 ⌇ ⦉ ⚫ ☐ ☀ ⼭ 🔋 🐕 ⊞ 🆃 💧 ㉿
🛁 🚿 🐎 ㉿
→ ∪ ► ◎ ⛲ ⚓ ☎ ♪

Credit Cards 💳 ▦ 🔄

○○○○○○○○○○○

CRANTOCK (NEAR NEWQUAY)

Trevella Tourist Park (SW801599)
TR8 5EW ☎ 01637 830308 Signposted

○○○○○○○○○○○

► ► ► ► De-Luxe Park ★ 🏕 £6.40-£10.60 🚐 £5.80-£9.80 ⛺ £6.40-£10.60
Open Etr-Oct Booking advisable bank hols & Jul-Aug
A well established and very well run family site, with outstanding floral displays. Set in rural area close to Newquay between Crantock and A3075. A 15-acre site with 295 touring pitches and 50 statics.
Crazy golf, fishing & badminton.
See advertisement under NEWQUAY

🔥 🐴 ⌑ ☉ ◙ 🦐 ⌇ ⚫ ☐ ☀ ⼭ 🔋 🐕 ⊞ 🆃 ✕ 💧 ㉿
🚿 🐎 ㉿
→ ∪ ► ◎ ⚓ ⛲ ☎ ♪

Credit Cards 💳 ▦ ▦ 🖼 🔄

○○○○○○○○○○○

Crantock Plains Touring Park (SW805589)
TR8 5PH ☎ 01637 830955 & 831273
Nearby town: Newquay
► ► ► Family Park ★ 🏕 £5.50-£8.50 🚐 £5.50-£8.50 ⛺ £5.50-£8.50
Open Etr/Apr-Sep Booking advisable Jul-Aug Last arrival 22.00hrs Last departure noon
A small farm site with level grassy touring pitches. From A3075 take 3rd turning right signed Crantock. Site on left along narrow lane. A 6-acre site with 40 touring pitches.

🔥 🐴 ⌑ ☉ ◙ 🦐 ⚫ ☀ ⼭ 🔋 🐕 ⊞ 💧 🚿 🐎 ㉿
→ ∪ ► ⚓ ☎ ♪

Treago Farm Caravan Site (SW782601)
TR8 5QS ☎ 01637 830277 & 830522 Signposted
► ► ► Family Park ★ 🏕 £6-£10 🚐 £6-£10 ⛺ £6-£10
Open mid May-mid Sep (rs Apr-mid May & Oct no shop or bar) Booking advisable Jun-Aug Last arrival 22.00hrs Last departure 18.00hrs
Grass site in open farmland in a south-facing sheltered valley; direct access to Crantock and Polly Joke beaches, National Trust Land and many natural beauty
contd.

spots. From A3075 W of Newquay turn right for ·
Crantock. Site signed beyond village. A 4-acre site with
92 touring pitches and 7 statics.

🔌📶☉📷📶🔦☐☀♀🛈🔌⌧Ⓣ🔲📶🍴
🐾⚡
➜∪🅿◎⚠✈🔧

CUBERT

Cottage Farm (SW786589)
Treworgans TR8 5HH ☎ 01637 831083 Signposted
▶ ▶ ▶ Family Park ★ 🚐 fr £3.75 🚐 fr £3.75 Å fr £3.75
Open Apr-Sep Booking advisable Last arrival 22.30hrs
Last departure noon ⚲
*A small grassy touring park nestling in the tiny hamlet
of Treworgans, in sheltered open countryside close to a
lovely beach. Leave A30 onto A392 towards Newquay,
turn left onto A3075 towards Redruth, and in 2m turn
right signed Holywell, Cubert and Penhalt Camp. Turn
right in 1.5m signed Crantock, and left in 0.5m past
school. Site in 300yds. A 2-acre site with 45 touring
pitches and 1 static.*

🔌📶☉📷📶☀🛈🔌⌧🔦⚡🔲
➜∪🅿◎⚠✈♟️

DAVIDSTOW

Inny Vale Holiday Village (SX170870)
PL32 9XN ☎ 01840 261248 & 261740 (on A395, 1m from
jct with A39)
Nearby town: Bude
▶ ▶ ▶ Family Park 🚐 £7-£12 🚐 £7-£12 Å £5-£10
Open Etr-Oct Booking advisable
*A level sheltered park with stream running through,
adjacent to and enjoying benefit from small holiday
bungalow village. Signed off A395 on single track rd to
Tremail, approx 1m from A39. A 2-acre site with 27
touring pitches.*
shop

🔌📶☉📷📶🔸🔍☀♀🚿🛈🔦⌧Ⓣ✕🔦📶🍴
🔲⚡
➜🅿🔧

DOWNDERRY

Carbeil Caravan & Camping Park (SX318544)
Treliddon Ln PL11 3LS ☎ 01503 250636 Signposted
Nearby town: Looe
▶ ▶ ▶ Family Park 🚐 🚐 Å

Open 31 Mar-Oct Booking advisable all year Last arrival
21.00hrs Last departure noon

A compact park in a sheltered valley with pitches tiered
into grass paddocks. Site at end of Downderry, up
narrow lane and signed. A 1.25-acre site with 20 touring
pitches and 8 statics.

🔌📶☉📷📶☀♀🚿✕🔦🚐📶🔲⚡
➜∪🔧

EDGCUMBE

Retanna Holiday Park (SW711327)
TR13 0EJ ☎ 01326 340643 (100m off A394) Signposted
Nearby town: Falmouth
▶ ▶ ▶ Family Park ★ 🚐 £5-£7.50 🚐 £5-£7.50 Å £5-£7.50
Open Apr-Oct (rs Apr & Oct limited shop facilities)
Booking advisable Jul & Aug Last arrival 22.00hrs Last
departure 11.00hrs
*A small rural site with limited amenities but central for
touring and 5m from Falmouth. Signed off the A394 4m
E of Helston. A 4-acre site with 24 touring pitches and
34 statics.*

🔌📶☉📷📶🔦☀🚿🛈🔌⌧Ⓣ🔦📶🐾🐕
➜∪🅿◎⚠✈🔧🔲
Credit Cards 💳 ⚏ 📇 ⑤

FALMOUTH

Maen Valley Holiday Park (SW789311)
Roscarrick Rd TR11 5BJ ☎ 01326 312190 Signposted

▶ ▶ ▶ ▶ De-Luxe Park 🚐 £8-£12 🚐 £8-£12 Å £8-£12
Open Etr-Oct Booking advisable Jul & Aug Last arrival
22.00hrs

Set in a picturesque valley with a stream, this site offers peace and quiet. 1.5m SW of Falmouth but within walking distance of Swanpool beach. Leave A39 at Hillhead rndbt on Penryn by-pass and follow signs to Maenporth and industrial estate. Site in 1.5m. A 4-acre site with 90 touring pitches and 94 statics. Crazy golf.

🔌🔦📻☉🎣🚲🔍⚓☀♀🏔🛡🚿❄🚮☎🕵️✂📞⚱
⛩⛺🐕🐴🛒
➜⛵🅿☉🔺⛱↩🎣

Credit Cards 💳 💳 💳 🏧

Tremorvah Tent Park (SW798313)
Swanpool TR11 5BA ☎ 01326 312103 Signposted
▶ ▶ ▶ Family Park 🏕 🅰
Open mid May-Oct Booking advisable Jul-Aug Last arrival 22.00hrs Last departure 10.00hrs
A secluded tent park in a meadowland setting overlooking Swanpool Beach. No towed caravans. In Falmouth follow signs to 'Beaches', and on to Swanpool; site signed on right. A 3-acre site with 72 touring pitches.
Dishwashing sinks & electric cooking hob.

🔦☉📻🍳🔍❄🛡🚮🕵️🐕🐴🛒
➜⛵🅿☉🔺⛱↩🎣

FOWEY

Penhale Caravan & Camping Park (SX104526)
PL23 1JU ☎ 01726 833425
▶ ▶ ▶ Family Park ★ 🏕 £5.50-£7 🅰 £5.50-£7 🅰 £5.50-£7
Open Etr/Apr-Oct Booking advisable for electric hook-ups
Set on a working farm 1.5 m from sandy beach and town of Fowey. Grassy park with lovely views, and direct access off A3082, 0.5m before junc with B3269. A 4.5-acre site with 56 touring pitches and 13 statics.

🔌🔦🔦☉📻📻🔍❄🛡🚮📞
➜❄↩🛒

GOONHAVERN

Silverbow Park (SW782531)
Perranwell TR4 9NX ☎ 01872 572347 Signposted
Nearby town: Truro

▶ ▶ ▶ ▶ De-Luxe Park ★ 🏕 £6-£13.50 🅰 £6-£13.50
🅰 £6-£13.50
Open mid May-mid Sep (rs mid Sep-Oct & Etr-mid May swimming pool & shop closed) Booking advisable Jul-Aug Last arrival 22.00hrs Last departure noon
A very well kept park in a rural setting, thoughtfully laid out and screened by mature shrubs and trees. Adjacent to A3075 .5m S of village. A 14-acre site with 100 touring pitches and 15 statics.
Badminton courts, short mat bowls rink.
See advertisement under PERRANPORTH

🔌🍴🔦☉📻📻🎣🍳🔍❄🏔🛡🚮🕵️☎↩🏕
🐕🛒🏪
➜⛵🅿↩

Perran Springs Touring Park (SW796535)
Bodmin Rd TR4 9QG ☎ 01872 540568 Signposted
Nearby town: Newquay
▶ ▶ ▶ Family Park 🏕 🏕 🅰
Open Etr or Apr-Oct Booking advisable Jul-Aug Last arrival anytime Last departure 10.00hrs
A brand new site with quality buildings and a good standard of facilities. Turn R off A30 on to B3285, signed Perranporth. Site on R in 1m. An 8-acre site with 120 touring pitches.

🔌🔦☉📻🍳❄🏔🛡🚮🕵️☎↩🐕🛒🏪
➜⛵🅿🔺↩🎣

Rosehill Farm Tourist Park (SW787540)
TR4 9LA ☎ 01872 572448 Signposted
Nearby town: Perranporth
▶ ▶ ▶ Family Park ★ 🏕 £5.25-£8.75 🅰 £5.25-£8.75
🅰 £5.25-£8.75
Open Whit-Oct (rs Etr-Whit shop) Booking advisable Jul-Aug Last arrival 21.30hrs Last departure 11.00hrs
A small, well-kept site set in hilly meadowland, .5m W of village on B3285. A 7-acre site with 65 touring pitches.
Off-licence in shop.
See advertisement under PERRANPORTH

🔌🔦☉📻📻🍳🔳❄🏔🛡🚮🕵️☎🐕🐴🛒
➜⛵🅿☉↩

GORRAN

Tregarton Park (SW984437)
PL26 6NF ☎ 01726 843666 Signposted
Nearby town: St Austell
▶ ▶ ▶ Family Park ★ 🏕 £6-£12.90 🅰 £6-£12.90
🅰 £6-£12.90

Open Etr-Sep Booking advisable Jul-Aug Last arrival 22.00hrs Last departure 11.00hrs
A sheltered park set in lovely countryside lying 2m from the sea and off minor road to Gorran Haven. From St Austell bypass turn left on B3273 for Mevagissey. At crossroads signed 'No caravans beyond this point', turn right on to unclass. road for Gorran. Site on right in 2.5m. A 12-acre site with 150 touring pitches.
Camping equipment for sale, Off Licence.

🔌🔦☉📻📻🎣☀❄🏔🛡🚮🕵️☎↩🏛🐕🛒
➜⛵🅿🔺❄↩

Credit Cards 💳 💳 💳 🏧

Treveor Farm Caravan & Camping Site (SW988418)
PL26 6LW ☎ 01726 842387 Signposted
Nearby town: St Austell
▶ ▶ ▶ **Family Park** ★ 🚐 £6.50-£12 🚐 £6.50-£12
🛆 £6.50-£12
Open Apr-Oct Booking advisable in Jan Last arrival
20.00hrs Last departure 11.00hrs
*A small family run camping park with good facilities,
situated on a working farm. From St Austell bypass turn
left onto B3273 for Mevagissey. On hilltop before
descent to village turn right on unclass rd for Gorran; in
3.5m fork right, and site signed on right. A 4-acre site
with 50 touring pitches.*
Coarse fishing.

🅿️ 🦮 ⊙ 🧺 ⚒ ❊ ⚠ 🖭 📞
➜ ⅄ ⤙ 🥾

GORRAN HAVEN

Trelispen Caravan & Camping Park (SX008421)
PL26 6HT ☎ 01726 843501 Signposted
Nearby town: St Austell
▶▶ **Town & Country Pennant Park** 🚐 🚐 🛆
Open Etr & Apr-Oct Booking advisable Last arrival
22.00hrs Last departure noon
*A very basic site in a beautiful, quiet location within
easy reach of beaches. From St Austell bypass take
B3273 for Mevagissey. At crossroads signed 'No
caravans beyond this point', turn right on unclass. rd,
continue through Gorran, and site on left towards
Gorran Haven. A 2-acre site with 40 touring pitches.*
A 30 acre nature reserve may be visited.

🅿️ 🦮 ⊙ 🖭 ❊ ⚠ 🖊 ⌀ 🥾
➜ ⅄ ⤙

CHALETS · CARAVANS · CAMPING

The Park is set in sand dunes which
run down to its own sandy beach.
Many units have superb sea views.
With a large indoor pool and 2
clubs on the Park what more could
you ask for? Except for our FREE
colour brochure.

*Call us on the number below
or write to us at*

St Ives Bay
Holiday Park, Upton
Towans, Hayle,
Cornwall TR27 5BH

ST IVES BAY
HOLIDAY PARK

right on the beach!

HAYLE

St Ives Bay Holiday Park (SW577398)
73 Loggans Rd, Upton Towans TR27 5BH
☎ 01736 752274
Signposted

✿✿✿✿✿✿✿✿✿✿✿✿✿✿✿✿✿✿✿✿✿

★ 🚐 £6-£20 🚐 £6-£20 🛆 £6-£20
Open 3 May 27 Sep (rs Etr-3 May & 27 Sep-25 Oct no
entertainment, pool, food & bar service) Booking
advisable Jan-Mar Last arrival 23.00hrs Last departure
09.00hrs
*An excellently maintained holiday park with a relaxed
atmosphere, built on sand dunes adjacent to a three-
mile long beach. The touring section forms a number of
separate locations in amongst the statics. Leave A30 at
first Hayle rndbt towards town centre, and in .25m turn
right at double rndbt signed Gwithian. Site on left. A 13-
acre site with 240 touring pitches and 250 statics.*
Crazy golf, video room.

🅿️ 🦮 ⊙ 🖭 🧺 🠊 🠊 ❅ ⚔ 🖵 ❊ 🍸 ⚠ 🖊 ⌀ 🖭 🅣 ✗
📞 🚿 🐴 🥾
➜ ∪ ▶ ⤙

Credit Cards 💳 💳

✿✿✿✿✿✿✿✿✿✿✿✿✿✿✿✿✿✿✿✿✿

Higher Trevaskis Caravan Park (SW611381)
Gwinear Rd, Conner Downs TR27 5JQ ☎ 01209 831736
Signposted
▶ ▶ ▶ **Family Park** ★ 🚐 £5-£10 🚐 £5-£10 🛆 £5-£10
Open mid Apr-mid Oct Booking advisable May-Sep Last
arrival 20.00hrs Last departure 11.00hrs
*Rural grassy park divided into sheltered paddocks, and
with views towards St Ives. Fluent German and
Swedish spoken. At Hayle rndbt on A30 take 1st exit
signed Connor Downs, in 1m turn right signed Carnhell
Green, and site is in 0.75m just past level crossing. A
6.5-acre site with 82 touring pitches.*

🅿️ 🦮 ⊙ 🖭 🧺 ❊ ⚠ 🖊 ⌀ 🖭 🅣 📞 🐴 🥾
➜ ▶ ⊚ ⌂ ⅄ ⤙

Parbola Holiday Park (SW612366)
Wall TR27 5LE ☎ 01209 831503 Signposted
Nearby town: St Ives
▶ ▶ ▶ **Family Park** ★ 🚐 £7.25-£12 🚐 £7.25-£12
🛆 £7.25-£12
Open Etr-Sep (rs Etr-spring bank hol & Sep shop &
takeaway closed) Booking advisable Jul-Aug Last arrival
22.00hrs Last departure noon 🐾
*A level grassy site in Cornish downland, with pitches in
both woodland and open grassy areas. Follow old A30
to Connor Downs, turn left on unclass rd for Wall, and
site in village on right. A 17.5-acre site with 110 touring
pitches and 20 statics.*
Crazy golf & bike hire.

🅿️ 🦮 ⊙ 🖭 🧺 🠊 ⚔ 🖵 ❊ ⚠ 🖊 ⌀ 🖭 🅣 📞 🚿 🏛
🥾 ♿
➜ ∪ ▶ ⊚ ⤙

Credit Cards 💳 💳 💳 ⑤

HELSTON

Trelowarren Chateau Park (SW721238)
Mawgan TR12 6AF ☎ 01326 221637 (3m S off B3293 to St Keverne) Signposted
▶ ▶ ▶ Family Park ⊞ ⊞ Å
Open Apr-16 Oct Booking advisable bank hols & Jul-Aug Last departure noon
A very attractive setting in the extensive park of Trelowarren House. From Helston on A3083 turn left past Culdrose Naval Air Station on to B3293. Signed on left in 1.5m. A 20-acre site with 225 touring pitches.

🖸 ➹ 🏌 ⊙ 🗑 ⬤ ❑ ⊹ 🔽 ⚕ 🛈 ⊘ 🖭 🖵 ✕ ⚲ ♨
🏧 🏛 🏠 🐎 🎱 ♿
→ ∪

HOLYWELL BAY

Trevornick Holiday Park (SW776586)
TR8 5PW ☎ 01637 830531
Signposted
Nearby town: Newquay

❀❀❀❀❀❀❀❀❀❀❀❀❀❀❀❀❀❀❀

★ ⊞ £6.50-£11.40 ⊞ £6.50-£11.40 Å £6.50-£11.40
Open Etr & mid May-mid Sep Booking advisable Jul-Aug Last arrival 21.00hrs Last departure 10.00hrs
A large seaside holiday complex with excellent facilities and amenities. From A3075 turn right near Rejerrah for Holywell Bay, and site on right. A 20-acre site with 450 touring pitches and 60 statics.
Fishing, golf course, entertainment.
See advertisement under NEWQUAY

🖸 ➹ 🏌 ⊙ 🗑 🔽 ❳ ✎ ⚲ ⬤ ⊹ 🔽 ⚕ 🛈 ⊘ 🖭 🖵 ✕
⚲ 🏧 🏠 🐎 🎱 ♿
→ ∪ ⮕ ◎ ⚠ ⚘ 🍴
Credit Cards 💳 🔲 🔲 🔲 §

❀❀❀❀❀❀❀❀❀❀❀❀❀❀❀❀❀❀❀

Holywell Bay Holiday Park (SW773582)
TR8 5PR ☎ 01637 871111 Signposted
Nearby town: Newquay

⬭⬭⬭⬭⬭⬭⬭⬭⬭⬭⬭

▶ ▶ ▶ ▶ De-Luxe Park ★ ⊞ £6.80-£12.20
⊞ £6.80-£12.20 Å £6.80-£12.20
Open Etr-30 Oct Booking advisable Jun-Aug Last arrival 21.00hrs Last departure 10.00hrs ⚘
Close to lovely local beaches in a rural location, this level grassy park borders on National Trust land, and is only a short distance from the Cornish Coastal Path. A 2.5-acre site with 75 touring pitches and 149 statics.

🖸 🏌 ⊙ 🗑 ❳ 🔽 ⚕ 🛈 ⊘ 🖭 🖵 ⚲ 🏧 🏛 🏠 🎱
→ ∪ ⮕ ◎ ⚠ 🍴
Credit Cards 💳 🔲

⬭⬭⬭⬭⬭⬭⬭⬭⬭⬭⬭

INDIAN QUEENS

Gnome World Touring Park (SW890599)
Moorland Rd TR9 6HN ☎ 01726 860812 Signposted
Nearby town: Newquay
▶▶ Town & Country Pennant Park ★ ⊞ £4-£7 ⊞ £4-£7
Å £4-£7

Open Etr-Oct (rs Nov-Mar) Booking advisable Jul-Aug Last arrival 22.00hrs Last departure noon
A level grassy park set in extensive farmland. Signed from slip road at A30 and A39 rndbt at village of Indian Queens - park is on old A30, now unclassified. A 4.5-acre site with 50 touring pitches.
Nature trail.

🖸 🏌 ⊙ 🔽 ⊹ 🔽 ⊘ 🖭 ⚲ 🖵 🐎 🎱 ♿
→ ∪ 🍴 🗑

JACOBSTOW

Edmore Tourist Park (SX187955)
Edgarrd, Wainhouse Corner EX23 0BJ ☎ 01840 230467 Signposted
Nearby town: Bude
▶ ▶ ▶ Family Park ⊞ ⊞ Å
Open Etr-Oct Booking advisable peak periods Last departure noon
Small, family run, rural campsite in good location, just off main A39 at Wainhouse Corner, and signed. A 3-acre site with 28 touring pitches and 2 statics.

🖸 🏌 ⊙ 🔽 ❑ ⊹ 🔽 🛈 ⊘ 🖭
→ 🎱

KENNACK SANDS

Gwendreath Farm Caravan Park (SW738168)
TR12 7LZ ☎ 01326 290666
Nearby town: Helston
▶ ▶ ▶ Family Park ⊞ £5.30-£6.50 ⊞ £5.30-£6.50
Å £5.30-£6.50
Open Etr-Oct Booking advisable all times Last departure 10.00hrs
A grassy park in elevated position with extensive sea and coastal views. A short walk through woods to the beach. From Helston on A3083 turn left past Culdrose Naval Air Station on to B3293, turn right past Goonhilly earth satellite station, signed Kennack Sands. Turn left in 1m. A 5-acre site with 10 touring pitches and 30 statics.

🖸 🏌 ⊙ 🗑 ⊹ 🔽 ⚕ 🛈 ⊘ 🖭 🖵 ⚲ 🍴 🏛 🖵 🐎 🎱
→ ∪ ⮕ ◎ ⚠ 🍴

Silver Sands Holiday Park (SW727166)
Gwendreath TR12 7LZ ☎ 01326 290631 Signposted
Nearby town: Helston
▶ ▶ ▶ Family Park ⊞ £6-£7.50 ⊞ £6-£7.50 Å £6-£7.50
Open May-Sep Booking advisable Jul-Aug Last arrival 22.00hrs Last departure 11.00hrs
A small, remote site adjacent to a beach and well maintained. Take A3083 from Helston, at Culdrose naval air station turn left on B3293 to Goonhilly earth station, and right at crossrds onto unclass rd. Site signed on left in 1m. A 9-acre site with 34 touring pitches and 16 statics.

🖸 🏌 ⊙ 🗑 ⊹ 🔽 ⚕ 🛈 ⊘ 🖭 ⚲ 🐎 🎱
→ ∪ ⚠ ⚘ 🍴

KILKHAMPTON

East Thorne Caravan & Camping Park (SS260110)
EX23 9RY ☎ 01288 321618 Signposted
▶ ▶ ▶ Family Park ★ ⊞ £4-£6.50 ⊞ £4-£6.50 Å £4-£6.50
Open Apr-Oct Booking advisable Last arrival 22.00hrs Last departure 11.00hrs

Small rural campsite situated adjacent to non-working farm, ideally positioned for touring Devon and Cornwall. In village centre follow B3254 Launceston road for approx .75m. A 2-acre site with 29 touring pitches.

🎵 🛱 ⊙ ⛏ ◆ ⚒ ⚙ 🛢 🖊 ⊞ 🏠
→ ∪ 🅿 ⚓ ⚲ 🏕 ♨ 🔱 🗽 🅱

LANDRAKE

Dolbeare Caravan & Camping Park (SX363616)
St Ive Rd PL12 5AF ☎ 01752 851332 Signposted
Nearby town: Plymouth
► ► ► **Family Park** 🚐 £7.50-£8.50 🚐 £7.50-£8.50
▲ £5.50-£8.50
Open all year Booking advisable peak periods only Last arrival 23.00hrs
A mainly level grass site with trees and bushes set in meadowland. Cross Tamar Bridge, stay on A38 for 4m, turn right immed after footbridge in Landrake village, and follow site signs for 0.75m. A 4-acre site with 60 touring pitches.
Volley ball pitch, Boules pitch, Info Centre.

🎵 🛱 ⊙ ⛏ ⚒ ⚙ 🛢 🖊 ⊞ 🅃 ♨ 🏕 🐕 🗽 🅱
→ 🅿 ⚲ 🏕 🔱

LAUNCELLS

Red Post Holiday Park (SS264052)
EX23 9NW ☎ 01288 381305 Signposted
Nearby town: Bude
► ► ► **Family Park** ★ 🚐 £4-£7.50 🚐 £4-£7.50 ▲ £3-£7.50
Open 31 Mar-Oct Booking advisable Jul & Aug Last arrival 23.00hrs Last departure 11.00hrs

A basic site at rear of a country inn, midway between Bude and Holsworthy on the A3072 at the junction with the B3254. A 4-acre site with 50 touring pitches.

🎵 🛱 ⊙ 🖥 ⚒ ⚙ 🛢 🖊 ⊞ 🅃 🗡 📞 ♨ 🅱
→ ∪ 🅿 🔱

LEEDSTOWN (NEAR HAYLE)

Calloose Caravan & Camping Park (SW597352)
TR27 5ET ☎ 01736 850431 Signposted
Nearby town: St Ives

◯◯◯◯◯◯◯◯◯◯

► ► ► ► **De-Luxe Park** 🚐 £6.50-£12.50 🚐 £6.50-£12.50
▲ £6.50-£12.50
Open Apr-Oct (rs Apr-mid May & late Sep swimming pool) Booking advisable Etr, May bank hols & Jun-Aug Last arrival 22.00hrs Last departure 11.00hrs
A comprehensively equipped leisure park in a remote rural setting in a small river valley. Follow B3302 from 'Duke of Leeds' public house in town centre for 0.5m. Winner of the Best Campsite for South-West England 1996/7. A 12.5-acre site with 120 touring pitches and 17 statics.
Crazy golf, skittle alley & fishing

🎵 🛱 ⊙ 🖥 ⛏ ⚓ ◆ 🔲 ⚒ ⚙ 🛢 🖊 ⊞ 🅃 🗡
📞 ♨ 🏕 🐕 🗽 🅱 ♿
→ 🔱

Credit Cards 💳 🆑 🆑 🆑 🅂

◯◯◯◯◯◯◯◯◯◯

LISKEARD

Pine Green Caravan & Camping Sitr (SX195646)
Doublebois PL14 6LE
☎ 01579 320183 & 01271 328981
Signposted
▶ ▶ ▶ Family Park ★ 🚐 £6-£10 🚐 £6-£10 ▲ £5-£8
Open Jan-Nov Booking advisable high season Last
arrival 22.00hrs Last departure noon
*A well-kept terraced site in a good touring location with
scenic views over surrounding countryside and Fowey
River Valley. Follow A38 through Dobwalls traffic lights,
and take 1st left in 0.5m; site signed. A 3-acre site with
50 touring pitches and 1 static.*

🔌📻⊙🗑🍳✳🚰🛉🍴🔥🐎
➔▶⛱🛝⛴🐕

LOOE

Tencreek Caravan & Camping Park (SX233525)
PL13 2JR
☎ 01503 262447 & 01831 411843
(take A387 1.75m from Looe site on left)
Signposted

ⓠⓠⓠⓠⓠⓠⓠⓠⓠⓠ

▶ ▶ ▶ ▶ De-Luxe Park 🚐 🚐 ▲
Open all year Booking advisable Jul & Aug Last arrival
23.00hrs Last departure 10.00hrs
*A mainly level grass site with good views. Signed off
A387 W of Looe. A 14-acre site with 254 touring pitches
and 62 statics.*

Nightly entertainment & solarium. 45m Flume in Pool

🔌📻⊙🗑🍳🔦✳🚰🛉🍴🔥🛉🍴💈🛝🐎
🏕🐕🐾♿
➔∪▶⛱🛝📹🎣

Credit Cards 💳 💳 💳 💳 💳

ⓠⓠⓠⓠⓠⓠⓠⓠⓠⓠ

Looe Valley Tourist Park (SX228536)
Polperro Rd PL13 2JS
☎ 01503 262425 (on A387 W of Looe 2.5m on right)
Signposted
▶ ▶ ▶ Family Park ★ 🚐 £8.90-£12.80 🚐 £8.90-£12.80
▲ £7-£10.90
Open Apr-Oct (rs May-Whit & mid-end Sep no
entertainment in club) Booking advisable last wk Jul-1st
2 wks Aug Last arrival 23.00hrs Last departure 11.00hrs
*A large holiday park under new ownership offering
many amenities. In a rural setting midway between
Looe and Polperro, offering a choice of beaches and
villages to visit. Signed off A387. A 30-acre site with 500
touring pitches and 36 statics.*
Dance hall/disco, crazy golf, off-licence, sinks.

🔌📻⊙🗑🍳🔦🚰📞✳🚰🛉🍴🔥🛉🍴🛝🍴🔥
🏕💈🐎🐕🐾
➔∪▶⛱🛝📹🎣

Credit Cards 💳 💳 💳 💳 💳 💳

See advertisement on p56.

Polborder House Caravan & Camping Park (SX283557)
Bucklawren Rd, St Martins PL13 1QR ☎ 01503 240265
(2.5m E, off B3253) Signposted
▶ ▶ ▶ **Family Park** ★ ⊕ £6-£8.50 ⊕ £6-£8.50 ▲ £6-£8.50
Open Etr or Apr-Oct Booking advisable Jul-Aug Last
arrival 22.00hrs Last departure noon
*A very neat and well-kept small grassy site on high
ground above Looe in a peaceful rural setting. Friendly
and enthusiastic owners. Site signed from A387. A 3-
acre site with 36 touring pitches and 5 statics.*
Washing up/food preparation sinks. Off-licence.

🄰 ⍾ ⊙ ◨ ⍟ ⚡ ⚹ 🅐 ⌀ ⊡ Ⓣ ⤟ ⛨ 🐾 ⚏ ⚼
➔ ∪ ⅃ ◎ △ ⅃ ⚌ ⌡

**Tregoad Farm Touring Caravan & Camping Park
(SX272560)**
St Martin's PL13 1PB ☎ 01503 262718 & 264777
Signposted
▶ ▶ ▶ **Family Park** ★ ⊕ £6.50-£10.50 ⊕ £6.50-£10.50
▲ £4-£10.50
Open Apr-Oct Booking advisable Jul & Aug Last arrival
21.00hrs
*A terraced grassy site with fine sea and rural views,
approx 1.5m from Looe. Signed with direct access from
B3253 & approaching Looe from E on A387 follow
B3253 for 1.75m towards Looe, and site on left. A 10-
acre site with 150 touring pitches and 4 statics.*
Fishing lake.

🄰 ⍾ ⊙ ◨ ⍟ ⚛ ⚹ ⛾ 🅐 🅐 ⌀ ⊡ Ⓣ ✘ ⚡ ⛩ 🏛
⛨ 🐾 ⚏
➔ ∪ ⅃ ◎ △ ⅃ ⚌ ⌡

Credit Cards 💳 💳 ◉ 💳 🖳 ⑤

LOSTWITHIEL

Powderham Castle Tourist Park (SX083593)
PL30 5BU ☎ 01208 872277 (1.5m SW on A390 turn right
at brown/white signpost in 400mtrs) Signposted
Nearby town: Fowey
▶ ▶ ▶ **Family Park** ★ ⊕ £6.60-£8.80 ⊕ £6.60-£8.80
▲ £6.60-£8.50
Open Apr-Oct Booking advisable peak periods Last
arrival 22.00hrs Last departure 11.30hrs
*A very quiet and well-run site in a good touring location,
set in mature parkland and well screened. 1.5m SW of
Lostwithiel, signed off A390 towards St Austell. A 12-
acre site with 70 touring pitches and 38 statics.*
Badminton, soft tennis, childrens paddling pool.

🄰 ⍾ ⊙ ◨ ⍟ ⚛ ⛾ ⚹ ⛾ 🅐 ⌀ ⊡ ⤟ ⚡ 🐕 ⚏
➔ ∪ ⅃ △ ⅃ ⌡ ⛨

LUXULYAN

Croft Farm Touring Park (SX044568)
PL30 5EQ ☎ 01726 850228
Nearby town: St Austell
▶ ▶ ▶ **Family Park** ★ ⊕ £5 ⊕ £5 ▲ £5
Open Apr-Oct Booking advisable Jul & Aug Last
departure noon
*A peaceful, picturesque setting at the edge of a wooded
valley. From A390 turn right past St Blazey level crossing
signed Luxulyan, turn right at T-junc, and right again at
next T-junc. From A30 turn left off Bodmin by-pass onto
A391, turn left at traffic lights at Bugle onto
B3374, turn left at Penwithick signed Trethurgy/ Luxulyan.
In 1.75m turn left at T-junc, and site on left in .5m. Do not
take any other routes signed Luxulyan or Luxulyan Valley.
A 5-acre site with 46 touring pitches and 6 statics.*

Mother & baby room, covered washing up area.

🄰 ⍾ ⊙ ◨ ⍟ ⚹ 🅐 🅐 ⌀ ⊡ Ⓣ ⤟ ⛨ 🐾 ⚏
➔ ⌡

Credit Cards 💳 💳 💳 ⑤

MAWGAN

See **Helston**

MAWGAN PORTH

Sun Haven Valley Caravan & Camping Site (SW861669)
TR8 4BQ ☎ 01637 860373 Signposted
Nearby town: Newquay

◯◯◯◯◯◯◯◯◯

▶ ▶ ▶ ▶ **De-Luxe Park** ⊕ ⊕ ▲
Open May-Sep (rs Etr & mid Sep no laundry or disabled
facilities) Booking advisable Jul-Aug Last arrival
22.00hrs Last departure 11.00hrs
*An attractive site set on the side of a river valley with a
camping area alongside the river. Exceptional floral
landscape and very high quality facilities. Situated .75m
from sea and fine sandy beach. Situated at Mawgan
Porth take unclass rd up Vale of Lanherne for 1m. Site on
left. A 5-acre site with 118 touring pitches and 36 statics.*

🄰 ⛟ ⍾ ⊙ ◨ ⍟ ⚛ ⤟ 🖵 ⚹ 🅐 🅐 ⌀ ⊡ Ⓣ ⤟ ⛩
⚏ ⅃
➔ ∪ ⅃ ◎ ⌡

Credit Cards 💳 💳

See advertisement on page 58.

◯◯◯◯◯◯◯◯

Trevarrian Holiday Park (SW853661)
TR8 4AQ ☎ 01637 860381 Signposted
Nearby town: Newquay
▶ ▶ ▶ **Family Park** ⊕ ⊕ ▲
Open Etr-Sep Booking advisable Jun-Aug Last arrival
22.00hrs Last departure 11.00hrs
*A well-established and well-run holiday park overlooking
Mawgan Porth beach. From A39 at St Columb rndbt turn
right onto A3059 towards Newquay. Fork left in approx
2m for St Mawgan to join B3276 coast road. Turn right
and site on left. A 7-acre site with 185 touring pitches.*
Sports field & pitch n putt.

🄰 ⛟ ⍾ ⊙ ◨ ⍟ ⚛ ⚛ ⚛ ⤟ 🖵 ⚹ ⛾ 🅐 🅐 ⌀ ⊡ Ⓣ
✘ ⤟ ⛨
➔ ∪ ⅃ ◎ ⅃ ⚌ ⌡

See advertisement on page 58.

MEVAGISSEY

See **Gorran, Boswinger & Pentewan & Advert on p 58.**

58

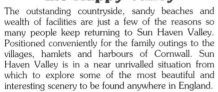
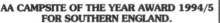

MULLION

Mullion Holiday Park (SW699182)
Lizard Peninsula, A3083 TR12 7LJ
☎ 01326 240000 & 240428
Signposted
Nearby town: Helston

★ ⚐ fr £5.75 ⚐ fr £5.75 ▲ fr £5.75
Open Etr & May-mid Sep Booking advisable Jul-Aug
Last arrival 21.00hrs Last departure 10.00hrs
A comprehensively equipped leisure park geared mainly for self-catering holidays, set in rugged moorland on the Lizard peninsula, adjacent to A3083 Helston road. A 10-acre site with 150 touring pitches and 347 statics.
Adventure playgrounds, sandpit, amusement & arcade.

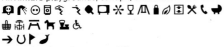

Credit Cards 💳 🌟 💳 💳 💳

See advertisement on page 59

'Franchis' Holiday Park (SW698203)
Cury Cross Lanes TR12 7AZ ☎ 01326 240301
Signposted
Nearby town: Helston
▶ ▶ ▶ **Family Park** ★ ⚐ £7-£8 ⚐ £7-£8 ▲ £7-£8

Open Wed before Etr-Sep (rs low season shop open on request) Booking advisable end Jul-Aug Last arrival 22.00hrs Last departure noon
This site is surrounded by hedges and coppices situated on the A3083 between Helston and The Lizard, an ideal position for exploring the Peninsula. A 4-acre site with 70 touring pitches and 12 statics.
Dive air to 3500 P.S.I. Dishwashing, Licensed shop

Credit Cards 💳 🌟 💳 💳 💳

Criggan Mill (SW670179)
Mullion Cove TR12 7EU ☎ 01326 240496 (follow signs to "The Cove")
Nearby town: Helston
▶ **Town & Country Pennant Park** ★ ⚐ £7-£9 ⚐ £7-£9
▲ £7-£9

Open Apr-Oct Booking advisable Jul-Aug Last arrival 22.00hrs Last departure 10.00hrs ⚒
A secluded site with level pitches in a combe near to Mullion Cove. From the A3083 Helston road take B3296 to Mullion. A 1-acre site with 5 touring pitches and 24 statics.

Credit Cards 💳 🌟 💳 💳 💳

NEWQUAY

Hendra Holiday Park (SW833601)
TR8 4NY ☎ 01637 875778 (2m SE)
Signposted

★ ⚐ £7.60-£11.30 ⚐ £7.60-£11.30 ▲ £7.60-£11.30
Open Etr or Apr-Oct (rs Apr-Spring bank hol) Booking advisable Jul-Aug Last arrival dusk Last departure noon
A large, long-established complex with mature trees and bushes set in downland, with superb leisure facilities. Situated 2m SE of Newquay, off Lane-Quintrell Downs road. A 46-acre site with 600 touring pitches and 160 statics.
Solarium, fish bar, sauna, kids club, train rides.

Credit Cards 💳 🌟 💳 💳

Newquay Holiday Park (SW853626)
TR8 4HS ☎ 01637 871111 (on A3059)
Signposted

★ ⚐ £7-£12 ⚐ £7-£12 ▲ £7-£12
Open 13 May-15 Sep Booking advisable Jun-Aug Last arrival 21.00hrs Last departure 10.00hrs ⚒
A well-managed and maintained site with a wide range of indoor and outdoor activities. Signed on B3059, 3m E of Newquay. A 14-acre site with 259 touring pitches and 137 statics.
Snooker/Pool tables,9hole pitch & putt, crazy golf.

Credit Cards 💳 🌟

See advertisement on page 62.

Trencreek Holiday Park (SW828609)
Higher Trencreek TR8 4NS ☎ 01637 874210 (A392 to Quintrell Downs, turn right in direction of Newquay, turn left at 2 mini rdbts into Trevenson rd to Trencreek)
Signposted

▶ ▶ ▶ ▶ **De-Luxe Park** ★ ⚐ £6.90-£10.50
⚐ £6.90-£10.50 ▲ £6.90-£10.50
Open Whit-mid Sep (rs Etr, Apr-May & late Sep swimming pool, cafe & bar closed) Booking advisable Jul-Aug Last arrival 22.00hrs Last departure noon ⚒
Slightly sloping grassy site with excellent facilities, set in meadowland in the village of Trencreek, 1.5m from
continued on p64.

NEWQUAY
CORNWALL

Excellent Camping & Touring Facilities
Luxury Static Caravans

Free Entertainment • Cabaret • Children's Pirate Den
Licensed Bars • Marios Bar • Fish and Chip Shop • Sauna
Supermarket • Food Bar • Amusements • Games Fields
Train Rides • Pitch n Putt • Heated Swimming Pools
and Waterslide • Adventure Playparks

To ensure everyones enjoyment,
Hendra Holiday Park caters exclusively
for families and couples only!

ROSE
AWARD

Hendra
HOLIDAY PARK

Brochure Hotline 0500 242523
Hendra Holiday Park, Newquay, Cornwall TR8 4NY
Tel: 01637 875778
e.mail: hendra.cornwall@dial.pipex.com
http://www.hendra-holidays.com

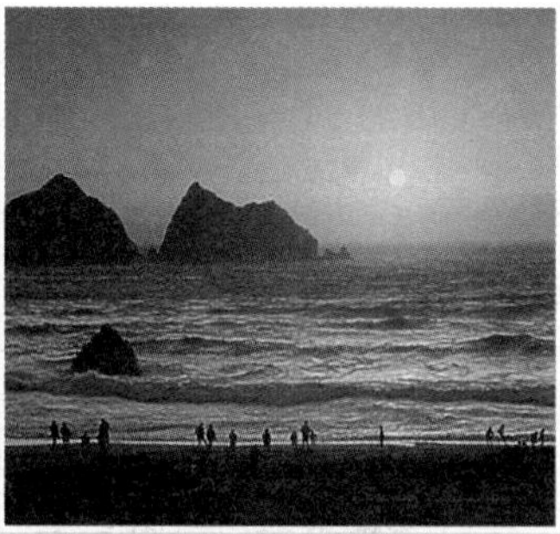

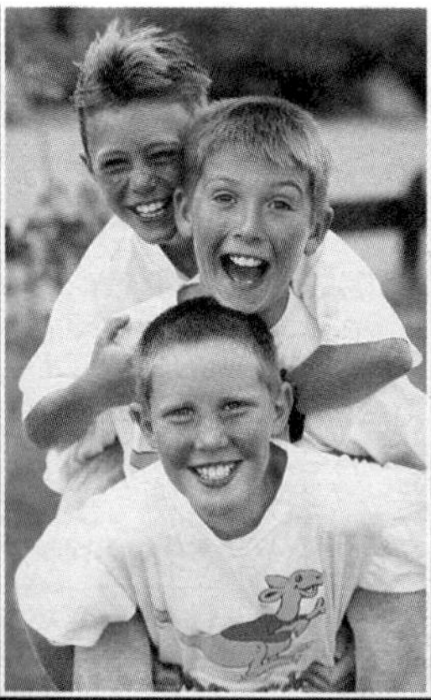

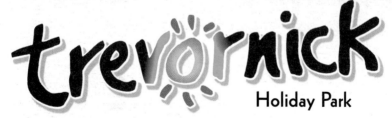

HOLIDAY PARK

A FAMILY-RUN PARK
WITH CAFE, BAR, SHOP, GAMES ROOM &
HEATED SWIMMING POOL.

SITUATED CLOSE TO BEACHES WITH
NEW MOBILE HOMES & EURO TENTS.
WELCOMING CAMPERS, TOURERS,
MOTOR CARAVANS & RALLIES!

Scotland Road, Rejerrah,
Newquay, CORNWALL TR8 5QL
Tel: 01872 572032 Fax: 01872 571298

Trencreek Holiday Park contd.
Newquay town centre. A 10-acre site with 194 touring pitches and 6 statics.
Coarse fishing on site.

😃 🎣 ⊙ 🗓 ⚡ ⚓ 🖵 ☀ ⚒ ⚠ 🛈 ⦿ ⊞ Ⓣ ✗ ☏ ⚓
🏛 🎢 🛅 ⚕
→ ∪ ► ◎ ⚠ ⚓ ♨ ♪

◠◠◠◠◠◠◠◠

Gwills Holiday Park (SW829592)
Ln TR8 4PE ☎ 01637 873617 (2m SE) Signposted
► ► ► Family Park 🚐 🚐 ⚊
Open Etr-Oct (rs Etr-Whitsun takeaway closed) Booking advisable Jul-Aug Last arrival 21.00hrs Last departure 10.00hrs
A lightly wooded, riverside site with level and sloping pitches. From A30 turn R at Indian Queens to A392 then follow unclass road between Lane and Newlyn East. An 11-acre site with 140 touring pitches and 30 statics. Fishing.

😃 🎣 ⊙ 🗓 ⚡ ⚓ 🖵 ☀ ⚒ ⚠ 🛈 ⊞ ☏ ⚕ 🐕
🛅
→ ∪ ► ◎ ⚠ ⚓ ♪

Credit Cards 💳 💳 💳 💳

Porth Beach Tourist Park (SW834629)
Porth TR7 3NH ☎ 01637 876531 (1m NE) Signposted
► ► ► Family Park ★ 🚐 £5.25-£22.95 🚐 £5.25-£22.95
⚊ £5.25-£22.95
Open Mar-Oct Booking advisable Jul-Aug Last arrival 21.00hrs Last departure 10.00hrs

Trevella & Newperran
CARAVAN AND CAMPING PARK   TOURIST PARK

Both parks have spotless facilities including modern toilet and shower blocks with individual wash cubicles, razor points, babies room, hairdressing room, hairdriers, launderette, crazy golf, games room, TV room, cafe, shop and off licence, free heated swimming pools and adventure play areas.

Our reputation for cleanliness, friendly and courteous service have earned each park the highest AA rating of 4 pennants and the Top AA Assessment of "Excellent" for Sanitary installations.

• Concessionary green fees at Perranporth's excellent links course.
• The well stocked lake at Trevella offers Free Fishing (no closed season).

TREVELLA PARK 15 CRANTOCK, NEWQUAY, CORNWALL TR8 5EW. TEL: 01637 830308
Trevella just outside Newquay and its seven golden beaches. A breathtakingly beautiful secluded family park. As well as touring pitches there are holiday caravans for hire with toilet, shower and colour Satellite TV.

VOTED TWO OF THE TOP 10 TOURING PARKS IN CORNWALL

NEWPERRAN TOURIST PARK 15 REJERRAH, NEWQUAY, CORNWALL TR8 5QJ.
TEL: 01872 572407
Newperran has been developed from a small Cornish farm in a picturesque, beautifully cared for setting. It is a level park with perimeter pitching ideal for caravans, tents, motor homes and the perfect family holiday.

TELEPHONE FOR COLOUR BROCHURES
01637 830308 (24 HOURS)
OR WRITE FOR BROCHURE TO THE SITE OF YOUR CHOICE.

A well-run site set in meadowland adjacent to sea and a fine sandy beach. Off B3276. A 6-acre site with 201 touring pitches and 12 statics.

🏠📞☉🗑☀⛰🏊◢🔌⛽🛁

➔∪▶☉⛰❄↖🎣

Credit Cards 💳 ▭ ▭ ▦ 🔁 Ⓢ

Rosecliston Park (SW815594)
Trevemper TR8 5JT ☎ 01637 830326 (2m S on A3075)
Signposted
▶▶▶ Family Park ★ 🏕 £7.80-£11.50 🚐 £7.80-£11.50
⛺ £7.80-£11.50
Open Whit-mid Sep Booking advisable Jul-Aug Last arrival 22.00hrs Last departure 10.00hrs
Small, well-organised site with attractively arranged pitches. From N on A3075 signed Redruth. On left in .5m. An 8-acre site with 130 touring pitches.
Sauna & solarium.

🏠📞☉🗑✉📶 ⚡◀🔌❄☂🔌◢⊞Ⓣ📞♿🛁

➔∪☉↖🎣

Credit Cards 💳 ▭ ▦ 🔁 Ⓢ

Trebellan Park (SW790571)
Cubert TR8 5PY ☎ 01637 830522
▶▶▶ Family Park 🚐 🚐 ⛺
Open Etr-Oct
A terraced grassy rural park within a picturesque valley with views of Cubert Common, and adjacent to the Smuggler's Den, a 16th-century thatched inn. 4m S of Newquay, turn W off A3075 at Cubert signpost, and turn
continued on p66.

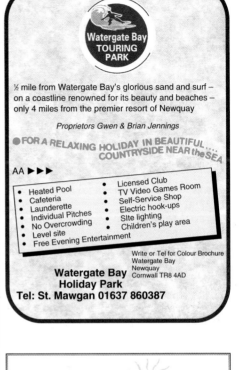

left in .75m onto unclass minor rd. An 8-acre site with 150 touring pitches.
Three well stocked coarse fishing lakes.

🔷 📻 ☉ 🗄 🏴 ⚡ ◀ 💢 ✳ 🏍 🎱 🦵

Treloy Tourist Park (SW858625)
TR8 4JN ☎ 01637 872063 & 876279 (just off A3059) Signposted
▶ ▶ ▶ Family Park ★ 🏕 £5-£9.80 🚐 £5-£9.80 ▲ £5-£9.80
Open Apr-Oct (rs Apr swimming pool & bar closed)
Booking advisable Jul-Aug Last arrival mdnt Last departure 11.00hrs
Attractive site with fine countryside views, within easy reach of resorts and beaches. From A3058 take A3059, and site signed on left. A 12-acre site with 119 touring pitches.
Golf, entertainment, childs club, fishing nearby.

🔷 📻 ☉ 🗄 🏴 ⚡ ◀ 💢 ✳ ⛱ 🏍 🖊 🔲 ✖ 🦵 🚐
🍴 🐕 🎱
➔ ∪ ⌐ ◎ 🔺 ✢ ✦
Credit Cards 💳 ▩ 🗒

See advertisement on page 65.

Trenance Caravan & Chalet Park (SW818612)
Edgcumbe Av TR7 2JY ☎ 01637 873447 Signposted
▶ ▶ ▶ Family Park ★ 🏕 £6.50-£11 🚐 £6.50-£11
▲ £6.50-£11
Open 26 May-Oct (rs Apr-25 May no showers or take-away restaurant) Booking advisable Jul-Aug Last arrival 22.00hrs Last departure 10.00hrs ✣
Principally a static park with a small, upgraded touring area on high ground, set within the urban confines of

Newquay. Off A3075 near viaduct. Entrance by boating lake rndbt. A 12-acre site with 50 touring pitches and 190 statics.
Dishwashing facilities.

🔷 📻 ☉ 🗄 🏴 ◀ ✳ 🖊 🔲 ✖ 🦵 🚩 ⛏ 🎱
➔ ∪ ⌐ ◎ 🔺 ✢ ✦
Credit Cards 💳 ▩ ▦ 🗒

Trethiggey Touring Park (SW846596)
Quintrell Downs TR8 4LG ☎ 01637 877672 (2m SE A392) Signposted
▶ ▶ ▶ Family Park ★ 🏕 £8.90 🚐 £8.90 ▲ £8.90
Open Mar-Dec Booking advisable Jul-Aug
A pleasant, improving site divided into paddocks with maturing trees and shrubs. On the A3058 3m from Newquay. A 15-acre site with 120 touring pitches and 12 statics.
Off licence & dishwashing sinks, recreation field.

🔷 📻 ☉ 🗄 🏴 ⚡ ◀ 💢 ✳ 🏍 🖊 🔲 🔲 ⓣ 🦵 ⛏ 🎱 🛖
🐕 🎱 ♿
➔ ∪ ⌐ ◎ 🔺 ✢ ✦
Credit Cards 💳 ▩ 🔳

NOTTER BRIDGE

Notter Bridge Caravan & Camping Park (SX384608)
PL12 4RW ☎ 01752 842318 (on A38, 3.5m W of Tamar Bridge) Signposted
Nearby town: Plymouth
▶ ▶ ▶ Family Park ★ 🏕 £4.50-£6.50 🚐 £4.50-£6.50
▲ £4.50-£6.50
Open Etr-Sep Booking advisable peak periods Last arrival 22.00hrs Last departure 11.00hrs
Small, level grassy riverside site in wooded Lynner Valley, adjacent to A38, 2m W of Saltash. Fishing licences available. A 6.25-acre site with 33 touring pitches and 23 statics.
Salmon & trout fishing.

🔷 📻 ☉ 🗄 ✳ 🏍 🖊 🦵 ⛏ 🐕
➔ ⌐ 🔺 ♨ ✦ 🎱

OTTERHAM

St Tinney Farm Holidays (SX169906)
PL32 9TA ☎ 01840 261274 (1m off A39) Signposted
Nearby town: Bude
▶ ▶ ▶ Family Park ★ 🏕 £5-£7.50 🚐 £5-£7.50 ▲ £5-£7.50
Open Etr-Oct Booking advisable Spring bank hol & Jul-Aug Last arrival 21.00hrs Last departure 11.00hrs
A family-run farm site in a rural area, with nature trails, lakes, valleys and complete seclusion. Take unclass rd off A39 signed Otterham, and site signed. A 5-acre site with 20 touring pitches and 9 statics.
Coarse fishing, horse & donkey rides, farm animals

🔷 📻 ☉ 🗄 ⚡ ◀ ✳ ⛱ 🏍 🖊 🔲 ✖ 🦵 ⛏ 🍴 🎱
➔ ∪ ♨ ✦
Credit Cards 💳 ▩

PADSTOW

Dennis Cove Camping (SW918743)
Dennis Farm, Dennis Cove PL28 8DR ☎ 01841 532349
Signposted
▶ ▶ ▶ Family Park ★ 🏕 £7.85-£11 🚐 £7.85-£11
▲ £7.85-£11

Open Whitsun-Sep (rs Etr-Whitsun & Sep onwards swimming pool & club closed) Booking advisable before Etr Last arrival 23.00hrs Last departure noon
Level and slightly sloping site with mature trees set in meadowland, overlooking Padstow Bay with access to River Camel estuary and Padstow Bay beach. Approach Padstow on A389 and turn right into Sarah's Lane. A 4.5-acre site with 63 touring pitches.

ſ⊙ ﮯ ✼ ♀ /ᐭ ▮ ⌀ ✸ ✕ ☚ ⛟ ⊡
→ ∪ ⌿ ⊚ ◬ ⅄ ☙ ✒ ⊡ ⛾

Trerethern Touring Park (SW913738)
PL28 8LE ☎ 01841 532061 (on A389 1m SSW town) Signposted
▶ ▶ ▶ **Family Park** ★ ♨ £6-£9 ♙ £6-£9 ▲ £6-£9
Open Apr-mid Oct Booking advisable Jul-Aug Last arrival 19.00hrs Last departure 16.00hrs
A rather open site situated 2m S of Padstow on eastern side of A389 Padstow-Wadebridge road. A 13.5-acre site with 100 touring pitches.
Motorvan hardstanding, electric & pumpout.

✿ ſ ⊙ ◙ ⚲ ✼ /ᐭ ▮ ⌀ ✸ ⊤ ☚ ⼮ ⛾ ⅄
→ ∪ ⌿ ◬ ⅄ ☙ ✒

PELYNT (NEAR LOOE)

Camping Caradon (SX218539)
Trelawne PL13 2NA ☎ 01503 272388 Signposted
Nearby town: Looe
▶ ▶ ▶ **Family Park** ★ ♨ £5-£8.50 ♙ £5-£7.50
▲ £4.50-£8.50
Open Etr-Oct Booking advisable Jul-Aug Last arrival 20.00hrs Last departure 11.00hrs
Established residential site with a level grass touring park in rural setting. Off B3359, between Looe and Polperro. A 4-acre site with 85 touring pitches and 1 static.
See advertisement under POLPERRO

✿ ſ ⊙ ◙ ⚲ ⌿ ✼ ♀ /ᐭ ▮ ⌀ ✸ ⊤ ✕ ☚ ⛟ ⛾
→ ∪ ⊚ ⅄ ☙ ✒

Trelay Farmpark (SX219545)
PL13 2JX ☎ 01503 220900 & 220993 (on B3359 towards Pelynt, 1m on right) Signposted
Nearby town: Liskeard
▶ ▶ ▶ **Family Park** ★ ♨ £7-£8.50 ♙ £7-£8.50
▲ £7-£8.50
Open Apr-Oct Booking advisable Jul & Aug Last arrival 21.00hrs
A slightly sloping, grass site in a rural area with extensive views. Signed off B3359, .5m S of Pelynt (on the Looe side). 3m from Looe and Polperro. A 3-acre site with 55 touring pitches and 20 statics.

✿ ſ ⊙ ◙ ⚲ ✼ ▮ ⌀ ✸ ☚ ⇖ ⼮ ⼎ ⅄
→ ∪ ◬ ⅄ ☙ ✒ ⛾

PENTEWAN

Sun Valley Holiday Park (SX005486)
Pentewan Rd PL26 6DJ ☎ 01726 843266 Signposted
Nearby town: St Austell

◯◯◯◯◯◯◯◯◯◯

▶ ▶ ▶ ▶ ▶ **Premier Park** ♨ £7.50-£20 ♙ £7.50-£20
▲ £7.50-£20

Open Apr (or Etr if earlier)-Oct Booking advisable May-Sep Last arrival 22.00hrs Last departure noon
A mainly static park in a woodland setting with a neat and well-maintained touring park. Sanitary facilities are outstanding. Situated 1m from sea, beach and river on B3273 St Austell-Mevagissey road. A 4-acre site with 22 touring pitches and 75 statics.

✿ ſ ⊙ ◙ ⚲ ⅏ ⚲ ◖ ✼ ♀ /ᐭ ▮ ⌀ ✸ ✕ ☚ ⛟
⼮ ⼎ ⼮ ⛾
→ ∪ ⌿ ◬ ⅄ ☙ ✒
Credit Cards ⬤ ▦ ▨ 🎵

◯◯◯◯◯◯◯◯◯◯

Penhaven Touring Park (SX008481)
PL26 6DL ☎ 01726 843687 Signposted
Nearby town: St Austell
▶ ▶ ▶ **Family Park** ★ ♨ £8-£17 ♙ £8-£17 ▲ £8-£13
Open Etr or Apr-Oct Booking advisable public hols & end Jul-Aug Last arrival 22.00hrs Last departure 10.00hrs
Level, landscaped site in wooded valley, with river running by and 1m from sandy beach at Pentewan. Situated on B3273. A 13-acre site with 105 touring pitches.
Off-licence.

✿ ſ ⊙ ◙ ⚲ ﮯ ✼ /ᐭ ▮ ⌀ ✸ ⊤ ☚ ⛟ ⼮ ⼎ ⅄
→ ∪ ⌿ ◬ ⅄ ☙ ✒
Credit Cards ⬤ ▦ ▨ ▨ 🎵

Pentewan Sands Holiday Park (SX018468)
PL26 6BT ☎ 01726 843485 (on B3273) Signposted
Nearby town: Mevagissey
▶ ▶ ▶ Family Park ★ 🛖 £6-£15 🚐 £6-£15 ▲ £6-£15
Open 15 May-14 Sep (rs Apr-14 May & 15 Sep-Oct shop,
snacks, pool, clubhouse ltd or closed) Booking advisable
Jul-Aug Last arrival 22.00hrs Last departure 10.30hrs ✵
*A large camping site on the dunes adjacent to a private
beach, well equipped for aquatic activities. 4m S of St
Austell on B3273. A 32-acre site with 480 touring pitches
and 120 statics.*
Mini golf, cycle hire, boat launching, water sports.

🔌�🐾⊙🍴🏴🪣⚡❀🍴🔍🏕🛖🛡🌿🔋⊡Ⓣ✗
📞🚿🛒♿
➜∪🅿◎⚠⌇🐾🎵

Credit Cards 💳 🆅🆉 💳 📇 🅖

PENZANCE

Bone Valley Caravan Park (SW472316)
Heamoor TR20 8UJ ☎ 01736 360313 Signposted
▶ ▶ ▶ Family Park ★ 🛖 £7-£9 🚐 £7-£8 ▲ £7-£9
Open Mar-7 Jan (rs Oct-Dec & Mar shop closed)
Booking advisable Jul-Aug Last arrival 22.00hrs Last
departure 11.00hrs ✵
*A compact grassy riverside site on the outskirts of
Penzance, with well maintained facilities. Follow A30 to
west Penzance and signs to Heamoor. At 1st crossroads
turn right, then 1st left; signed. A 1-acre site with 17
touring pitches and 1 static.*

🔌🐾⊙🍴🏴❀🪣🌿⊡🔋
➜∪◎⚠⌇🐾🎵

PERRANARWORTHAL

Cosawes Caravan Park (SW768376)
TR3 7QS ☎ 01872 863724 & 863717 (on A39)
Signposted
Nearby town: Truro
▶ ▶ ▶ Family Park ★ 🛖 £7.50-£9.50 🚐 £6.50-£8.50
▲ £6-£9
Open all year Booking advisable mid Jul-mid Aug
*A small touring park in a peaceful wooded valley,
midway between Truro and Falmouth. 6m W of Truro
on A39. A 2-acre site with 40 touring pitches and 100
statics.*
Squash court.

🔌🐾⊙🍴🏴❀🪣🌿⊡Ⓣ📞🏛🎄🐕🔋
➜∪🅿◎⚠⌇🎵🛒

PERRANPORTH

Perranporth Camping & Touring Site (SW768542)
Budnick Rd TR6 0DB ☎ 01872 572174 Signposted
▶ ▶ ▶ Family Park 🛖🚐▲
Open Whit-Sep (rs Etr-Whitsun & mid Sep-end Sep
shop & club facilities) Booking advisable Jul-Aug Last
arrival 23.00hrs Last departure noon
*A mainly tenting site with few level pitches but adjacent
to a fine sandy beach. .5m E off B3285. A 6-acre site
with 180 touring pitches and 9 statics.*

🔌�🐾⊙🍴🏴🪣⚡🍴⊡❀🍴🏕🛖🛡🌿⊡Ⓣ✗
📞🚿🏛🐕🛒♿
➜∪🅿⚠⌇🎵

Credit Cards 💳 🆅🆉

Perranporth ▶▶▶▶ Camping & Touring Park

The park, within easy walking distance (approx. 5 minutes) of beach and town, comprises seven acres of well drained sheltered grass land with tarmacadam access roads and all modern facilities.

Mini Supermarket • Swimming Pool • Launderette • Showers and Washrooms • Six berth luxury vans • Adjacent 'Failte Club' with licensed bar, overlooking heated swimming pool and children's paddling pool • Cafeteria.

Budnick Road, Perranporth, Cornwall
Tel: Perranporth (0187257) 2174

AA Camping Club, Caravan Club
British Tourist Authority listed site

Killigarth Manor Holiday Park

POLPERRO near LOOE, CORNWALL
EXCELLENT CAMPING & TOURING CARAVAN FACILITIES
★★ PLUS LUXURY SELF CATERING HOLIDAY HOMES ★★

Set in beautiful countryside close to picturesque Polperro and Talland Bay. Family run holiday park exclusively for families and couples.

★ Bars ★ Top class entertainment
★ Indoor swimming pool
★ Fitness room ★ Sauna
★ Sunbed ★ Amusement arcade
★ Mini cinema ★ Restaurant
★ Takeaway ★ Snooker ★ Pool
★ Darts ★ Mini market
★ Launderette ★ Tennis court

KIDS MEET PUGWASH AND POLLY-PERRO IN THE PIRATE CLUB

FOR BROCHURE & BOOKINGS
TEL: 01503 272216

EXCELLENT

KILLIGARTH MANOR HOLIDAY PARK
POLPERRO, LOOE, CORNWALL PL13 2JQ

AA AWARD FOR EXCELLENCE FOR LEISURE FACILITIES

ROSEHILL FARM TOURIST PARK

Perranporth

Our friendly 7 acre touring park offers level pitches in a rural setting with distant country views, yet only minutes from Perranporth's famous beach. Peace and quiet plus free hot showers, laundry room, shop, play area, electric hook-ups, dog walking field.

RING OR WRITE FOR BROCHURE
LES AND SUE ROLFE

200/153 ROSEHILL FARM TOURIST PARK
GOONHAVERN, TRURO, TR4 9LA
TELEPHONE: 01872 572448

Camping Caradon

Personally supervised family run touring park in peaceful, secluded location midway Looe/Polperro. With level pitches and good access for tourers, motor homes and tents. Licensed club house with evening social activities. Ideal for couples and families. Write or telephone for brochure.

Camping Caradon, Trelawne, nr. Looe, Cornwall PL13 2NA.
Tel: 01503-272388

POLPERRO

Killigarth Manor Holiday Estate (SX214519)
PL13 2JQ ☎ 01503 272216 & 272409
Signposted
Nearby town: Looe

⊙⊙⊙⊙⊙⊙⊙⊙⊙⊙⊙⊙⊙⊙⊙⊙⊙⊙⊙

★ ⊞ £8.80-£12.90 ⊞ £8.80-£12.90 ▲ £8.80-£12.90
Open Etr-Oct Booking advisable 3rd wk Jul-Aug Last
arrival 20.00hrs Last departure noon ⌧
*A well-ordered site on high ground on the approach to
a historic fishing village on the A 387. A large touring
and holiday complex with many amenities and facilities.
A 7-acre site with 202 touring pitches and 147 statics.
Amusement arcade, pool table & table tennis.*

🖾🖾⊙🖾🖾🖾 🖾🖾🖾🖾🖾🖾🖾🖾🖾🖾🖾🖾🖾
🖾🖾🖾🖾🖾🖾
➔🖾🖾🖾🖾🖾🖾

Credit Cards 🖾 🖾 🖾 🖾 🖾

See advertisement on page 69.

⊙⊙⊙⊙⊙⊙⊙⊙⊙⊙⊙⊙⊙⊙⊙⊙⊙⊙⊙

POLRUAN

Polruan Holiday Centre (SX133509)
Polruan-by-Fowey PL23 1QH ☎ 01726 870263
Signposted
Nearby town: Looe

►►► **Family Park** ★ ⊞ £6-£9 ⊞ £6-£9 ▲ £4-£9
Open Etr-Sep Booking advisable Jul, Aug & bank hols
Last arrival 21.00hrs Last departure noon
*A very rural and quiet site in a lovely elevated position
above the village, with good views. River Fowey
passenger ferry close by. Leave A390 at East Taphouse
and turn left onto B3359 after 4m. Turn right onto
unclass rd signed Polruan, and site signed. A 3-acre site
with 32 touring pitches and 11 statics.*
Tourist information.

🖾🖾⊙🖾🖾🖾🖾🖾🖾🖾🖾🖾🖾🖾🖾🖾🖾🖾
➔🖾🖾🖾🖾🖾

POLZEATH

South Winds Caravan & Camping Park (SW948790)
Polzeath Rd PL27 6QU ☎ 01208 863267 & 862646
Signposted
Nearby town: Wadebridge

►►► **Family Park** ★ ⊞ £8-£12 ⊞ £8-£12 ▲ £6-£12
Open Mar-Oct Booking advisable Jul & Aug Last arrival
23.00hrs Last departure 11.00hrs

*A peaceful site with beautiful sea and panoramic rural
views, within walking distance of new golf complex,*

*and 0.75m from beach and village. Leave B3314 on
unclassified road signed Polzeath, and park is on right
just past turn to New Polzeath. A 6-acre site with 50
touring pitches.*

🖾🖾⊙🖾🖾🖾🖾🖾🖾🖾🖾🖾🖾🖾🖾🖾🖾🖾
➔🖾🖾⊙🖾🖾🖾🖾🖾

Credit Cards 🖾 🖾

Tristram Caravan & Camping Park (SW936790)
PL27 6UG ☎ 01208 862215 & 863267 Signposted
Nearby town: Wadebridge

►►► **Family Park** ★ ⊞ £10-£20 ⊞ £10-£15 ▲ £10-£15
Open Mar-Oct Booking advisable Jul & Aug Last arrival
23.00hrs Last departure 10.00hrs
*An ideal family site, positioned on a gently-sloping cliff
with grassy pitches and glorious sea views. Direct gated
access to the beach, where surfing is very popular.
From B3314 take unclassified road signed Polzeath, go
through the village and up the hill, and site is 2nd
turning on right. A 10-acre site with 100 touring pitches.*

🖾🖾⊙🖾🖾🖾🖾🖾🖾🖾🖾🖾🖾🖾🖾🖾🖾🖾
🖾🖾
➔🖾🖾⊙🖾🖾🖾🖾🖾

Credit Cards 🖾 🖾 🖾 🖾 🖾 🖾 🖾

PORTHTOWAN

Porthtowan Tourist Park (SW693473)
Mile Hill TR4 8TY ☎ 01209 890256 & 890011 Signposted
Nearby town: Redruth

►►► **Family Park** ⊞ £5-£8.50 ⊞ £5-£8.50 ▲ £5-£8.50
Open Etr-Oct Booking advisable Jul-Aug Last departure
noon
*A neat, level grassy site on high ground above
Porthtowan, with maturing landscape providing shelter
from winds. Leave A30 at Redruth onto unclass rd
signed Portreath, and in 3m at T junc turn right for
Porthtowan. Site on left. A 5.5-acre site with 50 touring
pitches.*

🖾🖾⊙🖾🖾🖾🖾🖾🖾🖾🖾🖾🖾🖾🖾🖾🖾
➔🖾🖾⊙🖾🖾🖾🖾

Rose Hill Touring Park (SW693466)
Rose Hill TR4 8AR ☎ 01209 890802 Signposted
Nearby town: St Agnes

►►► **Family Park** ★ ⊞ £6.50-£9.50 ⊞ £6.50-£9.50
▲ £6.50-£9.50
Open end Mar-end Oct Booking advisable Jun-Aug Last
arrival 21.30hrs Last departure 11.00hrs ⌧
*A small, well-kept park in an attractive position, set into
the hillside and terraced. Site at bottom of descent to
port. A 2.5-acre site with 40 touring pitches.*
Tourist information.

🖾🖾⊙🖾🖾🖾🖾🖾🖾🖾🖾🖾
➔🖾🖾🖾🖾🖾🖾

PORTSCATHO

Treloan Farm Touring Park (SW876348)
Portscatho Ln TR2 5EF ☎ 01872 580989
►► **Town & Country Pennant Park** ⊞ ⊞ ▲
Open Apr-Oct Booking advisable Last departure
11.00hrs

A quiet and well-screened coastal site with mature trees and bushes, and three secluded nearby beaches. Take unclass rd to Gerrans off A3078 Tregony-St-Mawes rd. Immed after Gerrans church, road divides - take section beside Royal Standard pub. A 5-acre site with 49 touring pitches and 8 statics.

♀ ₨ ☉ ⓵
→ ◭ ⅃ ⴲ

REDRUTH

Cambrose Touring Park (SW684453)
Portreath Rd TR16 4HT ☎ 01209 890747 (take B3300 towards Portreath pass Gold Centre on left 1st rd on rght (Porthtowan Rd). Entrance to site 100yds on left) Signposted
Nearby town: Portreath
► ► ► Family Park ★ ⚘ £7-£9.50 ⚘ £7-£9.50 ▲ £7-£9.50
Open Apr-Oct Booking advisable Jul-Aug Last arrival 22.00hrs Last departure 11.30hrs
A mature park in a rural setting with trees and bushes. 2m from Redruth off B3300 (signposted 'Porthtowan and Portreath' from A30). A 6-acre site with 60 touring pitches.

♀ ₨ ☉ ⓵ ⚙ ⌇ ◖ ✳ ⋀ 🛈 ⌀ ⊞ Ⓣ ⓵ ⛲ ♞
ⴲ ও
→ ∪ ▶ ◎ ♨ 🎥 ✔

Lanyon Park (SW684387)
Loscombe Ln, Four Lanes TR16 6LP ☎ 01209 313474
► ► ► Family Park ★ ⚘ £4-£8.50 ⚘ £4-£8.50
▲ £3.50-£8
Open Mar-Oct & mid Jan-mid Feb Booking advisable Jul & Aug Last departure noon
Small, friendly rural park in elevated position with fine views to distant St Ives Bay. Signed 0.5m off B2397 on Helston side of Four Lanes village. A 10-acre site with 25 touring pitches and 49 statics.

♀ 🖴 ₨ ⓵ ⚙ ⌇ ✳ ⚲ ✗ ⓵ ⛲ ⋒ ♞
→ ∪

Tehidy Holiday Park (SW682432)
Harris Mill, Illogan TR16 4JQ ☎ 01209 216489 & 314558 (2m NW off B3300 on N side of A30) Signposted
► ► ► Family Park ⚘ £6.50-£7.50 ⚘ £6.50-£7.50
▲ £6.50-£7.50

Open Etr-Oct Booking advisable Jul-Aug Last arrival 20.00hrs Last departure 10.00hrs ⌕ no cars by caravans
An attractive wooded location in a quiet rural area only 2.5m from popular beaches. Mostly level pitches on tiered ground. Signed onto unclass rd off B3300 on

Redruth side of Cornish Gold Centre. A 1-acre site with 18 touring pitches and 32 statics.
Badminton, off-licence.

♀ ₨ ☉ 🖴 ⌇ ◖ ⟎ ✳ ⋀ 🛈 ⌀ ⊞ Ⓣ ⓵ ⋒ ⴲ
→ ∪ ▶ ◭ ⅃ ♨ ✔
Credit Cards ● 🔤 🔤 Ⓖ

REJERRAH

Newperran Tourist Park (SW801555)
TR8 5QJ ☎ 01872 572407 in season & 01637 830308 Signposted
Nearby town: Newquay

◯◯◯◯◯◯◯

► ► ► ► De-Luxe Park ★ ⚘ £6.40-£10.60
⚘ £5.80-£9.80 ▲ £6.40-£10.60
Open mid May-mid Sep Booking advisable Jul-Aug
A very good family site in a lovely rural position, central for several beaches and bays. In an airy location, but with some screening from wind. 4m SE of Newquay and 1m S of Rejerrah on A3075. A 25-acre site with 270 touring pitches.
Crazy golf, adventure playground, pool & badminton.

♀ 🖴 ₨ ☉ 🖴 ⌇ ◖ ⟎ ✳ ⛱ ⋀ 🛈 ⌀ ⊞ Ⓣ ✗
⓵ 🖴 ♞ ⴲ &
→ ∪ ▶ ◎ ◭ ⅃ ♨ ✔
Credit Cards ● 🔤 🔤 🔤 🔤 Ⓖ

◯◯◯◯◯◯◯

Monkey Tree Touring Park (SW803545)
TR8 5QL ☎ 01872 572032 Signposted
Nearby town: Newquay
► ► ► Family Park ⚘ ⚘ ▲
Open all year (rs Apr swimming pool weather permitting, shop) Booking advisable main season Last arrival 22.00hrs Last departure from 10.00
A quiet, open moorland setting, well-screened by mature hedges on high ground near the N Cornwall coast. Access from Rejerrah-Zelah road off A3075. A 12-acre site with 295 touring pitches and 6 statics.
Sauna, solarium, mountain bike hire & football pitch
See advertisement under NEWQUAY

♀ ₨ ☉ 🖴 ⌇ ◖ ⟎ ✳ ⛱ ⋀ 🛈 ⌀ ⊞ Ⓣ ✗ ◖
⋒ 🖴 ♞ ⴲ &
→ ∪ ▶ ◭ ⅃ ♨ ✔
Credit Cards ● 🔤 🔤 Ⓖ

RELUBBUS

River Valley Country Park (SW565326)
TR20 9ER ☎ 01736 763398 (from A30 signpost Helston A394, next rbdt 1st left signposted Relubbus) Signposted
Nearby town: St Ives

◯◯◯◯◯◯◯

► ► ► ► De-Luxe Park ★ ⚘ £6.50-£10 ⚘ £6.50-£10
▲ £6.50-£10
Open Mar-5 Jan (rs Nov-4 Jan hardstanding only) Booking advisable Jul-Aug Last arrival 20.00hrs Last departure 11.00hrs
A quiet, attractive, family-run site of quality in a picturesque river valley with direct access to shallow trout stream. Situated 4m from N and S coast sandy

contd.

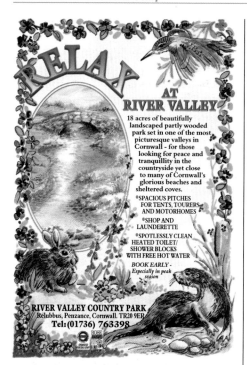

RELAX AT RIVER VALLEY

18 acres of beautifully landscaped partly wooded park set in one of the most picturesque valleys in Cornwall - for those looking for peace and tranquillity in the countryside yet close to many of Cornwall's glorious beaches and sheltered coves.

●SPACIOUS PITCHES FOR TENTS, TOURERS AND MOTORHOMES
●SHOP AND LAUNDERETTE
●SPOTLESSLY CLEAN HEATED TOILET/ SHOWER BLOCKS WITH FREE HOT WATER
BOOK EARLY - Especially in peak season

RIVER VALLEY COUNTRY PARK
Relubbus, Penzance, Cornwall. TR20 9ER
Tel: (01736) 763398

beaches, 3m from Marazion on B3280. An 18-acre site with 150 touring pitches and 27 statics.
Washing up sinks, fishing.

🔲 📞 ☉ 🔵 🍴 ☀ 🔩 🛢 ⊞ 🔲 T 📞 🐕 🐾
→ ∪ ► ⊙ ♨

Credit Cards

ROSUDGEON

Kenneggy Cove Holiday Park (SW562287)
Higher Kenneggy TR20 9AU ☎ 01736 763453
Signposted
Nearby town: Penzance
► ► ► Family Park ★ 🚐 £4.50-£7.50 🚐 £4.50-£7.50
▲ £4.50-£7.50
Open Apr-Nov Booking advisable Jul-Aug Last arrival 21.00hrs Last departure 11.00hrs
An attractive and neatly-kept site within a short walk of a sheltered, sandy beach and with lovely sea views. 6m W of Helston and 6m E of Penzance off A394, overlooking Mount's Bay. A 4-acre site with 60 touring pitches and 9 statics.

🔲 📞 ☉ 🔵 🍴 ☀ 🔩 🛢 ⊞ T 📞 ⛲ 🐕 🐾
→ ∪ ► ⊙ ♨

RUTHERNBRIDGE

Ruthern Valley Holidays (SX014665)
PL30 5LU ☎ 01208 831395 Signposted
Nearby town: Bodmin
► ► ► Family Park 🚐 £7.75-£10.90 🚐 £7.75-£10.90
▲ £7.75-£9.50

Open Apr-Oct Booking advisable high season Last arrival 21.00hrs Last departure noon
An attractive woodland site in remote, small river valley S of Bodmin Moor. From A30 just past W end of Bodmin bypass, site signed on right on unclass rd to Ruthernbridge. A 2-acre site with 29 touring pitches and 6 statics.
Off-licence.

🔲 📞 ☉ 🔵 ☀ 🔩 🛢 🔩 ⊞ 📞 🏠 🐾
→ ∪ ♨

ST AGNES

Beacon Cottage Farm Touring Park (SW705502)
Beacon Dr TR5 0NU ☎ 01872 552347 (left after St Agnes museum & follow signs)
Nearby town: Truro
► ► ► Family Park ★ 🚐 £5-£12 🚐 £5-£12 ▲ £5-£12
Open end May-Oct (rs Etr-Whitsun shop closed)
Booking advisable Jul-Aug Last arrival 20.00hrs Last departure noon
A neat and compact site utilizing a cottage and outhouses, an old orchard and adjoining walled paddock. Unique location on a headland looking NE along the coast. From A30 at Threeburrows rndbt take B3277 to St Agnes, then Beacon Rd left. A 4-acre site with 50 touring pitches and 1 static.

🔲 📞 ☉ 🔵 🍴 ☀ 🔩 🛢 ⊞ 📞 🐕 🐾
→ ∪ ► ⊙ △ ♨

Presingoll Farm Caravan & Camping Park (SW721494)
TR5 0PB ☎ 01872 552333 Signposted
► ► ► Family Park ★ 🚐 £6 🚐 £6 ▲ £6
Open Etr/Apr-Oct Booking advisable Jul & Aug Last departure 10.00hrs
A grassy park on a 200-acre working farm, in a scenic area approx 1m from village and beach. From A30 Chiverton rndbt (Little Chef) take B3277 towards St Agnes, and park on right in 3m. A 3-acre site with 90 touring pitches.

🔲 📞 ☉ 🔵 🍴 ☀ 🔩 ⊞ 📞 🏠 🐕 🔲 🐾 ♿
→ ∪ ♨

ST AUSTELL

River Valley Holiday Park (SX010503)
London Apprentice PL26 7AP ☎ 01726 73533
Signposted
► ► ► Family Park ★ 🚐 £8-£15 🚐 £8-£15 ▲ £8-£15
Open end Mar-Sep Booking advisable Jul-Aug Last arrival 22.00hrs Last departure 11.00hrs
A neat, well-maintained family-run park set in a pleasant river valley with cycle trail to Pentewan Beach alongside. Signed with direct access to park from B3273 from St Austell at London Apprentice. A 2-acre site with 45 touring pitches and 40 statics.
Cycle trail.

📞 ☉ 🔵 🍴 🔌 🚰 ☀ 🔩 📞 🐕 🐾
→ ► △ ♨ 🍽 ♨

Credit Cards

Holiday bungalows, caravans and a fully serviced touring park. All with country views and within easy reach of the sea. No bar or gaming machines, but a heated swimming pool, tennis court and fishing lake etc. We provide a supervised Kids Club in the main season and the park is safely situated a quarter of a mile off the main road, down our own private lane. **Special Offers:** Easter to mid July. Self catering: second week half price. Touring: **£42.00** per pitch, per week, including electric.

Trencreek Farm Holiday Park, Hewaswater, St Austell, Cornwall PL26 7JG
Telephone: 01726 882540

Trencreek Farm Holiday Park (SW966485)
Hewas Water PL26 7JG ☎ 01726 882540 Signposted
▶ ▶ ▶ Family Park ⚏ £5.50-£11 ⚏ £5.50-£11
▲ £5.50-£11
Open Spring bank hol-13 Sep (rs Etr-Spring bank hol & 14 Sep-Oct restricted shop hours & pool closed)
Booking advisable Jul-Aug Last arrival 21.00hrs Last departure noon
A working farm site with mature trees and bushes, close to river and lake. Off B3287, 1m from junction with A390. An 8-acre site with 184 touring pitches and 37 statics. Fishing, fitness & agility course & mini golf.

⚙🚋ſ⊙🎱🐟⤞👁🔦⌂⚱🔥▥🐕⚡🏕♿
➔∪👣⅄⛺♪
Credit Cards 💳 💳

Trewhiddle Holiday Estate (SX005512)
Trewhiddle PL26 7AD ☎ 01726 67011 Signposted
▶ ▶ ▶ Family Park ⚏ ⚏ ▲
Open all year Booking advisable
Secluded wooded site with well-kept gardens, lawns and flower beds, set in the grounds of a mature estate, and with country club facilities. From St Austell rndbt on A390 take B3273 towards Mevagissey, and site on right in 0.75m. A 10.5-acre site with 105 touring pitches and 74 statics.

ſ🎱🐟⚱🔥♀▥⚱⌂⚱🔦⌈T⌉✕👣🏕🏤🐑
➔∪👣⅄⛺♪
Credit Cards 💳 💳

ST BURYAN

Camping & Caravanning Club Site (SW378276)
Higher Tregiffian Farm TR19 6JB ☎ 01736 871588 (in season) & 01203 694995 (off B3306) Signposted
Nearby town: Penzance
▶ ▶ ▶ Family Park ★ ⚏ £10-£13 ⚏ £10-£13 ▲ £10-£13
Open end Mar-Sep Booking advisable bank hols & Jul-Aug Last arrival 21.00hrs Last departure noon
A level grassy park in a rural area with distant views of Carn Brae and the coast, situated just 2m from Land's End. Follow A30 from Penzance to Land's End, and site is signed off B3306 (St Just Airport road). Please see the advertisement on page 27 for details of Club Members' benefits. A 4-acre site with 75 touring pitches.

⚙ſ⊙🎱🐟✳⌂⚱🔦🐕🐑♿
➔♪
Credit Cards 💳 💳

Cardinney Caravan & Camping Park (SW401278)
Crows an Wra, Main A30 TR19 6HX ☎ 01736 810880 Signposted
Nearby town: Penzance
▶ ▶ ▶ Family Park ⚏ £4.50-£7.50 ⚏ £4.50-£7.50 ▲ £4.50-£11
Open Feb-Nov Booking advisable Jul & Aug Last arrival 23.30hrs Last departure noon
A pleasant grassy park set in farmland with an open aspect, midway between Penzance and Land's End. Site has direct access from A30, 4m from Penzance. A 4.5-acre site with 105 touring pitches and 2 statics.

⚙ſ⊙🎱🐟🔦⤞⌂✳♀⚱⚱🔥⌈T⌉✕👣🏤🐑
➔∪⛰⅄⛺♪
Credit Cards 💳 💳 💳 🔖 🔳

Lower Treave Caravan & Camping Park (SW388272)
Crows-an-Wra TR19 6HZ ☎ 01736 810559 Signposted
Nearby town: Penzance
▶ ▶ ▶ Family Park ⚏ £7-£9 ⚏ £7-£9 ▲ £7-£9
Open Apr-Oct Booking advisable Jul-Aug Last arrival 22.30hrs Last departure 11.00hrs
Terraced, grass site with trees and bushes, set in meadowland, 4m NE of Land's End off A30. A 5-acre site with 80 touring pitches and 5 statics.
See advertisement under PENZANCE

⚙ſ⊙🎱🐟✳⌂⚱🔥⌈T⌉🔦🐑
➔∪♪

Tower Park Caravans & Camping (SW406263)
TR19 6BZ ☎ 01736 810286 Signposted
Nearby town: Penzance
▶ ▶ ▶ Family Park ⚏ £6-£8.50 ⚏ £6-£8.50 ▲ £5-£8.50
Open 8 Mar-6 Jan (rs Mar-Whitsun shop & cafe closed)
Booking advisable Jul-Aug Last arrival 22.00hrs Last departure noon
A rural site sheltered by mature trees, and close to village amenities, near Land's End and 4m from Sennen Cove and Porthcurno. Off A30 and B3283. A 6-acre site with 102 touring pitches and 5 statics.

⚙ſ⊙🎱🐟⤞⌂✳⌂⚱🔥⚱⌈T⌉✕👣🏤🏕
🏕🐕🐑♿
➔♪

Treverven Touring Caravan & Camping Site (SW410237)
Treverven Farm TR19 6DL ☎ 01736 810221 (on B3315) Signposted
Nearby town: Penzance
▶▶▶ Family Park ★ ⊞ £6-£10 ⊞ £6-£10 ▲ £6-£10
Open Etr-Oct Booking advisable Jul-Aug Last departure noon
An isolated but well-maintained farm site set off B3315 with panoramic views and in sight of the sea. A 6-acre site with 115 touring pitches.

� icons 🔳 ⊙ 🖪 ⏚ ✳ 🔥 🗑 🐕 🐾 📺
→ ♩

ST COLUMB MAJOR

Southleigh Manor Tourist Park (SW918623)
TR9 6HY ☎ 01637 880938 Signposted
▶▶▶ Family Park ⊞ £10.50-£11.50 ⊞ £10.50-£11.50 ▲ £10.50-£11.50
Open mid Apr-mid Sep Booking advisable Jul & Aug Last arrival 20.00hrs Last departure noon
A very well maintained naturist park in the heart of the Cornish countryside, catering for families and couples only. Seclusion and security are very well planned, and the lovely gardens provide a calm setting. Leave A30 at sign to RAF St Mawgan and St Columb onto A3059, and park 3m on left. A 2.5-acre site with 50 touring pitches. Sauna, Spa bath & croquet lawn.

🔳 ⊙ 🖪 ⏚ ✳ 🏔 🗑 🐾 📋 🅣 🐕 🐾
→ ∪ ♩

ST DAY

Tresaddern Holiday Park (SW733422)
TR16 5JR ☎ 01209 820459 Signposted
Nearby town: Redruth
▶▶▶ Family Park ★ ⊞ £5.50-£6.50 ⊞ £5.50-£6.50 ▲ £5.50-£6.50
Open Etr & Apr-Oct Booking advisable Jul-Aug
A very friendly park in a good location. 2m NE of Redruth on B3298. A 2-acre site with 15 touring pitches and 17 statics.

🔳 ⊙ 🖪 ✳ 🗑 📋 🐕 🐾
→ ∪ ⌂ 🍴 ♩

ST GENNYS

Camping & Caravanning Club Site (SX176943)
Gillards Moor EX23 0BG ☎ 01840 230650 (in season) & 01203 694995 Signposted
Nearby town: Bude
▶▶▶ Family Park ★ ⊞ £11-£14 ⊞ £11-£14 ▲ £11-£14
Open end Mar-Sep Booking advisable bank hols & Jul-Aug Last arrival 21.00hrs Last departure noon
A well-kept, level grass site with good quality facilities. Signed off A39 1m S of Wainhouse Corner. Please see the advertisement on page 27 for details of Club Members' benefits. A 6-acre site with 100 touring pitches.

🔳 ⊙ 🖪 ⏚ 🖵 ✳ 🏔 🗑 📋 🐕 🐾
→ ∪ ⊙ ♩
Credit Cards 💳 💳 💳

ST HILARY

Wayfarers Caravan & Camping Park (SW558314)
Relebbus Ln TR20 9EF ☎ 01736 763326 (on B3280) Signposted
Nearby town: Penzance
▶▶▶ Family Park ⊞ £4.75-£8 ⊞ £4.75-£8 ▲ £4.75-£8
Open Etr/Mar-Oct Booking advisable Jul & Aug Last arrival 23.00hrs Last departure 11.00hrs
A quiet family park in a peaceful rural setting within 2.5m of St Michael's Mount. Turn left off A30 onto A394 towards Helston, turn left at rndbt onto B3280 in 2 miles, and site is 1.5miles on left. A 4.75-acre site with 54 touring pitches and 6 statics.

🔳 ⊙ 🖪 ⏚ ✳ 🏔 🗑 📋 🅣 🐕 🐾 📺
→ ∪ ⌂ ⊙ △ ＋ 🍴 ♩

ST ISSEY

Trewince Farm Holiday Park (SW937715)
PL27 7RL ☎ 01208 812830 Signposted
Nearby town: Wadebridge

▶▶▶▶ De-Luxe Park ★ ⊞ £6.50-£8.50 ⊞ £6.50-£8.50 ▲ £6.50-£8.50
Open Etr-Oct Booking advisable anytime Last departure 11.00hrs
A family-owned park run to high standards amongst rolling farmland close to the coast. From Wadebridge on A39 towards St Columb take A389 signed Padstow, and site on left in 2m. A 6-acre site with 120 touring pitches and 35 statics.
Crazy golf, farm rides in summer, near Camel trail
See advertisement under PADSTOW

🔳 🚿 🔥 ⊙ 🖪 ⏚ ✳ 🏔 🗑 🐕 🐾 🐾 ⚷
→ ∪ ⌂ ⊙ △ ＋ 🍴 ♩
Credit Cards 💳 💳 💳 💳

ST IVES

Polmanter Tourist Park (SW510388)
Halsetown TR26 3LX ☎ 01736 795640 (on holiday route into St Ives B3311) Signposted

▶▶▶▶ De-Luxe Park ⊞ £7-£15 ⊞ £7-£15 ▲ £7-£15
Open Whit-10 Sep (rs Etr-Whit & 12 Sep-Oct shop, pool, bar & takeaway food closed) Booking advisable Jul-Aug Last arrival 21.00hrs Last departure 10.00hrs
A well-developed touring park on high ground, with distant views of the sea in St Ives Bay. Signed off B3311 at Halestown. A 13-acre site with 240 touring pitches. Putting, sports field, two family shower rooms.

🔳 ⊙ 🖪 ⏚ ✳ 🔍 🔥 ✳ ♀ 🏔 🗑 📋 🅣 ✗ 🐕
🚿 🛁 🐕 🐾
→ ∪ ⌂ ⊙ △ ＋ 🍴 ♩
Credit Cards 💳 💳 💳 💳

St Ives ▶▶▶
Self Catering Holidays
E.T.B.

GRADING EXCELLENT

The only holiday park in St Ives itself, less than ½ mile from the harbour, town centre and beaches. Beautiful views over St Ives Bay. Holiday caravans and chalets, also touring van and tent pitches. Electric hook-ups, free showers, modern clean amenities. Signposted from B3306, ½ mile west of town centre.

For brochure, write to:
AA Baragwanath, Ayr Holiday Park, Ayr, St Ives, Cornwall TR26 1EJ. Telephone: (01736) 795855

Ayr Holiday Park (SW509408)
TR26 1EJ ☎ 01736 795855 Signposted
▶▶▶ Family Park ⚏ ⚏ ▲
Open Apr-Oct (rs Apr-mid May & Oct shop closed) Booking advisable Jul-Aug Last arrival 22.00hrs Last departure 10.00hrs
A well-established park on a cliffside overlooking St Ives Bay. From St Ives follow St Ives 'large vehicles' route via B3311 through Halestown on to B3306, and park signed in St Ives town centre direction. A 2-acre site with 40 touring pitches and 43 statics.

⚑ ⛄ ☉ ▣ ⚑ ◀ ☀ ⚒ ▯ ⌀ ⊡ Ⓣ ⛾ ↻
→ ∪ ▶ △ ┿ ⚏ ↗ ⚋

Credit Cards ⬤ 💳 ▨ 🆒

Trevalgan Family Camping Park (SW490402)
Trevalgan TR26 3BJ ☎ 01736 796433 Signposted
▶▶▶ Family Park ⚏ £7-£10.50 ⚏ £7-£10.50
▲ £7-£10.50
Open May-Sep Booking advisable mid Jul-mid Aug Last arrival 23.30hrs Last departure noon
An open, level grass site on a working farm with very good facilities. From St Ives take B3306; site signed on right. A 4.75-acre site with 120 touring pitches.
Farm trail, pets corner.

⚑ ⛄ ☉ ▣ ⚑ ◀ ▭ ☀ ⚒ ▯ ⌀ ⊡ Ⓣ ✕ ⛾ ⋔ ⌂
⍁ ⋔ ⚋
→ ∪ ▶ ⚏ ↗

Credit Cards ⬤ 💳 ▨ 🆒

Kelynack Caravan & Camping Park (SW374301)
TR19 7RE ☎ 01736 787633 Signposted
Nearby town: Penzance
▶▶▶ Family Park ★ ⚏ £5-£6 ⚏ £5-£6 ▲ £5-£6
Open Apr-Oct Booking advisable Jul-Aug Last arrival 22.00hrs Last departure noon
A small, secluded site in the grounds of an old walled garden, surrounded by open countryside. 1m from town on B3306 Land's End road. A 2-acre site with 20 touring pitches and 13 statics.
Wash-up room.

⚑ ⛄ ☉ ⚑ ◀ ☀ ▭ ⌀ ▯ ⊡ Ⓣ ⛾ ⛾ ⌂ ⋔ ⚋
→ ▶ ↗ ▣

Bosavern House Caravan Park (SW370305)
TR19 7RD ☎ 01736 788301 Signposted
Nearby town: Penzance
▶▶ Town & Country Pennant Park ★ ⚏ £7-£9 ⚏ £7-£9
▲ £6-£8
Open Mar-Oct Booking advisable Jul-Aug Last arrival 22.00hrs Last departure 14.00hrs
A small, neat site in a walled garden behind a guest house. Turn off A3071 near St Just onto B3306 Land's End Rd, and park on left in 0.5m. A 2-acre site with 12 touring pitches.

⚑ ⛄ ☉ ⚑ ▭ ☀ ⚐ ⊡ ⛾ ⛾
→ ∪ ▶ △ ↗ ⚋

Credit Cards ⬤ 💳 ▨ ▨ 🆒

Roselands Caravan Park (SW387305)
Dowran TR19 7RS ☎ 01736 788571 (1.25m E on unclass rd, off A3071)
Nearby town: Penzance
▶▶ Town & Country Pennant Park ★ ⚏ £5-£7 ⚏ £5-£7
▲ £5-£7
Open Jan-Oct Booking advisable Jun-Sep Last arrival 23.00hrs Last departure noon
A small site in an isolated rural setting with well-kept facilities and friendly owners. A 2-acre site with 12 touring pitches and 15 statics.

⚑ ⛄ ☉ ▣ ◀ ▭ ☀ ⚐ ▯ ⌀ ⊡ ⛾ ⛾ ⋔ ⚋
→ ∪ ▶ ↗

Trethem Mill Touring Park (SW860365)
TR2 5JF ☎ 01872 580504 Signposted

▶▶▶ Family Park ★ ⚏ £6.50-£10.50 ⚏ £6.50-£10.50
▲ £6.50-£10.50

contd.

Open Apr-Oct Booking advisable Jul-Aug Last arrival 21.00hrs Last departure 11.00hrs
A carefully tended and sheltered park in a rural setting. Take A3078 for St Mawes, and site signed on right 3m N of St Mawes. An 11-acre site with 80 touring pitches. Mountain bike hire & info centre.Wet suit hire.

🔌 📶 ⊙ 🗑 🗑 ◣ ◻ ☀ 🏔 ⓘ ⊘ 🚽 T ⌕ ➡ 🐕 🐾
➔ ∪ △ ⼥ ♪

Credit Cards 💳 💳 💳 💳 🗐

ST MABYN

Glenmorris Park (SX058733)
Glenmorris PL30 3BY ☎ 01208 841677 Signposted
Nearby town: Bodmin
▶ ▶ ▶ **Family Park** 🚐 £5-£7.50 🚐 £5-£7.50 ▲ £5-£7.50
Open Etr-Oct Booking advisable bank hols & Jul-Aug Last arrival 10.00hrs Last departure 10.30hrs
A very good park in a peaceful rural location. Signed on unclass road off B3266 towards St Mabyn, at Longstone village. A 10-acre site with 80 touring pitches and 6 statics.
Off licence

🔌 📶 ⊙ 🗑 🗑 ⟲ ◣ ☀ 🏔 ⓘ ⊘ ⌕ 🛖 ⚯ 🐕 🐾
➔ ∪ ▶ △ ♪

Credit Cards 💳 💳 💳

ST MERRYN (NEAR PADSTOW)

Carnevas Farm Holiday Park (SW862728)
Carnevas Farm PL28 8PN ☎ 01841 520230 & 521209 (take B3276 towards Porthcothan Bay, 2m) Signposted
Nearby town: Padstow
▶ ▶ ▶ **Family Park** ★ 🚐 £5.50-£8.50 🚐 £5.50-£8.50
▲ £5.50-£8.50

Open Apr-Oct (rs Apr-Whit & mid Sep-Oct shop closed) Booking advisable Jul-Aug
A rather open site in a rural setting near the North coast. Off B3276 Padstow-Newquay road 2m SW of village. An 8-acre site with 195 touring pitches and 14 statics.

🔌 📶 ⊙ 🗑 🗑 ◣ ☀ ⚲ 🏔 ⓘ ⊘ 🚽 T ⌕ 🐕 🐾 ⚹
➔ ∪ ▶ △ ⼥ 🍴 ♪

Tregavone Touring Park (SW898732)
Tregavone Farm PL28 8JZ ☎ 01841 520148 (1m off A389)
Nearby town: Padstow
▶ **Town & Country Pennant Park** ★ 🚐 fr £5 🚐 fr £5
▲ fr £5
Open Mar-Oct Booking advisable end Jul-beg Aug

A working farm site with better than average facilities. The very well converted farm buildings look purpose built. Situated .5 mile off A389 on unclass rd to church. A 3-acre site with 40 touring pitches.

🔌 📶 ⊙ 🗑 ☀ 🚽 🐕
➔ ∪ ▶ ◎ △ ⼥ 🍴 ♪ 🐾

Trevean Caravan & Camping Park (SW875724)
Trevean Ln PL28 8PR ☎ 01841 520772 (take B3276 for 1m, then turn left for Rumford, site .25m on right) Signposted
Nearby town: Padstow
▶ **Town & Country Pennant Park** ★ 🚐 £5.50-£6.50
🚐 £5.50-£6.50 ▲ £5.50-£6.50
Open Apr-Oct Booking advisable mid Jul-Aug Last arrival 22.30hrs Last departure noon
A small working farm site with level grassy pitches in rather open countryside. Signed on left off B3276, 1.5m S of St Merryn. A 1.5-acre site with 36 touring pitches and 3 statics.

🔌 📶 ⊙ 🗑 🗑 ☀ 🏔 ⓘ ⊘ 🚽 ⌕ 🛖 🐕 🐾
➔ ∪ ▶ ⼥ 🍴 ♪

ST MINVER

St Minver Holiday Park (SW965772)
PL27 6RR ☎ 01208 862305
Signposted
Nearby town: Wadebridge

ⓞⓞⓞⓞⓞⓞⓞⓞⓞⓞⓞⓞⓞⓞⓞⓞ
★ 🚐 £9-£21 🚐 £9-£21 ▲ £9-£21
Open Etr-5 Oct Booking advisable Jul-Sep Last arrival mdnt Last departure 10.00hrs
A large, mainly static holiday park set around St Minver House in sylvan surroundings. From A39 N of Wadebridge take Port Isaac rd B3314; site signed on left in 3m. A 5-acre site with 120 touring pitches and 99 statics.
Crazy golf, free evening entertainment, amusements.

🔌 📶 ⊙ 🗑 🗑 ⟲ ◣ ☀ ⚲ 🏔 ⓘ ⊘ 🚽 T ✕ ⌕ 🏛 🐕 🐾
➔ ▶ △ 🍴
Credit Cards 💳 💳 💳 🗐
ⓞⓞⓞⓞⓞⓞⓞⓞⓞⓞⓞⓞⓞⓞⓞⓞⓞ

Gunvenna Touring Caravan & Camping Park (SW969782)
PL27 6QN ☎ 01208 862405
Nearby town: Wadebridge
▶ ▶ ▶ **Family Park** ★ 🚐 £7-£12.50 🚐 £7-£12.50
▲ £7-£12.50
Open Apr-Oct Booking advisable Jul-Aug Last arrival mdnt Last departure 11.00hrs

Attractive site offering good facilities located 4m NE of Wadebridge on the B3314. Ideal position for touring North Cornwall. A 10-acre site with 75 touring pitches. Swimming lessons.

🏠📞☉🗄️🇶🇱 ◆☀️🍴/◐🏺🍽️∅✕📞◆🚿🏛️🐕🐎🐾

➔∪🏳️◭🌿🍽️🗡️

SCILLY, ISLES

(No map) No sites on the island hold AA classification. See Island Camping on page 00

SCORRIER

Wheal Rose Caravan & Camping Park (SW717449)
TR16 5DD ☎ 01209 891496 Signposted
Nearby town: Redruth
▶ ▶ ▶ **Family Park ★ 🏕️ £6-£9 🚐 £6-£9 ⚠️ £6-£9**
Open Mar-Dec Booking advisable Aug
A quiet, peaceful park in secluded valley setting, central for beaches and countryside. Leave A30 dual carriageway signed Scorrier, follow signs on unclass rd to Wheal Rose, and park in 0.5m on left. A 4-acre site with 50 touring pitches.

🏠📞☉🗄️🇶🇱◖◆☀️/◐🏺🍽️∅📧🛗🏛️🍴🐕

➔∪🏳️◉◭🍽️🗡️🐾

SUMMERCOURT

Resparva House Camping & Caravanning (SW881557)
Chapel Town TR8 5AH ☎ 01872 510332
▶ ▶ ▶ **Family Park ★ 🏕️ £6-£8 🚐 £6-£8 ⚠️ £6-£8**
Open Etr-Sep Booking advisable

Whitsand Bay Holiday Park

In Cornwall and only six miles from the historic city of Plymouth, and twelve miles from Looe. South East Cornwall's award winning holiday centre. Set in grounds of an historic hilltop ancient fortification with spectacular views over the Tamar estuary and Dartmoor. Minutes walk to unspoilt sandy beaches. Luxury self-catering chalets and caravans. Touring pitches for caravans and tents. Extensive range of facilities including heated pool; licensed family club with entertainment; cafe-bar; shop; playback; park; sauna; arcade; crazy golf and much more!!!!
New for 1999 season ... indoor heated pool and sun terrace!!
For free colour brochure
Tel: 01752 822597 Fax: 01752 823444

A small, grassy park with good facilities, almost in the centre of Cornwall. Signed off A30 to Chapel Town and Summerscourt, 1.5m past McDonald's and just past Kessels Volvo. Do not take 1st sign to Summerscourt. A 2-acre site with 15 touring pitches.

🏠📞☉🇶🇱☀️🏛️🍴

➔🐾

TINTAGEL

See **Camelford**

TORPOINT

Whitsand Bay Holiday Park (SX410515)
Millbrook PL10 1JZ ☎ 01752 822597 Signposted
Nearby town: Plymouth
▶ ▶ ▶ **Family Park 🏕️ 🚐 ⚠️**
Open all year (rs Oct-Feb some facilities closed)
Booking advisable Last arrival 24.00hrs Last departure 10.00hrs
A very well-equipped site with panoramic views from its tiered pitches, and plenty of on-site entertainment. Leave Torpoint on A374 and turn left at Anthony onto B3247 for 1.25m to T-junc. Turn left for .25m then right onto Cliff Rd, and site is 2m on left. A 27-acre site with 100 touring pitches and 40 statics.
Sauna, sunbed, entertainment, putting.

🏠📞☉🗄️🇶🇱◖◆🎱☀️🍴/◐🏺🍽️∅📧✕📞🏧

🏛️🍴🐕🐾♿

➔∪🏳️◉◭🌿🗡️

Credit Cards 💳 📧

TREGURRIAN

Camping & Caravanning Club Site (SW853654)
TR8 4AE ☎ 01637 860448 (in season) & 01203 694995
Signposted
Nearby town: Newquay
▶ ▶ ▶ **Family Park ★ 🏕️ £11-£14 🚐 £11-£14 ⚠️ £11-£14**
Open end Mar-end Sep Booking advisable bank hols & Jul-Aug Last arrival 21.00hrs Last departure noon
A level grassy site close to the famous beaches of Watergate Bay, with a modern amenity block. This upgraded club site is an excellent touring centre for the Padstow-Newquay coast. From A3059 fork right for St Mawgan, then join B3276 coast road and turn left for Watergate Bay. Please see the advertisement on page 27 for details of Club Members' benefits. A 4.25-acre site with 90 touring pitches.
Parent & child room, Motor caravan service area.

🏠📞☉🗄️🇶🇱☀️🏺∅📧🔲📞🍴♿

➔∪🗡️🐾

Credit Cards 💳 📧 📧 📧 📧

Watergate Bay Tourist Park (SW850653)
TR8 4AD ☎ 01637 860387 Signposted
Nearby town: Newquay
▶ ▶ ▶ **Family Park ★ 🏕️ £7-£11 🚐 £7-£11 ⚠️ £7-£11**
Open 22 May-12 Sep (rs Mar-21 May & 13 Sep-Nov restricted bar, cafe, shop & swimming pool) Booking advisable Jul-Aug Last arrival 22.00hrs Last departure noon
A well-established park on high ground above Watergate Bay. Situated on B3276 .5m from Watergate beach. A 24-acre site with 171 touring pitches.
contd.

Entertainment, free minibus to beach.
See advertisement under NEWQUAY

🔔 🚐 📻 ☉ 🗄 ◥ ⟲ ◀ 🖵 ❊ ⛱ 🅰 ⓘ ⊘ ⊞ Ⓣ ✗
📞 ⬚ ⛩ ⍭ 🐕 Ⓛ ⚿
→ ▶ ◉ ◿ ✈

Credit Cards 💳 ▦ 💳 ⑤

TRURO

Leverton Place (SW774453)
Greenbottom, Chacewater TR4 8QW ☎ 01872 560462
Signposted

◯◯◯◯◯◯◯◯◯◯

► ► ► ► De-Luxe Park ★ 🅿 £7.50-£15 🚐 £7.50-£15
🅰 £7.50-£15
Open all year (rs Oct-May not all facilities open all year
round) Booking advisable Spring bank hol & Jun-early
Sep Last arrival 22.00hrs Last departure noon
*An attractive park divided into paddocks, close to Truro
yet in a pleasant rural area 3.5m W of city, off A390 at
Threemilestone Roundabout. A 9.75-acre site with 107
touring pitches and 15 statics.*
Hairdrying room, childrens heated pool.

🔔 ⛩ ☉ 🗄 ◥ ⟲ ◀ 🖵 ❊ ⛱ 🅰 ⓘ ⊘ ⊞ Ⓣ ✗ 📞
⬚ ⛩ ⍭ ⚿
→ ∪ ▶ ☕ ✈

Credit Cards 💳 ▦ 💳 ⑤

◯◯◯◯◯◯◯◯◯◯

Ringwell Valley Holiday Park (SW805408)
Bissoe Rd, Carnon Downs TR3 6LQ ☎ 01872 862194 &
865409 (3m SW off A39) Signposted

◯◯◯◯◯◯◯◯◯◯

► ► ► ► De-Luxe Park 🅿 🚐 🅰
Open Etr-Oct Booking advisable Jul & Aug Last arrival
21.30hrs Last departure noon
*A well-run park nestling in a tranquil valley with open
countryside views. Turn off A39 at rndbt signed Carnon
Downs, then right onto Bissoe Rd in the village. Park
0.75m on right. A 4-acre site with 30 touring pitches and
30 statics.*

🔔 🚐 ⛩ ☉ 🗄 ◥ ⟲ ◀ 🖵 ❊ ⛱ 🅰 ⓘ ⊘ ⊞ Ⓣ ✗ 📞
⬚ 🐕 Ⓛ
→ ∪ ▶ ☗ ✈ ☕ ✈

Credit Cards 💳 ▦ 💳 🐾 ⑤

◯◯◯◯◯◯◯◯◯◯

Camping & Caravanning Club Site (SW934414)
Tretheake Manor, Veryon TR2 5PP ☎ 01203 501658
(from A390 turn onto A3078 signed St Mawes, site 6m
on left) Signposted
► ► ► Family Park ★ 🅿 £11-£14 🚐 £11-£14 🅰 £11-£14
Open end Mar-early Nov Booking advisable Jul-Aug
Last arrival 21.00hrs Last departure noon
*A quiet park situated on slightly undulating land with
pleasant views of the surrounding countryside. Turn left
off A3078 at filling stn, signed Veryan and Portloe, on
unclass road, and site signed on left. A 9-acre site with
150 touring pitches.*

🔔 ⛩ ☉ 🗄 ◥ ❊ ⛰ ⚿ 🐕 Ⓛ
→ ∪ ✈ ✈

Credit Cards 💳 ▦ 💳 🐾 ⑤

Carnon Downs Caravan & Camping Park (SW805406)
Carnon Downs TR3 6JJ ☎ 01872 862283 (3m off A39)
Signposted
► ► ► Family Park ★ 🅿 £7-£12 🚐 £7-£12 🅰 £6-£12
Open Etr or Apr-Oct Booking advisable Jul-Aug Last
arrival 23.00hrs Last departure 11.00hrs
*A mature park with a high standard of landscaping set
in meadowland and woodland just outside the urban
area, adjacent to A39 Falmouth-Truro road. An 11-acre
site with 150 touring pitches.*
Baby & children bathroom. Three family bathrooms.

🔔 🚐 ⛩ ☉ 🗄 ◥ 🖵 ❊ ⛰ 🅰 ⓘ ⊘ ⊞ Ⓣ 📞 🐕 Ⓛ
→ ∪ ▶ ☗ ✈ ☕ ✈

Credit Cards 💳 ▦ 💳 🐾 ⑤

Chacewater Park (SW740438)
Coxhill, Chacewater TR4 8LY ☎ 01209 820762
Signposted
► ► ► Family Park 🅿 £9 🚐 £9 🅰 £9
Open May-Sep Booking advisable May-Sep Last arrival
21.00hrs Last departure noon
*A level grassy site with young trees set in meadowland.
Along A30 towards Penzance, take A3047 to Scorrier,
400yds turn left at Crossroads Motel, continue to join
B3298 for 1.25m, at next crossroads turn left to
Chacewater and continue for 0.75m. A 4-acre site with
87 touring pitches and 12 statics.*
Family shower rooms.

🔔 ⛩ ☉ 🗄 ◥ 🖵 ❊ 🅰 ⓘ ⊘ ⊞ Ⓣ 📞 🐕 Ⓛ
→ ∪ ▶

Credit Cards 💳 ▦ 💳 🐾

Liskey Touring Park (SW772452)
Greenbottom TR4 8QN ☎ 01872 560274 (3m W off
A390) Signposted
► ► ► Family Park 🅿 £6.20-£10 🚐 £6.20-£10 🅰 £6.20-
£10
Open Apr-Sep Booking advisable Jul-Aug Last arrival
20.00hrs Last departure noon
*Small, south facing park, neat and well-maintained with
quality facilities, and enjoying a friendly relaxed
atmosphere. Off A390 at Threemilestone rndbt on to
unclass rd towards Chacewater. Signed on right in .5m.
A 4.5-acre site with 65 touring pitches.*

Serviced pitches, dish washing, undercover playbarn.

🚹 🚐 🐕 ☉ 🔲 🛒 ⛱ 🔥 ⚠ 🅿 ✉ 🔌 🚻 📱 🛒 🏇

➔ ∪ ⛷ ♨ ♪ 🐴

Credit Cards 💳 🔳 ▨ 🔲 🔷

Summer Valley (SW800479)

Shortlanesend TR4 9DW
☎ 01872 277878 (3m NW off B3284) Signposted
▶ ▶ ▶ Family Park 🚐 £6.50-£8.50 🚐 £6.50-£8.50
🛆 £6.50-£8.50
Open Apr-Oct Booking advisable Jul-Aug Last arrival
22.00hrs Last departure noon
*A very attractive and secluded site in a rural setting, and
very well-maintained. From A30 take B3284 signed Truro.
Site on right in 1.5m. A 3-acre site with 60 touring pitches.
Campers lounge.*

🚹 🐕 ☉ 🔲 🛒 ✲ ⚠ 🅿 ✉ 🔌 🔲 📱 🛒

➔ ∪ ⛷ ♨ ♪

Credit Cards 💳 🔳 🔷

Little Bodieve Holiday Park (SW995734)

Bodieve Rd PL27 6EG ☎ 01208 812323 (1m N off A39)
Signposted
▶ ▶ ▶ Family Park ★ 🚐 £6-£9 🚐 £6-£9 🛆 £6-£9
Open Apr-Oct (rs early & late season pool closed)
Booking advisable Jul-Aug Last arrival 20.00hrs Last
departure 11.00hrs

*An established and well-organised level grassy site 1m
from centre of Wadebridge on B3314 in quiet rural area,
with good touring facilities. Signed Rock and Port Isaac.
A 20-acre site with 195 touring pitches and 75 statics.
Crazy golf, water shute/splash pool & pets corner.*

🚹 🚐 🐕 ☉ 🔲 🛒 ⚡ 🔍 ✲ 🅿 ⚠ 🅿 🔌 🔲 📱 ✖ 🔌

🛒 🏇 🛒 ♿

➔ ∪ ⛷ ☉ ⚓ ♨ ♪

Credit Cards 💳 🔳 ▨ 🔷

White Acres Holiday Park (SW890599)

TR8 4LW ☎ 01726 860220 & 860999
Signposted
Nearby town: Newquay

🚐 🚐 🛆
Open Etr-Sep Booking advisable Jul-Aug Last arrival
22.00hrs Last departure 10.00hrs
*A large holiday complex, partially terraced, in a rural
setting, with one of the best coarse fishing centres in
the South West on site. From A30 at Indian Queens take
A392 signed Newquay. Site on right in 3m. A 44-acre
site with 200 touring pitches and 100 statics.
Entertainment, sauna, solarium, fishing lakes, gym.*

🚹 🐕 ☉ 🔲 🛒 ⚡ 🔍 🔌 ✲ 🅿 ⚠ 🅿 🔌 🔲 📱 ✖ 🔌

🚐 🛒 🛒 🏇 🛒 ♿

➔ ∪ ⛷ ♨ ♪

Summer Lodge Holiday Park (SW890597)

TR8 4LW ☎ 01726 860415 Signposted
Nearby town: Newquay
▶ ▶ ▶ Family Park ★ 🚐 £6.50-£18 🚐 £6.50-£18
🛆 £6.50-£18
Open Whitsun-Oct (rs Etr-Whitsun & Sep-Oct shop cafe
closed) Booking advisable Jul-Aug Last arrival 20.00hrs
Last departure noon
*Small holiday complex offering use of good facilities.
From Indian Queens on A30 take A392 signed*

contd.

Newquay, and site on left at Whitecross in 2.5m. A 26-acre site with 75 touring pitches and 106 statics.

🎮 📻 ⊙ 🖪 🢂 ⇃ ◖ ✳ ♀ 🏔 🛈 🖉 🖅 🔟 ✕ 📞 ⛟
🏛 🚻 🛒 ⓖ
➙ ∪ ⌁

Credit Cards 💳 ▭ 🔳 🅂

WIDEMOUTH BAY

 Widemouth Bay Caravan Parc (SS199008)
EX23 0DF ☎ 01288 361208 & 01271 866766
   (take Widemouth Bay coastal rd off A39)
Signposted
Nearby town: Bude

☉☉☉☉☉☉☉☉☉☉☉☉☉☉☉☉☉☉☉☉☉

★ 🎪 £11-£19 🚐 £11-£19 ▲ £7-£15
Open Mar-Oct Booking advisable Last arrival 23.00hrs
Last departure 10.00hrs
A partly sloping rural site set in countryside overlooking the sea and one of Cornwall's finest beaches. Nightly entertainment in high season. Leave A39 at Widemouth Bay sign, join coast road and turn left. Park on left, 3m from Bude. A 10-acre site with 100 touring pitches and 150 statics.
See advertisement under BUDE

🎮 📻 ⊙ 🖪 🢂 ⇃ ◖ ✳ ♀ 🏔 🛈 🖉 ✕ 📞 ⛟ 🏛 🏛
🐕 🛒
➙ ∪ ⌁ ◎ △ ⌖ 🎱 ⌁

Credit Cards 💳 ▭ 🔳 🅂

☉☉☉☉☉☉☉☉☉☉☉☉☉☉☉☉☉☉☉☉☉

Penhalt Farm Holiday Park (SS194003)
EX23 0DG ☎ 01288 361210 Signposted
Nearby town: Bude
► ► ► **Family Park** 🎪 £5.50-£10 🚐 £5.50-£10 ▲ £5-£9
Open Etr-Oct Booking advisable Jul & Aug
Splendid views of the sea and coast can be enjoyed from all pitches on this sloping but partly level site, set in a rural area on a working farm. From Bude take Widemouth Bay road off A39 4m S of town, turn left at end of road signed Millook onto Cornish coastal footpath, and site on left in .75m. An 8-acre site with 100 touring pitches and 2 statics.
Pool table.

🎮 📻 ⊙ 🖪 ◖ ✳ 🏔 🛈 🖉 🖅 📞 🐕 🛒
➙ ∪ ⌁ △ ⌖ 🎱 ⌁

CUMBRIA

AMBLESIDE

Skelwith Fold Caravan Park (NY355029)
LA22 0HX ☎ 015394 32277 Signposted

◎◎◎◎◎◎◎◎◎◎

► ► ► ► **De-Luxe Park** 🚐 🚐
Open Mar-15 Nov Booking advisable public hols & Jul-Aug Last departure noon
In the grounds of an old mansion, this park is in a beautiful setting close to Lake Windermere. On the B5286, 2m from Ambleside. A 10-acre site with 150 touring pitches and 300 statics.

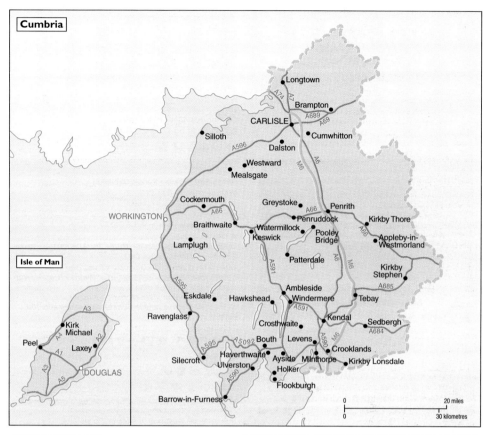

Cumbria

Isle of Man

Family recreation area.

Low Wray National Trust Campsite (NY372013)
Low Wray LA22 0JA ☎ 015394 32810 Signposted
▶▶▶ Family Park ▲
Open 1 wk before Etr-Oct Last arrival 23.00hrs
A site for tenters on banks of Lake Windermere, divided naturally into areas for families and for young people. 3m SW via A583 to Clappersgate, then B5286 and unclass road. A 10-acre site with 200 touring pitches and 6 statics.
Launching for sailing.

£3.50 pp
+ £2.00 car

Credit Cards 💳 💳 💳

APPLEBY-IN-WESTMORLAND

Wild Rose Park (NY698165)
Ormside CA16 6EJ ☎ 017683 51077 Signposted

▶▶▶▶▶ Premier Park ★ ⚐ £7.20-£11.80
⚐ £7.20-£11.80 ▲ £7.20-£11.80

Open all year (rs Nov-Mar shop, swimming pool & restaurant closed) Booking advisable bank & school hols Last arrival 22.00hrs Last departure noon
An excellent, well-maintained site with good views of surrounding countryside. Facilities are of a high standard. Site signed on unclass road to Great Ormside
contd.

*Friendly park in beautiful Eden Valley, twixt Lakes and Dales.
Excellent facilities include – Heated outdoor pools, play areas,
indoor TV and games rooms, mini-market and licensed
restaurant.
Luxury holiday homes for sale, but no letting, no bar, no
club. Brochure with pleasure.*

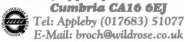
**Ormside, Appleby-in-Westmorland,
Cumbria CA16 6EJ**

Tel: Appleby (017683) 51077
E-Mail: broch@wildrose.co.uk
or visit our Website www.wildrose.co.uk

*off B6260 from Appleby-in-Westmorland. A 40-acre site
with 240 touring pitches and 240 statics.*
Tourist Information, bike hire & pitch and putt.

🔌 🐾 ⊙ 🖥 🚱 ⚡ ◉ ⬜ ☀ 🏔 🅰 ⌀ 🖃 🆃 ✗ 🔔 🍴
🚮 🐕 🐖 🦺 → ▶ 🎣
Credit Cards 💳 ▦ 💷 🈁 🗒

Low Moor Caravan Site (NY624259)
CA10 1XQ ☎ 017683 61231 (on A66, 5m NW)
▶ ▶ ▶ Family Park 🚐 £5 🚐 £5 🅰 £5
Open Apr-Oct Booking advisable high season Last
arrival 23.00hrs
*A small farm site with well cared for grounds and clean
sanitary facilities. 7m SE of Penrith on A66. A 2-acre site
with 25 touring pitches and 25 statics.*

🔌 🐾 ⊙ 🚱 ☀ 🏔 🅰 ⌀ 🖃 🔔 🐕 🎴 🦺 ♿

Hawkrigg Farm (NY659203)
Colby CA16 6BB ☎ 017683 51046 Signposted
▶▶ Town & Country Pennant Park ★ 🚐 £3 🚐 £3 🅰 £2-£3
Open all year Booking advisable Jul-Aug Last arrival
23.30hrs
*Attractive level farm site in a pleasant and quiet location
on the edge of the small village of Colby. On entering
village from Appleby turn left signed Kings Meadburn
and Newby, and site on right in 800 yards. A 1-acre site
with 15 touring pitches and 4 statics.*

🔌 🐾 ⊙ ☀ 🐕
→ ▶ 🎣 🖥

AYSIDE

Oak Head Caravan Park (SD389839)
LA11 6JA ☎ 015395 31475 Signposted
Nearby town: Grange-over-Sands
▶ ▶ ▶ Family Park 🚐 £9 🚐 £9 🅰 £7.50
Open Mar-Oct Booking advisable bank hols Last arrival
anytime Last departure noon
*A tiered grassy site with some hardstandings set in hilly
country with woodland, close to A590. A 3-acre site with
60 touring pitches and 71 statics.*

🔌 🐾 ⊙ 🖥 🚱 ☀ 🅰 ⌀ 🖃 🔔 🐕 ♿
→ 🛶 ⛵ 🦺 🎣 🐖

BARROW-IN-FURNESS

South End Caravan Park (SD208628)
Walney Island LA14 3YQ
☎ 01229 472823 & 471556
Signposted
▶ ▶ ▶ Family Park ★ 🚐 £8-£10 🚐 £8-£10
🅰 £8-£10
Open Mar-Oct Booking advisable Jul-Aug Last arrival
22.00hrs Last departure noon
*Mainly level grass site adjacent to sea, and close to a
nature reserve, on southern end of Walney Island. From
Barrow cross bridge onto island and turn L into council
estate and L again just before new private estate.
Signed. A 7-acre site with 60 touring pitches and 100
statics.*
Bowling green.

🔌 🐾 ⊙ 🖥 🚱 ⚡ 🔔 ⬜ ☀ 🅿 🏔 🅰 ⌀ 🖃 🔔
🚮 🐕 🦺
→ 🛶 ▶ ◉ 🍽 🎣
Credit Cards 💳 ▦ 🗒

BASSENTHWAITE LAKE

See map for locations of sites in the vicinity

BOUTH

Black Beck Caravan Park (SD335855)
LA12 8JN ☎ 01229 861274 Signposted
Nearby town: Newby Bridge
▶ ▶ ▶ Family Park 🚐 🚐 🅰
Open Mar-Nov Booking advisable bank hols Last arrival
20.00hrs Last departure 13.00hrs
*A quiet site surrounded by woods and fields close to S
Cumbria and the Lake District. N of A590. A 2-acre site
with 75 touring pitches and 235 statics.*

🔌 🐾 ⊙ 🖥 🚱 ☀ 🏔 🅰 ⌀ 🖃 🔔 🦺 ♿
→ 🛶 🎣

BOWNESS-ON-WINDERMERE

Sites are listed under **Windermere**

BRAITHWAITE

Scotgate Caravan Park (NY235235)
CA12 5TJ ☎ 017687 78343 Signposted
Nearby town: Keswick
▶ ▶ ▶ Family Park 🚐 🚐 🅰
Open Mar-Oct Last arrival 22.00hrs Last departure
11.00hrs

A pleasant rural site with dramatic views towards Skiddaw. Situated at junction of A66 and B5292, 2m from Keswick. An 8-acre site with 165 touring pitches and 35 statics.

🎪 🏠 ☉ 📺 🍽 ⚡ ✳ ⚠ 🚰 🖊 ⛽ 🛒

➔ ∪ ☉ ⊹ ☕ ✈

BRAMPTON

Irthing Vale Holiday Park (NY522613)
Old Church Ln CA8 2AA ☎ 016977 3600 Signposted
Nearby town: Carlisle
► ► ► Family Park ★ 🚐 £7.50 🚙 £7.50 ▲ £7.50

Open Mar-Oct Booking advisable public hols & Jul-Aug
Last arrival 23.30hrs Last departure noon
A grassy site on the outskirts of the market town on the A6071. Brampton now bypassed, so leave A69 into town to join A6071, and site .5m outside. A 4.5-acre site with 30 touring pitches and 26 statics.

🎪 🏠 ☉ ✳ ⚠ 🚰 🖊 ⊞ ⚡ ⛽

➔ ∪ ▶ ⊹ ✈

CARLISLE

Dandy Dinmont Caravan & Camping Park (NY399620)
Blackford CA6 4EA ☎ 01228 74611 due to change to 674611 (4m N on A7) Signposted
► ► ► Family Park 🚐 £7.25-£7.50 🚙 £7.25-£7.50
▲ £6-£6.50

Open Etr-Oct (rs Mar showers not available) Booking advisable high season Last arrival anytime Last departure 15.00hrs
A level, sheltered site, screened on two sides by hedgerows. Situated alongside A7 about 1m N of junction 44 of M6. A 4-acre site with 47 touring pitches and 15 statics.

🎪 🏠 ☉ 📺 ✳ 🚰 🖊 ⚡ 🏠

➔ ∪ ▶ ☉ ⛽

Green Acres Caravan Park (NY416614)
High Knells, Houghton CA6 4JW
☎ 01228 577403 & 75418 Signposted
► ► ► Family Park 🚐 £6 🚙 £6 ▲ £6
Open Etr-Oct Booking advisable Last arrival 21.00hrs
Last departure 14.00hrs
A small, newly-created family touring park in rural surroundings with distant views of the fells. Leave M6/A74 at junc 44, take A689 towards Brampton for 1m. Turn left signed Scaleby, and site 1m on left. A 1.5-acre site with 30 touring pitches.

🎪 🏠 ☉ ⚠ 🐕

➔ ⛽

Orton Grange Caravan & Camping Park (NY355519)
Orton Grange, Wigton Rd CA5 6LA ☎ 01228 710252
Signposted
Nearby town: Carlisle
► ► ► Family Park ★ 🚐 £6.50-£7 🚙 £6.50-£7 ▲ £6.50-£7
Open all year Booking advisable bank hols & Jul-Aug
Last arrival 22.00hrs Last departure noon
Mainly grassy site in rural surroundings close to A595, 4m from Carlisle. A 6-acre site with 50 touring pitches and 22 statics.
Cafe & Fast food facilities in Apr-Sep only.

🎪 🏠 ☉ 📺 ⚑ ↯ ⚡ 🖊 🚰 ✳ ⚠ 🚰 🖊 ⊞ Ⓣ ✖ ⚡
🍴 ⛴ 🏛 ⛽ 🛒 ♿

➔ ∪ ▶ ☕ ✈

Credit Cards 💳 💳 💳 💳 💳 💳 💳

CARTMEL

Greave Farm Caravan Park (SD391823)
Field Broughton LA11 6HR ☎ 015395 36329 & 36587
► ► ► Family Park 🚐 🚙 ▲
Open Mar-Oct Booking advisable
A small family-owned park close to working farm in peaceful rural area 3m from Windermere. Leave M6 junc 36 onto A590 signed Barrow. Approx 1m before Newby Bridge, turn left at crossroad signed Cartmel & Staveley, and site is 1.5m on left just before church. A 3-acre site with 10 touring pitches and 20 statics.

🎪 🏠 ⚑ ⚡

COCKERMOUTH

Violet Bank Holiday Home Park (NY126295)
Simonscales Ln, Lorton Rd CA13 9TG ☎ 01900 822169
Signposted
► ► ► Family Park ★ 🚐 £5.50-£6.50 🚙 £5.50-£6.50
▲ £5.50-£6.50
Open Mar-15 Nov Booking advisable Spring bank hol &
Jul-Aug Last arrival mdnt Last departure noon
Well-maintained site in a pleasant rural setting affording excellent views of Buttermere Hills. Approach by way of A5292 Lorton Road, via town centre. An 8.5-acre site with 30 touring pitches and 86 statics.

🎪 🏠 ☉ 📺 ✳ ⚠ 🚰 🖊 ⊞ ⚡ 🐕 ⛽

➔ ∪ ▶ ✈

CROOKLANDS

Waters Edge Caravan Park (SD533838)
LA7 7NN ☎ 015395 67708 & 67414
Nearby town: Kendal
▶ ▶ ▶ Family Park ⊞ £9.95-£14 ⊞ £9.95-£14
▲ £4.50-£13.50
Open Mar-14 Nov Booking advisable bank hols Last arrival 22.00hrs
A small rural site, close to junc 36 of M6 yet in a very peaceful setting. From M6 follow signs for Kirkby Lonsdale A65, at second roundabout follow signs for Crooklands/Endmoor. Site 1m on right. A 3-acre site with 30 touring pitches and 9 statics.

🔣 (icons)
→ ∪ ♪

Credit Cards ● ▨

CROSTHWAITE

Lambhowe Caravan Park (SD422914)
LA8 8JE ☎ 015395 68483 Signposted
Nearby town: Kendal
▶ ▶ ▶ Family Park ⊞ ⊞
Open Mar-Oct Booking advisable Etr, Spring bank hol & Jul-Aug Last arrival 21.00hrs Last departure noon
A secluded wooded site on A5074 between Lancaster and Windermere, ideal for touring the Lake District National Park. No tents. A 1-acre site with 14 touring pitches and 112 statics.

🔣 (icons)
→ ▶ 🖢

CUMWHITTON

Cairndale Caravan Park (NY518523)
CA4 9BZ ☎ 01768 896280
Nearby town: Carlisle
▶ ▶ ▶ Family Park ⊞ £5-£5.50 ⊞ £5-£5.50
Open Mar-Oct Booking advisable school & public hols Last arrival 22.00hrs
Lovely grass site set in tranquil Eden Valley with good views. Off A69 at Warwick Bridge on unclass road through Great Corby to Cumwhitton, turn left at village sign, then site in 1m. A 2-acre site with 5 touring pitches and 15 statics.

🔣 (icons)
→ ▶ ⌂ ⅃ ♪ 🖢

DALSTON

Dalston Hall Caravan Park (NY378519)
Dalston Hall Estate CA5 7JX ☎ 01228 710165
Signposted
Nearby town: Carlisle
▶ ▶ ▶ Family Park ⊞ ⊞ ▲
Open Mar-Oct Booking advisable Jul-Aug Last arrival 21.00hrs Last departure 13.00hrs
A neat, well-maintained site, on level grassy ground, situated in grounds of estate located between Carlisle and Dalston on B5299. Ideal position for touring northern Lake District, Carlisle and surrounding country. A 3-acre site with 60 touring pitches and 17 statics.
9 hole golf course & fly fishing.

🔣 (icons)
→ ▶ ⚬⚬ ♪

ESKDALE

Fisherground Farm Campsite (NY152002)
Fisherground CA19 1TF ☎ 019467 23319
▶ ▶ ▶ Family Park ★ ⊞ £8 ▲ £8
Open 8 Mar-14 Nov

A mainly level grassy site on farmland amidst beautiful scenery, in Eskdale Valley below Hardknott Pass, between Eskdale and Boot. Own railway halt on the Eskdale-Ravenglass railway, 'The Ratty'. A 3-acre site with 30 touring pitches and 5 statics.
Adventure playground and miniature railway.

🔣 (icons)
→ ♪ 🖢   ╳

FLOOKBURGH

 Lakeland Leisure Park (SD372743)
Moor Ln LA11 7LT ☎ 015395 58556
Nearby town: Grange over Sands

○○○○○○○○○○○○○○○○○○○○○

★ ⊞ £8-£14 ⊞ £8-£14 ▲ £8-£14
Open late Mar-early Nov Booking advisable May-Oct Last arrival 21.00hrs Last departure 11.00hrs
A complete leisure park with full range of activities and entertainments, making this flat, grassy site ideal for families. Approach on B5277 through Grange over Sands to Flookburgh, turn left at village square, and park is in 1 mile. A 105-acre site with 125 touring pitches and 740 statics.
Horse riding.

🔣 (icons)
⇿ 🔣 (icons)
→ ∪ ▶ ◎ ♪

Credit Cards ● ▨ ▨ ▨

○○○○○○○○○○○○○○○○○○○○○

GREYSTOKE

Hopkinsons Whitbarrow Hall Caravan Park (NY405289)
Berrier CA11 0XB ☎ 01768 483456 Signposted
Nearby town: Penrith
▶ ▶ ▶ Family Park ★ ⊞ £8.50 ⊞ £8.50 ▲ £8.50
Open Mar-Oct Booking advisable bank hols & for electric hook up Last arrival 22.00hrs Last departure 23.00hrs
A level grassy site, an ideal base for touring the Lake District National Park. Leave M6 at junc 40 onto A66 towards Keswick. Turn right in 8m at Sportsman's Inn onto unclass rd, signed Hutton Roof. Site in .5m. An 8-acre site with 81 touring pitches and 167 statics.

Table tennis, pool table & video games.

🕹️📻☉📼🍳🔦❄️🍷🎢🏧🛗⏹️🗂️📺📞🚿🐕🎯♿
→⛎▶️

HAVERTHWAITE

Bigland Hall Caravan Park (SD344833)
LA12 8PJ ☎ 01539 531702 Signposted
Nearby town: Grange-over-Sands
▶️▶️▶️ **Family Park** ★ 🚐 £7-£10 🚗 £7-£10
Open Mar-Oct Booking advisable public hols Last arrival
22.30hrs Last departure 13.00hrs
*A wooded site in lovely countryside with direct access
from B5278. 3m from the southern end of Lake
Windermere and near the Haverthwaite Steam Railway.
A 30-acre site with 86 touring pitches and 29 statics.*
Off-licence on site.

🕹️📻☉❄️🍳🔦🗂️⏹️📞
→⛎🏊🛗

HAWKSHEAD

Camping & Caravanning Club Site (SD337943)
Grizedale Hall LA22 0GL ☎ 01229 860257(in season) &
01203 694995
Nearby town: Ambleside
▶️ **Town & Country Pennant Park** ★ 🚗 £9.20-£11.60
▲ £9.20-£11.60
Open end Mar-Sep Booking advisable Spring bank hol
& Jul-Aug Last arrival 21.00hrs Last departure noon
*A peaceful, sloping site with level pitches set in
Grizedale Forest, with lots of marked walks. Close to the
famous theatre in the forest with its live shows. Take
A590 from Newby Bridge via Greenodd, then minor
road to right at Penny Bridge. Please see the
advertisement on page 27 for details of Club Members'
benefits. A 5-acre site with 60 touring pitches.*

🕹️📻☉📼🍳🔦❄️🍳🗂️⏹️📺📞
→🏊🛗

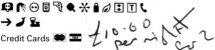

Credit Cards 💳 💳

HOLKER

Old Park Wood Caravan Park (SD335784)
LA11 7PP ☎ 015395 58266 Signposted
Nearby town: Grange-over-Sands
▶️▶️▶️ **Family Park** ★ 🚐 £12-£13.50 🚗 £12-£13.50
Open Mar-Oct Booking advisable bank hols Last
departure 17.30hrs
*Terraced park gently sloping towards the River Leven
estuary, surrounded on three sides by woodland; very
well maintained and with good facilities. 2m N of Cark
in Cartmel, off B5278; follow signs for Holker Hall. A 4-
acre site with 50 touring pitches and 325 statics.*

🕹️📻☉📼🍳🍹 🎢🍳🗂️❌📞🛗
→⛎▶️

KENDAL

Ashes Lane Caravan & Camping Park (SD478962)
Ashes Ln LA8 9JS ☎ 01539 821119 Signposted

▶️▶️▶️▶️ **De-Luxe Park** ★ 🚐 £8.50-£15.50 🚗 £8.50-
£15.50 ▲ £6-£15
Open mid Mar-mid Jan Booking advisable bank hols
Last arrival 22.00hrs Last departure noon

*Large, well-equipped park in naturally secluded Lake
District area with level grassy pitches. Signed off A591,
.75m from rndbt with B5284 towards Windermere. A 22-
acre site with 200 touring pitches and 68 statics.*

🕹️📻☉📼🍳🍳❄️🍷🎢🍳🖊️❌📞🛗🏧🍳
🐕🛗♿
→⛎▶️⛺🍳🎣

Credit Cards 💳 💳 💳 💳

Camping & Caravanning Club Site (SD526948)
Millcrest, Shap Rd LA9 6NY ☎ 01539 741363 (in season)
& 01203 694995 (on A6, 1.5m N) Signposted
▶️▶️▶️ **Family Park** ★ 🚐 £11-£14 🚗 £11-£14 ▲ £11-£14
Open end Mar-early Nov Booking advisable bank hols &
high season Last arrival 21.00hrs Last departure noon
*Sloping grass site, set in hilly wood and meadowland.
Situated on the A6, 1.5m N of Kendal. Please see
advertisement on page 27 for details of Club Members'
benefits. A 3-acre site with 53 touring pitches.*

🕹️📻☉📼🍳❄️🎢🍳🗂️⏹️📞🐕🛗
→⛎▶️🎣

Credit Cards 💳 💳 💳 💳

KESWICK

Camping & Caravanning Club Site (NY258234)
Derwentwater CA12 5EP ☎ 01768 772392 (in season) &
01203 694995 Signposted
▶️▶️▶️ **Family Park** ★ 🚐 £13-£14 🚗 £13-£14 ▲ £13-£14
Open early Feb-Nov Booking advisable all season Last
arrival 21.00hrs Last departure noon
*A well-situated lakeside site within walking distance of
the town centre. Please see advertisement on page 27
for details of Club Members' benefits. A 14-acre site
with 250 touring pitches.*

🕹️📻☉📼🍳❄️🎢🍳🗂️⏹️📞🐕🛗♿
→⛎🍳⛺🎣

Credit Cards 💳 💳 💳 💳

Castlerigg Hall Caravan & Camping Park (NY282227)
Castlerigg Hall CA12 4TE ☎ 017687 72437 Signposted
▶️▶️▶️ **Family Park** ★ 🚐 £8.50-£10 🚗 £7.50-£8
▲ £6.20-£7.40

Open Etr-mid Nov Last arrival 21.00hrs Last departure
11.30hrs

contd.

A family-run site with tiered pitches and spectacular views over Derwent Water to the mountains beyond. Situated about 300yds along unclass rd off A591, about 1.5m SE of Keswick in Ambleside direction, signed towards Heights Hotel. An 8-acre site with 173 touring pitches and 30 statics.

🕲 📻 ⊙ ⛷ ✳ 🏮 🖉 🖃 T ⤢ 🌉
➔ ▶ ◎ ◬ ☙ 🞉 🗖

Credit Cards 💳 ▨▨ ▨▨ 🖸

Derwentwater Caravan Park (NY257234)
Crowe Park Rd CA12 5EN ☎ 017687 72579 Signposted
▶ ▶ ▶ Family Park ★ 🚐 £8.80-£9.60 🚙 £8.80-£9.60
Open Mar-14 Nov Booking advisable at all times Last arrival 21.00hrs Last departure noon
A very well managed and maintained site which is divided into two areas for tourers. No tents or awnings. Signed off B5289 in town centre. A 4-acre site with 50 touring pitches and 160 statics.

🕲 📻 ⊙ 🖸 ⛷ 🕮 🏮 🖉 🖃 ⤢ 🏛 🗖 ⛷
➔ ∪ ▶ ◎ ◬ ⤣ ☙ 🞉 🌉

Gill Head Farm Caravan & Camping Park (NY380269)
Troutbeck CA11 0ST ☎ 017687 79652 Signposted
▶ ▶ ▶ Family Park ★ 🚐 £7-£10 🚙 £7-£10 ⤢ £7-£10
Open Apr-Oct Booking advisable bank hols

An attractive and well-maintained site, with spacious and comfortable facilities, set against a backdrop of Blencathra and the northern fells. From junc 40 of M6 avoiding Kirkstone Pass, site 200yds from A66/A5091. A 5.5-acre site with 42 touring pitches and 17 statics.

🕲 📻 ⊙ 🖸 ⛷ ✳ 🏮 🖉 ⤢ 🏛 🐕 🌉
➔ ∪ ▶ ◬ ⤣ 🞉

KIRKBY LONSDALE

Woodclose Caravan Park (SD618786)
Casterton LA6 2SE ☎ 01524 271597 Signposted

▶ ▶ ▶ ▶ De-Luxe Park ★ 🚐 £9-£14.50 🚙 £9-£14.50
⤢ £7-£14.50
Open Mar-Oct Booking advisable bank hols, Jul-Aug & Sep Last arrival 22.00hrs Last departure 14.00hrs
A pleasant site in a quiet, rural area. Situated off the A65, .5m SE of the town. A 9-acre site with 70 touring pitches and 50 statics.

🕲 📻 ⊙ 🖸 ✳ 🏮 🖉 🖃 ⤢ 🌉 ⛷
➔ ▶ 🞉

▶ ▶ ▶
Pennine View
Caravan & Camping Park
Station Road, Kirkby Stephen,
Cumbria CA17 4SZ. Tel: (017683) 71717

Pennine View Caravan & Camping Park is a family run site on the south side of the beautiful market town of Kirkby Stephen, one mile from the town centre. An ideal walking area, en route for the Coast to Coast walk, within easy reach of the Yorkshire Dales and the Lake District. Also within easy reach of the Settle to Carlisle railway line. Kirkby Stephen station 1 mile.
Amenities: *Modern toilet block with hot & cold water, showers, hair dryers and razor points. Dish washing area. Full laundry facilities. Chemical disposal point. Calor & Camping Gas. Children's play area. Milk & newspapers daily.*

Proprietors: Colin & Shiela Sim

New House Caravan Park (SD628774)
LA6 2HR ☎ 015242 71590 (1.5m S on A65)
▶ ▶ ▶ Family Park ★ 🚐 £5.50-£6 🚙 £5.50-£6 ⤢ £5.50-£6
Open Mar-Oct Booking advisable
A recently developed park around a former farm, set on part grass and part hardstanding in a rural area 1m SE of Kirkby Lonsdale. A 3-acre site with 50 touring pitches.

🕲 📻 ⊙ 🖸 ⛷
➔ ∪ ▶ 🞉 🌉

KIRKBY STEPHEN

Pennine View Caravan & Camping Park (NY772076)
Pennine View, Station Rd CA17 4SZ ☎ 01768 371717
Nearby town: Kendal
▶ ▶ ▶ Family Park ★ 🚐 £9.40-£10.30 🚙 £9.40-£10.30
⤢ £7.40-£8.80
Open Mar-Oct Booking advisable bank hols & Jul-Aug Last arrival 22.00hrs Last departure 12.30hrs
Once a railway goods yard on a now disused line, this is an attractive, level, well-maintained site with river walks, situated on the coast to coast path. 100 metres off A685 on the B6270. A 2.5-acre site with 43 touring pitches.

🕲 📻 ⊙ ⛷ 🕮 🏮 🖉 ⤢ ⛷
➔ 🞉 🌉

LAMPLUGH

Inglenook Caravan Park (NY084206)
Fitzbridge CA14 4SH ☎ 01946 861240 Signposted
Nearby town: Cockermouth
▶ ▶ ▶ Family Park ★ 🚐 £7.50-£8.50 🚙 £7.50-£8.50
⤢ £6.50-£8.50

Open all year Booking advisable bank hols Last arrival 20.00hrs Last departure noon

An ideal touring site, well-maintained and situated in beautiful surroundings, on left of A5086 in direction of Egremont. A 3.5-acre site with 30 touring pitches and 28 statics.

🔌🏪☉🏴❋🏔🛈🌿🅭✕🔌🦮🛒♿
➔🍴

LEVENS

Sampool Caravan Park (SD479844)
LA8 8EQ ☎ 015395 52265 Signposted
▶▶▶ **Family Park** ★ 🚐 £6-£8 🚐 £6-£8
Open 15 Mar-Oct Booking advisable bank hols & Jul-Aug

A pleasantly landscaped park adjacent to the River Kent. Turn off A6 at Levens Bridge onto A590, then left on unclassified lane to park in 1m. A 1.5-acre site with 20 touring pitches and 200 statics.

🏪☉🏴❋🏔🛈🦮🛒♿
➔🍴

LONGTOWN

Camelot Caravan Park (NY391666)
CA6 5SZ ☎ 01228 791248 Signposted
Nearby town: Carlisle
▶▶▶ **Family Park** ★ 🚐 £7 🚐 £7 🅰 £6
Open Mar-Oct Booking advisable Jul-Aug Last arrival 22.00hrs Last departure noon

Very pleasant level grassy site near junction 44 of M6. Ideal stopover site. A 1.5-acre site with 20 touring pitches and 1 static.

🔌🏪☉❋🛈🌿🅭🦮🛒
➔ ∪▶🍴

High Gaitle Caravan & Camping Park (NT675365)
High Gaitle Bridge CA6 5LU ☎ 01228 791819
▶▶▶ **Family Park**

A level grassy park with modern, spacious sanitary facilities. Situated 0.5m W of Longtown on A6071, not far from Gretna Green. Can be approached also from S at junc 44 of M6 and A7 through Longtown.

Oakbank Lakes Country Park (NY369700)
CA6 5NA ☎ 01228 791108
▶▶ **Town & Country Pennant Park** ★ 🚐 £8-£10.50
🚐 £8-£10.50 🅰 £5-£8
Open all year

Set alongside three fishing lakes, and adjacent to the River Esk, this park has many established and newly planted trees, and a bird sanctuary with a game bird breeding unit. Leave Longtown on A7 towards Langholm/Galashiels, turn left in 1m signed Corries Mill Chapelknowe, and site in 200yards. A 60-acre site with 20 touring pitches and 4 statics.
Fishing.

🔌🚐🏪☉🏴❋🅰🔌🗔❋🔲✕🏕🎋🦮🛒
➔🍴

MEALSGATE

Larches Caravan Park (NY205415)
CA5 1LQ ☎ 016973 71379 & 71803 Signposted
Nearby town: Wigton

◯◯◯◯◯◯◯◯

▶▶▶▶ **De-Luxe Park** ★ 🚐 £7-£9 🚐 £7-£9 🅰 £7-£9
Open Mar-Oct (rs early & late season) Booking advisable Etr Spring bank hol & Jul-Aug Last arrival 21.30hrs Last departure noon

Set in wooded rural surroundings on the fringe of the Lake District National Park. Situated on A595 Carlisle-Cockermouth road. A 5-acre site with 73 touring pitches and 100 statics.
Ensuite units with toilets, shower, washbasin.

🔌🏪☉🏴❋🗔❋🛈🌿🅭🆃🦮🛒♿
➔∪▶🍴

◯◯◯◯◯◯◯◯

MILNTHORPE

Fell End Caravan Park (SD505780)
Slackhead Rd, Hale LA7 7BS ☎ 015395 62122 & 64163 Signposted
Nearby town: Kendal

◯◯◯◯◯◯◯◯

▶▶▶▶ **De-Luxe Park** ★ 🚐 £12.50 🚐 £12.50 🅰 £9.50
Open all year Booking advisable school & bank hols

Well-kept site, constantly improving and with high standards being continually maintained. Pleasantly situated in a very picturesque natural setting surrounded by woodland. Within easy reach of the lakes and South Cumbria. 4.75m from junction 35 of M6, signed on left of A6 before Hale filling station. An 8-acre site with 68 touring pitches and 215 statics.
Off-licence, TV aerial hook ups, kitchen facility.

🔌🏪☉🏴❋🔲❋♀🏔🛈🌿✕🦮🏪🏕🛒♿
➔∪▶⚠🍴

Credit Cards 💳

◯◯◯◯◯◯◯◯

Hall More Caravan Park (SD502771)
Hale LA7 7BP ☎ 015395 63383 Signposted
▶ ▶ ▶ Family Park 🚐 🚐 ⚊
Open Mar-Oct Booking advisable bank hols & wknds
A mainly level grassy site in meadowland, adjacent to main road. Close to farm and stables, and fishing park. Leave M6 at junc 35 on to A6 towards Milnthorpe for 3.5m, take 1st left after crossing Cumbrian border, and site signed in .75m. A 3-acre site with 50 touring pitches and 65 statics.

🌐 🐾 ⊙ 📷 🗑️ 🅰 🛈 🖉 🚱 🔌 🔁
→ ∪ 🅿 🎣 🕹️ 🏋️

PATTERDALE

Sykeside Camping Park (NY403119)
Brotherswater CA11 0NZ ☎ 017684 82239
Signposted
Nearby town: Windermere
▶ ▶ ▶ Family Park ★ 🚐 £5.70-£8 ⚊ £7.60-£9.60
Open all year Booking advisable bank hols & Jul-Aug
Last arrival 22.30hrs Last departure 14.00hrs
A camper's delight, this family-run park is situated halfway up Kirkstone Pass, under the 2000ft Hartsop Dodd in a spectacular area with breathtaking views. Off A592 Windermere to Ullswater Road; not suitable for caravans. A 5-acre site with 86 touring pitches.

🌐 🐾 ⊙ 📷 🍳 ☀️ 🍴 🛈 🖉 🚱 🔲 🅣 ✗ 🔌 🏪 🏇 🏋️
→ ∪ 🛶 ⚓ 🕹️
Credit Cards 💳 🔲 💳 📶 🔄 ⑤

PENRITH

Lowther Caravan Park (NY527265)
Eamont Bridge CA10 2JB ☎ 01768 863631 Signposted

▶ ▶ ▶ ▶ De-Luxe Park ★ 🚐 🚐 ⚊ £11-£12
Open mid Mar-mid Nov Booking advisable bank hols
Last arrival 21.00hrs
A secluded natural woodland site with lovely on-site riverside walks and glorious surrounding countryside. Winner of the North of England Campsite of the Year Award for 1998/9. Site is 3m S of Penrith on A6. A 10-acre site with 150 touring pitches and 407 statics.

🌐 🐾 ⊙ 📷 🍳 ☀️ 🍴 🅰 🛈 🖉 🚱 🅣 ✗ 🔌
🏪 🏇 🏋️ ♿
→ ∪ 🅿 ⊙ 🎥 🕹️
Credit Cards 💳 🔲 💳 📶 ⑤

Thacka Lea Caravan Site (NY509310)
Thacka Ln CA11 9HX ☎ 01768 863319 Signposted
▶ ▶ ▶ Family Park 🚐 fr £6 🚐 fr £6
Open Mar-Oct Booking advisable public hols
A good, spotlessly clean site in urban area at the N edge of town, just off A6 and signed. A 2-acre site with 25 touring pitches.

🌐 🐾 ⊙ ☀️ 🛈 🖉 🚱
→ ∪ 🅿 🎥 🕹️ 🏋️

PENRUDDOCK

Beckses Caravan Park (NY419278)
CA11 0RX ☎ 01768 483224 Signposted
▶ ▶ ▶ **Family Park** ★ ⊕ £6.50 ⊕ £6.50 ▲ £5
Open Etr-Oct Booking advisable public hols Last arrival
20.00hrs Last departure 11.00hrs
*A small site on sloping ground with level pitches and
views of distant fells, on edge of National Park. From
A66 towards Keswick turn right onto B5288. A 4-acre
site with 23 touring pitches and 18 statics.*

🗦 ⋒ ⦿ ☉ ✳ ⋀ ⦙ ⌀ 🎕 🚻 📞 🐾
➜ ∪ ⏄ 📭

POOLEY BRIDGE

Park Foot Caravan & Camping Park (NY469235)
Howtown Rd CA10 2NA ☎ 017684 86309 Signposted
Nearby town: Penrith

▶ ▶ ▶ ▶ **De-Luxe Park** ★ ⊕ £12-£15 ⊕ £7.50-£11
▲ £7.50-£11
Open Mar-Oct Booking advisable bank hols Last arrival
22.00hrs Last departure noon
*A mainly tenting park on gently sloping ground, with
access to Lake Ullswater and lovely views. Leave M6
junc 40 onto A66 towards Keswick, then take A592 to
Ullswater. Turn left for Pooley Bridge, turn right at
church, and right at crossrds signed Howtown. Site 1m
on left. An 18-acre site with 323 touring pitches and 131
statics.*
Lake access with boat launch, pony treking.

🗦 ⋒ ⦿ ☉ 🞐 ⚲ ⚫ ⌖ ✳ ⚑ ⋀ ⦙ ⌀ 🎕 🚻 ✗ 📞
🛒 🏕 🐕 🐾 📭 ♿
➜ ∪ ⏄ ♿ ✚ 📭

Hillcroft Caravan & Camping Site (NY478241)

Roe Head Ln CA10 2LT ☎ 017684 86363 Signposted
Nearby town: Penrith
▶ ▶ ▶ **Family Park** ★ ⊕ £8-£11 ⊕ £8-£11 ▲ £8-£11
Open 7 Mar-14 Nov Booking advisable bank hols
*A pleasant rural site close to the village and Ullswater;
an ideal touring base. From A592 fork L just before
Pooley Bridge, and site is signed on L. A 10-acre site
with 125 touring pitches and 200 statics.*

🗦 ⋒ ⦿ 🞐 ⚲ ✳ ⋀ ⦙ ⌀ 🎕 🚻 📞 🐕 🐾 📭 ♿
➜ ∪ ♿ ✚ 📭

RAVENGLASS

Walls Caravan & Camping Park (SD087964)
CA18 1SR ☎ 01229 717250 Signposted
Nearby town: Whitehaven
▶ ▶ ▶ **Family Park** ★ ⊕ £8 ⊕ £7.50 ▲ £3.50-£8
Open Mar-15 Nov Booking advisable bank hols &
summer Last arrival 22.00hrs Last departure noon
*A well-maintained site in a woodland park with all
hardstandings. Situated off A595 close to Ravenglass-
Eskdale narrow railway service. A 5-acre site with 50
touring pitches.*
Washing up sinks with free hot water.

🗦 ⋒ ⦿ 🞐 ⚲ ✳ ⦙ ⌀ 🎕 📞 🏠 📭
➜ ♿ 📭

SEDBERGH

Pinfold Caravan Park (SD665921)
Garsdale Rd LA10 5JL
☎ 01539 620576 Signposted
▶ ▶ ▶ **Family Park** ★ ⊕ £9 ⊕ £8 ▲ £8
Open Mar-Oct Booking advisable bank hols & Jul-Aug
Last arrival 21.30hrs Last departure 13.30hrs
*A mature site amongst beautiful scenery on a river
bank; at edge of village on the Hawes road. A 4-acre site
with 40 touring pitches and 56 statics.*
barbeques are allowed

🗦 ⋒ ⦿ 🞐 🞒 ✳ ⦙ ⌀ 🎕 📞 📭
➜ ∪ ⏄ 📭

SILECROFT

Silecroft Caravan Site (SD124811)
LA18 4NX ☎ 01229 772659 Signposted
Nearby town: Millom
▶ ▶ ▶ **Family Park** ⊕ ⊕ ▲
Open Mar-15 Nov Booking advisable
*Quietly situated close to the shore 4m N of Millom, in a
beautiful, little-known area of the Lake District with
lovely beach nearby. A 5-acre site with 60 touring
pitches and 124 statics.*
Sauna, gym & Jacuzzi.

🗦 ⋒ ⦿ 🞐 🞒 ⚡ ⚫ ✳ ⋀ 🎕 📞 📭
➜ ∪ ⏄ 🛆 📭

SILLOTH

Stanwix Park Holiday Centre (NY108527)
Green Row CA5 4HH
☎ 016973 32666 (1m SW on B5300)
Signposted
Nearby town: Carlisle

★ ⊕ £7-£9.50 ⊕ £7-£9.50 ▲ £7-£9.50
Open Mar-Oct (rs Nov-Feb no mid week entertainment)
Booking advisable Etr, Spring bank hol & Jul-Aug Last
arrival 21.00hrs Last departure 11.00hrs
*A large well-run family park within easy reach of the
Lake District. Attractively laid-out, with lots of amenities
to ensure a lively holiday, including a 4-lane automatic
lo-pin bowling alley. On outskirts of Silloth on B5300.
A 4-acre site with 121 touring pitches and 212 statics.*
Pony trekking & entertainment.

🗦 🛒 ⋒ ⦿ 🞐 🞒 ⚡ ⚡ ⚲ ⚫ ⌖ ✳ ⚑ ⋀ ⦙ ⌀ 🎕
✗ 📞 🛒 📭
➜ ∪ ⏄ ⦿ 📭

Credit Cards 💳 ▨▨ 📇 📇 📇

See advertisement on page 90.

Tanglewood Caravan Park (NY131534)

Causewayhead CA5 4PE
☎ 016973 31253
Signposted
Nearby town: Wigton
▶ ▶ ▶ **Family Park** ⊕ £6 ⊕ £6 ▲ £6
Open Mar-Oct Booking advisable Etr, Whit & Jul-Aug
Last arrival 23.00hrs Last departure 10.00hrs
contd.

Mainly level grass site sheltered by a variety of trees and bushes, and set in meadowland adjacent to B5302 Wigton-Silloth road. A 7-acre site with 31 touring pitches and 58 statics.

♨ 🏍 ☉ 🗟 🍴 ◄ 🖵 ☀ ♀ ⚂ ⓘ ± 🔌 🐕
➜ ∪ ⚲ ◎ ♪ 🎱

TEBAY

Tebay Caravan Site (NY609060)
Orton CA10 3SB ☎ 015396 24511 Signposted
Nearby town: Kendal
► ► ► Family Park ★ 🚐 £6.50-£8.50 🚐 £6.50-£8.50
Open 14 Mar-Oct Booking advisable Jul-Aug Last departure noon

An ideal stopover site and good for touring the Lake District. Screened by high grass banks, bushes and trees. Site is adjacent to M6 at Tebay Service area .75m N of exit 38 for northbound traffic. Southbound traffic join northbound at junction 38, and can easily rejoin motorway with site warden's instructions. A 4-acre site with 77 touring pitches.

♨ 🏍 ☉ 🗟 🍴 ☀ ♀ ⚂ ✗ 🔌 🖛 🏕 🐎 🐕 🐾 ♿
➜ ∪ ♪

ULVERSTON

Bardsea Leisure Park (SD292765)
Priory Rd LA12 9QE ☎ 01229 584712 Signposted
► ► ► Family Park 🚐 🚐 Å

Open all year Booking advisable bank hols & Jul-Aug Last arrival 21.00hrs Last departure 18.00hrs
Attractively landscaped former quarry making a quiet and very sheltered site. On southern edge of town off the A5087, convenient for both the coast and the Lake District. A 5-acre site with 83 touring pitches and 73 statics.

♨ 🏍 ☉ 🗟 🍴 ☀ ⚂ ⓘ 🖉 ± T 🔌 🏕 🐎 🐾
➜ ∪ ⚲ 🍴 ♪

WATERMILLOCK

Cove Caravan & Camping Park (NY431236)
Ullswater CA11 0LS ☎ 017684 86549 (A592 to Ullswater, approx 4m to T jct, turn rught then rigth at Brackenrigg Inn, park 1.5m on left) Signposted
Nearby town: Penrith
► ► ► **Family Park** ★ 🚐 £8.50-£9 🚐 £6.80-£7.20
Å £6.80-£9
Open Etr-Oct Booking advisable bank & school hols Last arrival 21.00hrs Last departure noon
A family site in attractive rural setting amidst fells with views over the lake. Leave M6 at junction 40, turn W following signs for Ullswater (A592). Turn right at lake junction, then right at Brackenrigg Hotel. Site is 1.5m on left. A 3-acre site with 50 touring pitches and 38 statics. Dishwashing area, drinks machine.

🔌📻☉🔲🍴✳⚥🏔🛈🖉✚T🔦🏢🎋🐕🐾
➔ ∪ 🔱 🎣

The Quiet Site (NY431236)
Ullswater CA11 0LS ☎ 01768 486337 Signposted
Nearby town: Penrith
► ► ► **Family Park** ★ 🚐 £9-£11 🚐 £8-£10 Å £8-£10
Open Mar-Oct Booking advisable bank hols & Jul-Aug Last arrival 22.00hrs Last departure noon
A well-maintained site in a lovely, peaceful location, with very good facilities, including a charming olde-worlde bar. Leave M6 at junction 40, turn W following signs for Ullswater (A592). Turn right at lake junction, then right at Brackenrigg Hotel. Site is 1.5m on right. A 6-acre site with 60 touring pitches and 23 statics. Pets corner. Pool & darts (adults only).

🔌📻☉🔲🍴🔑✳⚥🏔🛈🖉✚T🔦🚐🐾
➔ ∪ 🔱 🎣

Ullswater Caravan Camping Site & Marine Park (NY438232)
High Longthwaite CA11 0LR ☎ 01768 486666 Signposted
Nearby town: Ullswater/Penrith
► ► ► **Family Park** ★ 🚐 £10 🚐 £9 Å £9
Open Mar-Nov Booking advisable public hols Last arrival 21.00hrs Last departure noon

A pleasant rural site with own nearby boat launching and marine storage facility. Leave M6 at junction 40, turn W following signs for Ullswater (A592) for 5 miles. Turn right alongside Ullswater for 2 miles, then turn right at telephone box signposted Longthwaite and Watermillock Church. Site .5 mile on right. A 9-acre site with 155 touring pitches and 55 statics.

Boat launching & moorings.

🔌📻☉🔲🔑✳⚥🏔🛈🖉✚T🔦❌🐕🐾♿
➔ ∪ 🔺 🔱 🎣
Credit Cards 💳 💳 💳 💳 📷

WESTWARD

Clea Hall Holiday Park (NY279425)
CA7 8NQ ☎ 016973 42880 Signposted
Nearby town: Wigton

◖◖◖◖◖◖◖◖◖

► ► ► ► **De-Luxe Park** ★ 🚐 £8-£10 🚐 £8-£10 Å £8-£10
Open Mar-Nov Booking advisable bank hols & Jul-Aug Last departure noon
A slightly sloping grassy site surrounded by woods, moorland and hills. 3.5m S of A595 from Red Dial, and signed. A 10-acre site with 16 touring pitches and 90 statics.

🔌📻☉🔲🍴🔑✳⚥🏔🔦🎋🐕🐾♿
◖◖◖◖◖◖◖◖◖

WINDERMERE

Fallbarrow Park (SD401973)
Rayrigg Rd LA23 3DL ☎ 015394 44428 Signposted

◖◖◖◖◖◖◖◖◖

► ► ► ► ► **Premier Park** 🚐 £11.40-£18.25
🚐 £11.40-£18.25
Open mid Mar-Oct Booking advisable bank hols & Jul-Aug Last arrival 23.00hrs Last departure 13.00hrs

contd. on p93

AA APPROVED

CLEA HALL Holiday Park

WESTWARD : WIGTON : CUMBRIA : CA7 8NQ
Telephone: WIGTON (016973) 42880
Quiet, privately owned park situated on the fringe of the Lake District National Park.
Facilities include:
heated outdoor swimming pool (May – September).
Childrens play area, tavern bar, showers and launderette.
Touring caravans and tents welcome.

A very high quality park with excellent facilities, a few minutes' walk from Bowness on shore of Lake Windermere. Winner of the 1996/97 Campsite of the Year Award. A 32-acre site with 83 touring pitches and 248 statics.
Boat launching facilities on shore Lake Windermere

Credit Cards

Limefitt Park (NY416032)
LA23 1PA ☎ 015394 32300 ext 41 Signposted

► ► ► ► ► **Premier Park** ⚐ £9.50-£13.50
⚐ £9.50-£13.50 ▲ £9-£12.50
Open 1 wk prior Etr-Oct Booking advisable bank hols & Jun-Sep Last arrival 22.30hrs Last departure noon ✍
A lovely family site with superb facilities in a beautiful location in the Lake District National Park. Direct access off A592 approach from Windermere but do not enter Troutbeck village. A 12-acre site with 165 touring pitches and 45 statics.
Riverpool for paddling & swimming (with beach)

Credit Cards

See advertisement on Inside Front cover.

Park Cliffe Farm Camping & Caravan Estate (SD391912)
Birks Rd, Tower Wood LA23 3PG ☎ 01539 531344 Signposted
► ► ► **Family Park** ★ ⚐ £11.20-£11.60 ⚐ £11.20-£11.60 ▲ £9.20-£11.60
Open 21 Mar-Oct Booking advisable bank hols & Aug Last arrival 22.00hrs Last departure noon
A lovely hillside site on level and sloping ground with trees, bushes, rocks and mountain stream. 3m S of Windermere off A592. A 25-acre site with 250 touring pitches and 50 statics.
Off-licence.

Credit Cards

DERBYSHIRE

For the map of this county
see STAFFORDSHIRE

ASHBOURNE

Rivendale Touring Caravan & Leisure Park (SK162566)
Buxton Rd, Alsop en le Dale DE6 1QU ☎ 01335 310311
► ► ► **Family Park** ⚐ ⚐ ▲
Open Mar-Jan Booking advisable

contd.

A sheltered site built in a long-closed quarry with all hardstandings. Off the Ashbourne-Buxton road, A515, opposite the turn to Biggin, N of Ashbourne. A 12-acre site with 105 touring pitches.

🖭 ℝ ☉ 🖥 /ⅅ ﹨ ⥁ ⅆ

Sandybrook Hall Holiday Park (SK179481)
Buxton Rd DE6 2AQ ☎ 01335 342679 (1m N of Ashbourne on A515) Signposted
Nearby town: Derby
▶▶ **Town & Country Pennant Park** ★ ⊕ £7.50-£9
⊕ £7.50-£9 ⅄ £7.50-£9
Open 26 Mar-Oct Booking advisable public hols & Jul-Aug
A family-run touring site on mostly sloping grass. Leave Ashbourne on A515 Buxton rd, and site on right in 2m opp sign for Thorpe and Dovedale. An 8-acre site with 70 touring pitches and 25 statics.
Bar meals, sand pit.

🖭 ℝ ☉ ♦ ⥁ ☐ ✳ ⅄ /ⅅ ⅆ ⅆ ⊕ ☐ ⥁ ⊞ ⅄ ⅄
→ ∪ ⎗ ◭ ◢

BAKEWELL

See also Youlgreave

Greenhills Caravan Park (SK202693)
Crow Hill Ln DE45 1PX ☎ 01629 813467 & 813052
(on A6, 2km NW) Signposted
▶▶▶ **Family Park** ★ ⊕ £10 ⊕ £9 ⅄ £9-£11.50
Open all year (rs Oct, Mar & Apr bar & shop closed)
Booking advisable Etr-Sep Last arrival 21.00hrs Last departure noon
Nicely kept and run site. Tenting field well cut with path of shorter grass to facilities block. 1 mile NW of Bakewell on A6, and site signed before Ashford in the Water, 50yds up unclass rd on right. An 8-acre site with 60 touring pitches and 60 statics.

🖭 ℝ ☉ 🖥 ⅊ ✳ ⅄ /ⅅ ⅆ ⅆ ⊞ ☐ ⥁ ⊞ ⅄ ⅄
→ ⎗

BUXTON

Limetree Holiday Park (SK070725)
Dukes Dr SK17 9RP ☎ 01298 22988 (1m S, between A515 & A6) Signposted

◯◯◯◯◯◯◯◯

▶▶▶▶ **De-Luxe Park** ★ ⊕ £7.50-£9 ⊕ £7.50-£9
⅄ £7.50-£9
Open Mar-Oct Booking advisable bank hols & Jul-Aug
Last arrival 21.00hrs Last departure noon
A most attractive and well-designed site, set on the side of a narrow valley in an elevated situation of gently sloping land with views. Leaving Buxton on A515 S, turn L after hospital and site is .25m on R. From A6, signed opposite Safeway. A 10.5-acre site with 99 touring pitches and 43 statics.

🖭 ℝ ☉ 🖥 ⅊ ♦ ⥁ ☐ ✳ /ⅅ ⅆ ⅆ ⊞ ☐ ⥁ ⅄ ⅄ ⅆ
→ ∪ ⎗ ◎ ◭ ⅄
Credit Cards 💳 ▨▨ ▨▨ ▨ ⅅ

◯◯◯◯◯◯◯◯

Cottage Farm Caravan Park (SK122720)
SK17 9TQ ☎ 01298 85330 (E on A6 for 6m then N on unclassified rd)
▶▶▶ **Family Park** ★ ⊕ £6 ⊕ £5.50 ⅄ £6
Open mid Mar-Oct Booking advisable Last arrival 21.30hrs
A small terraced site overlooking farm buildings with good views. Ideal for touring/walking in the Peak Park. 6m E of Buxton off A6 and B6049, signed Blackwell in the Peak. 30 touring pitches.

🖭 ℝ ☉ ✳ ⅆ /ⅅ ⊞ ⅄ ⅄

Thornheyes Farm Campsite (SK084761)
Thornheyes Farm, Longridge Ln, Peak Dale SK17 8AD
☎ 01298 26421
▶▶ **Town & Country Pennant Park** ★ ⊕ fr £10 ⊕ fr £8
⅄ fr £4
Open Etr-Oct Booking advisable bank hols & high season Last arrival 21.30hrs Last departure evenings
A pleasant farm site run by a friendly family team, in the central Peak District. 1.5m N of Buxton on A6 turn east for Peak Dale, and after .5m south at crossroads, site is on right up Longridge Lane. A 2-acre site with 10 touring pitches.

🖭 ℝ ✳ ⅆ ⊞
→ ∪ ⎗ 🖥 ⅄

CROWDEN

Camping & Caravanning Club Site (SK072992)
SK14 7HZ ☎ 01457 866057 (in season) & 01203 694995
(off A628) Signposted
Nearby town: Hyde
▶▶ **Town & Country Pennant Park** ★ ⅄ £9.20-£11.60
Open end Mar-early Nov Booking advisable bank hols & Jun-Aug Last arrival 21.00hrs Last departure noon
A beautifully located moorland site, overlooking the reservoirs and surrounded by hills. Tents only, with backpackers' dryng room. Off the A628. .5m from Glossop take B6105. Please see the advertisement on page 27 for details of Club Members' benefits. A 2.5-acre site with 45 touring pitches.

ℝ ☉ ⅊ ⅆ /ⅅ
→ ◢ ⅄
Credit Cards 💳 ▨▨

EDALE

Coopers Caravan Site (SK121859)
Newfold Farm, Edale Village S30 2ZD ☎ 01433 670372
▶▶ **Town & Country Pennant Park** ⊕ ⊕ ⅄
Open all year Booking advisable bank hols Last arrival 23.30hrs Last departure 15.00hrs
Rising grassland behind a working farm, divided by a wall into two fields, culminating in the 2062ft Edale Moor. Facilities converted from original farm buildings. Only 15 vans accepted. From A625 at Hope take minor rd for 4m to Edale, and site 800yds on the right. A 6-acre site with 135 touring pitches and 11 statics.

🖭 ℝ ☉ ⅊ ✳ ⅆ /ⅅ ⊞ ✕ ⥁ ⅄
→ ∪

FENNY BENTLEY

Bank Top Farm (SK181498)
DE6 1LF ☎ 01335 350250 (leave Ashbourne on A515 fro 2m, take B5056, 200yds on right)
Nearby town: Ashbourne
▶▶▶ Family Park ⚑⚑⅄
Open Mar/Etr-Sep Booking advisable peak periods Last arrival 22.00hrs Last departure 14.00hrs
Gently sloping grass site with some level pitches on working dairy farm, just off B5056. A 2-acre site with 36 touring pitches and 15 statics.
Working dairy farm with viewing gallery.

🏮📶⊙🔩☼🎱
➔▶⤵

HAYFIELD

Camping & Caravanning Club Site (SK048868)
Kinder Rd SK22 5LE ☎ 01663 745394 (in season) & 01203 694995 (off A624) Signposted
Nearby town: Stockport
▶▶ Town & Country Pennant Park ⚑⅄
Open end Mar-early Nov Booking advisable bank hols & peak periods Last arrival 21.00hrs Last departure noon
Pleasant site bordered by trees near the River Sett, off A624. Please see advertisement on page 27 for details of Club Members' benefits. A 7-acre site with 90 touring pitches.

📶⊙🔩☼🎱🗜📶
➔🎱
Credit Cards 💳 📶 📶

HOPE

Pindale Farm Outdoor Centre (SK163825)
Pindale Rd S33 6RN ☎ 01433 620111
▶▶ Town & Country Pennant Park

An ideal base for walking, climbing and various outdoor pursuits, offering good facilities for campers and with a self-contained bunkhouse for up to 60 people. From A625 in Hope turn into Pindale Lane between church and Woodroffe Arms. Pass cement works over bridge, and site in 1.5m and well signed.

MATLOCK

Darwin Forest Country Park (SK302649)
Darley Moor, Two Dales DE4 5LN ☎ 01629 732428 (3m NW off B5057) Signposted

▶▶▶▶▶ Premier Park ★ ⚑ £10-£12 ⚑ £10-£12
Open Mar-Dec Booking advisable bank hols & Jul-Aug Last arrival 21.00hrs Last departure 10.00hrs
A mostly level woodland site set amongst tall pines in the heart of the Derbyshire Dales. 3m NW off B5057. Approach from A632 to avoid very steep hill. A 44-acre site with 50 touring pitches.

🏮📶⊙🔩🗜↺🎱⊙🖥➔📶⌨⅄
🗄🏠🎱♿
➔∪▶⊙☼🎱⤵
Credit Cards 💳 📶 📶 📶

Wayside Farm Caravan Park (SK361620)
Chesterfield Rd, Matlock Moor DE4 5LF ☎ 01629 582967
▶▶▶ Family Park ★ ⚑ £7 ⚑ £7 ⅄ £7
Open all year (rs Nov-Feb showers turned off) Booking advisable all year Last arrival 22.00hrs Last departure flexible
A small hilltop farm overlooking Matlock with two camping fields and good facilities. From Matlock on A632 to Chesterfield, site on right in 2m opposite golf course. A 1.5-acre site with 30 touring pitches.

🏮📶⊙🔩☼📶🗄📶🖥🗒✕📶🗄🏠🎱♿
➔∪▶⊙🔺☼🎱⤵🖥

Packhorse Farm (SK323617)
Tansley DE4 5LF ☎ 01629 582781
▶▶ Town & Country Pennant Park ★ ⚑ £7 ⚑ £7 ⅄ £7
Open all year Booking advisable bank hols Last arrival 22.30hrs Last departure noon
A pleasant, well-run farm site in quiet situation with good views. 2m NE of Matlock off A632 at the Tansley signpost. A 2-acre site with 30 touring pitches.

🏮📶⊙☼🗒🏠
➔∪▶🎱⤵🖥🎱

Pinegroves Caravan Park (SK345585)
High Ln, Tansley DE4 5BG ☎ 01629 534815 & 534670
▶▶ Town & Country Pennant Park ★ ⚑ fr £6.50 ⚑ fr £6.50 ⅄ fr £6.50
Open Apr or Etr-Oct Booking advisable bank hols & Jul-Aug Last arrival 21.00hrs Last departure 16.00hrs
A beautiful hilltop location overlooking Matlock and Riber Castle. Very secluded site in a former plant nursery. From Matlock take A615 for 3m, then 2nd right at crossroads and site 400yds on left. A 23-acre site with 60 touring pitches and 14 statics.
Area of woodland for walks.

🏮📶⊙🖥☼🗗🗒📶🏠♿
➔∪▶☼🎱⤵

Sycamore Caravan & Camping Park (SK329615)
Lant Ln, Tansley DE4 5LF ☎ 01629 55760 (2.5m NE off A632)
Nearby town: Matlock
▶▶ Town & Country Pennant Park ★ ⚑ £7-£8 ⚑ £7-£8 ⅄ £8-£9
Open 15 Mar-Oct Booking advisable bank hols & summer hols Last arrival 21.00hrs Last departure noon

contd.

An open grassland site with mainly level touring pitches in two fields. 2.5m NE of Matlock off A632. A 6.5-acre site with 80 touring pitches and 35 statics.

🅰 📻 ⊙ ⚲ ☼ /Ⅱ\ 🔌 🕭 🖬 ⚓

→ ∪ ▶ ◬ ⅄ ⚏ ✄ 🖬 🐴

Credit Cards ●● ▣▣ ▨▨ 🔟

NEWHAVEN

Newhaven Holiday Camping & Caravan Park (SK167602)
SK17 0DT ☎ 01298 84300 (on A515 at Jct with A5012)
Signposted
Nearby town: Buxton
▶ ▶ ▶ **Family Park** ★ 🚐 £7-£8 🚐 £7-£8 🛆 £7-£8
Open Mar-Oct Booking advisable public hols Last arrival 23.00hrs Last departure anytime
Pleasantly situated within the Peak District National Park, between Ashbourne-Buxton on A515 at junction with A5012. Well-maintained and immaculate site. A 30-acre site with 95 touring pitches and 45 statics.

🅰 📻 ⊙ 🖬 ⚲ ⚫ ☼ /Ⅱ\ 🔌 🕭 🖮 ⊞ 🎢 🐴 🐕 ⚓

→ ∪ ◬ ⅄ ✄

ROWSLEY

Grouse & Claret (SK258660)
Station Rd DE4 2EL ☎ 01629 733233 Signposted
▶ ▶ ▶ **Family Park** ★ 🚐 £8.50-£11.50 🚐 £8.50-£11.50
🛆 £6
Open all year Booking advisable wknds, bank hols & peak periods Last arrival 20.00hrs Last departure noon
A well-designed site behind an eating house on A6 between Bakewell and Chatsworth. A flat grassy area running down to the river. A 2.5-acre site with 29 touring pitches.

🅰 📻 ⊙ ⚫ ☼ ⅄ /Ⅱ\ ✕ ⚓ 🖮 🎢

→ ∪ ▶ ✄ ⚓

Credit Cards ●● 🖸 ▣▣ ▨ ▨▨ 🔟

SHARDLOW

Shardlow Marina Caravan Park (SK444303)
London Rd DE72 2GL ☎ 01332 792832 Signposted
Nearby town: Derby
▶ ▶ ▶ **Family Park** ★ 🚐 £7-£10.75 🚐 £7-£10.75 🛆 fr £7
Open Apr-Oct Booking advisable bank hols Last arrival 20.00hrs Last departure 14.00hrs
A large marina site under new ownership, and being totally overhauled for 1999. Situated on the Trent/Mersey Canal near the A6 close to its junction with the M1. From junc 24 take turning for Shardlow. A 25-acre site with 70 touring pitches.

🅰 📻 ⊙ ☼ ⅄ /Ⅱ\ 🔌 🕭 ⊞ 🇹 ✕ ⚓

→ ⚏ ✄ 🖬

YOULGREAVE

Camping & Caravanning Club Site (SK206632)
c/o Hopping Farm DE45 1NA ☎ 01629 636555 (in season) & 01203 694995 Signposted
Nearby town: Bakewell
▶▶ **Town & Country Pennant Park** 🚐 £8-£9 🚐 £8-£9
🛆 £8-£9
Open end Mar-end Sep Booking advisable bank hols & peak periods Last arrival 21.00hrs Last departure noon
Ideal for touring and walking in the Peak District

National Park, this gently sloping grass site is accessed through narrow streets and along unadopted hardcore. Own sanitary facilities essential. Please see the advertisement on page 27 for details of Club Members' benefits. An 11.75-acre site with 100 touring pitches.

🅰 ☼ /Ⅱ\ 🕭 ⚓ 🐴

Credit Cards ●● ▣▣

DEVON

The total eclipse of the sun on 11th August at 11am is expected to attract thousands of visitors to Devon & Cornwall, where this once-in-a-lifetime phenomenon can be witnessed. While many extra touring pitches are being set up over the period to cater for the sudden influx, demand for places on parks listed in this guide is bound to be dramatically increased. To be sure of securing your holiday dates, please try to book well ahead for the period around 11th August.

ASHBURTON

Ashburton Caravan Park (SX753723)
Waterleat TQ13 7HU ☎ 01364 652552 (1.5m N towards moor) Signposted
Nearby town: Newton Abbot

⊙⊙⊙⊙⊙⊙⊙⊙⊙

▶ ▶ ▶ ▶ **De-Luxe Park** 🚐 🛆
Open Etr-Sep Booking advisable bank hols & Jul-Aug Last arrival 22.30hrs Last departure noon
A secluded park set in an attractive location amongst the trees in Dartmoor National Park, offering quality

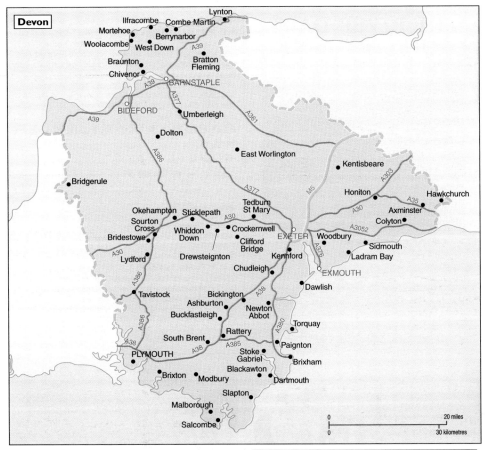

Devon

Lynton
Ilfracombe Combe Martin
Mortehoe Berrynarbor
Woolacombe West Down
Braunton Bratton Fleming
Chivenor
A39
BARNSTAPLE
BIDEFORD Umberleigh
A39 A386 A377 A361
Dolton
East Worlington
Kentisbeare
A303
Bridgerule
Honiton Hawkchurch
A35
M5
Okehampton Sticklepath Tedburn St Mary Axminster
Sourton Cross A30 Colyton
Whiddon Down Crockernwell A3052
Bridestowe Clifford Bridge EXETER Woodbury
A30 Kennford Sidmouth
Lydford Drewsteignton Ladram Bay
Chudleigh EXMOUTH
A386 Dawlish
Tavistock Bickington A38
Ashburton Newton Abbot
Buckfastleigh Torquay
A380
South Brent Rattery
A38 A385 Paignton
PLYMOUTH Stoke Gabriel Brixham
Blackawton
Brixton Modbury Dartmouth
Slapton
Malborough
Salcombe

0   20 miles
0   30 kilometres

---

facilities. From A38 in village centre turn right at T junc for Buckland on the Moor on unclass rd. Fork right at river bridge, and site 1.5m on left. A 2-acre site with 35 touring pitches and 40 statics.

🎎📻☉🗑️🍳❋🛉∅📞🛁⛿

➔∪▶♪🎿

Parkers Farm Holidays (SX779713)

Higher Mead Farm TQ13 7LJ ☎ 01364 652598
Signposted

▶ ▶ ▶ ▶ De-Luxe Park ★ 🚐 £4.50-£8.50 🚐 £4.50-£8.50
🅰 £4.50-£8.50
Open Etr-end Oct Booking advisable Whitsun & school hols Last departure 10.00hrs
A well-developed site terraced into rising ground, with maturing shrubs. Signed off A38, .75m E of Ashburton. An 8-acre site with 60 touring pitches and 25 statics.

🎎📻☉🗑️❋🍳♀🏔️🛉∅🆔❎📞🏺🎄🐴🐂⛿

➔♪

Credit Cards 💳 🎫 📰 🟢

River Dart Country Park (SX734700)

Holne Park TQ13 7NP ☎ 01364 652511 Signposted
Nearby town: Totnes

▶ ▶ ▶ ▶ De-Luxe Park ★ 🚐 £9-£12.50 🚐 £9-£12.50
🅰 £9-£12.50
Open May-Aug (rs Apr & Sep no evening facilities ie bar) Booking advisable Spring Bank Hol & Jul-Aug Last arrival 21.00hrs Last departure 10.00hrs
Mainly level site in a very attractive and quiet location in Holne Country Park just off the B3357. A 7-acre site with 117 touring pitches.

🎎📻☉🗑️🍳🏊🏸🎾📞🏸❋♀🏔️🛉∅🔼🆔❎

📞🏺🎄🐴🐂⛿ ➔∪▶♪

Credit Cards 💳 🎫 📰 🟢

See advertisement on page 98.

AXMINSTER

Andrewshayes Caravan Park (SY248088)

Dalwood EX13 7DY ☎ 01404 831225 (on A35)
Signposted

contd. on p98

Andrewshayes
▶ ▶ ▶ ▶ De-Luxe Park ⚑ £8-£9.50 ⚑ £7-£9.50 ⚑ fr £8
Open Mar-Jan (rs Apr-21 May & Oct shop hours restricted, pool closed) Booking advisable Spring bank hol & Jul-Aug Last arrival 22.00hrs Last departure noon
Slightly sloping site within easy reach of Lyme Regis, Seaton, Branscombe and Sidmouth. From Axminster take A35 W, and site on right 3m from town. A 4-acre site with 90 touring pitches and 80 statics.
Licenced Bistro May-Sep.

🔧🔦☉🖥🥄✒♦🗂☀🎡🅰🖊🎁✖🔌🚿🎋
🐴🐑♿
➔ ∪ ♩

Credit Cards 💳 ▦ ▦ ▦ 🔳

BERRYNARBOR

Napps Camping Site (SS561477)
Old Coast Rd EX34 9SW ☎ 01271 882557 & 882778
Signposted
Nearby town: Combe Martin
▶ ▶ ▶ Family Park ⚑ ⚑ ⚑
Open Etr-Oct (rs Etr-Whitsun & Sep-Nov shop closed)
Booking advisable always for caravans Last arrival 22.00hrs Last departure noon
Seclusion is guaranteed at this cliff top site adjacent to Combe Martin. Turn north off A399 W of Combe Martin at bottom of hill. An 11-acre site with 250 touring pitches and 2 statics.

Childrens paddling pool & slide.

🔧🔦☉🖥🥄✒♦🗂☀🅿🎡🅰🖊🎁🅣✖
✒🚿🎋🐴🐑
➔ ∪ ♩ ◉ ♦ ⚓ ⚑ ♩

Credit Cards 💳 ▦ ▦ ▦ 🔳

BICKINGTON (NEAR ASHBURTON)

The Dartmoor Halfway Caravan Site (SX804719)
TQ12 6JW ☎ 01626 821270
Nearby town: Newton Abbot

▶ ▶ ▶ ▶ De-Luxe Park ★ ⚑ £5.50-£6.50
⚑ £5.50-£6.50
Open all year Booking advisable high season & bank hols Last departure 10.00hrs
A recently developed site tucked away on the edge of Dartmoor, beside the River Lemon and adjacent to the Halfway Inn. Direct access off A383, 1m from A38

Exeter-Plymouth Rd. A 2-acre site with 22 touring pitches.

🔌 👣 ☉ ❄ ⚲ ⚠ ⊞ ✗ 👢 🏇 ♿
➔ ∪ ⌿ ◎ 🍴 🥤 ✒ 🔟 🐾

Credit Cards 💳 ▦ ▦ ◎ ▦ 🔌 🗒

◯◯◯◯◯◯◯◯◯◯

Lemonford Caravan Park (SX793723)
TQ12 6JR ☎ 01626 821242 Signposted
Nearby town: Ashburton

◯◯◯◯◯◯◯◯◯◯

► ► ► ► De-Luxe Park ★ 🚐 £5-£9 🚐 £5-£9 ⚑ £5-£9
Open Etr-Oct Booking advisable Whit & last wk Jul-1st wk Aug Last arrival 22.00hrs Last departure 11.00hrs
Small, secluded and well-maintained site. From Exeter along A38 take A382 turnoff, take 3rd exit on roundabout and follow site signs to Bickington. From Plymouth take A383 signed Newton Abbot, then turn left in 500m signed Bickington on right hand turn. A 7-acre site with 70 touring pitches and 18 statics.
Clothes drying area.
See advertisement under NEWTON ABBOT

🔌 🚿 👣 ☉ 🗒 ⚲ ❄ ⚠ 🛈 ⊘ ⊞ 📞 🏧 🎠 🏇 🐾
➔ ∪ ⌿ ◎ 🍴 ✒

◯◯◯◯◯◯◯◯◯◯

BLACKAWTON
Woodland Leisure Park (SX813522)
TQ9 7DQ ☎ 01803 712598 (signposted from A38)
Signposted
Nearby town: Dartmouth

◯◯◯◯◯◯◯◯◯◯

► ► ► ► De-Luxe Park 🚐 £6.50-£12.50 🚐 £6.50-£12.50
⚑ £6.50-£12.50
Open 15 Mar-15 Nov Booking advisable anytime Last departure 11.00hrs ⚘

An extensive woodland park with a terraced grass camping area, and facilities of a very high standard. A wildlife park is attached, with entry free to campers. Signed off A381 at Halwell. An 8-acre site with 225 touring pitches.

contd.

60 acre leisure park with animal farm complex.

🔊 🚖 🄬 ⊙ 🗂 🅡 ✳ 🄰 🎒 ⊞ 🎫 ❌ 🥄 🛁 🏛 🎏
🐂 ⚲

→ ∪ 🏻 ⅄ 🜃

Credit Cards 🔵 ▆ ▆ 🄂

BRATTON FLEMING

Greenacres Farm Touring Caravan Park (SS658414)
EX31 4SG ☎ 01598 763334 (2.5m N) Signposted
Nearby town: Barnstaple
▶ ▶ ▶ Family Park ★ 🅟 £3.50-£6 🅟 £3.50-£6
Open Apr-Oct Booking advisable all times Last arrival
23.00hrs Last departure 11.00hrs
*One of our best small sites with well-appointed facilities
and enthusiastic owners. On farmland, with good views
over North Devon. From A361 Tiverton/Barnstaple rd
take B3226 at 2nd rndbt N of South Molton, signed
Blackmoor Gate. Ignore all signs to Bratton Fleming.
Turn left at Stowford crossrds, and site on left. A 4-acre
site with 30 touring pitches.*

🔊 🄬 ⊙ 🅡 ✳ 🄰 🎒 🄴 🜃 🏛 🎋 ⚲

→ ∪ 🜃 🐂

BRAUNTON

Lobb Fields Caravan & Camping Park (SS475378)
Saunton Rd EX33 1EB ☎ 01271 812090 Signposted
Nearby town: Barnstaple
▶ ▶ ▶ Family Park ★ 🅟 £5-£8.50 🅟 £4-£7 ▲ £4-£7
Open 28 Mar-Oct Booking advisable Jul-Aug Last arrival
21.00hrs Last departure 10.30hrs

*Gently sloping grassy site on outskirts of Braunton, with
good wide entrance. Follow signs to Croyde Bay from
crossrds in Braunton, and site on right in 1m. A 14-acre
site with 180 touring pitches.*

🔊 🄬 ⊙ 🗂 🅡 ✳ 🄰 🎒 🎒 🄴 🜃 🎋 🐂

→ ∪ 🏻 ⚴ 🜃

BRIDESTOWE

Bridestowe Caravan Park (SX519893)
EX20 4ER ☎ 01837 861261 Signposted
Nearby town: Okehampton
▶ ▶ ▶ Family Park ★ 🅟 £6.50 🅟 £6.50 ▲ £6.50
Open Mar-Dec Booking advisable Last arrival 22.30hrs
Last departure noon
*A small, well-established mainly static park in a rural
setting close to Dartmoor National Park. Leave A30 at
Sourton Down junc with A386, join old A30 (now B3278)
signed Bridestowe, and turn left in 5m. At village centre*

*turn left down unclass rd and site 1m on left. A 1-acre
site with 13 touring pitches and 40 statics.*

🔊 🄬 ⊙ 🗂 🅡 🔍 ✳ 🄰 🎒 🄴 🜃 🐂

→ ∪ 🜃

BRIDGERULE

Hedleywood Caravan & Camping Park (SS262013)
EX22 7ED ☎ 01288 381404 Signposted
Nearby town: Bude
▶ ▶ ▶ Family Park 🅟 🅟 ▲
Open all year Booking advisable public hols & Jul-Aug
Last arrival anytime Last departure anytime
*An isolated site in a good location, with a considerable
amount of landscaping work in progress. From B3254
take Widemouth road (unclass) at the Devon/Cornwall
boundary. A 16.5-acre site with 120 touring pitches and
12 statics.*

Dog kennels, Nature Trail.

🔊 🄬 ⊙ 🗂 🅡 🔍 🄰 ✳ ⅄ 🄰 🎒 ⊞ 🎫 ❌ 🥄 🏛
🎏 🎋 🐂 ⚲

→ ∪ 🏻 💬 🜃

BRIXHAM

Galmpton Touring Park (SX885558)
Greenway Rd TQ5 0EP ☎ 01803 842066 Signposted
▶ ▶ ▶ Family Park 🅟 🅟 ▲
Open May-Sep (rs Apr shop closed) Booking advisable
Jul-Aug Last arrival 22.00hrs Last departure 11.00hrs

An excellent location on high ground overlooking the River Dart, with outstanding views of the river and anchorage. Signed off A3022 Torbay/Brixham road at Churston. A 10-acre site with 120 touring pitches.

🏪 🅿 ⊙ 🗄 🍴 ✳ 🏛 🌢 ⊘ 🎗 🚻 T 📞 ⊶ 🐕 🛒 ♿
→ ∪ ⍵ ◎ ⚠ ⅄ ☕ 🏊

Credit Cards 💳 ▰▰ 🟦 🟥 📊

Hillhead Holiday Camp (SX903535)
TQ5 0HH ☎ 01803 853204 & 842336 (2.5m SW)
Signposted
▶ ▶ ▶ **Family Park** 🚐 🚐 Å
Open Etr-Oct Booking advisable Whitsun-Aug Last arrival 21.00hrs Last departure 10.30hrs
Attractive, well laid out site with screening and landscaping to each pitch. Good views all around of countryside and sea. Amenities block well screened from touring park. On B3205 between Brixham and Kingswear. A 12.5-acre site with 330 touring pitches. Childrens clubroom & teenage disco room.

🏪 🅿 🗄 ⍳ 🍴 🖵 ✳ 🍸 🏛 🌢 ⊘ 📠 T ✂ 📞
🧹 🐕 🛒
→ ⍵ ⚠ ⅄ 🏊

BRIXTON

Brixton Caravan & Camping Park (SX550520)
Venn Farm PL8 2AX ☎ 01752 880378 Signposted
Nearby town: Plymouth
▶▶ **Town & Country Pennant Park** 🚐 🚐 Å
Open 15 Mar-14 Oct (rs 15 Mar-Jun & Sep-14 Oct no warden) Booking advisable Jul-Aug Last arrival 23.00hrs Last departure noon
A small site adjacent to a farm in the village, on A379. A 2-acre site with 43 touring pitches.

🏪 🧺 🅿 ⊙ ✳ 🗄
→ ∪ ⍵ ⅄ ☕ 🏊 🌢

BUCKFASTLEIGH

Beara Farm Caravan & Camping Site (SX751645)
Colston Rd TQ11 0LW ☎ 01364 642234 Signposted
▶▶ **Town & Country Pennant Park** ★ 🚐 £5.50-£6.25
🚐 £5 Å £5
Open all year Booking advisable peak periods Jul-Aug Last arrival anytime Last departure anytime
Level site, close to the River Dart and the Dart Valley steam railway line, within easy reach of sea and moors. Approach is narrow with passing places and needs care. Leave A38 at Buckfast A384 junc, and take B3380 (old A38) towards Buckfastleigh. Turn left on Old Totnes Rd in .25m after passing under bridge. Turn right into

---

Colston Rd, and follow single track for 2m. A 4-acre site with 30 touring pitches.

🏪 ⊙ ✳ 🗄 🐕
→ 🌢 🏊

Churchill Farm Campsite (SX743664)
TQ11 0EZ ☎ 01364 642844
Nearby town: Totnes
▶▶ **Town & Country Pennant Park** ★ 🚐 £5-£10 🚐 £5-£10
Å £5-£10
Open Mar-Nov Booking advisable Jul & Aug Last arrival 22.30hrs
A working family farm in a relaxed and peaceful setting with panoramic views. From A38 Dart Bridge exit for Buckfastleigh/Totnes head towards Buckfast Abbey. Turn left at mini rndbt, turn left at crossroads (Round Cross), and site opp Holy Trinity church. A 3-acre site with 25 touring pitches.

🏪 🅿 ⊙ ✳ 🗄
→ 🏊

BUDLEIGH SALTERTON

See **Ladram Bay**

CHIVENOR

Chivenor Caravan Park (SS501351)
EX31 4BN ☎ 01271 812217 Signposted
Nearby town: Braunton
▶ ▶ ▶ **Family Park** ★ 🚐 £6-£8 🚐 £6-£8 Å £5-£7
Open Mar-Nov Booking advisable Jul & Aug
Nicely laid out and well-maintained level site with good facilities. Adjacent to A361 and RAF Chivenor. A 3-acre site with 34 touring pitches and 10 statics.

🏪 🅿 ⊙ 🗄 ✳ 🏛 🌢 ⊘ 📞 🛒
→ ∪ ⍵ ☕ 🏊

Credit Cards 💳 ▰▰ 🟥

CHUDLEIGH

Finlake Holiday Park (SX855786)
TQ13 0EJ ☎ 01626 853833
Signposted
Nearby town: Newton Abbot

★ 🚐 £6.25-£14.50 🚐 £6.25-£14.50 Å £4.50-£11.25
Open Etr-Oct (rs Nov-Mar shop, tennis, golf, entertainment closed) Booking advisable bank hols & Jul-Aug Last arrival 22.00hrs Last departure 11.00hrs
A very well-appointed holiday centre situated in a wooded valley surrounded by 110 acres of wooded parkland. A wide range of leisure facilities and entertainment is available. Signed off A38 at Chudleigh exit. A 130-acre site with 410 touring pitches and 30 statics.
Fishing, horseriding, golf & fitness suite.

🏪 🧺 🅿 ⊙ 🗄 ⍳ ⍺ 🍴 ✳ 🍸 🏛 🌢 ⊘ T ✂ 📞 🧹
🎗 🐕 🛒 ♿
→ ∪ ⍵ 🏊

Credit Cards 💳 ▰▰ 🟦 🟥 📊

Holmans Wood Tourist Park (SX881812)
Harcombe Cross TQ13 0DZ ☎ 01626 853785 Signposted
Nearby town: Newton Abbot

◯◯◯◯◯◯◯◯◯◯

►►►► De-Luxe Park ★ 🚐 £6-£9.76 🚐 £6-£9.76
▲ £6-£9.75
Open mid Mar-Oct Booking advisable bank hols & Jul-Aug Last arrival 22.00hrs Last departure 11.00hrs

Delightful small, personally-managed touring site, set back in secluded wooded area off A38. Convenient location for touring South Devon and Dartmoor National Park. A 20-acre site with 144 touring pitches.
Caravan storage facilities.

🔌🏕☉🗑🍳✳️⚠️🍴🗑✉️⊺Ⓣ🔌🏠🐎🐄🛝
➜⋃🌳🎵

Credit Cards 💳 ▬ 🆑 🅹

◯◯◯◯◯◯◯◯◯◯

CLIFFORD BRIDGE

Clifford Bridge Park (SX780897)
EX6 6QE ☎ 01647 24226 Signposted
Nearby town: Moretonhampstead
►►► Family Park ★ 🚐 £7.25-£12.25 🚐 £6.40-£12.25 ▲ £7.25-£12.25
Open Etr-Sep Booking advisable school & bank hols Last arrival 22.00hrs Last departure 11.00hrs
A very attractive location in a deep wooded valley in the Dartmoor National Park. The approach roads are narrow and steep in parts, and care is needed in towing large units. Site signed from Cheriton Biship. Turn near Old Thatch Inn and follow brown signs for 2m. Turn right at crossrd signed Clifford Bridge, follow very narrow lane for 1m, go straight across junc, and over bridge to site on left. A 6-acre site with 65 touring pitches and 5 statics.
Fly fishing on site.

🔌🏕☉🗑🍳✹⚡✳️⚠️🍴🗑✉️⊺Ⓣ🔌🐎🐄
➜⋃🌳🎵

COLYTON

Leacroft Touring Park (SY217925)
Colyton Hill EX13 6HY ☎ 01297 552823 Signposted
Nearby town: Seaton

◯◯◯◯◯◯◯◯◯◯

►►►► De-Luxe Park ★ 🚐 £6-£11 🚐 £6-£11 ▲ £6-£11
Open 15 Mar-Oct Booking advisable Jul-Aug & Spring bank hol Last arrival 22.00hrs Last departure noon

A mostly level site with enthusiastic owners, offering good sanitary facilities. 1m from Stafford Cross on A3052 towards Colyton. A 10-acre site with 138 touring pitches.
Off-licence.

🔌🏕☉🗑🍳🍴✳️⚠️🍴🗑✉️⊺Ⓣ🔌🏠🐎🐄🛝
🐄🚿
➜⋃🌳◎⚠️🌡🎵

◯◯◯◯◯◯◯◯◯◯

COMBE MARTIN

Stowford Farm Meadows (SS560427)
Berry Down EX34 0PW ☎ 01271 882476 Signposted

◯◯◯◯◯◯◯◯◯◯

►►►►► Premier Park 🚐 🚐 ▲
Open Etr-Oct (rs Etr-Spring bank hol & Oct some amenities may be available ltd hrs) Booking advisable bank hols & Jul-Aug Last arrival 20.00hrs Last departure 10.00hrs
Very gently sloping, grassy, sheltered and south-facing site approached down a wide, well-kept driveway. From A399 turn left onto B3343 to T-junc. Turn left then right, and site in .5m. A 100-acre site with 570 touring pitches.
Horse rides, fun golf, mini zoo, snooker, cycle hire.
See advertisement under ILFRACOMBE

🔌🏕☉🗑🍳🍷⚡🍴✳️🍴⚠️⚠️✉️⊺Ⓣ✖🔌
🛒🐎🐄
➜⋃🌳◎🎵

Credit Cards 💳 ▬ 🆑 🅹

◯◯◯◯◯◯◯◯◯◯

CROCKERNWELL

Barley Meadow Caravan & Camping Park (SX757925)
EX6 6NR ☎ 01647 281629 Signposted
▶ ▶ ▶ Family Park ⚲ ⚲ ⚑
Open 15 Mar-15 Nov Booking advisable bank hols &
Jul-Aug Last arrival mdnt Last departure noon
*A small, very well-maintained site set on high ground in
the National Park with easy access. Off the old A30, now
bypassed, and isolated. From M5 take A30, leave by exit
for Tedburn; turn left through Cheriton Bishop and
Crockernwell, and site on left. A 4-acre site with 40
touring pitches.*
Picnic tables.

⚙ ⌂ ⊙ ⚑ ☀ ⌁ ⛟ ⬧ ⊞ Ⓣ ➡ ⌖ ⬛
➔ ⫩

DARTMOUTH

Little Cotton Caravan Park (SX858508)
Little Cotton TQ6 0LB ☎ 01803 832558

ⵔⵔⵔⵔⵔⵔⵔⵔ

▶ ▶ ▶ ▶ De-Luxe Park ★ ⚲ £5.50-£8.50 ⚲ £5.50-£8.50
⚑ £5.50-£8.50
Open 15 Mar-Oct Booking advisable Jul & Aug Last
arrival 22.00hrs Last departure noon
*A small, well-kept farm site on high ground above
Dartmouth, with quality facilities and park and ride to
the town from the gate. From Totnes take A381 signed
Kingsbridge, at Halwell take B3207 for Dartmouth, and
site on right before town. A 7.5-acre site with 95 touring
pitches.*

⚙ ⌂ ⊙ ⚑ ☀ ⛟ ⬧ ⊞ Ⓣ ➡ ⌖ ⬛

➔ ⚑ ⊙ ⛟ ⚙ ☀ ⬛ ⌁ ⛟ ⊞ Ⓣ ➡ ⌖ ⬛ ☀
➔ ⫩ ▶ ◎ ⟁ ⤭ ⫩

⚙ ⌂ ⊙ ⚑ ⚑ ☀ ⛟ ⬧ ⊞ Ⓣ ⌖ ⬛ ⌖ ⬛ ⬛ ☀
➔ ▶ ◎ ⟁ ⤭ ⫩
Credit Cards 💳 💳 💳 Ⓓ 🔲 🔲 📍

ⵔⵔⵔⵔⵔⵔⵔⵔ

Deer Park Holiday Estate (SX864493)
Stoke Fleming TQ6 0RF ☎ 01803 770253 (Stoke Fleming
2m S A379) Signposted
▶ ▶ ▶ Family Park ★ ⚲ £7.95-£9.95 ⚲ £7.95-£9.95
⚑ £7.25-£9.25
Open 15 Mar-Oct Booking advisable Jul-Aug Last arrival
anytime Last departure 11.00hrs
*A rather open, mainly level grass site on high ground
overlooking Start Bay. Direct access from A379 from
Dartmouth before Stoke Fleming. A 6-acre site with 160
touring pitches.*

⚙ ⌂ ⊙ ⚑ ⚑ ☀ ⚲ ⬧ ⌁ ⛟ Ⓣ ☀ ⌖ ⬛ ⬛ ☀
➔ ∪ ▶ ⟁ ⤭ ⫩
Credit Cards 💳 💳

DAWLISH

  Golden Sands Holiday Park (SX968784)
Week Ln EX7 0LZ ☎ 01626 863099
Signposted

❀❀❀❀❀❀❀❀❀❀❀❀❀❀❀❀

⚲ ⚲
Open Etr-Oct Booking advisable May-Sep Last arrival
22.00hrs Last departure 10.00hrs ⌖
*A mainly static park with a small touring area set
amongst trees, offering full family entertainment.*

contd. on p105

Signed off A379 Exeter/Dawlish road, 1m N of Dawlish. A 2.5-acre site with 60 touring pitches and 188 statics.

→ 🅿 ♨ ♪

Credit Cards 💳 💳 🅢

Cofton Country Holiday Park (SX967801)
Starcross EX6 8RP ☎ 01626 890111

▶ ▶ ▶ ▶ De-Luxe Park ⚐ ⚐ Å
Open Etr-Oct (rs Etr-Spring bank hol & mid Sep-Oct swimming pool closed) Booking advisable bank hols & Jul-Aug Last arrival 20.00hrs Last departure noon

A well-ordered grass site in a good holiday location 1m S of Starcross on A379. A 16-acre site with 450 touring pitches and 62 statics.
Coarse fishing, pub with family room.

→ 🅿 ⊙ ♨ ♪

Credit Cards 💳 💳 💳

Lady's Mile Touring & Caravan Park (SX968784)
EX7 0LX ☎ 01626 863411

▶ ▶ ▶ ▶ De-Luxe Park ⚐ ⚐ Å
Open 17 Mar-27 Oct Booking advisable bank hols & Jul-Aug Last arrival 20.00hrs Last departure 11.00hrs
A well-ordered, clean and tidy site, with all grass pitches, and indoor and outdoor pools with chutes. Fairly central for the surrounding beaches, and 1m N of Dawlish on A379. A 16-acre site with 286 touring pitches and 1 static.

→ ∪ 🅿 ⊙ △ ♨ ♪

Credit Cards 💳 💳 💳 🅢

See advertisement on page 106.

Peppermint Park (SX978788)
Warren Rd EX7 0PQ ☎ 01626 863436 & 862211
Signposted

▶ ▶ ▶ ▶ De-Luxe Park ★ ⚐ £5-£11 ⚐ £5-£11 Å £5-£11
Open Etr-Oct Booking advisable Spring bank hol & Jul-Aug Last arrival 20.00hrs Last departure 10.00hrs

Well-managed attractive site close to the coast, with excellent facilities including club and bar which are well away from pitches. From A379 at Dawlish follow signs for Dawlish Warren. Site on left in 1m. A 26-acre site with 250 touring pitches and 35 statics.
Licensed club & free entertainment.

→ 🅿 ↘ ♪

Credit Cards 💳 💳 🅢

See advertisement on page 107.

DOLTON

Dolton Caravan Park (SS573122)
Acorn Farm House, The Square EX19 8QF
☎ 01805 804536 Signposted
Nearby town: Great Torrington
▶ ▶ ▶ Family Park ⚐ £6-£8 ⚐ £6-£8 Å £6-£8
Open Etr-15 Nov Booking advisable Jul-Aug Last arrival 22.00hrs Last departure noon
A well-maintained, landscaped paddock with wide countryside views, at the rear of the Royal Oak Inn in the centre of Dolton. Take B3217 south at its junc with B3220 at Dolton Beacon. Site signed from Dolton. A 2-acre site with 25 touring pitches.

→ ∪ 🅿 ♪

DREWSTEIGNTON

Woodland Springs Touring Park (SX695912)
Venton EX6 6PG ☎ 01647 231695 Signposted
Nearby town: Okehampton
▶ ▶ ▶ Family Park ★ ⚐ £6.50-£8.50 ⚐ £6.50-£8.50
Å £6.50-£8.50
Open all year Booking advisable Last arrival 22.30hrs Last departure 11.00hrs ✇
An attractive site in a rural area within Dartmoor National Park. Leave A30 at Merrymeet rndbt, turn left onto A382 towards Mortonhampstead, and site 2m on left. A 4-acre site with 85 touring pitches.

→ ∪ 🅿 ♪

EAST WORLINGTON

Yeatheridge Farm Caravan Park (SS768110)
EX17 4TN ☎ 01884 860330
Nearby town: Witheridge

◯◯◯◯◯◯◯◯◯

▶▶▶▶ De-Luxe Park 🚐 £6.50-£8.25 🚐 £6.50-£8.25
Å £6.50-£8.25
Open Etr-Sep Booking advisable Etr, Spring bank hol & school hols Last arrival 22.00hrs Last departure 22.00hrs
Gently sloping grass site with young trees set in meadowland in rural Devon. On B3042 1.5m W of Thelbridge Arms Inn. Site is NOT in East Worlington village which is unsuitable for caravans. A 9-acre site with 85 touring pitches and 3 statics.
Horse riding, fishing & pool table.
See advertisement under TIVERTON

🔊📶☉◍🅀📶 ◖⊟☀♀⚠🛈⊘✚Ⓣ🕻🐴🐑
➜∪♪
Credit Cards ⬤ ▦

◯◯◯◯◯◯◯◯◯

EXETER

See **Kennford**

HAWKCHURCH

Hunters Moon Touring Park (SY345988)
EX13 5UL ☎ 01297 678402 Signposted
Nearby town: Axminster
▶▶▶ Family Park ★ 🚐 £6.50 🚐 £6.50 Å £6.50
Open all year Booking advisable Whitsun & Jul-Aug

contd. on p108

Last arrival 23.00hrs Last departure noon
An attractive site in wooded area with panoramic country views. From Charmouth take A35 W to B3165. Site on left in 1.5m. An 11-acre site with 150 touring pitches.
Bowling green, putting green & boules pitch.
See advertisement under AXMINSTER

🔌 📞 ⊙ 🗄 🦮 ✳ 🏴 🚿 ✕ ⚓ ⚾ 🏹 🛒

Credit Cards 💳 📧

HONITON

See also **Kentisbeare**

Camping & Caravanning Club Site (ST176015)
Otter Valley Park, Northcote EX14 8SP
📞 01404 44546 & 01203 694995 Signposted
▶ ▶ ▶ **Family Park** ★ 🚐 £10-£13 🚐 £10-£13 ⅄ £10-£13
Open end Mar-early Nov Booking advisable bank hols & Jul-Aug Last arrival 21.00hrs Last departure noon

A well run site just a short walk from the town. From Yeovil leave A30 at sign for A35 Dorchester, then turn left. Please see the advertisement on page 27 for details of Club Members' benefits. A 56-acre site with 90 touring pitches.
Dish washing sinks.

🔌 📞 ⊙ 🗄 ✳ 🦮 ⚓ 📞

Credit Cards 💳 📧

ILFRACOMBE

Watermouth Cove Holiday Park (SS558477)
Berrynarbor EX34 9SJ 📞 01271 862504 (towards Berrynarbor 2.5m E A361)

▶ ▶ ▶ ▶ **De-Luxe Park** 🚐 🚐 ⅄
Open Etr-Oct (rs Etr-Whit & Sep-Nov pool, takeaway, club & shop) Booking advisable Whit & Jul-Aug Last arrival anytime Last departure 11.00hrs

contd. on p110

A popular site in very attractive surroundings, set amidst trees and bushes in meadowland with access to sea, beach and main road. On A399 from Combe Martin, past Berrynarbor, A 6-acre site with 90 touring pitches.
Coastal headland fishing.

Ω ি ⊙ ⓹ ⛏ ⟩ ◀ 🛏 ✳ ⚑ ⚠ ⌷ ∂ ⊞ Ⓣ ✗ ℄
🚲 🏕 🎠 🐕 🔁
→ ∪ ▷ ◎ ♨ ⁀

Mullacott Cross Caravan Park (SS511446)
Mullacott Cross EX34 8NB
☎ 01271 862212 (Mullacott Cross 2.5m S A361) Signposted
▶ ▶ ▶ Family Park ★ ⊞ £6-£12 ⊞ £5.50-£10
Å £5.50-£10
Open Etr-Sep (rs Etr-Whit & Oct) Booking advisable Whit & Jul-Aug Last arrival 21.00hrs Last departure noon
This meadowland site is on gentle grass slopes with views over the Atlantic coastline, 2m S of Ilfracombe and 3m E of the sandy beach at Woolacombe. Located adjacent to A361 Braunton-Ilfracombe road. An 8-acre site with 115 touring pitches and 160 statics.
Caravan accessory shop.

Ω ি ⊙ ⓹ ⛏ ✳ ⚑ ⚠ ⌷ ∂ ⊞ Ⓣ ✗ ℄ 🔁 🔁
→ ∪ ▷ ♨ ⁀
Credit Cards ● ▬ ▬ ▬ ▨ 🦋

Kennford International Caravan Park (SX912857)
EX6 7YN ☎ 01392 833046 Signposted
Nearby town: Exeter

▶ ▶ ▶ ▶ De-Luxe Park ★ ⊞ fr £9.50 ⊞ fr £9.50
Å fr £9.50
Open all year Booking advisable public hols & Jul-Aug Last arrival mdnt Last departure 11.00hrs
A well-kept touring site on the A38, with mature landscaping. Mainly a transit site. An 8-acre site with 120 touring pitches and 6 statics.

Ω ⮕ ি ⊙ ⓹ ⛏ ◀ ✳ ⚑ ⚠ ⌷ ∂ ⊞ Ⓣ ✗ ℄ 🔁
🐕 ⬆
→ ∪ ▷ ♨ ⁀ 🔁
Credit Cards ● ▬ ▬ ▨ 🦋

Forest Glade Holiday Park (ST100075)
Cullompton EX15 2DT ☎ 01404 841381 Signposted
Nearby town: Honiton

▶ ▶ ▶ ▶ De-Luxe Park ⊞ £6-£11.50 ⊞ £6-£11.50
Å £6-£11.50
Open 2 wks before Etr-Oct (rs low season pool closed) Booking advisable school hols Last arrival 21.00hrs
A quiet, attractive site in a forest clearing with well-kept gardens and beech hedge screening, on top of the Black Down Hills. Tent traffic from A373 signed at Keepers Cottage Inn, 2.5m E of M5 junc 28. Touring caravans via Honiton/Dunkeswell road. Please telephone for route details. There is no need to enter Kentisbeare Village. A 10-acre site with 80 touring pitches and 57 statics.
Adventure play area & childrens paddling pool.
See advertisement under HONITON

Ω ি ⊙ ⓹ ⓺ ⛏ ⟩ ◀ ✳ ⚑ ⚠ ⌷ ∂ ⊞ Ⓣ ℄ 🔁 🐕
⬆ ⬆
→ ∪ ⁀
Credit Cards ● ▬ ▨ 🦋

Ladram Bay Holiday Centre (SY096853)
EX9 7BX ☎ 01395 568398 Signposted
Nearby town: Budleigh Salterton
▶ Town & Country Pennant Park ⊞ ⊞ Å
Open Spring bank hol-Sep (rs Etr-Spring Bank Hol pool closed no boat hire & entertainment) Booking advisable for caravans, school & Spring bank hols Last arrival 18.00hrs Last departure 10.00hrs
A large caravan site with many static vans and a separate camping area, set on terraced ground in wooded surroundings, overlooking rocky, shingle beach. A 5-acre site with 255 touring pitches and 369 statics.
Boat & canoe hire.

Ω ি ⊙ ⓹ ⓺ ✳ ⚑ ⚠ ∂ ✗ ℄ 🔁 ⬆
→ ∪ ▷ ♨ ⁀
Credit Cards ● ▬ 🦋

See advertisement on page 32.

LYDFORD

Camping & Caravanning Club Site (SX512853)
EX20 4BE ☎ 01822 820275 (in season) & 01203 694995
Signposted
Nearby town: Okehampton
►►► Family Park ★ ⊞ £10-£13 ⊞ £10-£13 ▲ £10-£13
Open end Mar-early Nov Booking advisable bank hols &
peak periods Last arrival 21.00hrs Last departure noon
Site on mainly level ground looking towards the
western slopes of Dartmoor at the edge of the village,
near the spectacular gorge. Leave A386 towards
Lydford village centre. Site signed on right. Please see
advertisement on page 27 for details of Club Members'
benefits. A 4-acre site with 70 touring pitches.

🔌📻☉⊡ʠ⚡※🅐🔋⊘⊞📞🏧
➜∪🅟⚓🎵
Credit Cards 💳 ⚡

LYNTON

Camping & Caravanning Club Site (SS700484)
Caffyns Cross EX35 6JS ☎ 01598 752379 (in season) &
01203 694995 Signposted
►►► Family Park ★ ⊞ £10-£13 ⊞ £10-£13 ▲ £10-£13
Open end Mar-early Nov Booking advisable bank hols &
peak periods Last arrival 21.00hrs Last departure noon
A level grassy site, with bushes, set below hill in well-
wooded countryside. 2m SW of Lynton off A39
Barnstaple-Minehead road. Please see the
advertisement on page 27 for details of Club Members'
benefits. A 5.5-acre site with 105 touring pitches.

🔌📻☉⊡ʠ⚡※🅐🔋⊘🗑🏧📞🎵
➜∪🅟⚓💈🎵🏧
Credit Cards 💳 ⚡ 🔳

Channel View Caravan Park (SS724482)
Manor Farm EX35 6LD ☎ 01598 753349 (off A39)
Signposted
Nearby town: Barnstaple
►►► Family Park ★ ⊞ £7.50-£10 ⊞ £7-£10 ▲ £7-£10
Open Etr-mid Oct Booking advisable Jul-Aug Last
arrival 22.00hrs Last departure noon
This well-placed site has panoramic views over Lynton
and the Channel. From Lynton take A39 E for .5m, and
site signed on left. A 6-acre site with 76 touring pitches
and 36 statics.

🔌📻☉⊡ʠ⚡※🅐🔋⊘🗑⊞Ⓣ📞🐕🔔🦮♿
➜∪◎⛟💈🎵
Credit Cards 💳 ⚡ 🔳 ⓖ

Sunny Lyn Holiday Park (SS719486)
Lynbridge EX35 6NS ☎ 01598 753384 Signposted
►►► Family Park ⊞ ⊞ ▲
Open Mar-Nov Booking advisable Etr, spring bank hol &
mid Jul-Aug Last arrival 20.00hrs Last departure
11.00hrs

Part-level, part-sloping site, bordering trout stream, in a
wooded combe within 1m of sea. On B3234. A 4.5-acre
site with 37 touring pitches and 31 statics.
Pool table & table tennis, trout fishing on site.

🔌📻☉⊡ʠ⚡※🔮🅐🔋⊘⊞✖📞🖥🐕🔔🦮
➜∪◎⚓💈🎵

MALBOROUGH

Higher Rew Caravan & Camping Park (SX714383)
Middle Rew TQ7 3DW ☎ 01548 842681 & 843681
Signposted
Nearby town: Salcombe
►►► Family Park ★ ⊞ £6-£8 ⊞ £6-£8 ▲ £6-£8
Open Mar-Nov Booking advisable Spring bank hol &
mid Jul-Aug Last arrival 22.00hrs Last departure noon
A long-established park in a remote location in sight of
the sea. Take A387 Salcombe Rd from Kingsbridge to
Malborough, turn sharp right in village and then fork
left along unclass rd with passing places signed Soar. A
5-acre site with 75 touring pitches.
Play Barn

🔌📻☉⊡ʠ※🅐🔋⊘⊞📞🐕🔔
➜∪⚓🎵

Sun Park Caravan & Camping Site (SX707379)
Soar Mill Cove TQ7 3DS ☎ 01548 561378 Signposted
Nearby town: Salcombe
▶ ▶ ▶ Family Park ★ ☎ £5-£9 Å £5-£9
Open Etr-Oct Booking advisable Jul-Aug Last arrival
20.00hrs Last departure 11.00hrs

*A level grassy park in a peaceful rural location. Approx
.75m from a safe sandy beach at Soar Mill Cove. Take
A381 from Kingsbridge, turn sharp right at Malborough
then take left fork to Soar Mill Cove. A 2.5-acre site with
65 touring pitches and 34 statics.*

🏴 ♠ ⊙ ᕻ ◀ ▭ ✳ ⋔ ⓘ ⌀ ⊡ ℃
→ ∪ ⚶ ⊹ ⏌ ⧰

MODBURY

Camping & Caravanning Club Site (SX705530)
California Cross PL21 0SG ☎ 01548 821297 (in season)
& 01203 694995 Signposted
Nearby town: Ivybridge
▶ ▶ ▶ Family Park ★ ☎ £10-£13 ☎ £10-£13 Å £10-£13
Open end Mar-early Nov Booking advisable Spring bank
hol & Jul-Aug Last arrival 21.00hrs Last departure noon
*A well-ordered site sloping gently and partially terraced
in rural surroundings, protected by high hedges. From
A38 at Wrangaton turn left onto B3210 signed Modbury.
At California Cross turn left signed Gara Bridge and site
signed on right. Please see advertisement on page 27
for details of Club Members' benefits. A 3.75-acre site
with 80 touring pitches.*

🏴 ♠ ⊙ 🔆 ⋔ ⓘ ⌀ ⊡ ℃ 🛒 ⛊ ♿
→ ∪

Credit Cards ⬤ ▭ ▭ ▭ 🔲

Moor View Touring Park (SX705533)
California Cross PL21 0SG ☎ 01548 821485 Signposted
▶ ▶ ▶ Family Park ★ ☎ £6.50-£9.50 ☎ £6.50-£9.50
Å £5.50-£9.50

Open Etr-Oct Booking advisable bank hols & mid Jul-
Aug Last arrival 21.00hrs Last departure noon
*A compact terraced site in picturesque South Hams,
with wide views of Dartmoor and quality services. From
A38 at Wrangaton take B3210 signed Modbury & site on
L past service stn. A 4-acre site with 68 touring pitches.*

🏴 ♠ ⊙ ◙ ᕻ ◀ ▭ ✳ ⋔ ⓘ ⌀ ⊡ ⊤ ℃ 🖐
🏕 ⛊ ⛊
→ ∪ ↾ ⏌

Credit Cards ⬤ ▭

Pennymoor Camping & Caravan Park (SX685516)
PL21 0SB ☎ 01548 830269 & 830542 (leave A38 at
Wrangton Cross. 1m to cross roads, continue for 4m,
pass petrol station then take 2nd left) Signposted
Nearby town: Kingsbridge
▶ ▶ ▶ Family Park ★ ☎ £5.50-£9 ☎ £4.50-£8
Å £5.50-£9
Open 15 Mar-15 Nov (rs 15 Mar-mid May 1 toilet &
shower block only open) Booking advisable Jul-Aug
Last arrival 22.30hrs Last departure noon
*A well-established rural grassy site on gently sloping
ground with good views. Leave A38 at Wrangaton
Cross, turn left, 1m to crossroads, straight across,
continue for approx 4m, pass petrol station on left then
take 2nd left, site 1m on right. A 12.5-acre site with 154
touring pitches and 70 statics.*
Dishwashing facilities.

🏴 ♠ ⊙ ◙ ᕻ 🔆 ⋔ ⓘ ⌀ ⊡ ⊤ ℃ 🏕 ⛊ ♿
→ ∪ ⏌

Southleigh Caravan & Camping Park (SX682515)
PL21 OSB ☎ 01548 830346 Signposted
► ► ► Family Park 🏕 🏕 Å
Open 15 May-20 Sep (rs 19 Mar-14 May & 20 Sep-Oct limited facilities) Booking advisable mid Jul-Aug Last arrival 23.00hrs Last departure noon

A rural site with a good variety of amenities including a new and extensive clubhouse and restaurant. From A38 at Wrangton take B3210 signed Modbury, after California Cross take 2nd fork left signed Aveton Gifford and Bigbury. Site 2nd on right. A 4-acre site with 100 touring pitches and 100 statics.
Family room with shower & toilet, entertainment.

🔌 🌂 ⊙ 🗗 🖳 ℥ ⭐ 🔦 ☀ ♀ ⋀ 🔋 ⌗ ✠ 🅣 ✗ 📞 ♨
🎋 🐾 ♿
➔ ∪ ▶ ♪

MORTEHOE

Easewell Farm Coastal Holiday Park (SS465455)
EX34 7EH ☎ 01271 870225 Signposted
► ► ► Family Park 🏕 🏕 Å
Open Etr-Sep (rs Etr no shop) Booking advisable Jul-Aug Last arrival 22.00hrs Last departure 10.00hrs
A clifftop site of varying terrain, well-run and maintained, and with a friendly atmosphere. From Mullacott Cross take B3343 to Mortehoe, turn right at unclass rd and site on right in 2m. A 17-acre site with 250 touring pitches.
9 hole golf on site.
See advertisement under WOOLACOMBE

🔌 🌂 ⊙ 🗗 🖳 ℥ 🔦 ☀ ♀ ⋀ 🔋 ⌗ 🅣 ✗ 📞 🛒
♨ 🐾 🐕 ♨
➔ ∪ ▶ ◉ ⌂ ⚓ ♨ ♪

Twitchen Park (SS465447)
EX34 7ES ☎ 01271 870476 Signposted
Nearby town: Woolacombe
► ► ► Family Park ★ 🏕 £7.50-£21 🏕 £7.50-£21
Å £5.50-£18
Open May-Sep (rs Apr & Oct outdoor pool closed, no entertainment) Booking advisable May bank hol & Jul-Aug Last arrival 23.00hrs Last departure 10.00hrs ⊗

AA members can call AA Hotel Booking Service on 0990 050505 to book at AA recognised hotels and B & Bs in the UK and Ireland, or through our Internet site: http://www.theaa.co.uk/hotels

---

A part-sloping grass site with trees and bushes, set in downland and wooded meadowland. From Mullacott Cross rndbt take B3343 Woolacombe Rd to Turnpike Cross junc, then right fork and site on left in 1.5m. A 45-acre site with 132 touring pitches and 274 statics.
Table tennis, snooker, putting green, teenage disco.

🔌 🌂 ⊙ 🗗 🖳 ℥ ⭐ 🔦 ☀ ♀ ⋀ 🔋 ⌗ 🅣 ✗
📞 🎋 🐾
➔ ∪ ▶ ⚓ ♨ ♪

Credit Cards 💳 💳 💳 💳 💳

Warcombe Farm Camping Park (SS478445)
Station Rd EX34 7EJ ☎ 01271 870690
► ► ► Family Park ★ 🏕 £5.50-£9.50 🏕 £4.50-£8.50
Å £3.50-£6.95
Open 15 Mar-Oct Booking advisable
An open site extending to the cliffs, with views over the Bristol Channel, and an attractive fishing lake. Travel N towards Mortehoe from Mullacot Cross rndbt at A361 junc with B3343. Site on right in 2m. A 19-acre site with 95 touring pitches.
Private fishing.

🔌 🌂 ⊙ 🗗 ℥ ⋀ 🔋 ⌗ 🅣 📞 ♨ 🎋 🐕 🐾
➔ ▶

MULLACOTT CROSS

See **Ilfracombe**

NEWTON ABBOT

Ross Park (SX845671)
Park Hill Farm, Ipplepen TQ12 5TT ☎ 01803 812983

Q Q Q Q Q Q Q Q

► ► ► ► Premier Park 🏕 🏕 Å
Open all year Booking advisable Last departure 10.00hrs
A top-class park in every way, with large pitches, secluded areas, high quality facilities and lovely floral displays throughout. Off A381, 3m from Newton Abbot in Totnes direction, signed opposite Jet garage towards 'Woodland'. A 26-acre site with 110 touring pitches.
Snooker, table tennis, bowling green, croquet.

🔌 🌂 ⊙ 🗗 ℥ 🔦 ☐ ⋀ ✗ 📞 🛒 🐕 🐾 ♿
➔ ▶

Q Q Q Q Q Q Q Q

Dornafield (SX838683)
Dornafield Farm, Two Mile Oak TQ12 6DD
☎ 01803 812732 Signposted

◯◯◯◯◯◯◯◯◯◯

► ► ► ► De-Luxe Park ★ ⚑ £8-£12.50 ⚑ £8-£12.50
⚑ £8-£12.50
Open Mar-Oct Booking advisable bank hols & Jul-Aug
Last arrival 22.30hrs Last departure 11.00hrs
*A quiet, very attractive and well-laid out site in a
secluded wooded valley setting. Take A381 (Newton
Abbot-Totnes) for 2m and at Two Mile Oak Inn turn
right, then in .5m at cross roads turn left for site on
right. A 30-acre site with 135 touring pitches.*
Wet weather room.

▣ ﾟ ⊙ ▣ ℀ ● ☀ /⅂ ▌ ⌀ ± T ╰ ⊢ ▦ ⅄
→ ∪ ▶ ☕ ♪

Credit Cards ●● ▨▨ ▨▨ ⑤

◯◯◯◯◯◯◯◯◯◯

Twelve Oaks Farm Caravan Park (SX852737)
Teigngrace TQ12 6QT ☎ 01626 352769
► ► ► Family Park ★ ⚑ £6-£7 ⚑ £6-£7 ⚑ £6-£7
Open all year Booking advisable Last departure 11.00hrs
*A newly created park with very good facilities, on a
working farm. Close to River Teign and Templar Way
walking route. Direct access from A38, signed
'Teigngrace only' in SW direction towards Plymouth. A
2-acre site with 35 touring pitches.*

▣ ﾟ ⟨ ╰
→ ∪ ▶

See also **Whiddon Down**

Moorcroft Leisure Park (SX603954)
Exeter Rd EX20 1QF ☎ 01837 55116 Signposted
► ► ► Family Park ⚑ ⚑ ⚑
Open all year Booking advisable Jul & Aug
*A level grassy field behind Moorcroft Inn with adequate
facilities. Leave A30 at sign for Belstone Services, and
follow signs for Okehampton. Site on left in 1m. A 3-
acre site with 35 touring pitches.*

▣ ﾟ ⊙ ▣ ⟨ ⟩ ☀ ▌ ⌀ T ✕ ╰ ▦
→ ∪ ▶ ♪ ▦

 **Beverley Parks Caravan & Camping Park
(SX886582)**
Goodrington Rd TQ4 7JE
☎ 01803 843887 (along A380/A3022, 2m S)
Signposted

◈◈◈◈◈◈◈◈◈◈◈◈◈◈◈◈◈

★ ⚑ £9-£15 ⚑ £9-£15 ⚑ £7.50-£13.50
Open Etr-Oct Booking advisable Jun-Sep Last arrival
22.00hrs Last departure 10.00hrs ⚘
*A high quality family-run park with extensive views of
the bay. From Exeter, signed off A380 ring road towards
Brixham onto unclassified Goodrington road. A 12-acre
site with 194 touring pitches and 197 statics.*
contd. on p116

*excellent by reputation . . .
. . . for the truly discerning caravanner.
We offer superb facilities in a lovely
location, our brochure is only a phone
call away.*

PETER DEWHIRST • DORNAFIELD FARM (AA)
TWO MILE OAK • NEWTON ABBOT • DEVON

01803 812732

Table tennis, pool, spa bath, crazy golf, sauna.fitnes

🔌 🚐 🅰️ ☉ 🔋 🥤 ⟨ ⟩ ♨ ⚙ ❄️ ♀ ⚠️ ⬛ ⌷ 🔳 ✖️
📞 ♿ 🏠 🚻
➜ ∪ ▶ ◎ ⚠ 🍴 ⛵ ☕ 🔩 🐋

Credit Cards 💳 📧 📧 📧 💲

◌◌◌◌◌◌◌◌◌◌◌◌◌◌◌◌◌

Grange Court Holiday Centre (SX888588)
Grange Rd TQ4 7JP
☎ 01803 558010 (S on A380 past jct A385, left at traffic lioghts into Goodrington rd, .75m turn left into Grange rd, site in 500 yds)
Signposted

◌◌◌◌◌◌◌◌◌◌◌◌◌◌◌◌◌

★ 🚐 £8-£21 🚐 £8-£21
Open 23 May-19 Sep (rs 15 Feb-22 May & 20 Sep-15 Jan club, entertainment) Booking advisable public hols & Jul-Aug Last arrival 22.00hrs Last departure 10.00hrs 🐕

Large grassy site situated amidst woodland near to sea, very well-equipped and maintained. 1.5m from Paignton on Brixham road. A 10-acre site with 157 touring pitches and 520 statics.
Crazy golf, sauna, steam room, snooker, volleyball.

🔌 🚐 🅰️ ☉ 🔋 🥤 ⟨ ⚫ ❄️ ♀ ⚠️ 🔩 ⌷ 🔳 ✖️ 📞
♿ 🐋
➜ ∪ ▶ ◎ ⚠ 🍴 ⛵ ☕ 🔩

Credit Cards 💳 📧 📧 📧 💲

◌◌◌◌◌◌◌◌◌◌◌◌◌◌◌◌◌

Byslades International Touring & Camping Park (SX853603)
Totnes Rd TQ4 7PY ☎ 01803 555072 (2m W on A385)
Signposted
Nearby town: Paignton

◯◯◯◯◯◯◯◯◯

▶▶▶▶ De-Luxe Park ★ 🚐 £6-£11 🚐 £5.50-£10
🛖 £5.50-£10
Open Jun-Sep (rs Mar-May & Oct bar & swimming pool closed) Booking advisable Jul-Aug Last arrival 22.00hrs Last departure 10.00hrs
A well-kept terraced site set in beautiful countryside only 2 miles from Paignton. Signed off A385 at entry to town. A 23-acre site with 170 touring pitches.

Ornamental lake, crazy golf.

🔌 🅰️ ☉ 🔋 🥤 ⟨ ⚫ 🛏️ ❄️ ♀ ⚠️ 🔩 ⌷ 🔳 ✖️
📞 ♿ 🏠 🐕 🐋 ♿
➜ ∪ ▶ ◎ ⚠ 🍴 ☕ 🔩

Credit Cards 💳 📧 📧 📧 💲

◯◯◯◯◯◯◯◯◯

Widend Camping Park (SX852619)
Berry Pomeroy Rd, Marldon TQ3 1RT
☎ 01803 550116
Signposted

◯◯◯◯◯◯◯◯◯

▶ ▶ ▶ ▶ De-Luxe Park 🚐 £5.50-£10 🚐 £5.50-£9.50
🛖 £5.50-£9.50
Open Apr-Oct (rs Apr-mid May & mid Sep Oct swimmimg pool, Club house May-Oct) Booking advisable Jul-Aug & Whit Last arrival 21.00hrs Last departure 10.00hrs
A terraced grass site paddocked and screened on high ground overlooking Torbay with views of Dartmoor. A well laid out and equipped site with high standards of maintenance. Signed off Torbay ring road. A 22-acre site with 207 touring pitches.

🔌 🅰️ ☉ 🔋 🥤 ⚫ ❄️ ♀ ⚠️ 🔩 ⌷ 🔳 📞
♿ 🐕 🐋 ♿
➜ ∪ ▶ 🍴 ☕ 🔩

Credit Cards 💳 📧 📧 📧 💲

◯◯◯◯◯◯◯◯◯

Marine Park Holiday Centre (SX886587)
Grange Rd TQ4 7JR ☎ 01803 843887 (2m S on A3022)
Signposted
▶ ▶ ▶ Family Park ★ ⚑ £7.50-£13.50 ⚑ £7.50-£13.50
Open Etr-Oct Booking advisable Jul-Aug Last arrival
22.00hrs Last departure 10.00hrs ✹
*A mainly static site catering for those who prefer peace
and quiet. Next door to sister site Beverley Park whose
amenities are available. Signed from ring road A3022
and B3198. A 2-acre site with 30 touring pitches and 66
statics.*

🔌 ➡ ｒ ⊙ ⬛ ⛏ ✳ ⚠ ⓘ ∅ Ⓣ 🔌 📻 🛇

➔ ∪ ⌐ ⊙ ⬙ ⤴ 📻 🛁

Credit Cards 💳 💳 📼 🖩 🖩 🅖

RIVERSIDE
CARAVAN PARK
Longbridge Road, Marsh Mills, Plymouth
Telephone: Plymouth (01752) 344122

PLYMOUTH

Riverside Caravan Park (SX515575)
Longbridge Rd, Marsh Mills, Plympton PL6 8LD
☎ 01752 344122 (.5m E off A38) Signposted

▶ ▶ ▶ ▶ De-Luxe Park ⚑ ⚑ ▲
Open Etr-Sep (rs Oct-Etr Bar, Restaurant & Take-away
closed) Booking advisable Jun-Aug Last arrival 22.00hrs
Last departure 10.00hrs
*A well-groomed site on the outskirts of Plymouth on the
banks of the R Plym. Approach by way of Longbridge
road, which is E of Marsh Mills roundabout. An 11-acre
site with 293 touring pitches.*

🔌 ｒ ⊙ ⬛ ⛏ ⌿ ◀ 🖵 ✳ ♀ ⚠ ⓘ ∅ Ⓔ Ⓣ ✗ 🔌
🛒 🐕 🔋

➔ ∪ ⌐ ⊙ ⬙ ⤴ 📻 🛁

Credit Cards 💳 💳 ▪ 📼 🅖

RATTERY

Edeswell Farm Country Caravan Park (SX731606)
Edeswell Farm TQ10 9LN ☎ 01364 72177 Signposted
Nearby town: Totnes
▶ ▶ ▶ Family Park ★ ⚑ £7.50-£9.50 ⚑ £7.50-£9.50
▲ £7.50-£9.50
Open Etr-Sep Booking advisable school hols Last arrival
20.30hrs Last departure noon
*Gently sloping, terraced grass site with mature trees, in
hilly country and near river, off A385. A 3-acre site with
46 touring pitches and 20 statics.*
Badminton, table tennis, adventure playground.

🔌 ｒ ⊙ ⬛ ⛏ ⚡ ◀ ✳ ♀ ⚠ ⓘ ∅ Ⓔ Ⓣ 🔌 ➡ 🎾
🛒 🐕 🔋 ♿

➔ ∪ ⌐ 🛁

Edeswell Farm Country
Caravan Park,
Rattery, South Brent, Devon TQ10 9LN
Telephone: 01364 72177
Small picturesque, family-run park set in beautiful
South Hams, on the edge of Dartmoor, ideally
situated for touring Devon and Cornwall. 20 holiday-
homes for hire, 46 terraced touring pitches. Indoor
heated swimming pool, games room and TV lounge.
Bar, shop, launderette, children's play areas and
covered floodlit badminton court.

SALCOMBE

Karrageen Caravan & Camping Park (SX686395)
Malborough TQ7 3EN ☎ 01548 561230 (from
Kingsbridge take A381 towards Salcombe, at
Malborough turn sharp right following signs to
Bolberry) Signposted
▶ ▶ ▶ Family Park ★ ⚑ £7-£10 ⚑ £7-£8.50 ▲ £6-£9
Open 15 Mar-15 Nov Booking advisable bank & school
hols Last arrival 23.30hrs Last departure 11.30hrs
contd.

A small, friendly, family-run park with terraced grassy pitches giving extensive sea and country views. One mile from the beach in the pretty hamlet of Hope Cove. At Malborough on A381, turn sharp right through village, follow Bolberry signs for 0.5 miles. Turn right to Bolberry and the park is one mile on right. A 7.5-acre site with 75 touring pitches and 20 statics.
Baby room, licensed shop, 2 play areas, takeaway.

🔌 🎣 ☉ 🗄 🥄 ✳ 🛡 📶 🗑 🚽 🐕 🚴 🏕 🐈 👶
→ ∪ 🛆 ✢ ✦

Bolberry House Farm Caravan & Camping Park (SX687395)
Bolberry TQ7 3DY ☎ 01548 561251 & 560926
Signposted
► ► ► Family Park
🚐 £7.50-£8.50 🚐 £7.50-£8.50 ⅄ £6-£8
Open Etr-Oct Booking advisable Jul & Aug Last departure noon

Oakdown
AA 4 Pennant De-luxe Park
SIDMOUTH'S AWARD WINNING TOURING & HOLIDAY HOME PARK

Whether holidaying in your own touring unit or in one of our luxurious caravan holiday homes, you'll always feel welcome at Oakdown. Oakdown is Sidmouth's multi award winning park

We offer:

► Level spacious 'standard' & 'super' pitches for tourers and tents
► Luxury heated caravan holiday homes to hire
► Closely mown landscaped park with easy access
► Centrally heated luxurious amenities
► Near East Devon Heritage coastline
► Fully alarmed touring caravan storage
► Field trail to famous Donkey Sanctuary
► 3 miles from the Regency town of Sidmouth
  Free colour brochure with pleasure

Tel: 01297 • 680387 Fax: 01395 • 513731

A level, well maintained family run park in peaceful setting on coastal farm with sea views, fine cliff walks and nearby beaches. At Malboroughon A381 turn right signed Hope Cove & Bolberry. Take L fork after village signed Soar & Bolberry, and site signed in .5m. Discount in low season for senior citizens. A 6-acre site with 70 touring pitches and 10 statics.
Childrens play area & play barn.

🔌 🎣 ☉ 🗄 🥄 ✳ 📶 🛡 📶 🗑 🚽 🐕 🏕 🐈
→ ∪ 🛈 ☉ 🛆 ✢ ✦

SAMPFORD PEVERELL

Minnows Caravan Park (SS042148)
Holbrook Ln EX16 7EN ☎ 01884 821770
► ► ► Family Park 🚐 🚐
Open 2 Mar-4 Jan
Attractive park bounded by Grand Western Canal, with good facilities and well positioned as a holiday base. From M5 junc 27 take A361 signed Tiverton and Barnstaple. Site signed on left almost immediately at 1st slip road. A 2-acre site with 41 touring pitches.

🔌 🎣 ☉ ✳ 📶 🛡 📶 🗑 🐕 🚴
→ ▶ ✦ 🗄 🐈

SEATON
See Colyton

SIDMOUTH

Oakdown Touring & Holiday Home Park (SY168901)
Weston EX10 0PH ☎ 01297 680387 (off A3052,2.5m E of junc with A375) Signposted

Q Q Q Q Q Q

► ► ► ► De-Luxe Park ★ 🚐 £7-£10.70 🚐 £7-£10.70
⅄ £7-£10.70
Open Apr-Oct Booking advisable Spring bank hol & Jul-Aug Last arrival 22.00hrs Last departure 10.30hrs
Friendly, well-maintained, level site with good landscaping. Reached by a short approach road off A3052, between Seaton and Sidmouth. A 13-acre site with 120 touring pitches and 46 statics.
Dishwashing sinks.

🔌 🚐 🎣 ☉ 🗄 🥄 ⬜ ✳ 📶 🛡 📶 🗑 🚽 🐕 🗑 🏕 🐈
🐈 🚴
→ ∪ 🛈 ☉ 🛆 ✢ 🍴 ✦ 🐈
Credit Cards 💳 💳 💳 💳 🅂

Q Q Q Q Q Q Q Q

Kings Down Tail Caravan & Camping Park (SY173907)
Salcombe Regis EX10 0PD ☎ 01297 680313 (off A3052 3m E of junc with A375) Signposted
► ► ► Family Park 🚐 🚐 ⅄
Open 15 Mar-15 Nov Booking advisable Whit, bank hols & mid Jul-Sep Last arrival 22.00hrs Last departure noon
A well-kept site on level ground on east side of Sid Valley in tree-sheltered position. Opposite Branscombe water tower on A3052. A 5-acre site with 100 touring pitches and 2 statics.
Off licence.

🔌 🎣 ☉ 🗄 🥄 ⬤ ✳ 📶 🛡 📶 🗑 🚽 🐕 🏕 🐈
→ ∪ 🛈 ☉ ✢ 🍴 ✦ 🗄
Credit Cards 💳 💳 🅂

Salcombe Regis Caravan & Camping Park (SY153892)
Salcombe Regis EX10 0JH ☎ 01395 514303 (off A3052
3m E of junc with A375) Signposted
▶ ▶ ▶ Family Park ★ 🚐 £6.25-£9.70 🚐 £6.25-£9.70
Å £6.25-£9.70
Open Etr-15 Oct Booking advisable bank hols & Jul-Aug
Last arrival 22.00hrs Last departure 10.00hrs
*Spacious level park with well-maintained facilities, on
the coastal path 1.5m from Sidmouth and .5m from the
sea. A 16-acre site with 110 touring pitches and 10
statics.*
Off licence, bike hire, putting & barbecue hire.

🖥️ 🚼 📻 ⊙ 🗗 🖑 ☼ 🕭 🔋 🖉 🎦 🖼 🔗 🖤 🐾 🐕 🖐
➔ ∪ ┣ ◎ 🔼 ⤴ ♨ 🍴

Credit Cards 💳 ▦ 🏦 🖊 🖇

SLAPTON

Camping & Caravanning Club Site (SX825450)
Middle Grounds TQ7 1QW ☎ 01548 580538 (in season)
& 01203 694995 Signposted
Nearby town: Kingsbridge
▶ ▶ ▶ Family Park ★ 🚐 £11-£14 Å £11-£14
Open end Mar-early Nov Booking advisable bank hols &
Jul-Aug Last arrival 21.00hrs Last departure noon
*A very attractive location and well-run site open to non-
members. The site overlooks Start Bay within a few
minutes' walk of the beach. Take A379 coast road
signed Dartmouth, after Tor Cross village turn left at
American War Memorial for Slapton. Site on right.
Please see the advertisement on page 27 for details of
Club Members' benefits. A 5.5-acre site with 115 touring
pitches.*

🖥️ 📻 ⊙ 🗗 🖑 ☼ 🕭 🔋 🖉 🖼 🔗 🖤 🐾 🖐
➔ ∪ 🍴 🖤

Credit Cards 💳 ▦ 🏦 🖊 🖇

SOURTON CROSS

Bundu Camping & Caravan Park (SX546916)
EX20 4HT ☎ 01837 861611 Signposted
Nearby town: Okehampton
▶ ▶ ▶ Family Park ★ 🚐 £7 🚐 £7 Å £4.50-£7
Open 15 Mar-15 Nov Booking advisable Jul & Aug
*A level grassy site in an ideal location, on the border of
the Dartmoor National Park and offering fine views.
Leave A30 at A386 signed Tavistock/Plymouth, and site
up first road on left. A 4-acre site with 38 touring
pitches.*

🖥️ 📻 ⊙ 🗗 🖑 ☼ 🕭 🔋 🖉 🖼 🐾 🖤
➔ ∪ ┣ 🖤

SOUTH BRENT

Webland Farm Holiday Park (SX715594)
Avonwick TQ10 9EX ☎ 01364 73273 (1m S of A38)
Signposted
Nearby town: Totnes
▶▶ Town & Country Pennant Park ★ 🚐 £5-£6.50
🚐 £5-£6.50 Å £5-£6.50
Open Etr-15 Nov Booking advisable school hols Last
arrival 22.00hrs Last departure noon
*A very rural park with extensive views, surrounded by
farmland, with sloping pitches mainly for tents. For
towed caravans, access can be awkward. Leave A38 at*
contd.

junc with A385 signed Marley Head, and site in 1m on unclass single track rd. A 5-acre site with 35 touring pitches and 50 statics.

🔌 🐾 ☉ 🗄 ✳ ⚠ ⊞ 🔌 🐾 🛒
➔ ∪ ▶ 🎵

STARCROSS

See **Dawlish**

STICKLEPATH

Olditch Caravan & Camping Park (SX645935)
EX20 2NT ☎ 01837 840734 Signposted
Nearby town: Okehampton
▶▶ **Town & Country Pennant Park** 🚐 🚐 Å
Open 14 Mar-14 Nov Booking advisable bank hols & Jul-Aug Last arrival 22.00hrs Last departure 16.00hrs
A basic farm site with trees and bushes set in Dartmoor National Park. Some pitches are now tiered. .5m E of village on A30, and 3m from Okehampton; follow signs for Sticklepath and South Zeal, and site 300 metres past garage at bottom of hill.. A 3-acre site with 32 touring pitches and 20 statics.
Small tourist information area

🔌 🐾 ☉ 🍴 ◀ ⊡ ✳ ⛱ ⚠ 🛢 🔌 ✕ 🔌 🎏 🛒
➔ ∪ ▶ 🍽 🎵

STOKE GABRIEL

Ramslade Touring Park (SX861592)
Stoke Rd TQ9 6QB ☎ 01803 782575 Signposted
Nearby town: Paignton

◯◯◯◯◯◯◯

▶▶▶▶ **De-Luxe Park** ★ 🚐 £8.80-£12.30
🚐 £8.80-£12.30 Å £8.80-£12.30
Open mid Mar-Oct Booking advisable Jul-Aug also Etr & Spring bank hol Last arrival 20.00hrs Last departure 11.00hrs

A high quality park in a rural setting next to the Dart Valley. Situated between Paignton and the picturesque village of Stoke Gabriel on the River Dart, .75 miles from Stoke Gabriel. An 8-acre site with 135 touring pitches.
Paddling pool and dishwashing room.

🔌 🚿 🐾 ☉ 🗄 🍴 ◀ ⊡ ✳ ⚠ 🛢 🔌 ⊞ Ⓣ 🔌 🔌 🎏
🎿 🛒 🛒 ♿
➔ ∪ ▶ ◎ ⛱ ⌇ 🍽 🎵

Credit Cards 💳 ▭ ▨ 🔲

◯◯◯◯◯◯◯

TAVISTOCK

Higher Longford Farm Caravan Site (SX520747)
Moorshop PL19 9JU ☎ 01822 613360 & 0585 166632
(2.5m from town along B3357) Signposted

◯◯◯◯◯◯◯

▶▶▶▶ **De-Luxe Park** ★ 🚐 £8-£9 🚐 £8-£9 Å £6-£9
Open all year Booking advisable Jun-Aug Last arrival 22.30hrs Last departure noon
A very pleasant small park on an isolated working farm in a moorland location. Adjacent to B3357 between Ashburton and Tavistock in the Dartmoor National Park. A 6-acre site with 52 touring pitches and 24 statics.
Farm animals.

🔌 🐾 ☉ 🗄 🍴 ✳ ⛱ ⚠ 🛢 🔌 ⊞ Ⓣ ✕ 🔌 🎏 🛒
➔ ∪ ▶ 🎵

◯◯◯◯◯◯◯

Langstone Manor Camping & Caravan Park (SX524738)
Moortown PL19 9JZ ☎ 01822 613371 (2.5m W off B3357) Signposted

◯◯◯◯◯◯◯

▶▶▶▶ **De-Luxe Park** ★ 🚐 £7-£8 🚐 £7-£8 Å £7-£8
Open 15 Mar-15 Nov Booking advisable bank hols & Jul-Aug Last arrival 23.00hrs Last departure 11.00hrs

A secluded site set in the well-maintained grounds of a manor house, within the National Park. Signed off B3357 Tavistock to Princetown road. A 5.5-acre site with 40 touring pitches and 25 statics.

🔌 🐾 ☉ 🗄 🍴 ◀ ✳ ⛱ ⚠ 🛢 🔌 ⊞ ✕ 🔌 🎏 🛒
➔ ∪ ▶ 🍽 🎵

◯◯◯◯◯◯◯

Harford Bridge Holiday Park (SX504768)
PL19 9LS ☎ 01822 810349 (off A386) Signposted
▶▶▶ **Family Park** 🚐 🚐 Å

Open 22 Mar-4 Nov Booking advisable Aug Last arrival 21.00hrs Last departure noon
Level, grassy site with mature trees, set in Dartmoor National Park, beside the River Tavy. 2m N of Tavistock on A386. A 10-acre site with 120 touring pitches and 80 statics.
Fly fishing.

🔌 📻 ⊙ 🖥 🍳 ♨ ● ☐ ☀ ⋀ 🐕 🧺 ✚ 🛁 ␥

🏛 📺 🐾 🐂

➜ ∪ ▶ ◎ △ ⅄ 🎾 ♦

Credit Cards 💳 ▩ 🅖

Woodovis Holiday Park (SX432744)
PL19 8NY ☎ 01822 832968 Signposted
▶ ▶ ▶ Family Park ★ 🏕 £8-£10 🚐 £8-£10 ▲ £8-£10
Open Mar-Jan Booking advisable Jul-Aug Last arrival 20.00hrs Last departure noon
A well-kept small park in a remote woodland setting. Take A390 Tavistock-Liskeard road, after 2m at Gulworthy crossroads turn right, for site in 1.5m. A 14.5-acre site with 54 touring pitches and 23 statics.
Mini-golf.

🔌 📻 ⊙ 🖥 🍳 ♨ ● ☀ ⋀ 🐕 🧺 ✚ 🛁 Ⓣ ␥

🏛 📺 🐾 🐂

➜ ∪ ▶ ◎ ⅄ ♦

Credit Cards 💳

Yeatheridge Farm
(Touring) Caravan Park
E. WORLINGTON, CREDITON, DEVON EX17 4TN
Telephone Tiverton (01884) 860 330
OFF THE A377 AND B3137 (OLD A373) ON THE B3042

WHY ARE WE DIFFERENT? We are a small Central Park with panoramic views on a genuine working farm with plenty of animals to see and some to touch! We also offer peace and space with freedom to roam the farm with its 2½ miles of woodland and river bank walks, coarse fishing lakes, 2 indoor heated swimming pools with 200 ft water flume, TV lounge, children's play area, hot and cold showers, wash cubicles – ALL FREE. Other amenities include horse riding from the park, electric hook-up points, campers' dish washing, laundry room, shop with frozen foods, fresh dairy products, ice pack service, a welcome for dogs H Summer parking in our storage area to save towing H Ideally situated for touring coast, Exmoor and Dartmoor. Golf and Tennis locally.
ALSO 3 CARAVANS TO LET –
PROPRIETORS/OWNERS – GEOFFREY & ELIZABETH HOSEGOOD
WRITE OR PHONE FOR FREE COLOUR BROCHURE

TEDBURN ST MARY

Springfield Holiday Park (SX788935)
Tedburn Rd EX6 6EW ☎ 01647 24242 (1.5m E of village off A30) Signposted
Nearby town: Exeter
▶ ▶ ▶ Family Park ★ 🏕 £5.50-£8.50 🚐 £5.50-£9.50
▲ £4.50-£8.50
Open 15 Mar-15 Nov Booking advisable Jul-Aug Last arrival 22.00hrs Last departure 14.00hrs
This terraced site offers panoramic views of the surrounding countryside, a tranquil atmosphere and useful facilities. Leave A30 at Tedburn St Mary exit, turn left onto old A30 towards Cheriton Bishop, and signed on right. A 9-acre site with 88 touring pitches and 14 statics.
Licensed shop.
See advertisement under EXETER

🔌 🛵 📻 ⊙ 🖥 🍳 ⅃ ● ☀ ⅄ ⋀ 🐕 🧺 ✚ 🛁 Ⓣ ✗ ␥
🚽 🏛 📺 🐾 🐂
➜ ∪ ▶ ♦

TIVERTON
See **East Worlington**

TORQUAY
See also **Newton Abbot**

Widdicombe Farm Tourist Park (SX880650)
Compton TQ3 1ST ☎ 01803 558325 Signposted

◯ ◯ ◯ ◯ ◯ ◯ ◯ ◯

▶ ▶ ▶ ▶ De-Luxe Park ★ 🏕 £5.50-£10 🚐 £5.50-£10
▲ £5.50-£10
Open mid Mar-mid Nov Booking advisable Whitsun & Jul-Aug Last arrival 21.30hrs Last departure 11.00hrs
Family-owned and run park on a working farm, with good quality facilities and extensive views. On A380 dual carriageway, midway between two rndbts on N-bound lane from Compton Castle, and signed. An 8-acre site with 200 touring pitches and 3 statics.

🔌 📻 ⊙ 🖥 🍳 ● ☐ ☀ ⅄ ⋀ 🐕 🧺 ✚ 🛁 Ⓣ ✗ ␥ 🛵
🚽 🏛 📺 🐾 🐂 ♿
➜ ∪ ▶ ◎ 🎾 ♦

Credit Cards 💳 ▩ ▦ 🅖

◯ ◯ ◯ ◯ ◯ ◯ ◯ ◯

UMBERLEIGH

Camping & Caravanning Club Site (SS606242)
Over Weir EX37 9DU ☎ 01769 560009 (in season) & 01203 694995 Signposted
▶ ▶ ▶ Family Park ★ 🏕 £10-£13 🚐 £10-£13 ▲ £10-£13
Open end Mar-early Nov Booking advisable bank hols & Jul-Aug Last arrival 21.00hrs Last departure noon ⌀
A compact site on high ground with fine country views adjacent to wooded area. Approached by metalled road, with wide entrance. Situated on the B3227, 200yds from the A377 at Umberleigh. Please see the advertisement on page 27 for details of Club Members' benefits. A 4-acre site with 60 touring pitches.
Fishing & tennis.

🔌 📻 ⊙ 🖥 🍳 ♨ ● ☐ ☀ ⋀ 🐕 🧺 ✚ 🛁 ␥ 🏛 🐾 🐂
➜ ▶ ♦

Credit Cards 💳 ▩ ▦

WEST DOWN

Hidden Valley Coast & Country Park (SS499408)
EX34 8NU ☎ 01271 813837 (on A361) Signposted
Nearby town: Ilfracombe

◯◯◯◯◯◯◯

▶▶▶▶▶ Premier Park 🚐 £3.50-£11 🚐 £3.50-£11
🛨 £3.50-£11
Open 15 Mar-15 Nov Booking advisable high season
Last departure 11.00hrs
A delightful, well-appointed family site set in a wooded valley, with superb facilities and a restaurant. Winner of the Best Campsite for the South West of England, 1997/8. 5m SW of Ilfracombe off A361. A 25-acre site with 135 touring pitches.
Lounge/bar.
See advertisement under ILFRACOMBE

🎮 📻 ☉ 🗄 🔍 ※ ♀ ⚠ ⓘ ⊘ ⊕ Ⓣ ✗ ℃ 🛒 ⊯ ⵣ
⊁ 🐕 🐾 &
➜ ∪ ⌁ ⵣ 😋 🏌

Credit Cards 💳 ▦ ⓞ ◼ 🔣 🅢

◯◯◯◯◯◯◯

WHIDDON DOWN

Dartmoor View Holiday Park (SX685928)
EX20 2QL ☎ 01647 231545 Signposted
Nearby town: Okehampton
▶▶▶ Family Park 🚐 £6.70-£9.10 🚐 £6.70-£9.10
🛨 £6.70-£9.10
Open Mar-Oct Booking advisable Etr, Whitsun & Jul-Aug Last arrival 22.30hrs Last departure 10-12.00hrs
A pleasant, informal site with modern facilities on high ground within the National Park. In rural location yet near to the main A30 West Country road, .5m from Whiddon Down. A 5-acre site with 75 touring pitches and 40 statics.
Off licence, cycle/hire service, games room, putting.

🎮 📻 ☉ 🗄 🔍 ⵜ ♦ ⊡ ※ ♀ ⚠ ⓘ ⊘ ⊕ Ⓣ ℃ ⵣ
⊁ 🐾
➜ ∪ 🏌

Credit Cards 💳 ▦ 🔣 🅢

WOODBURY

Webbers Farm Caravan Park (SY029878)
Castle Ln EX5 1EA ☎ 01395 232276 Signposted
Nearby town: Exmouth
▶▶▶ Family Park ★ 🚐 £7-£9.50 🚐 £7-£9.50
🛨 £7-£9.50
Open Etr-Sep Booking advisable all times Last arrival 21.00hrs Last departure 11.00hrs
Unspoilt farm site in two parts, with a fine view over River Exe towards Dartmoor. 4m from junction 30 of M5. Take the A376, then the B3179 to Woodbury Village, site is 500yds E of village. An 8-acre site with 115 touring pitches.
Pets corner, caravan storage facilities.

🎮 ♦ 📻 ☉ 🗄 🔍 ※ ⚠ ⓘ ⊘ ⊕ ℃ 🛒 ⊁ 🐾 &
➜ ∪ ⌁ 🏌

Credit Cards 💳 ▦ 🔣 🅢

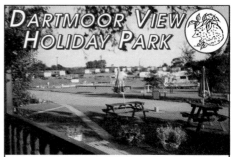

A quiet, friendly, family Park on the edge of Dartmoor. The ideal centre for a touring holiday in Devon and Cornwall. Easy access from M5 with level pitches for tents, tourers and motorhomes. Caravans for hire. Excellent facilities including heated pool, shop, bar, takeaway, games room, play area. Fishing, walking and riding nearby. Colour brochure.
Dartmoor View Holiday Park, Whiddon Down, Okehampton, Devon, EX20 2QL

Tel: 01647 231545 Fax: 01647 231654

WOOLACOMBE

 Golden Coast Holiday Village (SS482436)
Station Rd EX34 7HW ☎ 01271 870343
Signposted
Nearby town: Barnstaple

✿✿✿✿✿✿✿✿✿✿✿✿✿✿

★ 🚐 £10.70-£23.60 🚐 £10.70-£23.60 🛨 £7.20-£19.40
Open Etr-Nov Booking advisable Whitsun & mid Jul-end Aug Last arrival 23.30hrs Last departure 10.00hrs ✇
This holiday village includes villas and static caravans as well as the camping site. Woolacombe is surrounded by National Trust land. Follow road to Woolacombe Bay from Mullacott, and site in 1.5m on left. A 10-acre site with 155 touring pitches.
Sauna, solarium, jacuzzi, tennis, entertainment.

🎮 ♦ 📻 ☉ 🗄 🔍 ⵜ ⵣ ♦ ⊡ ※ ♀ ⚠ ⓘ ⊘ ⊕
Ⓣ ✗ ℃ 🛒 ⊯ 🍴 ⵣ 🐕 🐾 &
➜ ∪ ⌁ ☉ ⵏ ⌁ 😋 🏌

Credit Cards 💳 ▦ ◼ 🔣 🅢

See advertisement on page 4.

✿✿✿✿✿✿✿✿✿✿✿✿✿✿

Woolacombe Sands Holiday Park (SS471434)
Beach Rd EX34 7AF ☎ 01271 870569 Signposted
Nearby town: Ilfracombe
▶▶▶ Family Park ★ 🚐 £6.75-£16.50 🚐 £6.75-£16.50
🛨 £5.75-£15.50
Open Apr-Sep Booking advisable 18 Jul-30 Aug & 23-30 May Last arrival 22.00hrs Last departure 10.00hrs

A terraced site with level pitches and good facilities. From Woolacombe Bay go uphill towards Mullacott, and site in .25m on right. A 20-acre site with 200 touring pitches and 63 statics.

🔣 🔣 ⊙ 🔣 🔣 🔣 ⚡ ✳ 🍴 🏔 🛅 🖉 🔣 🥃 🧹 🐕 🔣
➔ ∪ ⌂ ◎ ♪

Credit Cards ●● ▬ ▬ 🔣

DORSET

BERE REGIS

Rowlands Wait Touring Park (SY842933)
Rye Hill BH20 7LP ☎ 01929 471958 (at Bere Regis take rd signposted to Wool/Bovington, about .75m at top of Rye Hill, turn right. Site about 200yds. Signposted
Nearby town: Dorchester

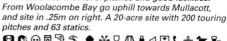

▶ ▶ ▶ ▶ De-Luxe Park ★ 🚐 £5.80-£8.80 🚐 £5.80-£8.80
▲ £5.80-£8.80
Open Mar-Oct Booking advisable bank hols & Jul-Aug
Last arrival 21.30hrs Last departure noon
This park lies in a really attractive setting overlooking Bere and the Dorset countryside, set amongst undulating areas of trees and shrubs. At the A35 roundabout E of village exit left for village. At the next roundabout exit left for Bovington Camp. Do not enter
contd.

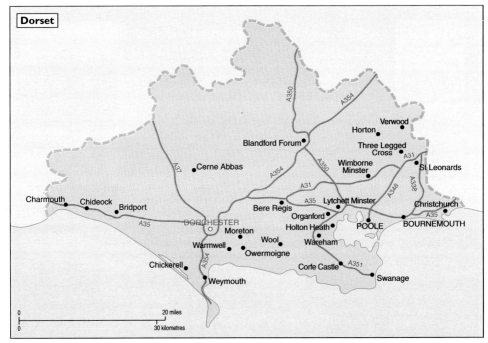

Dorset

Verwood
Horton
Blandford Forum
Three Legged Cross
St Leonards
Cerne Abbas
Wimborne Minster
A31
Charmouth
Chideock
Bridport
Bere Regis
Lytchett Minster
Christchurch
BOURNEMOUTH
DORCHESTER
Organford
Moreton
Holton Heath
POOLE
Wool
Wareham
Warmwell
Owermoigne
Chickerell
Corfe Castle
Swanage
Weymouth

0   20 miles
0   30 kilometres

village. Site signed on right approx 1.5m. An 8-acre site with 71 touring pitches.

🔌📞📶☉🗄🍳🔦✳⛰🚰📷🎂📺📞🔥🐎🐴

➔ ∪ ▶ 🎣

QQQQQQQQQQ

BLANDFORD FORUM

The Inside Park (ST869046)
Down House Estate DT11 0HG ☎ 01258 453719
Signposted

QQQQQQQQQQ

▶ ▶ ▶ ▶ **De-Luxe Park ★ 🚐 £7.45-£12.20**
🚐 £7.45-£12.20 ▲ £7.45-£12.20
Open Etr-Oct Booking advisable bank hols & Jul-Aug
Last arrival 22.00hrs Last departure noon
An attractive, well-sheltered and quiet site with some level pitches, in an isolated valley of woods and pasturelands. From town cross R Stour and follow signs to Winterbourne Stickland and site in 1.5m. A 12-acre site with 125 touring pitches.
Farm trips (main season). Kennels for hire.

🔌📞☉🗄🍳🔦✳⛰🚰📷🎂📺📞➡🐴🐎🐕

➔ ∪ ▶ 🎣

Credit Cards 💳 ▭ ▭

QQQQQQQQQQ

BOURNEMOUTH

Chesildene Touring Caravan Park (SZ107951)
2 Chesildene Av BH8 0DS ☎ 01202 513238 Signposted
▶ ▶ ▶ **Family Park 🚐 🚐**
Open Apr-Oct Booking advisable Spring bank hol & Jul-Aug

A well-maintained, level site in a quiet residential area close to the town centre and convenient for Poole. From Ringwood direction: 1m SW leave A31 and A338 signposted Bournemouth. In 7m at roundabout turn right onto A3060 then in 1m turn right at signpost. A 1.5-acre site with 35 touring pitches.

🔌📞☉🗄🍳🔦✳⛰🚰📷🎂📺📞

➔ ∪ ▶ ⚒ 🎂 🎣

BRIDPORT

Binghams Farm Touring Caravan Park (SY478963)
Melplash DT6 3TT ☎ 01308 488234

QQQQQQQQQQ

▶ ▶ ▶ ▶ **De-Luxe Park 🚐 🚐 ▲**
Open all year Booking advisable bank hols Last arrival 22.00hrs Last departure 11.00hrs
A very good site with good quality buildings, fittings and services, in a lovely rural setting. Take A3066 signed Beaminster, then left into farm road after 1.5m. A 5-acre site with 60 touring pitches.
Washing-up facilities.

🔌📞☉🗄🍳🔦✳⛰🚰📷🔦📷🔥🐎🐴

➔ ∪ ▶ ◎ 🔺 ⚒ 🎂 🎣 🎣

QQQQQQQQQQ

Freshwater Beach Holiday Park (SY493892)
Burton Bradstock DT6 4PT ☎ 01308 897317 (take B3517 towards Weymouth, park 1.5m on right)

QQQQQQQQQQ

▶ ▶ ▶ ▶ **De-Luxe Park ★ 🚐 £8.50-£18 🚐 £8.50-£18**
▲ £8.50-£18

Open 15 Mar-10 Nov Booking advisable Jul-Aug Last arrival 23.30hrs Last departure 10.00hrs
A well-maintained, typical holiday site with newly-built toilet block. On B3157, 1.5m E of Bridport. A 16-acre site with 400 touring pitches and 250 statics.

Credit Cards

Highlands End Farm Caravan Park (SY454913)
Eype DT6 6AR ☎ 01308 422139 (Eype, 1m W of A35)
Signposted

▶▶▶▶ De-Luxe Park ★ ⚘ £7.50-£11.75
⚘ £7.50-£11.75 ▲ £7.50-£11.75
Open mid Mar-mid Nov Booking advisable public hols & Jul-Aug Last arrival 22.00hrs Last departure 11.00hrs
contd.

A well-screened site with clifftop views over Channel and Dorset coast. Adjacent to National Trust land and overlooking Lyme Bay. From Bridport take A35 Lyme rd, and site on left in 2m. A 9-acre site with 195 touring pitches and 160 statics.
Solarium, gym, steam room, sauna & snooker room.

🖳 📞 ⊙ 🗄 🔧 🍴 🔍 🔦 ☀ ⛱ 🏔 🛢 🔊 🎁 T ✗ 📞
🔜 🖤 🐴 🛒 👤
➜ ∪ ▶ ⊁ ♨ 🍴

Credit Cards 💳 🎴

CACACACACACA

CERNE ABBAS

Giant's Head Caravan & Camping Park (ST675029)
Giants Head Farm, Old Sherborne Rd DT2 7TR
☎ 01300 341242 Signposted
Nearby town: Dorchester
▶ **Town & Country Pennant Park** 🚐 £5.50-£7 🚙 £5-£7
Å £5.50-£7
Open Etr-Oct (rs Etr shop & bar closed) Booking advisable Aug Last arrival anytime Last departure 13.00hrs
Part-level, part-sloping, grassy site set in Dorset downland near Cerne Giant (a figure cut into the chalk). A good stopover site ideal for tenters and back-packers on the Ridgeway route. Go into Dorchester avoiding by-pass. Take Sherborne road at town roundabout, after 500 yards take right fork at garage. A 4-acre site with 50 touring pitches.
Two holiday chalets.

🖳 📞 ⊙ 🗄 🔧 ⛱ ☀ 🛢 🔊 🎁 🏟 🐴
➜ ∪ ▶ ⊙ 🍴

CHARMOUTH

Monkton Wylde Farm Caravan Park (SY336964)
DT6 6DB ☎ 01297 34525 Signposted
Nearby town: Lyme Regis

CACACACACACA

▶ ▶ ▶ ▶ **De-Luxe Park** ★ 🚐 £6.25-£10.50
🚙 £6.25-£10.50 Å £6.25-£10.50
Open Etr-Oct (rs low & mid season site gate will be locked at 22.30hrs) Booking advisable after Xmas Last arrival 22.00hrs Last departure 11.00hrs

A pleasant family site in a secluded location yet central for Charmouth, Lyme and the coast. Situated on a 200 acre sheep and cereals farm. Leave A35 3m NW of Charmouth, and take B3165 signposted Marshwood. Site 0.25m on left. A 6-acre site with 60 touring pitches.
Family shower room.

🖳 📞 ⊙ 🗄 🔧 ⛱ 🏔 🛢 🔊 🎁 T 📞 🔜 🖤 🛒 🐴 👤
➜ ∪ ▶ ⊁ ♨ 🍴

CACACACACACA

Wood Farm Caravan & Camping Park (SY356940)
Axminster Rd DT6 6BT ☎ 01297 560697 Signposted
Nearby town: Lyme Regis

CACACACACACA

▶ ▶ ▶ ▶ **De-Luxe Park** ★ 🚐 £7.50-£12.50 🚙 £7.50-£12.50 Å £7.50-£12.50
Open Etr-Oct Booking advisable school hols Last arrival 19.00hrs Last departure noon
A pleasant, well-maintained terraced site adjoining the A35. From village centre travel W to A35 rndbt, and site entrance signed here. A 13-acre site with 216 touring pitches and 83 statics.
Coarse fishing lake.

🖳 📞 ⊙ 🗄 🔧 🍴 🔍 🔦 ☀ 🏔 🛢 🔊 T 📞 🔜 🖤 🐴
🛒 👤
➜ ∪ ▶ ⊙ ♨ ⊁ 🍴

Credit Cards 💳 💳 💳 🎴

CACACACACACA

CHICKERELL (NEAR WEYMOUTH)

Bagwell Farm Touring Park (SY627816)
DT3 4EA ☎ 01305 782575 Signposted
Nearby town: Weymouth
▶ ▶ ▶ **Family Park** 🚐 £6-£10.50 🚙 £6-£10.50 Å £5.50-£10
Open all year Booking advisable Jul-Aug Last arrival 21.30hrs Last departure 11.00hrs
Attractive terraced site set in hillside and valley leading to sea, with good views of Dorset downland. Situated 4m W of Weymouth on the B3157 Abbotsbury-Bridport road, 500yds past the 'Victoria Inn' public house. A 14-acre site with 320 touring pitches.
Wet suit shower, campers shelter.

🖳 🔜 📞 ⊙ 🗄 🔧 🔍 ☀ 🏔 🛢 🔊 🎁 T 📞 🖤 🏟 🐴
🛒 👤
➜ ∪ ▶ ⊁ ♨ 🍴

Credit Cards 💳 💳 🎴

CHIDEOCK

Golden Cap Caravan Park (SY422919)
Seatown DT6 6JX ☎ 01297 489341 & 01308 422139 (on A35) Signposted

CACACACACACA

▶ ▶ ▶ ▶ **De-Luxe Park** ★ 🚐 🚙 Å
Open mid Mar-early Nov Booking advisable public hols & Jul-Aug Last arrival 22.00hrs Last departure 11.00hrs
A grassy site, well-situated overlooking sea and beach and surrounded by National Trust parkland. Ideal base for touring Dorset and Devon. From A35 centre of Chideock follow signs. An 11-acre site with 130 touring pitches.

🖳 📞 ⊙ 🗄 🔧 ⛱ 🏔 🛢 🔊 🎁 T 📞 🔜 🖤 🏟 🐴 🛒 👤
➜ ∪ ▶ ⊁ ♨ 🍴

Credit Cards 💳 💳 🎴

CACACACACACA

CHRISTCHURCH

Hoburne Park (SZ194936)
Hoburne Ln, Highcliffe-on-Sea BH23 4HU
☎ 01425 273379

◯◯◯◯◯◯◯◯◯◯

▶ ▶ ▶ ▶ ▶ Premier Park 🏕 🏕
Open Mar-Oct

A large park with excellent facilities for family holidays.
Signed on A337 E of Christchurch. A 24-acre site with
285 touring pitches and 287 statics.

ℝ⚲

◯◯◯◯◯◯◯◯◯◯

Grove Farm Meadow Holiday Caravan Park (SZ136946)
Stour Way BH23 2PQ ☎ 01202 483597 Signposted
Nearby town: Bournemouth
▶ ▶ ▶ Family Park ★ 🏕 £8.50-£16 🏕 £8.50-£16
Open Mar-Oct Booking advisable peak periods Last
arrival 21.00hrs Last departure noon ✿
A well-maintained site in rural surroundings on the
banks of the River Stour, 1.5m from Christchurch and
3m from Bournemouth. From Christchurch travel W on
A35, then turn right just before ford bridge. Follow
signs. From Bournemouth, take A35 W towards Iford,
cross rndbt, take 1st left and follow signs. A 2-acre site
with 44 touring pitches and 180 statics.
Fishing on site.

🎮🔌🏕⊙🔲🍴🔦🛒🏔🏠🚿⊞⊤🔥
🏛🛋🐕🐾🔥
➔∪▶☉✚🍴♨🍴

Credit Cards 💳 💳 💳 🔳 🔳

CORFE CASTLE

Woodland Caravan & Camping Park (SY953818)
Glebe Farm, Bucknowle BH20 5NS ☎ 01929 480280
Signposted
Nearby town: Swanage
▶▶ Town & Country Pennant Park ★ 🏕 £8 🏕 £8 🏔 £8
Open Etr-Oct (weather permitting) Last arrival 21.00hrs
Last departure 11.00hrs
A gently sloping grass site set in the Purbeck Hills with
natural landscaping and lovely views. No short stays.
Adjacent to main A351 Swanage road. From Corfe
going N towards Wareham, take 1st left past castle, and
site on right in 1.5 miles. A 7-acre site with 65 touring
pitches.

🏕⊙🍴✳🏔🔦🍴🔲⊞🛋
➔∪▶🍴

DORCHESTER

See **Cerne Abbas**

HOLTON HEATH

Sandford Holiday Park (SY939916)
BH16 6JZ ☎ 01202 631600
Signposted
Nearby town: Wareham

◯◯◯◯◯◯◯◯◯◯

▶ ▶ ▶ ▶ De-Luxe Park 🏕 🏕 🏔
Open May-Oct (rs Nov-Apr) Booking advisable Jul-Aug
& bank hols Last arrival 22.00hrs Last departure
11.00hrs ✿
Good family site for those wanting entertainment, set in
wooded meadowland with direct access to A351 Poole-
Wareham road. From Wareham East on A351 turn left
after 2m at traffic lights, and site on left. A 60-acre site
with 481 touring pitches and 268 statics.
Hairdressers, entertainment, dancing, crazy golf.
See advertisement under POOLE

🎮🔌🏕⊙🔲🍴🔦🔍🔲☀🍴🏔🍴🔥⊞⊤✳
🛋🏛🏠🐕🐾🔥
➔∪▶☉✚♨🍴

Credit Cards 💳 💳 💳 🔳 🔳

◯◯◯◯◯◯◯◯◯◯

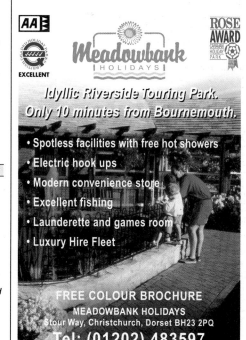

HORTON

Meadow View Touring Caravan Park (SU045070)
Wigbeth BH21 7JH ☎ 01258 840536
Nearby town: Ringwood
▶ ▶ ▶ Family Park ★ 🚐 £6 🚐 £6 ▲ £5.15
Open all year Booking advisable Last departure
11.00hrs
*A small, comfortable site in a secluded rural setting,
with level and gently sloping pitches. Follow unclass rd
from Horton, and site .5m from Druscilla pub. A 1.5-acre
site with 15 touring pitches.*
Coarse fishing.

🔌📻☉🖵🔍✳️⚠️⬆️❄️💂🚌

➔ ∪ ▶

LYME REGIS

See **Hawkchurch & Charmouth**

LYTCHETT MINSTER

South Lytchett Manor Caravan Park (SY954926)
BH16 6JB ☎ 01202 622577 (.5m E) Signposted
Nearby town: Poole
▶ ▶ ▶ Family Park ★ 🚐 £7.40-£9 🚐 £7.40-£9 ▲ £7.40-£9
Open 4 Apr-11 Oct Booking advisable bank hols & mid
Jul-Aug Last arrival 22.00hrs Last departure 11.00hrs
*A small, well-maintained site with mature trees set in
meadowland. On B3067, off A35, 1m E of Lytchett
Minster. An 11-acre site with 50 touring pitches.*
Four washing up sinks.

🔌📻☉🖵🔍🔲✳️⚠️⬆️❄️⬛️Ⓣ📞⛅♿

➔ ∪ ▶ 🏕️ 🔧

Credit Cards ●● 💳 💳 💳

See advertisement on page 130.

MORETON

Camping & Caravanning Club Site (SY782892)
Station Rd DT2 8BB ☎ 01305 853801 & 01203 694995
Signposted
▶ ▶ ▶ Family Park ★ 🚐 £11-£14 🚐 £11-£14 ▲ £11-£14
Open 16 Mar-Nov Booking advisable bank hols & peak
periods Last arrival 21.00hrs Last departure noon
*Modern purpose-built site on level ground with good
amenities. Located on B3390 Bere Regis to Weymouth
road. A 7-acre site with 130 touring pitches.*

📻☉🖵🔍✳️⚠️⬆️❄️⬛️Ⓣ📞🐕⛅♿

➔ ∪ 🔧

Credit Cards ●● 💳 💳 💳

ORGANFORD

Pear Tree Touring Park (SY938915)
BH16 6LA ☎ 01202 622434 Signposted
Nearby town: Poole

▶ ▶ ▶ ▶ De-Luxe Park ★ 🚐 £6.50-£9 🚐 £6.50-£9
▲ £6.50-£9
Open Etr & Apr-Oct Booking advisable Etr, Spring bank
hol & end Jul-Aug Last arrival 21.00hrs Last departure
11.00hrs

*An attractive park on fairly level grass. 6m W of Poole
off A351 at Holton Heath. A 7.5-acre site with 125
touring pitches.*
See advertisement under POOLE

🔌📻☉🖵🔍✳️⚠️⚠️⬆️❄️⬛️Ⓣ📞⛅🏠🐕♿
➔ ∪ ▶ ⬆️❄️🏕️🔧

Credit Cards ●● 💳 💳 💳

Organford Manor (SY943926)

BH16 6ES ☎ 01202 622202 & 623278 Signposted
Nearby town: Poole
▶ ▶ Town & Country Pennant Park ★ 🚐 £7-£8.50
🚐 £6-£7.50 ▲ £7-£8.50
Open 15 Mar-Oct Booking advisable peak periods Last
arrival 22.00hrs Last departure noon

*A quiet, secluded site in the grounds of the manor
house, with level grassy areas with trees and shrubs.
Take the first turning on left off A35 after the Lytchett
roundabout at the junction of A35/A351, site entrance is
a short distance on the right. An 8-acre site with 75
touring pitches and 45 statics.*

🔌📻☉🖵🔍✳️⚠️⬆️❄️⬛️📞⛅
➔ ∪ ▶

OWERMOIGNE

Sandyholme Caravan Park (SY768863)
Moreton Rd DT2 8HZ ☎ 01305 852677 Signposted
Nearby town: Dorchester
▶ ▶ ▶ Family Park ★ 🚐 £5.75-£11 🚐 £5.75-£11
▲ £5.75-£11
Open Etr-Oct Booking advisable peak periods Last
arrival 21.30hrs Last departure noon
*Level, grass site with trees and bushes set in woodland
near the coast at Lulworth Cove, about a mile outside
the village of Owermoigne. A 5-acre site with 60 touring
pitches and 45 statics.*
Restaurant/takeaway in peak season.

🔌📻☉🖵🔍🍷✳️🍴⚠️⬆️❄️⬛️Ⓣ✖️📞🍺⛅
➔ 🔧

Credit Cards ●● 💳 💳 💳

Remember that many parks in this guide may refuse
to take bookings from groups of young people or
groups of people of the same sex. Always check
before you go.

POOLE

Beacon Hill Touring Park (SY977945)
Blandford Rd North BH16 6AB ☎ 01202 631631 (off
A350, NW of junc A35) Signposted

► ► ► ► De-Luxe Park ★ ⊞ £7.40-£15 ⊞ £6.60-£15
Å £6.60-£15
Open Etr-Sep (rs low & mid season bar/take-
away/coffee shop, swimming pool) Booking advisable
Etr, Whit & Jul-Aug Last arrival 23.00hrs Last departure
11.00hrs
*Set in attractive, wooded area with conservation very
much in mind. Two large ponds are within the grounds
and the terraced pitches offer some fine views. From
Upton Cross rndbt take bridge over A35 towards
Blandford on A350. Site on right in 250yds. A 30-acre
site with 170 touring pitches.*
Fishing & view point.

🏕🛱☉🗑🍴 ⚡♻♨⚫⬜☀🍽⛰🛈🗑🎯🗑🆃✗
🔌🛁🐴🛒♿
➔∪🏳⬖↯⚫🍴♪

See advertisement on page 129.

Rockley Park (SY982909)
Hamworthy BH15 4LZ ☎ 01202 679393 Signposted
► ► ► Family Park ★ ⊞ £5-£16 ⊞ £9-£21 Å £5-£15
Open Mar-Oct Booking advisable Jul_Aug & bank hols
Last arrival 20.00hrs Last departure noon

POOLE DORSET

SOUTH LYTCHETT MANOR
CARAVAN PARK ► ► ►

Camping & Touring Caravan Park
LYTCHETT MINSTER ▪ POOLE
DORSET ▪ BH16 6JB
TELEPHONE: (01202) 622577

Popular rural site situated in lovely parkland
surroundings, just west of Poole. Ideal base
for sandy beaches, sailing and windsurfing
and for touring the Purbeck area, Poole,
Bournemouth etc, Well stocked shop,
modern washing facilities, free hot showers,
facilities for people with disabilities. Useful
overnight stop for the cross channel ferries.

FREE BROCHURE
ON REQUEST

Southern
Tourist Board

*A touring park within a static site, with all the
advantages of a holiday centre. Take A31 off M27 to
Poole centre, then follow signs to park. A 4.25-acre site
with 98 touring pitches and 1077 statics.*

🏕🛱☉🗑🍴⚡ ⚡♻⚫☀🍽⛰✗🔌
🔌🐴🛒♿
➔🏳☉⬖↯⚫🍴♪

Credit Cards 💳 💳 💳 💳 🔲

See advertisement on page 129.

ST LEONARDS

Camping International Holiday Park (SU104024)
Athol Lodge, 229 Ringwood Rd BH24 2SD ☎ 01202
872817 & 872742 (on A31) Signposted
Nearby town: Ringwood

► ► ► ► De-Luxe Park ★ ⊞ £7.70-£11.30
⊞ £7.70-£11.30 Å £7.70-£11.30
Open Mar-Oct (rs Mar-May & Sep-Oct (ex bank hols)
restaurant/take-away food not available) Booking
advisable school & bank hols Last arrival 22.30hrs Last
departure 10.30hrs

*Small, well-equipped, level camping site surrounded by
trees adjacent to A31. Travel W on A31 from Ringwood
through underpass to 2nd rndbt, turn left, and site on
left. An 8-acre site with 200 touring pitches.*
Football/basketball park.

🏕🛱☉🗑🍴⚡⚫⬜☀🍽⛰🛈🗑🆃✗🔌
🔪🔌🏛🐴🛒
➔∪🏳♪

Credit Cards 💳 💳 💳 💳 🔲

Oakdene Forest Park (SZ095023)
BH24 2RZ ☎ 01590 642513 & 01202 875422 (3m W of
Ringwood off A31) Signposted
Nearby town: Ringwood
► ► ► Family Park ★ ⊞ £4.50-£18 ⊞ £4.50-£18
Å £4.50-£18
Open Mar-5 Jan Booking advisable all times Last arrival
22.00hrs Last departure 10.00hrs
*An open site surrounded by forest, with good on-site
facilities. Travel W on A31(T) from Ringwood, and site
entrance next to hospital entrance, and signed. A 55-
acre site with 200 touring pitches and 207 statics.*

contd. on p132

Woodland walks, riding, mini bowling/crazy golf.

🔌 📻 ☉ 🗄 ⚓ ⚡ ◀ ✳ 🛱 🅿 ⚠ ⛽ 🚿 ◫ T ✕ ⚫ 🖤 🐎 🐕
➔ ∪ ♪

Credit Cards 💳 🏧 💳 💳 📶 🔛

Shamba Holiday Park (SU105029)
230 Ringwood Rd BH24 2SB ☎ 01202 873302
Signposted
Nearby town: Ringwood
▶ ▶ ▶ **Family Park ★ 🚐** £8-£11 **🚎** £8-£11 **Å** £8-£11
Open Mar-Oct Booking advisable bank hols & Jul-Aug
Last arrival 23.30hrs Last departure 11.00hrs
*Level grassy site in hilly wooded country. 3m W of
Ringwood off A31. A 7-acre site with 150 touring
pitches.*

🔌 📻 ☉ 🗄 ⚓ ⚡ ◀ ✳ 🛱 ⚠ 🚿 ◫ T ✕ ⚫
⚫ 🖤
➔ ∪ 🅿 ⛽ ♪

SWANAGE

Ulwell Cottage Caravan Park (SZ019809)
Ulwell Cottage, Ulwell BH19 3DG ☎ 01929 422823
Signposted
▶ ▶ ▶ **Family Park ★ 🚐** £10-£18 **🚎** £10-£18
Å £10-£18
Open Mar-7 Jan (rs Mar-spring bank hol & mid Sep-
early Jan takeaway closed, shop open variable hours)
Booking advisable bank hols & Jul-Aug Last arrival
23.00hrs Last departure 11.00hrs

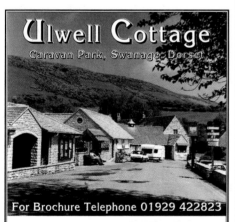

*Nestling under the Purbeck Hills surrounded by scenic
walks and only 2m away from the beach. A 13-acre site
with 77 touring pitches and 140 statics.*

🔌 📻 ☉ 🗄 ⚓ ✳ 🛱 🅿 ⚠ 🚿 ◫ ✕ ⚫ ⚫ 🛱 ⚫ ⚫
➔ ∪ 🅿 ☺ △ ⚡ 🎦 ♪

Credit Cards 💳 🏧 💳 💳 🔛

THREE LEGGED CROSS

Woolsbridge Manor Farm Caravan Park (SZ103050)
Three Legged Cross BH21 6RA ☎ 01202 826369 (2m off
A31,3m W of Ringwood)
Nearby town: Ringwood
▶ ▶ ▶ **Family Park 🚐** £7-£9 **🚎** £7-£9 **Å** £7-£9
Open Etr-Oct Booking advisable bank hols & Aug Last
arrival 22.00hrs Last departure 13.00hrs
*A flat quiet site with a very low density and clean, well-
maintained toilets. Situated 2m off A31, 3m W of
Ringwood. From Three Legged Cross continue S to
Woolsbridge, and site on left in 1.75m. A 6.75-acre site
with 60 touring pitches.*
See advertisement under RINGWOOD

🔌 📻 ☉ 🗄 ✳ ⚠ ⚠ 🚿 ◫ T ⚫ 🛱 🐎 ⚫ ⚫
➔ ∪ 🅿 ♪ 🗄

VERWOOD

Camping & Caravanning Club Site (SU069098)
Sutton Hill, Woodlands BH21 6LF ☎ 01202 822763 &
01203 694995 Signposted
▶ ▶ ▶ **Family Park ★ 🚐** £11-£14 **🚎** £11-£14 **Å** £11-£14
Open end Mar-early Nov Booking advisable Jul-Aug &
bank hols Last arrival 21.00hrs Last departure noon
*A popular site with pleasant wardens and staff. 7m
from Ringwood on B3081, 1.5m past Verwood on R.
Please see the advertisement on page 27 for details of
Club Members' benefits. A 12.75-acre site with 150
touring pitches.*
Recreation room, pool table, table tennis.

🔌 📻 ☉ 🗄 ⚓ ◀ ✳ ⚠ ⚠ 🚿 ⚫ 🐎 🐕 ⚫
➔ ∪ 🅿 ♪ ⚫

Credit Cards 💳 💳 💳 🔛

WAREHAM

Birchwood Tourist Park (SY917883)
Bere Rd, North Trigon BH20 7PA ☎ 01929 554763
Signposted
Nearby town: Poole
▶ ▶ ▶ **Family Park ★ 🚐** £6.50 **🚎** £6.50 **Å** £6.50
Open Mar-Oct Booking advisable bank hols & Jul-Aug
Last arrival 22.00hrs Last departure noon
*A well-maintained site which is maturing into a very
attractive park. Situated 3m N of Wareham on road
linking A351 at Wareham and Bere Regis. A 25-acre site
with 175 touring pitches.*
Riding stables, bike hire, pitch & putt, table tennis

🔌 📻 ☉ 🗄 ⚓ ⚡ ◀ ✳ ⚠ ⚠ 🚿 ◫ T ✕ ⚫ 🛱
🐎 ⚫ ⚫
➔ ∪ 🅿 ⚡ 🎦 ♪

Credit Cards 💳 🏧 💳 💳 🔛

Birchwood Tourist Park
North Trigon, Wareham,
Dorset BH20 7PA

Telephone 01929 554763

Family-run park, ideally situated
for exploring Dorset.
Well-stocked Shop, Off-Licence,
Take-Away, Free Hot Showers,
Children's Paddling Pool, Bike Hire,
Pony Riding, Fully Serviced Pitches,
Pitch and Putt, Large games field.

We accept VISA, DELTA
and MASTERCARD

Lookout Holiday Park (SY927858)
Stoborough BH20 5AZ ☎ 01929 552546 (on B3075 1m
S) Signposted
►►► Family Park ⛺ £9-£12 ⛺ £9-£12 ▲ £9-£12
Open Apr-Oct Booking advisable bank hols & Jul-Aug
Last arrival 22.00hrs Last departure noon ⊘

*Ideal family touring site on main road to Swanage 2m
from Wareham. The touring pitches are set well back
from the road. Turn right at exit for Wareham, and site
in 1.5 miles. 150 touring pitches and 90 statics.
9 hole crazy golf.*

🔊 📻 ⊙ 🗑 🔨 🔌 ✳ ⚠ 🔋 ⊘ ⊞ Ⓣ ⚓ 🧹 🏪
➔ ∪ ▶ ⤵ ☎ ✈

Credit Cards 💳 🔲 🔲 🔲 🔲

Manor Farm Caravan Park (SY872866)
1 Manor Farm Cottage, East Stoke BH20 6AW
☎ 01929 462870
►►► Family Park ⛺ ⛺ ▲
Open Etr-Sep Booking advisable school hols Last arrival
22.00hrs Last departure 11.00hrs
*An attractive, mainly touring site in a quiet rural setting.
From Wareham follow Dorchester road (A352) for 2m
then turn left onto B3070, at first crossroads turn right,
then next crossroads turn right; site is on the left. From
Wool take B3071 and follow Bindon Lane unclass, in
1.75m turn left. A 2.5-acre site with 40 touring pitches.*

🔊 📻 ⊙ 🗑 🔨 ✳ ⚠ 🔋 ⊘ ⊞ ⚓ 🏪 🧹 🏪 🛒
➔ ∪ ▶ ☎ ✈ 🗑

Warmwell Country Touring Park (SY764878)
DT2 8JD ☎ 01305 852313 Signposted
Nearby town: Dorchester

►►►► De-Luxe Park ★ ⛺ £3.30-£6.60 ⛺ £3.30-£6.60
▲ £3.30-£6.60
Open mid Mar-Jan Booking advisable Etr-Sep & Xmas
Last arrival dusk Last departure 11.00hrs
*A landscaped terraced site 5m from the Lulworth
beaches. Take B3390 1m N of Warmwell. A 15-acre site
with 190 touring pitches.*

🔊 📻 ⊙ 🗑 🔨 🔌 ✳ ⚑ ⚠ 🔋 ⊘ ⊞ Ⓣ 🛒 🧹 🏪 🛒
➔ ∪ ▶ ⊙ 🔺 ⤵ ✈

Credit Cards 💳 🔲 🔲 🔲 🔲

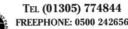

WEYMOUTH

Pebble Bank Caravan Park (SY659775)
Camp Rd, Wyke Regis DT4 9HF
☎ 01305 774844
► ► ► Family Park 🚐 🚐 Å
Open Etr- mid Oct bar open high season & wknds only Booking advisable peak times Last arrival 21.00hrs Last departure 11.00hrs
A sloping, mainly static site overlooking Lyme Bay and Chesil Beach. From Weymouth take Portland Rd, and at last rndbt turn right then 1st left to Army Tent Camp. Site opposite. A 4-acre site with 40 touring pitches and 80 statics.

🔲🖍⊙▣🆀✳️🍴🔔🅰️🗑️⊞📞🎱
➔∪🍴◎🔺🔆🎱♨️🎣

See advertisement on page 133.

WIMBORNE MINSTER

Merley Court Touring Park (SZ008984)
Merley BH21 3AA ☎ 01202 881488 (1m S A349) Signposted
Nearby town: Wimborne

◯◯◯◯◯◯◯

► ► ► ► ► Premier Park ★ 🚐 £6-£11.50 🚐 £6-£11.50 Å £6-£11.50
Open Mar-7 Jan (rs low season pool closed & bar/shop open limited hrs) Booking advisable bank hols & Jun-Sep Last arrival 22.00hrs Last departure 11.00hrs
A superb site in a quiet, rural position on the edge of Wimborne, with woodland on two sides and good access roads. Winner of the South of England Campsite of the Year Award 1998/9. From Wimborne take B3073 to rndbt, turn left to next rndbt with A31, turn right, and site signed. A 20-acre site with 160 touring pitches.
Badminton, mini football, table tennis, crazy golf.

🔲🚽🖍⊙▣🆀🔆🅿️🔍🔔✳️🍴🔔🅰️🗑️⊞⊞🅣✖️
📞🖨️🎋🐕🐾🦽♿
➔∪🍴◎🔆🎱♨️🎣

Credit Cards 💳 🈹 🈳 📇 📇

◯◯◯◯◯◯◯

Wilksworth Farm Caravan Park (SU004018)
Cranborne Rd BH21 4HW ☎ 01202 885467 Signposted
Nearby town: Wimborne

◯◯◯◯◯◯◯

► ► ► ► De-Luxe Park 🚐 🚐 Å
Open Mar-30 Oct (rs Mar no shop/coffee shop) Booking advisable Spring bank hol & Jul-Aug Last arrival 21.30hrs Last departure 11.00hrs
This popular and attractive site lies in the heart of Dorset, 1m N of the town on the B3078. It is well-maintained with good facilities. An 11-acre site with 85 touring pitches and 77 statics.
Paddling pool, volley ball, mini football pitch.

🔲🖍⊙▣🆀🔆🔍🔔✳️🅰️🔔🅰️🗑️⊞🅣✖️📞🖨️
🎋🐕🐾♿
➔∪🍴◎♨️🎣

◯◯◯◯◯◯◯

Charris Camping & Caravan Park (SY991988)
Candy's Ln, Corfe Mullen BH21 3EF
☎ 01202 885970 (2m W off A31) Signposted
Nearby town: Poole
►►► Family Park ★ ⊞ £6-£7 ⊞ £6-£7 ▲ £5-£6
Open Mar-Oct Booking advisable bank hols & Jul-Aug
Last arrival 21.00hrs Last departure 11.00hrs
A neat, clean, simple site enjoying a rural situation, with views of surrounding countryside. From Wimborne turn S on B3073 to rndbt, turn right onto A31, and site on left. A 3-acre site with 45 touring pitches.

🏳️ 🕯️ ⊙ ⛏️ ✳️ 🔲 🗓️ 📵 ⚡
➜ ∪ ► ᴊ ▣

Springfield Touring Park (SY987989)
Candys Ln, Corfe Mullen BH21 3EF ☎ 01202 881719
Signposted
Nearby town: Wimborne
►►► Family Park ★ ⊞ £7-£8 ⊞ £7-£8 ▲ £6-£8
Open mid Mar-Oct Booking advisable bank hols & Jul-Aug Last arrival 22.00hrs Last departure 11.00hrs
A small touring site with good facilities and hardworking owners. A quiet site overlooking the Stour Valley. Turn left off A31 at rndbt at W end of Wimborne bypass signed Corfe Mullen. Within .25m turn right into Candys Lane, and entrance 300yds past farm. A 3.5-acre site with 45 touring pitches.

🏳️ 🕯️ ⊙ ⛏️ ✳️ 🔲 🗓️ 📵 ⚡ ♿
➜ ∪ ► ᴊ

WOOL

Whitemead Caravan Park (SY841869)
East Burton Rd BH20 6HG ☎ 01929 462241 Signposted
Nearby town: Wareham
►►► Family Park ★ ⊞ £5.50-£9 ⊞ £5.50-£9
▲ £5.50-£9
Open mid Mar-Oct Booking advisable public hols & mid Jul-Aug Last arrival 22.00hrs Last departure noon

Well laid-out level site in valley of River Frome, 300yds W off A352. A 5-acre site with 95 touring pitches.

🏳️ 🕯️ ⊙ 🔲 ⛏️ ✳️ 🔲 🗓️ ⊤ 📵 ⚡
➜ ∪ ►

Summer weather can mean rain. It is a good idea to prepare for ground to be wet underfoot. Take something to amuse the children if they can't go outside

CO DURHAM

For the map of this county see NORTHUMBERLAND

BARNARD CASTLE

Camping & Caravanning Club Site (NZ025168)
Dockenflatts Ln, Lartington DL12 9DG
☎ 01833 630228 & 01203 694995
Signposted

〇〇〇〇〇〇〇〇
►►►► De-Luxe Park ★ ⊞ £11-£14 ⊞ £11-£14
▲ £11-£14
Open end Mar-beg Nov Booking advisable Jan-Mar Last arrival 21.00hrs Last departure noon
A peaceful site surrounded by mature woodland and meadowland, with first class facilities. Leave A66 by B6277 if approaching from S to avoid Barnard Castle. Park off B6277, 1.5m from junc with A67. A 10-acre site with 90 touring pitches.

🏳️ 🕯️ ⊙ 🔲 ⛏️ 🔲 📵 ⚡ ♿
➜ ∪ ⚠️ ⚡
Credit Cards 💳 ▭ ▭ ▭ ⑤

〇〇〇〇〇〇〇

BEAMISH

Bobby Shafto Caravan Park (NZ232545)
Cranberry Plantation DH9 0RY ☎ 0191 370 1776
Signposted
►►► Family Park ★ ⊞ £9-£10 ⊞ £9-£10 ▲ £9-£10
Open Mar-Oct Booking advisable school hols Last arrival 11.00hrs Last departure 11.00hrs
A tranquil rural site surrounded by mature trees, with well-organised facilities. Leave A1(M) at junc 63, follow A693 signed Beamish, and after 2 rndbts turn right in 1.25m. Turn immed left, then right onto unclass rd. After .75m take left fork, and after .75m turn left. Site in 500 metres on left. A 9-acre site with 20 touring pitches and 35 statics.

🏳️ 🕯️ ⊙ 🔲 ✴️ 🔲 ✳️ ♀ 📵 🗓️ ⊤ ⚡
➜ ∪ ► 🍴 📵 ᴊ ▣
Credit Cards 💳 ▭

CASTLESIDE

Allensford Caravan & Camping Park (NZ083505)
DH8 9BA ☎ 01207 591043 Signposted
►►► Family Park ⊞ ⊞ ▲
Open Mar-Oct Booking advisable Whit wknd Last arrival 22.00hrs Last departure noon
Level parkland with mature trees, in hilly moor and woodland country near the urban area adjacent to River Derwent and A68. Situated approx 2m SW of Consett, N on A68 for 1 mile then right at Allensford Bridge. A 2-acre site with 40 touring pitches and 46 statics. Tourist information centre.

🏳️ 🕯️ ⊙ 🔲 ⛏️ ✳️ 🔲 📵 ⊤ ⚡
➜ ∪ ► 🍴 ᴊ

WINSTON

Winston Caravan Park (NZ139168)
The Old Forge DL2 3RH ☎ 01325 730228
► ► ► Family Park ★ ⊕ £7.50-£9 ⊕ £7-£9
▲ £7-£9
Open Mar-Oct Booking advisable bank hols
Attractive tree-lined park with level sheltered pitches,
ideally located for exploring surrounding countryside.
Leave A67 Darlington/Barnard Castle rd into village
centre, and park signed here. A 2.5-acre site with 20
touring pitches and 11 statics.

🔒 🏕 🗂 ⛄ ✳ 🎁 ⊘ 🎫 🎏
→ ⛎ ⤵ 🦺

WYCLIFFE (NEAR BARNARD CASTLE)

Thorpe Hall (NZ105141)
DL12 9TW ☎ 01833 627230 (off unclass between
Wycliffe & Greta Bridge) Signposted
Nearby town: Barnard Castle
► ► ► Family Park ★ ⊕ £7.50 ⊕ £7.50
Open Mar-Oct Booking advisable bank hols & Jul-Aug
Last arrival 22.30hrs Last departure 13.00hrs
A very pleasant site with good facilities in the grounds
of a large country house. Lies S of River Tees and 5m
from Barnard Castle. From A66 1m SE of Greta Bridge
take unclassified road (signed Wycliffe). A 2-acre site
with 12 touring pitches and 16 statics.

🔒 🏕 ☺ 🗂 ✳ 🎁 🎫 🦺 🐾
→ ⤵ 🦺

ESSEX

BRENTWOOD

Camping & Caravanning Club Site (TQ577976)
Warren Ln, Frog St, Kelvedon Hatch CM15 0JG
☎ 01277 372773 Signposted
► ► ► Family Park ★ ⊕ £10-£13 ⊕ £10-£13 ▲ £10-£13
Open end Mar-early Oct Booking advisable bank hols &
Jul-Aug Last arrival 21.00hrs Last departure noon
A very pretty rural site with many separate areas
amongst the trees, and a secluded field for campers.
Head N on A128 out of Brentwood, and turn right at
Kelvedon Hatch. Signed. A 12-acre site with 90 touring
pitches.

🔒 🏕 ☺ 🗂 ✳ ⛄ 🎁 ⊘ 🎫 🦺 🐾 🚻 ⅙
→ ⤵ 🦺

Credit Cards 💳 🏧

CANEWDON

Riverside Village Holiday Park (TQ929951)
Creeksea Ferry Rd, Wallasea Island SS4 2EY
☎ 01702 258297 Signposted
Nearby town: Southend-on-Sea
► ► ► Family Park ⊕ £7-£9 ⊕ £7-£9 ▲ £4-£6
Open Mar-Oct Booking advisable public hols Last arrival
22.00hrs Last departure 17.00hrs

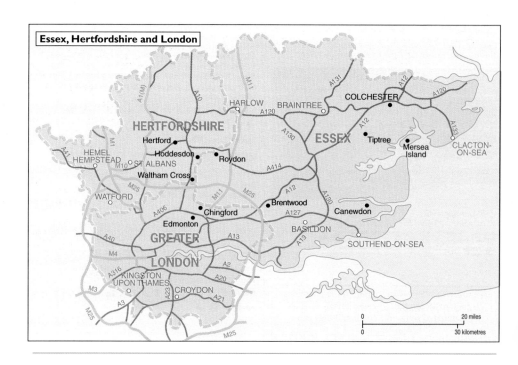

Essex, Hertfordshire and London

A pleasant and popular riverside site, well laid out and very neat. Signed off A127 near Southend. Approach from Rochford, not Canewelon Village. A 24-acre site with 60 touring pitches and 180 statics. Boule pitch.

🔌 📻 ☉ 🗑 ⛏ ☼ ⚲ ⚠ ⓘ ☒ ✕ ⛶ ⌂ 🐕

→ ∪ ▶ ◬ ⟋ ⚡

COLCHESTER

Colchester Camping Caravan Park (TL971252)

Cymbeline Way, Lexden CO3 4AG ☎ 01206 545551
Signposted

◯◯◯◯◯◯◯◯

▶ ▶ ▶ ▶ De-Luxe Park ★ ⚲ £7.50-£11.80
⚲ £7.50-£11.80 ⚶ £7.50-£11.80
Open all year Booking advisable public hols Last arrival 20.00hrs Last departure noon
A well-designed campsite on level grassland, on the west side of Colchester near the town centre. Close to main routes to London (A12) and east coast. A 12-acre site with 251 touring pitches.
Badminton court & putting green on site.

🔌 📻 ☉ 🗑 ⛏ ☼ ⚲ ⚠ ⓘ ⨀ ☒ ⓣ ⛶ ⌂ 🐕 ⚶ ♿

→ ∪ ▶ ◬ ♨ ⟋

Credit Cards

◯◯◯◯◯◯◯◯

MERSEA ISLAND

Waldegraves Holiday Park (TM033133)

West Mersea, Mersea Island CO5 8SE ☎ 01206 382898
Signposted

◯◯◯◯◯◯◯◯

▶ ▶ ▶ ▶ De-Luxe Park ★ ⚲ £8-£12 ⚶ £8-£12 ⚶ £8-£12
Open Mar-Nov Booking advisable bank hols Last arrival 22.00hrs Last departure noon
A spacious and pleasant site, located between farmland and its own private beach on the Blackwater Estuary. Facilities include two fresh water fishing lakes. Signed from Colchester. Follow signs through town to Mersey and military barracks. A 25-acre site with 60 touring pitches and 205 statics.
Boating and fishing on site.

🔌 📻 ☉ 🗑 ⛏ ⚓ ⚀ ☼ ⚲ ⚠ ⓘ ⨀ ☒ ⓣ ✕ ⛶ ⌂ 🐕 ⚶ ♿

→ ∪ ◎ ◬ ⟋ 🗑

Credit Cards

◯◯◯◯◯◯◯◯

ROYDON

Roydon Mill Leisure Park (TL403104)

CM19 5EJ ☎ 01279 792777 Signposted
▶ ▶ ▶ Family Park ⚲ £10-£11.20 ⚶ £10-£11.20
⚶ £10-£11.20
Open all year Booking advisable bank hols Last arrival 22.00hrs Last departure 22.00hrs ⚘
A busy complex with caravan sales and water sports. Facilities have recently been upgraded. Signed from A414 between A10 and Harlow. An 11-acre site with 120 touring pitches and 149 statics.

Large lake, clay pigeon shooting, waterski school.

🔌 📻 ☉ 🗑 ⚓ ☼ ⚲ ⚠ ⓘ ⨀ ☒ ⓣ ✕ ⛶ ⌂ 🌲 ⌂ ⚡

→ ∪ ▶ ◬ ♨ ♿ ⟋

Credit Cards

SOUTHMINSTER

Beacon Hill Leisure Park (TL959055)

St Lawrence Bay CM0 7LP ☎ 01621 779248
▶ ▶ ▶ Family Park ★ ⚲ £6.50-£10.50 ⚶ £6.50-£10.50
⚶ £5.50-£10.50
Open mid Mar-Oct Booking advisable
Small well-kept touring section of a large leisure park, on the banks of the River Blackwater, and offering swimming pool and clubhouse facilities. Signed off B1010 at Letchingdon, between Maldon and Bradwell-on-Sea. A 45-acre site with 130 touring pitches and 330 statics.
Boating lake, jacuzzi, childrens pool, sports field.

🔌 📻 ☉ 🗑 ⚀ ⚓ 🏳 ☼ ⚲ ⚠ ⓘ ⨀ ✕ ⛶ ⚡

→ ◬ ♨ ⟋

TIPTREE

Villa Farm (TL881155)

West End Rd CO5 0QN ☎ 01621 815217
Nearby town: Colchester
▶ Town & Country Pennant Park ⚲ ⚶ ⚶ ⚶
Open Apr-Sep Booking advisable mid Jun-mid Jul Last arrival 23.00hrs Last departure anytime
Grassland site on fruit farm, quiet except mid-June to mid-July (which is picking season (when booking is advisable). From Tiptree follow B1022, at pub fork right into West End Road. A 7-acre site with 5 touring pitches.

→ ∪ ▶ ⟋ ⚡

GLOUCESTERSHIRE

For the map of this county
see WILTSHIRE

CHELTENHAM

Briarfields (SO899215)

Gloucester Rd GL51 0SX ☎ 01242 235324 & 274440
Signposted

◯◯◯◯◯◯◯◯

▶ ▶ ▶ ▶ De-Luxe Park ⚲ £6.90 ⚶ £6.90 ⚶ £6.50
Open all year Booking advisable Last arrival mdnt Last departure 14.00hrs
A well-designed, comfortable site, well-positioned between Cheltenham and Gloucester. From Cheltenham take A40 to Golden Valley rndbt, then 3rd turning left and site well signed. A 6-acre site with 87 touring pitches.

🔌 📻 ☉ 🗑 ⛏ ☼ ⚠ ⓘ ⨀ ⛶ ⌂ 🐕

→ ∪ ▶ ◬ ♨ ♨ ⟋ ⚡

Credit Cards

◯◯◯◯◯◯◯◯

Longwillows Caravan & Camping Park (SO967278)
Station Rd, Woodmancote GL52 4HN ☎ 01242 674113
(3.5m N) Signposted
► ► ► Family Park ⊞ ⊞ Å
Open Mar-Oct Booking advisable bank hols & Jul-Aug
Last arrival 23.00hrs Last departure 18.00hrs
*Mostly level site with good quality, clean toilet facilities
in a remote situation. From Cheltenham take A438 to
Bishop Cleave, turn right for Woodmancote and follow
signs. A 4-acre site with 80 touring pitches.*
Separate games area.

⚐ ⏧ ⊙ ⊟ ⛏ ✻ ⵍ ⚠ ₤ ⌀ ⊡ ✕ ⛾ ⮲ ⛗ ⚲
→ ∪ ▶ ⼂ ♨ ⚏

CHRISTCHURCH

Bracelands Caravan & Camping Site (SO575129)
Bracelands GL16 7NN ☎ 01594 833376
Nearby town: Coleford
►► Town & Country Pennant Park ★ ⊞ £5.40-£9.40
⊞ £5.40-£9.40 Å £5.40-£9.40
Open Mar-Oct Booking advisable bank hols & peak
season Last arrival 22.00hrs Last departure noon
*A peaceful Forestry Commission park in lovely forest
surroundings. Approach from A4136 junc with unclass
rd at the Pike House Inn, Berry Hill, 1m N of Coleford.
Travel along Grove Rd for 0.5m, and turn left into
Braceland Drive. A 30-acre site with 520 touring pitches.*

⚐ ⏧ ⊟ ⚲ ⚠ ₤ ⌀ ⊡ ⊤ ⛾ ⛗ ⼂
→ ∪ ♨

Credit Cards ⊞ ▧ ▦ ▨ ⑤

FOREST OF DEAN

Come to the heart of Britain's
wonderful woodlands. Touring
caravan and camping sites in forests
throughout the UK. Three sites in the
Forest of Dean, including
Christchurch.

Bookings
01594 833 376

Forestry Commission

Brochure Hotline
0131 334 0066
Quote ref AA1

CIRENCESTER

Mayfield Touring Park (SP020055)
Cheltenham Rd, Perrott's Brook GL7 7BH
☎ 01285 831301 (2m N on A435) Signposted
► ► ► Family Park ★ ⊞ £6.80-£9.40 ⊞ £5.80-£9.40
Å £5.40-£9.40
Open all year Booking advisable public hols & Jun-Aug
Last arrival 22.30hrs Last departure noon
*Part-level, part-sloping grass site, in hilly meadowland
in the Cotswolds, an area of outstanding natural beauty.
Situated off A435, 2m from Cirencester. A 4-acre site
with 72 touring pitches.*
Dishwashing area.

⚐ ⏧ ⊙ ⊟ ⚲ ✻ ₤ ⌀ ⊡ ⊤ ⛾ ⛗ ⼂ ⚲
→ ▶ ♨

Credit Cards ⊞ ▧ ▦ ▨ ⑤

COLEFORD

Christchurch Caravan & Camping Site (SO575129)
Bracelands Dr GL16 7NN ☎ 01594 833376 (in season)
& 0131 314 6505 (1m N)
Signposted
► ► ► Family Park ★ ⊞ £5.40-£9.40 ⊞ £5.40-£9.40
Å £5.40-£9.40
Open Mar-Dec Booking advisable all times Last arrival
22.00hrs Last departure noon
*A well-appointed site in open forest with good
amenities. A good base for walking. From Coleford
follow signs for Symonds Yat to Berry Hill where
Forestry Commission site is signed. A 20-acre site with
280 touring pitches.*

⚐ ⏧ ⊙ ⊟ ⚘ ✻ ⵍ ⚠ ₤ ⌀ ⊤ ⛾ ⛗ ⼂ ⚲ ⚲
→ ∪ ▶ ♨ ⤫

Credit Cards ⊞ ▧ ▦ ▨ ⑤

GLOUCESTER

Red Lion Camping & Caravan Park (SO849258)
Wainlode Hill, Norton GL2 9LW
☎ 01452 730251
Signposted
► ► ► Family Park ★ ⊞ £7 ⊞ £7 Å £7
Open all year Booking advisable spring bank hol Last
arrival 22.00hrs Last departure 11.00hrs
*An attractive meadowland site opposite River Severn.
Ideal fishing centre and touring base. Turn off A38 at
Norton and follow road to river. A 13-acre site with 60
touring pitches and 20 statics.*
Bar snacks, hot & cold food.

⚐ ⏧ ⊙ ⚲ ✻ ⵍ ⚠ ₤ ⌀ ✕ ⛾ ⛗ ⮲ ⚲
→ ∪ ▶ ⤫

SEVERN BEACH

Salthouse Farm Caravan & Camping Park (ST543854)
BS12 3NH ☎ 01454 632274 & 632699 Signposted
Nearby town: Bristol
► ► ► Family Park ★ ⊞ £7.50-£8.50 ⊞ £7.50-£8.50
Å £7.50-£8.50
Open Apr-Oct Booking advisable public hols Last arrival
22.00hrs Last departure 14.00hrs
*Level, grassy site in meadowland adjacent to Severn
Estuary and beach, and well-protected from winds.
From M5 (London) from junc 17 take B4055 to Pilning.*

At crossrds turn left, cross mini rndbt in 0.25m, and in 0.5m take 1st right (signed). From M4 (London) change to M48 at junc 1, take A403 to Pilning, then as above. A 3-acre site with 40 touring pitches and 50 statics.

SLIMBRIDGE

Tudor Caravan & Camping (SO728040)
Shepherds Patch GL2 7BP ☎ 01453 890483 (from M5 Jct 13/14. Follow signs to Wildfowl Trust Site at rear of Tudor Arms PH 10yds before canal)
Signposted
Nearby town: Dursley

QQQQQQQQQ

▶ ▶ ▶ ▶ De-Luxe Park ☞ £7.50-£7.75 ☞ £7.50-£7.75 ▲ £5.25-£7.75
Open all year Booking advisable bank & school hols Last arrival 21.00hrs Last departure 18.00hrs

Level grass and gravel site with trees and bushes, set in meadow by canal, off A38. Nearby is the Wildlife Trust. Access through pub car park. An 8-acre site with 75 touring pitches.

QQQQQQQQQ

SOUTH CERNEY

Cotswold Hoburne (SU055958)
Broadway Ln GL7 5UQ ☎ 01285 860216
Signposted
Nearby town: Cirencester

❀❀❀❀❀❀❀❀❀❀❀❀❀❀❀❀❀❀

Open Good Fri-Oct Booking advisable public hols & high season Last arrival 21.00hrs Last departure 10.00hrs ✄

contd.

A large holiday centre on flat grassy ground and adjoining the Cotswold Water Park. From Cirencester take A419 for 3m. Turn right at sign, and right again in 1m. Site on left. A 70-acre site with 302 touring pitches and 211 statics.
Crazy golf, fishing & pedal-boat hire.

🔌 🐾 ⊙ 🖅 🔍   🔍 ⚲ ● ☐ ✳ ♀ ⚠ 🛈 ⊘ ✗ 🔧
🚿 🛒 🚻
➜ ∪ �ꕤ 🔺 ⅄ ♨ 🥢 🎵

Credit Cards 💳 ▭ ▭ 🔟

⚙⚙⚙⚙⚙⚙⚙⚙⚙⚙⚙⚙⚙⚙⚙⚙⚙

WINCHCOMBE

Camping & Caravanning Club Site (SP007324)
Brooklands Farm, Alderton GL20 8NX
☎ 01242 620259
▶ ▶ ▶ Family Park ★ ⚑ £11-£14 ⚑ £11-£14 ▲ £11-£14
Open mid Mar-early Nov Booking advisable
A pleasant site on B4077, ideal for touring this historic area between Cheltenham and Tewkesbury. From M5 junc 9 take A46 E to rndbt; road then becomes B4077. Site on right past Hobnails pub on left. A 20-acre site with 68 touring pitches.

🔌 🐾 ⊙ 🖅 🔍 ✳ ⚠ 🛈 ⊘ 🚿
Credit Cards 💳 ▭ ▭ 🔟 🔟

WOTTON-UNDER-EDGE

Canons Court Camp Site (ST742946)
Bradley Green GL12 7PN
☎ 01453 843128 Signposted
▶ Town & Country Pennant Park ★ ⚑ £11.50-£13.50 ⚑ £11.50-£13.50 ▲ £8-£11
Open Mar-Oct Booking advisable bank hols Jul & Aug Last arrival 21.00hrs Last departure noon
Attractive park in a pleasant valley with mature trees and bushes, 1m NW of town. 4m E of exit 14 (M5) by B4509. A 6-acre site with 35 touring pitches.
Bar snacks, golf.

🔌 🐾 ⊙ 🔍 ♀ ✗ 🔧
➜ ∪ ꕤ ♨ 🥢 🖅 🚻

GREATER MANCHESTER

For the map of this county see SHROPSHIRE

LITTLEBOROUGH

Hollingworth Lake Caravan Park (SD943146)
Round House Farm, Rakewood Rd, Rakewood OL15 0AT
☎ 01706 378661 & 373919
▶ ▶ ▶ Family Park ★ ⚑ £8-£10 ⚑ £6-£10 ▲ £4-£10
Open all year Booking advisable bank hols Last arrival 20.00hrs Last departure 14.00hrs
A popular park adjacent to Hollingworth Lake, at the foot of the Pennines, within easy reach of many local attractions. From either Littleborough or Milnrow (M62, junc 21), follow 'Hollingworth Lake Country Park' signs to the Fishermans Inn on the lakeside. Take 'no through

road to Rakewood, and site 2nd on right. A 3-acre site with 50 touring pitches and 13 statics.
Pony Treking.

🔌 🐾 ⊙ 🖅 🛈 ⊘ 🔧 🚻
➜ ꕤ 🥢 🎵

ROCHDALE

Gelder Wood Country Park (SD852127)
Ashworth Rd, Heywood OL11 5UP ☎ 01706 364858 & 620300 Signposted
Nearby town: Heywood
▶ ▶ ▶ Family Park ★ ⚑ £7 ⚑ £7 ▲ £7
Open Mar-Oct Booking advisable Etr Last departure 22.00hrs
A very rural site in a peaceful private country park with excellent facilities. All pitches have extensive views of the moor. Signed off B6222 midway between Bury and Rochdale. A 10-acre site with 34 touring pitches.

🔌 🐾 ⊙ 🛈 ⊘ 🔟 🔧 🐕 🚻
➜ ∪ 🥢 🖅 🚻

HAMPSHIRE

NEW FOREST

The New Forest covers 144 square miles and is composed of broadleaf and coniferous woodland, open commonland and heath. This unique area was originally a royal hunting forest and there are long established rights of access. It is not a 'Forest Park' but similar facilities for visitors are maintained by the Forestry Commission; these include caravan and camp sites, picnic sites, car parks, way-marked walks and an ornamental drive. The camp sites are open from the Friday before Easter until the end of September (two sites remain open in October). Information and camping leaflet available from the Forestry Commission, 231 Corstorphine Road, Edinburgh EH12 7AT. Telephone 0131 334 0066. Information also available from the Tourist Information Centre at Lyndhurst Car Park. Telephone Lyndhurst (01703) 282269. See Ashurst, Bransgore, Brokenhurst, Fritham, Lyndhurst and Sway for AA pennant classified sites.

ASHURST

Ashurst Caravan & Camping Site (SU332099)
Lyndhurst Rd SO4 2AA ☎ 0131 314 6505 (on A35) Signposted
Nearby town: Lyndhurst
▶ ▶ ▶ Family Park ★ ⚑ £6.70-£10.40 ⚑ £6.70-£10.40 ▲ £6.70-£10.40
Open Etr-Sep Booking advisable all times Last arrival 23.30hrs Last departure noon 🐾
Situated just off the A35 Southampton-Bournemouth road, this quiet, secluded Forestry Commission site is set amongst woodlands and heathland on the fringe of the New Forest. See under 'Forestry Commission' for further information. A 23-acre site with 280 touring pitches.

🐾 ⊙ 🔍 ✳ 🔟 🔧 🖅 🚻 🚻
➜ ∪ ꕤ

Credit Cards 💳 ▭ ▭ 🔟 🔟

See advertisement on page 142.

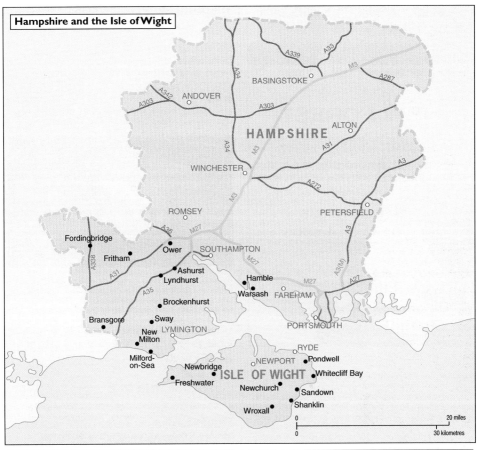

Hampshire and the Isle of Wight

BRANSGORE

Harrow Wood Farm Caravan Park (SZ194978)
Harrow Wood Farm, Poplar Ln BH23 8JE
☎ 01425 672487
Nearby town: Christchurch

► ► ► ► **De-Luxe Park** ★ 🚐 £9-£12.75 🚐 £9-£12.75
Open Mar-6 Jan Booking advisable bank & school hols
Last arrival 22.00hrs Last departure noon 🦌
*A very well laid out site in a pleasant rural position with
adjoining woodland and fields. Leave village from S,
and take last turning on left past shops. Site at top of
lane. A 6-acre site with 60 touring pitches.
Washing up facilities.*

🔌 🌮 ⊙ 🗑 🦞 ✳ 🔋 ⊘ 🖸 📞
➔ ✈ 🎱
Credit Cards 💳 💳 📷 🗾

See advertisement on page 142.

Holmsley Caravan & Camping Site (SZ215991)
Forest Rd, Holmsley BH23 7EQ ☎ 0131 314 6505 (off
A35) Signposted
Nearby town: New Milton
► ► ► **Family Park** ★ 🚐 £6.70-£10.40 🚐 £6.70-£10.40
⚑ £6.70-£10.40
Open Etr-Oct Booking advisable all times Last arrival
23.30hrs Last departure noon
*A large site in rural surroundings on the fringe of the
New Forest. See under Forestry Commission for further
information. From A35 S take Bransgore turn on right,
and right again in 1m. Site signed. An 89-acre site with
700 touring pitches.*

🔌 🌮 ⊙ 🦞 ✳ 🏔 🔋 ⊘ 🖸 📞 🛒 🔥 🎱 ♿
➔ ∪ ▶
Credit Cards 💳 💳 💳 📷 🗾

BROCKENHURST

Hollands Wood Caravan & Camping Site (SU303034)
Lyndhurst Rd SO42 7QH ☎ 0131 314 6505 (off A337)
Signposted
► ► ► **Family Park** ★ 🚐 £7.50-£11.50 🚐 £7.50-£11.50
⚑ £7.50-£11.50   *contd.*

NEW FOREST

Come to the heart of Britain's
wonderful woodlands. Touring
caravan and camping sites in forests
throughout the UK. Ten sites in the
New Forest.

BOOKINGS
0131 314 6505

 Forestry Commission

Brochure Hotline
0131 334 0066
Quote ref AA2

Open Etr-Sep Booking advisable all times Last arrival
23.30hrs Last departure noon
*Large and very popular secluded site, set amongst oak
and woodland, within the New Forest adjoining Balmer
Lawn. Take A337 Lyndhurst rd from Brockenhurst, and
site on right in .5m. See under 'Forestry Commission'
for further information. A 168-acre site with 600 touring
pitches.*

Credit Cards

Roundhill Caravan & Camping Site (SU332021)
Beaulieu Rd SO42 7QL ☎ 0131 314 6505 (off B3055, 2m
E) Signposted
▶▶ Town & Country Pennant Park ★ 🚐 £6-£9.30
🚐 £6-£9.30 ▲ £6-£9.30
Open Etr-Sep Booking advisable all times Last arrival
23.30hrs Last departure noon
*Large secluded Forestry Commission site amongst
gorse and birch within the New Forest, offering a
separate area for motorcyclists and also a lightweight
camping area. Take A3055 from Brockenhurst, and site
on right and signed in 2m. A 156-acre site with 500
touring pitches.*
Separate motorcycle field.

Credit Cards

 Sandy Balls Holiday Centre (SU167148)
Sandy Balls Estate Ltd, Godshill SP6 2JY
☎ 01425 653042 (take B3078 for
Cadnam, 1.25m E) Signposted
Nearby town: Salisbury

Open all year Booking advisable public hols & Jul-Aug
Last arrival 20.00hrs Last departure 11.00hrs

*A mostly wooded New Forest site with open fields, river
walks and fishing. Facilities and amenities constantly
improving. Cross bridge towards Godshill from
Fordingbridge, and site on left in 1m. A 30-acre site with
350 touring pitches and 250 statics.*
Jacuzzi, steam room, sauna, sunbeds, gym, fitness suite

Credit Cards

Longbeech Caravan & Camping Site (SU251119)
SO43 7HH ☎ 0131 314 6505 (take B3079 off A31 at
Cadnam) Signposted
Nearby town: Lyndhurst
▶▶ Town & Country Pennant Park ★ 🚐 £6.50-£8.70
🚐 £6.50-£8.70 ▲ £6.50-£8.70
Open Etr-Sep Booking advisable bank hols Last arrival
23.30hrs Last departure noon
*Large Forestry Commission site set attractively
amongst trees and close to a disused airfield bordering
the New Forest. Own sanitary facilities essential. Turn
off A37 at signs for Ocknell and Longbeach, 4m E of
Ringwood. A 20-acre site with 180 touring pitches.*

Credit Cards

Ocknell Caravan & Camping Site (SU251119)
SO43 7HH ☎ 0131 314 6505 (take B3079 off A31 at
Cadnam, through Brook & Fritham) Signposted
Nearby town: Lyndhurst
▶▶ Town & Country Pennant Park ★ 🚐 £6-£8.70
🚐 £6-£8.70 ▲ £6-£8.70
Open Etr-Sep Booking advisable all time Last arrival
23.30hrs Last departure noon
contd.

An open Forestry Commission site amid trees, shrubs and open heath. Turn off A37 at signs for Ocknell and Longbeach, 4m E of Ringwood. A 28-acre site with 300 touring pitches.

☺ ✳ T 📞 🎣 🗛 🐾 ♿
➔ ∪ ▶ ♪

Credit Cards 💳 ▨ ▦ ▧ 🔄

HAMBLE

Riverside Park (SU481081)
Satchell Ln SO31 4HR ☎ 01703 453220 Signposted
Nearby town: Southampton
▶ ▶ ▶ **Family Park** 🚐 £8-£10 🚐 £8-£10 ▲ £5-£10
Open Mar-Oct (rs Nov-Feb open wknds & bank hols for statics only) Booking advisable bank hols & peak season Last arrival 21.00hrs Last departure 11.00hrs
A slightly sloping, pleasant and peaceful site overlooking the R. Hamble. Located 1m north of Hamble just off the B3397. A 6-acre site with 60 touring pitches and 86 statics.
Bike hire.

🎮 📷 ☺ 🖥 🎿 ✳ 📶 🔔 📞
➔ ∪ ▶ ⛴ ↴ ♪ 🐾

Credit Cards 💳 ▨ ▧ 🔄

LYNDHURST

Denny Wood Caravan & Camping Site (SU334069)
Beaulieu Rd SO43 7FZ ☎ 0131 314 6505 (2m E off B3056) Signposted
▶▶ **Town & Country Pennant Park** ★ 🚐 £5.50-£6.70 🚐 £5.50-£6.70 ▲ £5.50-£6.70

RIVERSIDE
TOURING & HOLIDAY
PARK

ROSE AWARD
Set midway between Portsmouth, New Forest & Winchester Just 2 miles off Junc. 8 M27

⚓ Beautiful views over the marina and River Hamble
⚓ Serviced touring pitches
⚓ Free showers
⚓ Excellent sailing, walking, fishing and horse riding nearby
⚓ Luxurious self catering accommodation
⚓ Launderette
⚓ Lodges available all year including Xmas breaks

Satchell Lane, Hamble, Hants SO31 4HR
Ring now for your free colour brochure
FREEPHONE: 0500 575959

Open Etr-Sep Booking advisable all times Last arrival 23.30hrs Last departure noon ✍
Quiet Forestry Commission site in pleasant surroundings of mixed woodland, grass and gravel surface. Own sanitary facilities essential. From Lyndhurst take B3056, and site on right on bend in 2m. A 20-acre site with 170 touring pitches.

🔔 🎣 📞 💠
➔ ∪ ✦

Credit Cards 💳 ▨ ▦ ▧ 🔄

Matley Wood Caravan & Camping Site (SU332076)
Beaulieu Rd SO43 7FZ ☎ 0131 314 6505 (2m E off B3056) Signposted
▶▶ **Town & Country Pennant Park** ★ 🚐 £5.50-£6.70 🚐 £5.50-£6.70 ▲ £5.50-£6.70
Open Etr-Sep Booking advisable bank hols Last arrival 23.30hrs Last departure noon
A Forestry Commission park made up of clearings in pleasant partially wooded area. Own sanitary facilities essential. From Lyndhurst take B3056, and site on left in 1.5m. An 8-acre site with 70 touring pitches.

💠
➔ ∪

Credit Cards 💳 ▨ ▦ ▧ 🔄

MILFORD ON SEA

Lytton Lawn Touring Park (SZ293937)
Lymore Ln, Everton SO41 0TX ☎ 01590 642513 & 643339 (A337 from Lymington, turn left onto B3058) Signposted
Nearby town: Lymington

◗◗◗◗◗

▶ ▶ ▶ **De-Luxe Park** ★ 🚐 £9-£22 🚐 £9-£22 ▲ £9-£22
Open Mar-5 Jan Booking advisable at all times Last arrival 22.00hrs Last departure 10.00hrs
An ideal family site with refurbished facilities and plans for future improvements. From Lymington take A337 towards Christchurch for 2.5m, turn left on B3058 towards Milford-on-Sea. After .25m turn left into Lymore Lane. A 9.5-acre site with 126 touring pitches.
Dishwashing facilities.

🎮 📷 ☺ 🖥 🎿 ✳ 📶 🔔 🎣 T 📞 🛒 🎣 🗛 🐦 🐾 ♿
➔ ∪ ▶ ☺ 💠 ♪

Credit Cards 💳 ▨ ▦ ▧ 🔄

◗◗◗◗◗

South Coast
& New Forest

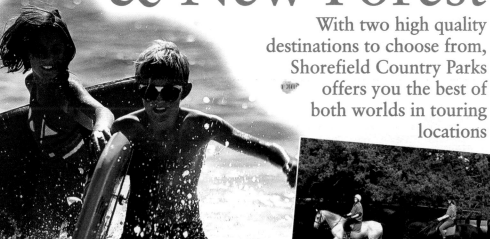

With two high quality destinations to choose from, Shorefield Country Parks offers you the best of both worlds in touring locations

LYTTON LAWN

...et in beautiful natural parkland close to ...ilford beach and the historic New Forest ...ith views to the Isle of Wight. Peaceful, ...nspoilt and relaxing. Electricity hook-up, ...owers, laundrette, shop, 'Premier ...tches' and a children's area. ...ptional Leisure Club facilities ...⁄2 miles away.

OAKDENE
FOREST PARK

Over 55 acres of beautiful parkland giving direct access to the Avon Forest, and only 9 miles from Bournemouth's sandy beaches. Indoor and outdoor pools, riding stables, adventure playground, sauna, solarium, gym, club with entertainment, cafeteria, takeaway, general store and launderette.

SHOREFIELD
COUNTRY PARKS

RALLIES WELCOME AT BOTH SITES

For further details telephone
01590 642513 Ref. AA

Oakdene Forest Park, St. Leonards, Ringwood, Hants BH24 2RZ
Lytton Lawn, Lymore Lane, Milford on Sea, Hants SO41 0TX
e-mail: holidays@shorefield.co.uk   Fax: 01590 645610   http//www.shorefield.co.uk

ENGLAND FOR EXCELLENCE
THE ENGLISH TOURIST BOARD
AWARDS FOR TOURISM

NEW MILTON

Bashley Park (SZ245972)
Sway Rd BH25 5QR ☎ 01425 612340

▶ ▶ ▶ ▶ ▶ Premier Park ★ 🚐 £9-£26.50 🚐 £9-£26.50
Open Mar-Oct Booking advisable

*A large, well-organised site in reasonably flat open fields
with hard gravel standings, bordered by woodland and
shrubbery. 1m N of New Milton on B3055. A 100-acre
site with 420 touring pitches and 380 statics.*

🛠 🐾 🗑 🍴 ⚡ 🎣 ⚲ 🏴 🛡 ⛱ 🍺 🚻 🚿 🐕 🛒
→ ∪ ⊹ ↯ ✈

Credit Cards 💳 ▨ 🏧 🔳

OWER

Green Pastures Farm (SU321158)
SO51 6AJ ☎ 01703 814444 Signposted
Nearby town: Romsey
▶ ▶ ▶ Family Park 🚐 £8 🚐 £8 🛖 £8
Open 15 Mar-Oct Booking advisable bank hols & peak
periods Last departure noon
*Open, level, grassy site in rural surroundings. Situated
on edge of New Forest W of Ower and off A31 between
Romsey and Cadnam. Take exit 2 off M27. A 5-acre site
with 45 touring pitches.*

🛠 🐾 ☉ ✳ 🛡 🖉 🖥 🛒 🐕 🏴 🍺 ♿
→ 🏴 ✈

RINGWOOD

See advertisement above.

ROMSEY

Doctors Hill Farm Caravan Park (SU287238)
Branches Ln, Sherfield English, ROMSEY SO51 6JX
☎ 01794 340402
▶ ▶ ▶ Family Park ★ 🚐 £8-£10 🚐 £8-£10 🛖 £8-£10
Open Mar-Oct Booking advisable
*A small, well sheltered site, peacefully located amidst
mature trees and fields. Signed off A27 Salisbury to
Romsey road, 4m NW of Romsey and M27 junc 2. A 3.5-
acre site with 45 touring pitches and 7 statics.
9 hole pitch 'n' putt.*

🛠 🐾 ☉ 🗑 ✳ ⚲ 🛡 🖉 🍺 ♿

SWAY

Setthorns Caravan & Camping Site (SU262003)
Wootton BH25 5UA ☎ 0131 314 6505 Signposted
Nearby town: New Milton
▶▶ Town & Country Pennant Park ★ 🚐 £5.20-£8
🚐 £5.20-£8 🛖 £5.20-£8
Open all year Booking advisable all times Last arrival
23.30hrs Last departure noon
*Pleasant level Forestry Commission site in woodland
with no sanitary facilities. Take Sway rd from
Brockenhurst to crossroads, turn left and site 1.5m on
left. A 60-acre site with 320 touring pitches.*

🛠 ✳ 🍺 🏕 ⛱ 🖾
→ ∪ 🏴

Credit Cards 💳 ▨ 🏧 🔳

WARSASH

Dibles Park (SU505060)
Dibles Rd SO31 9SA ☎ 01489 575232 Signposted
Nearby town: Fareham
▶ ▶ ▶ Family Park 🚐 £7 🚐 £7 🛖 £6
Open Mar-Nov Booking advisable bank hols & Jul-Aug
Last arrival 20.30hrs Last departure 13.00hrs
*Level, grass site with young trees and bushes, near
River Hamble and the Solent. Immaculate toilets. From
M27 junc 8 onto A27 signed Bursledon. Cross river
bridge and follow signs on right. A 0.75-acre site with
14 touring pitches and 46 statics.*

🛠 🐾 ☉ 🍴 ✳ 🛡 🖥 ⊤ 🍺 🏕
→ ∪ ✈ 🗑 🍺

Herefordshire, Warwickshire and Worcestershire

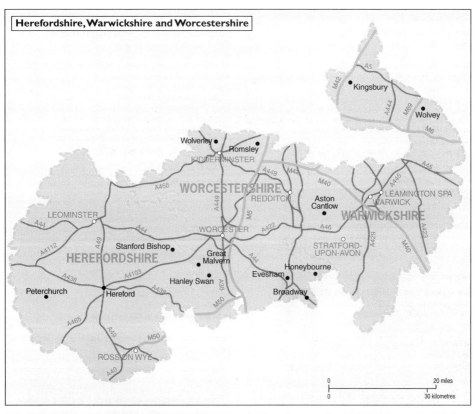

HEREFORDSHIRE

BIRCHER

Home Farm (SO478668)
HR6 0AX ☎ 01568 780525
▶▶ **Town & Country Pennant Park** 🏕 🏕 🅰
Open all year Booking advisable
*Level, grassy site on a working farm with lovely views
of the Welsh hills. On B4362, 4m N of Leominster,
midway between NT properties Croft Castle and
Berrington Hall. A 1.5-acre site with 30 touring pitches.*
🔌 🏕 ⊙

HEREFORD

Hereford Racecourse Campsite (SO500420)
Hereford Racecourse, Roman Rd HR4 9QN
☎ 01432 272364 Signposted
▶▶▶ **Family Park** ★ 🏕 £9.20-£11.60 🏕 £9.20-£11.60
🅰 £9.20-£11.60
Open mid Mar-Sep Booking advisable bank hols Last
arrival 20.00hrs Last departure noon
*Quiet, well-maintained sloping grass site with pitches
on the perimeter of the racecourse. Visitors must move
their units to adjacent pitches on racedays. Adjacent to*

*A49 Leominster road and A4103. A 5-acre site with 60
touring pitches.*
Free access to racing on race days.
🔌 🏕 ⊙ 🔋 ☐ ✳ 🔲 ☎
→ ∪ ▶ ⛰ ♨ 🥾
Credit Cards 💳 💳

PETERCHURCH

Poston Mill Caravan & Camping Park (SO355373)
HR2 0SF ☎ 01981 550225 & 01584 711280 (on B4348)
Nearby town: Hereford

▶▶▶▶ **De-Luxe Park** ★ 🏕 £6.50-£7.75 🏕 £6.50-£7.75
🅰 £4.75-£8.75
Booking advisable bank & summer hols Last departure
noon
*A level, grassy site with mature trees in hilly country
near River Dore, 11m W of Hereford on B4348. A 20-
acre site with 72 touring pitches and 50 statics.*
🔌 🏕 ⊙ 🔋 🍳 🔍 🍴 ✳ 🍺 🎢 🅱 🖊 📋 🔲 ✂ ☎ 🥢
🏛 🪑 🐕 🔲 ♿
→ ∪ ▶ ◎ 🔧 🥾

STANFORD BISHOP

Boyce Caravan Park (SO692528)
WR6 5UB ☎ 01885 483439 Signposted
Nearby town: Bromyard
▶ ▶ ▶ Family Park ★ ⊞ £7.50 ⊞ £7.50
Open Mar-Oct Booking advisable bank hols & Jun-Aug
Last arrival 18.00hrs Last departure noon
*A pleasant site on an Elizabethan farm with good
facilities. From B4220 Malvern road take sharp turn
opposite Herefordshire House Pub, R in .25m. A 10-acre
site with 30 touring pitches and 80 statics.*
Course fishing available.

🔌ſ☉◙🗟✳⚠🔲⊞🔦🛏🚿
➔⏝🏴

HERTFORDSHIRE

For the map of this county
see ESSEX

HERTFORD

Camping & Caravanning Club Site (TL334113)
Mangrove Ln SG13 8QF
☎ 01992 586696 Signposted

▶ ▶ ▶ ▶ De-Luxe Park ★ ⊞ £13-£14 ⊞ £13-£14
Å £13-£14
Open 24 Mar-3 Nov Booking advisable Last arrival
21.00hrs Last departure noon
*A well-landscaped site with immaculate new toilet
facilities, peacefully located off A414 S of Hertford. A
32-acre site with 250 touring pitches.*

🔌ſ☉◙🗟✳⚠🔲⊞⊤🔦🛏🚿
➔⏝🏴

Credit Cards 💳 🔲 🔲 🔲 🔳

HODDESDON

Lee Valley Caravan Park (TL383082)
Dobbs Weir, Essex Rd EN11 OAS ☎ 01992 462090
Signposted
▶▶ Town & Country Pennant Park ⊞ ⊞ Å
Open Etr-Oct Booking advisable public hols Last arrival
21.30hrs Last departure noon
*Neat, well kept site in a peaceful field surrounded by
hedges and tall trees, with a good play area and local
walks. Leave A10 at Hoddesdon junc, and follow signs
for Dobbs Weir; park 1m on right. An 8-acre site with
100 touring pitches and 100 statics.*
Fishing.

🔌ſ☉◙🗟⚠🔲⊤🔦🛏🚿
➔⌇🍴⏝

Credit Cards 💳 🔲 🔲

> AA pennant classification covers the touring section
> of a park, but not the static caravans available for
> rent, so we cannot deal with any complaints about
> static vans.

WALTHAM CROSS

Camping & Caravanning Club Site (TL344005)
Theobalds Park, Bulls Cross Ride EN7 5HS
☎ 01992 620604 Signposted
▶▶ Town & Country Pennant Park ★ ⊞ £9.20-£11.60
⊞ £9.20-£11.60 Å £9.20-£11.60
Open end Mar-beg Nov Booking advisable Last arrival
21.00hrs Last departure noon
*Lovely open site surrounded by mature trees, and set in
parkland at Theobalds Hall. From M25 take A10 S, then
1st right towards Crews Hill, and site signed in 0.5m. A
14-acre site with 150 touring pitches.*

🔌ſ☉◙🗟❀✳⚠🔲⊞🔦🛏
➔⏝⌇⏝🏴

Credit Cards 💳 🔲

KENT

ASHFORD

Broad Hembury Holiday Park (TR009387)
Steeds Ln, Kingsnorth TN26 1NQ
☎ 01233 620859 Signposted
Nearby town: Canterbury
▶ ▶ ▶ Family Park ★ ⊞ £10-£13 ⊞ £10-£13
Å £8-£13
Open all year Booking advisable Jul-Aug Last departure
noon
*Well-run and maintained small farm site surrounded by
open pasture, with pitches sheltered by mature hedges,
and all neatly landscaped. From junc 10 on M20 take
A2070 for 2m, then continue on A2042, following
camping signs to Kingsnorth. Turn left at 2nd crossrds
in village. A 5-acre site with 70 touring pitches and 25
statics.*
Sports field with football & volley ball.

🔌ſ☉◙🗟❀🔲✳⚠🔲⊞🔦🛏🚿
➔⏝⌇◎⚽⏝

Credit Cards 💳 🔲 🔲 🔳

BIDDENDEN

Woodlands Park (TQ867372)
Tenterden Rd TN27 8BT ☎ 01580 291216 Signposted
Nearby town: Tenterden
▶ ▶ ▶ Family Park ⊞ ⊞ Å

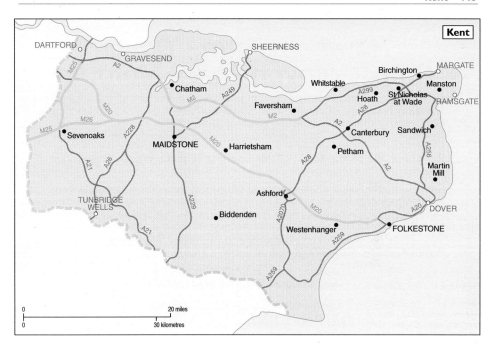

Open Mar-Oct (rs Mar-Apr weather permitting) Booking advisable bank hols & Jul-Aug Last arrival anytime Last departure anytime
A site of level grassland bordered by hedges and trees, with two ponds and a new toilet block. 1.5m S of Biddenden on northern side of A262. Ideal centre for Kent, Sussex and Channel ports. A 9-acre site with 100 touring pitches and 205 statics.
Camping accessory sales. Small site shop.

🕿 🎫 ☉ 🔟 🍳 ✳ ⚑ 🕅 🛆 🖎 ⊡ 🔟 🥤 🏥 🏧 🐄 👪

→ ∪ ⍴ ◎ 🎣

BIRCHINGTON

Quex Caravan Park (TR321685)
Park Rd CT7 0BL
☎ 01843 841273 Signposted
Nearby town: Margate

▶ ▶ ▶ ▶ De-Luxe Park ★ 🎫 £8.50-£11 🎫 £8.50-£11
Open Mar-Nov Booking advisable bank hols Last arrival anytime Last departure noon
Small parkland site, quiet and secluded, with very good sanitary facilities. From Birchington (A28) turn SE into Park Road, site in 1m. An 11-acre site with 88 touring pitches and 120 statics.

🕿 🎫 ☉ 🔟 🍳 ✳ 🕅 🛆 🖎 ⊡ 🔟 🥤 🏥 🐄

→ ∪ ⍴ ◎ 🛆 🌣 👪 🎣

⊖⊖⊖⊖⊖⊖⊖⊖

Two Chimneys Caravan Park (TR320684)
Shottendane Rd CT7 0HD ☎ 01843 841068 & 843157 Signposted
Nearby town: Margate
▶ ▶ ▶ Family Park ★ 🎫 £7-£14 🎫 £7-£14 Å £7-£14
Open Mar-Oct (rs Mar-May & Sep-Oct shop/bar/pool/takeaway restricted) Booking advisable bank & school hols Last arrival 23.00hrs Last departure noon
A good, well-managed site with a swimming pool and well-tended grounds. From A28 in Birchington turn right by church along Park Lane (B2048). Turn left at Manston Rd along Shottendane Rd, and site on R. A 9-acre site with 75 touring pitches and 65 statics.
Sauna, spa bath, solarium, amusement arcade.

🕿 🎫 ☉ 🔟 🍳 ⫞ ⚲ ⚫ ✳ ⚑ 🕅 🛆 🖎 ⊡ 🔟 🥤 🏥 🐄 👪

→ ∪ ⍴ ◎ 🛆 🌣 👪 🎣

Credit Cards 💳 ▭

CANTERBURY

See also **Petham**

Camping & Caravanning Club Site (TR172577)
Bekesbourne Ln CT3 4AB ☎ 01227 463216 (in season) & 01203 694995 (off A257) Signposted
▶ ▶ ▶ Family Park ★ 🎫 £13-£14 🎫 £13-£14
Å £13-£14

contd.

Open all year Booking advisable bank hols & peak periods Last arrival 21.00hrs Last departure noon
An attractive tree-screened site in pleasant rural surroundings. Off A257 Canterbury-Sandwich road. Please see the advertisement on page 27 for details of Club Members' benefits. A 20-acre site with 210 touring pitches.

🔌 🐾 ⊙ 🗄 ⚑ ✳ 🅰 ▲ 🚽 🎫 🚻 Ⓣ ⚓ 🐴 ⅙
➜ ∪ ▶ ⚌ 🔧
Credit Cards 💳 ▦ ▦ ▦ 🔟

QQQQQQQQ

CHATHAM
Woolmans Wood Caravan Park (TQ746638)
Bridgewood ME5 9SB ☎ 01634 867685
Signposted
▶▶ Town & Country Pennant Park 🚐 🚐 Å
Open all year Last departure 14.00hrs
Small site alongside the city airport and close to the London-Dover road. 3.25m S of Rochester. From M2 motorway leave at junction 3, then via A229 and B2097, .75m from junction 3. A 5-acre site with 60 touring pitches.
Caravan servicing, washing & valeting.

🔌 🐾 ⊙ ⚑ ✳ 🅰 🚽 🎫 🚻 Ⓣ ⚓ ⊞
➜ ∪ ▶ ⊁ ⚌ 🔧 🗑 🔧

DOVER
See **Martin Mill**

FAVERSHAM
Painters Farm Caravan & Camping Site (TQ990591)
Painters Forstal ME13 0EG ☎ 01795 532995 Signposted
▶▶ Town & Country Pennant Park 🚐 £6.60-£8.60
🚐 £6.60-£8.60 Å £6.60-£8.60
Open Mar-Oct Booking advisable bank hols Last arrival 23.59hrs
Delightful simple farm site in immaculately kept cherry orchard, with spotless toilets in converted farm buildings. Signed from A2 at Faversham. A 3-acre site with 45 touring pitches.

🔌 🐾 ⊙ ✳ 🅰 🚽 🎫 Ⓣ ⊞ 🐴
➜ ∪ ▶ ⚌

FOLKESTONE
Little Satmar Holiday Park (TR260390)
Winehouse Ln, Capel Le Ferne CT18 7JF
☎ 01303 251188 (2m W off A20 onto B2011)
Signposted
▶ ▶ ▶ Family Park ★ 🚐 £8.50-£11 🚐 £8.50-£11
Å £6.50-£11
Open Apr-Oct Booking advisable bank hols & Jul-Aug Last arrival 23.00hrs Last departure 14.00hrs
A quiet, well-screened site well away from the road. A useful base for touring Dover/Folkestone area, signed off B2011. A 5-acre site with 46 touring pitches and 80 statics.

🔌 🐾 ⊙ 🗄 ⚑ ⚙ ✳ 🅰 🚽 🎫 Ⓣ ⚓ 🔧
➜ ∪ ▶ ⚌ 🔧
Credit Cards 💳 ▦ ▦ ▦ 🔟

Camping & Caravanning Club Site (TR246376)
The Warren CT19 6PT
☎ 01303 255093 (in season) & 01203 694995 (signed from A20 rdbt) Signposted
▶▶ Town & Country Pennant Park ★ 🚐 £9.20-£11.60 Å £9.20-£11.60
Open end Mar-end Sep Booking advisable bank hols & peak periods Last arrival 21.00hrs Last departure noon
This site commands marvellous views across the Strait of Dover and is well located for the channel ports. It nestles on the side of the cliff and is tiered in some areas. Signed from A20 roundabout. Please see the advertisement on page 27 for details of Club Members' benefits. A 4-acre site with 82 touring pitches.

🗚⊙✳🛢🔧

Credit Cards 💳 🏧 💴

Little Switzerland Camping & Caravan Site (TR248380)
Wear Bay Rd CT19 6PS
☎ 01303 252168
Signposted
▶▶ Town & Country Pennant Park 🚐 🚐 Å
Open Mar-Oct Booking advisable from Mar Last arrival mdnt Last departure noon
A small site perched on the cliffs overlooking the Dover Straits, with cosy, sheltered pitches. Signed from A2 and A20 E of Folkestone. A 4-acre site with 18 touring pitches and 12 statics.

🗚🛒⊙🛢✳🍴🔋✕🕻🧺🐾🖳🗑🛢
➜∪ᑭ⊚◮🍼🥢

HARRIETSHAM

Hogbarn Caravan Park (TQ885550)
Hogbarn Ln, Stede Hill ME17 1NZ
☎ 01622 859648
Nearby town: Maidstone
▶▶▶ Family Park ★ 🚐 fr £8.50 🚐 fr £4.50 Å fr £8.50
Open Apr-Oct Booking advisable bank hols & Jul-Aug Last arrival 22.00hrs Last departure noon
A very good country site, with mainly large, fenced in pitches. Situated off A20, between Ashford and Maidstone, along a narrow lane at top of N Downs. A 5-acre site with 60 touring pitches and 70 statics. Coffee bar & Sauna.

🗚🗚⊙🛢🍶🥄🔌🗖✳🍴◮🔋🖉🛢🕻🖼🐾🛢🔥
➜∪ᑭ🍼🥢

HOATH

South View (TR205648)
Maypole Ln CT3 4LL
☎ 01227 860280 (off A291 & A28)
Signposted
Nearby town: Canterbury
▶▶▶ Family Park ★ 🚐 £9-£11 🚐 £9-£11 Å £9-£11
Open all year Booking advisable bank hols Last arrival 23.00hrs Last departure 22.00hrs
A small rural site, level and well secluded. Off A299 or A28. A 3-acre site with 45 touring pitches.

🗚🗚⊙🛢🍶✳◮🔌🖉🗖🖼🗂🔥🛢
➜∪ᑭ⊚◮🍼🥢🛢

MAIDSTONE

Pine Lodge Touring Park (TQ815549)
Ashford Rd, Bearsted, Hollingbourne ME17 1XH
☎ 01622 730018 (2m NW on A20, from junc 8 M20) Signposted

▶▶▶ De-Luxe Park ★ 🚐 £8.50-£9.50 🚐 £8.50-£9.50 Å £7-£9.50
Open all year Booking advisable bank hols Last arrival 22.00hrs Last departure 14.00hrs ✍
A very well laid out site close to Leeds Castle and the A20. Much planting of trees will result in good screening. A 7-acre site with 100 touring pitches. Waste disposal points.

🗚🗚⊙🛢🍶✳/◮🔌🖉🗖🕻🛢🔥
➜∪ᑭ🥢🍼🥢

Credit Cards 💳 🏧 💴 💶 🔗

MANSTON

Manston Caravan & Camping Park (TR348662)
Manston Court Rd CT12 5AU ☎ 01843 823442 (follow signs to Kent Int Airport. After passing entrance, turn left, opp garage, into Manston Court rd. Entrance 400yds on right) Signposted
Nearby town: Margate/Ramsgate
▶▶▶ Family Park 🚐 🚐 Å
Open Etr-Oct (rs Apr shop open weekends only (off-peak)) Booking advisable bank hols & Jul-Aug Last arrival 23.55hrs Last departure 11.00hrs
A level grassy site with mature trees situated near Manston Airport and convenient for the seaside resorts on the Isle of Thanet. Signed off B2150 in village. A 5-acre site with 100 touring pitches and 46 statics.

🗚🗚⊙🍶✳/◮🔌🖉🗖🕻🖼🔥🛢
➜∪ᑭ⊚◮🥢🍼🥢🛢
Credit Cards 💴 💶 🔗

Pine Meadows Tourer Park (TR357662)
Spratling Court Farm, Spratling St CT12 5AN
☎ 01843 587770 Signposted
Nearby town: Ramsgate
▶▶ Town & Country Pennant Park ★ 🚐 £8-£11.20 🚐 £8-£11.20 Å £8-£9.60
Open Apr-Sep Last arrival 19.00hrs ✍
A quiet family site screened by high hedges, on a working farm on the Isle of Thanet. Generous pitches and a pleasant atmosphere. Just off B2050, .5m E of Manston, opp Greensole Golf Range. A 3.5-acre site with 40 touring pitches.

🗚🗚⊙◮🕻🖼
➜∪ᑭ◮🥢🍼🥢🛢🛢

MARTIN MILL

Hawthorn Farm Caravan Park (TR342464)
Station Rd CT15 5LA ☎ 01304 852658 & 852914
Signposted
Nearby town: Dover

▶▶▶▶ De-Luxe Park ★ 🚐 £8.50-£10.50 🚐 £8.50-£10.50 Å £8.50-£10.50

contd.

Open Mar-mid Dec (water off if weather cold) Booking advisable bank hols & Jul-Aug Last arrival anytime Last departure noon

This pleasant rural site is screened by young trees and hedgerows, in grounds which include a rose garden and woods. Signed from A258. A 15-acre site with 250 touring pitches and 176 statics.

See advertisement under DOVER

🔲 📞 ☺ ⊡ 🔲 ⚡ ✳ 🛈 🖉 🗊 ✕ 👤 🐴 🛎

➜ ⋃ ⌓ ◎ 🔺 ⤴ ☎ 🗡

Credit Cards 💳 📇 📋 🆔

PETHAM

Yew Tree Caravan Park (TR137507)
Stone St CT4 5PL ☎ 01227 700306
Nearby town: Canterbury
▶ ▶ ▶ **Family Park** 🏕 🏕 🛈
Open Mar-Oct Booking advisable
Very attractive park set in rolling countryside with beautiful views over Chatham Downs. On the B2068, 4m S of Canterbury, 9m N of M42, jct 11. A 4.5-acre site with 45 touring pitches and 13 statics.

🔲 📞 ☺ ⊡ ➰ 🛎

Ashfield Farm (TR138508)
Waddenhall CT4 5PX ☎ 01227 700624 Signposted
Nearby town: Canterbruy
▶▸ **Town & Country Pennant Park** 🏕 £7-£9.50
🏕 £7-£8.50 🛈 £7
Open Apr-Oct Booking advisable Jul & Aug Last arrival anytime Last departure noon
Small rural site with new toilet block and well-drained pitches, located S of Canterbury. Signed off B2068. A 4.5-acre site with 20 touring pitches and 1 static.
Mini golf, short term kennelling.

🔲 📞 ☺ ✳ 🛈 🖉 🗄 🗊 👤 🐴 ♿

➜ ⋃ ⌓ 🛎

ST NICHOLAS AT WADE

St Nicholas at Wade Camping Site (TR254672)
Court Rd CT7 0NH ☎ 01843 847245 Signposted
Nearby town: Margate
▶▸ **Town & Country Pennant Park** ★ 🏕 £6.50-£9
🏕 £7-£8 🛈 £7.50-£9
Open Etr-Oct Booking advisable Jul-Aug Last arrival 22.00hrs Last departure 16.00hrs
A small field with a toilet block, close to village and shop, off A299 and A28. A 3-acre site with 75 touring pitches.

🔲 📞 ☺ ✳ ⚡ 🛈 🖉 🗊 🐴 🛎

➜ ⋃ 🗡 ⊡

SANDWICH

Sandwich Leisure Park (TR326581)
Woodnesborough Rd CT13 0AA
☎ 01304 612681 & 01227 771777 Signposted
▶ ▶ ▶ **Family Park** ★ 🏕 £6.80-£9.80 🏕 £6.80-£9.80
🛈 £6.80-£9.80
Open Mar-Oct Booking advisable Etr, Spring bank hol & Jul-Aug Last arrival 20.00hrs Last departure 11.00hrs

---

A useful touring site on the edge of Sandwich, with well laid out pitches and temporary toilets prior to development of full facilities. Signed from A256 at Sandwich. A 5.5-acre site with 100 touring pitches and 103 statics.
Washing-up area.

🔲 📞 ☺ ⊡ 🔲 ✳ ⚡ 🛈 🖉 👤 🐴 🛎

➜ ⋃ ⌓ 🔺 ⤴ ☎ 🗡

SEVENOAKS

Camping & Caravanning Club Site (TQ577564)
Styants Bottom Rd, Styants Bottom, Seal TN15 0ET
☎ 01732 762728 (in season) & 01203 694995
Signposted
▶ ▶ ▶ **Family Park** ★ 🏕 £10-£13 🏕 £10-£13 🛈 £10-£13
Open end Mar-early Nov Booking advisable bank hols & peak periods Last arrival 21.00hrs Last departure noon
A quiet park in the centre of NT woodlands, with buildings blending well into the surroundings. Signed from A25 just E of Seal. Please see the advertisement on page 27 for details of Club Members' benefits. A 4-acre site with 58 touring pitches.

🔲 📞 ☺ ⊡ 🔲 ✳ ⚡ 🛈 👤 🛎 ♿

Credit Cards 💳 📇

WESTENHANGER

Caravan Club Site (TR128371)
Folkestone Racecourse, Stone St CT21 4HX
☎ 01303 261761 & 266407 Signposted
Nearby town: Folkestone
▶▸ **Town & Country Pennant Park** 🏕 £10-£12 🏕 £10-£12
🛈 £7.50-£10
Open late Mar-mid Sep Booking advisable Jul-Aug Last arrival 20.00hrs Last departure noon
Situated in rural surroundings 7m W of Folkestone and 3m from nearest beach. Conveniently positioned for Channel ports. From junc 11 of M20 onto A261 at roundabout with A20, signed Sellinge. A 4-acre site with 55 touring pitches.

🔲 📞 ☺ ✳ 🛈 🖉 🗊 👤 ⛺ 🐴

➜ ⋃ ⌓ ◎ 🗡 ⊡ 🛎

Credit Cards 💳 📇 📋 📇 🆔

WHITSTABLE

Sea View Caravan Park (TR145675)
St John's Rd CT5 2RY ☎ 01227 792246
Signposted
Nearby town: Herne Bay
▶ ▶ ▶ **Family Park** 🏕 £8.50-£10.50 🏕 £8.50-£10.50
🛈 £8.50-£10.50
Open Etr-Oct Booking advisable all times Last arrival 21.30hrs
Pleasant open site on the edge of Whitstable, set well away from the static site. Signed off A229, 0.5m E of Whitstable. A 12-acre site with 20 touring pitches and 452 statics.
Amusements in games room & adventure trail.

🔲 📞 ☺ ⊡ 🔲 🔦 🔲 ✳ ⚡ 🏔 🛈 🖉 🗊 ✕ 👤 🛗 🎋
🛎 ♿

➜ ⋃ ⌓ ☎ 🗡

Lancashire

Map showing Lancashire towns and roads:

Silverdale, Capernwray, Bolton-le-Sands, Nether Kellet, Morecambe, Heysham, Middleton, LANCASTER, Glasson, Cockerham, FLEETWOOD, Thornton Cleveleys, Hambleton, Garstang, Gisburn, Clitheroe, Longridge, BLACKPOOL, Weeton, BURNLEY, Lytham St Anne's, PRESTON, BLACKBURN, Croston, Mere Brow, Ormskirk, SKELMERSDALE

Roads: A65, A6, M6, A683, A59, A682, A6068, M65, A671, A646, A677, A585, A583, M55, A56, A666, A565, A49, A6, M61, M58, A570, A59

0 — 20 miles
.0 — 30 kilometres

LANCASHIRE

BLACKPOOL

Marton Mere Holiday Village (SD347349)
Mythop Rd FY4 4XN
☎ 01253 767544

❀❀❀❀❀❀❀❀❀❀❀❀❀❀❀❀❀❀❀❀❀❀❀

🚐 🚐

Open Mar-Oct Booking advisable Last arrival 22.00hrs
Last departure noon
*A large holiday centre with plenty of on-site
entertainment, and a regular bus service into Blackpool.
Leave M55 at junc 4 onto A583 towards Blackpool, turn*

*right past windmill at 1st traffic lights into Mythop Rd,
and park is 150yds on left. A 30-acre site with 431
touring pitches and 921 statics.*

🔌 ❄ ⊙ 🗄 🍴 ⚲ ✎ ♦ ⊡ ☀ ♀ /Ⅲ 🔒 ⌀ ⊞ Ⓣ ✗
📞 🚾 🚿 🐕 🛒
→ ∪ ⊺ ⊚ ⚓ ☎ ↗

Credit Cards 💳 ▨▨ ▨▨ ▨▨ 🅂

❀❀❀❀❀❀❀❀❀❀❀❀❀❀❀❀❀❀❀❀❀❀❀

Pipers Height Caravan Park (SD355327)
Peel Rd, Peel ☎ 01253 763767

Ⓠ Ⓠ Ⓠ Ⓠ Ⓠ Ⓠ Ⓠ

▶ ▶ ▶ ▶ **De-Luxe Park** ★ 🚐 £10 🚐 £10 ▲ £10
Open Mar-Oct Booking advisable

contd.

Family owned and run park in a rural area, yet within 4m of the extensive beaches and entertainment of Blackpool and Lytham St Annes. Leave M55 at junct with A583 towards Preston; turn right at 1st traffic lighs, then sharp left; site 200yds on right, 0.5m from M'way. A 9-acre site with 137 touring pitches.

🔧 🐾 ⊙ 🗑 ⬜ ♀ ⚠ ✕ ⚓ ⏰ 🐕 ⛽ ♿

Mariclough Hampsfield Camping Site (SD356329)
Preston New Rd, Peel Corner FY4 5JR
☎ 01253 761034 (on A583 0.5m S of M55 Jct 4)
▶▶ Town & Country Pennant Park ★ ⚑ fr £6 ⚑ £4.80-£6
▲ fr £4.80
Open Etr-Nov Booking advisable high season bank hols (for caravans) Last arrival 22.30hrs Last departure noon
A small, tidy, family camping site located on A583 and on the outskirts of Blackpool, set in open countryside. A 2-acre site with 50 touring pitches and 2 statics.

🔧 🐾 ⊙ ✳ ⚠ ⚓ ⊘ ⊟ ⏰ ⚓ ⛽
→ ∪ ⏵ ✚ 🔔 ⤴

BOLTON-LE-SANDS

Detron Gate Farm (SD478683)
LA5 9TN ☎ 01524 732842 & 733617 (night)
Signposted
▶▶ Town & Country Pennant Park ⚑ £5-£6.50
⚑ £5-£6.50 ▲ £4.50-£6
Open Mar-Oct (rs Mar-May shop hours restricted) Booking advisable bank hols Last arrival 22.00hrs Last departure 18.00hrs
Rural grassy site overlooking Morecambe Bay off A6. A popular site on sloping ground with a small farm adjacent. A 10-acre site with 100 touring pitches and 42 statics.

🔧 🐾 ⊙ 🗑 🔍 ⬜ ✳ ⚠ ⚓ ⊘ ⊟ ⏰ ⚓ ⛽
→ ∪ ⏵ ✚ ⤴

Bolton Holmes Farm (SD481693)
Mill Ln LA5 8ES ☎ 01524 732854
Nearby town: Lancaster
▶▶ Town & Country Pennant Park ★ ⚑ fr £4.50
⚑ fr £4.50 ▲ fr £4.50
Open Apr-Sep Booking advisable peak periods
A gently sloping site forming part of a farm complex, offering good views across Morecambe Bay and to the hills of the Lake District. Site is signed off A6 between Morecambe and Carnforth. A 5-acre site with 30 touring pitches and 45 statics.

🔧 🐾 ⊙ ✳ ⚓ ⊟ ⚓
→ ∪ ✚ ⤴ 🗑 ⛽

CAPERNWRAY

Old Hall Caravan Park (SD533716)
LA6 1AD ☎ 01524 733276 & 735996
Nearby town: Carnforth
▶▶▶ Family Park ★ ⚑ £8.50-£10 ⚑ £8.50-£10
Open Mar-10 Jan Booking advisable bank hols & Jul-Aug
Set in a clearing in lovely secluded woods in a natural setting with marked walks. Off M6 at junc 35, towards

Over Kellet, turn left at village green, and site on right in 1.5m. A 3-acre site with 38 touring pitches and 128 statics.

🔧 🐾 ⊙ 🗑 ♀ ⚠ ⚓ ⊘ ⊟ ⏰ ⚓ 🐕 ⛽ ♿
→ ∪ ⚘ ✚ ⤴ ⛽

CLITHEROE

Camping & Caravanning Club Site (SD727413)
Edisford Bridge, Edisford Rd BB7 3LA
☎ 01200 425294 (in season) & 01203 694995
(1m W off B6243)
Signposted
▶▶▶ Family Park ★ ⚑ £9.20-£11.60 ⚑ £9.20-£11.60
▲ £9.20-£11.60
Open end Mar-early Nov Booking advisable bank hols & peak periods Last arrival 21.00hrs Last departure noon
Set on the banks of the River Ribble, this site is ideal for fishing and walking as well as enjoying the adjacent park. Situated 1m out of town on the B6243. Please see the advertisement on page 27 for details of Club Members' benefits. A 6-acre site with 80 touring pitches.

🔧 🐾 ⊙ 🗑 ✳ ⚠ ⚓ ⊘ ⊟ ⚓ ⛽
→ ⏵ 🔔 ⤴
Credit Cards 💳 💳

COCKERHAM

 Cockerham Sands Country Park (SD435529)
LA2 0BB ☎ 01524 751387
Signposted

🎪🎪🎪🎪🎪🎪🎪🎪🎪🎪🎪🎪🎪

★ ⚑ £10-£14.50 ⚑ £10-£14.50
Open Mar-14 Dec Booking advisable Last departure 10.00hrs
A small touring area close to all the amenities of a large holiday complex on the estuary of the River Lune. Leave Lancaster on A588 towards Cockerham, turn right at sign to Glasson Dock, and after 1.5m turn left following signs to Cockerham Sands. A 1-acre site with 15 touring pitches and 260 statics.

🔧 🐾 ⊙ 🗑 ⬜ ⚡ ♀ ⚠ ⚓ ⊟ ✕ ⚓ 🧹 ⛽
→ ∪ ⤴

🎪🎪🎪🎪🎪🎪🎪🎪🎪🎪🎪🎪🎪

Mosswood Caravan Park (SD456497)
Crimbles Ln LA2 0ES
☎ 01524 791041 (1m W along A588)
Signposted
Nearby town: Lancaster
▶▶▶ Family Park ⚑ ⚑ ▲
Open Mar-Oct Booking advisable bank hols & Jul-Sep Last arrival 20.00hrs Last departure 16.00hrs
A tree-lined grassy park with sheltered, level pitches, located on peaceful Cockerham Moss. Situated about 4m from A6/M6 junc 33, 1m W of Cockerham on A588. A 3-acre site with 25 touring pitches and 143 statics.

🔧 🐾 ⊙ 🗑 ♀ ✳ ⚠ ⚓ ⊘ ⚓ 🐕 ⛽
→ ∪ ⏵ ⤴
Credit Cards 💳 💳 💳 💳 📱

Relax, stay for a while...

Royal Umpire Touring Park

..appreciate our tranquil surroundings, for Touring and Camping alike, set in 60 acres in the heart of rural Lancashire

THE *Best of British*

Southport Road · Croston
Preston · Lancashire · PR5 7JB
Tel: 01772 600257 · Fax: 01772 600662

CROSTON

Royal Umpire Touring Park (SD504190)
Southport Rd PR5 7JB ☎ 01772 600257 (on the A581, between A59 & A49) Signposted
Nearby town: Chorley

► ► ► ► De-Luxe Park ★ ⊞ £7.70-£12.35
⊞ £7.70-£12.35 Å £6.20-£10.85
Open all year (rs 7 Nov-21 Dec only serviced pitches available) Booking advisable bank hols & peak season
Last arrival 22.00hrs Last departure noon
A pleasant, level site with good facilities and high standard of maintenance, set in open countryside, and signed off A581 from Chorley. A 10-acre site with 200 touring pitches.
Assault course, five a side football pitch.

Credit Cards 💳

GARSTANG

Claylands Caravan Park (SD496485)
Cabus PR3 1AJ ☎ 01524 791242 (2m N, off A6)
Signposted

► ► ► ► De-Luxe Park ★ ⊞ £9-£9.50 ⊞ £9-£9.50
Å £9-£9.50

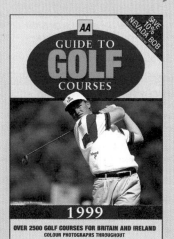

Open Mar-4 Jan (rs Jan & Feb) Booking advisable bank hols & Jul-Aug Last arrival 23.00hrs Last departure 14.00hrs
A well-maintained site with lovely river and woodland walks and good views, convenient for A6 and M6 between junctions 32 and 33. Signed off A6 down private rd on Lancaster side of Garstang. A 14-acre site with 55 touring pitches and 60 statics. Fishing.

Credit Cards

Bridge House Marina & Caravan Park (SD483457)
Nateby Crossing Ln, Nateby PR3 0JJ
☎ 01995 603207 (1m W on unclass rd)
Signposted
Nearby town: Preston
► ► ► Family Park ★ ⬛ £8.50 ⬛ £8.50
Open Mar-4 Jan Booking advisable bank hols Last arrival 22.00hrs Last departure 13.00hrs
A well-maintained site in attractive countryside by the Lancaster Canal, with good views towards the Trough of Bowland. Just off A6, on unclass rd signed Knott End. A 4-acre site with 50 touring pitches and 20 statics.

Credit Cards

GISBURN

Rimington Caravan Park (SD825469)
Hardacre Ln, Rimington BB7 4DS ☎ 01200 445355 & 447235 (off A682 1m S of Gisburn) Signposted
Nearby town: Clitheroe
► ► ► Family Park ★ ⬛ fr £8 ⬛ fr £8 ⚑ fr £8
Open Apr-Oct (rs Mar hardstanding available only) Booking advisable bank hols & Jul-3 Sep Last arrival 20.00hrs Last departure noon no cars by caravans no cars by tents
A well-cared for site set in an attractive rural valley close to the Pendle Hills and situated just off A682 Gisburn-Nelson road 1m from town centre. A 4-acre site with 30 touring pitches and 150 statics.

Todber Caravan Park (SD835469)
BB7 4JJ ☎ 01200 445322 Signposted
Nearby town: Nelson
► ► ► Family Park ⬛ £9 ⬛ £9 ⚑ £9
Open Mar-Oct (rs Mar-Etr clubhouse open wknds only) Booking advisable public hols & for electric hook-up Last arrival 20.00hrs Last departure 18.00hrs
A popular rural site on sloping ground with good views all round, off A682. A 5-acre site with 100 touring pitches and 250 statics.
Games field.

GLASSON

Marina Caravan Park (SD450561)
Conder Side LA5 3RD ☎ 01524 751787
► ► ► Family Park ⬛ ⬛ ⚑
Open Mar-Jan Booking advisable
Level touring pitches on hardstandings in a pleasant rurally-situated park. A short stroll to the waterside village of Glasson Dock, with its lock between Lancaster Canal and the sea. Off A588 at Condor Green; follow unclass road towards Glasson Dock, and park on left before village. A 2-acre site with 24 touring pitches and 123 statics.

HAMBLETON

Sunset Park (SD375437)
Sower Carr Ln FY6 9EQ ☎ 01253 700222 & 701888
Signposted
► ► ► Family Park ★ ⬛ £10-£12 ⬛ £10-£12
⚑ £10-£12
Open Mar-Oct Booking advisable wknds & bank hols Last departure noon
A pleasant rural park with plenty of children's entertainment on site, recently extensively upgraded. Take A588 turning off A585, cross Chard bridge, and site 1m on right through village. A 4-acre site with 30 touring pitches and 74 statics.
Pool tables, course fishing, sauna, spa.

Credit Cards

HEYSHAM

Ocean Edge Caravan Park (SD407591)
Moneyclose Ln LA3 2XA ☎ 01524 855657
► ► ► Family Park ⬛ ⬛ ⚑
Open Mar-Oct
A newly developed touring area of a large holiday complex adjacent to the sea. From junc 34 of M6, follow A683 to Heysham, and site signed at Heysham before ferry pont. A 10-acre site with 100 touring pitches and 629 statics.

LONGRIDGE

Beacon Fell View Caravan Park (SD618382)
110 Higher Rd PR3 2TF ☎ 01772 785434
► ► ► Family Park ★ ⬛ £7-£14 ⬛ £7-£14 ⚑ £7-£14
Open 8 Apr-28 Oct Booking advisable bank & school hols Last arrival 21.00hrs Last departure 18.00hrs
An elevated site with views over Beacon Fell. Leave A6 at Broughton on B5269 into Longridge and follow B6243 out of town centre, then take L fork signed Jeffrey Hill; site is .75m on R. A 7-acre site with 97 touring pitches and 397 statics.
Free evening entertainment, pool tables, darts.

Credit Cards

LYTHAM ST ANNES

Eastham Hall Caravan Site (SD379291)
Saltcotes Rd FY8 4LS ☎ 01253 737907 Signposted
Nearby town: Blackpool
► ► ► Family Park ♥ £10-£11.50 ♥ £10-£11.50
Open Mar-Oct Booking advisable bank hols & Jul Last
arrival 21.00hrs Last departure 15.00hrs
A level, secluded site with trees and hedgerows, in rural surroundings. From Preston on A584, turn right onto B5259 to site in .75m. A 15-acre site with 200 touring pitches and 200 statics.

🔊 🛒 ⊙ 🗒 🍳 ✳ ⚠ ⑧ ⊘ 📧 T ⎣ 🐴 🐾
➡ ∪ ⌐ ⚠

MERE BROW

Leisure Lakes (SD408176)
PR4 6JX ☎ 01772 813446 & 814502 (from Southport,
Take A565 for 3.5m, right turn on B5246 to site)
Signposted
Nearby town: Southport
► ► ► Family Park ★ ♥ £9.90 ♥ £9.90
Open all year Booking advisable bank hols, Jun-Aug &
wknds Last arrival 21.00hrs Last departure 16.30hrs
A level grassy site in spacious parkland with ample amenities including watersports, fishing and walking. Site is just off A565 Preston-Southport road approx 5 miles from Southport. A 30-acre site with 90 touring pitches.
Windsurfing, canoe hire, golf range, cycle hire.Horse

🔊 🛒 ⊙ 🗒 🍳 ✳ 🍺 ⚠ ⑧ ⊘ ✖ ⎣ ⎈ 🎯 🐴 🐾
➡ ∪ ⌐ ⚠ ⅄ ⊀ ✒ 🐾
Credit Cards 💳 ▬ ▬ ▬ 🔴 ⑤

MIDDLETON (NEAR MORECAMBE)

Melbreak Caravan Park (SD415584)
Carr Ln LA3 3LH
☎ 01524 852430 (in village turn right at church,
signed Middleton Sands, site .5m on left)
Signposted
Nearby town: Morecambe
► ► ► Family Park ★ ♥ £6.75-£7 ♥ £6.75-£7
⚑ £6.25-£6.50
Open Mar-Oct Booking advisable Jul-Aug Last arrival
22.00hrs Last departure noon
Small, well run, tidy site in open countryside S of Morecambe. Site on unclass rd from Heysham towards Middleton Sands. A 2-acre site with 22 touring pitches and 10 statics.

🔊 🛒 ⊙ 🗒 🍳 ✳ ⑧ ⊘ 📧 ⎈ 🐾
➡ ∪ ⌐ ✒

MORECAMBE

Regent Caravan Park (SD431629)
Westgate LA3 7DB ☎ 01524 413940
Signposted

✿✿✿✿✿✿✿✿✿✿✿✿✿✿✿✿✿✿✿✿✿

★ ♥ £10-£15 ♥ £10-£15
Open Mar-1 Jan Booking advisable Last arrival 21.00hrs
Last departure noon
A full entertainment complex for all ages, in a first class holiday centre, close to town and promenade. From

A589 turn left towards town centre at 3rd large rndbt,
and park on left in 1.5m. A 2-acre site with 24 touring
pitches and 330 statics.

🔊 🛒 ⊙ ⅄ ⚠ ✖ ⎣ ⎈ 🐴 🐾
➡ ∪ ⌐ ⓞ 😷 ✒

✿✿✿✿✿✿✿✿✿✿✿✿✿✿✿✿✿✿✿✿✿✿✿

Riverside Caravan Park (SD448615)
Snatchems LA3 3ER ☎ 01524 844193 (take unclass road
S off B5273) Signposted
Nearby town: Lancaster
► ► ► Family Park ♥ ♥ ⚑
Open Mar-Oct Booking advisable public hols & high
season Last arrival 22.00hrs Last departure noon
A nice level grassy site with views over River Lune and Morecambe Bay. On unclass road off B5273 near Heaton. A 2-acre site with 50 touring pitches.

🔊 🛒 ⊙ 🍳 ✳ ⚠ ⑧ 📧 T ⎣ 🐴 🎯 🐾 ⅋
➡ ∪ ⌐ ⚠ 😷 ✒ ⓞ
Credit Cards 💳 ▬ ▬

Venture Caravan Park (SD436633)
Langridge Way, Westgate LA4 4TQ
☎ 01524 412986 & 412585 Signposted
Nearby town: Lancaster
► ► ► Family Park ★ ♥ £9 ♥ £9 ⚑ £9
Open all year (rs Nov-Feb touring vans only, one toilet
block open) Booking advisable bank hols & peak
periods Last arrival 22.00hrs Last departure noon
Large, mainly static site off the A589, close to the centre of town. A 5-acre site with 56 touring pitches and 304 statics.
Amusement arcade & off licence.

🔊 ⇶ 🛒 ⊙ 🗒 🍳 ⚐ ☐ ✳ ⅄ ⚠ ⑧ ⊘ 📧 T ⎣ ⎈
🐾 ⅋
➡ ⌐ 😷 ✒

NETHER KELLET

Hawthorns Caravan & Camping Park (SD514686)
LA6 1EA ☎ 01524 732079 Signposted
Nearby town: Carnforth
► ► ► Family Park ★ ♥ £11.50 ♥ £11.50 ⚑ £8-£10
Open Mar-Oct Booking advisable bank hols Last arrival
22.00hrs Last departure noon
A very well-kept and planned site in a rural setting on the edge of the village. From junc 35 of M6 take B6254 towards Kirkby Lonsdale through village. A 10-acre site with 25 touring pitches and 62 statics.
Putting green, library, table tennis & darts.

🔊 🛒 ⊙ 🗒 🍳 🍺 ✳ ⚠ ⑧ 📧 ⎣ 🎯 🐴 🐴
➡ ∪ ⌐ ⓞ ⚠ ⊀ 😷 ✒ ⚠ 🐾

ORMSKIRK

Abbey Farm Caravan Park (SD434098)
Dark Ln L40 5TX ☎ 01695 572686 Signposted
Nearby town: Liverpool

► ► ► ► De-Luxe Park ★ ♥ £7.50-£10.50
♥ £7.50-£10.50 ⚑ £3.50-£9
Open all year Booking advisable public hols & Jul-Aug
Last arrival 22.00hrs Last departure 13.00hrs   *contd.*

A well-maintained rural site with level, grassy pitches close to town. In the grounds of Burscough Abbey, signed from the town centre on unclass rd to A5209 to Burscough. A 6-acre site with 56 touring pitches and 44 statics.
Undercover washing up area. Off-licence.

Credit Cards ●● ▬ 🔒

Shaw Hall Caravan Park (SD397119)
Smithy Ln, Scarisbrick L40 8HJ ☎ 01704 840298
Nearby town: Southport

►►►► De-Luxe Park ★ ⚑ £12-£15 ⚑ £12-£15
▲ £12-£15
Open Mar-7 Jan Booking advisable bank hols & peak periods
A quiet park with direct access to the Leeds-Liverpool Canal, offering good quality facilities. Situated 200yds S of canal bridge at Scarisbrick, 0.25m off A570 at Smithy Lane A 26-acre site with 43 touring pitches and 300 statics.

Credit Cards ●● ▬ ▬ 🔒

ROCHDALE

See **Greater Manchester**

SILVERDALE

Holgate's Caravan Park (SD455762)
Cove Rd LA5 0SH ☎ 01524 701508 Signposted
Nearby town: Lancaster

►►►►► Premier Park ★ ⚑ £15-£16.50 ⚑ £15-£16.50
▲ £15-£16.50
Open mid Feb-2 Nov (rs 22 Dec-mid Feb) Booking advisable school & public hols & wknds Last arrival 22.00hrs Last departure 14.00hrs

A superb family holiday park set in wooded countryside adjacent to the sea, this was the Regional Winner for Northern England of the AA's 1996 Campsite of the Year Award. From Carnforth centre take unclass Silverdale rd & follow tourist signs after Warton. A 10-acre site with 70 touring pitches and 350 statics.

Sauna, spa bath, steam room & mini-golf.

Credit Cards ●● ▬ ▬ 🔒

SOUTHPORT

See **Merseyside**

THORNTON CLEVELEYS

Kneps Farm Holiday Park (SD353429)
River Rd FY5 5LR ☎ 01253 823632 Signposted
Nearby town: Blackpool

►►►► De-Luxe Park ⚑ £8.50-£11 ⚑ £8.50-£11
▲ £8.50-£11
Open Mar-mid Nov Booking advisable at all times Last arrival 20.00hrs Last departure noon

A level stony and grassy site with mature trees near a river and with good facilities. 5m N of Blackpool. Leave A585 at roundabout onto B5412 to Little Thornton. Turn right at St Johns Church into Stanah Road, leading to River Road. A 10-acre site with 70 touring pitches and 80 statics.
Bird watching hide.

Credit Cards ●● ▬ ▬ ⊙ ▬ 🔒

WEETON

High Moor Farm Caravan Park (SD388365)
PR4 3JJ ☎ 01253 836273 (opposite Weeton Barracks) Signposted
Nearby town: Blackpool
►► Town & Country Pennant Park ★ ⚑ £10-£12 ▲ £2.50
Open Mar-Oct Booking advisable bank hols & Jul-Aug Last arrival 21.00hrs Last departure 14.00hrs
A small site in open farmland about 6m from Blackpool. Situated N of M55 (exit 3) off A585 Fleetwood road on B5260. A 4-acre site with 60 touring pitches.

LEICESTERSHIRE

For the map of this county
see NOTTINGHAMSHIRE

CASTLE DONINGTON

Donington Park Farmhouse Hotel (SK414254)
Melbourne Rd, Isley Walton DE74 2RN
☎ 01332 862409
Signposted
▶▶ Town & Country Pennant Park ★ ♥ £9-£12
♥ £9-£12 ▲ £7-£10
Open Mar-Dec (rs winter months hardstanding only)
Booking advisable summer season Last arrival 20.00hrs
Last departure noon
A developing site at rear of hotel beside Donington Park racecourse, .5m off A453 towards Melbourne. Booking essential on race days, but a quiet rural site at other times. A 6-acre site with 60 touring pitches.

Credit Cards

NORTH KILWORTH

Kilworth Caravan Park (SP605838)
Lutterworth Rd LE17 6JE ☎ 01858 880597
Nearby town: Lutterworth
▶▶▶ Family Park ♥ £6-£8 ♥ £6-£8
Open all year Booking advisable bank hols Last arrival 22.00hrs Last departure noon
Set in 12-acres of beautiful wooded estate with fishing lake and newly built facilities. On A4304, 3m from junc 20 of M1, and 1m W of North Kilworth. A 14-acre site with 40 touring pitches and 100 statics.
Lake for fishing.

Credit Cards

ULLESTHORPE

Ullesthorpe Garden Centre (SP515872)
Lutterworth Rd LE17 5DR ☎ 01455 202144
Nearby town: Leicester
▶▶ Town & Country Pennant Park ★
Open Mar-Oct Booking advisable
A pleasant site next to the garden centre, ideal for the self-contained caravanner, with nature walk and fishing on site. From M1 junc 20 take A4303 through Lutterworth, then B577 for 2m, and site just SE of Ullesthorpe village. A 7-acre site with 16 touring pitches.
Fishing & Nature Walks.

Credit Cards

LINCOLNSHIRE

ANDERBY

Manor Farm Caravan Park (TF533761)
Sea Rd PE24 5YB ☎ 01507 490372
Nearby town: Alford
▶▶▶ Family Park ★ ♥ £6 ♥ £6 ▲ £6
Open Mar-Nov Booking advisable bank hols no cars by caravans
A pleasant farm site in peaceful rural surroundings with newly-equipped toilet facilities. On unclass rd off A52 Skegness to Mablethorpe rd. A 3-acre site with 30 touring pitches.

Credit Cards

BARTON-UPON-HUMBER

Silver Birches Tourist Park (TA028232)
Waterside Rd DN18 5BA ☎ 01652 632509 (follow Bridge Viewing Point signs to Waterside rd, site just past Sloop pub) Signposted
Nearby town: Hull
▶▶▶ Family Park ★ ♥ £5.50 ♥ £5.50 ▲ £4-£5.50
Open Apr-Oct Booking advisable bank hols Last arrival 23.00hrs Last departure 20.00hrs
A very pleasant, well-screened site, convenient for Humber Bridge as well as Humberside and Lincolnshire. Situated S of bridge. Take A15 into Barton and site is clearly signed. A 2-acre site with 24 touring pitches.
Putting green.

BOSTON

Pilgrims Way (TF358434)
Church Green Rd, Fishtoft PE21 0QY
☎ 01205 366646 (A52, 1m from town)
Signposted

▶▶▶▶ De-Luxe Park ♥ £7.50 ♥ £7.50 ▲ £7.50
Open Etr & Apr-Sep Booking advisable Last arrival 20.00hrs Last departure noon
A very attractive site in the gardens of the Grange, with individually screened pitches and new purpose-built toilet facilities. From Boston travel N on A16(T), turn right onto A52, and right again at Ball House pub to Fishtoft 1m on left. A 1-acre site with 22 touring pitches.

Midville Caravan Park (TF386578)
Stickney PE22 8HW ☎ 01205 270316 Signposted
▶▶▶ Family Park ★ ♥ £5.50-£8.50 ♥ £5.50-£7
▲ £5.50-£7
Open Mar-Nov Booking advisable bank & school hols
Last arrival 22.00hrs contd.

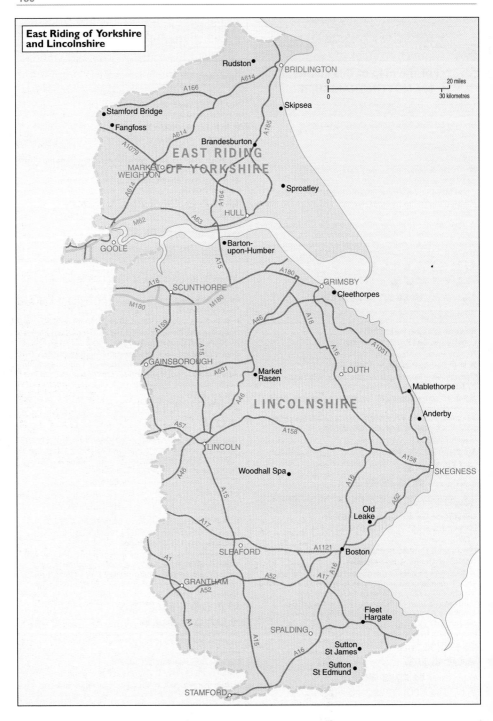

East Riding of Yorkshire and Lincolnshire

Rudston

BRIDLINGTON

A614

A166

20 miles

30 kilometres

Stamford Bridge

Skipsea

Fangfoss

A614

A165

A1079

Brandesburton

EAST RIDING

MARKET WEIGHTON

OF YORKSHIRE

A614

A164

Sproatley

A164

HULL

M62

A63

GOOLE

Barton-upon-Humber

A15

A180

SCUNTHORPE

GRIMSBY

A18

Cleethorpes

M180

M180

A46

A18

A159

A1031

A15

A16

GAINSBOROUGH

A631

Market Rasen

LOUTH

A46

Mablethorpe

LINCOLNSHIRE

Anderby

A57

A158

LINCOLN

A158

SKEGNESS

A46

Woodhall Spa

A16

A15

A52

Old Leake

A17

A1121

Boston

SLEAFORD

A1

A16

GRANTHAM

A52

A17

A52

Fleet Hargate

A1

SPALDING

A15

Sutton St James

A16

Sutton St Edmund

STAMFORD

A pleasant touring site in a quiet area. From A16(T) at Stickney travel E to Midville, turn left at bridge (Hobhole Drain), and site clearly signed. A 3-acre site with 24 touring pitches and 40 statics.

🔌📻☉🗑🏔🎣🍴🏕

➜🎣🛁

CLEETHORPES

Thorpe Park Holiday Centre (TA321035)
DN36 4HG ☎ 01472 813395
Signposted
Nearby town: Grimsby

◯◯◯◯◯◯◯◯◯◯◯◯◯◯◯◯

★ ⚑ £7-£13 ⚑ £7-£13 ⚑ £3-£9
Open Mar-Oct Booking advisable bank hols & school hols Last departure noon
A large static site with good touring facilities, and excellent recreational and leisure activities. Parts of the site overlook the sea and beach. Take unclassified road off A180 at Cleethorpes, signed Humberston and holiday Park. A 3.5-acre site with 115 touring pitches and 2500 statics.
Crazy golf & pets corner.

🔌📻🗑🥤 🔍🔦🌸🎾🏔🎱♿🖊🗑✖🗙📞

🎣🗳🛁♿

➜ ∪🏳◎🏊♨🛝🎣

Credit Cards 💳 ⬛ 💳 💳 💳 📱

◯◯◯◯◯◯◯◯◯◯◯◯◯◯◯◯

FLEET HARGATE

Delph Bank Touring Caravan & Camping Park (TF388248)
Main St PE12 8LL ☎ 01406 422910 Signposted
Nearby town: Holbeach
▶ ▶ ▶ **Family Park** ★ ⚑ £7.80 ⚑ £7.80 ⚑ £7.80
Open Mar-Oct Booking advisable 1-10 May Last arrival 22.30hrs Last departure noon
A well-kept and pretty site with some mature and many newly-planted trees. Off A17 midway between Long Sutton and Holbeach, signed. A 3-acre site with 45 touring pitches.

🔌📻☉🗑🥤 ✳🛁🔌🗑🐕🛁

MABLETHORPE

Camping & Caravanning Club Site (TF499839)
Highfield, Church Ln LN12 2NU ☎ 01507 472374 (in season) & 01203 694995 Signposted
▶ ▶ ▶ **Family Park** ★ ⚑ £11-£14 ⚑ £11-£14 ⚑ £11-£14
Open end Mar-end Sep Booking advisable bank hol & peak periods Last arrival 21.00hrs Last departure noon
Level, mainly grassy site off main road about 1m from sea. Take A1104 from Alford to Mablethorpe, turn R into Church Lane. Please see the advertisement on page 27 for details of Club Members' benefits. A 6-acre site with 105 touring pitches.

🔌📻☉🥤✳ 🏔🔌🗑🗑🅣📞🛁

➜ ∪🏳♨🎣

Credit Cards 💳 💳 📱

Golden Sands Holiday Park (TF501861)
Quebec Rd LN12 1QJ ☎ 01507 477871 & 472671
Nearby town: Skegness
▶ ▶ ▶ **Family Park** ⚑ ⚑ ⚑
Open 22 Mar-Oct Booking advisable May/spring bank hol & Jul-Sep Last departure 10.00hrs
A large, well-equipped seaside holiday park with separate touring facilities. 1m W of town off A1031 Cleethorpes road. 1st floor entertainment rooms are only accessible via stairs (no lifts). A 23-acre site with 350 touring pitches and 1300 statics.
Mini bowling alley, snooker/pool, indoor fun palace.

🔌📻🗑🥤 🔍🔦🌸🎱🏔🔌🗑🅣✖📞🛝🏓🎣

🛁♿

➜🏳♨🎣

Credit Cards 💳 💳 💳 📱 📱

Kirkstead Holiday Park (TF509835)
North Rd, Trusthorpe LN12 2QD
☎ 01507 441483 (on A52) Signposted
▶ ▶ ▶ **Family Park** ⚑ £6.50 ⚑ £6.50 ⚑ £6.50
Open Mar-Nov Booking advisable bank hols & Jul-Aug Last arrival mdnt Last departure 15.00hrs

A pleasant family-run site with a high quality toilet block. Situated 1m out of Mablethorpe towards Sutton-on-Sea, signed Kirkstead off Alford Rd. A 6-acre site with 60 touring pitches and 50 statics.
Snooker room, childrens room, evening bar meals.

🔌📻☉🗑🥤🎱🔦🌸🏔🔌🗑🛁📞🛝🏓🎣

🐕🛁♿

➜ ∪🏳◎♨🎣

MARKET RASEN

Racecourse Caravan Park (TF123883)
Legsby Rd LN8 3EA ☎ 01673 842307 & 843434
Signposted
Nearby town: Lincoln
▶ ▶ ▶ **Family Park** ★ ⚑ £9-£10.20 ⚑ £9-£10.20
⚑ £9.50-£10.70
Open 9 Apr-5 Oct Booking advisable bank hols & race days Last arrival 22.00hrs Last departure 15.00hrs
Well-run, mainly level, grass site on racecourse 1m SE of town centre off A63 Louth road. A 3-acre site with 55 touring pitches.
Reduced rate for racing.

🔌📻☉🥤✳🏔🔌🗑🗑🅣📞🐕🛁♿

➜ ∪🏳🗑

Credit Cards 💳 💳 📱

Walesby Woodlands Caravan Park (TF117906)
Walesby Rd LN8 3UN ☎ 01673 843285 Signposted
► ► ► Family Park ⚕ fr £7.50 ⚕ fr £7.50 ▲ fr £7.50
Open Mar-Oct Booking advisable public hols Last arrival
22.00hrs Last departure 17.00hrs
*A thoroughly well-planned, immaculate site. Out of
Market Rasen on B1203 and turn L for .75m. A 3-acre
site with 60 touring pitches.*

🖭 ♠ ☉ 🖥 ✳ 𝄞 🅰 🍴 ⌀ 🖶 🇹 📞 🐾 ♿
→ ∪ ▶ 🕤

OLD LEAKE

White Cat Park (TF415498)
Shaw Ln PE22 9LQ ☎ 01205 870121 Signposted
Nearby town: Boston
► ► ► Family Park ★ ⚕ £5.25-£6.25 ⚕ £5.25-£6.25
▲ £5.25-£6.25
Open mid Mar-mid Nov Booking advisable bank hols
Last arrival 22.00hrs Last departure 14.00hrs
*An efficient and pleasant site in quiet rural
surroundings just off A52, 7m NE of Boston. A 2.5-acre
site with 40 touring pitches and 4 statics.*

🖭 ♠ ☉ ✳ 𝄞 🍴 ⌀ 🖶 🇹 📞 🐾
→ 🕤

SUTTON ST EDMUND

Orchard View Caravan & Camping Park (TF365108)
Broadgate PE12 0LT ☎ 01945 700482 Signposted
Nearby town: Wisbech
► ► ► Family Park ★ ⚕ £5.50-£7.50 ⚕ £5.50-£7.50
▲ £4-£7.50

Open 31 Mar-Oct Booking advisable bank hols &
Spalding Flower Festival Last arrival anytime Last
departure anytime
*A well-maintained, level grassland site, showing signs
of general all-round improvement. 5m W of Wisbech,
signed N from B1166 or S from A17 at Long Sutton. A 2-
acre site with 35 touring pitches and 2 statics.*
Pot wash, pets corner & rally field.

🖭 ♠ ☉ 🖥 ✳ ♱ 𝄞 🍴 ⌀ 🖶 🇹 📞 🛒 🎏 🐕 🐾 ♿
→ ∪ ▶ 🕤

SUTTON ST JAMES

Foremans Bridge Caravan Park (TF409197)
PE12 0HU ☎ 01945 440346
Nearby town: Long Sutton
► ► ► Family Park ★ ⚕ £5.50-£7 ⚕ £5.50-£7 ▲ £5.50-£7
Open Mar-Dec Booking advisable Last arrival 21.00hrs
*A nicely-kept, trim site with good sanitary facilities.
Take B1390 Long Sutton to Sutton St James rd, and site
in 2m on L immediately after bridge. A 2.5-acre site with
40 touring pitches and 7 statics.*

🖭 ♠ ☉ 🖥 ♜ ✳ 🍴 ⌀ 🖶 📞 🐕 🐾
→ ▶ 🕤

WOODHALL SPA

 Bainland Country Park (TF215640)
Horncastle Rd LN10 6UX ☎ 01526 352903 &
353572 (1.5m from town, on B1191)
Signposted
Nearby town: Horncastle

❀❀❀❀❀❀❀❀❀❀❀❀❀❀❀❀❀❀❀❀❀

🏠 £9-£25 🏕 £9-£25 ⚑ £7-£22
Open all year Booking advisable all year Last arrival
20.00hrs Last departure 11.30hrs
*More a country club than a purely touring park, this is
one of the best equipped parks in the country with an
impressive array of leisure facilities, combined with
high standards of maintenance. On B1191 about 2m E
of town. A 12-acre site with 100 touring pitches and 10
statics.*
Jacuzzi, solarium, sauna, par 3 golf, putting, boule.

🔧🚗🌳⊙🦢🎵 🖇🔫⛁✳🍸⚠🛉⊘🚻🚰
✕🔥🚿🚽🎏🏪🐕🐾🛁🚾
➔∪🅿⊙🔺🎱🎵

Credit Cards 💳 ▨ ▨ ⑤

Camping & Caravanning Club Site (TF225633)
Wellsyke Ln, Kirkby-on-Bain LN10 6YU
☎ 01526 352911 (in season) & 01203 694995
Signposted
Nearby town: Boston
▶ ▶ ▶ **Family Park** ★ 🏕 £11-£14 🏕 £11-£14 ⚑ £11-£14
Open end Mar-early Nov Booking advisable bank hols &
Jul-Aug Last arrival 21.00hrs Last departure noon
*A pleasant site in silver birch wood and moorland. Take
B1191 towards Horncastle. After 5m turn right towards
Kirby-on-Bain. Signed. Please see the advertisement on
page 27 for details of Club Members' benefits. A 6-acre
site with 100 touring pitches.*

🔤🐾⊙🖇🦢✳🛉⊘🚻🚰🚗🐕🐾🛁
➔∪🅿🚻🎵🛁

Credit Cards 💳 ▨ ▨

LONDON

For the map see ESSEX

E4 CHINGFORD

Lee Valley Campsite (TQ381970)
Sewardstone Rd E4 7RA ☎ 0181 529 5689
Signposted

▶ ▶ ▶ ▶ **De-Luxe Park** ★ 🏕 £10 🏕 £10 ⚑ £10
Open Apr-Oct Booking advisable bank hols & Jul-Aug
Last arrival 22.00hrs Last departure noon
*Well-run useful North London site with excellent
modern facilities and a peaceful atmosphere, with easy
access to town. Overlooking King George's reservoir
and close to Epping Forest. From M25 junct 26 to A112
and signed. A 12-acre site with 200 touring pitches.*

🔤🐾⊙🖇🦢✳⚠🛉⊘🚻🚰🚗🐕🐾🛁🚾
➔∪🅿⊙🚻🎵

Credit Cards 💳 ▨ ▨ ▨ ⑤

See advertisement on page 164.

N9 EDMONTON

**Lee Valley Leisure Centre Camping & Caravan
(TQ360945)**
Meridian Way N9 0AS
☎ 0181 803 6900 & 0181 345 6666
Signposted
Nearby town: Edmonton/Enfield
▶ ▶ ▶ **Family Park** ★ 🏕 £8.50-£10.40 🏕 £8.50-£10.40
⚑ £8.50-£10.40
Booking advisable Jul-Aug Last arrival 22.00hrs Last
departure noon
*A pleasant open site tucked away behind a large
sporting complex with use of swimming pool, roller
skating and golf driving range. Very good toilet
facilities, and handy for London. 5m S of M25, signed
from A10. A 4.5-acre site with 160 touring pitches.*
Membership of adjacent sports complex.

🔤🐾⊙🖇🦢✳ ⚡🔫🔫✳🍸⚠🛉⊘🚻✕🔥
🚗🛁🐾🛁
➔🅿🔺🎱🚻🎵

Credit Cards 💳 ▨ ▨ ▨ ⑤

See advertisement on page 164.

MERSEYSIDE

For the map of this county
see SHROPSHIRE

SOUTHPORT

Hurlston Hall Country Caravan Park (SD398107)
Southport Rd L40 8HB ☎ 01704 841064
▶ ▶ ▶ **Family Park** 🏕 £8-£10 🏕 £8-£10 ⚑ £8-£10
Open Etr-Oct Booking advisable bank hols ✿
*New touring park at side of existing static park in
countryside about 10 mins drive from Southport. A
peaceful tree-lined park with fishing and golf nearby.
On A570, 3m from Ormskirk in Southport direction. A 5-
acre site with 60 touring pitches and 68 statics.*

🔤🐾🖇🦢🍸⚠🛉🚗🛁
➔🅿🛁

Willowbank Holiday Home & Touring Park (SD305110)
Coastal Rd, Ainsdale PR8 3ST ☎ 01704 571566
▶ ▶ ▶ **Family Park** ★ 🏕 £10 🏕 £10
Open Mar-Oct Booking advisable bank hols Last arrival
20.00hrs Last departure mdnt
*Set in a wooded clearing on a nature reserve, this brand
new site is just off the coastal road to Southport. Leave
A56(T) at traffic lights onto coastal road to Southport,
and site is 300 metres from traffic lights on left before
railway bridge. A 6-acre site with 54 touring pitches and
102 statics.*

🔤🐾⊙🖇🦢⚠🛉🚗🌳🐕🐾🛁
➔∪🅿🔺🎵🛁

Summer weather can mean rain. It is a good idea
to prepare for ground to be wet underfoot.
Take something to amuse the children if they
can't go outside.

BOTH WORLDS

Countryside settings with London on the doorstep

The Lee Valley Regional Park stretches from the edge of London's Docklands up to rural Hertfordshire and Essex. It boasts five camping and caravan sites for you to choose from, all with modern facilities, all in pleasant surroundings and all with their own local leisure attractions. Yet, each is within easy reach of Central London by public transport. So you can sleep under the stars and still enjoy the thrills of the West End.

Roydon Mill Leisure Park, Roydon, Essex: Children's adventure playground. Riverside Club with regular entertainment, 40-acre lake for water-based activities. Fast train service to London. Tel: 01279 792777.

Lee Valley Caravan Park, Hoddesdon, Herts: Delightful riverside site with good fishing, walking and boating nearby. Fast train service to London. Tel: 01992 462090.

Lee Valley Campsite, Chingford, Essex: On the edge of Epping Forest, close to the River Lee Country Park, easy access from the M25. Bus and tube to London. Tel: 0181 529 5689.

Lee Valley Leisure Complex, Edmonton, N. London: Large leisure centre, 18-hole golf course, 12-screen UCI cinema. Bus and tube to London. Tel: 0181 803 6900

Lee Valley Cycle Circuit, Leyton, E. London: Small site in 40 acres of open parkland, yet only 4 miles from the Tower of London. Adjacent to Lee Valley Sports Centre and off-road Cycle Circuit. Bus and tube to the West End. Tel:0181 534 6085.

NORFOLK

BARNEY

The Old Brick Kilns (TG007328)
Little Barney Ln, Barney NR21 0NL ☎ 01328 878305
Signposted
Nearby town: Fakenham

► ► ► ► De-Luxe Park 🚐 £8.75-£11.25 🚗 £8.75-£11.25
▲ £8.75-£11.25
Open Mar-Oct (rs low season bar food/takeaway
selected nights only) Booking advisable bank hols &
Jul-Aug Last arrival 22.00hrs Last departure noon
*A secluded and peaceful site with a small boating pool
and mature trees. Excellent, well-planned toilet
facilities. Approach from the A148 near Thursford
towards Barney village and in .25m turn into no-
through road. Site in .5m. A 6.5-acre site with 60 touring
pitches.*
Boules, outdoor draughts/chess, family games area.

🚐🐾☉📖🅀🔌🖵☀♀⚠🔌🥤🖩🇹🗙🔌🚿
🎋🐾🐾♿
→ 🍴
Credit Cards 💳

BELTON

Rose Farm Touring & Camping Park (TG488033)
Stepshort NR31 9JS ☎ 01493 780896 Signposted
Nearby town: Great Yarmouth
► ► ► Family Park ★ 🚐 £5-£6.50 🚗 £5-£6.50 ▲ £5-£6.50
Open all year (rs Dec & Jan repairs/decorating, please
telephone) Booking advisable Aug Last arrival 22.00hrs
*A very neat site with a good toilet block and tidy
facilities. Follow signs to Belton off A143, turn right at
the lane called Stepshort, and the site is first on right. A
6-acre site with 80 touring pitches.*
🚐🐾☉📖🅀🔌🖵☀⚠🔌🥤🖩🔌🎋🐾♿
→🍴🥤⛽☕🍴

Wild Duck Holiday Park (TG475028)
Howards Common NR31 9NE ☎ 01493 780268
Signposted
Nearby town: Great Yarmouth
► ► ► Family Park ★ 🚐 £7-£13 🚗 £7-£13 ▲ £7-£13
Open Mar-Oct Booking advisable Jun-Aug Last arrival
23.00hrs Last departure noon
*Level grassy site in forest with small cleared areas for
tourers and well laid out facilities. Signed from A143. A
60-acre site with 150 touring pitches and 309 statics.*
Sauna, solarium, jacuzzi & fitness room.
🚐🐾☉📖🅀🔌🖵☀♀🔌⚠🔌🥤🖩🇹🗙🔌🚿🎋🐾
→🍴🥤⛽☕🍴
Credit Cards 💳

CAISTER-ON-SEA

Grasmere Caravan Park (TG521115)
9 Bultitude's Loke, Yarmouth Rd NR30 5DH
☎ 01493 720382 (from A149 at Stadium rdbt after .5m sharp left turn just past petrol station)
Signposted
Nearby town: Great Yarmouth
► ► ► Family Park ★ ♣ £5.40-£8.70 ♣ £5.40-£8.70
Open Apr-Oct Booking advisable school & bank hols
Last arrival 22.00hrs Last departure 11.00hrs ♨
Mainly level grass and gravel site with mature trees. Set in meadowland in an urban area with access to A149. A 2-acre site with 46 touring pitches and 62 statics.

🎮 📶 ☉ 🖥 ☀ ⚠ ⓘ ✐ 🔾 📟 🎵 ⚿
→ ∪ ⏊ ⋎ 🎵 ✔

Credit Cards 💳 ▦ ▦ 🖅

Old Hall Leisure Park (TG521122)
High St NR30 5JL ☎ 01493 720400 (opposite church)
Signposted
Nearby town: Great Yarmouth
► ► ► Family Park ★ ♣ £6-£12 ♣ £6-£12
Open Spring bank hol wk & 22 Jun-1 Sep (rs Apr-21 Jun pool closed, bar/rest limited opening) Booking advisable Spring bank hol & Jul-Aug Last arrival mdnt Last departure 10.00hrs ♨
A small site at rear of hotel on main street (B1159) with a neat and attractive layout. Convenient for shops and beach. A 2-acre site with 35 touring pitches and 38 statics.

🎮 📶 ☉ 🖥 ⛏ 🔾 ☀ ⚠ ⚠ ⓘ ✐ ✖ ⚿
→ ∪ ⏊ ◎ △ ⋎ 🎵 ✔ 🖐

Credit Cards 💳 ▦ ▦ 🖅

CAWSTON

Haveringland Hall Caravan Park (TG153213)
NR10 4PN ☎ 01603 871302 Signposted
Nearby town: Alysham
►► Town & Country Pennant Park ★ ♣ £7.50-£8.50 ♣ £7.50-£8.50 ▲ £6.50-£8.50
Open Mar-Oct Booking advisable public hol wks & Jul-Aug Last arrival 22.00hrs Last departure noon
A very pleasant site set in woodland and meadowland with direct access to lake. Level pitches in different area with interesting mature trees. 10m N of Norwich on Cawston road. An 8-acre site with 65 touring pitches and 80 statics.
14 acre fishing lake.

🎮 📶 ☉ ☀ ⓘ ✐ 📟 🔾 🎵 🐕
→ ∪ ✔ 🖐

CLIPPESBY

Clippesby Holidays (TG423147)
NR29 3BL ☎ 01493 367800 Signposted
Nearby town: Great Yarmouth
► ► ► Family Park ♣ £8.50-£15.50 ♣ £8.50-£15.50 ▲ £8.50-£15.50
Open Etr wk, mid May-mid Sep (rs Mayday wknd some facilities may close) Booking advisable school hols Last arrival 17.30hrs Last departure 11.00hrs
A lovely country house estate with vans hidden among trees and a friendly welcome. From A1064 at Acle to

B1152 and signed. A 30-acre site with 100 touring pitches and 22 statics.
Putting, bowls, adult bicycle hire & tea room.

🎮 📶 ☉ 🖥 ⛏ ⚘ 🔾 ⚫ ☀ ⚠ ⚠ ⓘ ✐ 📟 🎵 ⚿
🎭 🎋 🐕 🖐 ♿
→ ∪ ◎ △ ⋎ 🎵

Credit Cards 💳 ▦ ▦ 🖅

CROMER

Seacroft Camping Park (TG206424)
Runton Rd NR27 9NJ ☎ 01263 511722
Signposted

► ► ► ► De-Luxe Park ★ ♣ £7.25-£9 ♣ £7.25-£9
▲ £7.25-£9
Open Mar-Oct Booking advisable school hols, 22-31 May & 4 Sep Last arrival 23.00hrs Last departure noon
A very good touring site, well laid out and landscaped. Toilets and showers tiled and spotless. 1m W of Cromer on A149 coast road. A 5-acre site with 120 touring pitches.
Baby change.

🎮 📶 ☉ 🖥 ⛏ 🔾 ⚫ 🔾 ☀ ⚠ ⚠ ⓘ ✐ 📟 🎵 ⚿
🎭 🎋 🐕 🖐 ♿
→ ∪ ⏊ ◎ △ 🎵 🎵

Credit Cards 💳 ▦ ▦ 🖅

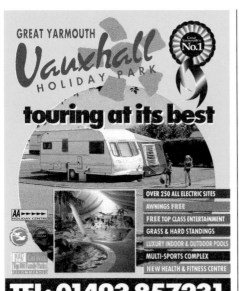

Forest Park Caravan Site (TG233405)
Northrepps Rd NR27 OJR ☎ 01263 513290 Signposted
▶▶▶ Family Park ♖ £6.50-£10 ♙ £6.50-£10 ▲ £6.50-£10
Open Apr-Oct Booking advisable Etr, Spring bank hol &
Jul-Aug Last arrival 22.00hrs Last departure 14.00hrs
Surrounded by forest, this gently sloping parkland offers
a wide choice of pitches. Signed from A149 and B1159.
An 85-acre site with 344 touring pitches and 372 statics.
BMX track.

🏠📶☉🗑🏕🍴 ♦☀♉⚙🖥🐟🅣✖🔔🐕
➜ ∪▶♃♨♪
Credit Cards 💳💳

FAKENHAM

Caravan Club Site (TF926288)
Fakenham Racecourse NR21 7NY ☎ 01328 862388
Signposted
▶▶▶ Family Park ★ ♖ £8.50-£14 ♙ £8.50-£14
▲ £8.50-£14
Open all year Booking advisable Etr & May-Aug Last
departure noon
A level grassy site with mature trees, three-quarters of a
mile SW of town off A1065 Swaffham road. Tourers
move on race days to centre of course, and have free
racing. An 11.5-acre site with 150 touring pitches.
TV aerial hook-ups & satellite channels.

🏠📶☉🗑🏕🍴☀♉⚙🖥🅣✖🔔🐕
♉⚙
➜ ∪▶♪
Credit Cards 💳💳💳💳 💹

GREAT YARMOUTH

See **Caister-on-Sea**

 Vauxhall Holiday Park (TG520083)
4 Acle New Rd NR30 1TB ☎ 01493 857231
Signposted

★ ♖ £12-£20 ♙ £12-£20 ▲ £12-£20
Open Etr then mid May-Sep Booking advisable mid Jul-
Aug Last arrival 21.00hrs Last departure 10.00hrs ⌖
A very large holiday complex with plenty of
entertainment and access to beach, river, estuary, lake
and main A47. A 16-acre site with 256 touring pitches
and 446 statics.
Childrens pool, entertainment. Multi Sports Arena.

🏠📶☉🗑🏕 ♦♦🗑☀♉🛖🏠🖥🅣✖🔔
♪♨♉🛖
➜ ∪▶☉♨♃♨♪
Credit Cards 💳💳💳💳 💹

HUNSTANTON

 Searles of Hunstanton (TF671400)
South Beach PE36 5BB ☎ 01485 534211 &
532342 ext 100
Signposted
Nearby town: Kings Lynn

♖♙▲
Open Etr/Mar-Nov (rs Mar-May & Oct-Nov outdoor pool
closed) Booking advisable bank hols & Jul-Aug Last
arrival 21.00hrs Last departure 11.00hrs
A large seaside holiday complex with well-managed
facilities, adjacent to sea and beach. Winner of the
Central England Campsite of the Year Award 1998/9. On
B1161, in South Hunstanton, off A149 King's Lynn road.
An 18-acre site with 350 touring pitches and 450 statics.
Stables, entertainment programme & hire shop.

🏠📶☉🗑🏕🍴 ♦♦♉☀♉⚙🖥🅣✖
🔔🛖🏠🐕♉⚙
➜ ∪▶☉♨♃♨♪
Credit Cards 💳💳💳💳 💹
See advertisement on page 168.

KING'S LYNN

See **Narborough**

MUNDESLEY

Links Caravan Site (TG305365)
Links Rd NR11 8AE ☎ 01263 720665 Signposted
Nearby town: North Walsham
▶▶ Town & Country Pennant Park ♖♙▲
Open Etr-1st wk Oct Booking advisable bank hols &
peak season Last arrival 22.00hrs Last departure noon
A pleasant site on a south-facing slope with level
pitches, offering distant rural views. From B1159 at
Mundesley turn into Church Road. A 2-acre site with 32
touring pitches.

🏠📶☉☀🖥
➜ ∪▶☉♪🗑🏠

NARBOROUGH

Pentney Park (TF742141)
Gayton Rd, Pentney PE32 1HU
☎ 01760 337479 & 709120
Signposted
Nearby town: Swaffham
▶ ▶ ▶ Family Park ★ ⊕ £8-£10.50 ⊕ £8-£10.50
▲ £8-£10.50
Open all year (rs Nov-Feb outdoor swimming pool closed) Booking advisable bank hols Last arrival 22.30hrs Last departure 11.00hrs
A large family touring site set in woods and meadowland adjacent to A47 Swaffham-King's Lynn Road. A 16-acre site with 200 touring pitches.

🔧 ⬚ ⊙ ⬚ ⬚ ⬚ ⬚ ⬚ ⬚ ⬚ ⬚ ⬚ ⬚ ⬚ ⬚ ⬚
⬚ ⬚ ⬚ ⬚
→ ⬚

Credit Cards 💳 💳 💳 💳 💳

NORWICH

Camping & Caravanning Club Site (TG237063)
Martineau Ln NR1 2HX
☎ 01603 620060 (in season) & 01203 694995
Signposted
▶ Town & Country Pennant Park ★ ⊕ £10-£13
⊕ £10-£13 ▲ £10-£13
Open end Mar-end Sep Booking advisable bank hols & Jul-Aug Last arrival 21.00hrs Last departure noon
A small site on the outskirts of Norwich close to a river and screened by trees from the city. From A47 take A146 left to traffic lights, then left and left again. Please

see the advertisement on page 27 for details of Club Members' benefits. A 2.5-acre site with 50 touring pitches.

🔧 ⬚ ⊙ ⬚ ⬚ ⬚ ⬚ ⬚ ⬚ ⬚ ⬚ ⬚ ⬚
→ ⬚ ⬚ ⬚ ⬚

Credit Cards 💳 💳 💳

SANDRINGHAM

Camping & Caravanning Club Site (TF683274)
The Sandringham Estate, Double Lodges PE35 6EA
☎ 01485 542555 (in season) & 01203 694995
Signposted
Nearby town: King's Lynn

▶ ▶ ▶ ▶ De-Luxe Park ★ ⊕ £13-£14 ⊕ £13-£14
▲ £13-£14
Open end Feb-1 Dec Booking advisable bank hols & high season Last arrival 21.00hrs Last departure noon
A prestige site, very well landscaped with toilets and other buildings blending in with the scenery. Well signed off A149 Hunstanton/Kings Lyn rd and A148. Please see the advertisement on page 27 for details of Club Members' benefits. A 22-acre site with 250 touring pitches.

🔧 ⬚ ⊙ ⬚ ⬚ ⬚ ⬚ ⬚ ⬚ ⬚ ⬚ ⬚ ⬚ ⬚
→ ⬚

Credit Cards 💳 💳 💳 💳 💳

SCOLE

Willows Camping & Caravan Park (TM146789)
Diss Rd IP21 4DH ☎ 01379 740271 (at Scole rdbt on A140 turn onto A1066, site 150yds on left) Signposted
Nearby town: Diss
▶ ▶ ▶ Family Park 🏕 🏕 ⅄
Open May-Sep Booking advisable Spring bank hol & school hols Last arrival 23.00hrs Last departure noon
Level, peaceful site on the banks of the River Waveney, bordered by willow trees. From A140 take A1066 at rndbt opp Scole Village access. Site signed in 300 yds. A 4-acre site with 32 touring pitches.
Washing-up sinks.

🏕 📻 ☉ ✳ 🏔 🛈 🖋 🔄 🔳 Ⓣ
➔ ▶ 🔧 🔲 🐌

SCRATBY

Scratby Hall Caravan Park (TG501155)
NR29 3PH ☎ 01493 730283 (off B1159) Signposted
Nearby town: Great Yarmouth
▶ ▶ ▶ Family Park ★ 🏕 £4.50-£9.90 🏕 £4.50-£9.90 ⅄ £4.50-£9.90
Open Spring bank hol-mid Sep (rs Etr-Spring bank hol & mid Sep-Oct reduced hours & shop closed) Booking advisable Spring bank hol wk & Jul-Aug Last arrival 10.00hrs Last departure noon

An immaculate grass site with very tidy toilet block and new children's play area, close to beach and the Norfolk Broads. Signed off B1159. A 5-acre site with 108 touring pitches.
Washing-up & food preparation room.

🏕 📻 ☉ 🔲 🛒 ✳ 🏔 🛈 🖋 🔳 Ⓣ 📞 🐌 ♿
➔ ∪ ▶ ✂ 🔧

SNETTISHAM

Diglea Caravan & Camping Park (TF656336)
Beach Rd PE31 7RB ☎ 01485 541367 (turn left at sign Snettisham beach, site on left 1.5m from turning) Signposted
Nearby town: Hunstanton
▶ ▶ ▶ Family Park 🏕 £5.50-£9 🏕 £5.50-£9 ⅄ £5.50-£9
Open Apr-Oct Booking advisable bank hols & mid Jul-Aug Last arrival 22.30hrs Last departure noon
Undulating pasture land, close to the sea and in rural surroundings. Signed from A149. A 15-acre site with 200 touring pitches and 150 statics.

🏕 📻 ☉ 🔲 🛒 ✳ 🍴 🏔 🛈 🖋 🔳 Ⓣ 📞 🔄 🐤 🐌
➔ ∪ △ 🔧

SYDERSTONE

The Garden Caravan Site (TF812337)
Barmer Hall Farm ☎ 01485 578220
Nearby town: Fakenham
▶ ▶ ▶ Family Park ★ 🏕 fr £8 🏕 fr £8 ⅄ fr £8
Open Mar-Nov Booking advisable Last departure noon
In the tranquil setting of a former walled garden beside a large farmhouse, with mature trees and shrubs, and surrounded by woodland, a brand new secluded site. Signed off B1454 at Barmer between A148 and Dorking, 1m NW of Syderstone. A 3.5-acre site with 30 touring pitches.

🏕 📻 ☉ 🍴 ✳ 🛈 🔳 📞 🐤 🐦
➔ ∪ ▶ 🐌

TRIMINGHAM

Woodlands Caravan Park (TG274388)
NR11 8AL ☎ 01263 579208 Signposted
Nearby town: Cromer
▶ ▶ ▶ Family Park 🏕 🏕
Open Apr-Oct Booking advisable public hols & Jul-Aug Last arrival 23.00hrs Last departure noon
A pleasant woodland site close to the sea but well sheltered from winds. Pitches in open areas among the trees. 4m SE on coast road, B1159. A 10-acre site with 85 touring pitches and 179 statics.

🏕 📻 ☉ 🍴 🍷 ♀ 🏔 🛈 🔳 ✖ 📞 🔄 ☰ 🐌 ♿
➔ ∪ ▶ 🍽 🔧
Credit Cards 💳 🈺 🈹 🈶 Ⓖ

WEST RUNTON

Camping & Caravanning Club Site (TG189419)
Holgate Ln NR27 9NW ☎ 01263 837544 (in season) & 01203 694995 Signposted
Nearby town: Cromer
▶ ▶ ▶ Family Park ★ 🏕 £13-£14 🏕 £13-£14 ⅄ £13-£14
Open end Mar-early Nov Booking advisable bank hols & peak periods Last arrival 21.00hrs Last departure noon
A lovely, well-kept site with some gently sloping pitches on pleasantly undulating ground. Surrounded by woodland. Approach from A148 about 2m SW of Cromer, signposted into unclass road and reached only by a narrow gravel bridleway. Please see the advertisement on page 27 for details of Club Members' benefits. An 11.75-acre site with 225 touring pitches.

🏕 📻 ☉ 🔲 🍷 ✳ 🏔 🔳 Ⓣ 📞 🔄 🐌 ♿
➔ ∪ ▶ 🍽 🔧
Credit Cards 💳 🈺 🈹 🈶 Ⓖ

WORTWELL

Little Lakeland Caravan Park (TM279849)
IP20 0EL ☎ 01986 788646 Signposted
Nearby town: Harleston

⭕⭕⭕⭕⭕⭕⭕

▶ ▶ ▶ ▶ De-Luxe Park 🏕 £7.40-£9.20 🏕 £7.40-£9.20
Open Mar-Oct (rs Mar-Etr restricted laundry facilities) Booking advisable bank hols & peak periods Last arrival 22.00hrs Last departure noon

A well-kept and pretty site built round a lake, with individual pitches in hedged enclosures, and brand new toilet facilities. 2m NE of Harleston. A 4.5-acre site with 40 touring pitches and 16 statics.
Library & fishing on site.

🔌 📻 ☉ 📺 ✳ ⚠ ➊ ⊘ ✚ 🅃 🅱 ♿
➜ ∪ ▶ ⅄ ☕ ✈

NORTHAMPTONSHIRE

For the map of this county
see BERKSHIRE

THRAPSTON

Mill Marina (SP994781)
Midland Rd NN14 4JR ☎ 01832 732850 Signposted
Nearby town: Kettering
▶▶ Town & Country Pennant Park 🏕 🏕 🛪
Open Apr-Dec (rs Jan-Mar) Booking advisable public hols & summer wknds Last arrival 21.00hrs Last departure 18.00hrs
Level riverside site with mature trees and bushes, with pleasure trips by boat from site. Take Thrapston exit from A14 or A605, signed. A 3-acre site with 45 touring pitches and 6 statics.
Slipway for boats & canoes;coarse fishing on site.

🔌 📻 ☉ 📺 ✳ ⚑ ➊ ⊘ ✚ 🅃 ✆ 🏕 🛪
➜ ∪ 🔺 ✈ 🅱

NORTHUMBERLAND

ALWINTON

Clennell Hall (NT928072)
Clennell NE65 7BG ☎ 01669 650341 Signposted
Nearby town: Rothbury
▶▶▶ Family Park 🏕 🏕 🛪
Open Mar-Jan (rs Feb by arrangement only) Booking advisable summer & bank hols Last arrival 23.00hrs Last departure 16.00hrs
A tranquil rural site on the fringe of the National Park NW of Rothbury. From B6341 take unclass rd signed Alwinton and caravan signs. A 14.5-acre site with 50 touring pitches and 18 statics.

🔌 📻 ☉ 📺 ● 🖵 ✳ ⚑ ⚠ ➊ ⊘ ✘ ✆ 🏕 🛪 ♿
➜ ∪ ✈

BAMBURGH

Glororum Caravan Park (NU166334)
Glororum Farm NE69 7AW ☎ 01668 214457 Signposted
▶▶▶ Family Park 🏕 🏕 🛪
Open Apr-Oct Booking advisable school hols Last arrival 22.00hrs Last departure 10.00hrs
A well-run site with good facilities, pleasantly situated off B1341, 1m W of Bamburgh. The open countryside setting gives views of Bamburgh Castle and

surrounding farmland. Leave A1 at junc B1341 (Purdy's Lodge), in 3.5m turn left onto unclass rd, and site on left in 300 yds. A 6-acre site with 100 touring pitches and 150 statics.

🔌 📻 ☉ 📺 ⚑ ✳ ⚠ ➊ ⊘ 🅃 ✆ 🐕 🛪 🅱
➜ ∪ ▶ ✈

Waren Caravan Park (NU155343)
Waren Mill NE70 7EE ☎ 01668 214366 Signposted
Nearby town: Berwick-on-Tweed
▶▶▶ Family Park ★ 🏕 £9.75-£13.50 🏕 £7.75-£11.50
🛪 £7.75-£11.50
Open Apr-Oct Booking advisable Spring bank hol & Jul-Aug Last arrival 20.00hrs Last departure noon
Attractive seaside site close to beach, surrounded by a slightly sloping grassy embankment affording shelter for caravans. Immaculate sanitary facilities. Situated 2m E of town on B1342. From A1 turn onto B1342 signed Bamburgh, and take unclassified road past Waren Mill, signed Budle. A 4-acre site with 120 touring pitches and 300 statics.
100 acres of private heathland.

🔌 📻 ☉ 📺 ⚑ ⚡ ● ✳ ⚑ ⚠ ➊ ⊘ 🅃 ✘ ✆ ♨
🏕 🛏 🛪 🅱 ♿
➜ ∪ ▶ ✈

Credit Cards 💳 ▬ ▬ ▬ ▬ 💷

BARDON MILL

Ashcroft Farm (NY782645)
NE47 7JA ☎ 01434 344409
Nearby town: Hexham
▶▶ Town & Country Pennant Park ★ 🏕 £3 🏕 £3 🛪 £2
Open Apr-Oct Booking advisable Last arrival 21.00hrs Last departure 13.00hrs
A small site in meadowland by a river, situated on a farm behind the war memorial in the village. Adjacent to A69, between Haltwhistle and Hexham. Leave A69 at Bardon Mill, and site at end of village. Own sanitary facilities essential. A 2-acre site with 20 touring pitches.
Fishing.

➜ 🅱

BEADNELL

Camping & Caravanning Club Site (NU231297)
NE67 5BX ☎ 01665 720586 (in season) & 01203 694995
▶▶ Town & Country Pennant Park ★ 🏕 £10-£13
🛪 £10-£13
Open end Mar-Sep Booking advisable bank hols & Jul-Aug Last arrival 21.00hrs Last departure noon
Level, grassy site set in coastal area with access to sea, beach and main road. From A1 follow B1340 signposted Seahouses-Bamburgh. Please see the advertisement on page 27 for details of Club Members' benefits. A 14-acre site with 150 touring pitches.

📻 ☉ 📺 ⚑ ✳ ➊ ⊘ ✆ 🅱
➜ ∪ ▶ ⅄ ✈

Credit Cards 💳 ▬

AA members can call AA Hotel Booking Service on 0990 050505 to book at AA recognised hotels and B & Bs in the UK and Ireland, or through our Internet site: http://www.theaa.co.uk/hotels

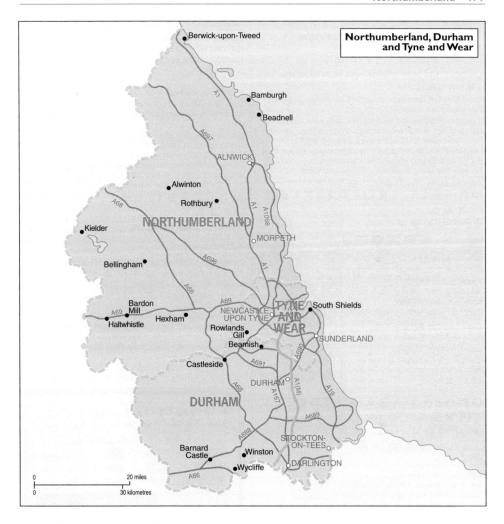

Berwick-upon-Tweed

Northumberland, Durham and Tyne and Wear

Bamburgh
Beadnell
ALNWICK
Alwinton
Rothbury
NORTHUMBERLAND
Kielder
MORPETH
Bellingham
Bardon Mill
A69
Haltwhistle
Hexham
NEWCASTLE UPON TYNE
TYNE AND WEAR
South Shields
Rowlands Gill
SUNDERLAND
Beamish
Castleside
DURHAM
DURHAM
Barnard Castle
Winston
Wycliffe
STOCKTON-ON-TEES
DARLINGTON

0   20 miles
0   30 kilometres

BELLINGHAM

Brown Rigg Caravan & Camping Park (NY835826)
NE48 2JY ☎ 01434 220175
Nearby town: Hexham

►►►► De-Luxe Park 🚐 £7-£8.50 🚐 £7-£8.50
▲ £6-£7.50
Open wk before Etr-Oct Booking advisable bank & school hols Last arrival 20.30hrs Last departure noon
This well laid out site is in a pleasant rural setting, run by enthusiastic resident owners. On B6320 .5miles S of Bellingham. A 5.5-acre site with 80 touring pitches.

🔧🐾☉🗑🍴◀🛒⚲❋🏔🚿🔌🎣T📞
🚰🐎⛴
➔►♪

BERWICK-UPON-TWEED

Berwick Holiday Centre (NU000540)
Magdalene Fields TD15 1NE
☎ 01289 307113 & 331700

★ ✿ £4-£10 ✿ £4-£10
Open Mar-Oct Booking advisable Last arrival 21.00hrs
Last departure noon
A large holiday centre with good touring facilities, and plenty of modern entertainment, shopping and sports facilities. Leave A1 N of Berwick, travel S on A1167 towards Berwick, and after crossing railway bridge turn left into Northumberland Ave, signed holiday centre. A 1.5-acre site with 35 touring pitches and 819 statics. Bowling green, arcade, basket ball & kiddies club.

🔌 🐕 ☉ 🍴 ♘ 🥤 ⚡ 🌳 🏪 🖥 🛒 🍳 ✕ 🔥 🎣

Credit Cards ⬤ ■ ▥ ▦ ▨ 🅂

Haggerston Castle (NU041435)
Beal TD15 2PA ☎ 01289 381333 & 381200
Signposted

★ ✿ £9.50-£21 ✿ £9.50-£21
Open Mar-Oct Booking advisable Last arrival 21.00hrs
Last departure 10.00hrs
A large holiday centre with a very well equipped touring park, offering comprehensive holiday activities. On A1, 5.5m S of Berwick on Tweed, and signed. A 7-acre site with 156 touring pitches and 1200 statics.

🔌 🐕 ☉ 🍴 ♘ 🥤 ⚡ 🌳 🏪 🖥 ✕ 🔥 🛒 🍳

Credit Cards ⬤ ▥ ▦ ▨ 🅂

Ord House Caravan Park (NT982515)
East Ord TD15 2NS ☎ 01289 305288 Signposted

▶ ▶ ▶ ▶ ▶ Premier Park ★ ✿ £7.25-£11.90
✿ £7.25-£11.90 ▲ £4.25-£11.90
Open Mar-9 Jan Booking advisable bank hols & Jul-Aug
Last arrival 23.00hrs Last departure noon
A very well-run site set in pleasant surroundings with mature trees and bushes. Situated on the A698, 1m from Berwick. A 6-acre site with 70 touring pitches and 200 statics.
Crazy golf, tabletennis,9 hole pitch/putt.

🔌 🐕 ☉ 🍴 ♘ ⚡ 🥤 🌳 🏪 Ⓣ ✕ 🔥 🛒 🍳

Credit Cards ⬤ ▦ ▨ 🅂

CRASTER

Dunstan Hill Camping & Caravanning Club Site (NU236214)
Dunstan Hill NE66 3TQ ☎ 01665 576310 (in season) & 01203 694995
Nearby town: Alnwick
▶ ▶ ▶ Family Park ★ ✿ £11-£14 ✿ £11-£14 ▲ £11-£14
Open end Mar-early Nov Booking advisable Spring bank hol & Jul-Aug Last arrival 21.00hrs Last departure noon
An immaculately maintained site with pleasant landscaping close to the beach and historic town of Alnwick, but in a countryside setting. From B1340 at Embleton take unclass rd signed Craster. Please see the advertisement on page 27 for details of Club Members' benefits. A 10-acre site with 150 touring pitches.

🔌 🐕 ☉ 🍴 ♘ ✳ ⚡ 🌳 🍳 🔥 🛒

Credit Cards ⬤ ▥ ▦ ▨ 🅂

HALTWHISTLE

Camping & Caravanning Club Site (NY685621)
Burnfoot, Park Village NE49 0JP ☎ 01434 320106 (in season) & 01203 694995 Signposted
▶ ▶ ▶ Family Park ★ ✿ £9.20-£11.60 ✿ £9.20-£11.60
▲ £9.20-£11.60
Open end Mar-early Nov Booking advisable bank hols & high season Last arrival 21.00hrs Last departure noon
An attractive site on the banks of the River South Tyne, amid mature trees, on the Bellister Castle Estate. From

A69 at Haltwhistle take unclass road signed Alston, and site 1.5m. Please see the advertisement on page 27 for details of Club Members' benefits. A 3-acre site with 60 touring pitches.

Fishing.

🔌📶☉🅿🚱✖🚻🛈⊘👝♿🐴🐕♿

➜⚠️🔩🏊

Credit Cards 💳 🔲

HEXHAM

Causey Hill Caravan Park (NY925625)
Benson's Fell Farm NE46 2JN ☎ 01434 604647
▶ ▶ ▶ **Family Park** 🚐 £8 🚐 £7.50 ▲ £5
Open Apr-Oct Booking advisable public hols & Jul-Sep Last arrival 22.00hrs Last departure noon
A well-maintained site on very sloping ground with some level pitches. Attractively screened by trees. To avoid steep hill out of Hexham, follow B6305, signed Allendale, turn left in 3m onto unclass rd, and left again 300yds past race course. Site in 100yds. A 2-acre site with 30 touring pitches and 105 statics.
Off Licence.

🔌📶☉✖🚠🛈⊘👝🐴

➜∪🅿🚾♨️🔩🏊

Hexham Racecourse Caravan Site (NY919623)
Hexham Racecourse NE46 3NN ☎ 01434 606847 & 606881 Signposted
▶ ▶ ▶ **Family Park** ★ 🚐 £8.50-£10 🚐 £8.50-£10
▲ £8.50-£10
Open May-Sep Booking advisable wknds & bank hols for electric hook-up Last arrival 20.00hrs Last departure noon
A part-level and part-sloping grassy site on racecourse overlooking Hexhamshire Moors. From Hexham take B6305 signed Allendale and Alston, turn left in 3m signed racecourse. In 1.5m on right. A 4-acre site with 60 touring pitches.

🔌📶☉🅿🛒🍴✖🚠🛈⊘⊞🅣👝🍴🐴

➜∪🅿◎♨️🎦🔩🏊

KIELDER

Kielder Caravan & Camping Site (NY626938)
NE48 1EJ ☎ 01434 250291 (in season) 0131 314 6505 Signposted
▶ ▶ ▶ **Family Park** ★ 🚐 £7-£8.50 🚐 £7-£8.50
▲ £7-£8.50
Open Etr-Sep Booking advisable bank hols & Jul-Aug Last arrival 22.00hrs Last departure noon
Forestry Commission site set in riverside fields with Kielder Water a few minutes' drive away. Proceed N from Kielder village towards the Scottish Border for approx 500yds, the site is on the right-hand side (E) of the road. A 10-acre site with 70 touring pitches.

🔌📶☉✖🍴🚠👝🍴🐴♿

➜∪⚠️♨️🔩

Credit Cards 💳 🔲 🔲 🔲

AA pennant classification covers the touring section of a park, but not the static caravans available for rent, so we cannot deal with any complaints about static vans.

ROTHBURY

Coquetdale Caravan Park (NU055007)
Whitton NE65 7RU ☎ 01669 620549 (.5m SW on Newtown rd) Signposted
▶ ▶ ▶ **Family Park** ★ £8-£11 🚐 £8-£11 ▲ £8
Open mid Mar/Etr-Oct Booking advisable bank hol wknds Last arrival anytime Last departure evening
Partly level and sloping grass site in hilly country adjacent to River Coquet, and overlooked by Simonside Hills and moorland; .5m SW of Rothbury on Newton road. A 2-acre site with 50 touring pitches and 180 statics.
Adventure playground.

🔌📶☉🅿✖🚠🛈⊘👝🍴🐴

➜∪🅿🔩🏊

NOTTINGHAMSHIRE

CLUMBER PARK

Camping & Caravanning Club Site (SK626748)
The Walled Garden S80 3BD ☎ 01909 482303 (in season) & 01203 694995 Signposted
Nearby town: Worksop
▶ **Town & Country Pennant Park** ★ 🚐 £9.20-£11.60
▲ £9.20-£11.60
Open end Mar-early Nov Booking advisable bank hols & Jul-Aug Last arrival 21.00hrs Last departure noon
Pleasant and peaceful site, well-maintained and situated in the splendid wooded surroundings of Clumber Park. Members only caravans. Follow signs for chapel and site signed beside cricket field. Please see the advertisement on page 27 for details of Club Members' benefits. A 2.5-acre site with 55 touring pitches.

🔌📶☉🅿✖🛈⊘⊞🅣👝🏊

➜∪🅿🔩

Credit Cards 💳 🔲 🔲

MANSFIELD WOODHOUSE

Redbrick House Hotel (SK568654)
Peafield Ln NG20 0EW ☎ 01623 846499
▶ ▶ ▶ **Family Park** 🚐 🚐
Open all year
A newly-established park in the secluded grounds of an hotel/restaurant, in the heart of Sherwood Forest. Off A6075, 1m NE of Mansfield Woodhouse. A 5-acre site with 30 touring pitches.

🔌📶☉🚠👝

NOTTINGHAM

See **Radcliffe on Trent** and **advert on p175.**

RADCLIFFE ON TRENT

Thornton's Holt Camping Park (SK638377)
Stragglethorpe Rd, Stragglethorpe NG12 2JZ
☎ 0115 9332125 & 9334204 Signposted
Nearby town: Nottingham
▶ ▶ ▶ **Family Park** ★ 🚐 £7-£8 🚐 £7-£8 ▲ £7-£8
Open Apr-1 Nov (rs 2 Nov-Mar limited facilities) Booking advisable bank hols & wknds mid May-Oct Last arrival 21.00hrs Last departure 13.00hrs
contd.

174

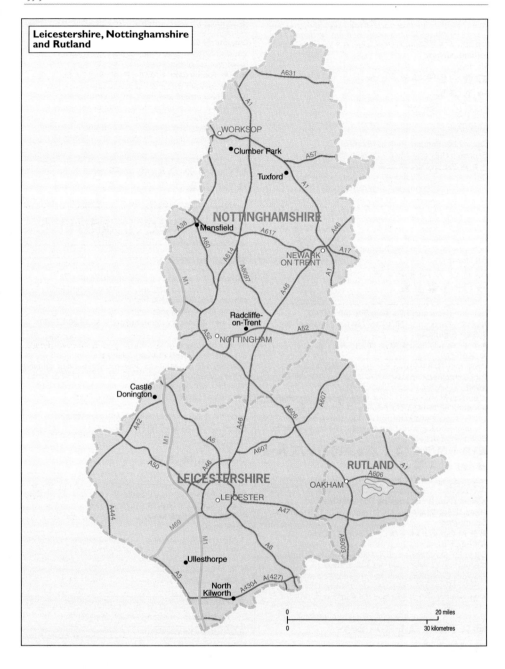

Leicestershire, Nottinghamshire and Rutland

Thorntons Holt
Camping Park ▶▶▶

Stragglethorpe, Radcliffe-on-Trent,
Nottingham NG12 2JZ
Tel: 0115 9332125   Fax: 0115 9333318

Situated off the A52, Nottingham to Grantham Road
**Where the peace of the countryside meets the
culture and entertainment of Nottingham**
13 acres of sheltered, landscaped, level grassland
and orchards for approximately 80 caravans or tents.
Open 1st April to 1st November with full facilities
2nd November to 31st March with limited facilites
★ 70 pitches with electric hook-ups ★
★ Pub and restaurants 100m away ★
★ Good toilet/shower/laundry ★
★ Indoor heated swimming pool ★
★ Shop and information centre ★
★ Play area and games room ★
★ Rallies catered for ★

*A level grass site with young trees and bushes, set in
meadowland .5m S of A52 and 2m N of A46. Nearby
(2m) is the National Water Sports Centre. A 13-acre site
with 84 touring pitches.*
Washing-up facilities.
See advertisement under NOTTINGHAM

🏵 📮 ⊙ 🗄 🍳 ≷ ❈ ✳ 🏔 🛈 🗷 🔁 🆃 ✗ 🍴 🏠 🐕
🐾 ♿
➔ ∪ ▶ 🔺 ⅃ ♨ 🐾 ⌁

TUXFORD

Greenacres Touring Park (SK751719)
Lincoln Rd NG22 0JW ☎ 01777 870264 Signposted
Nearby town: Retford
▶▶▶ Family Park ★ 📮 £6.75 🏕 £6.75 ▲ £6.75
Open Mar-Oct Booking advisable public hols Last arrival
23.00hrs Last departure 18.00hrs
*Level and slightly sloping grass site with trees, set in
rural area outside Tuxford, .75m E of A1 on A6075 over
railway bridge. A 4-acre site with 40 touring pitches and
14 statics.*
Playing field.

🏵 📮 ⊙ 🗄 🍳 ❈ 🏔 🛈 🗷 🔁 🆃 🔔 🍴 🐾 ♿
➔ ∪ ⌁

**Orchard Park Touring Caravan & Camping Park
(SK754708)**
Marnham Rd NG22 0PY ☎ 01777 870228 & 0402 433346
(1.25m SE of A1, off A6075 Lincoln rd) Signposted
Nearby town: Retford

▶▶▶ Family Park ★ 📮 £7-£7.50 🏕 £7-£7.50 ▲ £7-£7.50
Open mid Mar-Oct Booking advisable bank hols & Jul-
Aug Last arrival mdnt
*A very pleasant developing site with newly-built toilet
block. From Tuxford on A6075 .25m NE turn left to
Marnham. Site signed on right in 800yards. A 7-acre site
with 60 touring pitches.*
Family shower room.

🏵 📮 ⊙ ❈ 🏔 🛈 🗷 🔁 🆃 🔔 🍴 🐾 ♿
➔ ∪ ⌁

OXFORDSHIRE

For the map of this county
see BERKSHIRE

BANBURY

Barnstones Caravan & Camping Site (SP455454)
Great Bourton OX17 1QU ☎ 01295 750289 Signposted

🥚🥚🥚🥚🥚🥚🥚🥚🥚🥚

▶▶▶▶ De-Luxe Park ★ 📮 £5 🏕 £5 ▲ £3.50-£5
Open all year Booking advisable public hols
*An excellent, well-run and beautifully laid-out site.
Signposted from A423 (Coventry) Gt Bourton/Cropredy.
A 3-acre site with 49 touring pitches.*

🏵 📮 ⊙ 🗄 ❈ 🏔 🛈 🗷 🔁 🔔 🏠 🥨 🐕 ♿
➔ ∪ ▶ ◎ ♨ ♨ ⌁ 🐾

🥚🥚🥚🥚🥚🥚🥚🥚🥚🥚

Bo Peep Farm Caravan Park (SP481348)
Aynho Rd, Adderbury OX17 3NP ☎ 01295 810605

🥚🥚🥚🥚🥚🥚🥚🥚🥚🥚

▶▶▶▶ De-Luxe Park 📮 📮 ▲
Open Apr-Oct
*A delightful site with Cotswold stone facility buildings,
well planted with maturing shrubs and trees to provide
good shelter and screening. 1m E of Adderbury and the
A4260, on B4100 Aynho rd. A 13-acre site with 88
touring pitches.*

🏵 📮 🗄 🛈 🗷 🔁 🔔 🏠 🐾

🥚🥚🥚🥚🥚🥚🥚🥚🥚🥚

Mollington Touring Caravan Park (SP443477)
The Yews, Mollington OX17 1AZ ☎ 01295 750731
▶▶▶ Family Park 📮 £6-£7 🏕 £6-£7 ▲ £5-£6
Open Feb-Dec Booking advisable banks hols Last arrival
22.00hrs
*A neat, well-run small farm site with new brick-built
toilet facilities. On the edge of the village, adjacent to
A423. Leave M40 at junc 11 onto A422 signed Banbury,
take A423 signed Southam, and site on left in 3.5m. A 2-
acre site with 24 touring pitches.*
Field play area.

🏵 📮 ⊙ 🍳 🐕 ♿
➔ ∪ ◎ ⌁ 🐾

BENSON

Benson Camping & Caravanning Park (SU613917)
OX10 6SJ ☎ 01491 838304 Signposted
Nearby town: Wallingford
▶ Town & Country Pennant Park 🏕 🚐 ⋏
Open Apr-Oct Booking advisable bank hols & Jul-Aug
Last arrival 19.00hrs Last departure noon
An attractive riverside site close to a busy road. Signed from A4074 in Benson. A 1-acre site with 26 touring pitches and 25 statics.

🖪 🖍 ⊙ 🗑 ➰ ⊞ 🆃 ✕ ⚲ 🝙 ⅙
➔ ∪ 🏴 ⚑ ⚓ ⚽ 🖍
Credit Cards 🚇 ⚏

BLETCHINGDON

Diamond Farm Caravan & Camping Park (SP513170)
Islip Rd OX5 3DR ☎ 01869 350909 Signposted
Nearby town: Oxford

▶ ▶ ▶ ▶ De-Luxe Park 🚐 £7-£10 🏕 £7-£10 ⋏ £7-£10
Open all year (rs Oct-Mar shop, bar & swimming pool closed) Booking advisable bank hols & Jul-Sep Last arrival 22.00hrs Last departure noon
A well-run, quiet rural site in good level surroundings, and ideal for touring the Cotswolds. Situated alongside the B4027, 1m from the A43 and 7m N of Oxford in the heart of the Thames Valley. A 3-acre site with 37 touring pitches.
Snooker table.

🖪 🚙 🖍 ⊙ 🗑 ➰ ⋊ ⚲ ⚹ ⚲ 🅈 ⋀ 🝙 ⌀ ⊞ ⚲ 🝙
➔ 🏴 🖍

CASSINGTON

Cassington Mill Caravan Park (SP451099)
Eynsham Rd OX8 1DB ☎ 01865 881081 Signposted
Nearby town: Oxford
▶ ▶ ▶ Family Park ★ 🚐 £8-£9.50 🏕 £8-£9.50
⋏ £8-£9.50
Open Apr-Oct Booking advisable bank hols & Jun-Aug
Last arrival 21.00hrs Last departure noon
Secluded pretty site on the banks of the River Evenlode. First turn left 2.5m W of Oxford on A40 to Witney. A 4-acre site with 83 touring pitches and 50 statics.

🖪 🖍 ⊙ ⚹ ⋀ 🝙 ⌀ ⊞ 🆃 ⚲ 🏠 🝙 ⅙
➔ ⚑ 🖍 🗑
Credit Cards 🚇 ⚏ ⚏ 🆔 ⚏ ⚏ 🗗

CHARLBURY

Cotswold View Caravan & Camping Site (SP365210)
Enstone Rd OX7 3JH ☎ 01608 810314 Signposted
Nearby town: Witney
▶ ▶ ▶ Family Park 🏕 🚐 ⋏
Open Etr or Apr-Oct Booking advisable bank hols Last arrival 20.00hrs Last departure noon

A really first class Cotswold site, well-screened with attractive views. Signed from A44 on to B4022. A 7-acre site with 90 touring pitches.
Off-licence & cycle hire.

🖪 🚙 🖍 ⊙ 🗑 ➰ ⚲ ⚹ ⋀ 🝙 ⌀ ⊞ 🆃 ⚲ 🚙 🝙
🏠 🝙 ⅙
➔ 🖍
Credit Cards ⚏ 🗗

CHIPPING NORTON

Camping & Caravanning Club Site (SP315244)
Chipping Norton Rd OX7 3PE ☎ 01608 641993 & 01203 694995 Signposted
▶ ▶ ▶ Family Park ★ 🚐 £11-£14 🏕 £11-£14 ⋏ £11-£14
Open Mar-Nov Booking advisable bank hols & Jul-Aug
Last arrival 21.00hrs Last departure noon
A hilltop site surrounded by trees but close to a busy main road. Toilets very clean. Direct access off A361, but only from the road signed to Chadlington. Please see the advertisement on page 27 for details of Club Members' benefits. A 4-acre site with 75 touring pitches.

🖪 🖍 ⊙ 🗑 ➰ ⚹ ⋀ 🝙 ⌀ ⊞ ⚲ 🏠 🝙 ⅙
➔ ∪ 🏴 ⚽
Credit Cards 🚇 ⚏ ⚏ ⚏ 🗗

Churchill Heath Touring Caravan & Camp Site
Kingham OX7 6UJ ☎ 01608 658317
▶ ▶ ▶ Family Park 🏕 🚐 ⋏
Open all year Booking advisable bank hols & school hols Last arrival 22.00hrs Last departure noon
A peaceful little site on the Cotswold Way, with good views and sheltered pitches. On B4450 between Churchill and Kingham, 3m SW of Chipping Norton. A 7.5-acre site with 50 touring pitches.

🖪 🖍 ⊙ 🗑 ➰ ⚹ ⋀ 🝙 ⌀ 🆃 ⚲ 🗄 🝙 🏠 🝙
➔ ∪ 🏴 🖍

HENLEY-ON-THAMES

Swiss Farm International Camping (SU759837)
Marlow Rd RG9 2HY ☎ 01491 573419
Signposted
▶ ▶ ▶ Family Park ★ 🚐 £9 🏕 £9 ⋏ £9
Open Mar-Oct Booking advisable bank hols Last arrival 22.00hrs
Pleasantly screened rural site just outside Henley on A4155. A 6-acre site with 120 touring pitches and 6 statics.
Football pitch & fishing lake.

🖪 🚙 🖍 ⊙ 🗑 ➰ ⋊ ⚲ ⚹ 🅈 ⋀ 🝙 ⌀ ✕ ⚲ 🝙 🗄
🏠 🝙 ⅙
➔ ∪ 🏴 ⚑ ⚽ 🖍

OXFORD

Oxford Camping International (SP518041)
426 Abingdon Rd OX1 4XN
☎ 01865 246551 Signposted
▶ ▶ ▶ Family Park 🚐 £8.95 🏕 £8.95 ⋏ £8.95
Open all year Booking advisable bank hols & Jul-Aug
Last arrival 22.00hrs Last departure noon

A very busy town site with handy park-and-ride into Oxford. Situated on the south side of Oxford. Take A4144 to city centre from the ring road, site is .25m on left at rear of Texaco filling station. A 5-acre site with 129 touring pitches.

🏠 🌔 ⊙ 🖨 🍴 ☀ 🔋 🛈 ⊘ 🔲 📺 🌂 🐕 🐾 ⅋

→ ☂ ⛟ ⌥

Credit Cards 💳 ▆ 🏧 ▆ ▆ 🏧

STANDLAKE

Lincoln Farm Park (SP395028)
High St OX8 7RH ☎ 01865 300239
Nearby town: Witney

▶ ▶ ▶ ▶ ▶ **Premier Park ★** 🚐 £10-£12 🚐 £10-£12
⛺ £10-£12
Open Mar-Oct Booking advisable bank hols, Jul-Aug & most wknds Last arrival 21.00hrs Last departure noon
An attractively landscaped park, in a quiet village setting on A415, with superb facilities and excellent maintenance. A 9-acre site with 87 touring pitches and 19 statics.
Indoor leisure centre, putting green.

🏠 🌭 🌔 ⊙ 🖨 🍴 ⚡ ☀ 🏔 🛈 ⊘ 🔲 📺 🌂 🍽 🎋

🐕 🐾 ⅋

→ ☂ 🅿 △ ⌥

Credit Cards 💳 ▆ 🏧

Hardwick Parks (SP388047)
Downs Rd OX8 7PZ ☎ 01865 300501 (4.5m S of Witney)
Signposted
Nearby town: Witney
▶ ▶ ▶ **Family Park ★** 🚐 £7.50-£9.50 🚐 £7.50-£9.50
⛺ £7.50-£9.50
Open Apr-Oct Booking advisable bank hols Last arrival 21.00hrs Last departure 17.00hrs
A pleasant riverside site with views across the lake and its own water activities. Signed from A415 at Standlake. A 20-acre site with 250 touring pitches and 116 statics. Fishing, windsurfing, boating, jet ski, water skiing.

🏠 🌔 ⊙ 🖨 🍴 ☀ 🍸 🏔 🛈 ⊘ ⊞ 🔲 📺 ✗ 🔋

⛲ 🐕 🐾 ⅋

→ ⊍ ⌥

Credit Cards 💳 🏧 ▆ 🏧 🏧

SHROPSHIRE

BRIDGNORTH

Stanmore Hall Touring Park (SO742923)
Stourbridge Rd WV15 6DT ☎ 01746 761761 (E on A458)
Signposted

▶ ▶ ▶ ▶ **De-Luxe Park ★** 🚐 £10.40-£12.40
🚐 £10.40-£12.40 ⛺ £8.80-£10.40
Open all year Booking advisable bank hols & Jul-Aug Last arrival 20.00hrs Last departure noon
A top class site in peaceful surroundings offering outstanding facilities. Situated on the A458 2m E of Bridgnorth in the grounds of Stanmore Hall and adj to the Midland Motor Museum. National winner of the AA's 1995 Campsite of the Year Award. A 12.5-acre site with 131 touring pitches.

🏠 🌔 ⊙ 🖨 🍴 ☀ 🏔 🛈 ⊘ ⊞ 🔲 🔋 🍽 🎋 🐕 🐾 ⅋

→ 🅿 ⛟ ⌥

Credit Cards 💳 🏧 🏧

BROOME

Engine & Tender Inn (SO399812)
SY7 0NT ☎ 01588 660275
▶▶ **Town & Country Pennant Park ★** 🚐 £5 🚐 £5 ⛺ £5
Open all year Booking advisable bank hols Last departure 14.00hrs
A pleasant country pub site with gently sloping ground, in a rural setting with a good set of facilities. W from Craven Arms on B4368, fork left to B4367, and site in village on right in 2m. A 2-acre site with 30 touring pitches and 2 statics.

🏠 🌔 ⊙ 🍴 ☀ 🍸 🔲 ✗ 🔋 ⛲ 🎋

→ ⊍ 🅿 ⌥ 🖨 🐾

Credit Cards 💳 🏧 ▆ 🏧

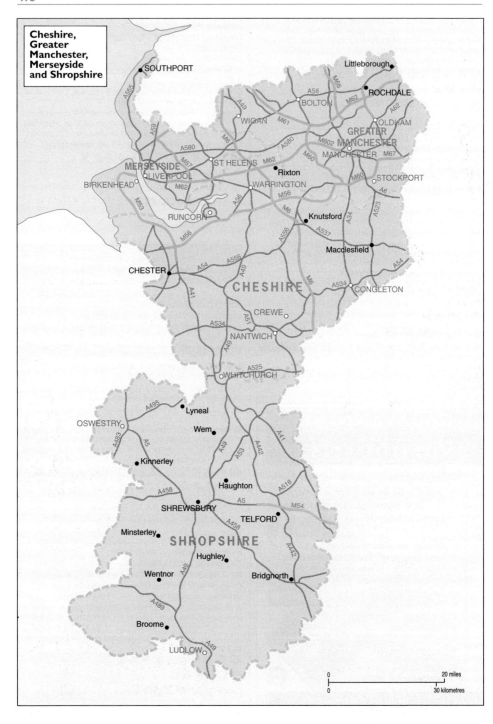

Cheshire, Greater Manchester, Merseyside and Shropshire

SOUTHPORT

Littleborough

A565

A58

M66

ROCHDALE

BOLTON

M62

A59

WIGAN

M61

A62

OLDHAM

GREATER MANCHESTER

A580

M6

A580

M602

A49

M60

MANCHESTER

M67

MERSEYSIDE

M57

ST HELENS

M62

Rixton

A580

LIVERPOOL

M69

STOCKPORT

BIRKENHEAD

M62

WARRINGTON

A6

M56

A53

M53

RUNCORN

M6

Knutsford

A34

A523

M56

A556

A537

Macclesfield

A54

CHESTER

A54

A556

A49

CHESHIRE

M6

A534

CONGLETON

A54

A41

CREWE

NANTWICH

A534

A51

A525

A49

WHITCHURCH

A495

Lyneal

OSWESTRY

Wem

A483

A5

A49

A53

A442

A41

Kinnerley

A458

Haughton

A518

SHREWSBURY

A5

M54

TELFORD

A458

Minsterley

SHROPSHIRE

A442

Hughley

Wentnor

A49

Bridgnorth

A458

Broome

A49

LUDLOW

| 0 | 20 miles |
| 0 | 30 kilometres |

ELLESMERE

See **Lyneal**

HAUGHTON

Camping & Caravanning Club Site (SJ546164)
Ebury Hill, Telford TF6 6BU ☎ 01743 709334 (in season)
& 01203 694995 Signposted
Nearby town: Shrewsbury
▶▶ **Town & Country Pennant Park** ★ ♠ £8-£9 ♠ £8-£9
▲ £8-£9
Open end Mar-early Nov Booking advisable bank hols &
high season Last arrival 21.00hrs Last departure noon
*A wooded hill fort with a central lake overlooking the
Shropshire countryside. Well-screened by very mature
trees. Own sanitary facilities essential. 4m NE of
Shrewsbury on B5062 Newport rd. Please see the
advertisement on page 27 for details of Club Members'
benefits. An 18-acre site with 160 touring pitches.
Fishing.*

🔲 ✳ ⛰ ⛵ ♞

Credit Cards 💳 ▒

HUGHLEY

Mill Farm Holiday Park (SO564979)
SY5 6NT ☎ 01746 785208 & 785255 Signposted
Nearby town: Much Wenlock
▶▶ **Town & Country Pennant Park** ★ ♠ £6 ♠ £6 ▲ £6
Open Mar-Oct Booking advisable peak periods Last
arrival 20.00hrs Last departure noon
*A well-established farm site set in meadowland
adjacent to river, with mature trees and bushes
providing screening, situated below Wenlock Edge..
A 7-acre site with 55 touring pitches and 85 statics.
Fishing & horse riding.*

🔲 ⛵ ⊙ 🔲 ⛰ ✳ 🅰 ⊘ ⊞ ⛵ ⛽ ⋈ ♞
➜ ∪ ✦

KINNERLEY

Cranberry Moss Camping & Caravan Park (SJ366211)
SY10 8DY ☎ 01743 741444 Signposted
Nearby town: Oswestry
▶▶ **Town & Country Pennant Park** ★ ♠ £5.75-£7.25
♠ £5.75-£7.25 ▲ £4.90-£6.25
Open Apr-Oct Booking advisable bank hols & Aug Last
departure noon
*A very pleasant, quiet site with a variety of trees. NW of
Shrewsbury off A5, take B4396 and site is 400yds on
left. A 4-acre site with 60 touring pitches.*

🔲 ⛵ ⊙ ✳ ⛰ 🅰 ⊘ ⊞ 🅃 ⛵ ⋈ ♞ ⛽

LYNEAL (NEAR ELLESMERE)

Fernwood Caravan Park (SJ445346)
SY12 0QF ☎ 01948 710221 Signposted
Nearby town: Ellesmere

○○○○○○○○

▶▶▶▶ **De-Luxe Park** ★ ♠ £6.50-£10.50
♠ £6.50-£10.50
Open Mar-Nov Booking advisable bank hols Last arrival
21.00hrs Last departure 17.00hrs
*A peaceful site set in wooded countryside, with
screened, tree-lined touring area and fishing lake. 4m E
of Ellesmere off B5063, signed on right. A 5-acre site
with 60 touring pitches and 165 statics.*

Lake for coarse fishing on site.

🔲 ⛵ ⊙ 🔲 ⛽ ✳ 🅰 🌳 ⊞ 🅃 ⛵ ⛽ ⅙
➜ ⋎ ✦

○○○○○○○○

MINSTERLEY

The Old School Caravan Park (SO322977)
Shelve SY5 0JQ ☎ 01588 650410 & 0777 1731631 (5m
SW on A488) Signposted
Nearby town: Bishop's Castle
▶▶ **Town & Country Pennant Park** ★ ♠ £7-£10.55
♠ £7-£10.55 ▲ £7-£10.55
Open Mar-Nov Booking advisable bank hols Last
departure 10.30hrs
*A well-designed site in a beautiful setting, 16miles S of
Shrewsbury on A488. A 1-acre site with 12 touring
pitches.*
Dish washing with hot water. CCTV over park.

🔲 ⛵ ⊙ ✳ ⛵ ⋈ ♞
➜ ∪ ✦ ⛽

SHREWSBURY

Beaconsfield Farm Caravan Park (SJ522189)
Battlefield SY4 4AA ☎ 01939 210370 & 210399 (A49,
1.5m N) Signposted

○○○○○○○○

▶▶▶▶ **De-Luxe Park** ♠ £9-£11 ♠ £9-£11
Open all year Booking advisable bank hols & Aug Last
arrival 19.00hrs Last departure 12.00hrs   *contd.*

A newly-built family-run park on a working farm in open parkland, with a fishing lake. Take A49 at Hadnall, signed Astley, and site 2m N of Shrewsbury. An 8-acre site with 50 touring pitches and 35 statics. Fly fishing.

🏳️🚐👤☉🗑️🅟❄️ ✳️🔌✕🔦🏕️🐴🐕♿
➔🅿☉🍽️🎣🎱

QQQQQQQQ

Oxon Touring Park (SJ455138)
Welshpool Rd SY3 5FB ☎ 01743 340868 Signposted

QQQQQQQQ

▶▶▶▶ De-Luxe Park ★ 🅟 £9.24-£11 🚐 £9.24-£11 Å £8.80-£10.40

Open all year Booking advisable high season Last arrival 21.00hrs

A brand new park with excellent facilities, offering grass and fully serviced pitches. Ideally located for Shrewsbury and the surrounding countryside. Leave A5 ring road at junct with A458. Park shares entrance with 'Oxon Park & Ride'. A 15-acre site with 130 touring pitches.

🏳️🅟☉🗑️🏔️🅿🎱🅣🔦🍴🏕️🐴🐕

QQQQQQQQ

Credit Cards 💳 💳 💳 🆔

Severn Gorge Caravan Site (SJ705051)
Bridgnorth Rd, Tweedale TF7 4JB ☎ 01952 684789 Signposted

▶▶▶ Family Park ★ 🅟 £8-£9.50 🚐 £8-£9.50 Å £8-£9.50

Open all year Booking advisable bank hols Last arrival 23.00hrs

A very pleasant wooded site in the heart of Telford, well screened and immaculately maintained. From junc 4 of M54 take Queensway rd A464, then A442 signed Tweedale. From A5 take Shifnal rd A4169, then A442 to site. A 16-acre site with 110 touring pitches and 1 static. Bike hire,3 golf hole, lake & fishing.

🏳️🅟☉🗑️🅟❄️🏔️🅿🎱🅣🔦🍴
🏕️🏕️🐴🐕♿
➔🅿🍽️🎣

Credit Cards 💳 💳 🆔

> Summer weather can mean rain. It is a good idea to prepare for ground to be wet underfoot. Take something to amuse the children if they can't go outside

Lower Lacon Caravan Park (SJ534304)
SY4 5RP ☎ 01939 232376 (3m from A49 on B5065 toward Wem) Signposted
Nearby town: Shrewsbury

▶▶▶ Family Park ★ 🅟 £9.50-£10 🚐 £9.50-£10 Å £9.50-£10

Open all year (rs Nov-Mar club wknds only, toilets closed if frost) Booking advisable public hols & Jul-Aug Last arrival 20.00hrs Last departure 19.00hrs

Level grass site set in meadowland with good sanitary facilities. 1.5m E of town centre on B5065. A 48-acre site with 270 touring pitches and 50 statics. Pony rides & crazy golf.

🏳️🚐🅟☉🗑️🅟❄️🔌🖥️❄️🍴🏔️🅿🎱🅣✕
🔦🛒🐴🐕♿
➔🅿🎣

Credit Cards 💳 💳 💳 💳 💳 🆔

The Green Caravan Park (S0380932)
SY9 5EF ☎ 01588 650605 Signposted
Nearby town: Bishop's Castle

▶▶▶ Family Park ★ 🅟 fr £6.50 🚐 fr £6.50 Å fr £6.50

Open Etr-Oct Booking advisable bank hols Last arrival 21.00hrs

A very pleasant spot with many recent improvments and more planned. Mostly level, grassy pitches. 1m NE of Bishops Castle to Lydham Heath on A489 turn rt, and site signed for 3m. A 15-acre site with 140 touring pitches and 20 statics.

🏳️🅟☉🗑️🅟❄️🏔️🅿🎱🔦🐴🐕
➔☾🎣

Credit Cards 💳 💳 💳 💳 🆔

SOMERSET

Bath Marina & Caravan Park (ST719655)
Brassmill Ln BA1 3JT ☎ 01225 428778 & 424301 (2m W) Signposted

QQQQQQQQ

▶▶▶▶ De-Luxe Park ★ 🅟 £12 🚐 £12

Open all year Booking advisable bank hols & Jun-Sep Last departure noon

A very pleasant site on the edge of Bath in park-like grounds among maturing trees and shrubs. From city head for suburb of Newbridge, and site is signed off A4, 1.5m W of Bath in Bristol/Wells direction. A 4-acre site with 88 touring pitches.

🏳️🅟☉🗑️🅟❄️🔌🏔️🅟🎱🅣🔦🍴🏕️🐴🐕♿
➔☾🅟☉🎣🍽️🎣

Credit Cards 💳 💳 💳 💳

QQQQQQQQ

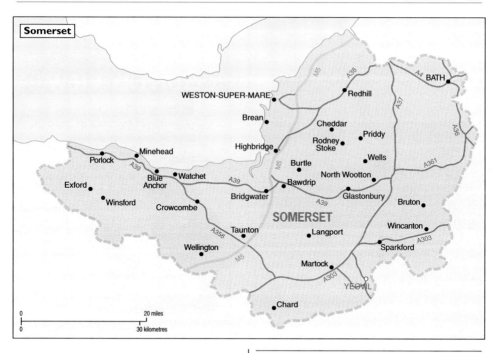

Somerset

WESTON-SUPER-MARE
Redhill
Brean
Cheddar
Priddy
Rodney Stoke
Highbridge
Minehead
Porlock
Wells
Burtle
Exford
Blue Anchor · Watchet
Bawdrip
North Wootton
Winsford
Bridgwater
Glastonbury
Bruton
Crowcombe
SOMERSET
Wincanton
Taunton
Langport
Sparkford
Wellington
Martock
YEOVIL
Chard

0   20 miles
0   30 kilometres

BATH MARINA & Caravan Park

BATH'S PREMIER PARK ON THE RIVER AVON

- This beautifully landscaped site overlooks the River Avon, only 1.5 miles from the attractions of the historic Roman spa city of Bath.
- Hard standing for 88 caravans.
- Electric points, flush toilets, showers, shaver points, laundry, children's playground, site shop, and tourist information. Dogs accepted on leash. Park & Ride bus.

 OPEN ALL YEAR ROUND

Telephone Bath (01225) 428778
or send for our brochure:
Bath Marina & Caravan Park, Brassmill Lane,
Bath, Avon BA1 3JT
Contact John and Gail Churchill

Newton Mill Caravan and Camping Park (ST715649)
Newton Rd BA2 9JF ☎ 01225 333909 (3m NW off A4)
Signposted

▶ ▶ ▶ ▶ De-Luxe Park ★ 🚐 £10.95-£13.50
🚐 £9.95-£11.95 ▲ £9.95-£10.95
Open all year Booking advisable public hols & Jul-Aug
Last arrival 21.00hrs Last departure noon
Tranquil terraced site with excellent facilities by trout stream and partially bordered by woodland. Situated within easy reach of main routes. From Bath travel W on A4(T) to A39 rndbt, turn immed left and site on left in 1m. A 42-acre site with 180 touring pitches.
Satellite T.V hook ups.

🖥️🐕☉🅿️🍴🔍☀️🚾⛰️🛈🚿📶⏣🅣✗🔌🚲🐎
🎱👥
➜∪▶🍴☕🎵
Credit Cards 💳 ■ 🚗 🏧 💳 📧 💷

BAWDRIP

Fairways International Touring Caravan & Camp (ST349402)
Woolavington Corner, Bath Rd TA7 8PP
☎ 01278 685569 (3m NE of Bridgwater
off B3141 jct A39) Signposted
Nearby town: Bridgwater

▶ ▶ ▶ ▶ De-Luxe Park ★ 🚐 £6-£9 🚐 £6-£9 ▲ £6-£9
Open Mar-15 Nov Booking advisable Spring bank hol & Jul-Aug Last departure noon   *contd.*

AA
▶▶▶▶

THE

INTERNATIONAL TOURING CARAVAN

Purpose built caravan situated on the edge of the Polden hills in rural Somerset. The park is level and occupies a 5½ acre site with a wide range of excellent facilities including disabled and children's area. 1½ miles off junction 23, M5. Easy reach local amenities, seaside and places of historical interest. Situated at junction A39 and B3141. 3½ miles east of Bridgwater.

"Loo of the Year Award Winner 1994, 1995, 1996 and 1997"

Bath Road, Bawdrip, Bridgwater, Somerset TA7 8PP.
Tel: 01278) 685569   Fax: (01278) 685569

A well-planned site offering good quality facilities. 100 yards off A39 on B3141, and 3.5m E of Bridgwater. A 5.5-acre site with 200 touring pitches.
Off-licence.

🔌♀🐕☉🔟🍳⬅🔲☀🏔🚿🎣🅣📶🏇🐶🐾♿
➜🔄💧⛱☎⚙🎵

QQQQQQQQ

BLUE ANCHOR

Blue Anchor Park (ST025434)
TA24 6JT ☎ 01643 821360 Signposted
Nearby town: Minehead

QQQQQ

▶▶▶▶ **De-Luxe Park** ★ 🏕 £5.50-£14 🚐 £5.50-£14
Open Mar-Oct (rs Mar & Oct shop & swimming pool limited) Booking advisable bank hols & Jul-Aug Last arrival 22.00hrs Last departure 10.00hrs ⌀

Large coastal site, partly wooded on level ground overlooking bay with individual areas screened. .25m E of West Somerset Railway Station on B3191. A 29-acre site with 103 touring pitches and 300 statics.
Crazy golf.

🔌♀🐕☉🔟🍳🎣 ☀🏔🚿⬅🔲✖️♿🚽⚙♿
➜🔄▶☀⚙🎵

Credit Cards 💳 💳 💳 💳 🆂

QQQQQQQQ

BREAN

Northam Farm Camping & Caravan Park (ST299556)
TA8 2SE ☎ 01278 751244 & 751222
Nearby town: Burnham-on-Sea
▶▶▶ **Family Park** ★ 🏕 £4-£8.50 🚐 £4-£8.50 ⛺ £4-£8.50
Open Etr-Sep (rs Oct shop & takeaway closed) Booking advisable bank & school hols Last arrival 22.00hrs Last departure noon
An attractive site a short walk from the sea with game, coarse and sea fishing close by. Take road to Brean, and site on left in 500yds. A 30-acre site with 299 touring pitches and 90 statics.
Pond fishing.

🔌♀🐕☉🔟🍳♿🍴🏔🚿🎣🅣☎⬅🏇
♿
➜🔄▶⚙🎵

Credit Cards 💳 💳 💳 💳 🆂

BRIDGWATER

Mill Farm Caravan & Camping Park (ST219410)
Fiddington TA5 1JQ ☎ 01278 732286

► ► ► ► De-Luxe Park ⚏ ⚏ Å
Established, mature site with helpful owners. From Bridgwater take A39 W, turn left at Cannington rndbt for 2m, and just past Apple Inn turn right towards Fiddington and follow camping signs. A 6-acre site with 125 touring pitches.

🔌 📶 ☉ 🖥 ⛏ ⚡ ⚽ ♀ ⛰ ✕ ℄ ⚒

BRUTON

Batcombe Vale Caravan & Camping Park (ST681379)
Batcombe Vale BA4 6BW ☎ 01749 830246 (off B3081 between Evercreech & Bruton)
Signposted
► Town & Country Pennant Park ⚏ ⚏ Å
Open May-Sep Booking advisable bank hols & Jul-Aug Last arrival 22.00hrs Last departure noon
A small, attractive and very quiet site in a secluded valley close to three lakes. Standards of maintenance remain high. Take Evercreech road from Bruton, signed. A 4-acre site with 30 touring pitches.
Coarse fishing, free boats for use.

🔌 📶 ☉ ☀ ⛰ 🔩 🛢 📧 ℄ 🎣 🐕
➔ ∪ ⚘ ✚ ✦ ⚒

BURTLE

Ye Olde Burtle Inn (ST397434)
Catcott Rd TA7 8NG ☎ 01278 722269
Nearby town: Glastonbury
► Town & Country Pennant Park ⚏ ⚏ Å
Open all year Booking advisable Jul-Aug Last arrival anytime
Tenting only site in a cider apple orchard. Situated beside pub in centre of village. A 0.75-acre site with 30 touring pitches.
Skittle alley, pool, darts & cycle hire.

☉ ⚽ ☀ ♀ ⛰ ✕ ℄ 🍺 🎏
➔ ∪ ✦ ⚒

Credit Cards 💳 💳 💳 💳 💳 💳 🆔

CHARD

South Somerset Holiday Park (ST279098)
Howley TA20 3EA
☎ 01460 62221 & 66036 (3m W on A30)
Signposted

► ► ► ► De-Luxe Park ★ ⚏ £5-£7 ⚏ £5-£7 Å £5-£7
Open all year Booking advisable bank hols & High Season Last arrival 23.00hrs Last departure noon
An immaculate site with impressive facilities and levels of maintenance. 3m W of Chard on A30. A 7-acre site with 110 touring pitches and 42 statics.

🔌 📶 ☉ 🖥 ⛏ ☀ ♀ ⛰ 🔩 🛢 📧 ✕ ℄ 🍺 🎏 🐕 ♿
➔ ✦

Alpine Grove Touring Park (SY342071)
Forton TA20 4HD ☎ 01460 63479 Signposted
► ► ► Family Park ⚏ £5-£7 ⚏ £5-£7 Å £5-£7
Open Etr-Sep Booking advisable bank hols & Jul-Aug Last arrival 23.00hrs
An attractive, quiet wooded site, close to Cricket St Thomas Park. Turn off A30 between Chard and Crewkerne towards Cricket St Thomas, follow signs from park, and site 2m on right. A 7.5-acre site with 40 touring pitches and 1 static.

🔌 📶 ☉ 🖥 ⛏ ⚡ ☀ ♀ ⛰ 🔩 🛢 🆃 ℄ 🎏 🐕 ⚒
➔ ∪ ► ✦

CHEDDAR

Broadway House Holiday Caravan & Camping Park (ST448547)
Axbridge Rd BS27 3DB ☎ 01934 742610 Signposted
Nearby town: Weston-Super-Mare

► ► ► ► ► Premier Park ★ ⚏ £5-£13.50 ⚏ £5-£10.50 Å £5-£13.50
Open end May-Sep (rs Mar-end May & Oct-Nov no bar & pool open, limited shop hours) Booking advisable bank hols & end Jul-Aug Last departure noon
A well-equipped family site on slopes of Mendips with exceptional adventure areas for children, jacuzzi and sun bed. Midway between Cheddar and Axbridge on A371. A 30-acre site with 200 touring pitches and 35 statics.

contd.

Sunbed, table tennis, crazy golf, full activity prog.

🔊 ➡ 🐾 ☉ 🔲 🎇 ⟍ ◀ 🏠 ✳ ♀ 🏔 🏮 🖉 🚻 🛈 ✗
📞 🖥 🏯 🎋 🛒 ♿
➔ ∪ ▶ ☉ 🎵

Credit Cards 💳 ▬ ▭ ⓪ ▦ 📶 🪙

QQQQQQQQQQ

Church Farm Caravan & Camping Park (ST460529)
Church St BS27 3RF ☎ 01934 743048 On entering
village. Along A371 Post Marked Cross & Church the
entrance is the first turning on the right. Signposted

QQQQQQQQQQ

▶ ▶ ▶ ▶ De-Luxe Park 🚐 🚐 ▲
Open Etr-Oct Booking advisable public hols Last arrival
22.00hrs Last departure noon
*Spacious, flat, grassy site, well-screened at rear of farm
and short walk from Cheddar. A 6-acre site with 44
touring pitches and 3 statics.*
Hairdryers.

🔊 🐾 🖥 🎇 ✳ 🏮 🖉 🛈 📞 🛒
➔ ∪ ☉ 🎵

QQQQQQQQQQ

Froglands Farm Caravan & Camping Park (ST462529)
BS27 3RH
☎ 01934 742058 & 743304 (150yds past Cheddar
church) Signposted
▶ ▶ ▶ Family Park ★ 🚐 £7.50-£8.50 🚐 £6.50-£7.50
▲ £6.50-£7.50
Open Etr or Apr-30 Oct Booking advisable Whitsun, Jul-
Aug & school hols Last arrival 23.00hrs Last departure
13.00hrs
*Farmland site on undulating ground with trees and
shrubs, located on A371 Weston-Super-Mare to Wells
road on SE outskirts of Cheddar. A 3-acre site with 68
touring pitches.*

🔊 🐾 ☉ 🖥 🎇 🏮 🖉 🛈 📞 🎋 🛒
➔ ∪ ▶ 🎵

CROWCOMBE

Quantock Orchard Caravan Park (ST138357)
TA4 4AW ☎ 01984 618618 Signposted
Nearby town: Taunton

QQQQQQQQQQ

▶ ▶ ▶ ▶ De-Luxe Park ★ 🚐 £6.90-£9.95 🚐 £6.90-£9.95
▲ £3.30-£9.95
Open all year Booking advisable bank hols & Jul-Aug
Last arrival 10.00hrs Last departure noon
*An attractive, quiet site at the foot of the Quantocks
with good views, and set back from the A358. A 3.5-acre
site with 65 touring pitches.*
Barbecues provided, off-licence on site.

🔊 ➡ 🐾 ☉ 🖥 🎇 ⟍ ◀ 🔲 ✳ 🏔 🏮 🖉 🛈 🇹 📞 ➡
🏯 🛒 ♿
➔ ∪ ▶ 🎵

Credit Cards 💳 ▬ ▦ 📶 🪙

QQQQQQQQQQ

QUANTOCK ORCHARD CARAVAN PARK

in the beautiful Quantock hills.
The small, clean and friendly Park for
Touring Caravans & Camping
Situated at the foot of the glorious Quantock hills, this
small, quiet, family-run Park is close to Exmoor and the
coast in the perfect location for touring Somerset and
North Devon.
Our full range of facilities include:
Immaculate timber and tiled washing facilities with free
showers (AA award for excellence winners 95/96 96/97) –
Large en-suite bathroom – Full laundry facilities – Mother
& Baby Room – Dishwashing room with microwave (free
use) – Beautiful heated swimming pool – Good children's
play area – Games room/TV room with Sky TV. Level
individual pitches, most with hook-ups, some on
hardstanding – tastefully landscaped – plenty of flowers –
level tent paddock. Mountain Bike hire.
Quality without quantity in a designed area of outstanding
natural beauty.
Dogs welcome on leads. Riding. Fishing. Steam Railway.
Good pub Food – all nearby.
Send for colour brochure and price guide to:
Mr & Mrs E C Biggs
QUANTOCK ORCHARD CARAVAN PARK,
Crowcombe, Taunton,
Somerset TA4 4AW

Excellent Graded   **Tel: (01984) 618618**   Deluxe Park
                    OPEN ALL YEAR   BHHPA Members

EXFORD

Westermill Farm (SS825398)
TA24 7NJ ☎ 01643 831238 & 831216 Signposted
Nearby town: Dulverton
▶ ▶ **Town & Country Pennant Park** 🚐 £8 ▲ £8
Open Apr-Oct (rs Mar-23 May shop closed) Booking
advisable Spring bank hol & Jul-Aug

*An idyllic site for peace and quiet, in sheltered valley in
the heart of Exmoor. Four waymarked walks over 500
acre working farm. Leave Exford on the Porlock road,
after .25m fork left. Continue for 2.25m along valley past
another campsite until 'Westermill' sign seen on tree,
then fork left. Not suitable for caravans. A 6-acre site
with 60 touring pitches.*
2.5m of shallow river for fishing & bathing.

🐾 ☉ 🖥 🎇 ✳ 🏮 🖉 📞 🛒
➔ ∪ 🎵

The Old Oaks
TOURING PARK

AA ⚬

SOUTHERN WINNER
AA's Best Camp Site of Year Award
1995/96

ANWB

A family run park in a delightfully tranquil and secluded setting with lovely views and walks, offering large level pitches and excellent facilities in an outstanding environment.

Centrally heated shower block, bathroom and disabled unit.

——— Telephone 01458 831437 ———
Wick Farm, Wick, Glastonbury, Somerset BA6 8JS.

An excellent, expanding and developing site of a very high standard close to town and an ideal touring centre. Signposted in town centre. An 8-acre site with 120 touring pitches.

🔷 ➡ ⊙ 🔲 🍳 ☀ ⚙ 🔋 🔌 ✜ 🔲 📞 🐕 ⚓
➡ ∪ ⛺ 🥤

○○○○○○○○

HIGHBRIDGE

New House Farm Caravan & Camping Park (ST338469)
Walrow TA9 4RA ☎ 01278 782218 & 783277
Signposted
Nearby town: Bridgwater

○○○○○○○○

▶ ▶ ▶ De-Luxe Park 🚐 🚐 Å
Open Mar-Oct Booking advisable Jul & Aug Last arrival 23.30hrs Last departure 18.30hrs
A very neat, quiet farm site with well-maintained facilities, sheltered by boundary hedging and trees. 3m from beaches. A 4-acre site with 30 touring pitches.

🔷 ➡ ⊙ 🔲 ☀ ⚙ 🔋 ✜ 🐕 🐕
➡ ∪ ▶ ⚠ ⛺ 🥤

○○○○○○○○

Edithmead Leisure & Park Homes (ST337459)
TA9 4HE ☎ 01278 783475 Signposted
Nearby town: Burnham-on-Sea
▶ ▶ ▶ Family Park 🚐 🚐 Å
Open 9 Feb-11 Jan Booking advisable bank hols & Jul-Sep Last arrival mdnt Last departure noon   *contd.*

GLASTONBURY

Old Oaks Touring Park (ST521394)
Wick Farm, Wick BA6 8JS ☎ 01458 831437 (take A361 towards Shepton Mallet in 1.75m turn left at sign Wick 1, site on left in 1m) Signposted

○○○○○○○○

▶ ▶ ▶ ▶ Premier Park 🚐 £7-£9 🚐 £7-£9 Å £7-£9
Open Mar-Oct Booking advisable bank hols & main season Last arrival 21.00hrs Last departure 11.00hrs
An ideal family park on a working farm on the east side of Glastonbury Tor with panoramic views towards the Mendip Hills. Glastonbury's two famous 1,000 year old oaks - Gog and Magog - are on site, hence the name. From Glastonbury take the Shepton Mallet road. A 2.5-acre site with 40 touring pitches.
Fishing & off-licence on site.

🔷 ➡ 🚐 ⊙ 🔲 🍳 ❀ ☀ ⚙ 🔋 ✜ 🔲 📞 🐕 ⚓ ♿
➡ 🥤

Credit Cards 💳 ▄▄ 💳 💳 ⑤

○○○○○○○○

Isle of Avalon Touring Caravan Park (ST494397)
Godney Rd BA6 9AF ☎ 01458 33618 Signposted

○○○○○○○○

▶ ▶ ▶ ▶ De-Luxe Park 🚐 🚐 Å
Open Mar-Oct Booking advisable mid Jul-mid Aug Last arrival 23.00hrs Last departure 18.00hrs

---

NEW HOUSE FARM
▶▶▶
Mark Road, Highbridge, Somerset TA9 4RA
Telephone: 01278 782218

A working farm, mostly sheep with new born lambs in the Spring and then shearing and haymaking. An ideal site for peace and tranquillity, level with easy access, no noisy club or bar but a lovely country pub within ¼ mile. Course fishing within 2 miles. Luxury toilet block with free showers. Small laundry and dish washing area. Children's play area.
Dogs welcome but must be kept on a lead at all times.

Level, compact site adjacent to M5. From Highcliffe
follow signs to M5 rndbt, and site on right. A 15-acre
site with 250 touring pitches and 65 statics.
Amusement arcade.

🎮🏪☉⊡🍴💺⚒💺⚠️🍴🚦

→🔄☉⚠️♨️♒

LANGPORT

Thorney Lakes Caravan Park (ST430237)
Thorney West Farm, Muchelney TA10 0DW
☎ 01458 250811
▶ ▶ ▶ Family Park ★ 🚐 £6 🚐 £6 Å £6
Open Mar-Nov Booking advisable
A small basic but very attractive site. From Langport
take Mucherley Rd, and site 3m on left. A 6-acre site
with 16 touring pitches.
Coarse fishing on site.

🎮🏪☉🖕

→▶♒💺

MARTOCK

Southfork Caravan Park (ST448188)
Parrett Works TA12 6AE ☎ 01935 825661 Signposted
Nearby town: Yeovil

▶ ▶ ▶ ▶ De-Luxe Park 🚐 £6-£9 🚐 £6-£9 Å £6-£9
Open all year Booking advisable bank hols & Jul-Aug
Last arrival 23.00hrs Last departure noon
Well-kept and equipped level site, 1.5m from centre of
Martock with good country views. An ideal touring
centre. From South Petherton follow rd N for 2m. Site
on left and signed. A 2-acre site with 30 touring pitches
and 3*statics.
Caravan service/repair centre & accessories shop.

🎮🏪☉⊡🍴💺⚠️🍴🚦

→🔄♒

Credit Cards 💳 💳 💳 🗝️

MINEHEAD

Camping & Caravanning Club Site (SS958471)
Hill Rd, North Hill TA24 5SF ☎ 01643 704138 (in season)
& 01203 694995 Signposted
▶ ▶ ▶ Family Park ★ 🚐 £9.20-£11.60 Å £9.20-£11.60
Open end Mar-end Sep Booking advisable bank hols &
Jul-Aug Last arrival 21.00hrs Last departure noon
A secluded site offering glorious views of the Bristol
Channel and Quantocks. The approach road is narrow
with sharp bends. From town centre follow camping
signs, and site on right at top of hill. Please see the
advertisement on page 27 for details of Club Members'
benefits. A 3.75-acre site with 60 touring pitches.

🏪☉🍴💺⚠️🍴💺

→🔄♒♒♒💺

Credit Cards 💳 💳

AA members can call AA Hotel Booking Service
on 0990 050505 to book at AA recognised hotels
and B & Bs in the UK and Ireland, or through our
Internet site: http://www.theaa.co.uk/hotels

Minehead & Exmoor Caravan Site (SS950457)
Minehead & Exmoor Caravan Park, Porlock Rd TA24
8SN ☎ 01643 703074 (1m W adj to A39)
Signposted
▶ ▶ ▶ Family Park ★ 🚐 £8 🚐 £8 Å £8
Open Mar-22 Oct Booking advisable bank hols & Jul-
Aug Last arrival 23.00hrs Last departure noon
Small, terraced, grassy site near the town with many
young trees and plants, on the edge of Exmoor.
Adjacent to A39. A 2.5-acre site with 50 touring pitches.

🎮🏪☉⊡🍴💺⚠️🍴💺♿

→🔄♒♨️💺♒

Credit Cards 💳

NORTH WOOTTON

Greenacres Camping (ST553416)
Barrow Ln BA4 4HL ☎ 01749 890497
Signposted
Nearby town: Wells
▶▶ Town & Country Pennant Park ★ 🚐 £8 Å £8
Open Apr-Oct Booking advisable school hols Last
arrival 21.00hrs Last departure noon ❄
An immaculately maintained site peacefully set within
sight of Glastonbury Tor. Mainly family orientated with
many thoughtful extra facilities provided. From North
Wootton follow signs for 1.5m. A 4.5-acre site with 30
touring pitches.

🏪☉🍴💺⚠️💺

→🔄♒♨️♒💺

PORLOCK

**Burrowhayes Farm Caravan & Camping Site
(SS897460)**
West Luccombe TA24 8HU
☎ 01643 862463 (SE of Porlock .25m off A39)
Nearby town: Minehead
▶ ▶ ▶ Family Park 🚐 🚐 Å
Open 15 Mar-Oct Booking advisable Etr, Spring bank
hol & Jun-Sep Last departure noon

A delightful site on the edge of Exmoor, on slope to the
river, and ideal for exploring surrounding area. From
Porlock take A39 E, in .25m turn right, and site on right
in 200yds. An 8-acre site with 140 touring pitches and
20 statics.
Pony-treking available.

🎮🏪☉⊡🍴💺⚠️🍴💺

→▶☉⚠️♨️♨️♒

PORLOCK CARAVAN PARK

Select family run site in the beautiful Exmoor National Park close to the sea, only 2 minutes walk from the quaint old village of Porlock. Situated in a vale at the foot of Porlock Hill. The site offers magnificent views all around. We have new modern well equipped caravans for hire all with mains sewage, electricity, gas cooker/heating, colour T.V., W.C., fridges, hot water, and showers.
Dogs allowed in some letting units.
Facilities include general shop, shower block, launderette, and public telephone. Tourers, dormobiles and tents welcome. Full facilities including electric hook-up.

▶▶▶

Porlock, Nr. Minehead, Somerset, TA24 8NS.
Tel: (01643) 862269
Proprietors: A. D. & D. A. Hardick
Last caravan park before Porlock Hill
Phone or Write for free colour brochure.

Porlock Caravan Park (SS882469)
TA24 8NS ☎ 01643 862269 Signposted
▶▶▶ Family Park ★ ♥ £6-£6.50 ♥ £5-£5.50 ▲ £5-£6.50
Open 15 Mar-Oct Booking advisable Etr, Whitsun & Jul-Aug Last arrival 23.00hrs Last departure noon
A well-planned site, in valley with shrubs and trees, and an ideal touring centre for Exmoor. In village by West car park. A 3-acre site with 40 touring pitches and 56 statics.

🔌 🐾 ⊙ 🗑 🍳 ✳ ⬛ ⊘ 🚽 T 📞 🐕 🐾
→ ∪ ↑ ⊁ ♨ ✔

PRIDDY

Mendip Heights Camping & Caravan Park (ST522519)
Townsend BA5 3BP ☎ 01749 870241 Signposted
Nearby town: Wells
▶▶▶ Family Park ★ ♥ £6.40-£7 ♥ £6.40-£7 ▲ £6.40-£7

Open Mar-15 Nov Booking advisable bank & school hols Last arrival 22.30hrs
Quiet family site in high open-countryside overlooking the Mendip Hills and valleys, signposted from A39 at Green Ore. A 4.5-acre site with 90 touring pitches and 1 static.
Archery, canoeing, absailing, caving, table tennis.

🔌 🐾 ⊙ 🗑 🍳 ✳ ⬛ ⊘ 🚽 T 📞 🐾
→ ∪

REDHILL

Brook Lodge Farm Camping & Caravan Park (ST486620)
Cowslip Green BS40 5RD ☎ 01934 862311 Signposted
Nearby town: Bristol
▶▶▶ Family Park ★ ♥ £8.50-£11 ♥ £8-£10.50
▲ £8-£10.50
Open Mar-Oct (rs Nov-Feb) Booking advisable 22 May-4 Sep & bank hols Last arrival 23.50hrs Last departure noon
A pleasant, well-screened touring site, hidden from the A38 by hedging and trees. 1.5m S of Redhill on A38. From M5 junc 19 follow signs to Bristol Airport, and site 2.5m on left. A 3-acre site with 29 touring pitches.

🔌 🐾 ⊙ 🍳 ✳ ⬛ ⊘ 🚽 T 📞 🎣 🐕 🐾
→ ∪ ↑ ✈ 🗑

RODNEY STOKE

Bucklegrove Caravan & Camping Park (ST487502)
Wells Rd BS27 3UZ ☎ 01749 870261 (midway between Cheddar & Wells) Signposted
Nearby town: Wells

QQQQQQQQQ

▶▶▶▶ De-Luxe Park ★ ♥ £4.50-£10 ♥ £4.50-£10
▲ £4.50-£10
Open Mar-Oct Booking advisable bank hols & peak periods Last arrival 22.00hrs Last departure noon ⊗

A well-sheltered site on the southern slopes of the Mendip Hills providing superb views of Somerset. An ideal touring base off A371. A 5-acre site with 125 touring pitches and 35 statics.
Large tourist information room.

🔌 ➡ 🐾 ⊙ 🗑 🍳 ⚡ ⬛ ✳ ⊘ ⬛ 🚽 ⬛ ⊘ 🚽 T 📞 ⛲
🎣 🐾 ♿
→ ∪ ↑ ◎ ♨ ✔

Credit Cards 💳 💳 💳 💳 🅾

QQQQQQQQQ

SPARKFORD

Long Hazel International Caravan & Camping (ST602262)
High St BA22 7JH ☎ 01963 440002 Signposted
Nearby town: Yeovil
▶ ▶ ▶ Family Park 🚐 £8-£10 🚐 £8-£10 ▲ £8-£10
Open Mar-Dec Booking advisable Last arrival 23.00hrs
Last departure noon
A very neat, smart site, situated next to the Sparkford Inn in the village High Street. A 3.5-acre site with 75 touring pitches and 3 statics.
Badminton & Croquet.

🔌🐾☉🍳☀️⛰️🚿🛁✦🎁🅃📞🚡🏕️🐴♿
➜∪🅿️♨️⚡

TAUNTON

Ashe Farm Camping & Caravan Site (ST279229)
Thornfalcon TA3 5NW ☎ 01823 442567 Signposted
▶ ▶ ▶ Family Park ★ 🚐 £6-£7.50 🚐 £6-£7.50 ▲ £6
Open Apr-Oct Booking advisable Jul-Aug
Attractive site with clean facilities. Situated off A358, 4m SE of Taunton, 3.5m from junc 25 of M5. A 3-acre site with 30 touring pitches and 2 statics.

🔌🐾☉🍳🎱🔍✦☀️⛰️🎁🅃📞🐕🏕️⚡
➜∪🅿️♨️⚡

Holly Bush Park (ST220162)
Culmhead TA3 7EA ☎ 01823 421515 (5m S on B3170, turn right at crossroads signed Wellington, right at T jct, site 100yds on left) Signposted
▶ ▶ ▶ Family Park ★ 🚐 £6-£7.50 🚐 £6-£7.50 ▲ £6-£7.50
Open all year Booking advisable bank hols & high season Last arrival 22.00hrs Last departure noon
A good basic site, ideal as overnight stop yet well positioned around attractive countryside with easy access to Wellington and Taunton. From Taunton take B3170 (Corfe), and at first crossrds in 5m turn right. Site on left past pub. A 2-acre site with 40 touring pitches.

🔌🐾☉🍳✦☀️🎁🅃📞🚡🏕️🐴⚡
➜∪🅿️⚡

WATCHET

Doniford Bay Holiday Park (ST095433)
TA23 0TJ ☎ 01984 632423
Nearby town: Minehead
▶ ▶ ▶ Family Park ★ 🚐 £9-£17 🚐 £9-£17 ▲ £9-£17
Open Etr-end Oct Booking advisable Jul-Aug & Whitsun Last departure 10.00hrs
A level site with some hardstanding pitches for caravans and surfaced internal roadways. E of Watchet off A39 and overlooking the sea (Minehead Bay). A 3-acre site with 75 touring pitches.
Free evening entertainment, amusements, Go-Karts.

🔌🐾☉🍳🍳🎱🔍🎱✦🍷⛰️🎁🔀✂️📞🛗
🏕️⚡♿
➜∪⚡
Credit Cards 💳 💳 💳

WELLINGTON

Gamlins Farm Caravan Park (ST083195)
Gamlins Farm, Greenham TA21 OLZ
☎ 01823 672596 (4m W)
Signposted
Nearby town: Taunton
▶ ▶ ▶ Family Park ★ 🚐 £6-£7 🚐 £6-£7 ▲ £5-£7
Open Apr-Sep Booking advisable bank hols Last arrival 20.00hrs Last departure noon
A well-planned site in a secluded position with panoramic views. Situated off the A38 on the Greenham road. A 3-acre site with 25 touring pitches.

🔌🐾☉🍳🎱☀️📞✦🏕️🐴
➜∪♨️⚡⚡

WELLS

See also **Priddy**

Homestead Caravan & Camping Park (ST532474)
Wookey Hole BA5 1BW ☎ 01749 673022
Signposted
▶ ▶ ▶ Family Park ★ 🚐 £8.80 🚐 £8.20 ▲ £9
Open Etr-Oct Booking advisable Last arrival 22.00hrs
Last departure noon
Attractive small site by stream with mature trees. Set in hilly woods and meadowland with access to river and Wookey Hole. .5m NW off A371 Wells-Cheddar road. A 2-acre site with 50 touring pitches and 28 statics.
Childrens fishing.

🔌🚗🐾☉🍳☀️🎁🚿📞⚡
➜∪🅿️♨️⚡🔲

WESTON-SUPER-MARE

Airport View Holiday Park (ST351611)
Moor Ln Worle ☎ 01934 622168
▶ ▶ ▶ Family Park 🚐 🚐 ▲
Open all year
A pleasant, well-cared for site with newly-built facilities. From A371 junc with A370 turn immediately east, and site signed. A 10-acre site with 135 touring pitches and 40 statics.

🔌🐾☉🍳🍷⛰️✂️📞🛗⚡
➜∪🅿️🔲⛰️🔀♨️⚡🔲

Country View Caravan Park (ST335647)
Sand Rd, Sand Bay BS22 9UJ ☎ 01934 627595
Signposted
▶ ▶ ▶ Family Park ★ 🚐 £6.50-£12 🚐 £6.50-£12
▲ £4-£12
Open Mar-Oct Booking advisable bank hols & peak periods Last arrival 21.00hrs Last departure noon
A pleasant, flat, open site in a country area not far from the coast. From Weston-super-Mare travel E to A35/M5 rndbt, turn left to Kewstoke/Sandy Bay, and follow signs; first caravan park on right. 3m N of town. An 8-acre site with 120 touring pitches and 65 statics.
See advertisement under BAWDRIP

🔌🐾☉🍳🎱🔍✦☀️🍷⛰️🎁🅃📞🚡⚡♿
➜∪🅿️🔀♨️⚡
Credit Cards 💳 💳

Purn International Holiday Park (ST332568)
Bridgwater Rd, Bleadon BS24 0AN ☎ 01934 812342
Signposted
► ► ► **Family Park** ★ 🚐 £7.50-£11.50 🚐 £7.50-£11.50
▲ £6.50-£9.50
Open Mar-7 Nov Booking advisable Last arrival mdnt
Last departure 10.30hrs
*A good flat site in a handy position for touring the
Somerset coast. Take A370 from Weston-super-Mare
towards Edithmead, and site on right by The Anchor
Inn, about 1m from 1st rndbt. An 11-acre site with 168
touring pitches.*
River with fishing.

🔳 📡 ⊙ 🔟 🖤 ⨯ ◕ ☀ ⦿ /⋀ ▯ ⌀ 🎚 🔟 🔌 ⛲ 🏕
🏓 📠
➔ ∪ �🇵 ◉ △ ⅄ ♨ 🎵

West End Farm Caravan & Camping Park (ST354600)
Locking BS24 8RH ☎ 01934 822529 (along A370, follow
signs for Helicopter Museum, after museum turn right
& follow site signs) Signposted
► ► ► **Family Park** ★ 🚐 £7-£9 🚐 £7-£9 ▲ £7-£9
Open all year Booking advisable peak periods Last
arrival 22.00hrs Last departure noon
*A flat, hedge-bordered site by helicopter museum with
good clean facilities and landscaping. Good access to
Weston-super-Mare and the Mendips. From Weston-
super-Mare take A370 N to junc with A371, turn right
then site in 1m on right, past Helicopter Museum. A 10-
acre site with 75 touring pitches and 20 statics.*

🔳 📡 ⊙ 🔟 🖤 ◕ ☀ /⋀ ▯ ⌀ 🎚 🔟 🔌 ⛲ 🐴 📠 ♿
➔ ∪ 🇵 ◉ △ ⅄ ♨ 🎵

Weston Gateway Caravan Site (ST370621)
West Wick BS24 7TF ☎ 01934 510344 Signposted
► ► ► **Family Park** ★ 🚐 £5-£9 🚐 £5-£9 ▲ £5-£9
Open Apr-Oct Booking advisable Jul-Aug Last arrival
23.30hrs Last departure noon
*A pleasant site set among trees and shrubs close to the
A370 and junc 21 of M5. Plenty of entertainment but
basic toilet block. A 15-acre site with 175 touring
pitches.*

🔳 📡 ⊙ 🔟 🖤 ◕ ☀ ◕ ☀ /⋀ ▯ ⌀ 🎚 🔟 🔌 🐴 📠 ♿
➔ ∪ 🇵 ♨ 🎵

WINCANTON

Wincanton Racecourse Caravan Club Site (ST708295)
BA9 8BJ ☎ 01963 34276 Signposted
►► **Town & Country Pennant Park** 🚐 🚐 ▲
Open late Apr-late Sep Booking advisable bank hols
Last arrival 20.00hrs Last departure noon
*A well-kept level grassy site on Racecourse Downs one
mile from the town centre on A303. Turn off main road
at Hunters Lodge to A3081 from either direction. A 2-
acre site with 50 touring pitches.*
9 hole golf course.

🔳 📡 ⊙ 🔲 ☀ ▯ ⌀ 🎚 🔟 🔌 🏕 🐴 ♿
➔ ∪ 🇵 ♨ 🎵 📠 🔟 📠
Credit Cards 💳 💳 💳 🗿

WINSFORD

Halse Farm Caravan & Camping Park (SS894344)
TA24 7JL ☎ 01643 851259 Signposted
Nearby town: Dulverton
► ► ► **Family Park** ★ 🚐 £5.50-£7.50 🚐 £5.50-£7.50
▲ £5.50-£7.50
Open 22 Mar-Oct Booking advisable bank hols & mid
Jul-Aug Last arrival 22.00hrs Last departure noon

*An Exmoor site overlooking a typical wooded valley
with glorious views. Midway between Minehead and
Tiverton. From Minehead take A396, turn right just
before Bridgetown towards Winsford, then left by pub
up narrow winding lane to top. Entrance over cattle
grid. A 3-acre site with 44 touring pitches.*

🔳 📡 ⊙ 🔟 🖤 ☀ /⋀ ▯ ⌀ 🔌 🐴 ♿
➔ 🎵 📠

STAFFORDSHIRE

CANNOCK CHASE

Camping & Caravanning Club Site (SK039145)
Old Youth Hostel, Wandon WS15 1QW
☎ 01889 582166 & 01203 694995 Signposted
► ► ► **Family Park** ★ 🚐 £10-£13 🚐 £10-£13 ▲ £10-£13
Open end Mar-early Nov Booking advisable bank hols &
Jul-Aug Last arrival 21.00hrs Last departure noon
*Very popular site in an excellent location in the heart of
the Chase. A gently sloping site with timber-built facility
blocks. From A460 take sign for Rawnsley/Hazleslade,
then left in 400yds, and site .5m past golf club.Please
see the advertisement on page 27 for details of Club
Members' benefits. A 5-acre site with 60 touring
pitches.*

🔳 📡 ⊙ 🔟 🖤 ☀ 🔌 🔙 🐴 ♿
➔ ∪ 🇵
Credit Cards 💳 💳

CHEADLE

Quarry Walk Park (SK045405)
Coppice Ln, Croxden Common, Freehay ST10 1RQ
☎ 01538 723495
► ► ► **Family Park** ★ 🚐 £7.50 🚐 £7.50 ▲ £6.50
Open all year Booking advisable bank hols Last arrival
23.00hrs Last departure noon *contd.*

190

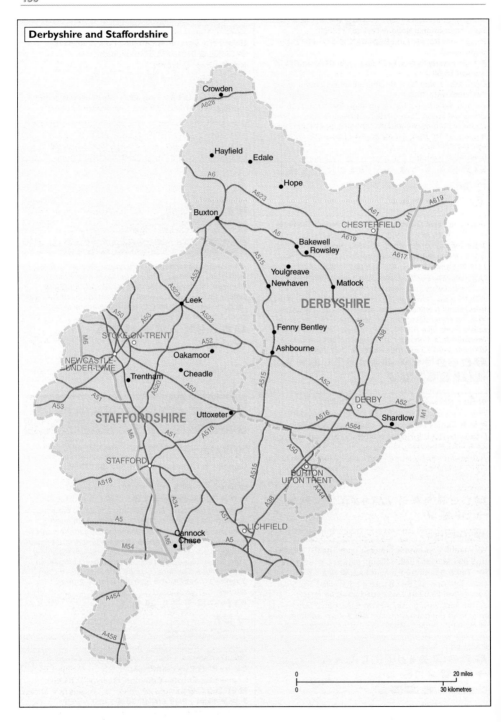

Derbyshire and Staffordshire

A pleasant park in an old quarry, well-screened with mature trees and shrubs. Situated 1m from A522 Cheadle-Uttoxeter Rd at Freehay. A 14-acre site with 40 touring pitches.
Off site pub owned by campsite used as clubhouse.

🔥 🛈 ⊙ 🗓 ✳ 🏔 🍴 🖉 ⊞ 🔌 🏕 🏠
→ ∪ ⅃ 🛁

LEEK

Camping & Caravanning Club Site (SK008599)
Blackshaw Grange, Blackshaw Moor ST13 8TL
☎ 01538 300285 & 01203 694995
▶ ▶ ▶ Family Park ★ 🚐 £10-£13 🚙 £10-£13
Å £10-£13
Open all year Booking advisable Jan-Mar Last arrival 21.00hrs Last departure noon
A beautifully located club site, with well-screened pitches. 2m NE of Leek on A53 to Buxton; site at Blackshaw Moor and signed. See advert on p27 for Club Members' benefits. A 6-acre site with 60 touring pitches.

🔥 🛈 ⊙ 🗓 ✳ 🏔 🍴 🖉 ⊞ 🔌 🏠 🛁 ♿
Credit Cards 💳 🔲 🔲 🔲 🔲 🔲

OAKAMOOR

Star Caravan & Camping Park (SK066456)
Cotton ST10 3BN
☎ 01538 702256 & 702219 (1.25m NE off B5417)
Signposted
Nearby town: Leek
▶▶ Town & Country Pennant Park ★ 🚐 £6 🚙 £6 Å £6
Open Feb-Dec Booking advisable anytime Last arrival 23.30hrs Last departure 19.00hrs

Trentham Gardens Caravan Park

Secluded 250 pitch site set in 750 acres of Ancestral Estate, Leisure Park, Gardens and Woodland.

The Perfect Caravan and Campsite.

Trentham Gardens, Trentham, North Staffordshire, ST4 8AX.
2 minutes from J15, M6. We are in easy travelling distance of Alton Towers and the Potteries.

For a Free Brochure and Details of Seasonal Discounts
Telephone (01782) 657519

A pleasant, well screened site situated within one mile of Alton Towers. !.25m N of Oakamoor off B5417, 1.5m S of A52. A 20-acre site with 120 touring pitches and 58 statics.

🔥 🛈 ⊙ 🗓 ✳ 🏔 🍴 🖉 ⊞ 🔌 🏕 🏠 🛁
→ ∪ ⅃ 🛁

STOKE ON TRENT

See **Trentham**

TRENTHAM

Trentham Gardens Caravan & Leisure Park (SJ864409)
Trentham Gardens, Stone Rd ST4 8AX
☎ 01782 657519 & 657341 Signposted
Nearby town: Newcastle-under-Lyme
▶ ▶ ▶ Family Park ★ 🚐 £5.50-£9.50 🚙 £5.50-£9.50
Å £5.50-£9.50
Open all year (rs Oct-Etr shop bar cafe closed) Booking advisable bank hols & during major events Last arrival 22.00hrs Last departure 18.00hrs
Wooded meadowland site by lakes. Access to A34 and exit 15 of M6. A 30-acre site with 250 touring pitches.
Shooting & fishing.
See advertisement under STOKE ON TRENT

🔥 🛈 ⊙ 🗓 ✳ ♀ 🏔 🍴 🖉 ⊞ ✗ 🔌 🏕 🏠 🛁 ♿
→ ∪ ↑ ◎ ⌂ ⤳ 🍴 ⅃
Credit Cards 💳 🔲 🔲 🔲 🔲

UTTOXETER

Racecourse Site (SK099334)
Uttoxeter Racecourse ST14 8BD
☎ 01889 564172 & 562561 Signposted
▶ ▶ ▶ Family Park 🚐 🚙 Å
Open Apr-Oct (rs Mar & Nov limited opening) Booking advisable bank hols & race meeting dates Last arrival 20.00hrs Last departure noon
Situated on SE edge of small market town, mainly level site in hilly country. Off B5017, ideal for Alton Towers and Peak District (5m). A 3-acre site with 83 touring pitches.

🔥 🛈 ⊙ ✳ 🍴 🖉 ⊞ 🔌 🏕 🏠
→ ∪ ↑ 🍴 ⅃ 🗓 🛁
Credit Cards 💳 🔲 🔲 🔲

SUFFOLK

For the map of this county see CAMBRIDGESHIRE

BUNGAY

Outney Meadow Caravan Park (TM333905)
Outney Meadow NR35 1HG ☎ 01986 892338
(signposted from rdbt at Jct of A143/A144) Signposted
▶ ▶ ▶ Family Park 🚐 £7-£11 🚙 £7-£11 Å £7-£11
Open Mar-Oct Booking advisable public hols Last arrival 22.00hrs Last departure 21.00hrs
A pleasant site with part river frontage and some watersports. Toilet facilities basic. W of village on A143,
contd.

adjoining the roundabout. A 6-acre site with 45 touring pitches and 30 statics.
Fishing, rowing boat and canoe hire.

🏠🐾⊙🗑🍳🏕🚿♿🆔🛈📞🐴🐎
➜⛵🏳💧✚🍴🎣♨

BURY ST EDMUNDS

The Dell Touring & Caravan Park (TL928640)
Beyton Rd, Thurston IP31 3RB ☎ 01359 270121
► ► ► **Family Park** ★ 🚐 £7.50 🚐 £7.50 ▲ £7.50
Open all year Booking advisable bank hols Last arrival anytime Last departure anytime
A small developing site with enthusiastic owners, making an ideal stopover or base for exploring picturesque area. Signed off A14 at Beyton/Thurston, 4m E of Bury St Edmunds. A 6-acre site with 60 touring pitches.

🏠🐾🍳🏕🚿♿📞🐴🐎♿
➜♨

BUTLEY

Tangham Campsite (TM355485)
IP12 3NP ☎ 01394 450707 Signposted
Nearby town: Woodbridge
► ► ► **Family Park** 🚐 £7.50-£9.50 🚐 £7.50 ▲ £7.50
Open Etr/Apr-10 Jan Booking advisable bank & school hols Last arrival 22.00hrs Last departure noon
Good, quiet, level grass site, situated on the edge of a deep forest with attractive walks. From Woodbridge take B1084, after 5m turn right into forest. A 7-acre site with 90 touring pitches.
Washing-up sinks.

🏠🐾⊙🍳✳🏕🚿♿🆔🛈📞🐎
➜⛵🏳
Credit Cards 💳 💳 💳 🅂

DUNWICH

Cliff House (TM475692)
Minsmere Rd IP17 3DQ ☎ 01728 648282 (from A12, follow sign to Dunwich Heath) Signposted
Nearby town: Southwold

► ► ► ► **De-Luxe Park** ★ 🚐 £8-£13 🚐 £8-£13 ▲ £8-£11
Open Etr or Apr-Oct Booking advisable all year Last arrival 21.00hrs Last departure 11.00hrs
A delightful woodland park on the cliffs near Minsmere Bird Reserve, centring on a large house with a walled garden.

A 30-acre site with 87 touring pitches and 93 statics.
Campers wash room, pool, table tennis.

🏠🐾⊙🗑🍳♨♿✳🍴🏕🚿♿🆔🛈❌📞🧹🐴🐎♿
➜♨

Credit Cards 💳 💳 💳 💳 🅂

EAST BERGHOLT

Grange Country Park (TM098353)
The Grange CO7 6UX ☎ 01206 298567 & 298912
Signposted
Nearby town: Manningtree

► ► ► ► ► **Premier Park** ★ 🚐 £8.50-£12.50
🚐 £8.50-£12.50 ▲ £8.50-£12.50
Open 31 Mar-Oct (rs Oct-Mar) Booking advisable for stays of 1 wk or more Last arrival 22.00hrs Last departure 18.00hrs
This level, grassy site is situated in hilly woodland with some moorland nearby. The park is sheltered by mature trees and bushes and provides first class sanitary facilities. 3m off A12 between Colchester and Ipswich. An 8-acre site with 120 touring pitches and 55 statics.

🏠🐾⊙🗑🍳🐟♨♿🖵✳🍴🏕🚿♿🆔🛈❌📞🧹
🏮🐴🐎♿
➜⛵💧✚♨

FELIXSTOWE

Peewit Caravan Park (TM290338)
Walton Av IP11 8HB ☎ 01394 284511 & 670217
Signposted
▶ ▶ ▶ Family Park 🚐 🚐 Å
Open Apr or Etr-Oct (rs early & late season shop closed)
Booking advisable school & bank hols Last arrival
21.00hrs Last departure 11.00hrs
*A useful town site, not overlooked by houses. The site is
neat and tidy with clean toilets, and the beach is a few
minutes away by car. Signed from A14 in Felixstowe. A
3-acre site with 65 touring pitches and 220 statics.*
Bowling green, washing up sink.

🔁 🌾 ⊙ 🗗 ⤢ ✳ ⚠ 🔋 ⊘ 🖃 📞 ⚡ ⚹
➔ 🍴 🎣

GISLEHAM

Chestnut Farm Touring Park (TM510876)
NR33 8EE ☎ 01502 740227 Signposted
Nearby town: Lowestoft
▶▶ Town & Country Pennant Park 🚐 £5.50-£7.50
🚐 £5.50-£7.50 Å £5.50-£7.50
Open Apr-Oct Booking advisable bank hols Last arrival
mdnt
*A nice little farm site with old but well-maintained
toilets in a peaceful setting. At southern roundabout of
Kessingland bypass go west signposted Rushmere,
Mutford and Gisleham. Take second turning on left. A 3-
acre site with 20 touring pitches.*
Fishing on site.

🔁 🌾 ⊙ ♈
➔ ∪ ⊮ ◎ △ 🔱 🍴 ⚹

IPSWICH

Low House Touring Caravan Centre (TM227425)
Bucklesham Rd, Foxhall IP10 0AU ☎ 01473 659437 (4m
E) Signposted
▶ ▶ ▶ Family Park ★ 🚐 £6.50 🚐 £6.50 Å £6.50
Open all year Booking advisable Last arrival anytime
Last departure anytime
*An appealing, secluded site with immaculate facilities
and very caring owners. From A45 south ring road take
slip road to A1156 signed East Ipswich. Turn right in 1m
and right again in .5m. Site on left. Tents accepted only
if room available. A 3.5-acre site with 30 touring pitches.*
Temporary membership of sports centre opposite.

🔁 🌾 ⊙ ✳ ✳ ⚠ 🔋 ⊘ 🖃 📞 ♈
➔ ∪ ⊮ ◎ 🍴 ⚹ 🗗

Priory Park (TM198409)
IP10 0JT ☎ 01473 727393 & 726373 Signposted
▶ ▶ ▶ Family Park 🚐 £15 🚐 £15 Å £15
Open all year (rs Oct-Apr limited number of sites,
club/pool closed) Booking advisable bank & school hols
Last arrival 21.00hrs Last departure noon
*Well-screened south-facing site with panoramic views
overlooking Orwell. Convenient for Ipswich southern
bypass. From bypass take Nacton exit then follow signs
Ipswich/Airport for 300yds to site entrance. An 85-acre
site with 75 touring pitches and 260 statics.*
9 hole golf, small boat launching, table tennis.

🔁 🛒 🌾 ⊙ 🗗 ⤢ ⬱ ℚ ✳ ⚲ ⚠ 🔋 ⊘ 🖃 ✕ 📞 🛁
♈ ♈
➔ ∪ ⊮ △ 🍴 ⚹ 🔋

PRIORY PARK
Ipswich, Suffolk IP10 0JT   Tel: (01473) 727393

Priory Park is a unique and magnificent property set in the middle of an area of
outstanding natural beauty. Its 100 acres of south facing wooded parkland enjoy
panoramic views over the River Orwell estuary. Surrounded by a woodland country
park, the river Orwell and rolling pastures, customers can enjoy ponds and walks
within the landscaped grounds stretching to the water's edge. Facilities include a 9
hole golf course, heated outdoor swimming pool, tennis courts, table tennis as well as
a licenced bar and restaurant.
There are 75 level touring pitches all with 5A electric supply.

KESSINGLAND

Heathland Beach Caravan Park (TM533877)
London Rd NR33 7PJ
☎ 01502 740337 Signposted

▶ ▶ ▶ ▶ **De-Luxe Park** ★ ♠ £10.50-£12.50
♠ £10.50-£12.50 ▲ £6-£12.50
Open Mar-6 Jan (rs Nov-6 Jan no bar, restaurant or swimming pool) Booking advisable peak periods Last arrival 22.00hrs
A well-run and maintained park offering superb toilet facilities. A level grass site with mature trees and bushes set in meadowland with direct access to sea, beach and A12, Lowestoft road via B1437. An 11-acre site with 106 touring pitches and 200 statics.
Freshwater/sea fishing.

🖾🖎☉🗹🗞☼🗜⚠🗎🖉🖭🇮🗓📞🚽🚿🚻🛒♿
➜ ∪🅿▲✚🍴🍼🥤

Kessingland Beach Holiday Village (TM535852)
Beach Rd NR33 7RN ☎ 01502 740636 & 740879
Signposted
Nearby town: Lowestoft

▶ ▶ ▶ **De-Luxe Park** ★ ♠ £7-£15 ♠ £7-£15
▲ £7-£13
Open Mar-Nov Booking advisable Jun-Aug Last arrival 21.00hrs Last departure 14.00hrs
A large seaside holiday park with plenty of entertainment for all ages. A 65-acre site with 90 touring pitches and 209 statics.
Bowling green, sauna, amusements, mini ten-pin bowls.

🖾🖎☉🗹🗞☼ ☼🗜🔍☼🗜⚠🗎🖉✗📞🚽
🚻🛒♿
➜ ∪▲✚🍴🥤
Credit Cards ● ▬ ▬ ▬ ▩ 🄢

Camping & Caravanning Club Site (TM520860)
Suffolk Wildlife Park, Whites Ln NR33 7SL
☎ 01502 742040 (in season) & 01203 694995
Signposted
Nearby town: Lowestoft
▶ ▶ ▶ **Family Park** ★ ♠ £10-£13 ♠ £10-£13 ▲ £10-£13
Open end Mar-eraly Nov Booking advisable bank hols & Jul-Aug Last arrival 21.00hrs Last departure noon
An open site next to a wildlife park, with beaches close by. Very tidy and well maintained. Concessions to wildlife park. Please see the advertisement on page 27 for details of Club Members' benefits. A 6.5-acre site with 90 touring pitches.

🖾🖎☉🗹🗞☼⚠🗎🖉🖭🇮📞🐕♿
➜ ∪🥤🍼🥤🐾
Credit Cards ● ▬ ▩ ▩ 🄢

LEISTON

Cakes & Ale (TM432637)
Abbey Ln, Theberton IP16 4TE
☎ 01728 831655 & 01473 736650 Signposted
Nearby town: Aldeburgh
▶ ▶ ▶ **Family Park** ♠ ♠ ▲
Open Apr-Oct (rs low season club, shop/reception open limited hours) Booking advisable public & school hols Last arrival 21.00hrs Last departure 16.00hrs
A large, well spread out site with many trees and bushes. Ideal centre for touring. From A12 at Saxmundham turn E onto B1119 for 3 miles. Then follow by-road over level crossing and signs to caravan park. A 5-acre site with 50 touring pitches and 200 statics.
Tennis, 5acre recreation ground, golf.

🖾🖎🖎☉🗹🗞🔍☼🗜⚠🗎🖉📞🐕🐾
➜ ∪🥤🍼
Credit Cards ● ▬

LOWESTOFT

See **Kessingland**

NEWMARKET

Camping & Caravanning Club Site (TL622625)
Rowley Mile Racecourse CB8 8JL
☎ 01638 663235 & 01203 694995 Signposted
▶ ▶ ▶ **Family Park** ★ ♠ £9.20-£11.60 ♠ £9.20-£11.60
▲ £9.20-£11.60
Open Mar-Sep Booking advisable Last arrival 21.00hrs Last departure noon
A level grassy site on Newmarket Heath with panoramic country views. From centre of Newmarket follow signs for Horse Museum and Hospital. Site 1m W of town centre at top of hill and signed. Please see the advertisement on page 27 for details of Club Members' benefits. A 10-acre site with 90 touring pitches.
Recreation room with TV.

🖾🖎☉🗹☼⚠🗎🖉📞
➜ ∪🅿🐾
Credit Cards ● ▬ ▩

SAXMUNDHAM

Whitearch Touring Caravan Park (TM379610)
Main Rd, Benhall IP17 1NA
☎ 01728 604646 & 603773 Signposted
▶ ▶ ▶ **Family Park** ★ ♠ fr £8.50 ♠ fr £8.50 ▲ fr £8.50
Open Apr-Oct Booking advisable bank hols Last arrival 22.00hrs
Attractive valley site with lake for coarse fishing and new, very clean toilet block. On the junction of A12 and B1121. A 14.5-acre site with 30 touring pitches.
Fishing lake

🖾🖎☉🔍☼⚠🗎🖉📞🛒🐾🐕🐾♿
➜🥤

Marsh Farm Caravan Site (TM385608)
Sternfield IP171HW ☎ 01728 602168 (1.5m S)
Signposted
▶▶ **Town & Country Pennant Park** ♠ ♠
Open all year Booking advisable Jun-Aug Last arrival 22.30hrs Last departure 22.30hrs

MOON & SIXPENCE
NEAR WOODBRIDGE, SUFFOLK

Secluded tourer sites and good choice of caravan holiday homes for sale owner occupiers, close friends and family. Superb, tranquil, landscaped parkland of 85 acres. Professionally managed lake, fishing Sept & Oct. Sandy beach, woods, meadows. Dog walks, cycle trails. Excellent restaurant serving local specialities. Attractive Lounge and bar. Located unspoilt Coastal Suffolk close Woodbridge and River Deben.

Full colour brochure from:
Moon & Sixpence, Waldringfield Woodbridge, Suffolk IP12 4PP.
Tel: 01473 736 650. Fax: 01473 736 270

Very attractive venture site with adjoining lakes offering coarse fishing, and no sanitary facilities. Take Aldburgh rd from A12, at Snape crossroads turn left signed Sternfield, and pick up sign for farm. A 6-acre site with 30 touring pitches.

SHOTTISHAM

St Margaret's House (TM323447)
Hollesley Rd IP12 3HD ☎ 01394 411247 Signposted
Nearby town: Woodbridge
▶▶ Town & Country Pennant Park 🏕 🏕 Å
Open Apr or Etr-Oct Booking advisable bank hols & Jul-Aug Last arrival 22.00hrs Last departure noon
A pleasant little family run site in attractive village setting. Turn off B1083 at village and in .25m find site to SE of church. A 3-acre site with 30 touring pitches.
Milk, dairy products & newspapers to order.

WOODBRIDGE

Moon & Sixpence (TM263454)
Newbourn Rd, Waldringfield IP12 4PP ☎ 01473 736650 (off A12) Signposted
▶▶▶ Family Park 🏕 £15 🏕 £15 Å £15
Open Apr-Oct (rs low season club/shop/reception open limited hours) Booking advisable school & bank hols Last arrival 20.00hrs Last departure noon
A splendid, well-planned site, with a lakeside sandy

beach. Tourers are in a valley around the lake. Signed from A12 at Martlesham. A 5-acre site with 90 touring pitches and 175 statics.
2 acre lake with sandy beach. Woodland cycle trail.

Credit Cards 💳

SURREY

For the map of this county see SUSSEX, EAST

CHERTSEY

Camping & Caravanning Club Site (TQ052667)
Bridge Rd KT16 8JX ☎ 01932 562405 & 01203 694995 Signposted

▶▶▶▶ De-Luxe Park ★ 🏕 £13-£14 🏕 £13-£14 Å £13-£14
Open all year Booking advisable Jul-Aug & bank hols Last arrival 21.00hrs Last departure noon
A pretty riverside site with many trees and shrubs, and well-looked after grounds. Fishing and boating allowed on the River Thames. Please see the advertisement on
contd.

page 27 for details of Club Members' benefits. A 12-acre site with 200 touring pitches.

Table tennis, fishing.

🔊📻☉🗑️🍴🚿🏍️🛢️🗑️📺🛎️🐕🛒👤

→▶🏌️

Credit Cards 💳 💳 💳 💳 🦋

EAST HORSLEY

Camping & Caravanning Club Site (TQ083552)
Ockham Rd North KT24 6PE ☎ 01483 283273 & 01203 694995 (between A3 & A246, on B2039) Signposted

▶ ▶ ▶ **De-Luxe Park** ★ 🚍 £11-£14 🚐 £11-£14
▲ £11-£14
Open end Mar-early Nov Booking advisable bank hols & Jul-Aug Last arrival 21.00hrs Last departure noon
Beautiful lakeside site with plenty of trees and shrubs, and separate camping fields. Well-organised, friendly wardens. Situated between A3 and A246, on the B2039. Please see the advertisement on page 27 for details of Club Members' benefits. A 12-acre site with 135 touring pitches.

Table tennis, fishing, dartboard.

🔊📻☉🗑️🍴🚿🏍️🛢️🗑️🛒👤🐕🛒👤

→🔙▶🏌️

Credit Cards 💳 💳 💳 💳 🦋

LINGFIELD

Long Acres Caravan & Camping Park (TQ368425)
Newchapel Rd RH7 6LE ☎ 01342 833205 & 834307 Signposted
Nearby town: East Grinstead
▶ ▶ ▶ **Family Park** 🚍 £8.50-£10.40 🚐 £8.50-£10.40
▲ £8.50-£10.40
Open all year Booking advisable bank hols & for electric hook ups Last arrival 22.30hrs Last departure noon
A pleasant ex-farm site, well-screened and well-maintained, with modern heated toilet facilities. Under Gatwick flight path. From A22 turn E into Newchapel Rd, signed. A 7-acre site with 60 touring pitches. Quad bikes, free fishing, bike tracks & Go-Karts.

🔊📻☉🗑️🚿🏍️🛢️🗑️📺🛎️🐕🛒👤🏓🛒

→🔙▶💒🏌️

SUSSEX, EAST

BATTLE

Whydown Farm Tourist Caravan & Camping Park (TQ782169)
Crazy Ln, Sedlescombe TN33 0QT ☎ 01424 870147 Signposted
▶ ▶ ▶ **Family Park** ★ 🚍 £7-£8.50 🚐 £7-£8.50 ▲ £7-£8.50
Open Mar-Oct Booking advisable bank hols

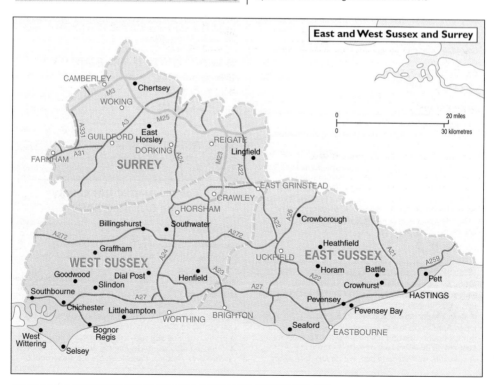

East and West Sussex and Surrey

A very good site on two levels amid attractive scenery and overlooking cider orchards. Signposted at junc of A229 and A21. A 3.5-acre site with 36 touring pitches.

🏴⊙✳️🅸⌀⊞🅃🍴&

→∪▶🔧🖼️

Senlac Park Caravan & Camping Site (TQ722153)
Main Rd, Catsfield TN33 9DU ☎ 01424 773969 & 752590
Signposted
Nearby town: Hastings
▶➤ **Town & Country Pennant Park** 🏕️🏕️ Å
Open Mar-Oct Booking advisable bank hols Last arrival 21.00hrs Last departure noon
A pretty woodland site with many secluded bays, well landscaped and attractively laid out. From Battle take A271, then turn left on to B2204 signed Bexhill. A 5-acre site with 32 touring pitches.

🏴⊙✳️🅸⊞🅃🌡️🦮

→∪▶🔧🐾

Credit Cards 💳 ▭

CROWBOROUGH

Camping & Caravanning Club Site (TQ520315)
Goldsmith Recreation Ground TN6 2TN
☎ 01892 664827 (in season) & 01203 694995
(just off A26) Signposted

ⓆⓆⓆⓆⓆⓆⓆⓆⓆ

▶▶▶ **De-Luxe Park** ★ 🏕️ £11-£14 🏕️ £11-£14
Å £11-£14
Open Feb-mid Dec Booking advisable bank hols & peak periods Last arrival 21.00hrs Last departure noon
A spacious terraced site with stunning views of the surrounding countryside. Situated next to an excellent leisure centre, just off A26 (well signed) and 200yds from town centre. Please see the advertisement on page 27 for details of Club Members' benefits. A 13-acre site with 88 touring pitches.

🏴🏴⊙🅾️🏴✳️/𝐌⌀🌡️🦮&

→∪▶✚📞🔧

Credit Cards 💳 ▭

ⓆⓆⓆⓆⓆⓆⓆ

CROWHURST

Brakes Coppice Park (TQ765134)
Forewood Ln TN33 9AB ☎ 01424 830322 (off A2100)
Signposted
Nearby town: Battle
▶▶▶ **Family Park** ★ 🏕️ £5-£7 🏕️ £5-£7 Å £5-£7
Open Mar-Oct Booking advisable public hols & Jul-Aug Last arrival dusk Last departure noon
Secluded farm site in meadow surrounded by woodland with small stream and fishing lake. Off A2100. A 3-acre site with 30 touring pitches and 1 static. Fishing.

🏴🏴⊙🅾️🏴✳️/𝐌🌡️⌀⊞🅃🌡️🚏📷🐾🐕

→∪▶🔧

HASTINGS & ST LEONARDS

Shearbarn Holiday Park (TQ842112)
TN35 5DX ☎ 01424 423583 & 716474
Signposted
▶▶▶ **Family Park** 🏕️🏕️ Å
Open Mar-15 Jan (rs Mar-Etr, early May & mid Sep-15 Jan facilities may be closed or reduced) Booking advisable bank hols & Jun-Aug Last arrival 22.00hrs Last departure 10.00hrs
A large touring site with sea views. All entertainments are available at the static site nearby. A 16-acre site with 450 touring pitches and 250 statics.
Entertainment & amusements on site.

🏴🏴⊙🅾️🏴🔍✳️🍸/𝐌🌡️⌀⊞🅃✖️📞🚵🐾

→∪▶📞🔧

Credit Cards 💳 ▭ ▭ ▭ 🔵

HEATHFIELD

Greenview Caravan Park (TQ605223)
Broad Oak TN21 8RT ☎ 01435 863531
Signposted
▶▶▶ **Family Park** 🏕️🏕️ Å
Open Apr-Oct Booking advisable Jul-Aug Last arrival 22.00hrs Last departure 10.30hrs ✏️
Small, attractive site adjoining main A265 at Broad Oak 1m E of Heathfield. A 3-acre site with 10 touring pitches and 51 statics.

🏴🏴⊙✳️🍸🌡️⌀🅃📞

HORAM

Horam Manor Touring Park (TQ579170)
TN21 0YD ☎ 01435 813662 (on A267, 3m S of Heathfield) Signposted
Nearby town: Heathfield

ⓆⓆⓆⓆⓆⓆⓆⓆⓆ

▶▶▶ **De-Luxe Park** ★ 🏕️ £11 🏕️ £11 Å £11
Open Mar-Oct Booking advisable peak periods
A well landscaped park in a peaceful location on former estate land, set in gently-sloping grassland surrounded by woods, nature trails and fishing lakes. Signed off A267 just S of Horam, and 3m S of Heathfield. A 7-acre site with 90 touring pitches.

🏴🏴⊙🅾️🏴✳️🌡️⌀⊞✖️📞🚵🐾🐕&

→∪▶🔧🐾

ⓆⓆⓆⓆⓆⓆⓆⓆⓆ

Woodland View Touring Park (TQ579170)
Horebeech Ln tn21 0hr
☎ 01435 813597
▶▶▶ **Family Park** ★ 🏕️ £8 🏕️ £8 Å £8
Open Etr-Sep Booking advisable Last departure 11.00hrs ✏️
Small, level grassy park behind owner's house, immaculately maintained and well-equipped. Signed off A267 in Horam, 3m S of Heathfield. A 3-acre site with 25 touring pitches.

🏴🏴⊙🅾️✳️/𝐌🌡️⌀🅃📞

→∪▶🔧🐾

PETT

Carters Farm (TQ887145)
Elm Ln TN35 4JD ☎ 01424 813206 & 812244
Signposted
Nearby town: Hastings
▶▶ Town & Country Pennant Park ★ ♠ £6-£8.50
♠ £6-£8.50 ▲ £6-£8.50
Open Mar-Oct Last arrival 21.00hrs Last departure noon
A very secluded, long-established working farm site in partly sloping meadow. The sea is only 15 mins walk away. From A259 from Hastings turn right after Guestling, signed Pett. A 12-acre site with 100 touring pitches and 85 statics.

🔌 🏕 ⏺ 🔧 ✳ 🎔 🌊 ⊞ Ⓣ ⬤ 🐾
➜ 🎣

PEVENSEY

Camping & Caravanning Club Site (TQ682055)
Normans Bay BN24 6PP
☎ 01323 761190 (in season) & 01203 694995
Signposted
Nearby town: Eastbourne

▶▶▶▶ De-Luxe Park ★ ♠ £11-£14 ♠ £11-£14
▲ £11-£14
Open end Mar-early Nov Booking advisable bank hols & peak periods Last arrival 21.00hrs Last departure noon
A well-kept site with immaculate toilet block, right beside the sea. Pass through Elborune, follow signs to Pevensey Bay, and take road signed Beachlands Only for 1m. Please see the advertisement on page 27 for details of Club Members' benefits. A 12-acre site with 200 touring pitches.

🔌 🏕 ⏺ 🔧 🎔 ✳ 🏔 🎔 🌊 ⊞ Ⓣ ⬤ 🐾 🎔 ⬤
➜ 🎣

Credit Cards 💳 ▭ ▭ ▭ 🇬

PEVENSEY BAY

Bayview Caravan and Camping Park (TQ648028)
Old Martello Rd BN24 6DX
☎ 01323 768688 (off A259)
Signposted
Nearby town: Eastbourne
▶▶▶ Family Park ♠ £8.15-£9.15 ♠ £8.15-£9.15
▲ £7.70-£8.40
Open Mar-Oct Booking advisable bank & school hols
Last arrival 22.00hrs Last departure noon
A level and flat site two minutes' walk from the sea-shore located E of the town centre off the A259 in an area known as "The Crumbles". A 3.5-acre site with 49 touring pitches and 5 statics.

🔌 🏕 ⏺ 🔧 🔧 ✳ 🏔 🎔 🌊 ⊞ Ⓣ ⬤ 🐾
➜ 🎔 ⏺ 🎔 ⬤ 🎣

SEAFORD

Buckle Caravan & Camping Park (TV469960)
Marine Pde BN25 2QR ☎ 01323 897801 Signposted
Nearby town: Newhaven
▶▶▶ Family Park ★ ♠ £7-£9 ♠ £7-£9 ▲ £7-£9
Open Mar-2 Jan Booking advisable bank hols & Jul-Aug
Last arrival 21.00hrs Last departure noon

A friendly, well-maintained site set alongside the sea wall. Signed off A259 on W side of Seaford towards Newhaven. A 9-acre site with 110 touring pitches.

🔌 🏕 ⏺ 🔧 ✳ 🏔 🎔 🌊 ⊞ ⬤ 🎔 🐾
➜ 🎔 ⏺ 🎔 ⬤ 🎣 🇬 🎔

SUSSEX, WEST

**For the map of this county
see SUSSEX, EAST**

BILLINGSHURST

Limeburner's Camping (TQ073255)
Newbridge RH14 9JA ☎ 01403 782311 Signposted
Nearby town: Horsham
▶▶ Town & Country Pennant Park ★ ♠ £7 ♠ £7 ▲ £7
Open Apr-Oct Booking advisable bank hols & Jul-Aug
Last arrival 22.00hrs Last departure 14.00hrs
Secluded rural site alongside the attractive 'Limeburner's Arms' public house. Located a short distance from the village of Billingshurst on the A272 Midhurst road and the River Arun. A 3-acre site with 42 touring pitches.

🔌 🏕 ⏺ ✳ 🎔 🏔 🎔 🌊 ⊞ ✖ ⬤
➜ ∪ 🎔 🎣 🎔

BOGNOR REGIS

Lillies Nursery & Caravan Park (SU964040)
Yapton Rd, Barnham PO22 0AY ☎ 01243 552081
Signposted
Nearby town: Chichester
▶▶ Town & Country Pennant Park ♠ £8 ♠ £8 ▲ £8
Open Mar-Oct Booking advisable Jul-Sep Last departure 11.00hrs
A friendly little site tucked behind the owner's nursery, in secluded peaceful countryside. On B2233 in Barnham, 2m off A27 and 6m from Bognor Regis. A 1-acre site with 10 touring pitches and 6 statics. Play area for ball games.

🔌 🏕 ⏺ ⊡ 🔧 ✳ 🎔 🌊 ⊞ Ⓣ ⬤ 🚮 🏔 🎔 ⬤
➜ ∪ 🎔 ⏺ 🎔 ⬤ 🎣

CHICHESTER

Southern Leisure Lakeside Village (SU875032)
Vinnetrow Rd PO20 6LB ☎ 01243 787715 Signposted
▶▶▶ Family Park ♠ ♠ ▲
Open Etr-early Oct (rs Etr-24 May & Sep-early Oct swim pool closed, bar wknds only(ex BH)) Booking advisable bank hols & Jul-Aug Last arrival 18.00hrs Last departure 16.00hrs
A large touring site in secluded rural setting surrounded by several lakes. Level, grassy and well laid out with modern toilets and good leisure facilities. Signed from A27. A 50-acre site with 400 touring pitches.

🔌 🏕 ⏺ ⊡ 🔧 ✳ 🎔 🏔 🎔 🌊 Ⓣ ⬤ 🚮 🎔
➜ ∪ 🎔 🌊 🎔 🎣

Credit Cards 💳 ▭ ▭ 🇬

WARNER FARM TOURING PARK

Warner Lane, Selsey, West Sussex, PO20 9EL
Tel: (01243) 604499
Fax: (01243) 604499
e-mail: john.bunn@btinternet.com

One of the most modern touring parks on the South Coast with great entertainment and two heated swimming pools. 250 pitches, 300 static caravans.

Open Mar-Oct.
Touring Caravans £6-£19.80
Tents £6-£17.50 per pitch per night.
Static caravans £150-£405 per week.

SOUTHERN LEISURE
LAKESIDE VILLAGE

▶▶▶

Vinnetrow Road, Chichester, Sussex PO20 6LB
Tel: Chichester (01243) 787715
24 hour answering service

Ideally situated for visiting the many places of interest. Flat, grassy pitches. Electrical hook ups. Free showers and toilet facilities. Ample mirrors and shaver points. Laundry room. Well stocked supermarket and off licence. Luxury lounge bar and separate family bar. Children's bar. Nightly free entertainment during high season. Heated outdoor swimming pool.

Windsurfing, water skiing and coarse fishing. Caravan sales area with wide selection of used vans. Dogs welcome on a lead. Family units only. Take away snack bar.

Free brochure on request.

DIAL POST

Honeybridge Park (TQ152183)
Honeybridge Ln RH13 8NX ☎ 01403 710923 Signposted
Nearby town: Horsham

►►►► De-Luxe Park ★ ⚑ £5-£6 ⚑ £5-£6 ⚠ £5-£6
Open all year Booking advisable bank hols Last arrival
22.00hrs Last departure 20.00hrs
*Gently sloping site surrounded by hedgerows and
mature trees off the A24 Worthing road, 6m S of
Horsham. A 15-acre site with 100 touring pitches.*

🔌📶☉🖥️🍳✳️⛰️🚿🚮🚽🎱🔦↑🐕🐾⛱️
➔∪⚠️↙

Credit Cards 💳 💳 💳 💳

GOODWOOD

Caravan Club Site (SU885111)
Goodwood Racecourse PO18 0PX ☎ 01243 774486
Signposted
Nearby town: Chichester
►►► Family Park ⚑ ⚑ ⚠
Open Apr-Sep (rs during race meetings site is closed)
Booking advisable public hols & Jul-Aug Last arrival
20.00hrs Last departure noon
*A neat and tidy level grassy site on Goodwood
Racecourse. Closed when race meetings are held. 5m N
of Chichester. A 3-acre site with 70 touring pitches.*

🔌📶☉⛰️🚿🚮🎱🔦🚽🔦↑⛱️
➔∪▶

Credit Cards 💳 💳 💳

GRAFFHAM

Camping & Caravanning Club Site (SU941187)
Great Bury GU28 0QJ ☎ 01798 867476 (in season) &
01203 694995 (5m S Petworth on unclass rd off A285)
Signposted
Nearby town: Midhurst
►►► Family Park ★ ⚑ £10-£13 ⚑ £10-£13 ⚠ £10-£13
Open end Mar-early Nov Booking advisable bank hols &
peak periods Last arrival 21.00hrs Last departure noon
*A superb wooded site, with each pitch occupying its
own private, well-screened area. From A285 towards
Petworth turn first left after Duncton. Please see the
advertisement on page 27 for details of Club Members'
benefits. A 20-acre site with 90 touring pitches.*

🔌📶☉🖥️🍳✳️🚿🎱🔦🚽🔦↑🛒🐾⛱️
➔∪↙

Credit Cards 💳 💳 💳 💳

HENFIELD

Harwoods Farm (TQ196153)
West End Ln BN5 9RF ☎ 01273 492820 Signposted
Nearby town: Brighton
►► Town & Country Pennant Park ⚑ ⚠
Open Etr-Oct Booking advisable bank hols Last arrival
mdnt Last departure eves
*A really unspoilt site with earth closets and a water tap
down a rough, narrow lane in good walking area.
Signed in Henfield, and 2m off A281. A 1.75-acre site
with 35 touring pitches.*

➔↙

LITTLEHAMPTON

White Rose Touring Park (TQ026041)
Mill Ln, Wick BN17 7PH ☎ 01903 716176 Signposted
►►► Family Park ⚑ £11-£15 ⚑ £11-£13 ⚠ £5-£13
Open 15 Mar-15 Jan Booking advisable bank hols & Jul-
Aug Last departure noon

*A well-maintained family run site providing level, well-
drained ground surrounded by farmland. Located close
to Arundel and Littlehampton which provide good local
facilities. From A284 turn left into Mill Lane. Winner of
the Best Campsite for South-East England 1996/7. A 7-
acre site with 127 touring pitches and 14 statics.*

🔌📶☉🖥️🍳✳️⛰️🚿🚮🎱🔦↑🐕🐾
➔∪▶☉⚠️✚☎️↙

Credit Cards 💳 💳 💳 💳 💳

SELSEY

Warner Farm Touring Park (SZ845939)
Warner Ln, Selsey PO20 9EL
☎ 01243 604121 & 604499 (turn right onto
School Lane & follow signs)
Signposted
Nearby town: Chichester

★ ⚑ £6.50-£18 ⚑ £6.50-£18 ⚠ £6.50-£18
Open Mar-Oct Booking advisable 3 wks prior to arrival
Last arrival 20.00hrs Last departure 10.00hrs
*A new touring site adjoining three static sites under
same ownership. A courtesy bus runs around the
complex to entertainment and supermarkets. A 10-acre
site with 200 touring pitches and 150 statics.*
See advertisement under CHICHESTER

🔌📶☉🖥️🍳 🎣🔍🍴🖥️✳️🍴⛰️🚿🚮🎱🔦🚽 ✖️
🔦🏪🍴🎣↑🐕🐾⛱️
➔∪▶☉↙

Credit Cards 💳 💳 💳 💳 💳 💳

SLINDON

Camping & Caravanning Club Site (SU958084)
Slindon Park BN18 0RG
☎ 01243 814387 (in season) & 01203 694995 Signposted
Nearby town: Chichester
►► Town & Country Pennant Park ★ ⚑ £8-£9 ⚠ £8-£9
Open end Mar-end Sep Booking advisable bank hols &
peak periods Last arrival 21.00hrs Last departure noon
*Beautiful former orchard, completely screened by NT
trees and very quiet. Turn off A27 at Aldingbourne*

Nurseries, take second right into Britten's Lane signed Eartham, then take 2nd right for Slindon; and entrance is on right. Please see the advertisement on page 27 for details of Club Members' benefits. Own sanitary facilities essential. A 2-acre site with 46 touring pitches.

🏴 ✳ 🔌 ✆ ⚡

Credit Cards 💳 ▨ ▧

SOUTHBOURNE

Camping & Caravanning Club Site (SU774056)
343 Main Rd PO10 8JH ☎ 01243 373202
Nearby town: Chichester

▶ ▶ ▶ ▶ De-Luxe Park ★ 🚐 £13-£14 🚐 £13-£14
⛺ £13-£14
Open all year Booking advisable bank hols, wknds & mid Jun-mid Sep Last arrival 22.00hrs Last departure 14.00hrs
Situated in open meadow and orchard, a very pleasant site with well looked after, clean facilities. Leave A27 at roundabout signed Bosham and Funtington, site 5m along A259. Please see the advertisement on page 27 for details of Club Members' benefits. A 3-acre site with 58 touring pitches.

🏴 📞 ☉ 🗑 🍴 ✳ ⚡

➔ ∪ ▶ 🥢 ⚡

Credit Cards 💳 ▨ ▧

SOUTHWATER

Raylands Park (TQ170265)
Jackrells Ln RH13 7DH ☎ 01403 730218 & 731822
Signposted
Nearby town: Horsham

▶ ▶ ▶ Family Park 🚐 🚐 ⛺

Open Mar-Oct Booking advisable bank hols & high season Last arrival 20.00hrs Last departure 14.00hrs
A very well run site in an excellent setting. Reasonably level ground, superb modern toilet blocks, a clubhouse and children's play area. Well maintained access roads. Signposted from the A24 in Southwater. A 6-acre site with 40 touring pitches and 60 statics.

🏴 📞 ☉ 🗑 🍴 🍷 🛒 ☐ ✳ ⚡ 🏔 🔌 ☐ ✗ ✆ 🐕 🐎 ⚡

➔ ∪ ▶ ⚠ ☎ 🥢 ⚡

WEST WITTERING

Wicks Farm Holiday Park (SZ796995)
Redlands Ln PO20 8QD ☎ 01243 513116 Signposted
Nearby town: Chichester

▶ ▶ ▶ Family Park 🚐 ⛺

Open 14 Mar-Oct Booking advisable peak periods Last arrival 21.00hrs Last departure noon
A pleasant rural site, well-screened by trees with good walks nearby and 2m from coast. Signed from B2179. A 14-acre site with 40 touring pitches.
Bicycle hire.

🏴 📞 ☉ 🗑 🍴 🍷 ✳ 🏔 🔌 ☐ ✆ 🐎 ⚡

➔ ∪ ▶ ☉ ⚠ ✚ 🥢

Credit Cards 💳 ▨ ▧ ▨ 🖊

TYNE & WEAR

For the map of this county
see NORTHUMBERLAND

ROWLANDS GILL

Derwent Park Caravan Site (NZ168586)
NE39 1LG ☎ 01207 543383 Signposted
Nearby town: Newcastle
▶ ▶ ▶ Family Park ★ 🚐 £8.10-£9 🚐 £8.10-£9
⛺ £5-£7.50
Open Apr-Sep Booking advisable public hols & Jul-Aug Last arrival 23.30hrs Last departure noon
A very pleasant and well-maintained municipal site. Situated on edge of Rowlands Gill at junc of A694 and B6314. A 3-acre site with 47 touring pitches and 25 statics.
Fishing, crazy golf, giant draughts & chess, bowling.

🏴 📞 ☉ 🗑 🍷 🍴 ✳ 🏔 🔌 ☐ ✆ 🚲 🛒 🐎 🐎

⚡ ♿

➔ ∪ ▶ ☉ ☎ 🥢

Credit Cards 💳 ▨ ▧ 🖊

SOUTH SHIELDS

Sandhaven Caravan & Camping Park (NZ376672)
Bents Park Rd NE33 2NL
☎ 0191 454 5594 & 0191 455 7411
Signposted
▶ ▶ ▶ Family Park ★ 🚐 £8.80-£9.90 🚐 £8.80-£9.90
⛺ £7.80-£8.90
Open Mar-Oct Booking advisable for complete wks Jul-5 Sep Last arrival anytime Last departure 11.00hrs
A spacious site adjoining the sea front, set in a well-screened and fenced area next to a public park. Situated on A183 .5 miles from the town centre with an entrance on Bents Park Road. A 3.5-acre site with 52 touring pitches and 46 statics.

🏴 📞 ☉ 🍷 ✳ 🔌 ✆ 🛒 🐎 ♿

➔ ∪ ▶ ✚ ☎ 🥢 🗑

Lizard Lane Caravan & Camping Site (NZ399648)
Lizard Ln NE34 7AB
☎ 0191 454 4982 & 0191 455 7411 Signposted
▶ Town & Country Pennant Park ★ 🚐 £6.70-£7.70
🚐 £6.70-£7.70 ⛺ £6.70-£7.70
Open Mar-Oct Booking advisable for complete wks Jul-5 Sep Last arrival anytime Last departure 11.00hrs
Sloping, grass site near beach, 2m S of town centre on A183 Sunderland road. Well-kept and maintained. A 2-acre site with 45 touring pitches and 70 statics.

📞 ☉ 🍷 ✳ 🏔 🔌 ☐ ✆ 🐎 ⚡

➔ ∪ ▶ ⚠ ✚ ☎ 🥢 🗑

Credit Cards ▨

WARWICKSHIRE

For the map of this county see HEREFORDSHIRE

ASTON CANTLOW

Island Meadow Caravan Park (SP137596)
The Mill House B95 6JP ☎ 01789 488273 (.25 W)
Signposted
Nearby town: Stratford-upon-Avon

▶ ▶ ▶ ▶ De-Luxe Park ★ ⚐ £9 ⚐ £9 Å £7
Open Mar-Oct Booking advisable peak periods Last arrival 21.00hrs Last departure noon
A small well-kept site bordered by the River Alne and its mill stream. Mature willows line the banks. .25m W of Aston Cantlow on the road to Alcester. A 3-acre site with 24 touring pitches and 56 statics.
Free fishing for guests.

🎇🏕☉🦃✳🅸🔳🆃🚻🎒♿
➔◟▶◎♪

KINGSBURY

Camping & Caravanning Club Site (SP202968)
Kingsbury Water Park, Bodymoor Heath B76 0DY
☎ 01827 874101 (in season) & 01203 694995 (off unclass rd joining A4097 & A4091)
Nearby town: Sutton Coldfield
▶ ▶ ▶ Family Park ★ ⚐ £9.20-£11.60 ⚐ £9.20-£11.60
Å £9.20-£11.60
Open end Mar-early Nov Booking advisable bank hols & Jul-Aug Last arrival 21.00hrs Last departure noon
A former gravel pit, now reclaimed and landscaped, the site is part of a level complex of lakes, canals, woods and marshland with good access roads. 2m SW on A5 take A4097 for 1m. Please see the advertisement on page 27 for details of Club Members' benefits. An 18-acre site with 120 touring pitches.

🎇🏕☉🦃🅸🔳🆃♿
➔♪

Credit Cards 💳 💳 💳

Tame View Caravan Site (SP209979)
Cliff B78 2DR ☎ 01827 873853 (1m N A51)
Signposted
Nearby town: Tamworth
▶▶ Town & Country Pennant Park ⚐ ⚐ Å
Open all year Booking advisable 1 month in advance
Last arrival 23.00hrs Last departure 23.00hrs
Enclosed level meadow on high bank overlooking River Tame, with minimal sanitary facilities. 400 yards off A51 Tamworth to Kingsbury road, 1m N of Kingsbury opposite restaurant. No through road sign. A 5-acre site with 55 touring pitches.
Fishing.

✳🔳🚻🎒♿
➔◟▶◎⚓⚒🍴♪🔳

WOLVEY

Wolvey Villa Farm Caravan & Camping Site (SP428869)
LE10 3HF ☎ 01455 220493 & 220630 Signposted
Nearby town: Hinckley
▶ ▶ ▶ Family Park ★ ⚐ £5.50-£5.70 ⚐ £5.50-£5.70
Å £5.40-£5.60
Open all year Booking advisable Spring bank hol-mid Aug Last arrival 23.15hrs Last departure noon
Level, grass site with mature trees and bushes set in meadowland. About 1m S of Wolvey. Ideally located to explore the Midlands area. From M6 junc 2, take B4056 (signed Ansty) to Wolvey for 3m. A 7-acre site with 110 touring pitches.
Fishing, putting green, off licence.

🎇🏕☉🦃🅸🔳🆃🚻🎒♿
➔◟▶♪

WIGHT, ISLE OF

For the map see HAMPSHIRE

ADGESTONE

BEMBRIDGE

See **Whitecliff Bay**

FRESHWATER

Heathfield Farm Camping (SZ335879)
Heathfield Rd PO40 9SH ☎ 01983 756756 & 752480
Signposted
Nearby town: Newport
► ► ► **Family Park** ★ ⊞ £5.50-£6.50 ⊞ £5.50-£6.50
▲ £5.50-£6.50
Open all year Booking advisable bank hols & Jul-Aug
Last arrival 22.30hrs Last departure 22.30hrs

*Pleasant and well-maintained small site on the edge of
Freshwater with views across the Solent. A 4-acre site
with 60 touring pitches.*

NEWBRIDGE

Orchards Holiday Caravan Park (SZ411881)
PO41 0TS ☎ 01983 531331 & 531350 (entrance opposite
Post Office) Signposted
Nearby town: Yarmouth

► ► ► ► ► **Premier Park** ★ ⊞ £7.15-£10.45
⊞ £7.15-£10.45 ▲ £7.15-£10.45
Open 5 Mar-3 Jan (rs Etr-Apr & late Sep-Oct) Booking
advisable Etr, Spring bank hol & late Jun-Aug Last
arrival 23.00hrs Last departure 11.00hrs
*An excellent, well-managed site set in downs and
meadowland adjacent to B3401 and near the sea.
Signed left at Horse and Groom pub on A3054. An 8-
acre site with 175 touring pitches and 65 statics.*
Coarse fishing, petanque.
See advertisement under YARMOUTH

Credit Cards ●● ▭ ▭ ▭ ▭

NEWCHURCH

Southland Camping Park (SZ557847)
PO36 0LZ ☎ 01983 865385 Signposted
Nearby town: Sandown

► ► ► ► **De-Luxe Park** ★ ⊞ £6.50-£9 ⊞ £6.50-£9
▲ £6.50-£9
Open Etr-Sep Booking advisable Jul-Aug Last arrival
22.00hrs Last departure 11.00hrs

*Beautifully maintained site, peacefully located on the
outskirts of the village in the Arreton Valley off A3056. A
7-acre site with 100 touring pitches.*
12 volt transformers available.

Credit Cards ●● ▭ ▭ ▭

PONDWELL

Pondwell Camp Site (SZ622911)
PO34 5AQ ☎ 01983 612330 Signposted
Nearby town: Ryde
► ► ► Family Park ⊕ £4-£7 ⊕ £4-£7 ▲ £4-£7
Open May-26 Sep Booking advisable Aug Last arrival
23.00hrs Last departure 11.00hrs ⊗
*A secluded site in quiet rural surroundings close to the
sea, slightly sloping with some level areas, and modern
toilet facilities. Signed from Ryde on B3330. A 9-acre
site with 250 touring pitches.*

🔌 🚐 🏠 ⊙ 🗃 🍳 🔦 ⌂ ✳ 🏍 🔥 🔌 🗄 🧺 🔪
→ ► ⚒ ☕ ✂

Credit Cards ⊕ ▦

SANDOWN

Adgestone Camping Park (SZ590855)
Lower Adgestone Rd PO36 OHL
☎ 01983 403432 & 403989 (2m NW)
Signposted

◯◯◯◯◯◯◯◯

► ► ► ► ► Premier Park ★ ⊕ £7.60-£11 ⊕ £7.60-£11
▲ £7.60-£11
Open Etr/mid Mar-Sep (rs Off peak limited opening of
takeaway) Booking advisable high season Last arrival
dusk Last departure 11.00hrs

*A well-managed site in a quiet location not far from the
town. The slightly sloping pitches are surrounded by
flower beds and trees. 2m NW of Sandown. A 15.5-acre
site with 200 touring pitches.*
River fishing, football pitch, petanque, volleyball.
See advertisement under ADGESTONE

🔌 🏠 ⊙ 🗃 🍳 ✂ ⚒ 🔦 ✳ 🏍 🔥 🔌 🗄 🖵 ⌂ 🚐 🚿 ▦
🏠 🐕 🧺 ♿
→ ∪ ► ◎ 🛆 ✈ ☕ ✂
Credit Cards ⊕ ▦ ▦ ▦ ◻

◯◯◯◯◯◯◯◯

Camping & Caravanning Club Site (SZ573833)
Cheverton Farm, Newport Rd, Apse Heath PO36 9PJ
☎ 01983 866414 & 01203 694995 (take A3056 from
Newport) Signposted
Nearby town: Shanklin

◯◯◯◯◯◯◯◯

► ► ► ► De-Luxe Park ★ ⊕ £11-£14 ⊕ £11-£14 ▲ £11-£14
Open end Mar-early Nov Booking advisable bank hols &
peak periods Last arrival 21.00hrs Last departure noon

*A terraced site with good quality facilities, bordering on
open farmland Off A3056 Newport Rd. A 5-acre site with
60 touring pitches.*

🔌 🏠 ⊙ 🗃 🍳 🔦 ⌂ ✳ 🔥 🔌 🗄 ⌂ 🐕 🚿
→ ∪ ► ☕ ✂

Credit Cards ⊕ ▦ ▦

◯◯◯◯◯◯◯◯

SHANKLIN

Landguard Camping Park (SZ577825)
Landguard Manor Rd PO37 7PH ☎ 01983 867028
Signposted

◯◯◯◯◯◯◯◯

► ► ► ► De-Luxe Park ★ ⊕ £6.30-£10.50
⊕ £6.30-£10.50 ▲ £6.30-£10.50
Open May-Sep Booking advisable school hols Last
arrival 22.00hrs Last departure noon ⊗
*Part of a holiday complex, the touring area is secluded
and surrounded by trees, in a rural setting. A 6-acre site
with 150 touring pitches.*
Horse riding.

🔌 🚐 🏠 ⊙ 🗃 🍳 ✂ ⚒ ✳ ♀ 🏍 🔥 🔌 🗄 🖵 ✂ 🔦
🚽 🧺 ♿
→ ∪ ► ◎ 🛆 ✈ 🌊 ✂
Credit Cards ⊕ ▦ ▦ ▦ ◻

◯◯◯◯◯◯◯◯

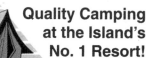

The ORCHARDS
Holiday Caravan & Camping Park
Isle of Wight

🍎 Special ferry inclusive package holidays for caravanners and campers

🍎 Holiday caravans to let and for sale

🍎 **Indoor & outdoor swimming pool complex with licensed cafe bar**

🍎 Superb self service shop / takeaway food bar

🍎 Coarse fishing

🍎 Small rallies welcome

🍎 Now Open: March - December

DIAL-A-BROCHURE ON
01983 531331

or write to the Proprietor
Malcolm A. Peplow
The Orchards, Newbridge,
Yarmouth, Isle of Wight, PO41 0TS

Ninham Country Holidays (SZ573825)
off Whitecross Ln PO37 7PL ☎ 01983 864243
Signposted
► ► ► Family Park ⚟ ⚟ ⚐
Open 15 May-15 Sep Booking advisable
Level, landscaped site in country park setting, near to sea and beach. Signed from A3056 via White Cross Lane. An 8-acre site with 88 touring pitches.

🔲🔲🔲🔲🔲🔲🔲🔲🔲🔲🔲🔲🔲🔲🔲🔲
🔲🔲
→ ∪ ⲓ ◎ ⊛ ⏃ ⚐ ⚐ ⌡

WHITECLIFF BAY

Whitecliff Bay Holiday Park (SZ637862)
Hillway PO35 5PL ☎ 01983 872671 Signposted

► ► ► ► De-Luxe Park ★ ⚟ £6.20-£9.40 ⚟ £6.20-£9.40
⚐ £6.20-£9.40
Open May-Oct (rs Mar-Apr limited entertainments)
Booking advisable Jul-Aug ⚘
A large seaside complex on two sites, with tourers and tents on one and tourers and statics on the other. Toilets of a very high standard. Many entertainments and easy access to beach. A 49-acre site with 400 touring pitches and 227 statics.
Leisure centre with fun pool, spa bath & sauna.

> Summer weather can mean rain. It is a good idea to
> prepare for ground to be wet underfoot. Take something
> to amuse the children if they can't go outside

See advertisement under BEMBRIDGE

🔲🔲🔲🔲🔲🔲🔲🔲🔲🔲🔲🔲🔲🔲🔲🔲🔲🔲
🔲🔲🔲🔲
→ ∪ ⲓ ⏃ ⌡
Credit Cards 💳 💳 🍥

🔲🔲🔲🔲🔲🔲🔲🔲🔲🔲

WROXALL

Appuldurcombe Gardens Caravan & Camping Park (SZ546804)
Appuldurcombe Rd PO38 3EP ☎ 01983 852597
Signposted
Nearby town: Ventnor
► ► ► Family Park ★ ⚟ £5.30-£10.30 ⚟ £5.30-£10.30
⚐ £5.30-£10.30
Open Spring bank hol-Aug bank hol (rs Mar-Spring bank hol & Aug bank hol-Oct pool & bar closed, shop restricted hrs) Booking advisable Jul-Aug Last arrival 23.00hrs Last departure noon
An attractive secluded site with a small stream running through it. Situated a few miles from Ventnor. A 12-acre site with 110 touring pitches and 42 statics.
Crazy golf & putting.

🔲🔲🔲🔲🔲🔲🔲🔲🔲🔲🔲🔲🔲🔲🔲🔲🔲🔲
→ ∪ ⲓ ◎ ⊛ ⏃ ⚐ ⌡
Credit Cards 💳 💳 🔳 🍥

YARMOUTH

See **Newbridge**

WILTSHIRE

CALNE

Blackland Lakes Holiday & Leisure Centre (ST973687)
Stockley Ln SN11 0NQ ☎ 01249 813672 Signposted

▶ ▶ ▶ De-Luxe Park 🏕 🚐 Å
Open all year (rs Nov-mid Mar bookings only) Booking advisable all year Last arrival 23.00hrs Last departure noon
A level, well-kept site in a rural area surrounded by Colstowe, and N and W Downs. Good outdoor facilities on site. From Calne take A4(T) E for 1.5m, turn right at camp sign, and site on left in 1m. A 17-acre site with 180 touring pitches.
Nature trail, wildfowl sanctuary, fishing facilities

CHIPPENHAM

Plough Lane Caravan Site (ST914761)
Kington Langley SN15 5PS ☎ 01249 750795 Signposted

▶ ▶ ▶ De-Luxe Park 🚐 🚐 Å
Open Mar-Oct Booking advisable Last arrival 22.00hrs
Attractive secluded park in immaculate surroundings, with an 'adults only' policy. On A350 2m S of M5, junc 17. A 2-acre site with 35 touring pitches.

DEVIZES

Bell Caravan Park (SU054580)
Andover Rd, Lydeway SN10 3PS ☎ 01380 840230
▶ ▶ ▶ Family Park 🚐 £7.50-£9 🚐 £7.50-£9 Å £7.50-£9
Open Etr or Apr-Sep Booking advisable bank hols & Jul-Aug Last arrival 22.00hrs
An attractive base for touring the area, with all level pitches. 3m S of Devizes on A342. A 3-acre site with 30 touring pitches.

Credit Cards

Lakeside (ST092626)
Rowde SN10 2LX ☎ 01380 722767 Signposted
▶ ▶ ▶ Family Park 🚐 🚐 Å
Open Apr-Oct Booking advisable bank hols & Jun-Aug Last arrival 22.00hrs Last departure noon

Pleasant level site on lakeside with attractive trees and shrubs set in countryside. From Devizes take A342 Calne rd N, take right fork at A342/A361, and site on right in 1m. A 4-acre site with 55 touring pitches.
Fishing.

LACOCK

Piccadilly Caravan Site (ST913683)
Folly Ln West SN15 2LP ☎ 01249 730260
Signposted
Nearby town: Chippenham
▶ ▶ ▶ Family Park 🚐 £7.50-£9 🚐 £7.50-£9
Å £7.50-£9
Open Apr-Oct Booking advisable school & bank hols Last arrival 22.00hrs Last departure noon
A good family site, well-established and overlooking Lacock village. 4m S of Chippenham. From Melksham on A350 towards Lacock for 3m, turn left at sign marked Gastard, and site on left in 200yds. A 2.5-acre site with 41 touring pitches.

MARSTON MEYSEY

Second Chance Caravan Park (SU140960)
SN6 6SZ ☎ 01285 810675 Signposted
Nearby town: Cricklade
▶ ▶ ▶ Family Park ★ 🚐 £7 🚐 £7 Å £7
Open Mar-Nov Booking advisable peak periods Last arrival 22.30hrs Last departure 13.30hrs ❀
A quiet and beautiful site with good toilet facilities, attractively situated near the source of the Thames. Situated 3m E of Cricklade off A419. A 1.75-acre site with 22 touring pitches and 4 statics.
Fishing on site, canoeing.

SALISBURY

Alderbury Caravan & Camping Park (SU197259)
Southampton Rd, Whaddon SP5 3HB
☎ 01722 710125
▶ ▶ ▶ Family Park ★ 🚐 £7.50 🚐 £7.50 Å £7.50
Open all year Booking advisable anytime Last arrival 22.00hrs Last departure 13.00hrs
A pleasant and friendly new site, set in the village of Whaddon just off A36, 3m from Salisbury. A 1.5-acre site with 39 touring pitches and 1 static.
Washing-up room.

Coombe Touring Park (SU099282)
Race Plain, Netherhampton SP2 8PN
☎ 01722 328451 (2m SW off A3094)
Signposted
▶ ▶ ▶ Family Park ★ 🚐 £6-£8 🚐 £6-£8 Å £6-£8
Open all year (rs Sep-Etr gas only, shop) Booking advisable bank hols (by letter only) Last arrival 21.00hrs Last departure noon

contd. on p208

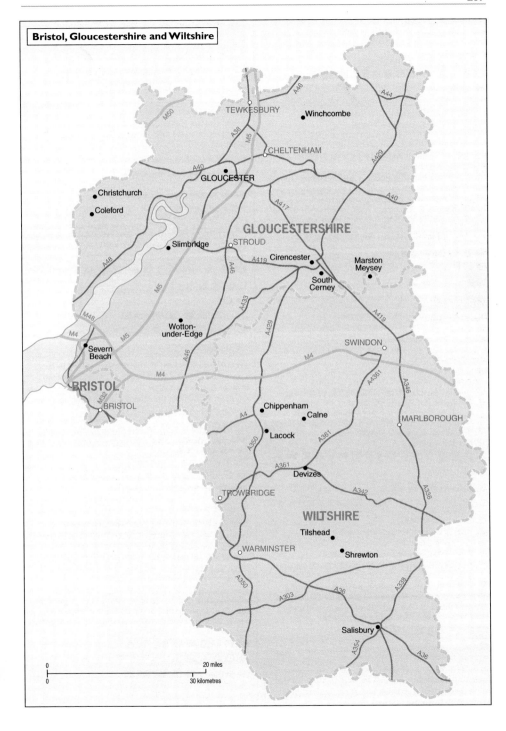

Bristol, Gloucestershire and Wiltshire

A very neat and attractive site adjacent to racecourse with views over the downs and outstanding flower beds. From Wilton take A3094 S, then first right on bend signed racecourse. Site at top of hill and signed. A 3-acre site with 50 touring pitches.

🔌 📞 ☉ 🗑 ᛩ ※ ⁄⊼ ᛜ ⁄∂ 🗓 Ⓣ ⌕ 🏊 ᕼ
→ ∪ ▶

Camping & Caravanning Club Site (SU140320)
Hudsons Field, Castle Rd SP1 3RR
☎ 01722 320713 (in season) & 01203 694995
Signposted
▶▶ **Town & Country Pennant Park** ★ 🚐 £11-£14
🚐 £11-£14 ▲ £11-£14
Open end Mar-beg Nov Booking advisable bank hols & peak periods Last arrival 21.00hrs Last departure noon
A well-kept site with friendly and helpful wardens. Take A345 Salisbury to Amesbury road, and Hudson's Field is close to Old Sarum Fort, 1m on L. Please see the advertisement on page 27 for details of Club Members' benefits. A 4.5-acre site with 150 touring pitches.

🔌 📞 ☉ 🗑 ᛩ ※ ᛜ ⁄∂
→ ∪ ▶

Credit Cards 💳 💳

SHREWTON

Stonehenge Touring Park (SU061456)
Orcheston SP3 4SH ☎ 01980 620304 Signposted
Nearby town: Amesbury
▶▶▶ **Family Park** ★ 🚐 £5.50-£9.50 🚐 £5.50-£9.50
▲ £5.50-£9.50
Open all year Booking advisable bank hols & Jul-Aug
Last arrival 21.00hrs Last departure 11.00hrs
A quiet site adjacent to the small village of Orcheston near the centre of Salisbury and 4m from Stonehenge. Site maturing and popular. From Shrewton take A360 N, then first right fork to Orcheston and follow site signs. A 2-acre site with 30 touring pitches and 6 statics.

🔌 📞 ☉ 🗑 ᛩ ※ ♀ ⁄⊼ ᛜ ⁄∂ 🗓 ✕ ⌕ ⛲ 🏛 ᕼ 🏊
→ ∪

Credit Cards 💳 💳 💳

TILSHEAD

Brades Acre (SU035477) ✗
SP3 4RX ☎ 01980 620402 Signposted
Nearby town: Salisbury
▶▶ **Town & Country Pennant Park** 🚐 🚐 ▲
Open all year Booking advisable public hols Last arrival 21.00hrs Last departure 11.00hrs
A small, pleasantly situated country site set among trees and shrubs in the heart of Salisbury Plain. From Tilshead turn S on A360 to end of village, and site on right. A 2-acre site with 25 touring pitches.

🔌 📞 ☉ ※ ᛜ ⁄∂ 🗓 🏛 ᕼ 🏊
→ ∪

WORCESTERSHIRE

For the map of this county
see HEREFORDSHIRE

BROADWAY

Leedon's Park (SP080384)
Childswickham Rd WR12 7HB ☎ 01386 852423
Signposted

〇〇〇〇〇〇〇〇〇

▶▶▶ **De-Luxe Park** 🚐 🚐 ▲
Open all year Booking advisable peak periods Last arrival 20.00hrs Last departure 11.00hrs
A large site on the edge of the Vale of Evesham, 1m from the historical village of Broadway; an ideal base from which to tour the Cotswolds. From A44 Evesham-Oxford road, take B4632 6m SE of Evesham. A 16-acre site with 450 touring pitches and 86 statics.
See advertisement under GLOUCESTER

🔌 🚗 📞 ☉ 🗑 ᛩ ⁀ ♀ ● ⊡ ※ ⁄⊼ ᛜ ⁄∂ 🗓 Ⓣ ✕
⌕ ⛲ ᕼ 🏊 ᕼ
→ ∪ ▶

Credit Cards 💳 💳 💳 💳 💳

〇〇〇〇〇〇〇〇〇

EVESHAM

Weir Meadow Holiday & Touring Park (SP047443)
Lower Leys WR11 5AB ☎ 01386 442417 Signposted
▶▶▶ **Family Park** 🚐 🚐
Open Etr or Apr-Oct Booking advisable bank hols Last arrival dusk Last departure noon
Although in the centre of town the site has a peaceful riverside setting. Turn off Port Street by Workmen's Bridge in Evesham, A44. A 10-acre site with 100 touring pitches and 120 statics.
Slipway, boating, fishing and sailing.

🔌 📞 ☉ 🗑 ᛩ ※ ⁄⊼ ᛜ ⁄∂ 🗓 Ⓣ ⌕ 🏛 🗓 🏊 ᕼ
→ ∪ ▶ ⅄ 🍴 ⚓

HANLEY SWAN

Camping & Caravanning Club Site (SO812440)
WR8 0EE ☎ 01684 310280 & 01203 694995 Signposted
Nearby town: Great Malvern
▶▶▶ **Family Park** ★ 🚐 £10-£13 🚐 £10-£13 ▲ £10-£13
Open end Mar-end Nov Booking advisable Jan-Mar Last arrival 21.00hrs Last departure noon
Well-established wooded park, ideally located for exploring the Malvern Hills and Worcester. From A38 take B4424 travelling S or B4211 N towards Hanley Swan, and site signed. A 12-acre site with 200 touring pitches.

🔌 📞 ☉ 🗑 ● ⁄⊼ ᛜ ⌕ ᕼ ᕼ ᕼ
→ ∪ △ ⅄ ⚓ 🏊

Credit Cards 💳 💳 💳 💳 💳

HONEYBOURNE

Ranch Caravan Park (SP113444)
WR11 5QG ☎ 01386 830744 (go through village
crossroads towards Bideford, entrance 400m on left
side) Signposted
Nearby town: Evesham

▶ ▶ ▶ ▶ De-Luxe Park ★ ⚲ £6.50-£13.75
⚲ £6.50-£13.75
Open Mar-Nov (rs Mar-May & Sep-Nov swimming pool
closed, shorter club hours) Booking advisable school
hols Last arrival 20.00hrs Last departure noon
*A clean, well-run site landscaped with trees and bushes,
set in farmland in the Vale of Evesham 2m from B4035.
A 12-acre site with 100 touring pitches and 180 statics.*

♬ ⌂ ☉ ⊙ 🖥 ☜ ⌇ ◖ ◻ ☀ ♀ ⚠ 🛈 ⌀ ⊞ Ⓣ ✕ ☾
⇩ ⚲ 🐾 ☙
➜ ∪ ♨

Credit Cards ⚫ ▭ ▧ ⑤

MALVERN

Riverside Caravan Park (SO833463)
Little Clevelode WR13 6PE ☎ 01684 310475 (on B4424)
Signposted
▶ ▶ ▶ Family Park ★ ⚲ £6 ⚲ £6 ᴀ £6
Open Mar-Dec (rs Nov, Dec & Mar water supply
depends on weather) Booking advisable bank hols &
end Jun-Aug Last arrival 21.00hrs Last departure noon
An open field site with some sloping pitches and a large

CARAVAN PARK
HOLIDAY CENTRE ✚

● Established family-run park
● Located in the vale of Evesham
● Tourers welcome
● Electric hook-ups available
● multi-service hook-ups
● Licensed club serving meals
● Heated outdoor swimming pool
● Shop
● Laundry

HONEYBOURNE
EVESHAM
WORCS
WR11 5QG

AA ➌

Tel: Evesham (01386) 830744

*play area. From A449 signed on to B4424. A 10-acre site
with 70 touring pitches and 130 statics.*
Slipway for boats, fishing on river.

♬ ⌂ ☉ ⊙ 🖥 ☜ ◖ ◻ ☀ ♀ ⚠ 🛈 ⌀ Ⓣ ☾ 🐾 ☙
➜ ∪ ♨ ⤢ ⚲

ROMSLEY

Camping & Caravanning Club Site (SO955795)
Fieldhouse Ln B62 0NH
☎ 01562 710015 (in season) & 01203 694995
Nearby town: Halesowen

▶ ▶ ▶ ▶ De-Luxe Park ★ ⚲ £11-£14 ⚲ £11-£14
ᴀ £11-£14
Open end Mar-early Nov Booking advisable bank hols &
peak periods Last arrival 21.00hrs Last departure noon
*A very pretty, well tended park surrounded by wooded
hills. Turn off B4551 at Sun Inn, then take 5th turn left,
and the park is 300 yds on. Please see the
advertisement on page 27 for details of Club Members'
benefits. A 6.5-acre site with 130 touring pitches.*

♬ ⌂ ☉ ⊙ 🖥 ☜ ◖ ☀ ⚠ 🛈 ⌀ ☾ ➜ 🐾 ☙ ⛰

Credit Cards ⚫ ▭ ▧ ⑤

WOLVERLEY

Camping & Caravanning Club Site (SO833792)
Brown Westhead Park DY10 3PX
☎ 01562 850909 & 01203 694995 Signposted
Nearby town: Kidderminster
▶ ▶ ▶ Family Park ★ ⚲ £10-£13 ⚲ £10-£13 ᴀ £10-£13
Open end Mar-early Nov Booking advisable bank hols &
Jul-Aug Last arrival 21.00hrs Last departure noon
*Very pleasant grassy site on edge of the village, with
good access to nearby motorways. At junction of A449
and B4189 take road signed Wolverley, and site .25m on
right. Please see the advertisement on page 27 for
details of Club Members' benefits. A 12-acre site with
120 touring pitches.*
Table tennis, darts.

♬ ⌂ ☉ ⊙ 🖥 ☜ ◖ ◻ ⚠ 🛈 ⌀ ⊞ ☾ 🐾 ☙ ⛰
➜ ∪ ♨ ⚲

Credit Cards ⚫ ▭ ▤ ▧ ⑤

YORKSHIRE, EAST RIDING OF

For the map of this county
see LINCOLNSHIRE

BRANDESBURTON

Dacre Lakeside Park (TA118468)
YO25 8RT ☎ 01964 543704 & 542372 Signposted
Nearby town: Hornsea
▶ ▶ ▶ Family Park ★ ⚲ £7-£7.50 ⚲ £7-£7.50 ᴀ £7-£7.50
Open Mar-Oct Booking advisable bank hols Last arrival
21.00hrs Last departure noon
contd.

EAST YORKSHIRE'S QUALITY SITE

Quiet, sheltered within kitchen garden
walls. Centrally heated toilet block.
Toilet and bathroom for disabled persons.
Dogs welcome. Own Coarse Fishery.
Thorpe Hall Caravan and Camping Site,
Rudston, Driffield, East Yorkshire YO25 4JE
Tel: 01262 420393 Fax: 01262 420588
Manager Mrs Jayne Chatterton
Residence: 01262 420574

*A pleasant, level grassy site beside a lake with good
adjacent sports facilities. Off the A165 bypass, midway
between Beverley and Hornsea. A 4-acre site with 120
touring pitches.*
Windsurfing, fishing, tennis & bowling green.

🔌📻☉🍳🦯✖️🍴🎣⌖⚡🅣🔌➤🏠⚽♿

➜ ∪ ▶ 🔺 ✚ 🗡

BRIDLINGTON

FANGFOSS

Fangfoss Old Station Caravan Park (SE747527)
Old Station House YO4 5QB ☎ 01759 380491
Signposted
Nearby town: York
▶ ▶ ▶ Family Park ★ 🚐 £7.50-£8 🚐 £7.50-£8
▲ £4-£8
Open Mar-Oct Booking advisable bank hols Last arrival
22.30hrs Last departure noon
*A well-maintained site in a pleasant rural area. The track
and sidings of the old railway station are grassed over
and provide excellent hardstanding with a level
landscaped field adjacent. Take A166 to Stamford
Bridge where site clearly signed. A 4.5-acre site with 45
touring pitches.*

🔌📻☉🍳🦯✖️⚡🅣🔌🚿
🎪🏠⚽♿
➜ ∪ 🗡

Credit Cards 💳

HULL

See **Sproatley**

RUDSTON

Thorpe Hall Caravan & Camping Site (TA108677)
Thorpe Hall YO25 0JE ☎ 01262 420393 & 420574 (on
B1253) Signposted
Nearby town: Bridlington
▶ ▶ ▶ Family Park 🚐 🚐 ▲
Open Mar-Oct Booking advisable bank hols & peak
periods Last arrival 22.00hrs Last departure noon
*A very attractive and well-ordered site in the walled
garden of a large estate on edge of village. 5m from
Bridlington on B1253. A 4.5-acre site with 90 touring
pitches.*
Covered outside washing up sinks with hot water.

🔌📻☉🍳⚡🦯✖️🍴❄️⚡🅣🔌📻
⌖⚡♿
➜ ∪ 🗡

SKIPSEA

   Far Grange Park (TA181530)
Hornsea Rd YO25 8SY
☎ 01262 468248 & 468293
Signposted
Nearby town: Hornsea

◉◉◉◉◉◉◉◉◉◉◉◉◉◉◉◉◉◉◉◉◉◉◉

★ 🚐 £10-£14 🚐 £10-£14 ▲ £10-£14
Open Mar-Oct Booking advisable bank & school hols
Last arrival 21.00hrs Last departure 11.00hrs

Far Grange Caravan Park

★ LOOKING FOR MORE THAN A HOLIDAY – TAKE A LOOK AT FAR GRANGE PARK ★

Full facilities for tourers, tents and motor homes, including all weather touring pitches with the "Superpitch" tower attachment, now available for weekend use OUT OF SEASON.

Luxury fully centrally heated and double glazed holiday homes for hire March to November.

Indoor Swimming Pool & Fully Equipped Gymnasium

Come and see for yourself that the facilities and standards set at Far Grange Park are exceptionally high.

A wide range of New and Pre-owned Holiday Homes for sale on both the Main park and our exclusive extended season WESTVIEW

Please telephone or write for a brochure to:
Far Grange Caravan Park Limited,
Skipsea, Driffield, East Yorkshire YO25 8SY
Tel: 01262 468293/468248

A well-developed holiday site with pleasing public buildings and well-laid out grounds of shrubs, hedges and trees. Adjacent to a private sandy beach on a fairly quiet part of the coast. On B1242, 2m S of village on seaward side next to golf course. A 30-acre site with 170 touring pitches and 500 statics.
Fishing, snooker, gym, sauna, solarium.

Credit Cards 💳 💳 💳

Low Skirlington Caravan Park (TA188528)
YO25 8SY ☎ 01262 468213 & 468466 (on B1242) Signposted
Nearby town: Bridlington
▶ ▶ ▶ Family Park ★ ⊞ £9-£12 ⊞ £9-£12 ⅄ £9-£12
Open Mar-Oct Booking advisable Jul-Aug
Part-level, part-sloping, grass site with young trees and bushes, set in meadowland adjacent to sea and beach 3m N of Hornsea on B1242. A 24-acre site with 285 touring pitches and 450 statics.
Sauna, sunbed, jacuzzi & bowls.
See advertisement under BRIDLINGTON

Credit Cards 💳 💳 💳

Burton Constable Caravan Park (TA186357)
Old Lodges HU11 4LN ☎ 01964 562508 Signposted
Nearby town: Kingston-upon-Hull
▶ ▶ ▶ Family Park ⊞ ⊞ ⅄
A beautiful site close to lakes in the grounds of Burton Constable Hall. Off A165 on B1328 to Sproatley.
Open Mar-Oct Booking advisable bank hols Last arrival 23.00hrs Last departure dusk
A 20-acre site with 109 touring pitches and 66 statics.

Weir Caravan Park (SE713557)
YO41 1AN ☎ 01759 371377 (A166 Bridlington rd) Signposted
▶ ▶ ▶ Family Park ★ ⊞ £8-£10.50 ⊞ £8-£10.50
⅄ £8-£10.50
Open Mar-Oct Booking advisable bank hols & Jul-Aug Last arrival 21.30hrs Last departure noon
Slightly sloping grass site near urban area and River Derwent. 50yds off A166 on entering village from York. An 8-acre site with 50 touring pitches and 125 statics.
Fishing & boating on site. Sauna & Solarium.

YORKSHIRE, NORTH

See also Yorkshire, South, Yorkshire, West, Yorkshire, East Riding

Chestnut Farm Caravan Park (SE589456)
YO2 1UQ ☎ 01904 704676 Signposted
Nearby town: York
▶ ▶ ▶ Family Park ★ ⊞ £11 ⊞ £11 ⅄ £8
Open Apr-Oct Booking advisable public hols & Jul-Aug Last arrival 23.00hrs Last departure noon
Level, grassy site with assorted trees and shrubs, adjacent to river. Leave A64 at Copmanthorpe, turning S signed Acaster Malbis. Site on unclass rd in 2m. A 5-acre site with 25 touring pitches and 56 statics.

Moor End Farm (SE589457)
YO2 1UQ ☎ 01904 706727 Signposted
Nearby town: York
▶▶ Town & Country Pennant Park ★ ⊞ £7.50 ⊞ £7
⅄ £6.50-£7.50
Open Etr or Apr-Oct Booking advisable bank hols & end Jul-early Aug Last arrival 22.00hrs Last departure 14.00hrs
Level, grassy site with hedges, well-drained and maintained. Set in meadowland adjacent to road. Leave A64 at Copmanthorpe, turning S signed Acaster Malbis. Site on unclass rd in 2m. A 1-acre site with 10 touring pitches and 5 statics.

contd.

North, South and West Yorkshire

Use of fridge/freezer.

🔌 📻 ☉ ⛄ ✳ 🔲 🧺
➔ 🍴 ⚒ 🐕 🎣 📼

ALLERSTON

Vale of Pickering Caravan Park (SE879808)
Carr House Farm YO18 7PQ ☎ 01723 859280
Signposted

QQQQQQQQQ

▶ ▶ ▶ ▶ De-Luxe Park 🚐 🚐 ⚑
Open Apr-Oct (rs Mar) Booking advisable anytime Last
departure noon
*A well-maintained modern site with good facilities set
in rolling countryside, and convenient for North
Yorkshire Moors and wolds. On the B1415, 1.75m off
the main Pickering to Scarborough road. An 8-acre site
with 120 touring pitches and 1 static.*

🔌 🚰 📻 ☉ ⛄ ✳ ⛰ 🚽 🗑 🧺 🔲 Ⓣ 🔥 🐕 🧺 ♿
➔ ∪ 🍴 ◎ 🎣

QQQQQQQQQ

ALLERTON PARK

Allerton Park Caravan Site (SE417576)
Allerton Mauleverer HG5 0SE
☎ 01423 330569 (0.25m E of A1 off the A59)
Signposted
Nearby town: Knaresborough

QQQQQQQQQ

▶ ▶ ▶ ▶ De-Luxe Park ★ 🚐 £8-£10.50 🚐 £8-£10.50
⚑ £8-£10.50
Open Feb-3 Jan Booking advisable bank hols Last
arrival 21.00hrs Last departure 17.00hrs
*An immaculately maintained site set in parkland
surrounded by mature trees, and offering peace and
quiet. Off A59, 400yards E of junc with A1(M). A 12-acre
site with 45 touring pitches and 80 statics.*

🔌 🚰 📻 ☉ ⛄ ✳ ⛰ 🚽 🗑 🔲 Ⓣ 🔥 🐕 🧺
➔ ∪ 🍴 🎣

QQQQQQQQQ

ARNCLIFFE

Hawkswick Cote Caravan Park (SD947703)
BD23 5PX ☎ 01756 770226 Signposted
Nearby town: Skipton

▶▶▶▶ De-Luxe Park ★ ⊞ £8-£12 ⊞ £8-£12 ▲ £8
Open Mar-14 Nov Booking advisable bank hols & Jul-Aug Last arrival 22.00hrs Last departure noon
A spacious site in the Dales, with mature landscaping and views of the surrounding fells. From B6160 1m N of Kilnsey, take unclassified road signed Arncliffe, and site on left in 1.5m. A 3-acre site with 50 touring pitches and 90 statics.

AYSGARTH

Westholme Caravan & Camping Park (SE016882)
DL8 3SP ☎ 01969 663268
Signposted
Nearby town: Leyburn
▶▶▶ Family Park ★ ⊞ £6.75-£9.25 ⊞ £6.75-£9.25 ▲ £6.75-£9.25
Open Mar-Oct Booking advisable bank hols & Jul-Aug Last arrival 22.00hrs Last departure noon
A beckside site with level grassy pitches in various paddocks set into the hillside. 1m E of Aysgarth on A684. A 4-acre site with 70 touring pitches and 44 statics.
Library, quiet room & fishing free on site.

BISHOP MONKTON

Church Farm Caravan Park (SE286658)
Knaresborough Rd HG3 3QQ
☎ 01765 677405
Nearby town: Ripon
▶▶ Town & Country Pennant Park ⊞ ⊞ ▲
Open Apr-Oct Booking advisable peak periods
Mainly level tree-lined field, adjacent to farm in picturesque village. From A61, 3.5m S of Ripon, take unclass rd signed Bishop Monkton. At crossrds in 1m turn right signed Knaresborough, and site on right in 500 metres. A 5-acre site with 30 touring pitches.

BOROUGHBRIDGE

Camping & Caravanning Club Site (SE384662)
Bar Ln, Roecliffe YO5 9LS
☎ 01423 322683 (in season) & 01203 694995
Signposted
▶▶▶ Family Park ★ ⊞ £10-£13 ⊞ £10-£13 ▲ £10-£13
Open all year Booking advisable bank hols & Jul & Aug Last arrival 21.00hrs Last departure noon
A quiet, riverside site with boating and riding available. Close to the dales and the market town of Boroughbridge. Leave A1(M) at S turn-off for

boroughbridge. Turn left to go N on A168 to unclass rd signed Roecliffe. Please see the advertisement on page 27 for details of Club Members' benefits. A 6-acre site with 80 touring pitches.
Fishing.

Credit Cards ⊞ ⊞ ⊞ ⊞ ⑤

CAWOOD

Cawood Holiday Park (SE563385)
Ryther Rd YO8 3TT ☎ 01757 268450 (0.5m NW on B1233) Signposted
Nearby town: York

▶▶▶▶ De-Luxe Park ★ ⊞ £8.50-£11 ⊞ £8.50-£11 ▲ £8.50-£11
Open Mar-Jan Booking advisable bank hols & Jul-Aug Last arrival 23.00hrs Last departure noon
A continually improving site with a very high level of maintenance and excellent toilet facilities. 0.5 miles NW of Cawood on B1223. An 8-acre site with 60 touring pitches and 10 statics.
Coarse fishing.

Credit Cards ⊞ ⊞ ⊞ ⊞ ⑤

CAYTON

Killerby Old Hall (TA063829)
Killerby YO11 3TW ☎ 01723 583799
▶▶▶ Family Park ★ ⊞ £7-£9 ⊞ £7-£9
Open Etr-Oct Booking advisable
A small secluded park well sheltered by mature trees and shrubs, located on the lawn at the rear of old hall. Direct access of B1261 at Killerby, near Cayton. A 1-acre site with 10 touring pitches.

CONEYSTHORPE (NEAR MALTON)

Castle Howard Caravan & Camping Site (SE705710)
YO60 7DD ☎ 01653 648366 & 648316 Signposted
Nearby town: Malton
▶▶▶ Family Park ★ ⊞ £7.20 ⊞ £7.20 ▲ £7.20
Open Mar-Oct Booking advisable public hols Last arrival 19.00hrs Last departure 14.00hrs
Tranquil grassy site adjacent to lake on Castle Howard Estate. A superb touring centre. Well signed from A64. A 13-acre site with 70 touring pitches and 122 statics.

AA pennant classification covers the touring section of a park, but not the static caravans available for rent, so we cannot deal with any complaints about static vans.

CONSTABLE BURTON

Constable Burton Hall Caravan Park (SE158907)
DL8 5LJ ☎ 01677 450428 Signposted
Nearby town: Leyburn

▶ ▶ ▶ ▶ De-Luxe Park ★ ⊞ £7.50-£8.50 ⊞ £7.50-£8.50
Open Apr-Oct Booking advisable public hols Last arrival
22.00hrs Last departure noon
*A part-level, part-sloping site within parkland of
Constable Burton Hall in farmland at entrance to
Wensleydale. Located off A684 but screened behind old
deer park wall. A 10-acre site with 120 touring pitches.*

🖸🛉☉🖬❄🛉🔗🖭🇹❌🕻🐕
➔ ∪ ⌐ ♨ ⏚ 🐾

CROCKEY HILL

Swallow Hall Caravan Park (SE657463)
YO1 4SG ☎ 01904 448219 (E off A19)
Nearby town: York
▶▶ Town & Country Pennant Park ★ ⊞ £7.50-£10.50
⊞ £7.50-£10.50 ▲ £7
Open Etr/Mar-Oct Booking advisable Etr & Spring bank
hol Last arrival 22.00hrs Last departure 16.00hrs
*A quiet site on meadowland at the edge of a forest
within easy reach of the centre of York. From A19 at
Crockey Hill turn E onto unclass rd, and site 2m on left.
A 5-acre site with 30 touring pitches.*
Golf driving range & 18 hole course.

🖸🛉☉⌐❄🖤🛉🖭🇹🕻🐾
➔⌐🗡🐾

CROPTON

Spiers House Campsite (SE756918)
YO18 8ES ☎ 01751 417591 (1m N on Rosedale rd)
Signposted
Nearby town: Pickering
▶ ▶ ▶ Family Park ⊞ ⊞ ▲
Open Etr-2 Oct Booking advisable bank & school hols
Last arrival 21.00hrs Last departure 16.00hrs
*Beautiful forest site in a clearing with good facilities and
peaceful surroundings. Walks are marked by Forestry
Commission. Approach by signs from A170, and 1m N
of Cropton on Rosedale Rd turn right into forest at
signpost A 15-acre site with 150 touring pitches.*

🖸🛉☉🖬🛉❄🖤🛉🔗🇹🕻🐕🐾🛒⛲
➔∪🗡

FILEY

  Flower of May Holiday Park (TA085835)
Lebberston Cliff YO11 3NU
☎ 01723 584311
(Lebberston 2.5m NW off A165)
Signposted
Nearby town: Scarborough

★ ⊞ £7-£11 ⊞ £7-£11 ▲ £7-£11
Open Etr-Oct (rs early & late season) Booking advisable
Spring bank hol wk & Jul-Aug Last arrival 22.00hrs Last
departure noon
A delightful family site with level grassy pitches,

*excellent facilities and direct access to the beach.
Signed off A165 on Scarborough side of Filey. Winner
of the 1995 Campsite of the Year Award for the North of
England. A 13-acre site with 270 touring pitches and 179
statics.*
Squash, gymnasium, bowling & 9-hole golf.
See advertisement under SCARBOROUGH

🖸🛉☉🖬🇷 ⌐❄🛉🖤🛉🔗🖭🇹❌🕻🛒
⛲🎋🐾🛒🐾🕭
➔∪⌐☉🛆⏚♨🗡

Crows Nest Caravan Park (TA086834)
Gristhorpe YO14 9PS ☎ 01723 582206
Nearby town: Scarborough

▶ ▶ ▶ ▶ De-Luxe Park ★ ⊞ £7-£12 ⊞ £8-£10.50
▲ £8-£10.50
Open Mar-Oct Booking advisable Last departure noon
*A beautifully situated park on the coast between
Scarborough and Filey, family owned and run to a high
standard. On the seaward side of A165, signed off
rndbt. A 2-acre site with 49 touring pitches and 217
statics.*

🖸🛉☉🖬🇷 ⌐❄🛉🖤🛉🔗🇹🕻🛒🐾🛒
➔∪⌐☉🛆🗡

Centenary Way Camping & Caravan Park (TA115798)
Muston Grange YO14 0HU ☎ 01723 516415
▶ ▶ ▶ Family Park ★ ⊞ £5.50-£7 ⊞ £5.50-£7
▲ £3.50-£7
Open Mar-Oct Booking advisable bank hols & Jul-Aug
Last arrival 21.00hrs Last departure noon
*A family-owned, mainly static park, with access to
footpath to nearby beach. On A1039 near its junc with
A165 on Bridlington side of Filey. A 3-acre site with 100
touring pitches.*

🖸🛉☉❄🛉🔗🖭🐾
➔∪⌐☉♨🗡🖬

Filey Brigg Touring Caravan & Country Park (TA115812)
North Cliff YO14 9ET ☎ 01723 513852 Signposted
Nearby town: Scarborough
▶ ▶ ▶ Family Park ★ ⊞ £4.90-£9.60 ⊞ £4.90-£9.60
▲ £4.90-£9.60
Open Etr/Apr-Oct Booking advisable bank hols & Jul-
Aug Last arrival 21.00hrs Last departure noon
*Level grassy park with some mature trees, near sea and
beach, and located within a country park. Signed via
unclassified road from A1039 on N of Filey. A 9-acre site
with 146 touring pitches.*

🖸🛉🖬❄🖤🛉🔗🖭❌🕻🛒🎋🐾🛒🐾
➔∪⌐☉♨🗡

Credit Cards 💳 ▭ ▭ ▭ 🅖

Muston Grange Caravan Park (TA113797)
Muston Rd YO14 0HU
☎ 01723 512167 & 01947 810415 winter
▶ ▶ ▶ Family Park ⊞ £5.50-£7.75 ⊞ £5.50-£7.75

WOOD NOOK
NEAR GRASSINGTON

Small secluded park in the heart of the
YORKSHIRE DALES
Tel/Fax: (01756) 752412
Caravan Holiday Homes for Hire
TOURING CARAVANS AND TENTS
TOILETS, SHOWERS, ELECTRIC HOOK-UPS,
SHOP, CHILDRENS PLAY AREA

AA ▶ ▶ ▶

Stamp for brochure to:

Mrs Thompson,
Wood Nook Caravan Park,
Skirethorns, Threshfield, Skipton,
N. Yorks BD23 5NU

Open Etr/Apr-20 Oct Booking advisable bank hols & Jul-Aug Last arrival 22.00hrs Last departure noon
A large touring park with views over the Yorkshire Wolds, with a footpath to Filey town and beach. Situated on A1039 near its junction with A165 on Bridlington side of Filey. A 10-acre site with 220 touring pitches.

🔲 ♋ ⊙ 🗑 ✳ /Ⅲ＼ 🛈 ✚ Ｔ 🚲
→ ∪ ▶ ◎ ♪

FYLINGDALES ('FLASK' INN)

Grouse Hill Caravan Park (NZ928002)
Flask Bungalow Farm YO22 4QH ☎ 01947 880543 Signposted
Nearby town: Whitby
▶ ▶ ▶ Family Park ★ ♋ £6.50-£7.50 ♋ £6.50-£7.50
⚠ £6.50-£7.50
Open Spring bank hol-Sep (rs Etr-May shop & reception restricted) Booking advisable public hols Last arrival 22.00hrs Last departure noon
Set in the midst of spectacular scenery in North Yorkshire Moors National Park adjacent to A171 Whitby-Scarborough road. A 14-acre site with 175 touring pitches.

🔲 ♋ ⊙ 🗑 ♦ ✳ /Ⅲ＼ 🛈 ⊘ ✚ Ｔ 🐕 🛖 🚲 ♿
→ ∪ ▶

GRASSINGTON

See **Threshfield**

GUISBOROUGH

Tockett's Mill Caravan Park (NZ626182)
Skelton Rd TS14 6QA ☎ 01287 610182 Signposted
▶ ▶ ▶ Family Park ★ ♋ £7.50-£9.50 ♋ £7.50-£9.50
Open Mar-Oct Booking advisable bank hols & high season Last arrival 21.00hrs Last departure noon
Situated in a private wooded valley alongside a stream, the site is centred around a preserved watermill. 1.5m E of Guisborough on A173. A 7-acre site with 30 touring pitches and 75 statics.

🔲 ♋ ⊙ 🗑 ✳ ⅄ /Ⅲ＼ 🛈 ✚ 🛖 ♿
→ ∪ 🚲

HARROGATE

Ripley Caravan Park (SE289610)
Knaresborough Rd HG3 3AU ☎ 01423 770050 Signposted

◯◯◯◯◯◯◯◯◯◯

▶ ▶ ▶ ▶ ▶ Premier Park ★ ♋ £6.75-£8 ♋ £6.75-£8
⚠ £6.75-£8
Open Etr-Oct Booking advisable bank hols Last arrival 21.00hrs Last departure noon
A superb, well-run rural site with easy access on B6165 .75m S of Ripley. An 18-acre site with 100 touring pitches and 10 statics.
Nursery playroom, sauna, sunbed, tennis net, football.

🔲 ♋ ⊙ 🗑 ✳ ♦ ✳ /Ⅲ＼ 🛈 ⊘ ⊡ Ｔ 🐕 🛖 🚲 ♿
→ ∪ ▶ ◎ ✚ 🍴 ♪

◯◯◯◯◯◯◯◯

where the country and enjoyment comes naturally …
This luxury touring caravan park in the beautiful North Yorkshire countryside, is within easy reach of Ripley Castle, village and only ten minutes north of Harrogate. First class facilities include amenities for the disabled; there is a shop, laundry, games room, telephone, childrens playground and nursery playroom, electric hook-up points and an indoor heated swimming pool. Dogs permitted.

For further information:
Peter & Valerie House, Ripley Caravan Park,
Ripley, Harrogate, HG3 3AU.
Tel: (01423) 770050

David Bellamy Bronze Award

TOURING CARAVANS and family camping

Award winning holiday park, situated in the North Yorkshire Dales 3 miles south of Harrogate, offering superb facilities for touring caravans and tents.
Set in beautiful parkland with lovely gardens and magnificent views; facilities include heated swimming pool, licensed bar serving meals, children's playground, games room and bicycle hire. Excellent amenities include centrally heated toilet blocks with free showers, electrical hook-up points, launderette, public telephones, park lighting and well stocked shop.
Supersites: Individual pitches, with hard standing for tourers, 16amp electricity, water, direct drainage, TV and satellite connections and picnic tables.

18 hole Golf Course available on a daily fee basis plus covered driving range

ROSE AWARD 1998

Please send for free brochure.

RUDDING holiday PARK

Follifoot, Harrogate, HG3 1JH. Tel:(01423) 870439.

Rudding Holiday Park (SE333531)
Follifoot HG3 1JH ☎ 01423 870439 (3m S) Signposted

QQQQQQQ

► ► ► ► ► **Premier Park** ★ ⊞ £9-£12 ⊞ £9-£12
Å £8-£12
Open 19 Mar-17 Nov (rs 1-21 Mar no hot water no shop) Booking advisable bank hols Last arrival 22.30hrs Last departure 18.00hrs
A spacious site set in mature parkland and walled gardens, situated 3m SE of Harrogate signed off A661. From A1 take A59 to A658, turn S signed Bradford, and in 4.5m turn right and signed. A 55-acre site with 141 touring pitches and 95 statics.
Golf course, driving range & cycle hire.

🔌 ➡ 🐕 ⊙ 🗓 🎱 ⚡ ❄ 🇶 Ⓜ 🛢 ⊞ Ⓣ ✖ 🔵
🚽 🔥 🐕 🐾 ♿
➜ ∪ 🏴 ✚ 🍽 🌙
Credit Cards 💳 🚗 📇 📶 🟢

QQQQQQQ

High Moor Farm Park (SE242560)
Skipton Rd HG3 2LT ☎ 01423 563637 & 564955 (4m W on A59) Signposted

QQQQQQQ

► ► ► ► **De-Luxe Park** ⊞ £9.50-£9.75 ⊞ £9.50-£9.75
Å £9.50-£9.75
Open Apr-Oct Booking advisable public hols Last arrival 23.30hrs Last departure 15.00hrs

An excellent site with first class facilities, set beside a small wood and surrounded by thorn hedges. On the A59, Harrogate-Skipton road. A 15-acre site with 320 touring pitches and 180 statics.
Course fishing, 9 hole golf course.

🔌 ➡ 🐕 ⊙ 🗓 🎱 ⚡ ❄ 🇶 Ⓜ 🛢 ⊞ Ⓣ ✖ 🔵
🚽 🔥 🐕 🐾
➜ ∪ 🏴 🍽 🌙
Credit Cards 💳 🚗 📇 📶 🟢

QQQQQQQ

Shaws Trailer Park (SE325557)
Knaresborough Rd HG2 7NE ☎ 01423 884432 & 883622 Signposted
► ► ► **Family Park** ★ ⊞ £8.50 ⊞ £7.50 Å £3
Open all year Booking advisable public hols Last arrival 21.00hrs Last departure noon
A level, grassy site with mature trees. On A59 Harrogate-Knaresborough road, 1m from town centre. An 11-acre site with 43 touring pitches and 146 statics.

🔌 ➡ 🐕 ⊙ 🗓 🛢 🔵 🐾
➜ ∪ 🏴 ✚ 🍽 🌙

HAWES

Bainbridge Ings Caravan & Camping Site (SD879895)
DL8 3NU ☎ 01969 667354 (approaching Hawes from Bainbridge on A684, turn left at signpost marked Gayle, 300yds on left) Signposted
► ► **Town & Country Pennant Park** ★ ⊞ £6.20-£6.50 ⊞ £5.70-£6 Å £5.70-£6
Open Apr-Oct Booking advisable school hols Last arrival 22.00hrs Last departure 14.00hrs
A family run site in open countryside, close to Hawes in the heart of Upper Wensleydale. Leave A684 on unclass rd signed Gayle. Site 440yds on left. A 5-acre site with 55 touring pitches and 14 statics.

🔌 🐕 ⊙ ❄ 🛢 🟢 ⊞
➜ 🌙

HELMSLEY

Golden Square Touring Caravan Park (SE604797)
Oswaldkirk YO62 5YQ ☎ 01439 788269 (2.5m S B1257 between Sproxton & Oswaldkirk) Signposted
Nearby town: Helmsley

► ► ► ► **De-Luxe Park** ★ ⊞ £6-£8 ⊞ £6-£8 Å £6-£8
Open Mar-Oct Booking advisable bank hols Last arrival 23.30hrs Last departure noon

FOXHOLME ▶▶▶
CARAVAN PARK

Campsite of the Year North Region Winner 1986
60 Touring Vans, Motor Caravans & Tents

Ryedale, North Yorkshire, (4 miles from Helmsley and the North York Moors National Park). A quiet site suitable for exploring North Yorkshire.
60 pitches set in individual clearings in the woodland. Luxury toilet blocks, AA graded Excellent for environment, wc's, hot water, showers, wash basins in cubicles and shaver points.
Reception, late arrival park, shop and mains hook-up points. Some pitches for tents.
Caravan Club approved. Camping Club listed.
For brochure, please send stamp to:

FOXHOLME CARAVAN PARK
(AA), Harome, Helmsley, York YO62 5JG
Tel. (01439) 770416

All-round excellent site with manicured grounds and first class toilets. Set in a quiet rural situation with lovely views over the N Yorks Moors. Off A170 on unclass road leading to B1257 near Ampleforth. A 12-acre site with 129 touring pitches.
Microwave oven.

🔵 🚐 👣 ☉ 🗄 🍴 ◀ ☀ 🏔 🛈 🖋 🔌 T 📞 ◀ 🎣 ⛹
⚑ 🔥
➔ ∪ ▶ ◎ 🗡

Foxholme Caravan Park (SE658828)
Harome YO62 5JG ☎ 01439 770416 & 771241 (follow A170from Helmsley in direction of Scarborough, turn right signposted Harome) Signposted
▶▶▶ Family Park 🚐 £7 🚐 £7 ▲ £7
Open Etr-Oct Booking advisable bank & school hols Last arrival 23.00hrs Last departure noon
A quiet site with mostly individual pitches divided by mature trees. Set in superb wooded countryside 1m S of Beadlam on unclass road. A 6-acre site with 60 touring pitches.

🔵 🍴 👣 ☉ 🗄 🍴 ☀ 🛈 🖋 🔌 T 📞 🐕 🎣 ⛹ 🚻
➔ ∪ ▶ 🗡

Wrens of Ryedale Caravan Site (SE656840)
Gale Ln, Nawton YO6 5SD ☎ 01439 771260 (3m E on A170) Signposted
Nearby town: Kirkbymoorside
▶▶▶ Family Park ★ 🚐 £5.75-£6.75 🚐 £5.75-£6.75
▲ £5.75-£6.75

Open Apr-16 Oct Booking advisable bank hols Last arrival 22.00hrs Last departure noon
A level, grassy site with mature trees and bushes, and open views, .5m S of Beadlam village off A170. A 2.5-acre site with 30 touring pitches.
Bike & caravan hire.

🔵 🍴 ☉ 🗄 🍴 ☀ 🏔 🛈 🖋 🔌 T 📞 🚻 ⛹
➔ ∪ ▶ 🗡

HIGH BENTHAM

Riverside Caravan Park (SD665688)
Wenning Av LA2 7HS ☎ 01524 261272 & 262163 Signposted
▶▶▶ Family Park ★ 🚐 fr £7.80 🚐 fr £7.80 ▲ fr £5
Open Mar-Oct Booking advisable bank hols Last arrival 20.00hrs Last departure 13.00hrs
This site is set on the banks of the River Wenning, in delightful countryside and screened by trees. Off B6480, and signed from town centre. A 12-acre site with 30 touring pitches and 170 statics.
Free fishing.

🔵 🍴 ☉ 🗄 🍴 🔍 ☀ 🏔 🛈 🖋 🔌 T 📞 🚻 🐕 🎣 ⛹
➔ ∪ ▶ 🗡

HUNMANBY

Orchard Farm Holiday Village (TA105779)
Stonegate YO14 0PU ☎ 01723 891582 Signposted
Nearby town: Scarborough

〇〇〇〇〇〇〇〇

▶▶▶▶ De-Luxe Park ★ 🚐 £5-£10 🚐 £5-£10 ▲ £5-£10
Open Etr-Oct (rs Nov-Mar no bar or pool facilities)
Booking advisable bank hols & peak season Last arrival 23.00hrs Last departure 11.00hrs
A level grassy site with pitches around lake and model railway, close to Hunmanby village, with coarse fishing on site. Signed from A1039. A 14-acre site with 91 touring pitches and 6 statics.
Veg prep area, boating lake, fishing.

🔵 🍴 ☉ 🗄 🍴 🔍 🍴 ☀ 🖐 🏔 🛈 🖋 🔌 📞 🚻 🚻
🍴 🐕 🎣 ⛹ 🔥
➔ ∪ ▶ ◎ ⛽ 🔱 🔌 🗡

Credit Cards 🔵 ▬ ▬ 🔵 ▬ 🔵

〇〇〇〇〇〇〇〇

KNARESBOROUGH

Scotton Holiday Park (SE327587)
New Rd, Scotton HG5 9HH ☎ 01423 864413 Signposted
▶▶▶ Family Park 🚐 🚐 ▲
Open Mar-7 Jan Booking advisable bank hols Last arrival 09.30hrs Last departure 13.00hrs
A very pleasant grassy park on the edge of the village and close to River Widd. From Knaresborough on B6165 towards Pateley Bridge, turn right immediately inside Scotton boundary. An 8.5-acre site with 65 touring pitches and 41 statics.

🔵 🍴 ☉ 🗄 🍴 ☀ 🍴 🏔 🛈 🖋 🔌 T ✕ 📞 🚻 🚻 🐕
⛹ 🔥
➔ ∪ ▶ ◎ 🗡

Credit Cards 🔵 ▬

Kingfisher Caravan Park (SE343603)
Low Moor Ln, Farnham HG5 9DQ ☎ 01423 869411
►►► Family Park ⚏ ⚏ Å
Open mid Mar/Etr-Oct Booking advisable bank hols &
15 Jul-1 Sep Last arrival 23.00hrs Last departure
16.00hrs
*A large grassy site with open spaces set in wooded area
in rural countryside. From Knaresborough take A6055,
after 1m turn L towards Farnham, and L again in village,
signed Scotton. Site 1m on L. A 4-acre site with 35
touring pitches and 30 statics.*

⚙ ☏ ⊙ 🗑 ⛏ ✳ ⚙ 🅟 ⌀ Ⓣ 🔔 🚿 🎪 🐕 🐂 ♿
➔ ∪ ⤬ 🍴 ➰

LEBBERSTON

Lebberston Touring Caravan Park (TA082823)
Manor View Rd YO11 3PB ☎ 01723 585723 Signposted
Nearby town: Scarborough
►►► Family Park ★ ⚏ £6-£8 ⚏ £6-£8
Open Mar-Oct Booking advisable bank hols
*A part-level and part-sloping grass site with saplings
and bushes. Off A165 Filey-Scarborough road. A 7.5-
acre site with 125 touring pitches.*
Washing up sinks.

⚙ ☏ ⊙ ✳ ⚙ 🅟 ⌀ ⚑ Ⓣ 🔔 🐕 🐂
➔ ∪ ▶ ◎ △ ⤬ 🍴 ➰ 🔋

NABURN

Naburn Lock Caravan & Camping Park (SE596446)
YO19 4RU ☎ 01904 728697 Signposted
►►► Family Park ★ ⚏ £9.50 ⚏ £9.50 Å £8
Open Mar-6 Nov Booking advisable anytime Last arrival
22.00hrs
*A meadowland site close to river in a rural area S of
York. Mainly level pitches divided by mature hedges.
From A64 head N on A19, turn left signed Naburn, and
site on right 0.5m past village. A 7-acre site with 100
touring pitches.*

⚙ ☏ ⊙ 🗑 ✳ 🅟 ⌀ ⚑ Ⓣ 🔔 🎪 🐕 🐂 ♿
➔ ▶ △ ⤬ 🍴 ➰
Credit Cards 💳 💳 💳 💳 💳 💳 💳

NORTH STAINLEY

Sleningford Water Mill Caravan Camping Park (SE280783)
HG4 3HQ ☎ 01765 635201 (5m NW of Ripon on A6108)
Signposted
Nearby town: Ripon
►►► Family Park ★ ⚏ £7-£8 ⚏ £7-£8 Å £7-£8
Open Etr & Apr-Oct Booking advisable bank hols &
school holidays Last arrival 22.00hrs Last departure
12.30hrs
*Level, grassy site with mature trees set in woods and
meadowland adjacent to River Ure and A6108. 4m N of
Ripon, and 1m N of North Stainley. A 14-acre site with
80 touring pitches.*
Off-licence, canoe access, fly fishing.

⚙ ☏ ⊙ 🗑 ⚈ ✳ ⚙ 🅟 ⌀ ⚑ Ⓣ 🔔 🚿 🐕 🐂 ♿
➔ ▶ △ ➰

OSMOTHERLEY

Cote Ghyll Caravan Park (SE461983)
DL6 3AH ☎ 01609 883425 (off A19 at junction A684, at
village cross turn left up hill) Signposted
Nearby town: Northallerton
►►► Family Park ★ ⚏ £6.50 ⚏ £6 Å £5.75
Open Apr-Oct Booking advisable bank hols & Jul-Aug
Last arrival 21.00hrs Last departure noon
*Quiet, peaceful site in pleasant valley on edge of moors,
close to village. From junction of A1/A684 take unclass
rd signed Osmotherley. In village turn left at T junc, and
site on right in 0.5 miles. A 4-acre site with 77 touring
pitches and 17 statics.*

⚙ ☏ ⊙ 🗑 ✳ 🅟 ⌀ ⚑ 🐕
➔ 🐂

PICKERING

Upper Carr Touring Park (SE804816)
Upper Carr Ln, Malton Rd YO18 7JP ☎ 01751 473115
►►► Family Park ⚏ ⚏ Å
Open Mar-Oct
*Attractive and well-maintained rural touring park set
amongst mature trees and hedges, with animal corner
and adjacent 9-hole golf course. Set off A169 Malton-
Pickering rd about 1.5m from Pickering; signed opposite
Black Bull pub. A 4-acre site with 80 touring pitches.*
Off-licence.

⚙ ☏ ⊙ 🗑 ⚈ ⚙ 🅟 🔔 🐕 🐂 ♿
➔ ▶

Wayside Caravan Park (SE764859)
Wrelton YO18 8PG ☎ 01751 472608 Signposted
►►► Family Park ★ ⚏ £8 ⚏ £7.50 Å £7
Open Etr-early Oct Booking advisable Etr, Spring bank
hol & Jul-Aug Last arrival 23.00hrs Last departure noon
*A level, grassy, well-maintained site divided up by mature
hedges into small areas off the A170 at Wrelton village. A
5-acre site with 75 touring pitches and 80 statics.*

⚙ ☏ ⊙ 🗑 ⚈ ✳ 🅟 ⌀ ⚑ Ⓣ 🔔 🐂 ♿
➔ ∪ ▶ 🍴 ➰

RICHMOND

Brompton-on-Swale Caravan & Camping Park (NZ199002)
Brompton-on-Swale DL10 7EZ ☎ 01748 824629 (1.5m
SE B6271 towards Brompton-on Swale) Signposted
Nearby town: Darlington

►►►► De-Luxe Park ★ ⚏ £7.25-£11.05
⚏ £7.25-£11.05 Å £5.50-£12.05

Open Etr or Mar-Oct Booking advisable school & bank hols Last arrival 22.00hrs Last departure 14.00hrs
A riverside site on former meadowland with mature trees and other natural features. Very well-equipped and maintained, adjacent to main road on the banks of the River Swale. Take B1263 off A1 signed Richmond, and site 1m on left. A 10.5-acre site with 150 touring pitches and 22 statics.
Fishing on site.

🔌 📻 ☉ 🗐 🏳 ⊡ ☀ ⚠ 🏋 ◎ ⊞ Ⓣ 🔔 ⛲ 🐕 🐾 ♿
➜ ∪ 🅿 ♪

Credit Cards 💳 ▬ ▬ ▩ 🔄

Swale View Caravan Site (NZ134013)
Reeth Rd DL10 4SF ☎ 01748 823106 Signposted
▶▶ **Town & Country Pennant Park** 🚐 £7.40 🚐 £7.10
🅰 £6.30-£7.40
Open Mar-Oct Booking advisable bank hols & summer hols Last arrival 21.00hrs Last departure noon
A level, grassy site shaded by trees, lying on the banks of the River Swale in picturesque country. From Richmond take B6270 signed Reeth for 2.5m. A 4-acre site with 60 touring pitches and 100 statics.

🔌 📻 ☉ 🗐 ⚓ ☀ ⚠ 🏋 ◎ ⊞ Ⓣ 🔔 🐕 🐾
➜ 🅿 ♪

RIPON

Riverside Meadows Country Caravan Park (SE317726)
Ure Bank Top HG4 1JD ☎ 01765 602964 Signposted
▶▶▶ **Family Park** ★ 🚐 £6.50-£10 🚐 £6.50-£10
🅰 £6.50-£10
Open Etr-Oct (rs Mar-Apr bar open wknds only) Booking advisable bank hols & high season Last arrival 22.00hrs Last departure noon
This pleasant and well-maintained site stands on high ground overlooking the River Ure, 1 mile from town centre. There is no access to the river from the site. Leave A1 at junc with A61 signed Ripon, at bypass rndbt turn right onto unclass rd, then 2nd left at 2nd rndbt. A 28-acre site with 200 touring pitches and 200 statics.

🔌 📻 ☉ 🗐 🏳 ⚓ 🏴 ☀ 🍴 ⚠ 🏋 ◎ ⊞ Ⓣ 🔔 🧹 🐕 🐾
➜ ∪ 🅿 🛆 ♪

ROBIN HOOD'S BAY

Middlewood Farm Holiday Park (NZ945045)
Middlewood Ln, Fylingthorpe YO22 4UF ☎ 01947 880414
Nearby town: Whitby
▶▶▶ **Family Park** ★ 🚐 £6.50-£8.50 🚐 £6.50-£7.50
🅰 £6.50-£8.50
Open Etr-Oct Booking advisable Last arrival 22.00hrs Last departure noon
A peaceful family park on a working farm, close to Robin Hood's Bay in a picturesque fishing village. Leave A171 towards Robin Hood's Bay, into Fylingthorpe village, and turn into Middlewood Lane to park. A 7-acre site with 140 touring pitches and 30 statics.

🔌 📻 ☉ 🗐 🏳 ☀ ⚠ 🏋 ◎ ⊡ 🔔 🐕
➜ ∪ 🅿 🍴 ♪ 🐾

SCARBOROUGH

Cayton Village Caravan Park (TA057837)
Mill Ln, Cayton YO11 3NN ☎ 01723 583171 & 01904 624630 (in winter) Signposted
▶▶▶ **Family Park** 🚐 £5-£9 🚐 £5-£9 🅰 £5-£9
Open Etr/Apr-1 Oct Booking advisable bank hols Last arrival 20.00hrs Last departure noon
A pleasant, landscaped site in an attractive rural area. Situated off A165 Scarborough to Filey Rd, adjoining Cayton Village. An 11-acre site with 200 touring pitches.

🔌 🍴 📻 ☉ 🗐 🏳 ☀ ⚠ 🏋 ◎ ⊡ Ⓣ 🔔 ⛲ 🐕 🐾 ♿
➜ ∪ 🅿 ◎ 🛆 🌿 🍽 ♪

Jacobs Mount Caravan Park (TA021868)
Jacobs Mount, Stepney Rd YO12 5NL ☎ 01723 361178 (2m in W on A170 Thirsk Road) Signposted
▶▶▶ **Family Park** ★ 🚐 £6-£9 🚐 £6-£9 🅰 £6-£9

contd.

Open Mar-Oct (rs Mar-May & Oct limited hours at shop/bar) Booking advisable bank hols & late Jun-early Sep Last arrival 21.00hrs Last departure noon
A gently sloping site situated in attractive countryside 2m from the coast, with direct access from A170. A 2.5-acre site with 56 touring pitches and 44 statics.
Dish wash & food preparation area.

🕮 ╟ ⊙ 🗟 ⚑ ◀ ⟈ ☼ ⚲ ⚞ 🛉 🖉 ⊞ Ⓣ ✕ 🕻 🏛
🐕 🎱
➜ ∪ 🏳 ⊚ △ ⋏ ⚇ ♪

Scalby Close Park (TA018925)
Burniston Rd YO13 0DA ☎ 01723 365908 Signposted
► ► ► Family Park ★ ⚏ £4.25-£8.75 ⚑ £4.25-£8.75
⚞ £4.25-£8.75
Open Mar-Oct Booking advisable bank hols & high season Last arrival 22.00hrs Last departure noon
A small family-run site situated 2m N of Scarborough on the A165. A 3-acre site with 42 touring pitches and 5 statics.

🕮 ╟ ⊙ 🗟 ☼ 🛉 🖉 ⊞ Ⓣ 🕻
➜ ∪ 🏳 ⋏ ⚇ ♪ 🎱
Credit Cards 💳 ▭

Scalby Manor Caravan & Camping Park (TA025911)
Burnston Rd YO13 0DA ☎ 01723 366212 Signposted
► ► ► Family Park ★ ⚏ £4.90-£9.60 ⚑ £4.90-£9.60
⚞ £4.90-£9.60
Open Etr-Oct Booking advisable bank hols Jul & Aug Last arrival 21.00hrs Last departure noon
Slightly undulating, grassy site in rural surroundings.

On the A165, 2m N of town centre. A 22-acre site with 300 touring pitches.
Off-licence.

🕮 ╟ ⋏ ⚞ 🛉 🖉 Ⓣ 🕻 🏛 ⟿ 🐕 ৬
➜ ∪ 🏳 ⋏ ⚇ ♪ 🗟 🎱
Credit Cards 💳 ▭ ▭ ▭ 🟥

SCOTCH CORNER

Scotch Corner Caravan Park (NZ210054)
DL10 6NS ☎ 01748 822530 & 822961 (winter)
Signposted
Nearby town: Richmond
► ► ► Family Park ★ ⚏ £8-£9.50 ⚑ £7.50-£9 ⚞ £7-£8.50
Open Etr-mid Oct Booking advisable public hols & Jul-Aug Last arrival 22.30hrs Last departure noon
A well-maintained site with excellent facilities. Off A6108, approach from Scotch Corner is towards Richmond for approx 200yds then make U-turn, crossing central reservation and proceed approx 160yds back towards Scotch Corner for site entrance. A 7-acre site with 96 touring pitches.

🕮 ╟ ⊙ 🗟 ⚑ ☼ ⚲ ⚞ 🛉 🖉 ⊞ Ⓣ ✕ 🕻 🐕 🎱 ৬
➜ ∪ 🏳 ♪
Credit Cards 💳 ▭ ▭ 🅾 ▭ 🟥

SEAMER

Arosa Caravan & Camping Park (TA011830)
Ratten Raw YO12 4QB ☎ 01723 862166 Signposted
Nearby town: Scarborough
► ► ► Family Park ★ ⚏ £8.50-£10.50 ⚑ £8.50-£10.50
⚞ £7.50-£10.50

contd.

Open Mar-4 Jan Booking advisable bank hols & Aug
Last arrival 18.00hrs Last departure mdnt
*A very well laid out site with screening from mature
trees, approx 4m from Scarborough. From junc with
unclass rd and A64 S of Seamer, travel N into village.
Site 250yards along Ratten Road. A 3.5-acre site with 92
touring pitches.*

🅟 ⊙ 回 🖳 🔍 ⚡ ✳ ♀ /ⁿ\ 🚶 🅐 ✅ T 🗓 ⬛ 🚿 ⚓ ☂ 🅣 🅽
🅛 ♿
→ ∪ 🅵 🛆 🏊 ⛹ 🚣

SHERIFF HUTTON

Camping & Caravanning Club Site (SE638652)
Bracken Hill YO6 1QG ☎ 01347 878660 (in season) &
01203 694995 Signposted
Nearby town: York
▶ ▶ ▶ **Family Park** ★ 🚐 £10-£13 🚗 £10-£13 ▲ £10-£13
Open end Mar-early Nov Booking advisable bank hols &
peak periods Last arrival 21.00hrs Last departure noon
*The site is within easy reach of York in a quiet rural
setting. From A1237 (York northern ring road) take
unclass rd signed Strensall and Sheriff Hutton, through
Strensall turn left on unclass rd signed Sheriff Hutton
and site 2m on right. Please see the advertisement on
page 27 for details of Club Members' benefits. A 10-acre
site with 176 touring pitches.*

🅟 🅟 ⊙ 回 🖳 ✳ /ⁿ\ 🚶 🅐 ✅ 🗓 ⚮ ♿
→ 🅛

Credit Cards 💳 🚫 📇 💱 🅶

SLINGSBY

Camping & Caravanning Club Site (SE699755)
Railway St YO6 7AA ☎ 01653 628335 (in season) &
01203 694995 Signposted
▶ ▶ ▶ **Family Park** ★ 🚐 £11-£14 🚗 £11-£14 ▲ £11-£14
Open end Mar-early Nov Booking advisable bank hols &
peak periods Last arrival 21.00hrs Last departure noon
*A part-grassy, part-hardstanding site near village
centre, offering first class facilities and signed from
B1257. Please see the advertisement on page 27 for
details of Club Members' benefits. A 3-acre site with 60
touring pitches.*

🅟 🅟 ⊙ 回 🖳 ✳ 🅐 ✅ 🗓 T ⚮ 🅛 ♿
→ ∪ 🅵

Credit Cards 💳 🚫

Robin Hood Caravan & Camping Park (SE701748)
Green Dyke Ln YO6 7AU ☎ 01653 628391 Signposted
Nearby town: Malton
▶ ▶ ▶ **Family Park** 🚐 🚗 ▲
Open Mar-Oct Booking advisable bank hols & 15 Jul-1
Sep Last arrival 22.00hrs Last departure 16.00hrs
*A pleasant, well-maintained grassy site, well-situated
for touring Yorks Dales. Situated on B1257. A 2-acre site
with 39 touring pitches and 7 statics.*
Caravan hire, washing up area. Off-license.

🅟 🅟 ⊙ 回 🖳 ✳ /ⁿ\ 🚶 🅐 ✅ 🗓 T ⚮ 🚿 🅣 🅛 ♿
→ ∪ 🚣

SNAINTON

Jasmine Caravan Park (SE928813)
Cross Ln YO13 9BE ☎ 01723 859240
Signposted
Nearby town: Scarborough
▶ ▶ ▶ **Family Park** 🚐 £6-£9 🚗 £6-£9 ▲ £6-£9
Open Mar-Dec Booking advisable 3 wks in advance for
bank hols Last arrival 22.00hrs Last departure noon
*A well-screened rural site on edge of the village, 1m off
A170 Pickering-Scarborough road; turn off opposite
school into Barker Lane. A 5-acre site with 90 touring
pitches and 10 statics.*

🅠 🅿 🅟 ⊙ 回 🖳 ✳ 🅐 ✅ 🗓 T ⚮ 🅛 ♿
→ ∪ 🅵 🚣

STAINFORTH

**Knight Stainforth Hall Caravan & Campsite
(SD816672)**
BD24 0DP ☎ 01729 822200 Signposted
Nearby town: Settle
▶ ▶ ▶ **Family Park** 🚐 fr £8.50 🚗 fr £8.50 ▲ fr £8.50
Open May-Oct Booking advisable bank hols & Jul-Aug
Last arrival 22.00hrs Last departure noon
*A very well-maintained site located near a river in the
Yorkshire Dales National Park. Approach only possible
from B6479 at Giggleswick. A 6-acre site with 100
touring pitches and 60 statics.*
Fishing on site.

🅠 🅟 ⊙ 回 🖳 🔍 ⚡ 🛏 ✳ /ⁿ\ 🚶 🅐 ✅ 🗓 T ⚮ 🅣 🅽 🅛
→ ∪ 🅵 🚣

Credit Cards 💳 🚫 📇 💱 🅶

STAXTON

Spring Willows Touring Caravan Park (TA026794)
Main Rd, Staxton Roundabout YO12 4SB
☎ 01723 891505 (jct A64/A1039)
Signposted
Nearby town: Scarborough

〇〇〇〇〇〇〇〇〇

▶ ▶ ▶ ▶ **De-Luxe Park** 🚐 🚗 ▲
Open Mar-Dec (rs Mar & Oct-Dec bar/pool/take-
away/restaurant restricted) Booking advisable bank
hols, Etr, Jul & Aug Last arrival 18.00hrs Last departure
11.00hrs
*A sheltered grassy site in a former sandpit, with level
pitches divided by shrubs and bushes, and offering a
wide variety of amenities. 6m from Scarborough at
junct of A64 and A1039. A 10-acre site with 184 touring
pitches.*
Washing-up facilities, sauna, solarium, coffee lounge

🅠 🅟 ⊙ 回 🖳 ⚡ 🔍 ⚡ 🛏 ✳ ♀ /ⁿ\ 🚶 🅐 ✅ 🗓 T ✕ ⚮
🚻 🚿 ⚓ 🅣 🅽 🅛 ♿
→ ∪ 🅵

〇〇〇〇〇〇〇〇〇

SUTTON-ON-THE-FOREST

Goosewood Caravan Park (SE595636)
YO61 1ET ☎ 01347 810829 (From A1237 outer York ring
rd, take B1363 signed Helmsley North, pass
Haxby/Wigginton jct & take next right) Signposted
Nearby town: York

◯◯◯◯◯◯◯◯

► ► ► ► De-Luxe Park ★ ⚑ £8.50-£10 ⚑ £8.50-£10
Open 22 Mar-Oct Booking advisable bank hols Last arrival 20.00hrs Last departure noon
An immaculately maintained site with its own lake and seasonal fishing, set in attractive woodland within the Vale of York. From A1237 (York northern ring road) take B1363, in 1.5m take unclass rd signed Eastmoor, and turn right in .25m. Take right turn in .5m, and site on right. A 12-acre site with 75 touring pitches.
Fishing lake.

🔌 ➡ 🐾 ⊙ 🗑 ⚖ ✳ ⋀ 🔋 ⌀ ⊞ T 🔌 �ↄ 🐕 🐎
➔ ∪ ▶ ♨ 🍴

◯◯◯◯◯◯◯◯

THIRSK

Sowerby Caravan Park (SE437801)
Sowerby YO7 3AG ☎ 01845 522753 (0.5m S off A168) Signposted
► ► ► Family Park ⚑ £6.50-£7 ⚑ £6.50-£7 ▲ £6.50-£7
Open Mar-Oct Booking advisable bank hols Last arrival 22.00hrs
A level grassy site, 1m from town on the Sowerby Road, with a tree-lined river bank. From junc A168/A19 S of Thirsk, follow A19 for 1m, turn right on unclass rd signed Sowerby. Site on left in 1m. A 1-acre site with 25 touring pitches and 85 statics.

🔌 🐾 ⊙ 🗑 🔍 ✳ ⋀ 🔋 ⌀ ⊞ T 🔌 ♨ ⚓
➔ ∪ ♨ 🍴

THRESHFIELD

Wood Nook Caravan Park (SD974641)
Skirethorns BD23 5NU ☎ 01756 752412 Signposted
Nearby town: Grassington

◯◯◯◯◯◯◯◯

► ► ► ► De-Luxe Park ★ ⚑ £8-£10.80 ⚑ £8-£10.80 ▲ £8-£9.80
Open Mar-Oct Booking advisable bank hols & peak periods Last arrival 22.00hrs Last departure noon
Gently sloping site in a rural setting, completely hidden by natural features of surrounding hills and woodland. Site on unclass rd 1m NW of Threshfield, off B6160. A 2-acre site with 48 touring pitches and 10 statics.
See advertisement under GRASSINGTON

🔌 🐾 ⊙ 🗑 ⚖ ✳ ⋀ 🔋 ⌀ ⊞ T 🔌 🐕 ⚓
➔ ∪ 🔺 🍴

Credit Cards 💳 ▓ ▓ ▓ 📖

◯◯◯◯◯◯◯◯

UGTHORPE

Burnt House Holiday Park (NZ784112)
YO21 2BG ☎ 01947 840448 Signposted
Nearby town: Whitby
► ► ► Family Park ★ ⚑ £8 ⚑ £8 ▲ £8
Open Mar-Oct Booking advisable bank hols & Jul-Aug Last arrival 21.00hrs Last departure noon

> Summer weather can mean rain. It is a good idea to prepare for ground to be wet underfoot. Take something to amuse the children if they can't go outside

Level grass site with trees and bushes set in moorland. 4.5m from sea and beach and 9m W of Whitby off A171 Teeside road. A 7.5-acre site with 99 touring pitches and 41 statics.

🔌 🐾 ⊙ 🗑 ⚖ ✳ ⋀ 🔋 ⌀ ⊞ 🔌
➔ ∪ ▶ 🔺 🍴

WHITBY

Northcliffe Holiday Park (NZ930076)
YO22 4LL ☎ 01947 880477 (3.5m S, off A171)
Signposted

◯◯◯◯◯◯◯◯

► ► ► ► De-Luxe Park ★ ⚑ £6-£11 ⚑ £6-£11 ▲ £6-£11
Open Etr or end Mar-Oct Booking advisable school & bank hols & Jul-Aug Last arrival 21.00hrs Last departure 11.00hrs ✾

A lovely little site in a peaceful position on the outskirts of Whitby, with clifftop views and country walks. Situated 3.5m S off A171. A 2-acre site with 30 touring pitches and 171 statics.
off-licence.

🔌 🐾 ⊙ 🗑 ⚖ 🔍 ✳ ⋀ 🔋 ⌀ ⊞ T ✖ 🔌 🛒 ⚓ 🚿
➔ ∪ ⊚ ♨ 🍴

Credit Cards 💳 ▓ ▓ ▓ 📖

◯◯◯◯◯◯◯◯

Ladycross Plantation Caravan Park (NZ821080)
Egton YO21 1UA ☎ 01947 895502
► ► ► Family Park ★ ⚑ £7.50-£10 ⚑ £7.50-£10
Open Etr-Oct Booking advisable bank hols & Aug Last arrival 20.30hrs Last departure noon
A sheltered and screened woodland park set on high ground with level, mainly grassy pitches. Signed and situated on unclass rd off A171 Whitby/Teeside Rd, 6m from Whitby centre. Only approach this way due to steep narrow roads from any other direction. A 12-acre site with 116 touring pitches.

🔌 🐾 ⊙ 🗑 ⚖ ✳ 🔋 ⌀ ⊞ T 🔌 🐕 ⚓
Credit Cards 💳 ▓

Rigg Farm Caravan Park (NZ915061)
Stainsacre YO22 4LP ☎ 01947 880430 (3.5m S on unclass off A171 at High Hawsker) Signposted
► ► ► Family Park ⚑ £8-£9 ⚑ £8-£9 ▲ £8-£9
Open Mar-Oct Booking advisable bank hols & Jul-Aug Last arrival 21.00hrs Last departure noon
A neat rural site with good views in peaceful surroundings. Site is off B1416 on unclass road. From A171 Scarborough rd turn L onto B1416 signed contd.

Ruswarp. In 3.25m turn R onto unclass road signed Sneatonthorpe-Hawsker-Stainsacre. In 1.25m turn L signed Hawsker-Robin Hoods Bay-Scarborough, site in .5m. A 3-acre site with 14 touring pitches and 15 statics.

🏠 📻 ⊙ 🔍 ✳ ⚠ 🎱 ⬛ ⚫ 🐾
➜ ∪ ⌐ ⅄ 📹 🎿

Sandfield House Farm (NZ875115)
Sandsend Rd YO21 3SR ☎ 01947 602660 Signposted
▶ ▶ ▶ **Family Park** ★ 🚐 £6.50-£8.90 🚐 £6.50-£8.90
Open mid Mar-Oct Booking advisable school hols Last arrival 21.00hrs Last departure 11.00hrs
Fine sea views can be enjoyed from this park, set in undulating countryside close to Whitby Golf Club. On A174, 1m N of Whitby. A 12-acre site with 50 touring pitches and 150 statics.

🏠 📻 ⊙ 🔲 ⚓ ✳ 🎱 ⬛ ⚫ 🐾
➜ ⌐ ◎ 🌢 ⅄ 🎿 🐕

York House Caravan Park (NZ926071)
YO22 4LW ☎ 01947 880354 (3.5m S, off A171) Signposted
▶ ▶ ▶ **Family Park** ★ 🚐 £6.50-£7.50 🚐 £6.50-£7.50 🅰 £6.50-£7.50
Open Mar-Oct Booking advisable Spring bank hol & mid Jul-Aug Last arrival 22.00hrs Last departure noon
A very well-kept site in an undulating position located south of Whitby, ideal for touring coast or moors. Just off A171 at Hawsker and signed. A 3-acre site with 59 touring pitches and 41 statics.
Open area for games.

🏠 📻 ⊙ 🔲 ⚓ ✳ ⚠ 🎱 ⚫ ⬛ ⚫ 🏠 🐕 🐕
➜ ∪ ⌐ ◎ 🌢 ⅄ 📹 🎿

Woodhouse Farm Caravan & Camping Park (SE241715)
HG4 3PG ☎ 01765 658309 Signposted
Nearby town: Ripon
▶ ▶ ▶ **Family Park** ★ 🚐 £6.50-£8 🚐 £6.50-£8 🅰 £6.50
Open Mar-Oct Booking advisable bank hols & mid Jul-Aug Last arrival 22.30hrs Last departure noon

An attractive rural site on a former working farm, with existing hedges used to screen pitches, and meadowland and mature woods surroundings. Friendly, knowledgeable owners. Situated 6m W of Ripon off B6265 Pateley Bridge road, 2.5m from Fountains Abbey.

A 16-acre site with 140 touring pitches and 62 statics.
Barbecue hire, coarse fishing lake.

🏠 📻 ⊙ 🔲 ⚓ ⚓ 🔍 ✳ ⚠ 🎱 ⚫ ⬛ ⚫ 🐾 🏠 🐕 🐕
➜ ∪ 🎿

Credit Cards 💳 💳 🔵

St Helens Caravan Park (SE967836)
St Helens in the Park YO13 9QD
☎ 01723 862771
Signposted
Nearby town: Scarborough

◯◯◯◯◯◯◯◯

▶ ▶ ▶ ▶ **De-Luxe Park** 🚐 🚐 🅰
Open Mar-Oct (rs Nov-Jan shop/laundry/main showerbathblock closed) Booking advisable bank hols & Jul-Aug Last arrival 22.00hrs Last departure 17.00hrs
Set on the edge of the North York Moors National Park this delightfully landscaped park is extremely well-maintained and thoughtfully laid out with strategically placed, top quality facilities. Situated on A170 in village 150yds on L past Downe Arms Hotel towards Scarborough. A 25-acre site with 250 touring pitches.
Caravan storage.
See advertisement under SCARBOROUGH

🏠 🛒 📻 ⊙ 🔲 ⚓ ⚓ ✳ ⚠ 🎱 ⚫ ⬛ 🆃 ✖ ⚫ 📮 ♿
🏠 🏠 🐕 🐕
➜ ∪ ⌐ ◎ 🌢 ⅄ 🎿

Credit Cards 💳 💳 💳 💳 🔵

◯◯◯◯◯◯◯◯

Rawcliffe Manor Caravan Site (SE583553)
Manor Ln, Shipton Rd YO3 6TZ
☎ 01904 624422
Signposted

◯◯◯◯◯◯◯◯

▶ ▶ ▶ ▶ **De-Luxe Park** 🚐 £8-£11.40 🅰 £4.40-£11.40
Open all year Booking advisable all times Last arrival 20.00hrs Last departure noon
A level site divided into hedged paddocks, with immaculate landscaping incorporating rose trees throughout. From A1273 York ring road turn towards York at junc with A19, take 1st left, and site in 0.5m. A 4.5-acre site with 120 touring pitches.
Petanque pitches & satellite TV.

🏠 🛒 📻 ⊙ 🔲 ⚓ ⚓ 🔍 🔲 ✳ 🍴 ⚠ 🎱 ⚫ ⬛ ✖ ⚫
♿ 🏠 🐕 ♿
➜ ∪ ⌐ ◎ ⅄ 📹 🎿 🎿

Credit Cards 💳 💳 💳 🔵

◯◯◯◯◯◯◯◯

YORKSHIRE, SOUTH

**For the map of this county,
see YORKSHIRE, NORTH**

DONCASTER
See **Hatfield**

HATFIELD

Hatfield Waterpark (SE670098)
DN7 6EQ ☎ 01302 841572 & 737343 Signposted
Nearby town: Doncaster
►►► Family Park ★ ⚏ fr £6.40 ⚏ fr £6.40
▲ £3.40-£6.40
Open Apr-Oct Booking advisable bank hols Last arrival
18.30hrs Last departure noon
*A clean, well-run site with fishing and good supervised
marina facilities, including windsurfing, sailing and
canoeing equipment for hire. Bunkhouse
accommodation for up to 32, handy for tenters in very
wet weather. Signed from Hatfield off A18. A 10-acre
site with 75 touring pitches.*
Canoeing, rowing, sailing, windsurfing & fishing.

🄿 📢 ⊙ ☀ /ⵎ ✕ ⌾ ➡ 🏠 🏕 🐎 ⓩ ♿
➜ ∪ ▶ ⌂ ⅄ ✦ ✔

SHEFFIELD
See **Worsbrough**

WORSBROUGH

Greensprings Touring Park (SE330020)
Rockley Abbey Farm, Rockley Ln S75 3DS
☎ 01226 288298 Signposted
Nearby town: Barnsley
►►► Family Park ★ ⚏ £6.50 ⚏ £6.50 ▲ £6.50
Open Apr-Oct Booking advisable when hook up is
required Last arrival 21.00hrs Last departure noon
*Part-level, part-sloping, grass site with young trees and
bushes, set in woods and meadowland with access to
river. From exit 36 off M1 turn along A61 to Barnsley,
then signposted. A 4-acre site with 65 touring pitches.*
Cycle hire. TV hook up.

🄿 📢 ⊙ ⅊ ☀ 🛈 🐕 🏕
➜ ∪ ▶ ☎ ✦ ⌿ 🎱 ⓩ

YORKSHIRE, WEST

**For the map of this county,
see YORKSHIRE, NORTH**

BARDSEY

Glenfield Caravan Park (SE351421)
Blackmoor Ln LS17 9DZ ☎ 01937 574657 Signposted
Nearby town: Leeds
►►► Family Park ⚏ £7-£9 ⚏ £7-£9 ▲ £6-£9
Open all year Booking advisable

*A rural site in a hedge-lined meadow with level pitches.
From A58 at Bardsey turn into Church Lane, continue
into Brickmoor Lane, and site on right in 0.5m. A 4-acre
site with 30 touring pitches and 1 static.*

🄿 📢 ⊙ 🛅 ☀ /ⵎ 🛈 ⅃ ⌾ ✖
➜ ∪ ▶ ☎ ⌿ ⅃

Moor Lodge Park (SE352423)
Blackmoor Ln LS17 9DZ ☎ 01937 572424
Signposted
Nearby town: Leeds
►►► Family Park ★ ⚏ £7.50-£8 ⚏ £7.50-£8
Open all year Booking advisable all times
*A neat, well-kept site in a peaceful and pleasant rural
location convenient to surrounding areas of interest.
From the Bracken Fox public house on the A58
Wetherby-Leeds rd, turn into Syke Lane, then right into
Blackmore Lane. Site signed on right. A 7-acre site with
12 touring pitches and 60 statics.*

🄿 📢 ⊙ 🛅 ⅊ ☀ /ⵎ 🛈 🐕 ⌾ ⅃ ⌾ ✖ 🏕
➜ ∪ ▶ ⌿ ⅃

LEEDS
See also **Bardsey**

Roundhay Park Site (SE339376)
Roundhay Park, Elmete Ln, Wetherby Rd LS8 2LG
☎ 0113 2652354 (in season) & 2661850
Signposted
►► Town & Country Pennant Park ★ ⚏ £8.25-£8.65
⚏ £8.25-£8.65 ▲ £4.10
Open 16 Mar-7 Nov Booking advisable Spring bank hol
& Jul-Aug Last arrival 21.00hrs Last departure noon
*On a south-facing hillside, adjacent to Roundhay Park,
3.5m from city centre. A very well-maintained site. An 8-
acre site with 60 touring pitches.*

🄿 📢 ⊙ ⅊ ☀ /ⵎ 🛈 🐕 ⌾ ⅃ ⌾ 🏕 🎱 ♿
➜ ∪ ▶ ⅄ ⌿ 🛅

SILSDEN

Dales Bank Holiday Park (SE036483)
Low Ln BD20 9JH ☎ 01535 653321 & 656523 (1m NW
on unclass rd) Signposted
►► Town & Country Pennant Park ★ ⚏ £6.50
⚏ £6.50-£7.50 ▲ £5-£6.50
Open Apr-Oct (rs Mar) Booking advisable public hols
Last arrival 22.00hrs Last departure 16.00hrs
*A pleasant farm site with very good facilities in open
countryside of typical Dales scenery. From A6034 in
town centre turn N, take left then right turns into
Bradley Rd, and after 1m turn right. Site in 500yds. A 3-
acre site with 40 touring pitches and 12 statics.*

🄿 📢 ⊙ 🛅 ✦ ☀ ⅄ /ⵎ 🛈 🐕 ⌾ ✖ ⌾ 🎱
➜ ∪ ▶ ⅄ ⌿ 🛅
Credit Cards 💳 🪙 📰

Remember that many parks in this guide may refuse
to take bookings from groups of young people or
groups of people of the same sex. Always check
before you go.

CHANNEL ISLANDS

There is no map of the Channel Islands

GUERNSEY

CATEL (CASTEL)

Fauxquets Valley Farm
CC GY5 7QA ☎ 01481 55460 Signposted
Nearby town: St Peter Port
► ► ► Family Park ▲ £9-£10
Open May-mid Sep (rs Apr no pool or farmhouse
kitchen use) Booking advisable last 2 wks Jul-
1st 3 wks Aug
*Beautiful, quiet farm site in a hidden valley yet close to
the sea. Friendly, helpful owners who understand
campers' needs. 3m W of St Peter Port, near German
Underground Hospital. A 3-acre site with 90 touring
pitches.*
Nature trail & bird watching.

🏺🐾☉📷🍳🏹🔫◀☐🌣⚠🚿🔌🖉⊞✕📞🏧🍴
🐕🦽
➔∪🅿◎⚠⅄♨🎵

Credit Cards 💳 💳 💳 💳

VALE

La Bailloterie Camping
Bailloterie Ln GY3 5HA ☎ 01481 43636 Signposted
Nearby town: St Sampsons
► ► ► Family Park ★ ▲ £7.10-£8.80
Open 15 May-15 Sep Booking advisable Jul-Aug Last
arrival 23.00hrs
*Pretty little site with one large touring field and a few
small, well-screened paddocks, on a working freesia
farm. 3m N of St Peter Port, take Vale Road to
Crossways and turn right into Rue du Braye. Site 1st left
at sign. An 8-acre site with 100 touring pitches.*
Volleyball net & boules pitch.

🏺🐾☉📷🍳🔫◀☐🌣⚠🚿🔌🖉⊞✕📞🚐🏧🍴
🏹🐕🦽
➔∪🅿◎⚠⅄♨🎵

JERSEY

ST BRELADE

Rose Farm
Route Des Genets JE3 8DE ☎ 01534 41231 Signposted
Nearby town: St Aubin

◯◯◯◯◯◯◯◯◯◯

► ► ► ► De-Luxe Park ▲
Open May-Sep Booking advisable as early as possible

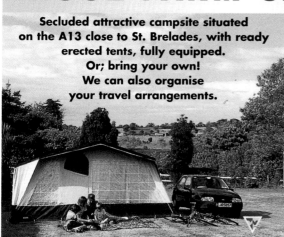

An attractive site set in a valley close to St Aubins, with friendly owners and secluded pitches. Facilities are of a very good standard. Located 1m W of St Aubin's village on A13; at junc with A57 turn right into Rose Farm Lane. A 5-acre site with 150 touring pitches.

🕿 📶 ⊙ 🗓 ⌇ ◀ ⊡ ☀ 🏔 🛈 ⌀ ✕ ℄ ⚡ ⌂
→ ∪ ┝ ◎ △ ⊹ ✍

ST MARTIN

Beuvelande Camp Site
Beuvelande JE3 6EG ☎ 01534 853575 & 852223

▶ ▶ ▶ ▶ **De-Luxe Park** ⚊ £10-£14
Open May-15 Sep Booking advisable Last arrival anytime
An old established site with refurbished facilities, in peaceful countryside close to St Martin. Take A6 from St Helier to St Martin, and follow signs. A 6-acre site with 150 touring pitches.

🕿 📶 ⊙ 🗓 ⌇ ◀ ⊡ ☀ 🏔 🛈 ⌀ ⊞ ✕ ℄ ⚡
→ ∪ ┝ ⊹ ✍

Rozel Camping Park
Summerville Farm JE3 6AX ☎ 01534 856797 & 851656
Nearby town: St Helier

▶ ▶ ▶ ▶ **De-Luxe Park** ★ ⚊ £7.40-£11.40
Open May-mid Sep (rs May & Sep snack bar closed) Booking advisable Jul-Aug Last departure noon ✍
An attractive and well-maintained secluded holiday site offering excellent amenities in a lovely farm location. From St Helier follow Bagatelle Road (A6) or St Saviour's Road (A7) then B38. Last arrival and departure time as soon as possible after car ferry docks. A 4-acre site with 70 touring pitches and 20 statics.

🕿 📶 ⊙ 🗓 ⌇ ◀ ⊡ ☀ 🏔 🛈 ⌀ ⊞ ⊤ ✕ ℄ ♨ ⚡ ⌂
→ ∪ ┝ △ ✍
Credit Cards 💳 🏧

ISLE OF MAN

For the map see CUMBRIA
Caravans are not allowed on the Island.

KIRK MICHAEL

Glen Wyllin Campsite (SC302901)
IM6 1AL ☎ 01624 878231 & 878836 Signposted
Nearby town: Peel
▶ ▶ ▶ **Family Park** ★ ⚐ £7 ⚊ £7
Open mid May-mid Sep Booking advisable end May-mid Jun

This tree-lined glen is divided by a tarmac road leading down to the beach. Just off A3 TT course at Kirk Michael, clearly signed on edge of village. A 9-acre site with 90 touring pitches.

📶 ⊙ 🗓 ⌇ 🏔 🛈 ⌀ ℄ ⌂ ⚡ ⌂
→ ∪ ┝

LAXEY

Laxey Commissioners Campsite (SC438841)
Quarry Rd, Minorca Hill ☎ 01624 861241 & 861816
Signposted
▶▶ **Town & Country Pennant Park** ★ ⚐ fr £7 ⚊ fr £7
Open Apr-Sep Booking advisable Apr-May Last arrival anytime
Level grassy site in hilly country with access to sea, beach and hills. Excellent facilities for tenters, including camper's kitchen. A 2-acre site with 50 touring pitches.

📶 ⊙ ⚡
→ ⊹ ✍ ⊡

PEEL

Peel Camping Park (SC252839)
Derby Rd IM5 1RG ☎ 01624 842341 & 843667 (on A20)
Signposted
▶▶ **Town & Country Pennant Park** ⚐ £7 ⚊ £7
Open mid May-mid Sep Booking advisable 1st & 2nd week Jun ✍

A pleasant grass site on the edge of town surrounded by hedges. On A20 .25m from Peel, past Clothmaker's School. A 4-acre site with 120 touring pitches.

🕿 📶 ⊙ ⊡ ℄ ♨ ⚡ ⌂
→ ┝ ✍ ⊡

SCOTLAND

The directory which follows has been divided into three geographical regions. Counties have not been shown against individual locations as recent legislation has created a number of smaller counties which will be unfamiliar to the visitor. The postal authorities have confirmed that it is no longer necessary to include a county name in addresses, provided a post code is shown. All locations appear on the regional maps in their appropriate counties.

HIGHLANDS & ISLANDS

This region includes the counties of Aberdeen City, Aberdeenshire, Highland, Moray, Orkney, Shetland and Western Isles.

ABERDEEN

Hazlehead Caravan Park & Campsite (NJ893057)
Groats Rd AB1 8BL ☎ 01224 647647 & 321268 (Apr-Sep) Signposted
► ► ► Family Park ★ ♥ £8.55 ♥ £8.55 ▲ £4.30
Open Apr-Sep Booking advisable Jun-Aug Last arrival 20.00hrs Last departure noon
A wooded, landscaped site close to park of the same name, on western outskirts of city off A944. From outer ring road A92 take A944 signed Alford, in 1m turn left into Groats Rd (signed camping), and site on right in 400 metres. A 6-acre site with 165 touring pitches.

🖼🖎⊙➩✳⚠🏕🛉⌀🔌🐕🛖🚾♿
➔∪➤🍴🔌

ABERLOUR

Aberlour Gardens Caravan Park (NJ282434)
AB38 9LD ☎ 01340 871586 Signposted
Nearby town: Elgin
► ► ► Family Park ★ ♥ £7-£8.50 ♥ £7-£8.50
▲ £6.50-£8.50
Open Apr-Oct Booking advisable bank hols & Jul-Aug
A quiet walled garden park with very clean modern facilities. Signed off A95 halfway between Aberlour and Craigellachie. Large motor vans should approach from A941, 0.5m E of Craigellachie, signed Blue Hill Quarry and 'Caravan' to avoid low bridge. A 5-acre site with 35 touring pitches and 26 statics.

🖼🖎⊙🗟✳⚠🏕🛉⌀🔌➕⊥🛖🚾♿
➔∪➤◎🔌

ABOYNE

Aboyne Loch Caravan Park (NO538998)
AB34 5BR ☎ 013398 86244 & 01330 811351 (1m E of Aboyne off A93) Signposted
Nearby town: Aberdeen

◯◯◯◯◯◯◯◯◯◯

► ► ► ► De-Luxe Park ★ ♥ £8-£9 ♥ £8-£9 ▲ £6-£9
Open 31 Mar-Oct Booking advisable Jul-Aug Last arrival 20.00hrs Last departure 11.00hrs

Attractively-sited caravan park set amidst woodland beside Aboyne Loch in scenic Deeside. On A93, 1m E of Aboyne. A 4-acre site with 55 touring pitches and 40 statics.
Coarse fishing.

🖼🖎⊙🗟🖎🔌✳⚠🏕🛉⌀🔌🔌⌕🛖🐕🚾
➔∪➤⚙🔌🔌

◯◯◯◯◯◯◯◯◯

ALVES

North Alves Caravan Park (NJ122633)
IV30 3XD ☎ 01343 85223 Signposted
► ► ► Family Park ♥ ♥ ▲
Open Apr-Oct Booking advisable peak periods Last arrival 23.00hrs Last departure noon
A quiet rural site in attractive rolling countryside within 3m of a good beach. From A96 take unclass rd signed Alves. A 10-acre site with 45 touring pitches and 12 statics.

🖼🖎⊙🗟🖎🔌➩✳⚠🏕🛉⌀➕⊥🔌🐕🚾
➔∪➤🔌⚙🔌

APPLECROSS

Applecross Campsite (NG714443)
IV54 8ND ☎ 01520 744268 & 744284 Signposted
Nearby town: Dingwall
► ► ► Family Park ♥ ♥ ▲
Open Etr-Oct (rs Apr, May, Sep & Oct only 1 toilet block open) Last arrival 22.00hrs

CAMPSITE
► ► ►

Applecross, Strathcarron, Ross-shire IV54 8ND
Tel & Fax: (01520) 744268 and
Tel: (01520) 744284 (out of season)
E:mail: applecross@sol.co.uk

Peaceful park in an area of outstanding scenic beauty
• Electric hook ups and water points
• Well equipped toilet blocks with showers.
• Launderette
• Shop
• Bakery
• Static vans
• Flower Tunnel, Licensed Restaurant

Open every day in season Easter - October

Highlands and Islands

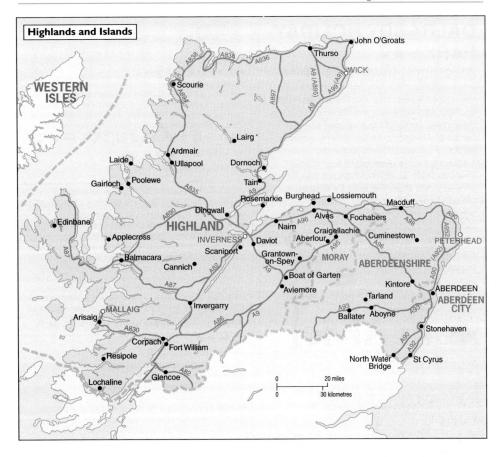

A quiet site in a lovely remote area close to mountains, moorland and beach. Caravans should approach via Shieldaig. On unclass rd off A896, 300yds from village. A 6-acre site with 60 touring pitches and 4 statics. Bakery.

🔌 🐈 ⊙ ✳ 🅿 🖉 🗄 🚽 ✗ 🔧

➜ 🗡

Credit Cards ▒▒▒

ARDMAIR

Ardmair Point Caravan Park (NH108983)
IV26 2TN ☎ 01854 612054 (3m N of Ullapool on A835)
Signposted
Nearby town: Ullapool

○○○○○○○○

▶▶▶▶ De-Luxe Park ★ 🚐 £7.50-£9.50 🚙 £7.50-£9.50 ⛺ £7.50-£9.50
Open May-Sep Booking advisable Jul-Aug Last arrival 22.00hrs Last departure noon
An excellent touring site on small peninsula 3.5m N of Ullapool on A835, with superb views of surrounding mountains and sea lochs. A 4-acre site with 45 touring pitches.

Boats, fishing, canoes, windsurfers for hire.

🔌 🐈 ⊙ 🖥 🗑 ✳ 🎡 🅿 🖉 🗄 🚽 ✗ 🔧 🔧 ♿

➜ 🅄 ▶ 🛆 ⅄ 🗡

Credit Cards ●● ▒▒ ▒▒ 🖏

○○○○○○○○

ARISAIG

Camusdarach Campsite (SS664916)
Camusdarach PH39 4NT ☎ 01687 450221
Signposted

○○○○○○○○

▶▶▶▶ De-Luxe Park ★ 🚐 £8 🚙 £8 ⛺ £6
Open 15 Mar-15 Oct Booking advisable Jul-Aug Last arrival 22.00hrs Last departure 18.00hrs no cars by tents
Very attractive secluded park with new sanitary facilities, and access to sandy beach. On A830 4m N of Arisaig village. A 2.75-acre site with 42 touring pitches.

🔌 🐈 ⊙ 🗑 ✳ 🅿 🗄 🔧 🖥 ♿

➜ ▶ ⅄ 🗡 🔧

○○○○○○○○

DALRADDY HOLIDAY PARK ►►►

Aviemore, Inverness-shire

A beautiful country park set amongst birch trees and heather near the River Spey with spectacular views over the Cairngorms. Only three miles south of the Highland holiday centre of Aviemore. Tents, tourers, holiday statics. 7 Luxury Chalets available, 1 catering for the disabled. A well-stocked licensed shop, launderette, public telephone, showers, hair dryers, children's play area, electric hook-ups. Activities include clay pigeon shooting, river and loch fishing, horse riding and much more. Plenty of space.

For further information, brochure or bookings.

Phone Aviemore (01479) 810330

Very Good

Fax: (01540) 651380

Gorten Sands Caravan Site (NM640879)
Gorten Farm PH39 4NS ☎ 01687 450283
Signposted
Nearby town: Mallaig
►►► **Family Park** 🚲 £9 🚐 £7.50-£9 ⛺ £7.50-£9.50
Open Etr-Sep Booking advisable Jul-Aug Last arrival 23.00hrs Last departure 13.00hrs
A well-run site with mainly modern facilities. 2m NW of Arisaig on A830, turn left at sign "Back of Keppoch" and follow to end of road. A 6-acre site with 42 touring pitches and 3 statics.

Portnadoran Caravan Site (NM651892)
Bunacaimbe PH39 4NT ☎ 01687 450267 (2m N on A830) Signposted
Nearby town: Mallaig
►►► **Family Park** 🚲 £6-£8 🚐 £5-£8 ⛺ £5-£8
Open Apr-Oct Booking advisable Jul-Aug Last arrival 23.00hrs Last departure noon
Small, level, grassy site situated close to sandy beach overlooking the Islands of Eigg, Rhum and Skye. Very welcoming. Signed .25m off A380, 1.5m N of Arisaig. A 2-acre site with 55 touring pitches and 9 statics.

Dalraddy Holiday Park (NH859083)
PH22 1QB ☎ 01479 810330 (3.5m S on B9152) Signposted
►►► **Family Park** 🚲 🚐 ⛺
Open all year (rs Nov open 10am-4pm) Booking advisable Jul-Aug Last arrival 19.00hrs Last departure noon
A secluded site off the A9, 3.5m S of Aviemore, set amidst heather and young birch trees, with mountain views. A 25-acre site with 30 touring pitches and 94 statics.

Credit Cards

Glenmore Caravan & Camping Site (NH976097)
Glenmore PH22 1QU ☎ 01479 861271 & 0131 314 6505 (at town turn right onto B970) Signposted
►►► **Family Park** ★ 🚲 £7.70-£8.70 🚐 £7.70-£8.70 ⛺ £7.70-£8.70
Open Dec-Oct Booking advisable bank hols & Jul-Aug Last arrival 22.00hrs Last departure noon
An attractive Forestry Commission site with grassy areas, landscaped with mature trees, and close to the eastern end of Loch Morlich at the head of Glenmore. There are sandy beaches close by. Signed off B970 on Cairngorms rd. A 17-acre site with 220 touring pitches.

Credit Cards

Rothiemurchus Camping & Caravan Park (NH916108)
Coylumbridge PH22 1QU ☎ 01479 812800 (1.5m E on A951) Signposted
►►► **Family Park** ★ 🚲 £9-£12 🚐 £9-£12 ⛺ £6-£10
Open all year Booking advisable Jul-Aug Last arrival 22.00hrs Last departure 11.00hrs no cars by tents
A secluded site in tree-studded undulating ground off approach road to the Cairngorm Mountains. An attractive natural site offering good facilities. A 4-acre site with 39 touring pitches and 50 statics.

Credit Cards

Anderson Road Caravan Site (NO371955)
Anderson Rd AB3 5QW ☎ 013397 55727 (in season) & 01569 762001 Signposted

►►►► **De-Luxe Park** 🚲 🚐 ⛺
Open Apr-mid Oct Booking advisable anytime Last arrival 20.00hrs Last departure 10.00hrs
This well-equipped site is in a beautiful setting bordered by the River Dee with wooded hills behind. From A93 turn W into Victoria Rd, and left into Braiche Rd. Near town centre. A 5-acre site with 66 touring pitches and 93 statics.

BALMACARA

Reraig Caravan Site (NG815272)
IV40 8DH ☎ 01599 566215 (on A87) Signposted
Nearby town: Kyle

► ► ► ► De-Luxe Park ⚏ £7 ⚏ £7 ▲ £7
Open mid Apr-Sep Last arrival 22.00hrs Last departure
noon
*Set on level, grassy ground surrounded by trees, the
site looks south towards Loch Alsh and Skye. Very
nicely organised with a high standard of maintenance.
On A87 at rear of Balmacara Hotel. A 2-acre site with 45
touring pitches.*
Hard standings available & dish washing sinks.

🔌 🛒 ☉ 🍴 🍊

Credit Cards 💳 💳 💳

Balmacara Caravan & Camping Site (NG803279)
IV40 8DN ☎ 01599 566374 (in season) & 0131 314 6505
Signposted
Nearby town: Kyle of Lochalsh
►► Town & Country Pennant Park ★ ⚏ £4.20-£5.30
⚏ £4.20-£5.30 ▲ £4.20-£5.30
Open Etr-Sep Booking advisable Last arrival 22.00hrs
Last departure noon
*An attractive and sheltered Forestry Commission site
situated 3.5m E of Kyle of Lochalsh, off the A87
(signposted Balmacara Square). A 7-acre site with 60
touring pitches.*
Forest walks.

🔌 🛒 🍊 ☂
➔ ∪ ▶ ✚ 🍴

Credit Cards 💳 💳 🔲

BOAT OF GARTEN

Campgrounds of Scotland (NH939191)
PH24 3BN ☎ 01479 831652 Signposted
Nearby town: Aviemore
► ► ► Family Park ★ ⚏ £7.50-£11.50 ⚏ £7.50-£11.50
▲ £5.50-£9
Open all year Booking advisable 26 Dec-2 Jan & 25 Jul-
7 Aug Last arrival 22.00hrs Last departure 11.00hrs
*Level, grass site with young trees and bushes set in
mountainous woodland in the village itself, near the
River Spey and Loch Garten, off A95. A 3.5-acre site
with 37 touring pitches and 60 statics.*

🔌 🔦 ☉ 📗 🍴 ✳ ⚂ ❶ ⌀ ⊞ Ⓣ ✗ 🔧 🔋 ♿
➔ ▶ 🍴

BURGHEAD

Red Craig Hotel Caravan & Camping Park (NJ124689)
Mason Haugh IV30 2XX
☎ 01343 835663
Signposted
Nearby town: Elgin
► ► ► Family Park ⚏ ⚏ ▲
Open Apr-Oct Booking advisable Jul & Aug Last arrival
22.30hrs Last departure noon

*A slightly sloping site with level pitches, overlooking
the Moray Forth. On outskirts of Burghead at junc of
B9012 and B9040. A 3-acre site with 30 touring pitches
and 8 statics.*

🔌 🔦 ☉ 🍴 ✳ ⚏ ⚂ ❶ ⊞ ✗ 🔧 🔋 🍊
➔ ▶ 🍴 🔋

Credit Cards 💳 💳

CANNICH

Cannich Caravan and Camping Park (NH345317)
IV4 7LN ☎ 01456 415364 & 415263 Signposted
Nearby town: Inverness
► ► ► Family Park ★ ⚏ £5.50-£7.50 ⚏ £5.50-£7.50
▲ £3.50-£6.50
Open Mar-Nov Booking advisable Jul & Aug Last arrival
23.00hrs Last departure noon
*A well-run site with plenty of potential, situated on A831
200 yards SE of Cannich Bridge. A 12-acre site with 140
touring pitches and 9 statics.*
Mountain bike hire & fishing.

🔌 🔦 ☉ 📗 🍴 ⚏ 🍴 ✳ ⚂ ❶ ⌀ ⊞ Ⓣ 🔧 🔋 🍊 ♿
➔ ∪ ▶ 🔺 ✚ 🍴 🔋

CORPACH

Linnhe Caravan & Chalet Park (NN074771)
PH33 7NL ☎ 01397 772376 (on A830, 1m W of village,
5m from Fort William) Signposted
Nearby town: Fort William

► ► ► ► ► Premier Park ⚏ £10-£13 ⚏ £10-£13
▲ £7.50-£9   *contd.*

Caravan & Chalet Park

Corpach, Fort William, Highlands PH33 7NL
Tel: 01397-772376   Fax: 01397-772007

Enjoy one of the best and most beautiful lochside parks in
the Highlands. Magnificent scenery and beautiful views
from well-tended and peaceful surroundings. Hard standing
and electric hook-ups to all pitches. Well-stocked shop and
superb amenity block.
Fully equipped launderette and toddlers' playroom.
Playgrounds, private beach and free fishing.
Holiday caravans and luxury pine chalets for hire.
Pets accepted. Colour brochure sent with pleasure.

Open Etr-Oct (rs 15 Dec-Etr shop & main toilet block closed) Booking advisable school hols & peak periods Last arrival 21.00hrs Last departure 11.00hrs no cars by tents

An excellently maintained site in a beautiful setting. Situated 1m W of Corpach on A830 on shores of Loch Eil with Ben Nevis to E and mountains to Sunart to W. A 5.5-acre site with 73 touring pitches and 100 statics. Launching slipway, private beach, free fishing.

🔌 ⛽ ♠ ☉ 🗑 ⚲ ☼ ⟐ ⓘ ⟐ ⊡ Ⓣ 🔦 ⛲ 🏕 🐴 🛒
→ ∪ ▶ ♪

Credit Cards 💳 🔲 🔲 🔲 ⑤

CRAIGELLACHIE

Camping & Caravanning Club Site (NJ257449)
Elchies AB38 9LS ☎ 01340 810414 (in season) & 01203 694995 (travel N on A941, site 2.5m on left) Signposted
▶ ▶ ▶ **Family Park** ★ ⚘ £11-£14 ⚘ £11-£14 ▲ £11-£14
Open all year Booking advisable bank hols & Jul-Aug Last arrival 21.00hrs Last departure noon
A rural site with views across meadowland towards Speyside, and the usual high Club standards. From Craigellachie travel N on A941, turn left onto B9102 (signed Archiestown), and site is 2.5m on left. Please see the advertisement on page 27 for details of Club Members' benefits. A 10-acre site with 75 touring pitches.

🔌 ♠ ☉ 🗑 ⚲ ☼ ⟐ 🔦 🐴 ♿
→ ▶ ♪

Credit Cards 💳 🔲

CUMINESTOWN

East Balthangie Caravan Park (NJ841516)
East Balthangie AB53 5XY ☎ 01888 544261 & 544921
Nearby town: Turriff
▶➤ **Town & Country Pennant Park** ★ ⚘ £7.50-£8.50 ⚘ £7.50-£8.50 ▲ £6
Open Mar-Oct Booking advisable Jul & Aug Last arrival 22.00hrs Last departure noon
A small farm site with level pitches, sheltered by trees to N and with extensive views to the S. A remote rural setting. From N leave A98 to head S on A9027 to New Byth, then unclass rd signed New Deer to junc with farm rd in 2.25m. A 2-acre site with 12 touring pitches and 1 static.

🔌 ♠ ☉ 🗑 ⚲ ● ⟐ ☼ ⊡ 🔦 ⛲ 🏕 🐴 🛒
→ ∪ ▶ ✚ ♪

DAVIOT

Auchnahillin Caravan & Camping Centre (NH742386)
IV1 2XQ ☎ 01463 772282 (A9 to Daviot off onto B9154 1.5m) Signposted
Nearby town: Inverness
▶ ▶ ▶ **Family Park** ⚘ £7-£9 ⚘ £7-£9 ▲ £5.50-£8
Open Etr-Oct Booking advisable Jun-Aug Last arrival 22.00hrs Last departure noon
Level grassy site with clean and spacious facilities, surrounded by hills and forest. Situated 7m SE of Inverness on B9154 off A9; follow Daviot East signs. A 10-acre site with 65 touring pitches and 35 statics.

🔌 ♠ ☉ 🗑 ⚲ ☼ ⟐ ⓘ ⟐ ⊡ Ⓣ ✖ 🔦 🐴 🛒 ♿
→ ♪

DINGWALL

Camping & Caravanning Club Site (NH555588)
Jubilee Park IV15 9QZ ☎ 01349 862236 (in season) & 01203 694995 Signposted

▶ ▶ ▶ ▶ **De-Luxe Park** ★ ⚘ £11-£14 ⚘ £11-£14 ▲ £11-£14
Open end Mar-early Nov Booking advisable bank hols & Jul-Aug Last arrival 21.00hrs Last departure noon
An attractive site with well-equipped facilities and a high standard of maintenance, close to the town centre. Cross bridge at Dingwall rlwy stn then turn L past football ground. Please see the advertisement on page 27 for details of Club Members' benefits. A 10-acre site with 85 touring pitches.

🔌 ♠ ☉ 🗑 ⚲ ☼ ⓘ ⟐ ⊡ Ⓣ 🔦 🛒 ♿
→ ∪ ♪

Credit Cards 💳 🔲 🔲

DORNOCH

 Grannie's Heilan Hame Holiday Park (NH818924)
Embo IV25 3QD ☎ 01862 810383 & 810753 (A949 to Dornoch, turn left in square & follow signs for Embo)
Signposted
Nearby town: Inverness

★ ⚘ £7.50-£16 ⚘ £7.50-£16 ▲ £7.50-£16
Open all year Booking advisable Jun-Aug Last arrival 23.30hrs Last departure 14.00hrs
An ideal Highland touring centre set on the beach. Signed off unclass rd at Embo. A 60-acre site with 300 touring pitches and 121 statics. Spa bath, sauna, solarium & mini ten-pin bowling.

🔌 ♠ ☉ 🗑 ⚲ ⟐ ● ● ☼ ⟐ ⓘ ⟐ ⊡ Ⓣ ✖ 🔦
⛲ 🐴 🛒
→ ▶ ◎ ♪

Credit Cards 💳 🔲 🔲 🔲 🔲 ⑤

FOCHABERS

Burnside Caravan Site (NJ350580)
Keith Rd IV32 7PF ☎ 01343 820511 & 820362
Signposted
Nearby town: Elgin
▶ ▶ ▶ **Family Park** ★ ⚘ £8-£9.50 ⚘ £8-£9.50 ▲ £5.50-£9.50
Open Apr-Oct Booking advisable Jul-Aug Last departure noon
Attractive site in tree-lined sheltered valley with footpath to the village. .5m E of town off the A96. A 5-acre site with 110 touring pitches and 60 statics.

🔌 ♠ ☉ ⚲ ● ⟐ ⟐ 🔦 🐴 🛒
→ ∪ ▶ ♪

FORDOUN

Brownmuir Caravan Park (NO740772)
AB30 1SL ☎ 01561 320786
Nearby town: Stonehaven
▶▶ Town & Country Pennant Park ★ 🚐 £6 🚐 £6
Open Apr-Oct Booking advisable Last departure noon
*A mainly static site set in a rural location with level
pitches and good touring facilities. From N on A90 take
B966 signed Fettercain, and site on left in 1.5m. From S
take unclass rd signed Fordoun. A 2-acre site with 15
touring pitches and 45 statics.*

🔲📞☉🔲☀/Ⓜ🅰️📞🏠🌲
➡️▶️🎣🍴

FORT WILLIAM

**Glen Nevis Caravan & Camping Park
(NN124722)**
Glen Nevis PH33 6SX
☎ 01397 702191 & 705181
Signposted

▶▶▶▶▶ Premier Park ★ 🚐 £7.50-£10.80
🚐 £7.20-£10.50 🅰️ £7.20-£10.50
Open 15 Mar-Oct (rs Mar & mid-end Oct limited shop &
restaurant facilities) Booking advisable Jul-Aug Last
arrival 22.00hrs Last departure noon
*A tasteful site with well-screened enclosures, at the foot
of Ben Nevis, in the midst of some of the Highlands'
most spectacular scenery. 2m off A82 on Glen Nevis rd.
A 30-acre site with 380 touring pitches and 30 statics.*

This award-winning
environmental park –
1998 Best Park in
Scotland and David
Bellamy Gold
Conservation Award –
situated at the foot of Ben Nevis, Britain's
highest mountain, offers modern, clean and
well equipped facilities, including Motor
Caravan Service Point. Many pitches are fully
serviced with electricity, water and drainage.
Showers, laundry, scullery, gas, licensed shop
and play areas are all on par with our own
spacious restaurant and lounge only a few
minutes walk. Colour brochure available.

AA
▶▶▶▶
Brochure from:
Glen Nevis Caravan
and Camping Park, Glen Nevis,
Fort William, Inverness-shire PH33 6SX.
Telephone: (01397) 702191
holidays@glen-nevis.demon.co.uk
http//www.lochaber.co.uk/glenevis/

Licensed club/bar adjacent to site.

🔲📞☉🔲🎣☀/Ⓜ🅰️🖊️🔲Ⓣ✖️📞🏠🌲🐕🐾
🐾👦
➡️▶️🍴🎣

Credit Cards 💳 💳 💳 🅾️

GAIRLOCH

Gairloch Caravan & Camping Park (NG798773)
Strath IV21 2BT ☎ 01505 614343 & 01445 712373
Signposted
▶▶▶ Family Park ★ 🚐 £8 🚐 £8 🅰️ £7
Open Apr-15 Oct Booking advisable bank hols & Jul-
Aug Last arrival 21.30hrs Last departure noon
*A clean, well-maintained site on flat coastal grassland
close to Loch Gairloch, signed off A832. A 6-acre site
with 70 touring pitches and 3 statics.*
Adjacent cafe, restaurant, activity centre & bar.

🔲📞☉🔲🎣📞📺☀️🍴📞🐾
➡️▶️🍴🎣

Sands Holiday Centre (NG758784)
IV21 2DL ☎ 01445 712152 (take B8021 to Melvaig for
4m) Signposted
▶▶▶ Family Park ★ 🚐 £8-£9 🚐 £8-£8.50 🅰️ £8-£8.50
Open 20 May-10 Sep (rs Apr-19 May & 11 Sep-mid Oct
no shop or laundry some toilets closed) Booking
advisable Jul-Aug Last arrival 22.00hrs Last departure
noon
*Part-level site close to sandy beach with a panoramic
outlook towards Skye. 3m W of Gairloch on B8021. A
51-acre site with 360 touring pitches and 20 statics.*
Boat slipway.

🔲📞☉🔲🎣☀/Ⓜ🅰️🖊️🔲Ⓣ📞🏠🌲🐕🐾
➡️🎣

Credit Cards 💳 💳 🅾️

GLENCOE

Invercoe Caravan Site (NN098594)
PA39 4HP ☎ 01855 811210 Signposted
Nearby town: Fort William

▶▶▶▶ De-Luxe Park 🚐 £9-£12 🚐 £9-£12 🅰️ £8-£10
Open Etr-mid Oct Booking advisable Jul-Aug for electric
hook ups Last departure noon
*Level, grass site set on the shore of Loch Lever with
excellent mountain views. Located on the Kinlochleven
road on the edge of Glencoe village, signed .25m N of
A82 on B863.. A 5-acre site with 60 touring pitches and
5 statics.*

🔲📞☉🔲🎣☀/Ⓜ🅰️🖊️🔲Ⓣ📞🐾👦👦
➡️🍴🎣

Glencoe Campsite (NN111578)
Carnoch PA39 4LA ☎ 01855 811397 & 811278 (out of
season) (1m E on A82) Signposted
Nearby town: Fort William
▶▶▶ Family Park 🚐 🚐 🅰️

contd.

Open Etr/Apr-Oct Booking advisable Jul-Aug Last arrival 22.00hrs Last departure 17.00hrs
Part-level, part-sloping, grass, gravel and sand site with young trees and bushes in mountainous woodland. Direct access to river and main A82 road. A 40-acre site with 150 touring pitches.

🔊📻☉🗄🍴✳🛈🔧🚰⛱🐕🛒♿
➜🛆⤴🍴

GRANTOWN-ON-SPEY

Grantown on Spey Caravan Park (NJ028283)
Seafield Av PH26 3JQ ☎ 01479 872474 (from town turn N at Bank of Scotland Park, straight ahead from .25m) Signposted
Nearby town: Aviemore

▶▶▶▶ **De-Luxe Park** ★ 🚐 £7-£9.25 🚐 £7-£9.25 🔺 £6-£6.75
Open Etr-Sep Booking advisable Etr, May day, Whitsun & Jul-Aug Last arrival 22.00hrs
Attractive site with mature trees and bushes near river, and set amidst hills, mountains, moors and woodland. Good standards and personal attention. Signed .5m off main street in town. A 15-acre site with 100 touring pitches and 45 statics.
Picnic tables, football pitch. Free dishwashing.

🔊📻☉🗄🍴🔍✳🛗🛈🔧🎛️🆃🔧🐕
➜ ∪ 🍴 ⤴ 🛒
Credit Cards 💳💳💳💳💳

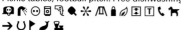

INVERGARRY

Faichemard Farm (NH288016)
PH35 4HG ☎ 01809 501314 Signposted
Nearby town: Fort William
▶▶▶ **Family Park** 🚐 £6 🚐 £6 🔺 £6
Open Apr-Oct Booking advisable Last arrival 22.00hrs Last departure 11.30hrs
Attractive park with clean, well-maintained facilities and spacious pitches. Situated 1m W of Invergarry off A87. A 10-acre site with 40 touring pitches.

🔊📻☉🗄✳🎛️🔧⛱🐕
➜🛆⤴🍴🛒

Faichem Park (NH285023)
Ardgarry Farm, Faichem PH35 4HG ☎ 01809 501226 Signposted
Nearby town: Fort Augustus
▶▶▶ **Family Park** ★ 🚐 £6.50-£7 🚐 £6.50-£7 🔺 £6.50-£7
Open 15 Mar-15 Oct Booking advisable Jul-Aug Last arrival 22.00hrs Last departure noon
Small, quiet touring site with good, clean facilities and panoramic views. Meticulously maintained. The site is located just off the A87 about 1m W of Invergarry, signed Faichem. A 2-acre site with 30 touring pitches.

🔊📻☉🔍✳🛈🔧🎛️🔧
➜🛆⤴🍴🛒

JOHN O'GROATS

John O'Groats Caravan Site (ND382733)
KW1 4YS ☎ 01955 611329 (at end of A99) Signposted
Nearby town: Wick
▶▶▶ **Family Park** ★ 🚐 £7-£8 🚐 £7-£8 🔺 £4-£6
Open Apr-Oct Booking advisable Last arrival 22.00hrs Last departure noon
Good clean and attractive site in open position above the seashore and looking out towards the Orkney Islands, at the end of A9. Passenger ferry nearby. A 4-acre site with 90 touring pitches.

🔊📻☉🗄🍴✳🛈🔧🎛️🔧🛒♿
➜🍴

KINTORE

Hillhead Caravan Park (NJ777163)
AB51 0YX ☎ 01467 632809 Signposted
Nearby town: Inverurie
▶▶▶ **Family Park** 🚐 £6.10-£7.70 🚐 £6.10-£7.70 🔺 £6.10-£7.70
Open 26 Mar-Oct Booking advisable at all times Last arrival 22.00hrs Last departure 13.00hrs
An attractive, peaceful site in the R Don Valley, about 1m from the village and A96. Follow B994 (signed Kemnay), turn right in 0.5m onto unclass rd (signed Kintore). A 1.5-acre site with 24 touring pitches and 5 statics.
Caravan repair service & caravan storage, shop.

🔊📻☉🗄✳🛗🛈🔧🎛️🆃🔧🐕🛒♿
➜🍴☕⤴
Credit Cards 💳💳💳

LAIDE

Gruinard Bay Caravan Park (NG903918)
Laide IV22 2ND ☎ 01445 731225 (from A835 Signposted
Nearby town: Aultbea
▶▶▶ **Family Park** 🚐 £8.50 🚐 £8.50 🔺 £8.50
Open Apr-Oct Booking advisable Jul-Aug Last arrival 22.00hrs Last departure 11.00hrs

Campers receive a warm welcome at this spotless, lovingly managed site on the outskirts of Laide. On A832, 300yds N of village. A 3.25-acre site with 43 touring pitches and 14 statics.
Dishwashing sinks/free hot water. Laundry service.

🔊📻☉🗄✳🛈🔧🎛️🆃🐕🛒
➜🛆🍴

LAIRG

Dunroamin Caravan Park (NC585062)
Main St IV27 4AR ☎ 01549 402447
Signposted
▶ ▶ ▶ Family Park ★ ⊞ £5-£8 ⊞ £5-£8 Å £5-£7
Open Apr-Oct Booking advisable anytime Last arrival
23.00hrs Last departure noon
*A small, attractive and well laid out site on A839 in
village. A 10-acre site with 50 touring pitches and 10
statics.*

🅟 👣 ⊙ 🖥 🗑 ✳ 🍴 ⊘ 🔲 🆃 ✗ ℃ 🚗 🏧 🐾
➜ 🛆 ⅄ 🕭

Credit Cards 💳 ▦

Woodend Caravan & Camping Site (NC551127)
Achnairn IV27 4DN ☎ 01549 402248 (A836 turn left onto
A838 then 1st right signposted) Signposted
▶ ▶ ▶ Family Park ⊞ £6.50-£7.50 ⊞ £6.50-£7.50
Å £6-£7
Open Apr-Sep Booking advisable Last arrival 23.00hrs
*A clean, fresh site set in hilly moors and woodland with
access to sea, beach, river and Loch Shin. 4m N of Lairg
off A838, signed at Achnairn. A 4-acre site with 60
touring pitches and 5 statics.*

🅟 👣 ⊙ 🖥 🗑 ✳ 🕭 🍴 ⊘ 🔲 ℃ 🐾
➜ ⅄ 🕭

LOCHALINE

Fiunary Camping & Caravanning Park (NM614467)
Morvern PA34 5XX
☎ 01967 421225 (A884 to Lochaline, turn right onto
B849 at top of village. Site on left (4.5m at Fiunary)
Signposted
Nearby town: Fort William
▶ ▶ ▶ Family Park ★ ⊞ £5.50-£7 ⊞ £5.50-£7
Å £5.50-£7
Open May-Oct (rs Apr hot water & showers not
available) Booking advisable Last arrival 22.00hrs
Last departure noon
*A small, carefully maintained site with beautiful
lochside views, quiet and secluded and in an area of
great interest to naturalists. Signed 5m W of Lochaline
and ferry on Loch Shore at Fiunary. A 3.5-acre site with
25 touring pitches and 2 statics.*

🅟 👣 ⊙ ✳ 🔲 ℃ 🏧 🏟 🐾
➜ ⅄ 🕭 🖥 🐾

LOSSIEMOUTH

Silver Sands Leisure Park (NJ205710)
Covesea, West Beach IV31 6SP
☎ 01343 813262 (2m W B9040)
Signposted

◯◯◯◯◯◯◯◯

▶ ▶ ▶ ▶ De-Luxe Park ★ ⊞ £7.55-£11.20
⊞ £7.55-£11.20 Å £7.55-£11.20
Open Jun-Sep (rs Apr, May & Oct shops &
entertainment restricted) Booking advisable Jul-Aug
Last arrival 23.00hrs Last departure noon
*A holiday park with entertainment for all during the
peak season. From Lossiemouth follow B9040 to site.
A 7-acre site with 140 touring pitches and 180 statics.*

DUNROAMIN CARAVAN PARK
*A warm Highland
welcome awaits you*

Lew Hudson, his wife Margaret and their family welcome you
to Dunroamin Caravan Park. A small family run park situated in
the picturesque village of Lairg by Loch Shin. Lairg is the ideal
base for touring the whole of Sutherland and Caithness.
Pony trekking, fishing, walking and water sports all nearby with
golf just 10 miles away. Outstandingly well maintained grounds
with Crofters licensed restaurant on site. Launderette with full
facilities. 200 yards from pub, bank, shops, post office etc.
Holiday Caravans for Hire. Tourers and Tents welcome.
Electric hook-ups available.
**Main Street, Lairg, Sutherland IV27 4AR
Tel: 01549 402447**

| Scottish Tourist Board Listed | | |

Childrens entertainment.

🅟 🚗 👣 ⊙ 🖥 🗑 🔍 ❦ 🔲 ✳ 🍴 🕭 🍴 ⊘ 🔲 🆃 ✗
℃ 🏧 🏟 🍴 🐾 🐾
➜ ∪ ⌐ ⊙ 🛆 ⅄ 🕭
Credit Cards 💳 ▦

◯◯◯◯◯◯◯

MACDUFF

Wester Bonnyton Farm Site (NJ741638)
Gamrie AB45 3EP ☎ 01261 832470
▶▶ Town & Country Pennant Park ⊞ ⊞ Å
Open Mar-Oct Booking advisable
*A farm site in a screened meadow, with level touring
pitches enjoying views across Moray Firth. From A98
1m S of Macduff join B9031, signed Rosehearty, and
site on right in 1.25m. A 1-acre site with 10 touring
pitches and 18 statics.*

👣 ⊙ 🖥 🕭 ℃

NAIRN

 Nairn Lochloy Holiday Park (NH895574)
East Beach IV12 4PH ☎ 01667 453764
Signposted

✿✿✿✿✿✿✿✿✿✿✿✿

★ ⊞ £9-£15 ⊞ £9-£15 Å £7-£13
Open Mar-Oct Booking advisable Jun-Aug Last arrival
22.00hrs Last departure 14.00hrs
*A level site bordered by the beach, the River Nairn and
golf course. Signed off A96 in Nairn close to town
centre. A 15-acre site with 45 touring pitches and 230
statics.* contd.

Discount on adjacent golf course.

🕿 📞 ☉ 🏕 ⛏ 🍴 🛒 ⚡ ✕ 🍽 🛆 🏠 🚽 🅃 ✕ ⚓ ⛲ ♨ 🏊

→ ∪ ↑ ◎ △ ↳ ✦

Credit Cards 💳 ▬ ▬ ▬ ▬ 🅂

◎◎◎◎◎◎◎◎◎◎◎◎◎◎◎◎◎◎

Spindrift Caravan & Camping Site (NH863537)
Little Kildrummie IV12 5QU ☎ 01667 453992 (take B9090 S for 1.5m, turn right at sharp left hand bend signposted Little Kildrummie, site 400yds on left)

◯◯◯◯◯◯◯◯

▶▶▶▶ De-Luxe Park ★ 🚐 £5.50-£8.50 🚗 £5.50-£8.50 ▲ £5.50-£7.50
Open Apr-Oct Booking advisable Jul-Aug Last arrival 22.00hrs Last departure noon
An informal site in attractive setting with good facilities and first class maintenance. Signed off B9090, 2m S of Nairn. A 3-acre site with 40 touring pitches.
Fishing permits available from reception.

🕿 📞 ☉ 🏕 ⛏ ✳ 🍴 ⚡ 🛆 🍽 ⚓ 🏊

→ ∪ ↑ ◎ △ ↳ ✦

◯◯◯◯◯◯◯◯

Delnies Woods Caravan Park (NH852552)
Delnies Wood IV12 5NX ☎ 01667 455281 (2m W on A96)
Signposted
▶▶▶ Family Park ★ 🚐 £7.50-£9.50 🚗 £7.50-£9.50 ▲ £7.50-£9.50
Open Etr-Oct Booking advisable end Jun-early Aug Last arrival 22.00hrs Last departure noon
An attractive site amongst pine trees. Situated about 3m W of Nairn on the A96. A 7-acre site with 50 touring pitches and 16 statics.

🕿 📞 ☉ 🏕 🍴 ✳ 🛆 🍴 ⚡ 🛒 🏠 🅃 ⚓ ⛲ 🏠 🏊

→ ∪ ↑ ✦

Credit Cards 💳 ▬

NORTH WATER BRIDGE
Dovecot Caravan Park (NO648663)
AB30 1QL ☎ 01674 840630 Signposted
▶▶▶ Family Park 🚐 £7-£8 🚗 £7-£8 ▲ £7-£8
Open Apr-Oct Booking advisable Jul & Aug for hook up Last arrival 20.00hrs Last departure noon
A level grassy site in a country area close to the A90, with mature trees screening one side and the R North Esk on the other. A handy overnight stop in a good touring area. Leave A90 at North Water Bridge on unclassified road signed Edzell/RAF Edzell, and site on left in 0.25m. A 6-acre site with 25 touring pitches and 44 statics.

🕿 📞 ☉ ⛏ 🍴 🖵 ✳ 🍴 🛆 🅃 ⚓ 🏠 🏊 ♿

POOLEWE
Camping & Caravanning Club Site (NG862812)
Inverewe Gardens IV22 2LF ☎ 01445 781249 (in season) & 01203 694995 (on A832, .25m N) Signposted
▶▶▶ Family Park ★ 🚐 £11-£14 🚗 £11-£14 ▲ £11-£14
Open end Mar-early Nov Booking advisable bank hols & Jul-Aug Last arrival 21.00hrs Last departure noon
A well-run site located in Loch Ewe Bay, not far from

Inverewe Gardens. On A832, .25m N of Poolewe village. Please see the advertisement on page 27 for details of Club Members' benefits. A 3.5-acre site with 55 touring pitches.

🕿 📞 ⛏ ✳ 🍴 🛆 🐕 ⚓

→ ✦

Credit Cards 💳 ▬

RESIPOLE (LOCH SUNART)
Resipole Farm (NM725639)
PH36 4HX ☎ 01967 431235
Signposted
Nearby town: Ardnamurchan

◯◯◯◯◯◯◯◯

▶▶▶▶ De-Luxe Park ★ 🚐 £8.50-£9.50 🚗 £8.50-£9.50 ▲ £8.50-£9.50
Open Apr-Sep (rs Oct shop closed) Booking advisable bank hols Last arrival 22.00hrs Last departure 11.00hrs
A well-managed site in beautiful surroundings, with deer frequently sighted. On A861 5m W of Strontian and 2m E of Salen. An 8-acre site with 45 touring pitches and 15 statics.
Private slipway, 9 hole golf.

🕿 📞 ☉ 🏕 ⛏ 🍴 ✳ 🍴 🛆 🍴 ⚡ 🛒 🅃 ✕ ⚓ 🐕 🏊 ♿

→ ↳ ✦

Credit Cards 💳 ▬

◯◯◯◯◯◯◯◯

ROSEMARKIE
Camping & Caravanning Club Site (NH739569)
IV10 8UW ☎ 01381 621117 (in season) & 01203 694995
Signposted
Nearby town: Fortrose
▶▶ Town & Country Pennant Park ★ 🚐 £9.20-£11.60 🚗 £9.20-£11.60 ▲ £9.20-£11.60
Open end Mar-Sep Booking advisable bank hols & Jul-Aug Last arrival 21.00hrs Last departure noon
A very clean and well-maintained site. At Rosemarkie turn right onto Promenade, and site is in 100 yards, or turn right at Fortrose police station and follow signs. Please see the advertisement on page 27 for details of Club Members' benefits. A 5-acre site with 60 touring pitches.

📞 ☉ 🏕 ✳ 🐕 ♿

→ ↳ ✦ 🏊

Credit Cards 💳 ▬

ST CYRUS
East Bowstrips Caravan Park (NO745654)
DD10 0DE ☎ 01674 850328
Signposted
Nearby town: Montrose

◯◯◯◯◯◯◯◯

▶▶▶▶ De-Luxe Park ★ 🚐 £6.50-£7.50 🚗 £6.50-£7.50 ▲ £5-£7.50
Open Etr or Apr-Oct Booking advisable Jun-Aug Last arrival 22.00hrs Last departure noon
A quiet, rural site close to seaside village, with thoughtfully modernised facilities and a particular welcome for the disabled. From A92 travelling N turn left after post office and hotel, follow unclass road, then

take first L and second R. A 2-acre site with 30 touring pitches and 18 statics.

🔌 🛱 ☉ 🗑 ╲ ✳ 🏔 🛈 🔲 🔦 ☎ 🔦 🐾 🛒 ♿

→ ♪

◎◎◎◎◎◎◎◎◎◎

SCANIPORT

Scaniport Caravan & Camping Park (NH628398)
IV1 2DL ☎ 01463 751351
Nearby town: Inverness
▶▶ Town & Country Pennant Park 🏠 🏠 Å
Open Etr-Sep Last arrival 23.45hrs Last departure 20.00hrs
A simple, pleasant site with some trees, set in hills, woods and moorland near canal. On B862 Inverness-Foyers road about 5m S of Inverness. Entrance to site is opposite shop at Scaniport. A 2-acre site with 30 touring pitches.
Dish washing sinks.

🔦 ☉ ✳ 🛈 ⊘ 🔦 🐾

SCOURIE

Scourie Caravan & Camping Park (NC153446)
Harbour Rd IV27 4TG
☎ 01971 502060 & 502061
Signposted
▶▶▶ Family Park ★ 🏠 £8 🏠 £8 Å £8
Open Etr-Sep Last arrival 22.00hrs Last departure noon
An attractive and well-equipped site adjacent to beach and sea in centre of village off the Ullapool-Durness road A894. A 4-acre site with 60 touring pitches.

🔌 🛱 ☉ 🗑 ╲ ✳ ⚲ 🔲 ✕ 🔦 🧺 🐾 ♿

→ ✚ ♪

SKYE, ISLE OF

EDINBANE

Loch Greshornish Caravan Site (NG343524)
Borve, Arnisort IV51 9PS ☎ 01470 582230
Signposted
Nearby town: Portree
▶▶▶ Family Park 🏠 🏠 Å
Open Apr-Oct Booking advisable Jul-Aug Last arrival 22.00hrs Last departure noon
A pleasant, open site, mostly level and with a high standard of maintenance. Situated by the loch-shore at Edinbane, approx 12m from Portree on the A850 Dunvegan road. A 5-acre site with 130 touring pitches.

🔌 🛱 ☉ ╲ ✳ ⊘ 🔲

→ ♪

STONEHAVEN

Queen Elizabeth Caravan Site (NO875866)
AB39 2NH ☎ 01569 764041(in season) & 762001
Signposted
▶▶▶ Family Park 🏠 🏠
Open Apr-mid Oct Booking advisable anytime Last arrival 20.00hrs Last departure 10.00hrs
A gently sloping grass site offering a good range of recreational facilities, situated between a main road and seafront adjoining a public park. Leave A90 N of Stonehaven at junc with B979. Site on left after joining A957 at N end of Stonehaven. A 4.5-acre site with 35 touring pitches and 76 statics.

Site adjacent to Leisure Centre & outdoor pool.

🔌 🛱 ☉ 🗑 ╲ 🛈 ⊘ 🔲 🔲

→ ∪ 🏃 ✚ ♪ 🐾

TAIN

Meikle Ferry Caravan & Camping Park (NH748844)
IV19 1JX ☎ 01862 892292 2 miles north of Tain on A9.
At roundabout take A836. In 200 yds turn right for park.
Signposted
▶▶▶ Family Park 🏠 £6-£7 🏠 £6-£7 Å £4.50-£5
Open all year Booking advisable Jul-Aug Last arrival 22.00hrs Last departure noon
A pleasant family site with meticulously maintained facilities, on A9 N of Tain, at S end of Dornoch Firth Bridge. A 2-acre site with 30 touring pitches and 15 statics.
Restaurant adjacent to site.

🔌 🛱 ☉ 🗑 ╲ ✳ 🏔 🔲 🔦

→ ∪ 🏃 ♪ 🐾

TARLAND

Camping & Caravanning Club Site (NJ477044)
Drummie Hill AB34 4UP
☎ 01339 881388
Signposted
Nearby town: Aboyne
▶▶▶ Family Park ★ 🏠 £9.20-£11.60 🏠 £9.20-£11.60 Å £9.20-£11.60
Open early Apr-early Nov Booking advisable Jul-Aug
Last arrival 23.00hrs Last departure noon   *contd.*

Broomfield ▶
Holiday Park

Ullapool, Ross & Cromarty
Telephone: (01854) 612020 & 612664

This is the only caravan and camping park in Ullapool

Situated on the sea front at the West End of Ullapool and extends to some 12 acres of level grass overlooking the Summer Isles, famous for marvellous sunsets. The site has 2 large toilet blocks with flush toilets and hot & cold wash basins, shaving points, hairdryers and hand dryers, hot & cold showers, coin operated, and coin operated washing machines and tumble dryers. Power hook-ups. Children's playground. Within 5 minutes walk from the park entrance are super-markets, bars, restaurants, cafes, bus stops, post office, telephone and boat hire. Also 9-hole golf course, tennis courts, leisure centre and covered swimming pool.

A level, sheltered site screened by mature trees. Enter Tarland on B9119, bear left before bridge and continue for 600yds. Site is on left. A 4-acre site with 40 touring pitches.

🔲 🐾 ☉ ⓥ ✦ ☀ 🏔 🛈 ⌀ 🚻 🔊 🎐 🐾
➔ ∪ ▶ ⚓

Credit Cards 💳 ▭

THURSO

Thurso Caravan & Camping Site (ND111688)
Smith Ter, Scrabster Rd KW14 7JY
☎ 01847 894631 & 01955 607776 Signposted
▶▶ **Town & Country Pennant Park** 🚐 fr £6.25 🚙 fr £6.25
🛆 £4.50-£6.50
Open May-Sep Booking advisable 14 days in advance
Last arrival 22.00hrs Last departure noon
Exposed grassy site, set high above the coast on the W side of town with panoramic views out to sea. Signed on A882 on W edge of Thurso. A 4.5-acre site with 117 touring pitches and 10 statics.

🔲 🐾 ☉ ⓥ ▭ 🏔 ✗ 🔊 👜 🐕 🐾 ♿
➔ ▶ 🛆 ⚓ ⚓

ULLAPOOL

Broomfield Holiday Park (NH123939)
West Shore St IV26 2UR ☎ 01854 612020 & 612664
Signposted
Nearby town: Inverness
▶▶▶ **Family Park** ★ 🚐 £10 🚙 £9 🛆 £8
Open Apr-Oct Last departure noon
A level grass site by the shore of Loch Broom close to the harbour and town centre. A 10-acre site with 140 touring pitches.

🔲 🐾 ☉ ⓥ 🛐 🏔 🛒 🎐 🐾 ♿
➔ ∪ ▶ ☺ ⚓ ⚓

CENTRAL SCOTLAND

This region includes the counties of Angus, Argyll & Bute, City of Edinburgh, Clackmannanshire, Dundee City, East Lothian, Falkirk, Fife, Inverclyde, Midlothian, Perthshire & Kinross, Stirling and West Lothian.

ABERFELDY

Aberfeldy Caravan Park (NN858495)
Dunkeld Rd PH15 2AQ ☎ 01887 820662 & 475211
▶▶▶ **Family Park** ★ 🚐 £7.90-£8.90 🚙 £7.90-£8.90
🛆 £7.60-£8.90
Open late Mar-late Oct Booking advisable Jul-mid Sep
Last arrival 20.00hrs Last departure noon   .
A very well-run and well-maintained site, with good facilities and some landscaping, at the eastern end of the town and lying between main road and banks of the River Tay. Good views from site of surrounding hills. Off A827 on E edge of town. A 4-acre site with 92 touring pitches and 40 statics.

🔲 🐾 ☉ ⓥ 🛐 🏔 🔊 🛒 🎐 🐕 🐾
➔ ▶ 🛆 ⚓
Credit Cards 💳 ▭ 🔳 🔊

ABERFOYLE

Trossachs Holiday Park (NS544976)
FK8 3SA ☎ 01877 382614 (access on E side of A81 1m S of junc A821) Signposted
Nearby town: Stirling

◯◯◯◯◯◯◯◯

▶ ▶ ▶ ▶ **Premier Park** 🚐 🚙 🛆
Open Mar-Oct Booking advisable anytime Last arrival 21.00hrs Last departure noon
An imaginatively designed terraced site offering a high degree of quality all round, with fine views across Flanders Moss. Sited off A81, 3m S of Aberfoyle. A 40-acre site with 45 touring pitches and 38 statics.
Cycle hire.

🔲 🐾 ☉ ⓥ 🛐 ✦ ☀ 🏔 🛈 🎐 🚻 🅣 🔊 🐕 🐾
➔ ▶ 🛆 ⚓
Credit Cards 💳 ▭ 🔳 🔊

◯◯◯◯◯◯◯◯

Cobleland Caravan & Camping Site (NS531988)
FK8 3UX ☎ 01877 382392 (in season) & 0131 314 6505
(access on E side of A81 1m S of junc A821) Signposted
▶ ▶ **Family Park** ★ 🚐 £7.50-£8.40 🚙 £7.50-£8.40
🛆 £7.50-£8.40
Open Etr-29 Oct Booking advisable bank hols & Jul-Aug
Last arrival 20.00hrs Last departure noon
Set within the Queen Elizabeth Forest Park, this grass and tree-studded site offers seclusion, views, forest walks and free fishing on the River Forth which borders the camping area. Signed on unclass road off A81 approx 1.5 miles S of Aberfoyle. An 8-acre site with 100 touring pitches.

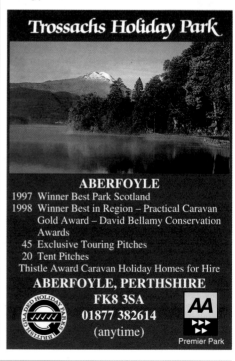

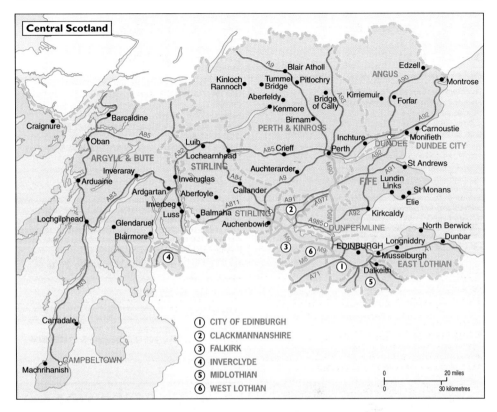

Central Scotland

- Blair Atholl
- Edzell
- ANGUS
- Kinloch Rannoch
- Tummel Bridge
- Pitlochry
- Montrose
- Aberfeldy
- Kirriemuir
- Forfar
- Kenmore
- Bridge of Cally
- Craignure
- Barcaldine
- Birnam
- Carnoustie
- PERTH & KINROSS
- Oban
- Luib
- Crieff
- Inchture
- Monifieth
- DUNDEE
- DUNDEE CITY
- ARGYLL & BUTE
- Lochearnhead
- Perth
- St Andrews
- STIRLING
- Inveraray
- Auchterarder
- FIFE
- Lundin Links
- Arduaine
- Inveruglas
- St Monans
- Ardgartan
- Aberfoyle
- Callander
- Elie
- Inverbeg
- Kirkcaldy
- Lochgilphead
- Luss
- Balmaha STIRLING
- Glendaruel
- Auchenbowie
- DUNFERMLINE
- North Berwick
- Blairmore
- Longniddry
- Dunbar
- EDINBURGH
- Musselburgh
- EAST LOTHIAN
- Dalkeith
- Carradale
- ① CITY OF EDINBURGH
- ② CLACKMANNANSHIRE
- ③ FALKIRK
- Machrihanish
- CAMPBELTOWN
- ④ INVERCLYDE
- ⑤ MIDLOTHIAN
- ⑥ WEST LOTHIAN

0   20 miles
0   30 kilometres

Fishing & swimming in river.

🔌📻☉🍳✳🏕🖊🔲🆃🔌🚐🛒🎪🏇⛺♿
➜∪►↳🎣

Credit Cards 💳 💳 💳 💳 🅖

ARDGARTAN

Ardgartan Caravan & Camping Site (NN275030)
G83 7AL ☎ 01301 702293 (in season)
0131 314 6505 Signposted
Nearby town: Helensburgh
► ► ► **Family Park** ★ 🚐 £5.80-£7 🚐 £5.80-£7
⛺ £5.80-£7
Open Etr-Oct Booking advisable public hols & Jul-Aug
Last arrival 22.30hrs Last departure noon
*Situated on a small promontory alongside Loch Long
with access to shingle beach; a grassy Forestry
Commission site on two levels. Direct access from A83
beside Loch Long at Ardgartan before road turns to
climb. A 17-acre site with 160 touring pitches.*
Slip-way for launching small boats.

🔌📻☉🍳🏕🖊🛒🎪🏇⛺♿
➜∪↳🎣

Credit Cards 💳 💳 💳 💳 🅖

See advertisement on page 240.

ARDUAINE

Arduaine Caravan & Camping Park (NM800101)
PA34 4XA ☎ 01852 200331 Signposted
Nearby town: Kilmelford
► **Town & Country Pennant Park** 🚐 🚐 ⛺
Open Mar-Oct Booking advisable Spring bank hol & Jul-
Aug Last arrival 22.00hrs Last departure noon
*Gently sloping grass site pleasantly situated by the
seashore beside a small jetty with views of Shuna,
Scarba, Jura and Luing. Access is from the A816. A 5-
acre site with 40 touring pitches.*
Free dinghy launching into sea.

🔌📻☉🍳✳🔲🔌
➜∪🔺↳🎣🖼🛒

AUCHENBOWIE

Auchenbowie Caravan & Camping Site (NS795880)
FK7 8HE ☎ 01324 822141
Nearby town: Stirling
► ► ► **Family Park** 🚐 🚐 ⛺
Open Apr-Oct Booking advisable mid Jul-mid Aug Last
departure noon
*A mainly level, grassy site in quiet rural location .5m S
of junction 9 of M9. Turn right off A872 for half a mile,
signposted. A 3.5-acre site with 60 touring pitches and 7
statics.*

contd.

Paddling pool.

🔣🔣☺🔣🔣🔣🔣🔣🔣🔣🔣
➔🔣🔣🔣🔣🔣🔣🔣

Credit Cards 💳 🔲

AUCHTERARDER

Auchterarder Caravan Park (NN964138)
Nether Coul PH3 1ET ☎ 01764 663119 (1m E off B8062)
Signposted
Nearby town: Perth
▶▶▶ Family Park 🏕 🏕 Å
Open all year Booking advisable Jul-Aug Last arrival
22.00hrs Last departure noon
*A small, level touring site, well-run and well-
maintained. From N turn right off A9 on A823 to
Auchterarder, after 2 miles turn left onto B8062 signed
Dunning. Turn left after 100m into site. A 4-acre site
with 23 touring pitches.*
Private fishing.

🔣🔣☺🔣🔣🔣🔣🔣🔣🔣🔣🔣🔣🔣🔣🔣🔣
➔🔣🔣🔣

BALMAHA

Camping & Caravnning Club Site (NN407927)
Milarrochy Bay G63 0AL ☎ 01360 870236 Signposted
▶▶▶ Family Park ★ 🏕 £11-£14 🏕 £11-£14 Å £11-£14
Open mid Mar-beg Nov Booking advisable Last arrival
21.00hrs Last departure noon
*Situated on the quieter side of Loch Lomond next to the
75,000 acre Queen Elizabeth Forest. Leave A811 at S
end of loch by the B837 to Balmaha, through village for
1.5m. A 14-acre site with 150 touring pitches.*

Boat launching & fishing.

🔣🔣☺🔣🔣🔣🔣🔣🔣🔣🔣🔣🔣
➔🔣

Credit Cards 💳 🔲 🔲 🔲 💲

Cashel Caravan & Camping Site (NS395940)
G63 0AW ☎ 01360 870234 (in season) & 0131 314 6505
(on B837)
Nearby town: Drymen
▶▶▶ Family Park ★ 🏕 £7.50-£8.60 🏕 £7.50-£8.60
Å £7.50-£8.60
Open Etr-Oct Booking advisable public hols & Jul-Aug
Last arrival 22.00hrs Last departure noon
*An attractive and well-wooded Forestry Commission
site, lying on the eastern shores of Loch Lomond within
the Queen Elizabeth Forest Park, offering seclusion to
campers and splendid views over the loch. Caravanners
should beware of a steep hill at a quick right hand turn
when leaving Balmaha. Situated 3m beyond Balmaha
village on A837 Drymen-Rowardennan road. A 12-acre
site with 100 touring pitches.*
Boating on Loch Lomond.

🔣🔣☺🔣🔣🔣🔣🔣🔣🔣🔣🔣🔣🔣🔣🔣
➔🔣🔣🔣

Credit Cards 💳 🔲 🔲 💲

BARCALDINE

Camping & Caravanning Club Site (NM966420)
PA37 1SG ☎ 01631 720348 (in season) & 01203 694995
Signposted
Nearby town: Oban

◯◯◯◯◯◯◯◯◯

▶▶▶▶ De-Luxe Park ★ ⊞ £10-£13 ⊞ £10-£13
Å £10-£13
Open end Mar-early Nov Booking advisable bank hols &
Jul-Aug Last arrival 21.00hrs Last departure noon
*A sheltered site within the grounds of a former walled
garden, bordered by Barcaldine Forest, close to Loch
Creran, situated 10m N of Oban off A828. Winner of the
1995 Campsite of the Year Award for Scotland. Please
see the advertisement on page 27 for details of Club
Members' benefits. A 4-acre site with 90 touring pitches.*

🔌 🛞 ⊙ 🖥 🗞 ◀ 🖵 ☀ ⛱ ⚠ 🛉 🖉 🖃 🅣 ✕ 🌡

➔ ∪ ↖ ✦ 🛎

Credit Cards 💳 ▦ ▦ ▦ 🗐

◯◯◯◯◯◯◯◯◯

BIRNAM

Erigmore House Holiday Park (NO036416)
PH8 9XX ☎ 01350 727236 Signposted
Nearby town: Perth

◯◯◯◯◯◯◯◯◯

▶▶▶▶ De-Luxe Park ⊞ ⊞
Open Mar-Oct Booking advisable all times Last arrival
23.30hrs Last departure noon
*A predominantly touring site in the grounds of 18th-
century Erigmore House which has a wide variety of
unusual trees including Japanese maple and cherry. Site
well-secluded from the main road and a considerable
degree of privacy can be found. Situated on B898. An 18-
acre site with 24 touring pitches and 183 statics.*
Sauna, solarium & spa bath.

🔌 🛞 🛞 ⊙ 🖥 🗞 ⚡ ◀ ☀ ⛱ ⚠ 🛉 🖉 ✕ 🌡 ⚗ 🏛 🛎

➔ ↖ ✦

Credit Cards 💳 ▪ ▦ ▦ ▦ 🗐

◯◯◯◯◯◯◯◯◯

BLAIR ATHOLL

River Tilt Caravan Park (NN875653)
PH18 5TE ☎ 01796 481467 & 0738 149184 Signposted
Nearby town: Pitlochry

◯◯◯◯◯◯◯◯◯

▶▶▶▶ De-Luxe Park ★ ⊞ £8-£12 ⊞ £7-£11
Å £4-£15

Open mid Mar-Nov Booking advisable Jul-Aug Last
arrival 21.00hrs Last departure 11.00hrs
*Level, grass site with trees and bushes set in hilly
woodland country on the banks of the River Tilt, next to*

*golf course. 7m N of Pitlochry on A9, take B8079 to Blair
Atholl, and site at rear of Tilt Hotel.. A 2-acre site with
37 touring pitches and 92 statics.*
Multi-gym, sauna & solarium.Steam room, spa pool.

🔌 🛞 ⊙ 🖥 🗞 🗞 ⚡ ☀ ⛱ ⚠ 🛉 🖉 🖃 🅣 ✕ 🌡 🏛

🖵 🛉

➔ ∪ ↖ 🛞 ✦ 🛎

Credit Cards 💳 ▦

◯◯◯◯◯◯◯◯◯

Blair Castle Caravan Park (NN874656)
PH18 5SR ☎ 01796 481263 Signposted
Nearby town: Pitlochry

◯◯◯◯◯◯◯◯◯

▶▶▶▶ De-Luxe Park ⊞ £8.50-£10 ⊞ £8.50-£10
Å £7-£10
Open Apr-late Oct (rs Apr-Jun & Sep-mid Oct
restaurant) Booking advisable bank hols & Jul-Aug Last
arrival 21.30hrs Last departure noon
*Attractive site set in impressive seclusion within the Atholl
estate, surrounded by mature woodland and the R Tilt.
From A9 junc with B8079 At Aldclune, travel NE to Blair
Atholl, turn on right after crosing bridge in village. A
32-acre site with 283 touring pitches and 112 statics.*

🔌 🛞 🛞 🛞 ⊙ 🖥 🗞 ⚡ ◀ 🖵 ☀ ⚠ 🛉 🖉 🖃 🅣 ✕ 🌡 ⚗

🖵 🛉 🛎 ♿

➔ ∪ ↖ ✦

Credit Cards 💳 ▦ ▦ ▦ 🗐

◯◯◯◯◯◯◯◯◯

BLAIRMORE

Gairletter Caravan Park (NS193845)
PA23 8TP ☎ 01369 810208 & 810220
Nearby town: Dunoon
▶ ▶ ▶ Family Park ★ ⚘ £9.50 ⚘ £9.50
Open Mar-Oct Booking advisable Last arrival 22.00hrs
A quiet lochside site, family run and long established, with a good toilet block and recreation facilities. From Dunoon take A885 to Ardbeg, then A880 to Blairmore. Site at water's edge on right in .5m. A 1.5-acre site with 12 touring pitches and 28 statics.
Pool table.

🎏🐾⊙🔦☼🗚🛈🔲🗪
➜▶🛥

BRIDGE OF CALLY

Corriefodly Holiday Park (NO134513)
PH10 7JG ☎ 01250 886236 Signposted
Nearby town: Blairgowrie

▶ ▶ ▶ ▶ De-Luxe Park ★ ⚘ £8.50-£9 ⚘ £8.50-£9
⚘ £5-£7
Open early Dec-early Nov Booking advisable bank hols & Jul-Aug Last arrival 22.00hrs Last departure noon
A secluded riverbank site in a wooded area 150 yards N of Bridge of Cally on A924. A 17.5-acre site with 38 touring pitches and 32 statics.
Bowling green & fishing on site.

🎏🐾⊙🔲🏴🔦☼♀🗚🛈🌳🔦🔲⚿
➜🔵🌙🛥

CALLANDER

Callander Holiday Park (NN615073)
Invertrossachs Rd FK17 8HW ☎ 01877 330265
Signposted

▶ ▶ ▶ ▶ De-Luxe Park ⚘ £11.50 ⚘ £11.50
Open 15 Mar-Oct Booking advisable Jun-Aug Last arrival 22.00hrs Last departure noon
An attractive terraced park with glorious views over the surrounding countryside. From A84 in centre of Callander take A81 Glasgow road over bridge, then turn right in 200 yards towards Invertrossachs road, and site in .5 mile. A 10-acre site with 28 touring pitches and 110 statics.
Fishing on site.

🎏🐾⊙🔲☼🗚🛈🔲⚿🎠🐕🔲🔳♿
➜🔵🛒✂🌙🛥

Gart Caravan Park (NN643070)
The Gart FK17 8LE ☎ 01877 330002 Signposted

▶ ▶ ▶ ▶ De-Luxe Park ⚘ £12 ⚘ £12
Open Etr or Apr-15 Oct Booking advisable Last arrival 22.00hrs Last departure noon
A well-screened site bordered by trees and shrubs and with helpful owners. 1m E of Callander on A84. A 25-acre site with 122 touring pitches and 66 statics.

Fishing on site.

🎏🐾⊙🔲☼🗚🛈🔦🐕🔲♿
➜🔵🛒✂🌙🛥
Credit Cards 💳 💳 🕗

CARNOUSTIE

Woodlands Caravan Park (NO560350)
Newton Rd DD7 6HR ☎ 01241 854430 & 853246
Signposted
▶ ▶ ▶ Family Park ⚘ ⚘ 🔥
Open late Mar-early Oct Booking advisable Jul-mid Aug Last arrival 21.00hrs Last departure noon
An excellent, well-maintained site with good facilities. Set in a quiet area of town, well-signed from A930. A 5.5-acre site with 108 touring pitches and 4 statics.

🎏🐾⊙🔲🗚🛈🔦🔳🎠🐕♿
➜🔵🛒🔺🌙🛥

CARRADALE

Carradale Bay Caravan Site (NR815385)
PA28 6QG ☎ 01583 431665 Signposted
Nearby town: Campbeltown
▶ ▶ ▶ Family Park ★ ⚘ £7.50-£12.80 ⚘ £7.50-£12.80
🔥 £7.50-£12.80
Open Etr-Sep Booking advisable bank hols & Jul-Aug Last arrival 22.00hrs Last departure noon
A beautiful, natural site on the sea's edge with superb views over Kilbrannan Sound to Isle of Arran. Approach from north is via Tarbert, leaving by A83 Campbeltown road; within 5m turn onto B8001, then B842 Carradale road. This is a single-track road with passing places. In Carradale take road to the pier, site is in .5m. An 8-acre site with 75 touring pitches and 3 statics.
Canoe use.

🎏🐾⊙🔲🏴☼🔳⚿🔦🛥
➜▶🔺✂🌙

CRIEFF

Crieff Holiday Village (NN857225)
Turret Bank PH7 4JN ☎ 01764 653513 Signposted
Nearby town: Perth
▶ ▶ ▶ Family Park ★ ⚘ £7-£9.50 ⚘ £7-£9.50 ⚘ £6-£9
Open all year Booking advisable Jul-Aug Last arrival mdnt
A level site by the riverside, 1m W of Crieff on A85. A 3-acre site with 40 touring pitches and 40 statics.

🎏🐾⊙🔲🏴🔦🔲☼🗚🛈🔦🔳🔳🔲⚿
🏠🐕🛥
➜🔵🛒✂🌙
Credit Cards 💳 💳

DALKEITH

Fordel (NT359668)
Lauder Rd EH22 2PH
☎ 0131 663 3046 & 0131 660 3921
Signposted
▶ ▶ ▶ Family Park ⚘ ⚘ 🔥
Open Apr-Sep Booking advisable Jul-Aug Last departure noon

A small, tree lined, grassy site on A68 1.5m S of Dalkeith. A 3-acre site with 35 touring pitches.

🎯 ⬅ ⊙ 🗄 🍴 ✳ 🍷 ⛰ 🎱 🖊 ✗ ⟍ 🍴 🎏 ⊞ 🎱
➜ ∪ ▶ ⊚ ♪

Credit Cards 💳 ▬ 💳 ⓪ 💳 🔢

DUNBAR

Thurston Manor Holiday Home Park (NT712745)
Innerwick EH42 1SA
☎ 01368 840643 (.5m from A1)
Signposted

○○○○○○○○○

▶ ▶ ▶ ▶ ▶ **Premier Park** ★ ♨ £10-£12 ♨ £10-£12
▲ £7-£12
Open Mar-Oct Booking advisable Etr,
bank hols & high season Last arrival 9.00hrs
Last departure noon
A developing site with good facilities and level pitches. From A1, 6m N of Cockburnspath, take unclass rd signed Innerwick, in .5m turn R, and site in .5m on R. A 250-acre site with 100 touring pitches and 300 statics. Private lake, pony treking, fitness room, sauna/steam

🎯 ⬅ ⊙ 🗄 🍴 🔱 ◀ 🖥 ✳ 🍷 ⛰ 🎱 🖊 ⊞ ⊤ ✗ ⟍
🍴 🎏 ⊞ 🐴 🎱 ♿
➜ ∪ ▶ ⚠ ♪

Credit Cards 💳 ▬ 🔢 🔢

○○○○○○○○○

DRUM MOHR CARAVAN PARK
Near Edinburgh

East Lothian's premier touring park for caravanners and campers. A secluded, well landscaped site on the edge of East Lothian's beautiful countryside, yet only 20 minutes from Princes Street, Edinburgh.
Facilities are of an exceptionally high standard, and the toilet blocks include showers, laundry room, dishwashing area and chemical waste disposal.
120 pitches (most with electric hook-up and a few fully serviced), children's play area, well stocked shop, plus tourist information at reception.

Best of British.

CAMPSITE OF THE YEAR

AA

SCOTLAND 1993

Send for brochure to: Drum Mohr Caravan Park
Levenhall, Musselburgh, Nr Edinburgh EH21 8JS
Tel: 0131-665 6867 Fax: 0131-653 6859

Camping & Caravanning Club Site (NT723773)
Barns Ness EH42 1QP
☎ 01368 863536 (in season) & 01203 694995 (4m E)
Signposted
▶ ▶ ▶ **Family Park** ★ ♨ £9.20-£11.60 ♨ £9.20-£11.60
▲ £9.20-£11.60
Open end Mar-early Nov Booking advisable bank hols & high season Last arrival 21.00hrs Last departure noon
A grassy, landscaped site close to the foreshore and lighthouse on a coastline noted for its natural and geological history. 4m E of Dunbar, approached off A1. Please see the advertisement on page 27 for details of Club Members' benefits. A 10-acre site with 90 touring pitches.

🎯 ⬅ ⊙ 🗄 🍴 ✳ ⛰ 🎱 🖊 ⊞ ⊤ ⟍
➜ ∪ ▶ 🔱 ♪

Credit Cards 💳 ▬

DUNKELD

See **Birnam**

DUNOON

See **Blairmore**

EDINBURGH

Mortonhall Caravan Park (NT265680)
38 Mortonhall Gate, Frogston Rd East EH16 6TJ
☎ 0131 664 1533 Signposted

○○○○○○○○○

▶ ▶ ▶ ▶ **De-Luxe Park** ♨ ♨ ▲
Open mid Mar-Oct Booking advisable Jul-Aug Last arrival 22.00hrs Last departure noon
Located on the S side of Edinburgh within 20 minutes' car ride of the city centre, this site is part of a 200-acre estate surrounding the 18th-century Mortonhall mansion designed by Robert Adam. A large site with high standards. Take the new city bypass to junction with A702 and follow signs to Mortonhall. A 22-acre site with 250 touring pitches and 19 statics.

🎯 ⬅ ⊙ 🗄 🍴 ◀ 🖥 ✳ 🍷 ⛰ 🎱 🖊 ⊞ ⊤ ✗ ⟍ 🐴
🎱 ♿
➜ ∪ ▶ 🍴

Credit Cards 💳 ▬ 🔢 🔢 🔢

○○○○○○○○○

EDZELL

Glenesk Caravan Park (NO602717)
DD9 7YP ☎ 01356 648565 & 648523 (1m NW off B966)
Signposted
Nearby town: Brechin
▶ ▶ ▶ **Family Park** ★ ♨ £6.50-£9 ♨ £6.50-£9
▲ £5-£6
Open Apr-Oct Booking advisable public hols & mid Jun-Aug Last arrival 22.00hrs Last departure 16.00hrs
A carefully improved and maintained woodland site surrounding a small fishing lake. Situated on unclass road to Glen Esk, 1m N of the B966. An 8-acre site with 45 touring pitches and 10 statics.

🎯 ⬅ ⊙ 🗄 🍴 ◀ 🖥 ⛰ 🎱 🖊 ⊞ ⊤ ⟍ 🍴 🎏 🔢
➜ ∪ ▶ 🔱 ♪ 🎱

ELIE

Shell Bay Caravan Park (NO465005)
Kincraig Hill KY9 1HB
☎ 01333 330283 & 330334
Signposted
Nearby town: Leven
▶▶▶ Family Park ★ 🚐 £9-£11.50 🚐 £9-£11.50
🏕 £8-£9
Open 21 Mar-Oct Booking advisable Jul-Aug Last arrival 21.00hrs Last departure noon
Large, mainly static holiday site utilizing natural coastal area of a secluded bay. 1.5m NW of Elie off A917, signed off unclass road, with direct access to beach. A 5-acre site with 120 touring pitches and 250 statics.

🔌🚿⊙🅿️🍳🔥🍴☀️⚲⛰🛉🛢🗑❌📞🚽🏛
🎫🎱♿
➔∪🅿️🎯△⚓🏹 ✔

Credit Cards 💳 💳 💲

FORFAR

Lochside Caravan Park (NO450505)
Forfar Loch Country Park DD8 1BT
☎ 01307 464201 & 468917
Signposted

◯◯◯◯◯◯◯◯◯

▶▶▶▶ De-Luxe Park 🚐🚐🏕
Open late Mar-early Oct Booking advisable mid Jun-Aug Last arrival 21.00hrs Last departure noon
A pleasant, well laid out site close to the loch and

leisure centre. Well-signed off ring road (A94). A 4.75-acre site with 74 touring pitches.

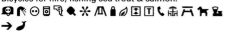

GLENDARUEL

Glendaruel Caravan Park (NR005865)
PA22 3AB ☎ 01369 820367 Signposted
▶ ▶ ▶ Family Park ★ ⊞ £8-£10 ⊞ £8-£10 ▲ £8-£10
Open Apr-Oct Booking advisable Spring bank hol & mid Jul-Aug Last arrival 22.00hrs Last departure noon
Attractive, grassy, level site in 23 acres of wooded parkland in a valley surrounded by mountains. Situated off A886, with many rare species of trees on site. A 3-acre site with 45 touring pitches and 30 statics.
Bicycles for hire, fishing sea trout & salmon.

Credit Cards ●● ▦

INCHTURE

Inchmartine Caravan Park & Nurseries (NO263277)
Dundee Rd PH14 9QQ ☎ 01821 670212 & 686251 Signposted
Nearby town: Perth
▶▶ Town & Country Pennant Park ⊞ £8.50 ⊞ £8.50
Open Mar-Oct Last arrival 20.00hrs Last departure noon
A quiet site with excellent toilet facilities, adjacent to A85 Perth-Dundee road. An 8-acre site with 45 touring pitches.

INVERARAY

Argyll Caravan Park (NN075055)
PA32 8XT ☎ 01499 302285 Signposted

▶ ▶ ▶ ▶ De-Luxe Park ⊞ ⊞ ▲
Open Apr-Oct Last arrival anytime Last departure noon
A mainly grassy site with some hardstandings on the shores of Loch Fyne, with ample on-site facilities and indoor sports hall. 2.5m S of Inveraray on A83. A 6-acre site with 140 touring pitches and 240 statics.
Mini football pitch.

Credit Cards ●● ▦ ▢

INVERBEG

Inverbeg Holiday Park (NS348983)
G83 8PD ☎ 01436 860267 & 0131 654 0142 Signposted
Nearby town: Luss
▶ ▶ ▶ Family Park ⊞ ⊞
Open Mar-Oct Booking advisable Spring bank hol, Jul-Aug & hol wknds Last arrival 23.00hrs Last departure noon

A well-maintained site on a small promontory alongside Loch Lomond with direct access to shingle beach and a small marina. No tents, and all pitches hardstanding, with no grass. Signed with access off A82, 4m N of Luss. Very fast section of road and great care should be taken. A 4-acre site with 35 touring pitches and 120 statics.
Sailing & fishing.

INVERUGLAS

Loch Lomond Holiday Park (NN320092)
G83 7DW
☎ 01301 704224 (3.5m N of Tarbet)
Signposted
Nearby town: Helensburgh

▶ ▶ ▶ ▶ De-Luxe Park ★ ⊞ £7-£12.50 ⊞ £7-£12.50
Open Mar-Oct (rs Dec-Jan main amenity building restricted hours) Booking advisable May-Aug Last arrival 21.00hrs Last departure 11.45hrs
A lovely setting on the shores of Loch Lomond with views of forests and mountains, and boat hire available. Situated on A82 between Tarbet and Ardlui. A 6-acre site with 18 touring pitches and 72 statics.
Satellite TV, pool tables, boat hire.

Credit Cards ●● ▦

KENMORE

Kenmore Caravan & Camping Park (NN772458)
PH15 2HN ☎ 01887 830226
Signposted
Nearby town: Aberfeldy

▶ ▶ ▶ ▶ De-Luxe Park ★ ⊞ £8.50-£9.50 ⊞ £8.50-£9.50 ▲ £7.50-£8.50
Open 25 Mar-Oct Booking advisable mid Jul-mid Aug Last arrival 22.00hrs Last departure 14.00hrs

A pleasant riverside site with an air of spaciousness and a very good licensed bar/restaurant. On A827 opposite Loch Tay 8.5 miles W of Aberfeldy. A 14-acre site with 160 touring pitches and 60 statics. contd.

KENMORE CARAVAN & CAMPING PARK

STB
✓✓✓✓✓   ▶▶▶▶

Taymouth Holiday Centre
Kenmore, Aberfeldy, Perthshire PH15 2HN
Telephone: 01887 830226

Pleasant site by the River Tay. Ideal touring centre. Beautiful forest and hill walks or mountain treks. Excellent golf course on site (par 70) with others nearby. Fishing on the river or Loch Tay. Most water activities available and a swimming pool 6 miles away in Aberfeldy. Pony trekking also nearby. There are new modern facilities with family washing rooms, laundry, dish washing areas and two children's play parks. The Byre Bistro offers excellent bar and restaurant facilities with families welcome, there are also a variety of places to eat well locally. The site is quiet at night and owner supervised.

Cycle hire, 9 hole golf, games & TV room.
🖤 🕏 ⊙ 🗗 🗟 🔦 ⎁ ✲ ♀ ⚠ 🛆 🖋 ⊞ Ⓣ ✕ 🕻 🚐
🚽 🚿 🐕 🐾 ♿
➔ ∪ ⏻ ◭ ⅄ ♨ ⬗
Credit Cards 💳 🆅🆂🅰 💳 💳

KINLOCH RANNOCH

Kilvrecht Campsite (NN623567)
PH17 ☎ 01350 727284
▶▶ **Town & Country Pennant Park** ★ 🐛 £5 🐛 £5 ⅄ £5
Open Etr-Oct Last arrival 22.00hrs
A basic site in a large clearing in the forest, about .75 mile from Loch Rannoch shore, with no hot water. Approach along unclass road along loch shore with Forestry Commission signs. A 17-acre site with 60 touring pitches.
🐕 🐾
➔ ⅄ ⬗

KIRKCALDY

Dunnikier Caravan Park (NT283940)
Dunnikier Way KY1 3ND
☎ 01592 275563 & 266701
Signposted

▶▶▶▶ **De-Luxe Park** ★ 🐛 £7-£9 🐛 £7-£9 ⅄ £5.50-£8
Open Mar-Jan Booking advisable peak periods Last arrival 19.00hrs Last departure noon

A level site set in mature parkland adjacent to the B981 but screened by trees. From A92 (signed Kirkcaldy) travel S, at 1st rndbt turn W onto B891, and site on right in 500 yds after Asda store. An 8-acre site with 60 touring pitches and 24 statics.
🖤 🕏 ⊙ 🗗 🗟 ✲ 🛆 🖋 ⊞ 🕻 🚿 🐕 🐾 ♿
➔ ∪ ⏻ ◉ ◭ ⅄ ♨ ⬗

KIRRIEMUIR

Drumshademuir Caravan Park (NO381509)
Roundyhill DD8 1QT
☎ 01575 573284
Signposted
Nearby town: Forfar

▶▶▶▶ **De-Luxe Park** ★ 🐛 £8.25-£9 🐛 £8.25-£9
⅄ £5-£6.50
Open mid Mar-end Oct Booking advisable public hols & Jun-Aug Last arrival 23.00hrs Last departure 16.00hrs
Part-sloping grass site in valley overlooking farmland, 2.5m S of Kirriemuir on A928. A 7.5-acre site with 80 touring pitches and 34 statics.
Bar food & putting.
🖤 🕏 ⊙ 🗗 ✲ ♀ ⚠ 🛆 🖋 ⊞ Ⓣ ✕ 🕻 🚽 🚿 🐕 🐾 ♿
➔ ∪ ⏻ ◭ ⬗

LOCHEARNHEAD

Balquhidder Braes Caravan Park (NN581218)
Balquhidder Station FK19 8NX
☎ 01567 830293 & 384320
Signposted
Nearby town: Callander
▶▶▶ **Family Park** 🐛 £7-£8 🐛 £7-£8
⅄ £4-£8
Open Mar-Oct Booking advisable bank hols & Jul-Aug Last arrival 22.00hrs Last departure noon
A level grass site with some trees for shelter, a good base for hill walking and water sports. 10m N of Callander on A84, 1m before Lochearnhead. A 4-acre site with 50 touring pitches and 10 statics.
Dish washing room.
🖤 🕏 ⊙ 🗗 🗟 ✲ ⚠ 🛆 🖋 ⊞ 🕻 🚿 🐕 🐾
➔ ◭ ⅄ ⬗ 🐾

LOCHGILPHEAD

Lochgilphead Caravan Site (NR859881)
PA31 8NX ☎ 01546 602003 Signposted
▶▶▶ **Family Park** ★ 🐛 £6.50 🐛 £6.50 ⅄ £6.50
Open Apr-Oct Booking advisable Jul-Aug
Mainly level, grassy site close to the shore of Loch Gilp, an inlet of Loch Fyne. Situated beside the A83 and convenient to the town centre facilities. Fishing and sailing available on the Loch. A 7-acre site with 70 touring pitches and 30 statics.
Mountain bike hire.
🖤 🕏 ⊙ 🗗 🗟 🔦 ✲ ⚠ 🛆 🖋 ⊞ Ⓣ 🕻 🚿 🐕 🐾 🐾
➔ ∪ ⏻ ⬗
Credit Cards 💳 💳 💳

LONGNIDDRY

Seton Sands Holiday Village (NT420759)
EH32 0QF ☎ 01875 813333 &
0345 508508
Nearby town: Port Seton

❀❀❀❀❀❀❀❀❀❀❀❀❀❀❀❀❀❀❀

★ 🚐 £8-£18 🚐 £8-£18
Open Mar-Oct Booking advisable Last arrival 23.00hrs
Last departure noon
A large, mainly static park, with reasonable touring facilities on a grassy paddock near the road. Take A1 to Tranent slip road, then B6371 to Cockenzie, and right onto B1348. Park 1m on left. A 1.75-acre site with 60 touring pitches and 120 statics.

🔊 ⌂ ⊙ 📅 ⚲ ⤢ ✆ ◀ 🍴 ⋒ 🚽 ⓘ T ✕ ✆ ⊞
🚿 🎋 🐕 🐎
→ ∪ ▶ ◎ ♨ ⤴

Credit Cards 💳 💳 💳 💳 ⑤

❀❀❀❀❀❀❀❀❀❀❀❀❀❀❀❀❀❀❀

LUIB

Glendochart Caravan Park (NN477278)
FK20 8QT ☎ 01567 820637
Signposted
Nearby town: Stirling
▶ ▶ ▶ Family Park 🚐 🚐 ▲
Open Etr-Oct (rs Mar-Etr no showers) Booking advisable Jul & Aug Last arrival 22.00hrs Last departure noon
A small, well-maintained site with imaginative landscaping. Set on hillside in Glendochart with glorious mountain and hill-country views, 5m E of Crianlarich on the A85. A 7-acre site with 45 touring pitches and 40 statics.

🔊 ⌂ ⊙ 📅 🚿 ⤢ 🍴 ⤴ ⓘ T ✆ ⋒ 🐕 🐎
→ ∪ ▶ ◎ ⚑ ⤴ ⤴

LUNDIN LINKS

Woodland Gardens Caravan & Camping Site (NO418031)
Blindwell Rd KY8 5QG ☎ 01333 360319 (turn off A915 at E end of town, signposted on A915) Signposted
Nearby town: Leven
▶ ▶ ▶ Family Park 🚐 £7.50-£10.70 🚐 £7.50-£10.70
▲ £7.50-£10.70
Open Mar-Oct Booking advisable Jul-Aug Last arrival 22.00hrs Last departure noon
A secluded and sheltered site off the A917 coast road at Largo. Approach along narrow, well signed road. A 1-acre site with 20 touring pitches and 5 statics.

🔊 ⌂ ⊙ ⚲ ◀ ⤢ 🚿 ⤢ 🍴 ⤴ ⓘ ✆ 🎋 🐎
→ ∪ ▶ ⚑ ⤴

LUSS

Camping & Caravanning Club Site (NS360936)
G83 8NT ☎ 01436 860658 (in season) & 01203 694995
(.25m N on A82) Signposted
Nearby town: Dumbarton

◯◯◯◯◯◯◯◯◯◯

▶ ▶ ▶ ▶ De-Luxe Park ★ ▲ £1-£14
Open end Mar-early Nov Booking advisable bank hols & Jul-Aug Last arrival 21.00hrs Last departure noon

Lovely grass tenting site on W shore of Loch Lomond, with excellent toilets and laundry facilities. Motorvans and caravans of Club members only permitted. .25m N of Luss village on A82 Glasgow-Fort William road. Please see the advertisement on page 27 for details of Club Members' benefits. A 10-acre site with 90 touring pitches.

🔊 ⌂ ⊙ 🚿 ⤢ ⤢ ✆ 🐕 🐎
→ ⤴ ⤴

Credit Cards 💳 💳 💳 💳 ⑤

◯◯◯◯◯◯◯◯◯◯

MACHRIHANISH

Camping & Caravanning Club Site (NR647208)
East Trodigal PA28 6PT ☎ 01586 810366 (in season) &
01203 694995
Nearby town: Campbeltown
▶ ▶ ▶ Family Park ★ 🚐 £9.20-£11.60 🚐 £9.20-£11.60
▲ £9.20-£11.60
Open end Mar-Sep Booking advisable bank hols & high season Last arrival 21.00hrs Last departure noon
A very open site with superb sea views, situated adjacent to the golf course. On B843 .75m before village. Please see the advertisement on page 27 for details of Club Members' benefits. A 10-acre site with 90 touring pitches.

🔊 ⌂ ⊙ 🚿 ◀ 🍴 ✆ ♿
→ ▶ ⤴

Credit Cards 💳 💳 💳

MONIFIETH

Riverview Caravan Park (NO502322)
Marine Rd DD5 4NN ☎ 01382 535471 Signposted
Nearby town: Dundee
▶ ▶ ▶ Family Park 🚐 🚐 ▲
Open Apr-Oct Booking advisable Jul-Aug Last arrival 22.00hrs Last departure 12.30hrs
A seafront site in a quiet location with direct access to the beach, and close to town centre and amenities. Signs from A930 when approaching from north. No signs on south approach but follow signs for Barry Links. An 8-acre site with 165 touring pitches and 2 statics.
Indoor dishwashing/veg prep area, tourist info.

🔊 ⌂ ⊙ 📅 ⚲ ◀ 🚿 ⤢ ⓘ ✆ ⋒ 🎋 🐕 🐎 ♿
→ ∪ ▶ ◎ ⚑ ♨ ⤴

Credit Cards 💳 💳 💳 💳 💳 ⑤

MONTROSE

South Links Caravan Park (NO725575)
Traill Dr DD10 8EJ ☎ 01674 72026 & 72105 Signposted
▶ ▶ ▶ Family Park 🚐 🚐 ▲
Open late Mar-early Oct Booking advisable mid Jun-Aug Last arrival 21.00hrs Last departure noon
A well-maintained site with good facilities, partly overlooked by a processing plant. From A92 follow signs for golf course. A 10.75-acre site with 172 touring pitches.

🔊 ⌂ ⊙ ⤢ ✆ 🎋 🐕 ♿
→ ▶ ⤴ 🐎

MOTHERWELL

See **Bothwell**

MULL, ISLE OF

CRAIGNURE

Shieling Holidays (NM724369)
PA65 6AY ☎ 01680 812496 Signposted
Nearby town: Tobermory
► ► ► **Family Park** ⊞ £10 ⊞ £10 ▲ £10
Open Apr-Oct Booking advisable Spring bank hol & Jul-Aug Last arrival 22.00hrs Last departure noon
A lovely site on the water's edge with spectacular views. Less than 1m from ferry landing. A 7-acre site with 30 touring pitches and 12 statics.
Adventure playground, boat hire.

🔌 🏕 ⊙ 🖥 ☜ ⬤ ☐ ✳ 🏔 🔋 ⌀ 🔥 🛖 🏠 ♞ 🐾 ⛫
➔ ▶ ⌂ ⅄ 🗡

Credit Cards 💳 💳 💳 🅂

MUSSELBURGH

Drum Mohr Caravan Park (NT373734)
Levenhall EH21 8JS ☎ 0131 665 6867 (1.5m E between B1361 & B1348) Signposted

► ► ► **De-Luxe Park** ⊞ £8-£10 ⊞ £8-£10 ▲ £8-£10
Open Mar-Oct Booking advisable Jul-Aug Last arrival 22.00hrs Last departure noon
This attractive park is set 2 miles east of Musselburgh between the A198 and B1348. Leave A1 at junc with A199 heading towards Musselburgh, at at rndbt turn right onto unclass road signed Prestonpans, take 1st left, and site in 400yds. A 9-acre site with 120 touring pitches.
See advertisement under EDINBURGH

🔌 🏕 ⊙ 🖥 ☜ ✳ 🏔 🔋 ⌀ 🖃 ⊺ ☐ ⌂ 🐾 ⛫
➔ ▶ ☕

Credit Cards 💳 💳 💳 🅂

NORTH BERWICK

Tantallon Caravan Park (NT570850)
Dunbar Rd EH39 5NJ ☎ 01620 893348 (on A198) Signposted
Nearby town: Edinburgh
► ► ► **Family Park** ⊞ ⊞ ▲
Open Mar-Oct Booking advisable Jul-Aug Last arrival 20.00hrs Last departure noon
Level grass site in meadowland in urban area with direct access to sea and beach. Located off A198 Dunbar road. A 10-acre site with 147 touring pitches and 60 statics.

🔌 🏕 ⊙ 🖥 ☜ ⬤ ☐ ✳ 🏔 🔋 ⌀ 🖃 ⌂ 🐕 🏠 🐾 ⛫
➔ ∪ ▶ ⊙ 🗡

Credit Cards 💳 💳 💳 💳 🅂

OBAN

Oban Divers Caravan Park (NM841277)
Glenshellach Rd PA34 4QJ ☎ 01631 562755 Signposted

► ► ► ► **De-Luxe Park** ⊞ £7-£9 ⊞ £7-£9 ▲ £7-£9
Open 15 Mar-Oct Booking advisable Etr, Whit & Jul-Aug
🎿

A well-maintained site amidst mountain scenery with a stream running through. The site specialises in facilities for divers. S out of Oban on the one-way system signed for ferry. Before ferry turn go left for Glenshellach, signed in .5m. A 4-acre site with 50 touring pitches.

🔌 🏕 ⊙ 🖥 ☜ ✳ 🏔 🔋 ⌀ 🖃 ⊺ ⌂ 🔥 🛖 🐾 ⛫
➔ ∪ ▶ ⌂ ⅄ ☕ 🗡

Oban Caravan & Camping Park (NM831277)
Gallanachmore Farm, Gallanach Rd PA34 4QH
☎ 01631 562425 Signposted
► ► ► **Family Park** ★ ⊞ £8-£9 ⊞ £8-£9 ▲ £8-£9
Open Etr/Apr-Oct Last arrival 23.00hrs Last departure noon
A well-equipped tourist park in an attractive location close to sea and ferries. Signed from centre of Oban. A 15-acre site with 140 touring pitches and 12 statics.

🔌 🏕 ⊙ 🖥 ⬤ ✳ 🏔 🔋 ⌀ 🖃 ⊺ ⌂ 🐕 🐾
➔ ∪ ▶ ⌂ ⅄ ☕ 🗡

PERTH

Cleeve Caravan Park (NO097227)
Glasgow Rd PH2 0PH ☎ 01738 639521 & 475211

► ► ► **De-Luxe Park** ★ ⊞ £7.85-£8.90 ▲ £7.60-£8.90
Open late Mar-late Oct Booking advisable Jul-mid Aug Last arrival 21.00hrs Last departure noon
Mature woodland surrounds this park, which offers pitches on terraced levels or in a walled garden. All facilities immaculately maintained. Adjacent to the A93 Perth to Glasgow road, 2m W of Perth. A 5.5-acre site with 100 touring pitches.
Free use of microwave.

🔌 🏕 ⊙ 🖥 ☜ ✳ 🏔 🔋 ⌀ ⊺ ⌂ 🍴 🔥 🛖 🐕 🐾 ⛫
➔ ∪ ▶ ⊙ ⌂ ⅄ ☕ 🗡

Credit Cards 💳 💳 💳 🅂

Faskally Caravan Park

Pitlochry, Perthshire PH16 5LA
Tel: (01796) 472007 & 473202

This park is situated outside the town and on the banks of the River Garry, which is bordered on one side by the main road. It is on gently sloping grassland dotted with trees and with splendid views. Indoor Leisure Pool with Spa Bath, Sauna and Steam Room.
Turn off A9 Pitlochry by-pass ½ mile north of town then proceed 1 mile north on B8019.
Bar and Restaurant.

Camping & Caravanning Club Site (NO108274)
Scone Racecourse, Scone PH2 6BB
☎ 01738 552323 (in season) & 01203 694995 (adjacent to racecourse off A93)
Signposted
▶ ▶ ▶ Family Park 🇶 🇶 Å
Open end Mar-early Nov Booking advisable bank hols & peak periods Last arrival 21.00hrs Last departure noon
A sheltered site in wooded area adjacent to the racecourse off A93, 1m N of Perth. Please see the advertisement on page 27 for details of Club Members' benefits. A 12-acre site with 150 touring pitches and 20 statics.
Recreation room.table tennis.
🎛 🐾 ⊙ 🖫 🏕 ◀ ☀ 🗠 🛆 🖪 🎛 Ⓣ ⬗ 🛏 🛃 🕭
➔ ⋃ ▶ ♨ ✈
Credit Cards 💳 💳 💳 🌀

PITLOCHRY

Faskally Caravan Park (NN916603)
PH16 5LA ☎ 01796 472007
Signposted

▶ ▶ ▶ De-Luxe Park 🇶 🇶 Å
Open 15 Mar-Oct Booking advisable Jul-Aug Last arrival 23.00hrs
A secluded riverbank site in sloping meadowland surrounded by trees. 1.5 miles N of Pitlochry on B8019. A 23-acre site with 255 touring pitches and 65 statics.

Steam room, spa, sauna & mini golf.
🎛 🐾 ⊙ 🖫 🏕 ☀ ◀ ☀ ☥ 🗠 🛆 🖪 🕭 Ⓣ ✖ ⬗ 🛃 🕭
➔ ⋃ ▶ ♨ ✈
Credit Cards 💳 💳

Milton of Fonab Caravan Site (NN945573)
PH16 5NA ☎ 01796 472882 (.5m S) Signposted

▶ ▶ ▶ De-Luxe Park ★ 🇶 £9-£9.50 🇶 £9-£9.50
Å £9-£9.50
Open Apr-Oct Booking advisable Jul-Aug Last arrival 21.00hrs Last departure 13.00hrs
Level, grass site with mature trees on banks of River Tummel, .5m S of town off A924. A 12-acre site with 154 touring pitches and 36 statics.
Mountain bike hire, free trout fishing.
🎛 🐾 🐟 ⊙ 🖫 🏕 ☀ 🛆 🖪 🕭 🛏 🛃 🕭
➔ ⋃ ▶ ⊙ ♨ ✈

ROSLIN

Slatebarns Caravan Club Site (NT277632)
EH25 9PU ☎ 0131 440 2192 Signposted

▶ ▶ ▶ De-Luxe Park ★ 🇶 £7.50-£10 🇶 £7.50-£10
Å £7.50-£10
Open Etr-Oct Booking advisable Jul & Aug Last arrival 20.00hrs Last departure noon
A newly developed site with good modern facilities and marked pitches, within easy access of Edinburgh. From A720 (city bypass) take A701, signed Penicuik and Peebles, S to B7006, turn left signed Roslin, and take unclass rd at end of village. A 2.5-acre site with 30 touring pitches.
🎛 🐾 ⊙ 🖫 🏕 ☀ 🛆 🖪 🕭 🛏 🛏
➔ ⋃ ▶ 🛃

ST ANDREWS

Craigtoun Meadows Holiday Park (NO482150)
Mount Melville KY16 8PQ ☎ 01334 475959 Signposted

▶ ▶ ▶ ▶ Premier Park 🇶 £12.50-£17 🇶 £12.50-£17
Å £12.50-£13.50
Open Mar-Oct Booking advisable bank hols & Jun-Aug Last arrival 21.00hrs Last departure 13.00hrs

contd.

Craigtoun Meadows
►►►►►Holiday Park
Mount Melville, St Andrews Fife. KY16 8PQ.
Tel: 01334 475959 Fax: 01334 476424

Quiet Award-winning Park with spacious fully serviced pitches including some with patio pitches with their own summerhouse. Carefully landscaped with ornamental trees and shrubs. Open Mar-Oct inclusive. Play areas, restaurant, launderette, shop. In a rural setting and just one mile from St Andrews. An ideal base to explore the Kingdom of Fife.

KINKELL BRAES
CARAVAN PARK
ST ANDREWS, FIFE, KY16 8PX
Tel: (01334) 474250 ►►►►

A beautiful location overlooking the sea, the beaches and the spires of St Andrews. Ideal for families and of course the home of Golf. Facilities include a Lounge Bar with Fast Food Service, Free Entertainment, Laundry, Free Hot Showers, Electric Hook-ups, Games Room and a Bus Service to the site entrance. The Beautiful Harbours of Crail, Anstruther, St Monans and Elie are close by.
New Leisure Complex nearby.
Hire caravans also available.

An attractive site set unobtrusively in mature woodlands with large pitches in hedged paddocks, 2m from sea and sandy beaches. 2m from St Andrews on the Craigtoun road. A 32-acre site with 98 touring pitches and 143 statics.
Adult mini-gymnasium.

Credit Cards 💳 🪙 🅂

Kinkell Braes Caravan Site (NO522156)
KY16 8PX ☎ 01334 474250
►►► Family Park 🚐 🚐
Open 21 Mar-Oct Booking advisable Jun-Aug Last departure noon
A mainly static site with touring area giving views across St Andrews and the Eden estuary. On A917 1m S of St Andrews. A 4-acre site with 100 touring pitches and 392 statics.

Credit Cards 💳 🪙 🅂

ST MONANS

St Monans Caravan Park (NO529019)
KY10 2DN ☎ 01333 730778 & 310185 (on A917 east end of town) Signposted
Nearby town: St Andrews
►►► Family Park ★ 🚐 £9 🚐 £9 🅰 £7-£9
Open 21 Mar-Oct Booking advisable Jul-Aug Last arrival 22.00hrs Last departure noon
Mainly static site on fringe of coastal village adjacent to main road and public park. On A917, 100yds E of St Monans. A 1-acre site with 18 touring pitches and 112 statics.

STIRLING

See **Auchenbowie**

TUMMEL BRIDGE

Tummel Valley Holiday Park (NN764592)
PH16 5SA ☎ 01882 634221 Signposted
Nearby town: Pitlochry

►►►► De-Luxe Park ★ 🚐 £10-£17 🚐 £10-£17
Open Mar-Oct Booking advisable bank hols & Jun-Aug Last arrival 21.00hrs Last departure 10.00hrs
Well-developed site amongst mature forest in this attractive valley. From A9 N of Pitlochry turn W on B8019. A 55-acre site with 40 touring pitches and 153 statics.
Bicycle hire, crazy golf, fishing rod hire.

Credit Cards 💳 ⬛ 🪙 🟥 🅂

SOUTHERN LOWLANDS & BORDERS

This region includes the counties of City of Glasgow, Dumbarton & Clydebank, Dumfries & Galloway, East Ayrshire, East Dunbartonshire, East Renfrewshire, North Ayrshire, North Lanarkshire, Renfrewshire, Scottish Borders, South Ayrshire, South Lanarkshire and West Dunbartonshire.

ANNAN

Galabank Caravan Park (NY192676)
North St DG12 5BQ ☎ 01461 203311 & 01556 502521 Signposted
►► Town & Country Pennant Park ★ ⊞ £6.10 ⊞ £6.10 ⊼ £3.75
Open May-early Sep Last departure noon
A tidy, well-maintained grassy little site close to the centre of town but with pleasant rural views, and skirted by River Annan. Follow B721 into town centre, turn rt at traffic lights into Lady St and site 500yds on left. A 1-acre site with 30 touring pitches.

⌂ ℝ ⊓ ⟍ ➔ ⏻ ⚎ ⏌

ARRAN, ISLE OF

LAMLASH

Middleton Caravan & Camping Park (NS027301)
KA27 8NN ☎ 01770 600251 & 600255 Signposted
►►► Family Park ⊞ fr £5 ⊞ fr £5 ⊼ £3-£5
Open late Apr-mid Oct Booking advisable Jul-Aug (for static caravans only) Last arrival 21.30hrs Last departure noon no cars by caravans
A grassy site sheltered by hills and mature trees, with lovely views. Close to sea and village amenities in a very pleasant location. A 3.5-acre site with 70 touring pitches and 60 statics.

⌂ ℝ ⊙ ⎙ ⟍ ✳ ⎕ ⌀ ⟍ ➔ ⏌ ⊚ ⌓ ⏌
See advertisement on page 252.

AUCHENMALG

Cock Inn Caravan Park (NX238518)
DG8 0JT ☎ 01581 500227 Signposted
Nearby town: Stranraer
►►► Family Park ★ ⊞ £6.50-£8.25 ⊞ £6.50-£8.25 ⊼ £6-£7
Open Mar-Oct Booking advisable bank hols & Jul-Aug Last arrival 22.00hrs Last departure 11.00hrs
A grassy site in meadowland, close to sea, beach and main (A747 Glenluce-Port William) road. Overlooks Luce Bay. A 2-acre site with 40 touring pitches and 80 statics.

⌂ ➡ ℝ ⊙ ⎙ ⟍ ✳ ⏛ ⚠ ⌀ ⊡ ⏉ ✕ ⏌ ⏖ ⚐ ➔ ⏻ ⊚ ⌓ ⏌

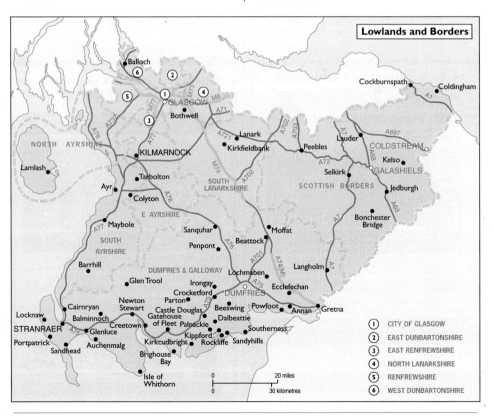

Lowlands and Borders

① CITY OF GLASGOW
② EAST DUNBARTONSHIRE
③ EAST RENFREWSHIRE
④ NORTH LANARKSHIRE
⑤ RENFREWSHIRE
⑥ WEST DUNBARTONSHIRE

AYR

Heads of Ayr Leisure Park (NS300184)

Dunure Rd KA7 4LD ☎ 01292 442269 Signposted

► ► ► Family Park ★ ⚤ £8.50-£11.50 ⚤ £7.50-£9.50
Å £7.50-£9.50

Open Mar-Nov Booking advisable bank hols & Jul-Aug
Last arrival 23.30hrs Last departure 15.00hrs

A small family-run site with attractive, well-screened pitches, .5m from beach overlooking Firth of Clyde. On R of A719 Ayr to Dunure road, 5m S of Ayr. An 8-acre site with 36 touring pitches and 126 statics.

🔥 🐾 ⊙ 🗑 ❄ ● ⚂ 🍴 ⚑ Å 🕯 ◫ T ✗ ✆
🛒 🐕 🗜
→ ∪ ▶ ☺ ✈

BALLOCH

Tullichewan Caravan Park (NS383816)

Old Luss Rd G83 8QP ☎ 01389 759475 Signposted

► ► ► Family Park ⚤ ⚤ Å

Open all year Booking advisable bank hols & Jul-Aug
Last arrival 22.00hrs Last departure noon

A popular, well-equipped site at S end of Loch Lomond, surrounded by woodland and hills. Close to the A82. A 13-acre site with 120 touring pitches and 35 statics. Leisure suite - sauna, spa bath, sunbeds.Bike hire.

🔥 🛏 🐾 ⊙ 🗑 ❄ ● ⬜ ✳ ⚑ Å 🕯 ◫ T ✆ 🐕
🗜 ♿
→ ∪ ▶ ⏏ ✚ ✈
Credit Cards 💳 💳 🖪

BALMINNOCH

Three Lochs Holiday Park (NX272655)

DG8 0EP ☎ 01671 830304
Nearby town: Newton Stewart

► ► ► ► De-Luxe Park ★ ⚤ £9-£10 ⚤ £9-£10 Å £6-£9

Open Etr-mid Oct Booking advisable bank hols & Jul-Aug Last arrival 22.00hrs Last departure 11.00hrs

A spacious, well-maintained site in moorland close to lochs, N off A75, with lovely views. Signed off B7027 on an unclass road in Glenluce direction. A 45-acre site with 45 touring pitches and 90 statics.

Games room & snooker.

🔥 🐾 ⊙ 🗑 ❄ ≋ ● ❄ ⚑ Å 🕯 ◫ T ✆
🍴 ⊞ 🗜 ♿
→ ✚ ✈

BARRHILL

Windsor Holiday Park (NX216835)

KA26 0PZ ☎ 01465 821355 (on A714 between Newton Stewart & Girvan, 1m north of village of Barrhill) Signposted

Nearby town: Girvan

► ► ► Family Park ⚤ £7.50-£8.50 ⚤ £7.50-£8.50
Å £5-£7.50

Open all year (rs Nov-Feb open wknds only) Booking advisable Jun-Aug Last arrival 22.00hrs Last departure 16.00hrs

---

A small site in a rural location, well-screened from A714 by small, mature trees. 1m NW of village. A 6-acre site with 30 touring pitches and 26 statics.

🔥 🐾 ⊙ ❄ ✳ ⚑ 🍴 ⚂ ⊞ T ✆ 🐕 ▣
→ ▶ ✈ 🗜

Credit Cards 💳 💳 🖪

BEATTOCK

Beattock House Hotel Caravan Park (NT079027)

DG10 9QB ☎ 01683 300403 & 300402 Signposted
Nearby town: Moffat

►► Town & Country Pennant Park ⚤ ⚤ Å

Open Mar-Oct (rs winter parking limited) Booking advisable

Pleasant, well-maintained level touring site set amongst trees in the grounds of a country house, adjacent to A74. A 2-acre site with 35 touring pitches.

Fishing.

🔥 🐾 ⊙ ❄ ✳ ⚑ ✗ ✆ 🛒 🍴 🐕
→ ∪ ▶ ✈

BEESWING

Beeswing Caravan Park (NX885485)

Kirkgunzeon DG2 8JL ☎ 01387 760242 (off A711)
Nearby town: Dumfries

► ► ► Family Park ⚤ ⚤ Å

Open Mar-Oct Booking advisable

A delightful park in open countryside, with lovely rural views in a peaceful setting. Midway between Dumfries and Dalbeattie on A711, 0.5m S of Beeswing. A 6-acre site with 25 touring pitches and 3 statics.

🔥 🐾 ⊙ 🗑 ❄ ⚑ 🍴 ⚂ 🍴 ✆ 🐕 ♿
→ ∪ ▶ ✈

BONCHESTER BRIDGE

Bonchester Bridge Caravan Park (NT586123)

Fernbank TD9 8JN ☎ 01450 860676
Nearby town: Edinburgh

► ► ► Family Park ★ ⚤ £6.50-£8 ⚤ £6.50-£8 Å £5-£6.50

Open Apr-Oct Booking advisable Jul-Aug Last arrival 22.00hrs Last departure noon

Neat little country village site close to Bure Water, on A6088 N of village centre. A 3-acre site with 25 touring pitches.

🔥 🐾 ⊙ ❄ ⚑ 🍴 ⚂ ⊞ ✆ 🍴 🍴 🐕 🗜
→ ✈

BOTHWELL

Strathclyde Country Park Caravan Site (NS717585)

366 Hamilton Rd ML1 3ED ☎ 01698 266155 Signposted
Nearby town: Hamilton

► ► ► Family Park ⚤ £8 ⚤ £8 Å £3.60-£6.90

Open Apr-Oct Booking advisable Jun-Aug Last arrival 10.30hrs Last departure noon

A level grass site situated in a country park amidst woodland and meadowland with lots of attractions. Direct access to park from junc 5 of M74. 250 touring pitches.

See advertisement under BOTHWELL

🔥 🐾 ⊙ 🗑 ⚑ 🍴 ⚂ ✗ ✆ 🍴 🐕 🗜 ♿
→ ∪ ▶ ⏏ ✚ ☺ ✈

See advertisement on page 254.

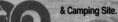
BRIGHOUSE BAY

Brighouse Bay Holiday Park (NX628453)
DG6 4TS ☎ 01557 870267 Signposted
Nearby town: Kirkcudbright

▶▶▶▶▶ **Premier Park** ★ ⚲ £8.75-£11.75
⚲ £8.75-£11.75 ▲ £8.75-£11.75
Open all year Booking advisable Etr, Spring bank hol & Jul-Aug Last arrival 21.30hrs Last departure 11.30hrs
This grassy site enjoys a marvellous coastal setting adjacent to the beach and with superb sea views. Pitches have been imaginatively sculpted into the meadowland with stone walls and hedges blending in with the site's mature trees. These features together with the large range of leisure activities available make this an excellent holiday centre. Turn left off B727 4 miles S of Kircudbright at signpost to Brighouse Bay on unclass rd. Winner of the 1997/8 Campsite of the Year Award, and Best Campsite for Scotland. A 30-acre site with 190 touring pitches and 120 statics.
Mini golf, riding, fishing, quad bikes,18 hole golf.

Credit Cards

CAIRNRYAN

Cairnryan Caravan & Chalet Park (NX075673)
DG9 8QX ☎ 01581 200231 (5m N of Stranraer on A77)
Signposted
Nearby town: Stranraer
▶ ▶ ▶ Family Park ⌂ £8.50 ⊞ £8.50 ▲ £4.50
Open Etr/Mar-Oct (rs Apr-21 May restricted pub hours)
Booking advisable Jul-Aug Last arrival 23.00hrs Last
departure noon
*Mainly static site immediately opposite ferry terminal
for N Ireland (Larne). Ideal stopover site with good
views of Loch Ryan. A 7.5-acre site with 15 touring
pitches and 83 statics.*
Snooker & pool tables.

CASTLE DOUGLAS

Lochside Caravan & Camping Site (NX766618)
Lochside Park DG7 1EZ ☎ 01556 502949 & 01556
502521 (off A75) Signposted
▶ ▶ ▶ Family Park ★ ⌂ £7.50-£9 ⊞ £7.50-£9 ▲ £7.50-£9
Open Etr-mid Oct Last departure noon
*Municipal touring site incorporating park with
recreational facilities, on southern edge of town in
attractive setting adjacent to Carlingwark Loch. Situated
off B736 Auchencairn road. A 5.5-acre site with 161
touring pitches.*
Putting, rowing boats (wknds & high season)

COLDINGHAM

Scoutscroft Holiday Centre (NT906662)
St Abbs Rd TD14 5NB ☎ 018907 71338
Nearby town: Berwick on Tweed
▶ ▶ ▶ Family Park ★ ⌂ £6-£11.50 ⊞ £6-£11.50
▲ £6-£8
Open Mar-Oct Booking advisable bank hols & Jul-Aug
Last arrival mdnt Last departure noon
*A large grassy site on edge of village. 0.75m from the
sea. From A1 take B6438 signed Coldingham and St
Abbs, and site on edge of Coldingham village. A 16-acre
site with 70 touring pitches and 120 statics.*
Sub Aqua Centre.

Credit Cards

COYLTON

Sundrum Castle Holiday Park (NS405208)
KA6 6JM ☎ 01292 570057 Signposted
Nearby town: Ayr

▶ ▶ ▶ De-Luxe Park ★ ⌂ £9-£15 ⊞ £9-£15 ▲ £7-£13
Open Mar-Oct Booking advisable all times Last arrival
23.30hrs Last departure 14.00hrs no cars by tents
*A large family holiday centre, with plenty of on-site
entertainment, just a 10 min drive from the centre of
Ayr. Set off the A70. A 30-acre site with 52 touring
pitches and 250 statics.*

Amusement arcade.

Credit Cards

CREETOWN

Castle Cary Holiday Park (NX475576)
DG8 7DQ ☎ 01671 820264 Signposted

▶ ▶ ▶ ▶ Premier Park ★ ⌂ £8.45-£10.75
⊞ £8.45-£10.75 ▲ £8.45-£10.75
Open all year (rs Oct-Mar reception/shop, no heated
outdoor pool) Booking advisable Bank hols & Jul-Aug
Last arrival anytime Last departure noon
*This attractive site in the grounds of Cassencarie House
is sheltered by woodlands, and faces south towards
Wigtown Bay. The park is in a secluded location with
beautiful landscaping and excellent facilities. A 6-acre
site with 50 touring pitches and 26 statics.*
Mountain bike hire, crazy golf & snooker.

See advertisement on page 36.

Creetown Caravan Park (NX474586)
Silver St DG8 7HU ☎ 01671 820377 (turn down between
Ellangowan Hotel & clock tower) Signposted
▶ ▶ ▶ Family Park ⌂ ⊞ ▲
Open Mar-Oct Booking advisable Jul & Aug Last arrival
22.30hrs Last departure 14.00hrs
*Neat and well-maintained park set in village centre with
views across the estuary. Off A75 into village of
Creetown, turn between clock tower and hotel, then
turn left along Silver Street. A 2-acre site with 15
touring pitches and 50 statics.*

CROCKETFORD

Park of Brandedleys (NX830725)
DG2 8RG ☎ 01556 690250 Signposted
Nearby town: Dumfries

▶ ▶ ▶ ▶ Premier Park ⌂ ⊞ ▲
Open Etr-Oct (rs Mar-Etr some facilities restricted)
Booking advisable public hols & Jul-Aug Last arrival
22.00hrs Last departure noon
*A well-maintained site in an elevated position off the
A75, with fine views of Auchenreoch Loch and beyond.
Excellent on-site amenities. A 9-acre site with 80 touring
pitches and 27 statics.*
Putting, badminton court & outdoor draughts.

Credit Cards

See advertisement on page 256.

PARK OF
BRANDEDLEYS

ADAC 'BEST PARK OF THE YEAR' 1997 & 1998
CALOR AWARD BEST PARK SCOTLAND 1995

- INDOOR POOL
- OUTDOOR POOL
- GAMES ROOM
- TENNIS COURTS
- BADMINTON
- PLAY AREAS
- RESTAURANT/BAR

CROCKETFORD, DUMFRIES DG2 8RG
TELEPHONE 01556 690250

DALBEATTIE

Islecroft Caravan & Camping Site (NX837615)
Colliston Park, Mill St DG5 4HE
☎ 01556 610012 & 502521 Signposted
►► Town & Country Pennant Park ★ ⊞ £5.80-£6.90
⊞ £5.80-£6.90 ▲ £5.80-£6.90
Open Etr-Sep Last departure noon
A neat site in two sections tucked away to rear of town, close to local park. Access is via Mill Street. A 3.5-acre site with 74 touring pitches.

🔯 🏕 ⊙ 🇳 🌂
➜ ▶ ⤺ ♫ 🏊

ECCLEFECHAN

Hoddom Castle Caravan Park (NY154729)
Hoddom DG11 1AS ☎ 01576 300251 Signposted
Nearby town: Lockerbie

► ► ► ► Premier Park ★ ⊞ £6-£11 ⊞ £6-£11
▲ £5-£8.50
Open Etr or Apr-Oct (rs early season cafeteria closed)
Booking advisable bank hols & Jul-Aug Last arrival
21.00hrs Last departure 15.30hrs
A beautiful site within the grounds of Hoddom Castle, with amenities housed in the keep and outhouses. 2m SW of Hoddom Bridge which carries B725 over River Annan. Winner of the Best Campsite for Scotland Award 1996/7. A 12-acre site with 170 touring pitches and 29 statics.
Nature trails, visitor centre & 9 hole golf course.

See advertisement under LOCKERBIE
🔯 🇳 ⊙ 🇳 🇳 🍴 ♦ 🌂 ⚲ 🏛 🇮 🖊 🔲 🇹 🗙 🍴 🛒
🏛 🇭 🐕 🇾 🦮 🔯
➜ ▶ ◎ ♫
Credit Cards 🔲 🔲 🔲 🔲

Cressfield Caravan Park (NY196744)
DG11 3DR ☎ 01576 300702 Signposted
Nearby town: Lockerbie

► ► ► ► De-Luxe Park ★ ⊞ £6.30-£7.50 ⊞ £6.30-£7.50
▲ £6
Open all year Booking advisable bank hols Last arrival
23.00hrs Last departure 13.00hrs
An open, spacious park with views to the hills, ideal as a stopover or for touring the area. Take loop service road from A74(M) to Ecclefechan, and site is at S end of town. A 12-acre site with 65 touring pitches and 48 statics.
Sports enclosure, golf nets, petanque, giant chess.

🔯 🏕 🇳 ⊙ 🇳 🇳 🌂 🏛 🇮 🍴 🐕 🦮 🔯
➜ ▶ ◎ ♫

GATEHOUSE OF FLEET

Auchenlarie Holiday Farm (NX536522)
DG7 2EX ☎ 01557 840251 (4m W on main A75)

► ► ► ► De-Luxe Park ★ ⊞ £6-£10 ⊞ £6-£10 ▲ £6-£10
Open Mar-Oct Booking advisable all year
A well-organised family park with good facilities, set on cliffs overlooking Wigtown Bay towards the Isle of Whithorn, and with its own sandy beach. Direct access off A75, 5m W of Gatehouse-of-Fleet. A 5-acre site with 35 touring pitches and 202 statics.

🔯 🇳 ⊙ 🇳 🇳 ♦ 🌂 🇾 🇮 ⚲ 🔲 🗙 🍴 🛒 🏛 🇭
🐕 🦮 🔯
➜ ▶ ◎ 🍴 ♫
Credit Cards 🔲 🔲 🔲 🔲 🔲 🔲

Anwoth Caravan Site (NX595563)
DG7 2JU ☎ 01557 814333 & 840251 Signposted
► ► ► Family Park ⊞ £6-£10 ⊞ £6-£10
Open Mar-Oct Booking advisable Jul-Aug Last arrival
22.00hrs Last departure noon
A sheltered touring site close to the town centre, signed from town centre, on right towards Stranraer direction. A 2-acre site with 28 touring pitches and 38 statics.

🔯 🇳 ⊙ 🇳 🌂 🇮
➜ ▶ ♫ 🏊
Credit Cards 🔲 🔲 🔲 🔲 🔲

Mossyard Caravan & Camping Park (NX546518)
Mossyard DG7 2ET ☎ 01557 840226 (4m W of town)
► ► ► Family Park ★ ⊞ £7-£8 ⊞ £7 ▲ £6-£8
Open Etr/Apr-Oct Booking advisable

A grassy park with its own beach, located on a working farm, and offering an air of peace and tranquility. Located 0.75m off A75 on private tarmaced farm road, 4.5m W of Gatehouse-of-Fleet. A 6.5-acre site with 35 touring pitches and 15 statics.

🔲 ⌐⊙ 回 ◥ 自 ⊘ 🗉 📞
➔ ⤴ 🐾

GLENLUCE

Glenluce Caravan & Camping Park (NX201576)
DG8 0QR ☎ 01581 300412 Signposted
Nearby town: Stranraer
▶ ▶ ▶ Family Park ★ 🏕 £7.50-£9 🏕 £7.50-£9
Å £6.50-£8
Open Mar-Oct Booking advisable Jul-Aug Last arrival 22.00hrs Last departure noon
A neat, well-maintained site situated beside a small river close to the village centre. Off A75 Stranraer road. Concealed entrance at telephone kiosk in centre of main street. A 5-acre site with 30 touring pitches and 30 statics.

🔲 ⌐⊙ 回 ◥ ⋇ 🏔 自 ⊘ 🗉 📞 🏛 🛒 🐕 🐾
➔ ∪ ▶ ⤴

Whitecairn Farm Caravan Park (NX225599)
DG8 0NZ ☎ 01581 300267 Signposted
Nearby town: Stranraer
▶ ▶ ▶ Family Park 🏕 £8-£8.50 🏕 £8-£8.50 Å £8-£8.50
Open Mar-Oct Booking advisable all times Last arrival 22.00hrs Last departure 11.00hrs
A well-maintained farmland site, in open countryside with extensive views. 1.5m N of Glenluce village on Glenluce-Glassnock Bridge Rd. A 3-acre site with 10 touring pitches and 40 statics.

🔲 ⌐⊙ ◥ ⋇ 🏔 自 ⊘ 📞 🏛 🐾
➔ ∪ ▶

GLEN TROOL

Caldons Caravan & Camping Site (NX400790)
DG8 6SU ☎ 01671 840218 (in season) & 0131 314 6505 Signposted
Nearby town: Newton Stewart
▶ ▶ ▶ Family Park ★ 🏕 £6.50-£7 🏕 £6.50-£7
Å £6.50-£7
Open Etr-Sep Booking advisable bank hol & Jul-Aug Last arrival 22.00hrs Last departure noon
Secluded Forestry Commission site amidst fine hill, loch and woodland scenery in Galloway Forest Park. 13m N of Newton Stewart. A 25-acre site with 160 touring pitches.

🔲 ⌐⊙ ◣ ⋇ 🏔 自 ⊘ 📞 🏛 🛒 🐾 ⬇
➔ ⤴
Credit Cards 💳 💳 💳 💳 💳

Glen Trool Holiday Park (NX400790)
DG8 6RN ☎ 01671 840280 Signposted
Nearby town: Newton Stewart
▶ ▶ ▶ Family Park ★ 🏕 £8-£9 🏕 £8-£9 Å £8-£9
Open Mar-Oct Booking advisable Jul-Aug Last arrival 21.00hrs Last departure noon
A small compact site close to the village of Glen Trool and bordered by the Galloway National Park. 9m N of

Newton Stewart. A 1-acre site with 14 touring pitches and 26 statics.
Trout pond for fly fishing, bikes for hire.

🔲 ⌐⊙ ◥ ◣ ⋇ 自 ⊘ 🗉 📞 🐾 ⬇
➔ ∪ ⤴
Credit Cards 💳 💳 💳

GRETNA

Braids Caravan Park (NY313674)
Annan Rd DG16 5DQ ☎ 01461 337409 Signposted
Nearby town: Annan
▶ ▶ ▶ Family Park ★ 🏕 £7.50 🏕 £7.50 Å £6-£8
Open all year Booking advisable Jul-Sep Last arrival 24.00hrs Last departure noon

A well-maintained grassy site in centre of the village just inside Scotland. Situated on B721 .5m from village on right, towards Annan. A 4-acre site with 70 touring pitches and 8 statics.

🔲 ⌐⊙ ◥ ⋇ 🏔 自 ⊘ 🗉 T 📞 🏛 🐾 ⬇
➔ ▶ ⤴

IRONGRAY

Barnsoul Farm (NX876778)
DG2 9SQ ☎ 01387 730249 Signposted
Nearby town: Dumfries
▶▶ Town & Country Pennant Park ★ 🏕 £5-£8 Å £5-£8
Open Apr-Oct (rs Mar) Booking advisable Jul & Aug Last arrival anytime Last departure anytime

A scenic farm site set in 250 acres of woodland, parkland and ponds. Leave A75 between Dumfries and Crocketford at brown site sign onto unclass rd signed Shawhead at T-junc. Turn right and immed left signed Dunscore, and site 1m on left. A 4-acre site with 30 touring pitches and 6 statics.

🔲 ⌐⊙ 回 ◥ ⋇ 🗉 📞 🏛 🐕
➔ ∪ ⤴ 🐾

ISLE OF WHITHORN

Burrowhead Holiday Village (NX450345)
DG8 8JB ☎ 01988 500252 Signposted
Nearby town: Stranraer
►►► Family Park ★ 🚐 £6.50 ⛺ £6.50 ▲ £6.50
Open Mar-Oct Booking advisable high season
*Large holiday park in 100 acres on coast of Solway
Firth, about 2m from old-fashioned harbour at Isle of
Whithorn. Leave A75 at Newton Stewart on A714, take
A746 to Whithorn, then road to Isle of Whithorn. A 100-
acre site with 100 touring pitches and 400 statics.
Sauna, jacuzzi, swimjet, spa, splash pool.*

🖪 📞 ⊙ 🗗 🖳 🖐 ⊀ ☀ 🏋 🗛 🛈 ⊘ ✗ 📞 🧹 🗛 🐓
➔ ◎ ♪ 🏖
Credit Cards 💳 🈹 🈯 🔅 🅹

JEDBURGH

Camping & Caravanning Club Site (NT658219)
Elliot Park, Edinburgh Rd TD8 6EF
☎ 01835 863393 (in season) & 01203 694995
Signposted
►►► Family Park ★ 🚐 £9.20-£11.60 ⛺ £9.20-£11.60
▲ £9.20-£11.60
Open end Mar-early Nov Booking advisable bank hols &
Jul-Aug Last arrival 21.00hrs Last departure noon
*A touring site on northern edge of town, nestling at foot
of cliffs close to Jed Water. From S on A68 bypass
town, take 1st right over bailey bridge. From N A68, 1st
left past "Welcome" sign, following signs. Please see
the advertisement on page 27 for details of Club
Members' benefits. A 3-acre site with 55 touring
pitches.*

🖪 📞 ⊙ 🗗 🖳 ☀ 🖃 📞 ⛬
➔ ♪ 🏖
Credit Cards 💳 🈹

Jedwater Caravan Park (NT665160)
TD8 6QS ☎ 01835 840219 (4.5m S of Jedburgh off A68
on unclass rd) Signposted
►►► Family Park ★ 🚐 £8-£9 ⛺ £8-£9 ▲ £7-£9
Open Etr-Oct Booking advisable high season Last arrival
mdnt Last departure noon
*A quiet riverside site 4.5m S of Jedburgh, close to A68
but unaffected by traffic noise. Ideal for touring Borders
and Northumberland. A 10-acre site with 30 touring
pitches and 60 statics.
Bike hire, trampoline, football field.*

🖪 📞 ⊙ 🗗 🖳 🖐 ⛆ ☀ 🗛 ⊘ 🖃 🅃 📞
🏮 🗛 🐓 🏖
➔ ∪ 🏴 ♪

KELSO

Springwood Caravan Park (NT720334)
TD5 8LS ☎ 01573 224596 (1m S on A699)
Signposted

◯◯◯◯◯◯◯◯

►►►► De-Luxe Park 🚐 £9-£11 ⛺ £9-£11 ▲ £10
Open end Mar-mid Oct Booking advisable bank hols &
Jul-Aug Last arrival 23.00hrs
*A very well-maintained site with a pleasant atmosphere.
Set in a secluded position close to the tree-lined River*

*Teviot about 1m W of town. Winner of the Campsite of
the Year Award for Scotland 1998/9. On A699 (signed
Newton St Boswells). A 4-acre site with 50 touring
pitches and 260 statics.*

🖪 📞 ⊙ 🗗 🖳 🖐 ☀ 🗛 🛈 📞 🐓 ⛬
➔ ∪ 🏴 ⛺ ♪ 🏖
Credit Cards 💳 🈹 🔅

◯◯◯◯◯◯◯◯

KILMARNOCK

Cunningham Head Estate Caravan Park (NS370418)
Cunningham Head, Irvine KA3 2PE ☎ 01294 850238
Signposted
►► Town & Country Pennant Park ★ 🚐 £7-£8.50
⛺ £7-£8.50 ▲ £6-£8.50
Open Apr-Sep Booking advisable Jul-Aug Last arrival
22.00hrs Last departure noon
*A rural site in the grounds of a farmland estate, 3.5m
NE of Irvine on B769. From Irvine take A736 Glasgow
road, at Stanecastle roundabout turn E on to B769
Stewarton road. Park is 3m on left. A 7-acre site with 50
touring pitches and 50 statics.*

🖪 📞 ⊙ 🗗 🖳 🖐 🗛 ⊘ 🖃 📞
➔ ⛺ ♪ 🏖

KIPPFORD

Kippford Caravan Park (NX844564)
Kippford Caravan Park DG5 4LF ☎ 01556 620636
Signposted
Nearby town: Dalbeattie
►►► Family Park 🚐 £9-£11 ⛺ £9-£11 ▲ £6-£11
Open Mar-Oct Booking advisable Last arrival 21.00hrs
Last departure 11.00hrs
*Part-level, part-sloping grass site surrounded by trees
and bushes, set in hilly country adjacent to Urr Water
estuary and stony beach. On A710. An 18-acre site with
45 touring pitches and 119 statics.
Childrens adventure playground.*

🖪 📞 ⊙ 🗗 🖳 🗛 🛈 🖃 📞 🐓 🏖
➔ ∪ 🏴 ⛆ ♪

KIRKCUDBRIGHT

Seaward Caravan Park (NX662494)
Dhoon Bay DG6 4TJ ☎ 01557 870267 & 331079 (2m SW
off B727 Borgue Road) Signposted

◯◯◯◯◯◯◯

►►►► De-Luxe Park ★ 🚐 £7.20-£10.30
⛺ £7.20-£10.30 ▲ £7.20-£10.30

Open Mar-Oct (rs Mar-mid May & mid Sep-Oct swimming pool closed) Booking advisable Spring bank hols & Jul-Aug Last arrival 21.30hrs Last departure 11.30hrs
This very attractive elevated site has outstanding views over the Dee estuary. Facilities are well organised and neatly kept. On B727 from Kirkcudbright towards Borgue. An 8-acre site with 26 touring pitches and 30 statics.
TV aerial hook-up, mini golf. Dishwashing.

🔋 🚮 🦴 ⊙ 🗑 🗑 🔦 ⊰ 🔌 🖵 ☼ 🛒 ⚙ 🛆 🏕 🔦 🥢
🐕 🝙 ♿
→ ∪ ⟋ 🛆 🝙 ♪

Silvercraigs Caravan & Camping Site (NX686508)
Silvercraigs Rd DG6 4BT ☎ 01557 330123 & 01556 502521 Signposted
▶▶ Town & Country Pennant Park ★ 🚗 £6.90-£8.50 🚐 £6.90-£8.50 ▲ £6.90-£8.50
Open Etr-mid Oct Last departure noon
A well-maintained municipal site overlooking town and harbour, just a short stroll to the town centre. A 6-acre site with 50 touring pitches.

🔋 🦴 ⊙ ☼ ⚙ 🔦
→ ∪ ⟋ 🛆 ♪ 🝙

KIRKFIELDBANK

Clyde Valley Caravan Park (NS868441)
ML11 9TS ☎ 01555 663951 Signposted
▶▶ Town & Country Pennant Park 🚗 🚐 ▲
Open Apr-Oct Booking advisable anytime Last arrival 23.00hrs Last departure noon

Level, grass site with trees and bushes set in hilly country with access to river. From Glasgow on A72, cross river bridge at Kirkfieldbank and site is on left. From Lanark on A72, turn right at bottom of very steep hill before going over bridge. A 5-acre site with 50 touring pitches and 115 statics.

🔋 🦴 ⊙ 🗑 ⚙ 🦴 🛆 ⊙ 🔦 🛒 🔦 🝙
→ ∪ ⟋ ✕ 📷 ♪

LANARK

Newhouse Caravan & Camping Park (NS926456)
Ravenstruther ML11 8NP ☎ 01555 870228 Signposted
▶▶▶ Family Park 🚗 £7.50 🚐 £7.50 ▲ £7.50
Open mid Mar-mid Oct Booking advisable Jul-Aug Last arrival 22.00hrs Last departure noon
Pleasant level grass and gravel site, with young trees and bushes, situated on A70 Ayr-Edinburgh road, 3m E of Lanark. A 5-acre site with 45 touring pitches and 3 statics.
Caravan storage compound.

🔋 🦴 ⊙ 🗑 🔦 ☼ ⚙ 🦴 🛆 ⊙ 🔦 🛒 🦴 🏕 🔦 🝙 ♿
→ ∪ ⟋ ✕ ♪

LANGHOLM

Ewes Water Caravan & Camping Park (NY365855)
Milntown DG13 0BG ☎ 013873 80386 & 80358
▶▶▶ Family Park ★ 🚗 fr £7 🚐 fr £7 ▲ fr £4
Open Apr-Sep
A recently developed park in sheltered wooded valley close to unspoilt Borders town. Directly off A7T approx .5m on Hawick side of town centre. A 2-acre site with 24 touring pitches.

🔋 🦴 ⊙ 🦴 ⚙ 🦴 🏕 ♿
→ ⟋ ♪ 🝙

LAUDER

Thirlestane Castle Caravan & Camping Site (NT536473)
Thirlestane Castle TD2 6RU ☎ 01578 722254 & 0976 231032 Signposted
▶▶▶ Family Park 🚗 £8 🚐 £8 ▲ £8
Open Etr-Oct Booking advisable Jul-Aug Last arrival anytime Last departure anytime
Mainly level grass site set in the grounds of the impressive Thirlestane Castle. Set off the A697, S of the village. A 5-acre site with 60 touring pitches.

🔋 🦴 ⊙ 🗑 🔦
→ ⟋ ♪ 🝙

LOCHMABEN

Halleaths Caravan Site (NY098818)
DG11 1NA ☎ 01387 810630 Signposted
Nearby town: Lockerbie
▶▶▶ Family Park 🚗 🚐 ▲
Open Mar-Nov Booking advisable bank hols & Jul-Aug Last arrival 22.00hrs Last departure noon
Level, grassy site in a sheltered position with a wood on one side and a high hedge on the other. From Lockerbie on A74(M) take A709 to Lochmaben - .5m on right after crossing River Annan. An 8-acre site with 70 touring pitches and 12 statics.
Fishing (charged).

🔋 🦴 ⊙ 🗑 🔦 ☼ ⚙ 🦴 🛆 ⊙ 🔦 🏕 🔦 🝙
→ ⟋ ✕ 📷 ♪

Kirkloch Brae Caravan Site (NY082825)
☎ 01461 203311 & 01556 502521 Signposted
▶▶ Town & Country Pennant Park ★ ⚙ £6.10 ⚙ £6.10
▲ £3.75
Open Etr-Oct Last departure noon
A grassy lochside site with superb views and well-maintained facilities. Signed from centre of town. A 1.5-acre site with 30 touring pitches.

🔲 📻 ☉ ⛉ ⚠
→ ▶ ⤳ ⚱

LOCHNAW

Drumlochart Caravan Park (NW997634)
DG9 0RN ☎ 01776 870232 Signposted
Nearby town: Stanraer

▶▶▶▶ De-Luxe Park ★ ⚙ £8.50-£10 ⚙ £8.50-£10
Open Mar-Oct Booking advisable bank hols & Jul-Aug
Last arrival 22.00hrs Last departure noon
A peaceful rural site in hilly woodland, adjacent to Loch Ryan and Luce Bay, offering coarse fishing. 5m NW of Stranraer on B7043. A 9-acre site with 30 touring pitches and 96 statics.
10 acre Loch for coarse fishing & rowing boats.

🔲 📻 ☉ 🖥 ⛉ ⚡ ⚠ ❗ 🕯 ⚱
→ ∪ ▶ ⤴ ⤳

LOCKERBIE

See **Ecclefechan**

MAYBOLE

The Ranch (NS286102)
Culzean Rd KA19 8DU ☎ 01655 882446
Nearby town: Ayr

▶▶▶▶ De-Luxe Park ★ ⚙ £7.50-£9.50 ⚙ £7.50-£9.50
▲ £5-£8
Open Mar-Oct & wknds in winter Booking advisable
bank hols & Jul-Sep Last arrival 20.00hrs Last departure
noon
A small well run touring site with good views and many on site amenities. Situated on the L of B7023, 1m S of Maybole towards Culzean. A 9-acre site with 40 touring pitches and 68 statics.
Mini gym, sauna & sunbed.

🔲 📻 🖥 ⛉ ⚡ ⚡ ✴ ⚠ ❗ ⊞ ✕ 🕯 ⛲ 🛏 🐕 ▣
⚱ ♿
→ ∪ ▶ ◎ ⤴ ⤳

Camping & Caravanning Club Site (NS247103)
Culzean Castle KA19 8JK ☎ 01655 760627 (in season) &
01203 694995 (on A719) Signposted

AA pennant classification covers the touring section of a park, but not the static caravans available for rent, so we cannot deal with any complaints about static vans.

▶▶▶▶ De-Luxe Park ★ ⚙ £7-£10 ⚙ £7-£10 ▲ £7-£10
Open end Mar-early Nov Booking advisable bank hols &
Jul-Aug Last arrival 21.00hrs Last departure noon
A mainly level, grassy site situated at the entrance to the castle and country park, surrounded by trees on three sides and with lovely views over Culzean Bay. Signed at entrance to Culzean Castle on A719. Please see the advertisement on page 27 for details of Club Members' benefits. A 6-acre site with 90 touring pitches.

🔲 📻 ☉ 🖥 ⛉ ✴ ⚠ ❗ ⌀ 🖽 🕯 🛏 🐕
→ ∪ ▶ ⚱

Credit Cards 💳 💳 💳 💳 🗐

MOFFAT

Camping & Caravanning Club Site (NT085050)
Hammerlands Farm DG10 9QL ☎ 01683 220436 (in season) & 01203 694995 Signposted
▶▶▶ Family Park ★ ⚙ £11-£14 ⚙ £11-£14 ▲ £11-£14
Open end Mar-early Nov Booking advisable Spring bank hol & peak periods Last arrival 21.00hrs Last departure noon
Well-maintained level grass touring site. Leave A74 onto A701 to Moffat centre, take A708 and site is signed. Please see the advertisement on page 27 for details of Club Members' benefits. A 14-acre site with 200 touring pitches.

🔲 📻 ☉ 🖥 ⛉ ✴ ⚠ ❗ ⌀ ⊟ 🕯 🛏 ♿
→ ∪ ▶ ⤴ ⚱

Credit Cards 💳 💳 💳 💳 🗐

NEWTON STEWART

Creebridge Caravan Park (NX415656)
Minnigaff DG8 6AJ ☎ 01671 402324 & 402432
Signposted
▶ ▶ ▶ Family Park ★ 🚐 fr £7.80 🚐 £7.40-£7.80
🛆 £2.30-£3
Open Apr-Oct (rs Mar only one toilet block open)
Booking advisable Jul-Aug Last arrival 20.00hrs Last
departure noon
*A level urban site a short walk from the amenities of
town. .25m E of Newton Stewart at Minnigaff on the
bypass, signed off A75. A 4.5-acre site with 36 touring
pitches and 50 statics.*
Security street lighting.

🖾 🕅 ⊙ 🗟 🦒 🔦 ☀ 𝐴 🅸 🖉 🔁 🎕 📞 🚿 🎝
➔ ∪ 🏲 ◎ 😋 🎝

Talnotry Campsite (NX492719)
Queens Way, New Galloway Rd DG8 7BL ☎ 01671
402420 & 402170 (7m NE off A712) Signposted
▶▶ Town & Country Pennant Park 🚐 🚐 🛆
Open Apr-Sep Booking advisable Etr
*An attractive open grassy site set amidst the superb
scenery of Galloway Forest Park close to A712 and the
picturesque Queens Way. Owned and run by the
Forestry Commission. A 15-acre site with 60 touring
pitches.*

𝐴 📞 🎕 🎕 🛆
➔ 🎝

Credit Cards 💳 💳

PALNACKIE

Barlochan Caravan Park (NX819572)
DG7 1PF ☎ 01556 600256 & 01557 870267 Signposted
Nearby town: Dalbeattie
▶ ▶ ▶ Family Park ★ 🚐 £7-£9.75 🚐 £7-£9.75 🛆 £7-£9.75
Open Apr-Oct (rs Apr-mid May & mid Sep-end Oct
swimming pool) Booking advisable Spring bank hol &
Jul-Aug Last arrival 21.30hrs Last departure 11.30hrs

*An attractive terraced site in a sheltered position but
with fine, open views. On A711. A 9-acre site with 20
touring pitches and 40 statics.*
Fishing, pitch & putt. Dishwashing facilities.

🖾 🕅 ⊙ 🗟 🦒 ⏚ 🔦 🖳 ☀ 𝐴 🅸 🖉 🔁 🎕 📞 🎕 🎕
🛆 ⏚
➔ 🏲 🎝

PARTON

Loch Ken Holiday Park (NX687702)
DG7 3NE ☎ 01644 470282 (on A713) Signposted
Nearby town: Castle Douglas
▶ ▶ ▶ Family Park ★ 🚐 £8-£10 🚐 £8-£10 🛆 £7-£9
Open mid Mar-mid Nov (rs Mar/Apr (ex Etr) & late Sep-
Nov restricted shop hours) Booking advisable Etr,
Spring bank hol & Jun-Aug Last arrival 20.00hrs Last
departure noon
*An attractive touring site on eastern shores of Loch Ken,
with superb views. Off A713. A 7-acre site with 52
touring pitches and 33 statics.*
Bike, boat & canoe hire, fishing on loch.

🖾 🕅 ⊙ 🗟 🦒 ☀ 𝐴 🅸 🖉 🔁 🎕 📞 🚿 🎕 🎕 🛆
➔ 🛆 ⌁ 🎝

PEEBLES

Crossburn Caravan Park (NT248417)
The Glades, 95 Edinburgh Rd EH45 8ED
☎ 01721 720501 (.5m N on A703) Signposted

〇〇〇〇〇〇〇〇〇

▶ ▶ ▶ De-Luxe Park 🚐 £9-£10 🚐 £8.50-£9.50
🛆 £8-£10
Open Apr-Oct Booking advisable Jul-Aug Last arrival
23.00hrs Last departure 14.00hrs
*A level site in a peaceful and relatively quiet location,
despite the proximity of the main road which partly
borders the site, as does the Eddleston Water. Facilities
maintained to a high standard. A 6-acre site with 35
touring pitches and 95 statics.*
9 hole putting course & mountain bikes for hire.

🖾 🌢 🕅 ⊙ 🗟 🦒 🔦 ☀ 𝐴 🅸 🖉 🔁 🎕 📞
🚿 🎕 🎕 🎕 🛆
➔ ∪ 🏲 🎝
Credit Cards 💳 💳 🔒

〇〇〇〇〇〇

Rosetta Caravan & Camping Park (NT245415)
Rosetta Rd EH45 8PG ☎ 01721 720770
Signposted
▶ ▶ ▶ Family Park 🚐 🚐 🛆
Open Apr-Oct Booking advisable public & bank hols
Last arrival 23.00hrs Last departure 15.00hrs
*A pleasant parkland site set in hilly woodland country.
From N signed from A703, 1m S of Redscarhead, 2m N
of Peebles. A 25-acre site with 160 touring pitches and
29 statics.*
Bowling & putting greens.

🖾 🕅 ⊙ 🗟 🦒 🔦 🖳 ☀ 🍷 𝐴 🅸 🖉 🔁 🎕 📞 🎕 🎕
➔ ∪ 🏲 ⌁ 🎝

PENPONT

Penpont Caravan and Camping Park (NX852947)
DG3 4BH ☎ 01848 330470 Signposted
Nearby town: Thornhill
▶ ▶ ▶ Family Park 🚐 £7.50 🚐 £6.50-£7.50
🛆 £6.50-£7.50
Open Etr or Apr-Oct Booking advisable Jul-Aug Last
arrival 23.00hrs Last departure 14.00hrs
*Peaceful, grassy, slightly sloping site in a rural area,
excellently situated for touring. From Thornhill on the*
contd.

A702, site on left 0.5 miles before Penpont village. A 1.5-acre site with 20 touring pitches and 20 statics.

🏨 📞 ⊙ 🖥 ⚙ 🔌 ▮ ∅ ⊟ 📞 🐕
➔ ► ⚓

PORTPATRICK

Galloway Point Holiday Park (NX005537)
Portree Farm DG9 9AA ☎ 01776 810561 Signposted
Nearby town: Stranraer
► ► ► **Family Park** 🚐 £10-£12 🚐 £9-£12 ▲ £7-£10
Open Etr-Oct Booking advisable Mar, & May-Oct Last arrival 23.00hrs Last departure 14.00hrs
Strung out along gorse-clad downland, the holiday park looks out on the North Channel 1m S of town. Approach on A77, then take 1st unclass rd on left after entering village. Galloway Point is the second caravan park from the top of the steep hill; park at sign and walk to reception. An 18-acre site with 100 touring pitches and 60 statics.

🏨 📞 ⊙ 🖥 ⚙ 🍴 ⚔ ▮ ∅ ⊟ T ✖ 📞 🐾 🐕 🔥
➔ ∪ ► ⊙ ⚓ ⚓

Sunnymeade Caravan Park (NX005540)
DG9 8LN ☎ 01776 810293
Nearby town: Stranraer
► ► ► **Family Park** ★ 🚐 £7-£8.50 🚐 £7-£8.50 ▲ £7-£8.50
Open mid Mar-Oct Booking advisable
A mainly static park with mostly grass touring pitches, and views of the coast and Irish Sea. Approach on A77, then 1st unclassified road on left after entering village. First caravan park on left at top of hill. An 8-acre site with 15 touring pitches and 75 statics. Private coarse fishing pond on site.

🏨 📞 ⊙ 🖥 ⚙ ▮ ⊟ 📞
➔ ∪ ► ⚓ ⚓ ⚓

POWFOOT

Queensberry Bay Caravan Park (NY135653)
DG12 5PU ☎ 01461 700205 Signposted
Nearby town: Annan
► ► ► **Family Park** 🚐 🚐 ▲
Open Etr-Oct Booking advisable Jul-Aug Last arrival 20.00hrs Last departure noon
A flat, mainly grassy site in a quiet location on the shores of the Solway Firth with views across the estuary to Cumbrian hills. Follow sign to Powfoot off B724 and drive through village past golf club on single track road on shore edge to site. .75m. A 5-acre site with 100 touring pitches and 60 statics.
See advertisement on page 252

🏨 📞 ⊙ 🖥 ▮ ∅ ⊟ 📞 ⚓
➔ ► ☕ ⚓

ROCKCLIFFE

Castle Point Caravan Park (NX851539)
DG5 4QL ☎ 01556 630248 Signposted
Nearby town: Dalbeattie

Remember that many parks in this guide may refuse to take bookings from groups of young people or groups of people of the same sex. Always check before you go.

► ► ► **Family Park** 🚐 £7.50-£10.50 🚐 £7.50-£10.50
▲ £7.50-£10.50
Open Etr-Sep (rs Mar-Etr & 1-30 Oct limited supervision)
Booking advisable Whit wk & Jul-Aug Last arrival 23.00hrs Last departure 11.00hrs
A level, grassy site with superb views across the estuary and surrounding hilly countryside. Leave A710 onto unclass rd to Rockcliffe, site signed on left before descent into village. A 3-acre site with 29 touring pitches and 8 statics.

🏨 📞 ⊙ ⚙ ▮ ∅ ⊟ 🐕 ⚙
➔ ∪ ► ⊙ △ ⚓ ⚓ 🖥 ⚓

SANDHEAD

Sands of Luce Caravan Park (NX103510)
D69 9JR ☎ 01776 830456 (entrance off A716)
Signposted
Nearby town: Stranraer

◯◯◯◯◯◯◯◯◯

► ► ► ► **De-Luxe Park** 🚐 £7-£9 🚐 £6.50-£8.50 ▲ £7-£9
Open mid Mar-Oct Booking advisable Jul-Aug Last arrival 22.00hrs Last departure noon
A friendly site on a beautiful sandy beach, with lovely views across Luce Bay. Facilities are well-maintained and clean. Turn left off A75 onto B7084 2m from Glenluce, signed Sandhead and Drummore, and site signed on left in 5m. A 3-acre site with 50 touring pitches and 40 statics.
Boat launching, dishwashing sinks.

🏨 📞 ⊙ 🖥 🍴 ✎ ⚙ 🔌 ▮ ∅ ⊟ 📞 ⚓ ⚙
➔ ⚓

◯◯◯◯◯◯◯◯◯

SANDYHILLS

Sandyhills Bay Leisure Park (NX892552)
DG5 4NY ☎ 01557 870267 & 01387 780257 (7m from Dalbeattie, 6.5m from Kirkbean) Signposted
Nearby town: Dalbeattie
► ► ► **Family Park** ★ 🚐 £7-£10.30 🚐 £7-£10.30
▲ £7-£10.30
Open Apr-Oct Booking advisable Spring bank hol & Jun-Aug Last arrival 21.30hrs Last departure 11.30hrs

A flat, grassy site adjacent and with access to south-facing Sandyhills Bay and beach, sheltered by woods and hills with superb views. Site on A710 coast road. A 6-acre site with 26 touring pitches and 34 statics.
Dishwashing facilities.

🏨 📞 ⊙ 🖥 🔌 ⚔ ⚙ ▮ ∅ ⊟ T 📞 🔥 🐕 ⚓
➔ ∪ ► ⚓

SANQUHAR

Castleview Caravan & Camping Park (NS787095)
Townfoot DG4 6AX
☎ 01659 50291 & 50125
▶ ▶ ▶ Family Park ★ ♠ £7 ♠ £7 ▲ £7
Open Etr-Oct
A very good little park on edge of olde worlde village, with lovely views and close to Southern Upland Way coast to coast walk. Located with direct access of A76 at S end of town. A 2-acre site with 15 touring pitches.

Credit Cards

SELKIRK

Victoria Park Caravan & Camping Park (NT465287)
Victoria Park, Buccleuch Rd TD7 5DN ☎ 01750 20897
Signposted
▶ ▶ ▶ Family Park ♠ ♠ ▲
Open Apr-Oct (rs 10-18 Jun site closed) Booking advisable Jul-Aug Last arrival 21.00hrs Last departure 14.00hrs
A consistently well-maintained site with good basic facilities forming part of public park and swimming pool complex close to River Ettrick. From A707/A708 N of town, cross river bridge, take first left then left again. A 3-acre site with 60 touring pitches.
Mini gymnasium, sauna, sunbed.

SOUTHERNESS

Southerness Holiday Village (NX976545)
DG2 8AZ ☎ 01387 880256 & 880281
Signposted
Nearby town: Dumfries

♠ ♠ ▲
Open Mar-Oct Booking advisable Last departure 16.00hrs
A large family campsite with plenty of on-site entertainment situated close to sandy beach. Near centre of Southerness. An 8-acre site with 200 touring pitches and 350 statics.
Amusement centre, disco, videos.

Credit Cards

STRANRAER

Aird Donald Caravan Park (NX075605)
London Rd DG9 8RN ☎ 01776 702025 Signposted

▶ ▶ ▶ ▶ De-Luxe Park ♠ £8.50 ♠ £8.50 ▲ £3.70-£7.90
Open all year Booking advisable Last departure 16.00hrs
A spacious touring site, mainly grass but with tarmac hard-standing area. On the fringe of town screened by

mature shrubs and trees. Ideal stopover en route to N.I. ferry ports. A 12-acre site with 100 touring pitches.

TARBOLTON

Middlemuir Park (NS439263)
KA5 5NR ☎ 01292 541647 Signposted
Nearby town: Ayr
▶ ▶ ▶ Family Park ♠ ♠ ▲
Open all year Booking advisable bank hols & Jul-Aug Last arrival 18.00hrs Last departure noon
A rural site in the partly-walled garden where Montgomerie House used to stand. Set in rolling farmland off the B743 Ayr-Mauchline road. A 17-acre site with 25 touring pitches and 45 statics.

WALES

The directory which follows has been divided into three geographical regions. Counties have not been shown against individual locations as recent legislation has created a number of smaller counties which will be unfamiliar to the visitor. The postal authorities have confirmed that it is no longer necessary to include a county name in addresses, provided a post code is shown. All locations appear on the regional maps in their appropriate counties.

NORTH WALES

This region includes the counties of Conwy, Denbighshire, Flintshire, Gwynedd, Isle of Anglesey and Wrexham.

ABERGELE

See **Betws-Yn-Rhos**

ABERSOCH

Bryn Cethin Bach Caravan Park (SH304290)
Lon Garmon LL53 7UL ☎ 01758 712719 & 712156
Nearby town: Pwllheli

▶ ▶ ▶ ▶ De-Luxe Park ★ ♠ £9-£11 ♠ £9-£11
Open Apr-Oct (rs Mar-May shop closed) Booking advisable Spring bank hol & Jul-Aug Last arrival 18.00hrs Last departure noon
A well-run family site within .5m of sandy beaches, the harbour and all the facilities of Abersoch, offering lovely views and a first class toilet block. On entering Abersoch take unclass rd signed Aberdaron, and site on right at top of hill. A 2-acre site with 15 touring pitches and 53 statics.
Lake & fishing.

North Wales

[Map of North Wales showing towns and roads including Amlwch, Dulas, Marian-glas, Brynteg, Pentraeth, Llanbedrgoch, HOLYHEAD, ISLE OF ANGLESEY, Rhosneigr, Llandudno, Conwy, Llanddulas, Towyn, Rhuallt, Brynsiencyn, BANGOR, Betws-yn-Rhos, FLINTSHIRE, Tal-y-Bont, Trefriw, CONWY, Caernarfon, Llanrwst, RUTHIN, Dinas Dinlle, Betws Garmon, BETWS-Y-COED, Llandwrog, Pontlyfni, Beddgelert, DENBIGHSHIRE, GWYNEDD, Corwen, WREXHAM, Eyton, Bangor-on-Dee, Llanystumdwy, Porthmadog, Llangollen, Llandrillo, Criccieth, Morfa Bychan, Talsarnau, Bala, Abersoch, Tal-y-bont, DOLGELLAU, Barmouth, Bryncrug, Tywyn. Scale: 0–20 miles, 0–30 kilometres]

Seaview (SH305262)
Sarn Bach LL53 7ET ☎ 01758 712052 & 713256
Signposted
Nearby town: Pwllheli
▶▶ Town & Country Pennant Park ★ ⊕ £8-£11 ⊕ £7-£9
Å £7-£9
Open Mar-Oct Booking advisable from March Last
arrival 23.00hrs Last departure noon
*Gently sloping family site in quiet elevated position
near to Abersoch, on the Lleyn Peninsula. Very sharp
turn opposite the telephone kiosk in Sarn Bach for site
200yds on right. A 4-acre site with 97 touring pitches.*

🖪 🖍 ⊙ 🖾 🖻 ☀ ▤ ⊘ 🖃 📞 ➡ 🌲 ⌂ 🖃 🥾
➡ ∪ ⌶ △ ↳ ☷ ♪
Credit Cards ● ▨ ▨

ANGLESEY, ISLE OF

AMLWCH

Point Lynas Caravan Park (SH474930)
Llaneilan LL68 9LT ☎ 01407 831130 & 01248 852423
▶▶ Town & Country Pennant Park ★ ⊕ £6-£8 ⊕ £6-£8
Å £5-£8
Open Mar-Oct Booking advisable bank hols Last arrival
22.00hrs Last departure noon
*This first-class site is near a sheltered rocky cove, safe
for swimming. 1 mile N of Penysarn on A5025; turn
right at garage on to unclass rd to Llaneilian. Site on left
just before beach. A 2-acre site with 6 touring pitches
and 44 statics.*

Childrens sandpit & climbing bars.

🎭 🛉 ⊙ 🛢 🄿 ⊡ 🔔 � 🛆
→ 🇵 ✒ ⊡ 🛒

BRYNSIENCYN

Fron Caravan & Camping Site (SH472669)
LL61 6TX ☎ 01248 430310 Signposted
Nearby town: Bangor
▶ ▶ ▶ Family Park 🚐 £9 🚐 £8 ▲ £8
Open Etr-Sep Booking advisable Spring bank hol & Jul-Aug Last arrival 23.00hrs Last departure noon
Quiet family site in pleasant rural area, ideally situated for touring Anglesey and North Wales. Off A4080 Llanfair PG-Newborough road, 1m W of Brynsiencyn. A 5.5-acre site with 60 touring pitches.

🎭 🛉 ⊙ ⊓ ʒ ⦿ ✳ ⋀ 🛢 🄿 ⊡ 🅣 🔔 � 🛆
→ ∪ 🇵 🛆 ✒

BRYNTEG

Nant Newydd Caravan Park (SH485814)
LL78 8JH ☎ 01248 852842 & 852266
Signposted
Nearby town: Bangor

▶ ▶ ▶ De-Luxe Park 🚐 🚐 ▲
Open Mar-Oct (rs May & Sep pool restricted) Booking advisable Jul-Aug Last arrival mdnt Last departure 17.00hrs
Gently sloping grass site with mature trees and bushes set in meadowland adjacent to main road, 1m from Brynteg on B5110 towards Llangefni. A 4-acre site with 30 touring pitches and 83 statics.
Satalite TV & licensed shop.

🎭 🛉 ⊙ ⊡ ⊓ ʒ ⦿ 🗖 ✳ ⋀ 🛢 🄿 ⊡ 🅣 🔔 ⌗ 🍴
� ⟺ &
→ ∪ 🇵 🛆 ⚎ ✒

Ysgubor Fadog Caravan & Camping Site (SH497820)
Ysgubor Fadog, Lon Bryn Mair LL78 8QA
☎ 01248 852681 Signposted
Nearby town: Bangor
▶▶ Town & Country Pennant Park 🚐 £5.50-£6
🚐 £5.50-£6 ▲ £5.50-£6
Open Etr-Sep Booking advisable Whitsun & school hols
Last arrival 20.00hrs Last departure 18.00hrs
A peaceful and remote site reached along a narrow lane where care is needed. From Benllech take B5108, and after sports field take 3rd on left. A 2-acre site with 15 touring pitches and 1 static.

🎭 🛉 ⊙ ✳ ⊡ 🍴 🛆
→ ∪ 🇵 ⊚ ✒ ⊡ 🛒

DULAS

Tyddyn Isaf Caravan Park (SH486873)
Lligwy Bay LL70 9PQ ☎ 01248 410203 (.5m off A5025
between Benllech & Amlwch) Signposted
Nearby town: Benllech

▶ ▶ ▶ ▶ De-Luxe Park ★ 🚐 £8-£12 🚐 £8-£12 ▲ £6-£10
Open Mar-Oct (rs Mar-Etr & Oct clubhouse limited, shut from mid Sept) Booking advisable May bank hol & Jun-Aug Last arrival 22.00hrs Last departure 11.00hrs
A lovely site located on gently rising ground adjacent to sandy beach affording magnificent views. A 16-acre site with 80 touring pitches and 50 statics.

🎭 🛉 ⊙ ⊡ ⊓ ✳ ⦿ ⋀ 🛢 🄿 ⊡ 🅣 ✕ 🔔 ⌗ 🍴
⟺ ⟺
→ ∪ 🇵 🛆 ✢ ✒

LLANBEDRGOCH

Ty Newydd Leisure Park (SH508813)
LL76 8TZ ☎ 01248 450677 Signposted
Nearby town: Benlech
▶ ▶ ▶ Family Park ★ 🚐 £7-£17 🚐 £7-£17 ▲ £7-£17
Open Whit-mid Sep (rs Mar-Whit & mid Sep-Oct club/shop wknds only outdoor pool closed) Booking advisable Etr, Whit & Jul-Aug Last arrival 23.30hrs Last departure 10.00hrs
A low density site with many facilities including a health centre. Site N of village on unclass rd between A5025 and B5108. A 4-acre site with 40 touring pitches and 60 statics.
Health centre.
See advertisement under BENLLECH BAY

🎭 🛉 ⊙ ⊡ ⊓ ʒ ⦿ ✳ ⦿ ⋀ 🛢 🄿 ⊡ 🅣 ✕ 🔔
⟺ &
→ ∪ 🇵 🛆 ⚎ ✒

Credit Cards 💳 🆅🆂🅰 ⬛ ⬛ 🅖

MARIANGLAS

Home Farm Caravan Park (SH498850)
LL73 8PH ☎ 01248 410614

▶ ▶ ▶ ▶ De-Luxe Park ★ 🚐 £7.50-£12.50 🚐 £7.50-£11
▲ £7.50-£10.50
Open Apr-Oct Booking advisable bank hols Last arrival 21.00hrs Last departure noon
A first class site with friendly, helpful owners. On A5025, 2m N of Benllech, with park entrance 300 metres beyond church. Winner of the Best Campsite for Wales Award 1996/7. A 6-acre site with 61 touring pitches and 72 statics.
Indoor adventure playground.

🎭 🛉 ⊙ ⊡ ⊓ ⦿ 🗖 ✳ ⋀ 🛢 🄿 ⊡ 🅣 🔔 ⌗ ⟺ 🔔 &
→ ∪ 🇵 🛆 ✒

Credit Cards 💳 ⬛ 🆅🆂🅰 ⓘ ⬛ 🅖

PENTRAETH

Rhos Caravan Park (SH517794)
LL75 8DZ ☎ 01248 450214 (.75m N on A5025)
Signposted
Nearby town: Benllech
▶ ▶ ▶ Family Park 🚐 £6-£8 🚐 £6-£8 ▲ £6
Open Etr-Oct (rs Mar shop & showers restricted) Booking advisable Spring bank hol & Jul-Aug Last arrival 22.00hrs Last departure 16.00hrs

contd.

TOURING & CAMPING PARK
Llangynog Road, Bala LL23 7PH
Tel: 01678 520549

OUR TOP 10 FOR YOUR ENJOYMENT
1. FREE, NEW Hot Showers of CONTINENTAL Standard
2. FREE, NEW Spacious Private VANITY Cubicles with Individual Lights, Mirrors & Shaving Points
3. NEW Laundry with Washer, Drier, Iron & Deep Sink
4. FREE, NEW Disabled Facilities and Baby Room
5. NEAREST Park to Bala (a gentle 10 minutes walk)
6. CLOSEST Park to Sailing Club & Small Gauge Railway
7. SHOP Stocking Provisions and CALOR GAS
8. DOGS Welcome on our Dog Walk Area
9. NEW Hard Standing Parking Strips – All Electric
10. MODERN UNDERCOVER Dish Washing Facilities

For brochure or advance bookings phone 01678 520549. or fax: 01678 520006

Site on level, grassy ground off main road to Amlwch. On left side of A5025, 1m N of Pentraeth. A 15-acre site with 98 touring pitches and 60 statics.

🔌📻☉🅿☀⚠🛈🚿♿🛅🇹🔌🕇🐕🐎🎣
➜⋃🅿✚☕♨🎵

BALA

Camping & Caravanning Club Site (SH962391)
Crynierth Caravan Park, Cefn-Ddwysarn LL23 7IN
☎ 01678 530324 (in season) & 01203 694995 (3.25m NE off A494) Signposted

▶▶▶▶ De-Luxe Park ★ 🚐 £11-£14 🚐 £11-£14
Å £11-£14
Open end Mar-end Oct Booking advisable bank hols & peak periods Last arrival 21.00hrs Last departure noon
A quiet pleasant site with interesting views and high class facilities. Situated just off A494 4m E of Bala. Please see the advertisement on page 27 for details of Club Members' benefits. A 4-acre site with 50 touring pitches.

🔌📻☉🅿☀✳⚠🛈♿🕇🐕🐎🎣♿
➜⋃🅿✚☕♨🎵

Credit Cards 💳 💳 💳 💳 💳

Pen Y Bont Touring & Camping Park (SH932350)
Llangynog Rd LL23 7PH
☎ 01678 520549 & 0589 987499 (from A494 in Bala take B4391, site .75m along on right)
Signposted

▶▶▶▶ De-Luxe Park ★ 🚐 £8.45-£9.45 🚐 £7.95-£8.95
Å £7.45-£8.45
Open Apr-Oct Booking advisable all year Last arrival 24.30hrs Last departure 13.00hrs
Partly-sloping, grass and gravel site with trees and bushes set in woodland country, almost adjacent to river Dee and Bala Lake. 0.5m from Bala on side of B4391. A 7-acre site with 85 touring pitches. Dish washing & vegetable preparation area.

🔌📻☉🅿🔾☀✳🛈🛅🇹🔌🕇🐕♿
🏕🔥🐕🐎♿
➜⋃🅿☀✚☕♨🎵

Pen-y-Garth Caravan & Camping Park (SH940349)
Rhos-y-Gwaliau LL23 7ES
☎ 01678 520485 & 0850 773642 Signposted

▶▶▶ Family Park ★ 🚐 £6.95-£8.25 🚐 £6.95-£8.25
Å £6.95-£8.25
Open Mar-Oct Booking advisable bank hols & Jul-Aug Last arrival 22.00hrs Last departure noon
A level site with well-laid out pitches for tourers, amidst attractive scenery. From Bala take B4391 and in 1m follow unclass rd signed YH/Lake Vyrnwy. Site on right at top of hill. A 20-acre site with 63 touring pitches and 54 statics.
Table tennis,10acres recreation, dish washing room

🔌📻☉🅿🔾✳🛈🛅🇹✗🔌🏕🔥🐕🐎♿
➜⋃🅿☀✚☕♨🎵

BANGOR-ON-DEE

Camping & Caravanning Club Site (SJ385448)
The Racecourse, Overton Rd LL13 0DA
☎ 01978 781009 (in season) & 01203 694995
Signposted

▶▶▶ Family Park ★ 🚐 £9.20-£11.60 🚐 £9.20-£11.60
Å £9.20-£11.60
Open end Mar- beg Nov Booking advisable bank hols & peak periods Last arrival 21.00hrs Last departure noon
A mainly level, grassy site within the racecourse which lies in a bend of the River Dee. Please see the advertisement on page 27 for details of Club Members' benefits. A 6-acre site with 100 touring pitches.

🔌📻☉🅿🔾☀✳🛈🛅🇹🔌🐕🐎♿
➜⋃🔾

Credit Cards 💳 💳

BARMOUTH

Hendre Mynach Caravan Park (SH605170)
Llanaber Rd LL42 1YR
☎ 01341 280262 (.5m N on A496)
Signposted

▶▶▶▶ De-Luxe Park ★ 🚐 £6-£12 🚐 £6-£10 Å £5-£10
Open Mar-Nov (rs Mar-Etr & Oct-Nov (ex half term) shop) Booking advisable bank hols & Jul-Aug Last arrival 23.00hrs Last departure noon
A lovely site with immaculate facilities, situated off the A496 on the northern outskirts of Barmouth and near to railway, with almost direct access to promenade and beach. A 10-acre site with 205 touring pitches.

TV & satellite hook ups.

🔌 ⌂ ☉ 回 ᛩ ☼ ⚠ 🅿 ⊘ 🆃 ✗ ☎ 🛒 🐕 ➤ ∪ ♨ ⚓ ⚶

Ọ Ọ Ọ Ọ Ọ Ọ Ọ Ọ

Trawsdir Touring & Caravan Park (SH596198)
Llanaber LL42 1RR ☎ 01341 280999 & 280611 (2.5m N on A496)
▶ ▶ ▶ **Family Park** ★ 🚐 £10-£15 🚍 £10-£15 ▲ £5-£7
Open Mar-Oct Booking advisable Etr, Whitsun & Jul-Aug Last arrival 21.00hrs Last departure noon
A new park on a working sheep farm with views to sea and hills, and very accessible to motor traffic. 3m N of Barmouth on A496. 50 touring pitches.

🔌 ⌂ ☉ 回 ᛩ ☼ 🅿 ⊘ ☎ 🐕 ⚶ ➤ ∪ ◎ ⚓ ⚶ ⚶

BEDDGELERT

Beddgelert Caravan & Camping Site (SH578490)
LL55 4UU ☎ 01766 890288 (2m N on A4085) Signposted
▶ ▶ ▶ **Family Park** ★ 🚐 £7-£8 🚍 £7-£8 ▲ £7-£8
Open all year Booking advisable bank hols & Jul-Aug Last arrival 22.00hrs Last departure noon
Well-run and very popular Forestry Commission site amidst trees and bushes. Set in mountainous woodland country near to river and main road. Site in 1m N of Beddgelert on A4085. A 25-acre site with 280 touring pitches.

🔌 ⌂ ☉ ᛩ ☼ ⚠ 🅿 ⊘ ⊞ 🆃 ☎ 🏕 ⚶ ⚶ ➤ ⚓ 回

Credit Cards 💳 💳 💳 💳 💳

BENLLECH BAY

See **Brynteg & Llanbedrgoch** under **Anglesey, Isle of**

BETWS GARMON

Bryn Gloch Caravan & Camping Park (SH534574)
LL54 7YY ☎ 01286 650216 Signposted
Nearby town: Caernarfon

Ọ Ọ Ọ Ọ Ọ Ọ Ọ Ọ

▶ ▶ ▶ ▶ **De-Luxe Park** ★ 🚐 £7.50-£9 🚍 £7.50-£9 ▲ £7.50-£9
Open all year Booking advisable school & bank hols Last arrival 23.00hrs Last departure 17.00hrs
An excellent family-run site with new and improved toilets, and all level pitches in beautiful surroundings. Site on A4085 between Beddgelert and Caernarfon. A 12-acre site with 92 touring pitches and 14 statics. Family bathroom & mother & baby room.
See advertisement under CAERNARFON

🔌 🛒 ⌂ ☉ 回 ᛩ ⚫ 🛒 ☼ 🍴 ⚠ 🅿 ⊘ ⊞ 🆃 ✗ ☎ 🏕 🏕 🐕 ⚶ ⚶ ➤ ∪ 🅿 ◎ ⚶ ⚓

Credit Cards 💳 💳

See advertisement on page 268.

Ọ Ọ Ọ Ọ Ọ Ọ Ọ Ọ

WITHIN SNOWDONIA NATIONAL PARK

Caravan & Camping Park
Betws Garmon, Nr. Caernarfon
Gwynedd LL54 7YY
Tel/Fax: (01286) 650216

On A4085 Beddgelert to Caernarfon road our 28 acre picturesque park is bounded partly by the river Gwyrfai in the Vale of Betws and is overlooked by the Welsh mountains of Mynydd Mawr and Moel Eilio.
We have 10 Dragon Award Caravans for hire, four level well drained fields for Touring Caravans and tents with continental type serviced and superpitches. Pitches are generally marked to avoid overcrowding.
★ LICENSED BAR & RESTAURANT ★ CHILDREN'S PLAY AREA ★ LUXURY TOILET & SHOWER BLOCKS ★ MOTHER / BABY ROOM ★ FAMILY BATHROOM ★ ELECTRIC HOOK-UPS ★ LAUNDERETTE ★ SHOP / OFF-LICENCE ★ TAKE-AWAY ★ GAMES ROOM ★ FISHING ★ MINI GOLF. Campsite of the year awards '91 & '92.
For further details of our excellent facilities send S.A.E. for brochure.
OPEN ALL YEAR (limited facilities in winter)

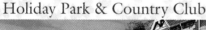

🕹 🕭 ⊙ 🗟 ⍾ 🗞 ☐ ⅄ ⚠ ⅰ ✕ 📞 🏛 ⊓ 🖭 🛒
➔ ∪ 🏳 ⊚ ◔ ♒ 🎣
Credit Cards 💳 🏧

See advertisement on page 268.

CAERNARFON

Bryn Teg Holiday Park (SH524636)
Llanrug LL55 4RF
☎ 01286 871374 & 01492 532197 (3m E A4086)

○○○○○○○○○

► ► ► ► De-Luxe Park ★ 🚐 £6.50-£13 🚐 £6.50-£13
🛏 £6.50-£13
Open Mar-14 Jan (rs mid Oct-Etr pool, bar & shop closed) Booking advisable bank hols & peak season Last arrival 20.00hrs Last departure noon
A large site set in undulating countryside, with mostly level pitches. Signed off A4086 near Llanrug, behind Bryn Bras Castle. A 50-acre site with 168 touring pitches and 287 statics.
12 acre lake with coarse & trout fishing.

🕹 🕭 ⊙ 🗟 ⍾ 🗞 ⚡ ☐ ❄ ⅄ ⚠ ⅰ ⊘ Ⓣ ✕ 📞 ↩
🏛 ⊓ 🐕 🐾 🛒 ♿
➔ ∪ 🏳 ⊚ ◔ ♒ 🎣
Credit Cards 💳 🏧 💳

○○○○○○○○○

Cadnant Valley Caravan Park (SH487628)
Cadnant Valley Park, Llanberis Rd LL55 2DF
☎ 01286 673196 Signposted
► ► ► Family Park 🚐 🚐 🛏
Open 15 Mar-Oct Booking advisable bank hols & Jul-Aug Last arrival 22.00hrs Last departure noon
Situated close to the main Caernarfon-Llanberis road and conveniently near the town. Level, terraced pitches in a secluded, landscaped, wooded valley with some near a stream. On the outskirts of Caernarfon on B4086 to llanberis. A 4.5-acre site with 69 touring pitches. Outdoor table tennis.

🕹 🕭 ⊙ 🗟 ⍾ ❄ ⚠ ⅰ ⊘ ⊞ 📞 🏛 ⊓ 🐕 🛒
➔ ∪ 🏳 ♒ 🎣 🎣

Glan Gwna Holiday Park (SH502622)
Caeathro LL55 2SG
☎ 01286 673456 & 676402
► ► ► Family Park 🚐 £7-£12 🛏 £7-£12   *contd.*

Open Etr-Oct (rs mid Apr-May & mid Sep-Oct some
facilities are closed) Booking advisable bank hols & Jul-
Aug Last arrival 23.00hrs Last departure noon
*Beautifully situated on a bend in the Afon Seiont, and
part of a large holiday complex with excellent facilities.
Take A4085 signed Beddgelert, 1m from Caernarfon. A
7-acre site with 100 touring pitches and 130 statics.*
Horse riding & fishing.

🔌 🐾 ⊙ 回 🖙 ⌘ 𝄇 ♀ ⚡ Ⓧ 🔍 ☕ ⛏ 🐕 🦮
➜ ∪ ▶ ◢ ♪

Riverside Camping (SH505630)
Caer Glyddyn, Pont Rug LL55 2BB ☎ 01286 672524 &
678781 eves (2m E on A4086) Signposted
▶▶▶ Family Park 🚐 £9-£11.50 🚗 £8-£10.50 ▲ £6-£8
Open Etr-end Oct Booking advisable Jul-Aug Last
arrival anytime Last departure 20.00hrs
*A secluded park divided up by shrubs and trees,
adjacent to the small River Seiont, 2m E of Caernarfon
on A4086. Entrance to site at Seiont Nurseries and
Garden Centre. A 4.5-acre site with 55 touring pitches.*
River swimming.

🔌 🐾 ⊙ ✳ ⚡ ◿ 🏠 🐕 🔍 ⚓
➜ ∪ ▶ ◎ ◢ ⚴ ♪ 回 🦮

**Ty'n yr Onnen Mountain Farm Caravan & Camping
(SH534588)**
Waunfawr LL55 4AX ☎ 01286 650281 Signposted
▶▶▶ Family Park ★ 🚐 £7-£8.50 🚗 £6-£7 ▲ £6-£7.50
Open Spring bank hol-Oct (rs Etr & Mayday bank hol open
if weather premitting) Booking advisable Spring bank hol
& Jul-Aug Last arrival 21.00hrs Last departure 10.00hrs
*A gently sloping site on a 200-acre sheep farm, set in
magnificent surroundings with mountain views. At
Waunfawr on A4085, turn down unclass rd opposite
church, and signed. A 4-acre site with 20 touring pitches
and 4 statics.*
Fishing.

🔌 🚮 🐾 ⊙ 回 🖙 ◀ 🖵 ✳ ⚡ 𝄇 ◿ ⊞ Ⓣ 🔍 🏠 ⛏
🐕 🦮
➜ ∪ ▶ ◢ ⚴ 😊 ♪
Credit Cards 💳

Conwy Touring Park (SH779757)
LL32 8UX ☎ 01492 592856 (1.5m S on B5106)
Signposted
▶▶▶ Family Park ★ 🚐 £4.85-£10.25 🚗 £4.85-£10.25
▲ £4-£10.25
Open Etr-Oct Booking advisable public hols & Jul-Aug
Last arrival 20.00hrs Last departure noon
*An excellent site, with informally sited pitches set high
up above the Conway Valley, and a good range of
facilities. A 70-acre site with 319 touring pitches.*
Indoor playground monitored by staff.

🔌 🐾 ⊙ 回 ◀ ✳ ♀ ⚡ 𝄇 ◿ Ⓣ 🔍 🐕 🦮 ⚓
➜ ∪ ▶ ♪
Credit Cards 💳 💳 💳 🅶

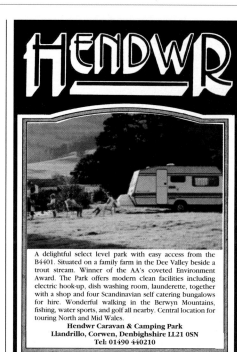

CORWEN

Glan Ceirw Caravan Park (SJ067454)
Ty Nant LL21 0RF ☎ 01490 420346
Nearby town: Bala
▶ ▶ ▶ **Family Park** ★ ⚘ £6-£7 ⊞ £6-£7 ▲ £5-£6
Open Mar-Oct no cars by tents
*A small riverside site in a rural location, 300yds off A5.
On unclass loop rd off A5 between Corwen and Betws-
y-Coed, 1.5m from Cerrigydruidion. A 1.5-acre site with
15 touring pitches and 29 statics.*

🏕🅿📶🏳🍴🅰🛁🔌🆔🔱⛲🚽🐕
➜🔺🧺🛍

Llawr-Betws Farm Caravan Park (SJ016424)
LL21 0HD ☎ 01490 460224 & 460296
Signposted
Nearby town: Bala
▶▶ **Town & Country Pennant Park** ★ ⚘ £6-£8 ⊞ £5-£6
▲ £4-£6
Open Mar-Oct Booking advisable bank hols & Jul-Aug
Last arrival 23.00hrs Last departure noon
*Mainly level site with grass and mature trees, 3m W of
Corwen off A494 Bala road. A 35-acre site with 35
touring pitches and 72 statics.
Fishing.*

🏕📶☀️⛽🔋🎣🍴☀️🏳🅰🛁🔌🆔🔱🐕♻️🛍
➜🔌▶🍴🚲🧺

CRICCIETH

Llwyn-Bugeilydd Caravan & Camping Site (SH498398)
LL52 0PN ☎ 01766 522235
Signposted
▶▶ **Town & Country Pennant Park** ★ ⚘ £7-£8 ⊞ £7-£8
▲ £5-£6.50
Open Etr/Apr-Oct Booking advisable Etr, Whit & Jul-Aug
Last arrival anytime Last departure 11.00hrs
*A beautiful little site, well-maintained and in excellent
condition, with sea and mountain views. Situated 1m N
of Criccieth on B4411, and first site on right. A 6-acre
site with 45 touring pitches.*

🏕📶☀️🔋☀️🅰🛁⛲🚽🐕🔱
➜🔌▶🔘🔺🍴🧺🛍

Tyddyn Cethin Farm (SH492404)
LL52 0NF ☎ 01766 522149
▶▶ **Town & Country Pennant Park** ★ ⚘ £7-£9.50 ⊞ £7-
£9.50 ▲ £6-£7
Open Mar-Oct Booking advisable Feb-Mar Last arrival
22.00hrs Last departure noon
*A very good quiet family holiday site with enthusiastic
proprietors, on banks of River Dwyfor. Travel N from
Criccieth on B4411 and Tyddyn Cethin is 4th site on right.
An 8-acre site with 60 touring pitches and 40 statics.
Fishing on site.*

🏕🚐📶☀️🔋☀️🅰🛁⛲🚽🐕
➜🔌▶🔘🔺🍴🧺🛍

Tyddyn Morthwyl (SH488402)
LL52 0NF ☎ 01766 522115 (1.25m N on B4411)
Signposted
▶▶ **Town & Country Pennant Park** ★ ⚘ £5 ⊞ £5 ▲ £5
Open Etr-Oct (rs Mar & Oct) Booking advisable Spring
bank hol & Jul-Aug Last departure 14.00hrs

*A quiet, sheltered site with good level grassy pitches,
ideal for families. Conveniently situated N of B4411,
1.5m from centre of Criccieth. A 10-acre site with 60
touring pitches and 22 statics.*

🏕📶☀️☀️🆔🔌
➜🔌▶🚲🧺🛍

DINAS DINLLE

Dinlle Caravan Park (SH443568)
LL54 5TW ☎ 01286 830324 (2m W of Dinas Dinlle coast)
Signposted
Nearby town: Caernarfon

⬭⬭⬭⬭⬭⬭⬭⬭

▶ ▶ ▶ ▶ **De-Luxe Park** ★ ⚘ £5-£10.50 ▲ £5-£10.50
Open May-Aug (rs Mar-Apr & Sep-Nov club, shop,
swimming pool restricted hours) Booking advisable
Spring bank hol & Jul-Aug Last arrival 23.00hrs Last
departure noon
*A very accessible, well-kept grassy level site, adjacent
to sandy beach, with good views to Snowdonia. Turn
right off A499 at sign for Caernarfon Airport An 11-acre
site with 200 touring pitches and 138 statics.
See advertisement under CAERNARFON*

🏕📶☀️⛽🔋🎣🔦☀️🍴🏳🅰🛁🆔🔌🧺♿
➜🔌🧺

Credit Cards 💳 💳 💳 💳 🅶

⬭⬭⬭⬭⬭⬭⬭⬭

EYTON

The Plassey Leisure Park (SJ353452)
The Plassey LL13 0SP ☎ 01978 780277 Signposted
Nearby town: Wrexham

⬭⬭⬭⬭⬭⬭⬭⬭

▶ ▶ ▶ ▶ **De-Luxe Park** ⚘ £10.50-£12.50 ⊞ £10.50-
£12.50 ▲ £10.50-£12.50
Open Mar-Oct Booking advisable bank hols & school
hols Last arrival 20.00hrs Last departure 18.00hrs

*A lovely level grassy site set in 247 acres of quiet farm
and meadowland. Adjoining the Plassey Craft Centre,
off the B5426 and signed from A483. A 10-acre site with
120 touring pitches and 40 statics.
Sauna, sunbed, badminton, table tennis,9 hole golf.*

🏕📶☀️⛽🔋🎣🔦🔦☀️🍴🏳🅰🛁🆔🔱✖️🔌🛎
⛲🐕🧺♿
➜🔌▶🔘🧺

Credit Cards 💳 💳 💳 🅶

⬭⬭⬭⬭⬭⬭⬭⬭

LLANDDULAS

Bron Y Wendon Caravan Park (SH904786)
Wern Rd LL22 8HG ☎ 01492 512903 (A55 heading west, turn at sign for Llanddulas (A547) then sharp right, continue for 200 yds under A55 bridge, park on left) Signposted
Nearby town: Colwyn Bay

► ► ► ► De-Luxe Park ♥ £8-£9 ♥ £8-£9
Open 21 Mar-30 Oct Booking advisable bank hols Last arrival anytime Last departure 11.00hrs
A good quality site with sea views from every pitch and excellent purpose-built ablution block. Located between main railway line and new N Wales coast highway (A55). Leave this road at the Llanddulas interchange (A547). An 8-acre site with 130 touring pitches.

Credit Cards 🏧

LLANDRILLO

Hendwr Caravan Park (SJ035386)
LL21 0SN ☎ 01490 440210 Signposted
Nearby town: Corwen
► ► ► Family Park ★ ♥ £7-£8.75 ♥ £7-£8.75 ▲ £7-£8.75
Open Apr-Oct (rs Nov-Mar no toilet facilities during this period) Booking advisable bank & school hols Last arrival 22.00hrs Last departure 16.00hrs
Level grass site with mature trees near river, hills, woods and moorland. SW of Corwen on A5, left onto B4401 for 4m. A 10-acre site with 40 touring pitches and 80 statics.
Wet weather camping facilities.
See advertisement under CORWEN

LLANDWROG

White Tower Caravan Park (SH453582)
LL54 5UH ☎ 01286 830649 & 0802 562785 Signposted
Nearby town: Caernarfon

► ► ► ► De-Luxe Park ★ ♥ £5-£8.75 ♥ £5-£8.75 ▲ £5-£8.75
(rs Mar-mid May & Sep-Oct swimming pool & bar wknds only) Booking advisable bank hols & Jul-Aug Last arrival 23.00hrs Last departure noon

A level, well-maintained site with lovely Snowdonia views, 1.5m from village along Tai'r Eglwys Road. From Caernarfon take A487 signed Porthmadog, cross over rndbt, then take 1st right and site on right in 3 miles. A 3-acre site with 52 touring pitches and 53 statics.

LLANGOLLEN

Ty-Ucha Caravan Park (SJ232415)
Maesmawr Rd LL20 7PP ☎ 01978 860677 Signposted
► ► ► Family Park ★ ♥ fr £7 ♥ fr £6
Open Etr-Oct (rs Mar toilet block closed) Booking advisable public hols Last arrival 22.00hrs Last departure 14.00hrs
A very well-run site in beautiful surroundings conveniently placed close to A5, 1m E of Llangollen. Ideal for country and mountain walking, with small stream on its southern boundary. A 4-acre site with 40 touring pitches.

LLANRUG

See **Caernarfon**

LLANRWST

Bodnant Caravan Site (SH805609)
Nebo Rd LL26 0SD ☎ 01492 640248 (S, turn off A470 opp Birmingham garage for B5427 signed Nebo, site 300yds on right) Signposted
► ► ► Family Park ♥ £7.50-£9 ♥ £7.50-£9 ▲ £7.50-£9
Open Mar-end Oct (rs Mar toilet blocks closed if weather very bad) Booking advisable Etr, May Day, Spring bank hol & Jul-Aug Last arrival 22.00hrs Last departure 11.00hrs
Small, well-maintained, level touring site, S of village off A470. Twelve times winner of 'Wales in Bloom' competition for best kept touring caravan site in Wales. A 5-acre site with 54 touring pitches and 2 statics.
Two outside dishwashing sinks.

Maenan Abbey Caravan Park (SH790656)
LL26 0UL ☎ 01492 660630 Signposted
► ► ► Family Park ♥ £4.50-£9.50 ♥ £4.50-£9.50
Open Mar-Oct Booking advisable peak periods Last arrival 22.30hrs Last departure noon
An excellent site, level, grassy and well-screened, in the beautiful Conwy Valley. Site on A470 2m N of Llanrwst. A 3-acre site with 26 touring pitches and 72 statics.

LLANYSTUMDWY

Camping & Caravanning Club Site (SH469384)
Tyddyn Sianel LL52 0LS
☎ 01766 522855 (in season) & 01203 694995 Signposted

Nearby town: Criccieth

◯◯◯◯◯◯◯◯

▶ ▶ ▶ ▶ De-Luxe Park ★ ⚘ £11-£14 ⚘ £11-£14
▲ £11-£14
Open end Mar-early Nov Booking advisable bank hols &
peak periods Last arrival 21.00hrs Last departure noon
*Well-maintained, attractive grassy site on slightly
sloping land alongside the A497 with a good range of
facilities. Please see the advertisement on page 27 for
details of Club Members' benefits. A 4-acre site with 70
touring pitches.*
Playfield

🔌 🕯️ ☉ 📖 🍴 ✳️ 🔨 🎏 🥤 ⬆️ 🐕 🐂 ♿
➜ ∪ ▶ ꜜ ✈

Credit Cards 💳 ▭ ▨

◯◯◯◯◯◯◯◯

MORFA BYCHAN

Gwyndy Caravan Park (SH543371)
Black Rock Sands LL49 9YB ☎ 01766 512047
Signposted
Nearby town: Porthmadog
▶ ▶ ▶ Family Park ★ ⚘ £6.50-£8.50 ⚘ £6.50-£8.50
▲ £6.50-£8.50
Open Mar-Oct Booking advisable bank hols & Jul-Aug
Last departure 11.00hrs
*A quiet family site a minute's walk to the beach at Black
Rock Sands. Signed in the centre of Morfa Bychan. A 5-
acre site with 15 touring pitches and 44 statics.*

🔌 🕯️ ☉ 📖 🍴 ✳️ 🔨 ⬆️ 🥤
➜ ∪ ▶ ☉ ⛟ ꜜ 🍴 ✈

PONTLLYFNI

St Ives Touring Caravan Park (SH432524)
Lon-Y-Wig LL54 5EG ☎ 01286 660347 Signposted

◯◯◯◯◯◯◯◯

▶ ▶ ▶ ▶ De-Luxe Park ★ ⚘ £7-£9 ⚘ £7-£9 ▲ £5-£9
Open Mar-Oct Booking advisable all times Last arrival
21.00hrs Last departure noon
*An immaculate little site with good facilities, within
easy walking distance of beach. Off A499 along lane
towards beach from village centre. A 1-acre site with 20
touring pitches.*

🔌 🕯️ ☉ 📖 ✳️ 🔨 ⬆️ 🥤 ⊞ 👕 🛁 🔲 🍴
➜ ∪ ▶ ☉ ⛟ ꜜ 🍴 ✈

◯◯◯◯◯◯◯◯

Llyn-y-Gele Farm & Caravan Park (SH432523)
LL54 5EL ☎ 01286 660283 & 660289 Signposted
Nearby town: Caernarfon
▶▶ Town & Country Pennant Park ★ ⚘ £7-£8 ⚘ £6-£7 ▲
Open Etr-Sep Booking advisable Jul-Aug Last arrival
22.00hrs Last departure 13.00hrs
*Quiet farm site within 5-7 minutes' walking distance of
the beach in the centre of the village. Centrally situated
for touring the Lleyn Peninsula, Anglesey and
Snowdonia, off A499. A 4-acre site with 6 touring
pitches and 24 statics.*

🔌 🕯️ ☉ ✳️ ⟋ 🔨 🐕
➜ ∪ ✈ 🥤

PONT-RUG

See **Caernarfon**

PORTHMADOG

Tyddyn Llwyn Caravan Park & Camping Site (SH561384)
Black Rock Rd LL49 9UR ☎ 01766 512205 & 514196

◯◯◯◯◯◯◯◯

▶ ▶ ▶ ▶ De-Luxe Park ★ ⚘ £8 ⚘ £6-£8 ▲ £6-£8
Open Mar-Oct Booking advisable school hols Last
arrival 23.00hrs Last departure noon

*Set in an amphitheatre of wooded hills, with both level
and slightly sloping pitches in beautiful countryside.
Turn S (signed Black Rock Sands) in centre of
Porthmadog, and site entrance in 0.5m. A 14-acre site
with 150 touring pitches and 53 statics.*

🔌 🕯️ ☉ 📖 🍴 🛒 ✳️ 🔨 ⟋ ⬆️ 🔲 🔳
✖ 🍴 🐕 🥤
➜ ∪ ▶ ☉ ⛟ ꜜ 🍴 ✈

◯◯◯◯◯◯◯◯

RHUALLT

Penisar Mynydd Caravan Park (SJ093770)
Caerwys Rd LL17 0TY ☎ 01745 582227 (2m NE)
Signposted
Nearby town: Dyserth
▶▶ Town & Country Pennant Park ★ ⚘ £6 ⚘ £6
Open Etr or Apr-Oct Booking advisable bank hols
*A beautifully situated site, close to seaside resort of
Rhyl. 2m NE of Penisar. From Chester take A55 westerly
beyond Prestatyn exit, and take second right turn in 2
miles. From Llandudno take first left at top of Rhuallt
Hill. A 2-acre site with 30 touring pitches.*

🔌 🕯️ ☉ 📖 ✳️ ⟋ 🔨 ⬆️ 🍴
➜ ▶ ☉ ✈

TALSARNAU

contd.

Barcdy Touring Caravan & Camping Park (SH623368)
LL47 6YG ☎ 01766 770736 Signposted
Nearby town: Harlech

▶ ▶ ▶ ▶ De-Luxe Park 🚐 £7-£10 🚐 £7-£10 ⋀ £7-£10
Open Spring bank hol-mid Sep (rs Etr-Spring bank hol
& mid Sep-Oct only two fields open, food shop closed)
Booking advisable from Feb ⌦
*A quiet picturesque site on the southern edge of the
Vale of Ffestiniog near Dwryd estuary. Very well-run
and maintained. On A496 N of Talsarnau. A 12-acre site
with 68 touring pitches and 30 statics.*
Dishwashing sinks hot water charged.

🛈📻☉🗑⛽☼ 🚻🛈📶 🎱🆔🔢🚽 🔦🎏🛒
➜ 🎣
Credit Cards 💳 🈹 📶 🈸

TAL-Y-BONT

Benar Beach Camping & Touring Park (SH573226)
LL43 2AR ☎ 01341 247571 & 247001
Nearby town: Barmouth
▶➤ Town & Country Pennant Park ★ 🚐 £5-£12
🚐 £5-£12 ⋀ £4-£8
Open Mar-3 Oct Booking advisable peak periods
*Friendly family site 1 mile from A496 halfway between
Harlech and Barmouth. Adjacent to sandy beach with
view of mountains. A 5-acre site with 40 touring pitches.*
Satellite & TV hook-ups.

🛈📻☉☼🔦🐕
➜ 🚽 🎣 🛒

TAL-Y-BONT (NEAR CONWY)

Tynterfyn Touring Caravan Park (SH768692)
LL32 8YX ☎ 01492 660525 (5m S of Conwy on B5106, rd
sign Tal-y-Bont, 1st on left)
Nearby town: Conwy
▶➤ Town & Country Pennant Park 🚐 £4.80 🚐 £4.80
⋀ £3.50-£5.50
Open Mar-Oct Booking advisable bank hols & Jul-Aug
Last arrival 22.00hrs Last departure noon
*Small, family site on level ground situated in the lovely
Conwy Valley. On the B5106, .25m N of village. A 2-acre
site with 15 touring pitches.*

🛈📻☉🗑☼🛝🛈📶🆔🐕
➜ 🚽🛟🌿🎣🛒

TOWYN (NEAR ABERGELE)

Ty Mawr Holiday Park (SH965792)
Towyn Rd LL22 9HG ☎ 01745 832079 (on A548, .25m W
of town)
Nearby town: Rhyl
▶ ▶ ▶ Family Park 🚐 🚐 ⋀
Open Etr-Oct (rs Apr (excluding Etr)) Booking advisable
at all times Last departure 10.00hrs
*A well laid out coastal site with very good leisure
facilities, on the A548 .25m west of Towyn village. An
18-acre site with 348 touring pitches and 352 statics.*

Free evening entertainment, sauna, solarium.

🛈📻☉🗑🍴🎣 🍺☼🍸🛝🛈📶✂🔦
♿🐕🛒♿
➜🚽🛟
Credit Cards 💳 🈹

TREFRIW

Plas Meirion Caravan Park (SH783630)
Gower Rd LL27 0RZ ☎ 01492 640247 (on B5106, turn
left opposite Woollen Mill, site 200mtrs on left)
Nearby town: Betws-y-Coed
▶ ▶ ▶ Family Park ★ 🚐 £6.50-£9.50
🚐 £6.50-£9.50
Open Etr-Oct Booking advisable school hols Last arrival
22.00hrs Last departure 10.30hrs ⌦
*A level site with mature trees set in the Conwy Valley.
Off B5106. A 2-acre site with 5 touring pitches and 26
statics.*

🛈🚐📻☉🗑☼🛈🆔🚿🎏🛒
➜🚽🛟🌿🎣

TYWYN

See **Bryncrug**

Ynysymaengwyn Caravan Park (SH601021)
LL36 9RY ☎ 01654 710684 (on A493, 1m heading
towards Dolgellau)
▶ ▶ ▶ Family Park ★ 🚐 £6-£9 ⋀ £6-£7
Open Etr or Apr-Oct Booking advisable Jul-Aug Last
arrival 23.00hrs Last departure noon
*This site is ideally situated with the full amenities of the
seaside on one hand and beautiful countryside and hills
on the other. On right of A493 almost halfway between
Bryncrug and Tywyn. A 4-acre site with 80 touring
pitches and 115 statics.*

🛈📻☉🗑🎣☼🛝🛈📶🔦🖳🛒♿
➜🚽🛟◉🛟🍴🎣

WREXHAM

MID WALES

This region includes the counties of Ceredigion,
Carmarthenshire, Pembrokeshire and Powys.

ABERAERON

Aeron Coast Caravan Park (SN462633)
North Rd SA46 0JF ☎ 01545 570349 (on A487)
▶ ▶ ▶ Family Park 🚐 £7-£10 🚐 £7-£10 ⋀ £7-£10
Open Etr or Apr-Oct Booking advisable bank & school
hols Last arrival 20.00hrs Last departure noon
*A large site sloping gently towards the sea, run by
enthusiastic owners. On A487 at entrance to Aberaeron
from the N, turn right near petrol stn. An 8-acre site
with 50 touring pitches and 150 statics.*
Disco & indoor leisure rooms.

🛈📻☉🗑🎣🍴🍽🍴🛒☼🍸🛝🛈📶🆔🔢🚽🔦♿
🛒♿
➜🚽◉🛟🌿🎣

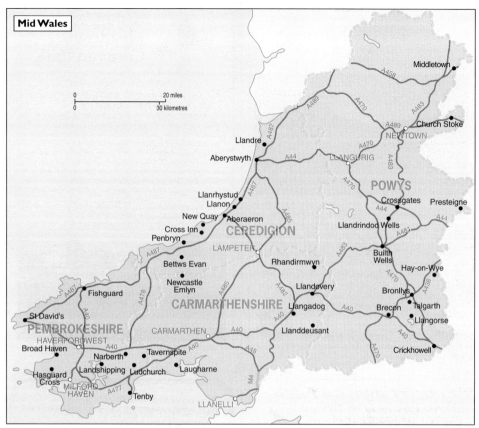

Mid Wales

Ocean View Caravan Park (SN592842)
North Beach, Clarach Bay SY23 3DT ☎ 01970 828425 & 623361 (off A487, N) Signposted
► ► ► **Family Park ★ ⊞** £6.50-£8.50 **⊞** £6.50-£8.50 **Å** £6.50-£8.50
Open Apr-Oct Booking advisable bank hols Last arrival 22.00hrs Last departure noon
A neat and tidy site on gently sloping ground in a sheltered valley with views to the sea. Follow unclass rd signed Clarach from S end of Bow St on A487. A 2-acre site with 24 touring pitches and 50 statics.

🔌 🐾 ⊙ ⚠ 🅱 🖊 🛒 ⬆ 🔧 🛁 🅑 🐴 🐕 ♿
➜ ∪ ▶ ◎ ⛺ 🎣 🗑

BETTWS EVAN

Pilbach Caravan Park (SN306476)
SA44 5RT ☎ 01239 851434 (S on A487, turn left onto B4333) Signposted
Nearby town: Aberporth
► ► ► **Family Park ★ ⊞** £7.75-£10.25 **⊞** £7.75-£10.25
Å £7.75-£10.25
Open Spring bank hol-Sep (rs Mar-Spring bank hol & Oct swimming pool closed) Booking advisable Spring bank hol & Jul-Aug Last arrival 22.00hrs Last departure 10.30hrs

An exceptionally well-run small site set in secluded countryside. 3m N of Newcastle Emlyn and 7m E of Cardigan. A 3-acre site with 65 touring pitches and 70 statics.

🔌 🐾 ⊙ 🅱 ⚡ ⚓ ⚒ 🔦 ☀ 🛒 ⚠ 🅱 🖊 🛁 🔧 🅣
✗ ∖ 🐴 📶
➜ ∪ ▶ ⚠ ⛺ 🎣

Credit Cards 💳 💳

BRECON

Brynich Caravan Park (SJ071279)
Brynich LD3 7SH ☎ 01874 623325 (1m E ON a470 near Jct wih A40) Signposted

◯ ◯ ◯ ◯ ◯ ◯ ◯ ◯ ◯ ◯

► ► ► ► **De-Luxe Park ★ ⊞** £8-£9 **⊞** £8-£9
Å £8-£9
Open Etr-Oct Booking advisable bank & school hols
Very attractive and well-appointed site offering commanding views of the Brecon Beacons. Ideal as a touring base or for longer stays. Winner of the Campsite of the Year Award for Wales, 1998/9. Adjacent to the A470, 1m E of Brecon. A 20-acre site with 130 touring pitches.

contd.

276

Adventure playground, off-licence, dish washing.

🕻🕻⊙🖪🖳✳️🏔🛈🖉🖭🕙🕻🕳🍴🐕🐾🔥

➔🅤🎏🛠️🏕️🎣

Credit Cards 💳 🏧 🏧 🏧 ⑤

⊙⊙⊙⊙⊙⊙⊙⊙⊙⊙⊙

Bishops Meadow Caravan Park (SO060300)
Bishops Meadow, Hay Rd LD3 9SW
☎ 01874 610000 & 622392 (on B4602)
Signposted
► ► ► Family Park ★ 🚐 fr £9 🚐 fr £9 Å £5-£9
Open Etr-Oct Booking advisable bank hols
Part of a large leisure complex with a wide range of facilities. On B4062 between Brecon and Hay-on-Wye. A 3.5-acre site with 82 touring pitches.

🕻🚐🕻⊙🕳🔍✳️🅈🏔🛈🖉🖭🕙✖️🕻
🍴🐕🐾🏕️
➔🅤🎏🛠️🏕️🎣🔥

Credit Cards 💳 🏧 🏧 ⓪ ⤴ ⑤

BROAD HAVEN

Creampots Touring Caravan & Camping Park (SM882131)
Havenway SA62 3TU ☎ 01437 781776 Signposted
Nearby town: Haverfordwest
►► Town & Country Pennant Park 🚐 £5.65-£7.95
🚐 £5.15-£7.45 Å £4.15-£5.95
Open Etr or Mar-Oct Booking advisable mid Jul-Aug
Last arrival 23.00hrs Last departure noon

Cenarth Falls
HOLIDAY PARK
CENARTH · NEWCASTLE EMLYN ·
CARDIGANSHIRE · SA38 9JS
TELEPHONE: 01239 710345

Family-run Park ideally situated for exploring the coast and countryside of this unique and unspoilt area of West Wales. Superb award winning touring caravan and camping facilities. Luxury caravans also available for hire. Excellent leisure facilities include out door heated pool. Country Club, shop and children's play area. Telephone for free brochure.
AA "Best Campsite of the year for Wales 97/98"

Large, well-maintained fields with a good toilet block. Turn L off B4341 Haverfordwest-Broad Haven road at Broadway, and Creampots is second park 500 yards on R. A 5-acre site with 72 touring pitches and 1 static. Milk, eggs & papers daily.

🕻🕻⊙✳️🏔🛈🖭🕳
➔🅤🔍🛠️🎣🔥

South Cockett Caravan & Camping Park (SM879135)
SA62 3TU ☎ 01437 781296 & 781760 (1.5m E off B4341)
Signposted
Nearby town: Broadhaven
►► Town & Country Pennant Park ★ 🚐 £5.25-£7.20
🚐 £4.75-£6.70 Å £3.75-£5.45
Open Etr-Oct Booking advisable Jul-Aug Last arrival 13.00hrs
Small farm-style campsite rurally located and offering high standards of modern toilet facilities. Conveniently positioned close to the coastline and is a good touring base. A 6-acre site with 70 touring pitches and 1 static.

🕻🕻⊙🖪✳️🛈🖉🖭🕳
➔🅤🛠️🎣🔥

BRONLLYS

Anchorage Caravan Park (SO142351)
LD3 0LD ☎ 01874 711246 & 711230 (8m NE of Brecon on A438) Signposted
Nearby town: Brecon
► ► ► Family Park 🚐 🚐 Å
Open all year (rs Nov-Mar TV room closed) Booking advisable bank hols Last arrival 23.00hrs Last departure 18.00hrs
A well-maintained site. Touring pitches are on grassy slopes and level ground with good mountain views of the Brecon Beacons National Park. 8m NE of Brecon, on A438. An 8-acre site with 110 touring pitches and 101 statics.
Baby bath room.

🕻🚐🕻⊙🖪🖳🖵✳️🏔🛈🖉🖭🕙🕻🔥🐕
🐾🕳
➔🅤🎣

BUILTH WELLS

Fforest Fields Caravan & Camping Park (SO100535)
Hundred House LD1 5RT ☎ 01982 570406 & 570220 (from town follow to 'New Radnor' on A481, 4m signed entrance on right) Signposted
► ► ► Family Park ★ 🚐 £7.50 🚐 £6.50 Å £3-£6.50
Open Etr & Apr-Oct Booking advisable bank hols & Jul-Aug Last arrival 23.00hrs Last departure 18.00hrs

contd.

A sheltered site in a hidden valley, with wonderful views. On A481, 5 miles E of Builth Wells. A 7-acre site with 40 touring pitches.

🔧📞☉🖲☀⚠🚿🛢🔲♿🐕
➡🚩◎⛱⛲🍴🔔

Llewelyn Leisure Park (SO003514)
Cilmery LD2 3NU ☎ 01982 552838 & 0831 101052 (2m W on A483) Signposted
▶ **Town & Country Pennant Park** ★ ⚏ £4.50-£8.50 ⚏ £4.50-£8.50 ▲ £4.50-£8.50
Open Etr-Oct (rs Nov-Etr toilet/shower facilities in house) Booking advisable Jul-Aug Last arrival 22.00hrs Last departure 11.00hrs
A small site with great potential situated 2m W of Builth Wells, on S of A483 in Cilmery Village. A 0.75-acre site with 25 touring pitches and 26 statics.
Free library service.

🔧📞☉🖲🎣☕🍴🚿⚠🛢🔲🔲🕅🔔🏧🎪🍴
➡🚶🚩🍴♨
Credit Cards 💳 💳 💳 🔳

CARDIGAN

CHURCH STOKE

Daisy Bank Caravan Park (SO303929)
SY15 6EB ☎ 01588 620471 (on A489 between Lydham & Churchstoke) Signposted
Nearby town: Bishops Castle

▶▶▶▶ **De-Luxe Park** ★ ⚏ £6-£7.50 ⚏ £6-£7.50
Open Feb-Nov Booking advisable bank hols Last arrival 21.00hrs Last departure 19.00hrs
A first-rate park, well-landscaped with quality facilities. Marvellous views and welcoming owners. From A49 at Craven Arms take A489 to Churchstoke. Turn off 1.5m after Bishops Castle. A 4-acre site with 40 touring pitches.

🔧📞☉☀⚠🛢🔲🏧🍴🐕♿
➡🚶♨🍴

Bacheldre Watermill Touring & Camping Park (SO243928)
Bacheldre Watermill SY15 6TE ☎ 01588 620489 (turn left 2.50m W of Church Stoke on A489, signed Bacheldre Mill) Signposted
Nearby town: Welshpool
▶ **Town & Country Pennant Park** ⚏ £6 ⚏ £6 ▲ £6
Open Etr-Oct Booking advisable bank hols
Secluded little site in the grounds of a working water mill. On A489, 2.5m W of Church Stoke. A 2-acre site with 25 touring pitches.

🔧📞☉☀🔲🏧🍴
➡♨

CRICKHOWELL

Riverside Caravan & Camping Park (SO215184)
New Rd NP8 1AY ☎ 01873 810397 Signposted
▶▶▶ **Family Park** ★ ⚏ £6-£11 ⚏ £5.50-£8 ▲ fr £8
Open Mar-Oct Booking advisable for stays over 1 wk Last arrival 23.00hrs
A clean and well-maintained site, adjacent to the River Usk, in lovely tranquil surroundings. The site does not take children. On A40, and well signed from A40. A 3.5-acre site with 35 touring pitches and 20 statics.

🔧📞☉☀🛢⚠🔲🔔♿⚙
➡🚶🍴♨♨

CROSSGATES

Greenway Manor (SO081651)
LD1 6RF ☎ 01597 851230
▶▶▶ **Family Park** ⚏ ⚏ ▲
Open May-Oct
A small secluded site in the wooded and lawned grounds of a newly-refurbished hotel. Immediately off A44, 0.5m W of Crossgates. A 2-acre site with 13 touring pitches.

The Park Motel (SO081651)
Rhayader Rd LD1 6RF ☎ 01597 851201
Nearby town: Llandrindod Wells
▶ **Town & Country Pennant Park** ★ ⚏ £6-£7.50 ⚏ £6-£7.50 ▲ £3.50-£4
Open Mar-Oct Booking advisable bank hols Last arrival 22.30hrs Last departure noon
This quiet rural site, set in beautiful countryside, has flat pitches and is well-sheltered by trees. It is an ideal touring centre, situated off A44. A 1-acre site with 10 touring pitches and 15 statics.

🔧📞☉🎣☀🍴⚠🛢⚠🔲❌🔔🏧🍴♨
➡🚶🍴◎♨♨🍴🖲

CROSS INN

Camping & Caravanning Club Site (SN383566)
Llwynhelyg SA44 6LW ☎ 01545 560029 (in season) & 01203 694995 Signposted
Nearby town: Cardigan
▶▶▶ **Family Park** ★ ⚏ £10-£13 ⚏ £10-£13 ▲ £10-£13
Open end Mar-early Nov Booking advisable bank hols & peak periods Last arrival 21.00hrs Last departure noon
An excellent, attractive touring site in an elevated rural position. From A487 at Synod take A486, signed New Quay, then left in centre of Cross Inn village with site in 1mile. Please see the advertisement on page 27 for details of Club Members' benefits. A 13.5-acre site with 90 touring pitches.

🔧📞☉🖲🎣☀⚠🛢🔲🔲🕅🔔🐕🍴♿
➡🚶♨
Credit Cards 💳 💳

FISHGUARD

Fishguard Bay Caravan & Camping Park (SM984383)
Dinas Cross SA42 OYD ☎ 01348 811415 (2m E off A487) Signposted
▶▶▶ **Family Park** ★ ⚏ £8-£10 ⚏ £8-£10 ▲ £7-£9
Open Mar-9 Jan Booking advisable Jul-Aug Last departure noon

Well-run part level and sloping grass site with bushes, high up on cliffs with excellent views and close to the sea. 1m N of A487. A 3-acre site with 50 touring pitches and 50 statics.
View point.

🛉 🐾 ☉ 🗗 🎅 ◀ ⌷ ☀ ⋀ 🛈 ⌀ ⊞ 🆃 📞 🛂
➜ ∪ ⅍ ☃ ♨ 🥄

Credit Cards 💳 💳 💳 💳 🗗

Gwaun Vale Touring Park (SM977356)
Llanychaer SA65 9TA ☎ 01348 874698 (1.5m SE on B4313) Signposted
▶ ▶ ▶ Family Park ★ 🚐 £6-£7 🚐 £6-£7 Å £6-£7
Open Mar-9 Jan Booking advisable Jul-Aug
A beautiful and immaculate site run by an enthusiastic owner. 1.5m from Fishguard on the B4313 Llanychaer/Gwaun Valley road. A 1.75-acre site with 30 touring pitches.
Free loan of Boules, video films, guide books.

🛉 🐾 ☉ 🎅 ☀ ⋀ 🛈 ⌀ ⊞ 🆃 📞 🌳 🐴 🛂
➜ ∪ △ ⅍ ☃ 🥄 🗗

Hasguard Cross Caravan Park (SM850108)
SA62 3SL ☎ 01437 781443 Signposted
Nearby town: Haverfordwest
▶ ▶ ▶ Family Park ★ 🚐 £6-£8 🚐 £6-£8
Open all year Booking advisable Spring bank hol & Jun-Aug Last arrival 23.00hrs Last departure 11.00hrs
A very clean, efficient and well-run site in Pembrokeshire National Park with views of surrounding hills. 1.5m from sea and beach at Little Haven. Approach to B4327 from Haverfordwest to Dale, after 7m turn right at crossroads and site is first entrance on right. A 3-acre site with 25 touring pitches and 35 statics.

🛉 🐾 ☉ ☀ 🍸 🛈 ⊞ ✕ 📞 🌳
➜ ∪ ▶ △ ⅍ 🥄 🛂

Hollybush Inn (SO205406)
HR3 5PS ☎ 01497 847371 (Off B4350) Signposted
▶ Town & Country Pennant Park 🚐 🚐 Å
Open Good Fri-Oct Booking advisable bank hols Last arrival 23.00hrs Last departure 13.00hrs
A neat little site adjacent to a small inn and close to the R Wye. 2m from Hay-on-Wye off B4350. A 3-acre site with 22 touring pitches and 5 statics.
Canoe launch.

🛉 🐾 ☉ ☀ 🍸 ✕ 📞 🌳 🐴
➜ ∪ ▶

New Park Farm (SN026111)
SA67 8BG ☎ 01834 891284
Nearby town: Narberth
▶ Town & Country Pennant Park 🚐 🚐 Å

> Summer weather can mean rain. It is a good idea to prepare for ground to be wet underfoot. Take something to amuse the children if they can't go outside

---

Open May Day wknd-Oct Booking advisable peak periods Last arrival 20.00hrs Last departure noon
A nice, quiet site on a smallholding with basic but adequate facilities. 7m W of Narberth, along unclass rd off A4075. A 2-acre site with 5 touring pitches and 30 statics.

🛉 🐾 ☉ 🗗 ☀ 🛈 ⌀ ⊞ 🆃 📞 🏛
➜ ∪ ⅍ 🥄 🛂

Ants Hill Caravan Park (SN299118)
SA33 4QN ☎ 01994 427293 Signposted
Nearby town: Carmarthen
▶ ▶ ▶ Family Park 🚐 🚐 Å
Open Etr-Oct Booking advisable Jul-Aug & public hols Last arrival 23.00hrs Last departure 10.30hrs
A small, well-run touring site on sloping grass, located near the village, on the Taff estuary. Care should be taken on descent into Laugharne on A4066 as site entrance is on minor road to left. A 4-acre site with 60 touring pitches and 60 statics.

🛉 🐾 ☉ ⋜ ◀ ⌷ ☀ 🍸 ⋀ 🛈 ⌀ ⊞ 🆃 📞 🌳 🛂
➜ ∪ ▶ 🥄 🗗

See **Hasguards Cross**

Cross Inn & Black Mountain Caravan Park (SN773259)
SA19 9YG ☎ 01550 740621 Signposted
Nearby town: Llandeilo
▶ Town & Country Pennant Park 🚐 🚐 Å
Open all year Booking advisable bank hols Last departure 10.30hrs
A very pleasant small site in a secluded position. Take unclassified road south out of Trecastle, pass Castle Hotel and continue for approx seven miles. A 5-acre site with 40 touring pitches and 20 statics.

🛉 🐾 ☉ 🎅 ☀ 🍸 ⋀ 🛈 ⌀ ✕ 📞 🌳 🛏 🐴 🛂
➜ ∪ ▶ 🥄

Erwlon Caravan & Camping Park (SN776343)
Brecon Rd SA20 0RD ☎ 01550 720332 (1m on A40) Signposted
Nearby town: Carmarthen
▶ Town & Country Pennant Park ★ 🚐 £5 🚐 £5 Å £5
Open all year Booking advisable bank hols Last arrival anytime Last departure noon
Long established family-run site set beside a brook in the Brecon Beacons foothills. On the A40, 1 mile E of Llandovery. An 8-acre site with 40 touring pitches.

🛉 🐾 ☉ 🗗 🎅 ☀ ⋀ 🛈 ⌀ ⊞ 📞 🛏 🐴 🛂 ♿
➜ ∪ ▶ 🥄

Riverside Park (SN634878)
Lon Glanfred SY24 5BY ☎ 01970 820070 Signposted
Nearby town: Borth
▶ ▶ ▶ Family Park 🚐 🚐 Å
Open Mar-Oct Booking advisable bank & school hols Last arrival 23.30hrs Last departure noon

contd.

A quiet site with good quality facilities and easy access to the seaside. Set amongst well-wooded hills and bounded by a stream. On A487, 4m north of Aberystwyth, take B4353 and turn right at second turning. A 4-acre site with 24 touring pitches and 76 statics.
River fishing on site.
See advertisement under ABERYSTWYTH

🏢 🐾 ⊙ 🔲 🥤 ✳ ⚠ 🔒 🗑 ➕ T 📞 ➰
🏛 🏠 🐕 🐾 ♿
➔ ∪ ► ◎ ⚠ ⊁ ♪

LLANDRINDOD WELLS

Disserth Caravan & Camping Park (SO035583)
Disserth, Howey LD1 6NL ☎ 01597 860277
Signposted
▶ ▶ ▶ **Family Park** ★ 🚐 £6.50-£7.75 🚐 £6.50-£7.75
▲ £6.50-£7.75
Open Mar-Oct Booking advisable early as possible Last arrival 22.00hrs Last departure noon
A peaceful site nestling in a beautiful valley on the banks of R Ithon, a tributary of the R Wye. Take A470 from Aberystwyth towards Builth Wells, turn left at Newbridge on Wye, and right towards Disserth. A 2.5-acre site with 25 touring pitches and 21 statics.
Private trout fishing.

🏢 🐾 ⊙ 🔲 🥤 ✳ 🔒 🗑 ➕ 📞 🏛 🐾
➔ ∪ ► ◎ ⚠ ⊁ 🐕‍🦺 ♪
Credit Cards 💳 💳 💳 💳 🅂

Dalmore Camping & Caravanning Park (SO045568)
Howey LD1 5RG ☎ 01597 822483 (Howey 3m S A483)
Signposted
▶▶ **Town & Country Pennant Park** ★ 🚐 £6-£7 🚐 £6-£7
▲ £6-£7
Open Mar-Oct Booking advisable Jun-Aug Last arrival 22.00hrs Last departure noon
A clean, tidy site on A483 but screened from road and traffic noise by hedgerow. Wonderful views. 1.5m S of village. A 2-acre site with 20 touring pitches and 20 statics.

🏢 🐾 ⊙ ✳ 🔒 🗑 ➕ 📞 🏛 🐕
➔ ∪ ► ◎ ⊁ 🐕‍🦺 ♪ 🔲 🐾

LLANGADOG

Abermarlais Caravan Park (SN695298)
SA19 9NG
☎ 01550 777868 & 777797 (on A40 6m W of Llandovery)
Signposted
Nearby town: Llandovery
▶ ▶ ▶ **Family Park** ★ 🚐 £7 🚐 £7 ▲ £7
Open Apr-Oct (rs Nov, Dec & Mar 1 wc, water point no hot water if frosty) Booking advisable bank hols & 15 Jul-Aug Last arrival 23.00hrs Last departure noon
An attractive, well-run site with a welcoming atmosphere. Part-level, part-sloping grass in a wooded valley on edge of Brecon Beacons National Park. It is by the River Marlais and off A40 Llandeilo-Llandovery road. A 17-acre site with 88 touring pitches.
Volleyball, badminton court & softball tennis net.

🏢 🐾 ⊙ ✳ ⚠ 🔒 🗑 ➕ T 📞 🐕 🐾
➔ ∪ ♪

LLANGORSE

Lakeside Caravan Park (SO128272)
LD3 7TR ☎ 01874 658226
Nearby town: Brecon
▶ ▶ ▶ **Family Park** ★ 🚐 £6.50-£8.50 🚐 £6.50-£8.50
▲ £6.50-£8.50
Open Jun-Sep (rs Apr, May & Oct swimming pool clubhouse & restaurant) Booking advisable peak periods Last arrival 21.30hrs Last departure noon
A much improved site with an enthusiastic warden, located next to Llangorse Lake. An ideal centre for water sports enthusiasts. A 2-acre site with 40 touring pitches and 72 statics.
Boat hire & launching, windsurfing, fishing.

🏢 🐾 ⊙ 🥤 ⚡ ✳ 🍴 ⚠ 🔒 🗑 T ✕ 📞 🏤 🏛 🐕 🐾
➔ ∪ ⚠ ⊁ ♪
Credit Cards 💳 💳

LLANON

Woodlands Caravan Park (SN511668)
SY23 5LX ☎ 01974 202342 & 202454
Signposted
Nearby town: Aberaeron
▶ ▶ ▶ **Family Park** 🚐 £8-£9.50 🚐 £8-£9.50 ▲ £8-£9.50
Open Apr-Oct (rs Mar toilet block closed) Booking advisable school hols Last arrival 21.30hrs Last departure noon
A level grass site surrounded by mature trees and shrubs near woods and meadowland, adjacent to a stoney beach. 11m from Aberstwyth on A487. A 4-acre site with 80 touring pitches and 60 statics.

🏢 🐾 ⊙ 🔲 🥤 ✳ 🔒 🗑 ➕ T 📞 🐕 🐾
➔ ∪ ► ◎ ⊁ ♪

LLANRHYSTUD

Pengarreg Caravan Park (SN539697)
SY23 5DJ ☎ 01974 202247 Signposted
Nearby town: Aberystwyth
▶▶ **Town & Country Pennant Park** ★ 🚐 £5-£6 🚐 £5-£6
▲ £4.50-£6
Open Mar-Jan Booking advisable Last arrival mdnt Last departure 10.00hrs
A gently sloping site fronted by a pebble beach, with cliff walks and boat launching facilities. On A487 W of Llanrhystud at S end of village. A 7-acre site with 50 touring pitches and 155 statics.
Slipway to beach for sailing.

🏢 🐾 ⊙ 🔲 🥤 🍷 ✳ 🍴 ⚠ 🔒 🗑 T ✕ 📞 🐕 🐾
➔ ► ♪

LUDCHURCH

Woodland Vale Caravan Park (SN140113)
SA67 8JE ☎ 01834 831319
▶ ▶ ▶ **Family Park** 🚐 🚐
Open Mar-Oct Booking advisable bank hols & Jul-Aug Last arrival 21.00hrs Last departure 14.00hrs ✂
Site with informally sited pitches set between areas of water created in an old quarry. N of Ludchurch on unclass rd, the continuation S of B4314. A 1.5-acre site with 30 touring pitches and 80 statics.

🏢 🐾 ⊙ 🔲 🥤 🍷 ⚡ ✳ 🍴 ⚠ 🔒 ➕ 📞 🐾
➔ ∪ ► ♪

MIDDLETOWN

Bank Farm Caravan Park (SJ293123)
SY21 8EJ ☎ 01938 570526 & 570260 Signposted
Nearby town: Welshpool
▶▶ **Town & Country Pennant Park** ⚐ £7.50-£8.50
⚑ £7.50-£8.50 ▲ fr £5
Open May-Oct Booking advisable bank hols Last arrival
20.00hrs
*A grass site with two different areas - one gently
sloping and the other mainly level. Immediate access to
hills, mountains and woodland. On A458 W of
Middletown. A 2-acre site with 20 touring pitches and
33 statics.*
Trout pool.

🔌📶⊙🔲🔍🔦🏔🛈🔋🔌🎣🐕♿
➜▶🔪🚲

NARBERTH

Noble Court Caravan & Camping Park (SN111158)
Redstone Rd SA67 7ES
☎ 01834 861191 (.5m off A40 on B4313) Signposted
Nearby town: Tenby

▶▶▶ **De-Luxe Park** ★ ⚐ £8-£13.50 ⚑ £8-£13.50
▲ £8
Open Mar-Nov (rs early & late season swimming pool
closed) Booking advisable Jul-Aug Last arrival 23.30hrs
Last departure 11.00hrs
*Mostly sloping site with good views and a high
standard of service. On B4313 between Narberth & A40.
A 14-acre site with 92 touring pitches and 60 statics.*
30 Acres of adjoining land for walks & picnics.

🔌📶⊙🔲🔍🔦🔍🔦🏔🛈🔋🔌✖🔦⛲🏕
🔦🐕♿
➜∪▶🔪🚲
Credit Cards 💳 🈹 🈺

NEWCASTLE EMLYN

Afon Teifi Caravan & Camping Park (SN338405)
Pentrecagal SA38 9HT ☎ 01559 370532 (2m E A484)

▶▶▶ **De-Luxe Park** ★ ⚐ £7-£8 ⚑ £7-£8 ▲ £7-£8
Open Apr-Oct (rs Nov-Mar when facilities limited, no
toilet block) Booking advisable peak periods Last arrival
23.00hrs
*Very attractive and well-managed site in secluded
valley. Signed off A484, 2m E of Newcastle Emlyn.
A 6-acre site with 110 touring pitches and 3 statics.*
15 acres of woodland, fields & walks.

🔌🚿📶⊙🔲🔍🔍🔦🏔🛈🔋🔌🔋🔌🔌
⛲🔦🐕🚲♿
➜∪▶🔺⛺🔪

Summer weather can mean rain. It is a good idea
to prepare for ground to be wet underfoot.
Take something to amuse the children if they
can't go outside

Cenarth Falls Holiday Park (SN265421)
Cenarth SA38 9JS ☎ 01239 710345 (just off A484 on
outskirts of Cenarth) Signposted
Nearby town: Cardigan

▶▶▶▶ **De-Luxe Park** ★ ⚐ £8-£13 ⚑ £8-£13 ▲ £8-£13
Open Mar-9 Jan (rs Mar-mid May & mid Sep-9 Jan
swim pool closed, clubhouse wknds only) Booking
advisable bank hols & Jul-Aug Last arrival 20.00hrs Last
departure noon
*A very well run, delightful park with excellent facilities.
Signed immed off A484, .5m W of Cenarth. A 2-acre site
with 30 touring pitches and 89 statics.*
Clubhouse with bar meals, pool table, video games.
See advertisement under CARDIGAN

🔌📶⊙🔲🔍🔦🔍🔦🔲🔦🏔🛈🔋🔌🔋🔌
🔌🐕🚲♿
➜⛺🔪
Credit Cards 💳 🈹 🈺 🈺

See advertisement on page 277.

NEW QUAY

Cei Bach Country Club (SN409597)
Parc-y-Brwcs, Cei Bach SA45 9SL ☎ 01545 580237 (off
A487 onto B4342 signed to Cei Bach) Signposted
Nearby town: Aberaeron

contd.

*Cei Bach Country Club, Cei Bach,
New Quay, Ceredigion SA45 9SL*
Cei Bach lies 1½ miles from the fishing
village of New Quay, off the A487 coast
road. The park overlooks Cei Bach Bay with
pathway leading to sheltered sandy beach
with safe bathing.

On park facilities include:
★ Modern toilet & shower block ★ Club House
★ 48 electric points ★ Shop – 100 yards
★ Chemical waste point ★ Take Away Food
★ Games room ★ Ball park ★ 17 water points
★ Camping gas ★ AA Best Campsite
in Wales Award for 1996
★ Washing sinks
★ Launderette
★ Children's play area

Telephone: 01545 580237

▶ ▶ ▶ ▶ **De-Luxe Park** ★ 🏠 £6-£12.50 🚐 £6-£12.50
🔺 £6-£12.50
Open Good Fri-last Sun in Sep Booking advisable Etr,
Spring bank hol & school hols Last arrival 22.00hrs Last
departure 11.00hrs
*A very good site in a beautiful situation overlooking
Cardigan Bay with views of the distant cliffs. The
Wynne family are very welcoming, and this park was
the winner of the 1996 Campsite of the Year Award for
Wales. Turn off A487 onto B4342 road to New Quay,
then follow signs for Cei Bach. A 3-acre site with 60
touring pitches.*

🖿 📻 ⊙ 🗖 🍴 ✳ 🍸 ⋀ 🕯 ⌀ 🗓 ✕ 📞
💷 🎋 🐓 🖼 🐾
➜ ∪ ▶ 🛆 ⅄ 🎱 🎣

Credit Cards 💳 💳 📶 🖫

PENBRYN

**Talywerydd Touring Caravan & Camping Park
(SN297507)**
SA44 6QY ☎ 01239 810322 Signposted
Nearby town: Cardigan

▶ ▶ ▶ ▶ **De-Luxe Park** ★ 🏠 £6-£10 🚐 £6-£10 🔺 £6-£10
Open Mar-Oct Booking advisable bank hols & Jul-Aug
Last arrival 22.00hrs Last departure 11.00hrs
*Small family site with seaviews from every pitch, off
A487. Take 2nd turn off A487 signed Penbryn, and site
500yds on left. A 4-acre site with 40 touring pitches.
9 hole pitch & putt, microwave available*

🖿 📻 ⊙ 🗖 🍴 🐟 🍴 🗖 ✳ 🍸 ⋀ 🕯 ⌀ 🗓 ✕ 📞 💷
🎋 🎋 🐓 🖼
➜ ∪ ▶ ◎ 🛆 ⅄ 🎣

PRESTEIGNE

Rock Bridge Park (SO294654)
LD8 2NF ☎ 01547 560300 Signposted
▶ ▶ ▶ **Family Park** ★ 🏠 £9.50-£11 🚐 £8.50-£10
🔺 £4-£10
Open Apr-Sep Booking advisable public & school hols
Last arrival 21.30hrs Last departure noon 🐾
*Part-level, part-sloping grass site with trees and bushes,
set in meadowland with access to River Lugg. 1m W of
Presteigne off B4356. A 3-acre site with 35 touring
pitches and 30 statics.*

🖿 📻 ⊙ 🗖 ✳ 🕯 🗓 🎋 🖼 🐾
➜ ▶ 🎣

RHANDIRMWYN

Camping & Caravanning Club Site (SN779435)
SA20 0NT ☎ 01550 760257 (in season) &
01203 694995
Signposted
Nearby town: Llandovery

▶ ▶ ▶ ▶ **De-Luxe Park** ★ 🏠 £11-£14 🚐 £11-£14
🔺 £11-£14

Open end Mar-early Nov Booking advisable bank hols &
peak periods Last arrival 21.00hrs Last departure noon
*Set on the banks of the Afon Tywi near the Towy Forest
and the Llyn Brianne reservoir, this first class site has
superb views on all sides. Take A40 through
Llandovery, turn right immediately after crossing river
at sharp left-hand bend, signed Rhandirmwyn. At T
junction turn right recrossing river, and then left. In
approx 6m at Royal Oak Inn site signed on left. Please
see the advertisement on page 27 for details of Club
Members' benefits. An 11-acre site with 90 touring
pitches.*

🖿 📻 ⊙ 🗖 🍴 ✳ ⋀ 🕯 ⌀ 🗓 📞 🎋 🖼 🐾
➜ 🎣

Credit Cards 💳 💳 💳 📶 🖫

ST DAVIDS

Caerfai Bay Caravan & Tent Park (SM759244)
SA62 6QT ☎ 01437 720274
Signposted
▶ ▶ ▶ **Family Park** 🏠 £6-£11 🚐 £5-£7 🔺 £5-£6
Open Etr-Oct Booking advisable school hols Last arrival
21.00hrs Last departure 11.00hrs
*Gently sloping meadows with magnificent coastal
scenery overlooking St Brides Bay - bathing beach
300yds from park entrance. Off A487, end of unclass
road to Caerfai Bay. A 7-acre site with 82 touring pitches
and 33 statics.*

🖿 📻 ⊙ 🗖 🍴 ✳ 🕯 ⌀ 🗓 📞 🖼
➜ ▶ 🛆 ⅄ 🎣

Hendre Eynon Camping & Caravan Site (SM773280)
SA62 6DB ☎ 01437 720474 Signposted
▶ ▶ ▶ **Family Park** 🏠 🚐 🔺
Open May-Sep (rs 27 Mar-Apr one toilet block &
showers only) Booking advisable school hols Last
arrival 21.00hrs Last departure noon
*A country site on a working farm with a modern toilet
block including family rooms. 2m NE of St Davids on
unclassified road leading off B4583. A 7-acre site with
48 touring pitches and 2 statics.*

🖿 📻 ⊙ 🗖 ✳ 🕯 🗓 📞 🐾 🎋 🖼 🐾
➜ ∪ ▶ 🛆 ⅄ 🎣 🖼

Camping & Caravanning Club Site (SM805305)
Dwr Cwmdig, Berea SA62 6DW ☎ 01348 831376 (in
season) & 01203 694995 Signposted
▶▶ **Town & Country Pennant Park** ★ 🏠 £10-£13
🚐 £10-£13 🔺 £10-£13
Open end Mar-end Sep Booking advisable bank hols &
peak periods Last arrival 21.00hrs Last departure noon
*Immaculately kept small grassy site in open country
near the Pembrokeshire Coastal Path. Situated at the
junction of two unclass roads 1.5m W of Croesgoch on
the A487 St David's-Fishguard road. Please see the
advertisement on page 27 for details of Club Members'
benefits. A 4-acre site with 40 touring pitches.*

🖿 📻 ⊙ 🗖 🍴 🕯 ⌀ 🗓 🆃 📞 🖼
➜ ∪ 🎣

Credit Cards 💳 💳

Tretio Caravan & Camping Park (SM787292)
SA62 6DE ☎ 01437 720270 & 781359 (on leaving St David's keep left at Rugby Football Club & carry straight on for 3m) Signposted
Nearby town: Haverfordwest
▶▶ **Town & Country Pennant Park** ★ ⊕ £4.75-£7.50
⊕ £4.25-£7 ▲ £4.25-£7
Open 14 Mar-14 Oct Booking advisable bank hols & mid Jul-Aug Last arrival 23.00hrs Last departure 17.00hrs
A gently sloping touring site with well-converted facilities. On minor rd linking St David's with Croesgoch, 4m from St David's. A 4.5-acre site with 40 touring pitches and 10 statics.
4.5 acre pitch & putt, small animal farm corner.

🔧🚰🛠☉🔩🍴⚡🏠🛡🚿⊞🔟🎣⛽🏠🐕🐾♿
➜∪🅿◎⛴⚠✚🗡

Riverside International (SO148346)
Bronllys LD3 0HL ☎ 01874 711320 & 712064 (on A479 opposite Bronllys Castle) Signposted
Nearby town: Brecon
▶▶▶ **Family Park** ★ ⊕ £8-£9 ⊕ £8-£9 ▲ £8-£9
Open Etr-Oct Booking advisable bank hols & Jul-Aug Last arrival 22.00hrs Last departure 16.00hrs ⊘
Well-appointed touring site with pitches available on riverside. Elevated position with magnificent views of the Black Mountains. Off A479. A 9-acre site with 80 touring pitches.
Leisure facilities, sauna, jacuzzi, sunbed & gym.
See advertisement under BRECON

🔧🚰🛠☉🔩🍴🎣 🔦🖥✱🍽🏠🛡⚡⊞🔟✗
🔥🏠🐾♿
➜∪⚠✚🗡

Pantglas Farm Caravan Park (SN175122)
SA34 0NS ☎ 01834 831618 Signposted
Nearby town: Whitland
▶▶▶ **Family Park** ⊕ £5-£6.50 ⊕ £5-£6.50 ▲ £4-£5.50
Open Etr-15 Oct Booking advisable Spring bank hol & Jul-Aug Last arrival 23.00hrs Last departure 11.00hrs

A quiet, family-run site in a rural setting, with a welcoming attitude towards children. On B4328 between Ludchurch and Tavernspite; at village pump take middle turning, and site signed on right. A 7-acre site with 75 touring pitches.

Year round caravan weekly storage £2.

🔧🚰🛠☉🔩🍴✱🏠🛡⚡⊞🔟🎣🏠🖥♿
➜∪🗡🐾

 Kiln Park Holiday Centre (SN119002)
Marsh Rd SA70 7RB
☎ 01834 844121 & 0345 433433
★ ⊕ £5-£12 ⊕ £5-£12 ▲ £3-£6.50

Open Mar-Oct (rs Mar-mid May & Oct) Booking advisable all times Etr-Sep Last arrival noon Last departure 10.00hrs no cars by caravans
A large, commercial, touring, camping and static holiday site, situated on level ground on the town's outskirts. A short walk through dunes leads to the sandy south-facing beach. On A4139. A 103-acre site with 240 touring pitches and 620 statics.
Entertainment complex.

🔧🚰🛠☉🖥🔩🎣 🔦🔍🔦✱🍽🏠🛡⚡🔟✗
⚡🔥🏠🐕🐾
➜∪🅿◎⚠✚📺🗡
Credit Cards 💳 💳 💳

Rowston Holiday Park (SN133024)
New Hedges SA70 8TL ☎ 01834 842178
Signposted
contd. on p285

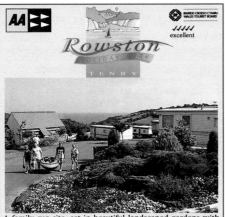

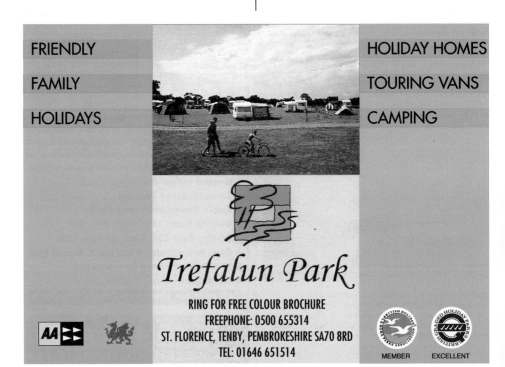

▶ ▶ ▶ ▶ De-Luxe Park ★ ⚐ £10-£16 ⚐ £10-£16 ▲ £5-£16
Open Apr-mid Oct (rs Oct-Jan 10 no site shop &
laundry) Booking advisable May & Jul-Aug Last arrival
21.00hrs Last departure 10.00hrs
*A really top class site in all ways, commanding views
over woodland and Carmarthon Bay. On left at top of
New Hedges bypass. A 10-acre site with 100 touring
pitches and 136 statics.*
Dishwashing sinks under canopy.

🔌 🍴 📵 ☉ 🗑 🎣 🔍 ✳ 〽 🏧 ⓘ ✐ ⬛ ✕ 📞 🦆 🛒 🚿
🛖 🐕 🐾 ♿
➔ ∪ 🏴 ☉ ✢ 🍴 ☕ 🎵

Trefalun (SN093027)
Devonshire Dr, St Florence SA70 8RH ☎ 01646 651514
& 0500 655314 Signposted

▶ ▶ ▶ ▶ De-Luxe Park ★ ⚐ £6-£10 ⚐ £6-£10 ▲ £5-£7
Open Etr-Oct Booking advisable bank hols & Jul-Aug
Last arrival 20.00hrs Last departure noon
*A well-maintained level grass site with bushes and trees
W of St Florence 3m off B4318. A 7-acre site with 35
touring pitches.*

🔌 🚰 ☉ 🗑 🎣 ✳ 〽 🏧 ⓘ ✐ ⬛ 🐾 🛖
➔ ∪ 🏴 ☉ ✢ 🍴 ☕ 🎵 🐾
Credit Cards 💳 💳

Well Park Caravan & Camping Site (SN128028)
SA70 8TL ☎ 01834 842179 (on right hand side of A478)
Signposted

▶ ▶ ▶ ▶ De-Luxe Park ★ ⚐ £5-£12 ⚐ £5-£12 ▲ £5-£9
Open Apr-Oct (rs Apr-mid May & mid Sep-Oct shop
closed) Booking advisable Spring bank hol & Jul-Aug
Last arrival 22.00hrs Last departure 11.00hrs
*An excellent, well-run site with trees and bushes. 1.5m
N of Tenby off A478 New Hedges by-pass. A 7-acre site
with 100 touring pitches and 42 statics.*
Off-licence in shop.

🔌 🚰 ☉ 🗑 🎣 🔍 🛒 ✳ 🍴 〽 🏧 ⓘ ✐ ⬛ 🇹
📞 🦆 🐕 🐾
➔ ∪ 🏴 ✢ 🍴 ☕ 🎵

Wood Park Caravans (SN128025)
New Hedges SA70 8TL ☎ 01834 843414 Signposted

▶ ▶ ▶ ▶ De-Luxe Park ★ ⚐ £5.50-£10 ⚐ £5.50-£10
▲ £5-£8.50
Open Spring bank hol-Sep (rs Etr-Spring bank hol &
Sep-Oct bar shop & launderette may not open) Booking
advisable Spring bank hol & Jul-Aug Last arrival
22.00hrs Last departure 10.00hrs
*A well-run, slightly sloping, part-level grass site with
trees and bushes. 1.5m N of Tenby off A478 New*

---

*Hedges by-pass. A 10-acre site with 60 touring pitches
and 90 statics.*
Outside dish/clothes washing area.

🔌 🚰 🦆 ☉ 🗑 🎣 🔍 ✳ 🍴 〽 🏧 ⓘ ✐ ⬛ 🐕 🛖 🐾
➔ ∪ 🏴 ✢ 🍴 ☕ 🎵

SOUTH WALES

This region includes the counties of Blaenau Gwent,
Bridgend, Caerphilly, Cardiff, Merthyr Tydfil,
Monmouthshire, Neath Port Talbot, Newport, Rhondda
Cynon Taff, Swansea, Torfaen and Vale of Glamorgan.

CARDIFF

Cardiff Caravan Park (ST171773)
Pontcanna Fields CF1 9JJ ☎ 01222 398362 & 471612

▶ ▶ ▶ ▶ De-Luxe Park ★ ⚐ £11.25-£13.75
⚐ £11.25-£13.75
Open Mar-Oct Booking advisable Last arrival telephone
Last departure noon
*An excellent site with good amenities, and very close to
centre of Cardiff. Take A48 turn off M4 through Cardiff,
turn left at lights at Llandaff, and follow signs to Sophia
Gardens and the Welsh Institute of Sport. A 2-acre site
with 43 touring pitches.*

🔌 🚰 ☉ 🗑 🎣 ⓘ 📞 ♿
➔ ∪ 🏴 ☉ ✢ 🍴 ☕ 🎵 🐾

CHEPSTOW

St Pierre Camping & Caravan Site (ST509901)
Portskewett ☎ 01291 425114
▶ ▶ ▶ Family Park ★ ⚐ £11 ⚐ £11 ▲ £8
Open Mar-Oct Booking advisable bank hols Last
departure 18.00hrs
*Well-established site with immaculately kept facilities
and a peaceful atmosphere, overlooking the Severn
Estuary. From Chepstow take A48 towards Newport,
turn left at first rndbt, then immed left. A 4-acre site
with 50 touring pitches.*
Boule, croquet.

🔌 🚰 ☉ 🗑 🎣 ⓘ 📞 🛖 🐕 🐾

DINGESTOW

Bridge Caravan Park & Camping Site (SO459104)
Bridge Farm NP5 4DY ☎ 01600 740241 Signposted
Nearby town: Monmouth
▶ ▶ ▶ Family Park ⚐ £8-£10.50 ⚐ £8-£9.50 ▲ £8-£9.50
Open Etr-Oct Booking advisable bank hols Last arrival
22.00hrs Last departure 16.00hrs
*An excellent site in a quiet village setting, signposted
from Raglan and located off the A449, South Wales-
Midlands road. A 4-acre site with 94 touring pitches.*
Fishing.

🔌 🚰 ☉ 🗑 🎣 ✳ ⓘ ✐ ⬛ 🇹 📞 🐕 🐾 ♿
➔ ∪ 🏴 ✢ 🍴 ☕ 🎵

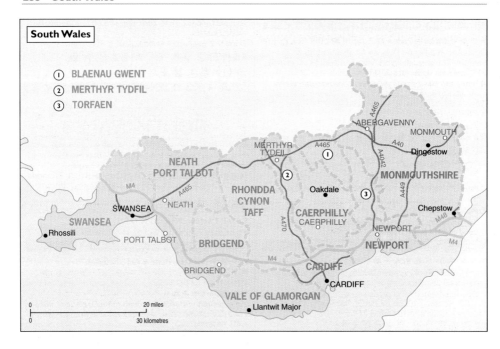

LLANTWIT MAJOR

Acorn Camping & Caravan Site (SS973678)
Ham Ln South CF61 1RP ☎ 01446 794024 & 0589
421112 Signposted
Nearby town: Cardiff
► ► ► Family Park ★ 🚐 £6-£7 🚐 £6-£7 ▲ £6-£7
Open Etr or 1st Feb - 8th Dec Booking advisable bank
hols & Aug Last arrival 23.00hrs Last departure noon
A quiet country site on meadowland, with individual
pitches marked out by hedges and shrubs. From
Llantwit Major follow B4265 south. Approach site
through Ham Manor residential park. A 4.5-acre site
with 90 touring pitches and 15 statics.
🔧 🛒 ⊙ 🦘 🔍 ✳ ⚠ 🗄 ⊘ 🎁 ⊤ 🔌 🎵 👤
➜ ∪ 🎵

Llandow Touring Caravan Park (SS956713)
Marcross CF7 7PB ☎ 01446 794527 & 792426 (2m NW)
Signposted
Nearby town: Cowbridge
► ► ► Family Park 🚐 🚐 ▲
Open Feb-Nov Booking advisable bank hols & end Jun
Last arrival 10.00hrs Last departure noon
A large level touring park with a new purpose-built
toilet block, within easy reach of Glamorgan's Heritage
Coast, and a short distance from Cardiff and Porthcawl.
Signed off B4270. A 6-acre site with 100 touring pitches.
Caravan Storage
🔧 🛒 ⊙ 🗄 🦘 ✳ ⚠ 🗄 ⊘ 🎁 🔌 🎪 🐎 🎵
➜ ∪ 👟 🎵

MONMOUTH

Monmouth Caravan Park (SO498135)
Rockfield Rd NP5 3BA ☎ 01600 714745
► ► ► Family Park 🚐 🚐
Open Mar-Oct Booking advisable
Level grassy site adjacent to Offa's Dyke footpath and
within easy distance of town. From A40 take B4233 S of
Monmouth, leading into Rockfield Rd, and site is
opposite fire station. A 3-acre site with 40 touring
pitches.
🔧 🛒 ⊙ 🔌 🎵

OAKDALE

Penyfan Caravan & Leisure Park (SO189012)
Manmoel Rd NP2 0HY ☎ 01495 226636 (off B4251)
Signposted
Nearby town: Blackwood
► ► ► Family Park 🚐 🚐 ▲
Open all year Booking advisable bank hols
A constantly improving site with good facilities for the
whole family, including a licensed bar with bar meals.
From junc 28 on M4 follow A467 to Crumlin, turn left on
to B4251, and follow signs towards site. A 4-acre site
with 75 touring pitches and 12 statics.
🔧 🛒 ⊙ 🗄 🦘 🖵 ✳ ⚘ ⚠ ✕ 🍺 🏛 ⴲ 🐎
➜ 🏴 👟 🎵 🎵

Credit Cards 💳 💳

RHOSSILI

Pitton Cross Caravan & Camping Park (SS434877)
SA3 1PH ☎ 01792 390593 & 390593 (2m W of Scurlage on B4247)
Nearby town: Swansea
▶ ▶ ▶ Family Park ★ ⚲ £7.50-£9.50 ⚏ £7.50-£9.50 ▲ £7.50-£9.50
Open Etr-Oct (rs Apr-early May & Sep-Oct some facilities may be closed) Booking advisable Spring bank hol & Jul-Aug Last arrival 21.00hrs Last departure noon
Constantly improving farm site within walking distance of the coast, with enthusiastic proprietors. On B4247, 1 mile inland from Rhossili. A 6-acre site with 100 touring pitches.
Motor caravan service bay, pets corner.

🖾 ⚟ ⊙ ◧ ⚱ ❊ ⋀ ⓘ ⌀ ⊞ Ⓣ ☎ ⚘ ⋔ ⚲ 占
➜ ∪ ▶ △ ♪
Credit Cards ● ▥ ▦ ▨ ⑤

SWANSEA

Riverside Caravan Park (SS679991)
Ynys Forgan Farm, Morriston SA6 6QL
☎ 01792 775587 (1m NE of A48/A4067 unclass 1m M4 junc 45) Signposted
▶ ▶ ▶ Family Park ★ ⚲ £9-£11 ⚏ £9-£11 ▲ £5-£11
Open all year (rs winter months pool) Booking advisable bank hols & main school hols Last arrival mdnt Last departure noon
A large site close to the M4, an ideal base for touring Mumbles, Gower beaches and Brecon National Park. Signed directly off junc 45 of M4. A 70-acre site with 120 touring pitches and 132 statics.
Fishing on site by arrangement.

🖾 ⚟ ⊙ ◧ ⚱ ⚡ ⬟ ◻ ❊ ⚲ ⋀ ⓘ ⌀ ⊞ Ⓣ ☎ 曲
⊓ ⋔ ⚲ 占
➜ ∪ ▶ ◉ ⚹ ⚏ ♪
Credit Cards ● ▥ ▦ ▨ ⑤

NORTHERN IRELAND

CO ANTRIM

BALLYCASTLE

Silver Cliffs Holiday Village
21 Clare Rd BT54 6DB ☎ 012657 62550 (0.25m W off A2) Signposted
▶ ▶ ▶ Family Park ★ ⚲ £10-£12 ⚏ £10-£12 ▲ £10-£12
Open 17 Mar-Oct Booking advisable 11-25 Jul & 22-25 Aug Last arrival 20.00hrs Last departure 17.00hrs
A typical large seaside site with a swimming pool and bar. Close to the beach and River Glenshesk, .25m W of Ballycastle off B15. A 2-acre site with 50 touring pitches and 250 statics.
Sun beds, sauna, spa & snooker.

🖾 ⚟ ⊙ ◧ ⚱ ⚡ ◻ ❊ ⚲ ⋀ ⓘ ⌀ ⊞ Ⓣ ✗ ☎ 曲 ⌂
⊓ ⚲ 占
➜ ∪ ▶ ⚹ ♪
Credit Cards ● ▥

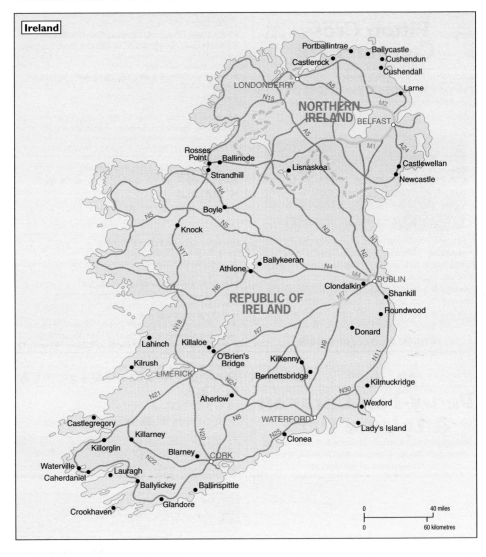

Ireland

Please note that caravan and camping parks are listed county by county and under alphabetical order of place name within each county. Northern Ireland counties are listed first, followed by those in the Republic. Place names are highlighted on the location map, but no map references are given against the directory entries.

Prices given in the Republic of Ireland entries are in Irish Punts (IR£) Please consult yur bank for the current exchange rate

See p303 for changes to phone numbers

CUSHENDALL

Cushendall Caravan Camp
62 Coast Rd BT44 0QW ☎ 012667 71699 Signposted
▶ Town & Country Pennant Park ☎ ☎ ⚑
Open mid Mar-mid Oct Booking advisable peak periods
Last arrival 23.00hrs Last departure 14.00hrs
*A pleasant site next to the beach and sailing club on the
A2, 1m S of town. A 1-acre site with 14 touring pitches
and 55 statics.*

CUSHENDUN

Cushendun Caravan Park
14 Glendun Rd BT44 0PX ☎ 01266 761254 Signposted
Nearby town: Ballycastle
▶ Town & Country Pennant Park ★ ☎ £8.30 ☎ £8.30
⚑ £4.90-£8.30
Open Etr-Sep Booking advisable Jul-Aug Last arrival
22.00hrs Last departure 12.30hrs
*A small touring site with mostly level pitches next to
larger static site. From A2 take B52 for 1m, clearly
signed. A 0.5-acre site with 15 touring pitches and 50
statics.*

LARNE

Curran Caravan Park
131 Curran Rd ☎ 01574 260088 Signposted
▶ ▶ ▶ Family Park ★ ☎ £7 ☎ £7 ⚑ £4.50
Open Apr-Sep Booking advisable main season
*A tidy and very clean council site ideal for the ferry. Site
on A2 .25m from ferry, and clearly signed. A 3-acre site
with 40 touring pitches.*
Bowling & putting greens.

PORTBALLINTRAE

PortBallintrae Caravan Park
Ballaghmore Av BT57 8RX ☎ 012657 31478 Signposted
Nearby town: Bushmills
▶ Town & Country Pennant Park ☎ ☎ ⚑
Open Apr-Sep Booking advisable Etr & Jul-Aug Last
arrival 20.30hrs Last departure 14.00hrs
*Very tidy site, popular for Giants Causeway. In
Portballintrae village clearly signed from A2, .25m from
Bushmills Distillery. A 12-acre site with 53 touring
pitches and 150 statics.*

CO DOWN

CASTLEWELLAN

Castlewellan Forest Park
Dept of Agriculture, Forest Service BT31 9BU
☎ 013967 78664 Signposted
Nearby town: Newcastle

▶ ▶ ▶ Family Park ☎ £6.50-£10 ☎ £6.50-£10
⚑ £6.50-£10
Open all year Booking advisable wknds & Jul-Aug Last
arrival 22.00hrs Last departure 15.00hrs
*Attractive forest park site, situated down a long drive with
views of the castle. Site broken up into smaller areas by
mature trees and shrubs. Joint Winner of Best campsite
for Northern Ireland 1998/9. Off A25 in Castlewellan; turn
right at Upper Square and turn into Forest Park, clearly
signed. A 5-acre site with 90 touring pitches.*
Lake, arboretum, fishing on site. First aid.

NEWCASTLE

Tollymore Forest Park
☎ 01396 722428 Signposted
▶ ▶ ▶ Family Park ☎ ☎ ⚑
Open 15 Mar-15 Nov (rs 16 Nov-14 Mar) Booking
advisable Jul & Aug & wknds Apr-Sep Last arrival
21.00hrs Last departure 17.00hrs
*Popular site with family field and large tent area. Set in
a large and beautiful forest park. Joint Winner of Best
campsite for Northern Ireland 1998/9. From A2 at
Newcastle take B180, and site clearly signed on right. A
7.5-acre site with 100 touring pitches.*

CO FERMANAGH

LISNASKEA

Lisnaskea Caravan Park
BT92 0NZ ☎ 01365 721040 Signposted
Nearby town: Enniskillen
▶ Town & Country Pennant Park ★ ☎ £10-£11 ☎ £10-
£11 ⚑ £6-£7
Open Apr-Sep Booking advisable Jul-Aug Last arrival
21.00hrs Last departure noon
*A pretty riverside site set in peaceful countryside. From
A34 turn onto B514 for Lisnaskea, and site signed .5m
before town. A 4-acre site with 43 touring pitches.*

CO LONDONDERRY

CASTLEROCK

Castlerock Holiday Park
24 Sea Rd ☎ 01265 848381 Signposted
▶ ▶ ▶ Family Park ☎ ☎ ⚑
Open Etr-Oct Booking advisable Jul-Aug Last arrival
21.00hrs Last departure noon
*A mainly static site at the seaside with a tidy touring
area, 2 minutes from the beach. From A2 to Castlerock,
turn right before the rlwy stn into site; signed. A 2-acre
site with 40 touring pitches and 210 statics.*

REPUBLIC OF IRELAND

CO CLARE

KILLALOE

Lough Derg Caravan and Camping Park
☎ 061 376329 Signposted

QQQQQQQ

► ► ► ► ► Premier Park 🚐 🚐 Å
Open 29 Apr-Sep Last arrival 21.00hrs Last departure
noon ⊘
*A 4.5-acre site with 57 touring pitches and 15 statics.
Boats for hire, boat slipway, fishing.*
🔌 🏠 ☉ 🗄 🎣 🔧 🔍 ✳ ⚠ ⊘ 🖭 T ✕ 📞 🛒 🅿
➜ ∪ 🅿 ⚠ ⌇ 🎵

QQQQQQQ

KILRUSH

Aylevarroo Caravan and Camping Park
☎ 065 51102 (off N67) Signposted
► ► ► Family Park 🚐 🚐 Å
Open 24 May-13 Sep Booking advisable Last arrival
22.00hrs Last departure noon ⊘
*A 7.5-acre site with 36 touring pitches and 10 statics.
Basketball court.*
🔌 🏠 ☉ 🔍 🔍 ⚠ 🗄 ✳ ⚠ 🅿 ⊘ 📞
➜ ∪ 🅿 ◎ ⚠ ⌇ 🎵 🗄 🛒

LAHINCH

Lahinch Camping and Caravan Park
☎ (065) 81424 Signposted

QQQQQQQ

► ► ► ► De-Luxe Park 🚐 🚐 Å
Open May-Sep Booking advisable mid Jul-mid Aug Last
arrival 23.00hrs Last departure noon
*A 5-acre site with 115 touring pitches and 12 statics.
Bicycle hire.*
🔌 🏠 ☉ 🗄 🎣 🔍 🔍 ✳ ⚠ 🗄 📞 🛒
➜ ∪ 🅿 ◎ ⚠ ⌇ 🎵

QQQQQQQ

CO CORK

BALLINSPITTLE

Garrettstown House Holiday Park
☎ 021 778156 Signposted

QQQQQQQ

► ► ► ► De-Luxe Park 🚐 🚐 Å

GARRETTSTOWN HOUSE HOLIDAY PARK ► ► ► ►

**Garrettstown, Kinsale, Co Cork
Tel: 00 353 21 778156/775286**

Top class spacious park in old world setting of
Garrettstown estate near beach and forest. Ideally
located for touring, scenic, historic and amenity
areas of the south. Kinsale, gourmet centre of
Ireland is 6 miles. Cork/Ringaskiddy ferryport 25
miles. Numerous facilities and activities on site or
within 16 km.
*Recommended by all main camping clubs
including BFE 4 star*

Open 19 May-16 Sep (rs Etr-18 May) Last arrival
22.00hrs Last departure noon
*A 7-acre site with 60 touring pitches and 80 statics.
Disco, ceilidh, campers' kitchen*
🔌 ☉ 🗄 🔍 🔍 ✳ ⚠ 🗄 ⊘ 🖭 T ✕ 📞 🛒
➜ 🎵 🗄

QQQQQQQ

BALLYLICKEY

Eagle Point Caravan and Camping Park
☎ 027 50630 Signposted
Nearby town: Bantry

QQQQQQQ

► ► ► ► ► Premier Park 🚐 🚐 Å
Open May-Sep Last arrival 23.00hrs Last departure
noon ⊘
A 20-acre site with 125 touring pitches.
🔌 🏠 ☉ 🗄 🔍 🔍 ✳ ⚠ 🗄 📞 🛒 ♿
➜ ∪ 🅿 🎵

Credit Cards 💳 💳

QQQQQQQ

BLARNEY

Blarney Caravan & Camping Park
Stone View ☎ 021 385167 & 382051 Signposted
▶ ▶ ▶ Family Park ★ ⊕ IR£8-IR£9 ⊕ IR£8-IR£9
⅄ IR£7-IR£8
Open all year Booking advisable anytime Last arrival
mdnt Last departure noon
A 3-acre site with 40 touring pitches.
Mini golf.

🏕 🦷 ☉ 🍳 ⛽ ⚡ 🔥 ⛺ 🐕 🏪
➔ ∪ ▶ ◎ 🎣 ▣

CROOKHAVEN

Barley Cove Caravan Park
☎ 028 35302 & 021 346466 Signposted
Nearby town: Schull

◯ ◯ ◯ ◯ ◯ ◯ ◯ ◯

▶ ▶ ▶ ▶ Premier Park ⊕ ⊕ ⅄
Open Etr & Jun-1 Sep (rs May & Sep) Booking advisable
7 Jul-17 Aug Last arrival 21.00hrs Last departure noon
⌀
A 9-acre site with 100 touring pitches and 50 statics.
Pitch & putt, children's playhouse

🏕 🦷 🦷 ☉ ⊙ ▣ 🍳 ⚡ ⚓ ⛽ ☀ ⚡ ⛺ 🚻 ⊞ Ⓣ ✗ 🦷
🦷 🏪 🦷 ♿
➔ ∪ ▶ 🔺 🎣

◯ ◯ ◯ ◯ ◯ ◯ ◯ ◯

GLANDORE

Meadow Camping Park
Kilfinnin ☎ 028 33280 Off N71 at Leap or Rosscarbery.
Take R597 to Glandore. For 5 Kms. Site is on R597 2kms
Rosscarbery side of Glanmore. Signposted
Nearby town: Skibbereen
▶▶ Town & Country Pennant Park ⊕ IR£7-IR£8 ⅄ fr IR£7
Open 16 Mar-15 Sep Booking advisable Jul-Aug Last
arrival 22.30hrs Last departure noon ⌀ no cars by tents
A 1.5-acre site with 19 touring pitches.
Dining room.

🏕 🦷 ☉ ▣ ☀ 🦷 🍼
➔ ∪ ◎ 🔺 ⚓ 🎣 🏪

CO DUBLIN

CLONDALKIN

Camac Valley Tourist Caravan & Camping Park
Corkagh Park ☎ 01 4640644 Signposted

◯ ◯ ◯ ◯ ◯ ◯ ◯ ◯

▶ ▶ ▶ ▶ De-Luxe Park ⊕ ⊕ ⅄
Booking advisable Jul & Aug Last arrival anytime Last
departure noon
A 15-acre site with 163 touring pitches.

🏕 🦷 ☉ ▣ 🍳 ☀ ⚡ ⚡ ⊞ 🦷 🐕 🏪 ♿
➔ ∪ 🚻
Credit Cards 💳

◯ ◯ ◯ ◯ ◯ ◯ ◯ ◯

SHANKILL

Shankill Caravan Park
☎ 01 2820011
▶ ▶ ▶ Family Park ⊕ ⊕ ⅄
Open all year Last departure noon
A 7-acre site with 82 touring pitches and 9 statics.

🏕 🦷 ☉ ☀ ⚡ ⚡ ⊞ 🦷 🏪
➔ ∪ ▶ ⚓ 🚻 🎣 ▣

CO KERRY

CAHERDANIEL

Wave Crest Caravan and Camping Park
☎ 066 75188 Signposted

◯ ◯ ◯ ◯ ◯ ◯ ◯ ◯

▶ ▶ ▶ ▶ De-Luxe Park ★ ⊕ IR£6.50-IR£7.50
⊕ IR£6.50-IR£7 ⅄ IR£6.50-IR£7.50
Open 17 Mar-12 Oct Last arrival 22.00hrs
Last departure noon
A 4.5-acre site with 45 touring pitches and 2 statics.
Boat anchorage, fishing & pool room.

🏕 🦷 ☉ ▣ 🍳 ⚓ ⛺ ☀ ⚡ ⛽ ⚡ ⊞ Ⓣ ✗ 🦷 🦷
🐕 🏪 ♿
➔ ∪ ▶ 🔺 🦷 🎣
Credit Cards 💳

◯ ◯ ◯ ◯ ◯ ◯ ◯ ◯

CASTLEGREGORY

Anchor Caravan Park
☎ 066 39157 Signposted
Nearby town: Tralee

◯ ◯ ◯ ◯ ◯ ◯ ◯ ◯

▶ ▶ ▶ ▶ De-Luxe Park ⊕ IR£9-IR£10 ⊕ IR£9-IR£10
⅄ IR£7-IR£10
Open Etr-Sep Last arrival 22.00hrs Last departure noon
A 5-acre site with 24 touring pitches and 6 statics.
Camper kitchen.

🏕 🦷 ☉ ▣ ⚓ ⛺ ☀ ⚡ ⊞ 🦷 🦷 🐕 🏪
➔ ∪ ▶ ◎ 🔺 🦷 🎣

◯ ◯ ◯ ◯ ◯ ◯ ◯ ◯

KILLARNEY

Fossa Caravan Park
Fossa ☎ 064 31497 (2.5m SW on R562)
★ ⊕ IR£9-IR£9.50 ⊕ IR£9-IR£9.50
⅄ IR£8.50-IR£9.50

Open Etr-Sep (rs Sep, Oct & Mar/Apr restaurant &
takeaway closed) Booking advisable Jul-Aug Last arrival
23.00hrs Last departure noon
A 6-acre site with 100 touring pitches and 20 statics.

contd.

Campers kitchens & bikes for hire.

Credit Cards 💳 💳

Flesk Muckross Caravan & Camping Park
Muckross Rd ☎ 064 31704 & 35794 (1m S)
Signposted

▶ ▶ ▶ ▶ **De-Luxe Park** 🚐 🚐 ▲
Open mid Mar-end Oct Booking advisable Last arrival
21.00hrs Last departure noon
A 7-acre site with 72 touring pitches
Bike hire.Bar/club, tennis, pool all within 50 mtrs.

Credit Cards 💳 💳 💳

KILLORGLIN

West's Caravan Park
Killarney Rd ☎ 066 61240 (1m on Killarney rd)
Signposted
▶ ▶ ▶ **Family Park** ★ 🚐 IR£8-IR£8.50 🚐 IR£8-IR£8.50 ▲
IR£8-IR£8.50
Open Apr-Oct Booking advisable Last departure noon
A 5-acre site with 20 touring pitches and 40 statics.
Salmon/Trout fishing, volleyball.

Credit Cards 💳 💳

LAURAGH

Creveen Park
Healy Pass Rd ☎ 064 83131 (1m SE on R574)
Signposted
▶▶ **Town & Country Pennant Park** 🚐 IR£8 🚐 IR£8
▲ IR£8
Open Etr-Oct Booking advisable Aug bank hol Last
arrival mdnt Last departure noon
A 2-acre site with 20 touring pitches and 2 statics.

WATERVILLE

Waterville Caravan and Camping
Spunkane ☎ 066 74191 1 Kilometre. N of Waterville just
off main N70 "Ring of Kerry" road. Signposted

▶ ▶ ▶ ▶ **De-Luxe Park** 🚐 IR£9.50-IR£10
🚐 IR£9.50-IR£10 ▲ IR£8.50-IR£9
Open Etr-Sep Booking advisable Jul-Aug Last departure
noon

A 4.5-acre site with 59 touring pitches and 22 statics.
Playroom, cycle hire, campers kitchen.

CO KILKENNY

BENNETTSBRIDGE

Nore Valley Park
☎ 056 27229
Nearby town: Kilkenny
▶ ▶ ▶ **Family Park** ★ 🚐 IR£9.50 🚐 IR£8.50 ▲ IR£5-IR£9
Open Mar-Oct Booking advisable bank hols & Jul Last
arrival 22.00hrs Last departure 16.00hrs
A 4-acre site with 70 touring pitches and 4 statics.
Bread & farm produce, river walks, crazy golf.

KILKENNY

Tree Grove Caravan & Camping Park
Danville House ☎ 056 70302
▶▶ **Town & Country Pennant Park** 🚐 🚐 ▲
Open Apr-Oct Booking advisable
A 7-acre site with 30 touring pitches.
Campers kitchen & sinks.

CO MAYO

KNOCK

Knock Caravan and Camping Park
Claremorris Rd ☎ 094 88100 & 88223 Signposted
Nearby town: Claremorris
▶ ▶ ▶ **Family Park** 🚐 🚐 ▲
Open Mar-Nov Booking advisable Aug Last arrival
22.00hrs Last departure noon
An 8-acre site with 58 touring pitches and 8 statics.

CO ROSCOMMON

ATHLONE

Hodson Bay Caravan & Camping Park
Hodson Bay ☎ 0902 92448 Signposted
▶▶ **Town & Country Pennant Park** ★ 🚐 IR£9 🚐 IR£9 ▲
IR£8.50

Open 9 May-Aug Booking advisable bank hols & last wk Jul-1st wk Aug Last arrival 22.30hrs Last departure noon ⌖
A 2-acre site with 34 touring pitches.

BOYLE

Lough Key Forest Park
☎ 079 62363 & 62212 Signposted

◯◯◯◯◯◯◯◯◯◯

► ► ► ► **De-Luxe Park** 🚐 🚐 Å
Open 27 Mar-6 Apr & May-1 Sep Booking advisable 3 wks before arrival Last arrival 22.00hrs Last departure noon no cars by tents
A 15-acre site with 72 touring pitches.

◯◯◯◯◯◯◯◯◯◯

CO SLIGO

BALLINODE

Gateway Caravan & Camping Park
(.75m from town at traffic lights on N16)

◯◯◯◯◯◯◯◯◯◯

► ► ► ► **De-Luxe Park** 🚐 🚐 Å
Open all year
A 2.5-acre site with 40 touring pitches and 10 statics.

◯◯◯◯◯◯◯◯◯◯

ROSSES POINT

Greenlands Caravan & Camping Park
☎ 071 77113 & 45618 Take R291 (L16) NW from SLIGO 5m. Site golf club and beach. Signposted

◯◯◯◯◯◯◯◯◯◯

► ► ► ► **De-Luxe Park** 🚐 IR£8.50-IR£10.50 🚐 IR£8.50-IR£10.50 Å IR£8.50-IR£10.50
Open 21 May-17 Sep & Easter Last arrival 20.00hrs Last departure noon
A 4-acre site with 78 touring pitches and 12 statics.

◯◯◯◯◯◯◯◯◯◯

STRANDHILL

Strandhill Caravan Park
☎ 071 68120 Signposted
►► **Town & Country Pennant Park** 🚐 🚐 Å
Open May-14 Sep Booking advisable Jul-26 Aug Last arrival 23.00hrs Last departure 14.00hrs
A 10-acre site with 28 touring pitches and 12 statics.

CO TIPPERARY

AHERLOW

Ballinacourty House Camping and Caravan Park
☎ 062 56230 Signposted
Nearby town: Tipperary

◯◯◯◯◯◯◯◯◯◯

► ► ► ► **De-Luxe Park** 🚐 🚐 Å
Open Etr-end Sep Booking advisable high season & bank hols Last arrival 22.00hrs Last departure noon
A 5-acre site with 58 touring pitches.
Mini-golf.

◯◯◯◯◯◯◯◯◯◯

CO WATERFORD

CLONEA

Casey's Caravan Park
☎ 058 41919 Signposted
Nearby town: Dungarvan
► ► ► **Family Park** 🚐 🚐 Å
Open 2 May-7 Sep Booking advisable May-Jun Last arrival 22.00hrs Last departure noon
A 4.5-acre site with 108 touring pitches and 170 statics.
Crazy golf & games room.

CO WESTMEATH

BALLYKEERAN

Lough Ree Caravan and Camping Park
☎ 0902 78561 & 74414 Signposted
Nearby town: Athlone
►► **Town & Country Pennant Park** ★ 🚐 IR£7.50 🚐 IR£7 Å IR£7
Open Apr-2 Oct Booking advisable bank hols
A 5-acre site with 40 touring pitches and 2 statics.
Pool table & campers kitchen.

Summer weather can mean rain. It is a good idea to prepare for ground to be wet underfoot. Take something to amuse the children if they can't go outside

Stay at

FERRYBANK Caravan Park

►►►

Ferrybank, Wexford, Co Wexford
Telephone: 00 353 53 44378/43274

OPEN EASTER TO SEPTEMBER

Location: 16kms from Rosslare ferry port.
Just 5 minutes walk from Wexford town on
Dublin road at end of bridge on sea front.

On site facilities include:
★ Heated indoor swimming pool ★ Sauna
★ Shop ★ Toilets ★ Showers ★ TV room
★ Recreation hall ★ Laundry
★ Facilities for disabled
★ Hard pitches and grass pitches
★ Many electric hook ups

24 hour supervision

Recommended by AA, ADAC, ANWB

Facilities close by
★ Fishing ★ Sailing ★ Tennis ★ Golf
★ Pony trekking ★ Walks etc.

CO WEXFORD

KILMUCKRIDGE

Morriscastle Strand Caravan & Camping Park
Morriscastle ☎ 053 30124 & 01 4535355 (off-season)
Signposted
Nearby town: Gorey
►►► Family Park ⊞ ⊞ Å
Open Jul-27 Aug (rs May-Jun & 28 Aug-Sep shop,
reception, games room, take-away food) Booking
advisable Whitsun wknd & mid Jul-mid Aug Last arrival
22.00hrs Last departure 16.00hrs ⬠
A 16-acre site with 100 touring pitches and 150 statics.
Dish washing room, indoor cooking facilities.

⊞ ⋔ ⊙ ⊡ ⚲ ⬤ ⋇ ⋀ 🌡 ⬚ 📞 🖽 ✠ ⓖ
➔ ∪ ⥀ ◎ ⛺ 𝆔

LADY'S ISLAND

St Margaret's Beach Caravan & Camping Park
St Margarets ☎ 053 31169 Signposted
Nearby town: Wexford
►► Town & Country Pennant Park ⊞ ⊞ Å
Open Mar-Oct Booking advisable Jul & Aug Last arrival
23.00hrs Last departure noon
A 4-acre site with 30 touring pitches and 20 statics.

⊞ ⋔ ⊙ ⊡ ⍨ ⋇ 🌡 ⬚ ✠ 🖽 ⓖ
➔ ∪ ⥀ ◎ ⛄ 𝆔 𝆔

WEXFORD

Ferrybank Caravan Park
Ferrybank ☎ 053 44378 & 43274 Signposted
►►► Family Park ⊞ ⊞ Å
Open Apr-Sep (rs Etr & Sep no shop) Booking advisable
Whit wknd & Aug bank hol Last arrival 22.00hrs Last
departure 16.00hrs
A 4.5-acre site with 130 touring pitches.

⊞ ⋔ ⊙ ⊡ ⍨ ⬤ ⬚ ⋇ ⋀ ⋈ 📞 🖽 🖽 ✠ ⓖ
➔ ∪ ⥀ ◎ ⛄ ⛺ 𝆔

CO WICKLOW

DONARD

Moat Farm Caravan & Camping Park
☎ 045 404727 Signposted
Nearby town: Baltinglass
►►► Family Park ⊞ ⊞ Å
Open all year Booking advisable bank hols & Jun-Aug
Last arrival 22.30hrs Last departure noon
A 2.75-acre site with 40 touring pitches.

⊞ ⋔ ⊙ ⊡ ⍨ ⬚ ⋇ ⋀ 🌡 ⬚ 📞 ⓖ ✠ 🖽 🖽 ✠ 🖽 🦅
🖽 ⓖ
➔ ∪ ⥀ ◎ 𝆔

ROUNDWOOD

Roundwood Caravan Park
☎ 01 2818163 Signposted
Nearby town: Bray

►►►► De-Luxe Park ⊞ IR£7-IR£8 ⊞ IR£7-IR£8
Å IR£6-IR£8
Open Apr-Sep Booking advisable Jun-Aug Last arrival
11.00hrs Last departure noon
A 5-acre site with 45 touring pitches and 33 statics.
Campers kitchen & dining room.

⊞ ⋔ ⊙ ⊡ ⍨ ⬤ ⬚ ⋇ ⋀ 🌡 ⬚ 📞 ✠ 🖽 ⓖ
➔ ∪ ⥀ 𝆔

This is the checklist compiled by one of our campsite inspectors to ensure that he leaves nothing behind when he sets off either from home or from park visits with a towed caravan. We thought you might like to share his handy hints, and save yourself from embarassment ... or worse.

Before You Go

- Check that all interior caravan items are safely stored, cupboards are closed, loos not full of moveable objects, all interior electrics set correctly. Remember that vase of flowers!

- Check roof lights are closed and windows secure.

- Corner steadies should be up tightly, blocks cleared away, steps stowed.

- Disconnect electric hook-ups to site and check that gas bottles are turned off.

- Make sure electrics to car are secure.

- Check that the tow-hook safety wire is clipped on, and, if used, that the anti-snake device is fitted correctly.

- Visually check that caravan number plate is secure - and that it reads the same as the one on the car.

- Using a second person to stand behind the caravan, check that all lights and indicators are working correctly.

- Move forward about 15 metres, then stop, get out and inspect your pitch for any items which have been left under the caravan.

- Check that the caravan door is locked and secure.

- Another useful and potentially life-saving tip is to travel always with a small fire extinguisher, fire blanket or both. Fires in caravans and tents are all too commonplace, and once started can take hold very quickly. By the time help has come, or you have gone to find the site's fire-fighting equipment, a tent in particular can already have burned down completely. Never treat fire lightly.

- If you use Calor Gas, they issue a free directory of stockists and dealers. Simply call free on 0800 626 626.

Useful Addresses

CAMPING AND CARAVANNING CLUB
Greenfields House
Westwood Way
Coventry CV4 8JH
Tel 01203 694995

CARAVAN CLUB
East Grinstead House
East Grinstead
West Sussex RH19 1UA
Tel 01342 326944

BRITISH HOLIDAY & HOME PARKS ASSOCIATION LTD
6 Pullman Court
Great Western Road
Gloucester GL1 3ND
Tel 01452 526911

NATIONAL CARAVAN COUNCIL LTD
Catherine House
Victoria Road
Aldershot
Hampshire GU11 1SS
Tel 01252 318251

Please write to: Campsites Editor, AA Camping and
Caravanning Guide, Publishing Division,
The Automobile Association, Fanum House,
Basingstoke RG21 4EA

Use this form to recommend any caravan and camping park with
good touring pitches where you have stayed which is not already
in our guide.

If you have any comments about your stay at a touring park listed
in the guide, we shall be grateful if you will let us know, as
feedback from readers helps us to keep our guide accurate and up
to date. Please note, however, that the AA only inspects and
classifies parks for their touring facilities. We do not inspect or
grade static caravans.

If a problem arises during your stay on a park, we do recommend
that you discuss the matter with the park management there and
then so that they have a chance to put things right before your
holiday is spoilt.

Please note that the AA does not undertake to arbitrate between
you and the park management, or to obtain compensation or
engage in protracted correspondence.

Readers
Report form

Your name (block capitals) . . . .

. . . .

. . . .

Your address (block capitals) . . . .

. . . .

. . . .

. . . .

. . . .

. . . .

Comments . . . .

. . . .

. . . .

. . . .

. . . .

. . . .

CARAVAN AND
CAMPING
GUIDE 1999

....
....
....
....
....
....
....
....
....
....
....
....
....
....
....
....
....
....
....
....
....
....
....
....

....
....
....
....

Please write to: Campsites Editor, AA Camping and
Caravanning Guide, Publishing Division,
The Automobile Association, Fanum House,
Basingstoke RG21 4EA

Use this form to recommend any caravan and camping park with good touring pitches where you have stayed which is not already in our guide.

If you have any comments about your stay at a touring park listed in the guide, we shall be grateful if you will let us know, as feedback from readers helps us to keep our guide accurate and up to date. Please note, however, that the AA only inspects and classifies parks for their touring facilities. We do not inspect or grade static caravans.

If a problem arises during your stay on a park, we do recommend that you discuss the matter with the park management there and then so that they have a chance to put things right before your holiday is spoilt.

Please note that the AA does not undertake to arbitrate between you and the park management, or to obtain compensation or engage in protracted correspondence.

Readers
Report form

Your name (block capitals) . . . .
. . . .
. . . .

Your address (block capitals) . . . .
. . . .
. . . .
. . . .
. . . .
. . . .

Comments . . . .
. . . .
. . . .
. . . .
. . . .
. . . .

CARAVAN AND
CAMPING
GUIDE 1999

....
....
....
....
....
....
....
....
....
....
....
....
....
....
....
....
....
....
....
....
....
....
....
....
....
....
....
....

CARAVAN AND
CAMPING
GUIDE 1999

Please write to: Campsites Editor, AA Camping and
                    Caravanning Guide, Publishing Division,
                    The Automobile Association, Fanum House,
                    Basingstoke RG21 4EA

Use this form to recommend any caravan and camping park with
good touring pitches where you have stayed which is not already
in our guide.

If you have any comments about your stay at a touring park listed
in the guide, we shall be grateful if you will let us know, as
feedback from readers helps us to keep our guide accurate and up
to date. Please note, however, that the AA only inspects and
classifies parks for their touring facilities. We do not inspect or
grade static caravans.

If a problem arises during your stay on a park, we do recommend
that you discuss the matter with the park management there and
then so that they have a chance to put things right before your
holiday is spoilt.

Please note that the AA does not undertake to arbitrate between
you and the park management, or to obtain compensation or
engage in protracted correspondence.

Readers
Report form

Your name (block capitals) . . . .
. . . .
. . . .

Your address (block capitals) . . . .
. . . .
. . . .
. . . .
. . . .
. . . .

Comments . . . .
. . . .
. . . .
. . . .
. . . .
. . . .

CARAVAN AND
CAMPING
GUIDE 1999

....
....
....
....
....
....
....
....
....
....
....
....
....
....
....
....
....
....
....
....
....
....
....
....
....
....
....
....
....
....

CARAVAN AND
CAMPING
GUIDE 1999

REPUBLIC OF IRELAND -
TELEPHONE NUMBER CHANGES

Some telephone codes will change during the currency of this guide. From August 1998, both old and new telephone numbers can be dialled. From December 1998, calls to the old numbers will be connected to a recorded announcement which will advise the caller of the new number, which the caller will then have to redial. From August 1999, only the new number can be dialled.

National Dialling Code (NDC)	Numbering Area	Leading Digits of Current Numbers	New Prefix
41	Drogheda	2, 3, 4, 7, 8	98
41	Ardee	5, 6	68
42	Dundalk	2, 3, 5, 7, 8	93
42	Carrickmoss	6, 90, 91, 92, 94, 98	96
42	Castleblayney	4, 95	97
49	Cavan	3, 6, 7	43
49	Cootehill	5	55
49	Oldcastle	4	85
49	Belturbet	2	95
65	Ennis	2, 3, 4, 6	68
65	Ennistymon	7, 8	70
65	Kilrush	5	90
66	Tralee	2, 3, 4, 8	71
66	Dingle	5	91
66	Cahirciveen	7	94
66	Killorglin	6, 9	97

NUMBER CHANGES IN THE CORK AREA

In the Cork area there will be a two-phase process. Local numbers beginning with 40, 43 or 33 will be prefixed with a 2 or a 7 (see Phase 1 below). In phase two, these new 2 or 7 numbers will be prefixed with a 4 (see Phase 2 below), as will the other first digits.

National Dialling Code (NDC)	Numbering Area	Leading Digits of Current Numbers	New Prefix
PHASE 1			
21	Cork	40	2
21	Coachford	43, 33	7
PHASE 2			
21	Cork	2, 3, 5, 8, 9	4
21	Midleton	6	4
21	Kinsale	7	4

IN CASE OF DIFFICULTIES, PLEASE CONSULT DIRECTORY ENQUIRIES

Symbols & Abbreviations

▶ AA pennant classification (see p 11)
☎ Site telephone number
🐕 No dogs
★ 1998 prices
🚐 Touring caravans
🚐 Motor caravans
🛖 Tents
⚡ Electric hook up
🛁 Bath(s)
🚿 Shower(s)
⊙ Electric shaver point(s)
▣ Launderette
Hairdryer
Indoor swimming pool
Outdoor swimming pool
Tennis court
Games room
Separate TV room
Ice pack facility
Licensed bar
Children's playground
Calor Gas
Camping Gaz
Battery charging
Toilet fluid
Café/restaurant
Disabled facilities
Public telephone
Shop on site or within 200 yds (except where it appears after ➜)
Mobile shop calls at the site at least 5 days a week

➜ Facilities within three miles of site
U Stables
9 hole/18 hole golf course
Boats for hire
Cinema
Fishing
Baby care
Barbeque area
Picnic area
Fast food/take away
Dog exercise area on site
Mini golf
Watersports
all year Site open all year
C Century
cdp Chemical closet disposal point
Etr Easter
fr From
hrs Hours
m Mile
mdnt Midnight
nc No children (with age limit)
rs Restricted service
Sign-posted Officially prescribed sign to site
supervised Site supervised 24hrs a day
wk Week
wknd Weekend
Credit/charge cards